WED
2 MARCH
1430

RIS
LIBERTY } CNET
JUSTICE

Bonnie Caldwell
850 Davis St
186 466 201

1672
$ 14?0
NOV   1983

PHILOSOPHICAL ETHICS

PHILOSOPHICAL ETHICS
An Introduction to Moral Philosophy

234567890 HDHD 898765432

This book was set in Times Roman by University Graphics, Inc. The editors were
Kaye Pace and Susan Gamer; the designer was Joseph Gillians; the production
supervisor was Leroy A. Young.

Library of Congress Cataloging in Publication Data

Beauchamp, Tom L.
    Philosophical ethics.

    Includes bibliographies and index.
    1. Ethics.   I. Title.
BJ1012.B4   170   81-2748
ISBN 0-07-004203-9   AACR2

Philosophical Ethics

An Introduction to Moral Philosophy

Tom L. Beauchamp

Georgetown University

McGraw-Hill Book Company

New York   St. Louis   San Francisco   Auckland
Bogotá   Hamburg   Johannesburg   London
Madrid   Mexico   Montreal   New Delhi   Panama
Paris   São Paulo   Singapore   Sydney   Tokyo   Toronto

For Karine, Ruthie, and Petey,
who make life come alive

Contents

PART TWO   CLASSICAL ETHICAL THEORIES

PART THREE   TOPICS IN MORAL AND SOCIAL PHILOSOPHY

Chapter 6 Rights

Chapter 7 Justice

PART FOUR   MORAL JUSTIFICATION

Preface

The structure of this book is as follows:

This structure and the design of each chapter were developed over a five-year period. My conviction is as firm now as it was when I began that virtually all introductory ethics texts suffer one or two of three substantial limitations: they are either embarrassingly thin in substantive philosophical material, are composed entirely of lengthy scholarly articles originally addressed to professional philosophers, or are utterly removed from application to public and private problems of the moral life. My hope has been to avoid these limitations by creating a pedagogically sound work that presents substantive arguments, readable materials, and practical applications.

Another unfortunate feature of many ethics texts is that they immerse students into the intricacies of philosophical works by such authors as Aristotle, Kant, and Mill without providing an explanation of the broader systematic implications of these writings. In presenting Aristotelian, Kantian, and classical utilitarian ethical theories, I have eschewed treatment of them as mere historical curiosities. All three are presented as viable, defensible theories, despite the powerful objections that must be faced by each. One reviewer of the manuscript believes that I have been too harsh on utilitarianism. This would come as a shock to those who have been exposed to my philosophical opinions, and I take this review as evidence that I have at least succeeded in liberating the volume from an unduly biased presentation. I do not, however, regard this attempt at fairness as a forced contrivance merely useful in introducing students to moral theory. I believe that each of these three classical theories *is* an eminently defensible, living option in contemporary ethics.

Some friends have asked why I reordered history by presenting Mill first (in Chapter 3), Kant second (in Chapter 4), and Aristotle third (in Chapter 5). The reason is uncomplicated: I believe that utilitarianism is the least intricate of these theories and that Kantianism is best learned and appreciated as a reaction to certain alleged deficiencies in utilitarianism. Finally, Aristotelianism—at least in its form as a type of virtue ethics—is best presented as providing alternatives to the obligation-based utilitarian and Kantian accounts. I have thus allowed pedagogy to override history in the ordering of these three chapters.

Ethics courses in philosophy departments tend nowadays to be courses either in traditional ethical theory or in so-called applied ethics. (The latter explores problems of public policy, dilemmas of private morality, and issues of professional ethics in such fields as medicine, business, law, journalism, social science, and engineering.) Students tend to be attracted to applied ethics, while their teachers gravitate by training and interest to more theoretical and historical materials.* Because I reject the mentality of compartmentalization that underlies this entrenched division, I move freely in this book from case studies and issues in private, professional, and public ethics to various more traditional concerns in ethical theory. I am convinced of the importance of training students to reason both without fear of theoretical irrelevancies and without disdain for practical applications. I am equally convinced that the method of analyzing case studies in terms of ethical principles, and vice versa, is an aid in such training, not a hindrance. For this reason, every chapter in this text begins with a case study and contains numerous practical applications.

Many friendly critics helped improve this book. Will Aiken, Tom Auxter, Ruth Faden, Hugh LaFollette, and R. Jay Wallace, Jr., deserve special mention for their penetrating and thorough commentaries on every chapter. Their influence has been enormous, as has the impact of many discussions over the years with James Childress,

---

* This distinction and others, as well as the arguments that surround them in contemporary philosophy, are intelligently explored in Bernard Rosen and Arthur L. Caplan, *Ethics in the Undergraduate Curriculum* (Hastings-on-Hudson, N.Y.: The Hastings Center, 1980), pp. 12ff.

Arnold Davidson, and Donald Seldin. For some comments on earlier materials that led to Chapters 2, 6, 7, and 8, I am indebted to Dick Wasserstrom, Alasdair MacIntyre, Robert L. Simon, Joel Feinberg, William T. Blackstone, Burton Leiser, Norman Daniels, Norman Bowie, and Louis Katzner. For comments on several chapters in later drafts I owe thanks to Raymond Herbenick, Thomas Mappes, LeRoy Walters, and Jane Zembaty.

Several students and members of the Kennedy Institute of Ethics at Georgetown University also aided me immeasurably. Abigail Evans, Sally Finnerty, Rolland Pack, and Dorle Vawter contributed in numerous ways by proposing reconstructions, checking references, reading proofs, and making helpful suggestions regarding style and substance. William Pitt prepared the index with his customary facility. Most important, I am grateful to Mary Ellen Timbol for guiding the manuscript through all its stages. Without her assistance, together with that of Mary Baker, Kyle Ward, and Emilie Dolge, the book would have been long delayed. Finally, generous support from the Kennedy Foundation has made long stretches of work on the manuscript possible, and I am pleased to acknowledge this source of support.

T. L. B.

PHILOSOPHICAL ETHICS

PART ONE

Fundamental
Questions

CHAPTER ONE

Morality and Moral Philosophy

In this book we shall encounter many perplexing moral problems together with ethical theories that indicate how these problems should be handled. Each chapter begins with a case study that is analyzed in the subsequent pages. The following case introduces several matters discussed in this chapter. In particular, it helps us understand how moral behavior can be studied by social scientists, how moral problems can arise unexpectedly and require one to take a moral position, how moral controversies can arise as a result, and how moral philosophy can be used to guide evaluation of such problems.

In 1971 Philip G. Zimbardo, a professor at Stanford University, constructed a mock prison environment in the basement of a laboratory at the university. He solicited two dozen male student volunteers from several colleges throughout the United States and Canada to act out the roles of prisoners and guards in those surroundings for a daily wage of $15. The experiment was designed to explore the effects of an extreme and rigid institutional situation on individual attitudes and behavior. It had been planned to run for two weeks; but, after six days, Zimbardo decided to discontinue it prematurely. The reason for this premature termination was surprising: the student subjects randomly assigned to play the role of prisoners suffered abuse at the hands of subjects acting as guards. As Zimbardo himself put it, "Volunteer prisoners suffered physical and psychological abuse hour after hour for days. . . . Many of the 'prisoners' were in serious distress, and many of the 'guards' were behaving in ways which brutalized and degraded their fellow subjects."

Once inside the mock prison environment, differences in uniform and power helped to segregate the two groups of subjects. The simulation was realistic enough to elicit what Zimbardo describes as "pathological reactions" from the majority of the participants. The guards were both verbally and physically abusive, readily assuming "dehumanizing" postures with respect to those acting as prisoners.

Zimbardo's results allegedly showed that the prison environment exerts a powerful effect on the actions and attitudes of people situated within it, a conclusion that in his opinion provides a critical insight into the degrading effects of institutional roles and rules. Zimbardo stressed the influence and importance of his findings and argued that his research was socially beneficial. He cited both the publicity that his project attracted in the popular press and the frequency with which government and community officials consulted him about prison reform as evidence that his results were reaching a wide audience and were directly affecting public policymaking. There were no reported long-term negative reactions due to the study, and a majority of the subjects said that it was a "valuable didactic experience" for them.

Critics disputed Zimbardo's claims about the overall beneficial consequences of his results, contending that they revealed nothing about prison environments that had not already been known. Objections focused on the harmful consequences of the study for the subjects. These consequences included high levels of emotional stress and even a certain amount of physical discomfort and abuse that were introduced in order to produce a highly realistic prison setting. Subjects who assumed the role of prisoners suffered humiliation and physical degradation at the hands of the guards, while the guards found it severely trying to come to terms with their capacity for inflicting such harms. Many commentators considered these harmful consequences sufficient to outweigh the benefits of the results, and concluded that the research was therefore morally unjustifiable.

However, prior to the experiment, Zimbardo did inform his subjects of his purposes and of the possibility that the methods employed would pose certain risks. To the extent that the subjects consented to participate in an experiment whose purposes and some of whose dangers they understood beforehand, it could be argued that the project was morally justifiable despite the subsequent harmful effects on the subjects. By being informed in advance, the subjects were given an opportunity to exercise their right to self-determination; and by stopping the experiment when it became clear that the stressful effects far exceeded anything the subjects had consented to experience, Zimbardo signaled his willingness to respect their expressed wishes and intentions. Nonetheless, the subjects were not informed that some of them would be "arrested" by local police as the first step in the simulation study, and in general the advance specification of possible harms gave subjects little indication of the intensity of the stress they were to experience. Zimbardo explained the lapse by arguing that members of the project staff had no reason to anticipate such high levels of intensity before initiating the study. For example, none of the student profiles, which had been carefully collected in advance, indicated that there might be such reactions.*

*This case study is developed from Philip G. Zimbardo, "On the Ethics of Intervention in Human Psychological Research: With Special Reference to the Stanford Prison Experiment," *Cognition,* **2**: 2 (1973), 243–256; Donald P. Warwick, "Types of Harm in Social Research," in *Ethical Issues in Social Science Research* (Baltimore: Johns Hopkins University Press, 1982); and P. G. Zimbardo, C. Haney, W. C. Banks, and D. Jaffe, "The Mind as a Formidable Jailor: A Pirandellian Prison," *The New York Times Magazine* (April 8, 1973), section 6, 38–60.

While this case is hardly typical of our everyday experience, certain aspects of it can help us understand both everyday morality and moral philosophy.

THE CONCEPT OF MORALITY

As we reflect on Zimbardo's study, we inevitably encounter moral questions. Is what Zimbardo did really wrong? Was his experiment right or wrong from the start, or did it just turn out right or wrong—or is that question even sensible? We may go on to ponder whether our moral rules are equipped to handle the complexities involved in this case and thus whether we can reach any satisfactory moral conclusions about Zimbardo's motives and actions. These questions may in turn lead us to wonder whether our moral rules fit together in a unified system and whether inconsistencies and conflicts among rules are avoidable.

Such questions and reflections are philosophical, and we shall meet them many times in this book. However, both this case and our everyday knowledge of the English language indicate that the words "ethics" and "morality" cannot be confined to *philosophical* contexts. In its broadest and most familiar meaning, morality is concerned with many forms of belief about right and wrong human conduct. These normative beliefs are expressed through such general terms as "good," "bad," "virtuous," "praiseworthy," "right," "ought," and "blameworthy." On the other hand, there are many social institutions in which these same terms are used to evaluate human endeavors, and these institutions are sometimes remarkably similar to morality. Religion, law, etiquette, economics, and politics are all similar in this respect, for they all involve the evaluation of conduct, and they all use a similar vocabulary of action-directing terms. We may ask, then, "What is distinctive about morality?" or, more generally, "How is morality as an institution distinct from all other areas of human endeavor in which normative judgments occur?" Since this is a book about morality, we need at least a rough and ready answer to this question. Once we have explored it in Part One and have arrived at a general idea of what morality is, we can proceed in Part Two to questions about the nature of a "moral position." The object or purpose of morality is examined in Part Three; and finally, in Part Four, different approaches that have been taken to the study of morality are discussed, including the approaches found in the later chapters of this book.

Some problems involved in answering the question "What is morality?" can be illustrated by a tale told by John Dean in his testimony before Congress regarding the Watergate scandal that led to the resignation of President Richard Nixon. According to Dean, when the Watergate burglars were arrested, the intent of higher officials at the White House was immediately to effect a cover-up. That is, in his judgment there was never really any question whether the full story of a burglary in the offices of an opposition party should be made public. It was simply assumed that these facts must be concealed. There were different reasons for this view—some in the White House feared prosecution, some feared impeachment, and some feared the overthrow of the country by radicals—but the imperative to cover up was, according to Dean, accepted spontaneously and unanimously. Millions of people who followed this testimony, and Dean himself, subsequently argued that the burglars had done something *morally* wrong, whether or not it was illegal. It is now well established that at least some of their actions were *illegal,* and that the whole affair was politically ill-advised, but nothing obviously follows from these judgments about the *immorality* of the actions. Indeed, one of the early witnesses in the congressional hearings (Bernard Barker) defended the burglary itself as both patriotic and morally proper, whatever its legality.

The question we are investigating is *not* the one that was directly on the minds of millions who followed Dean's testimony in the Watergate scandal. They were asking whether certain actions were "moral" in the sense of *morally correct* or "not moral" in the sense of *morally incorrect.* We are asking the very different question, "Why are such actions, motives, or judgments categorized as *moral* at all?" We can ask the same question about Zimbardo's experiment: "Why does it present *moral* issues at all?" This sense of "moral" is the opposite of the word "nonmoral," not the opposite of "immoral." When Dean was testifying, he was of course using "moral" as the opposite of "immoral," a word used evaluatively to categorize an action as morally incorrect by condemning the action or the person who performs it. In this sense, the word "moral" means "morally good" or "morally right" or "morally virtuous"; in the first sense, it is used only to distinguish the moral from that which is not moral. We are asking, then, what it is about certain actions or judgments that places them in the sphere of morality as contrasted with the other-than-moral (not the *im*moral).

Morality as a Social Institution

In attempting to answer the question, "What is morality?" we may be tempted to reply that morality is a concept, or perhaps a set of rules. If we are influenced by social-scientific approaches such as the one used by Zimbardo, we might answer that morality is a type of psychological reaction or a distinctive form of learned behavior; and if we are influenced by religion, perhaps we will hold that morality is properly a set of divine commands. Morality may be connected in some way with all these matters, but most obviously it seems to be a social institution with a code of learnable rules. Like political constitutions and languages, morality exists before we are instructed in its relevant rules and regulations; we learn these existing requirements and their appropriate applications as we grow up. As we develop beyond infancy, we learn moral rules alongside other important social rules, and this is one reason why it later becomes difficult to distinguish the two. For example, we are constantly bombarded in our early years with rules such as, "Don't swim near the rocks," "Don't cross the street without looking both ways," and "See your physician for an annual checkup." Most of these rules are instructions in our own interest, teaching us about the various kinds of *prudent behavior.* We are also taught rules of a different kind. We are told by parents, teachers, and peers that certain things ought or ought not to be done because they affect the interests of other people: "Don't color your sister's photographs." "Don't lie to your father and mother." "It is better to give than to receive." "Respect the rights of others." These are elementary instructions in morality, for they express what society expects of us in terms of taking the interests of other people into account. We thus learn about *moral* behavior.

Morality is usually contrasted with prudence or self-interest *because* morality does require taking account of the interests of others. (In Chapter 2 we shall encounter one theory, ethical egoism, that challenges this claim.) Yet, is this not also true of such social institutions as law, etiquette, and religion? These institutions are both social and action-guiding; they tell us what we must do or ought to do, and they demand that we pay attention to the interests of others. They have also seemed to some people to be the source or foundation of many of our moral beliefs. How, then, can they be distinguished from morality?

One important answer to this question is that many such social institutions, especially law and etiquette, can be distinguished from morality only by the degree of their social importance, and that these institutions do *not* differ in kind or in substantive content. The English philosopher John Hartland-Swann defends this thesis in the following illuminating article by arguing that the concept of morality refers to the keeping or violating of customs considered to be socially important.

JOHN HARTLAND-SWANN

The Moral and the Non-Moral*

First of all, it is clear enough that the terms "moral" and "ethical" respectively derive from Latin and Greek words meaning "pertaining to *custom* or *customs*." Anyone can reassure himself on this point by consulting a Latin dictionary and a Greek lexicon, or, if neither of these is handy, the *Shorter Oxford English Dictionary*. It remains true, however, that not all, and not even perhaps the majority of customs in any given community are regarded as moral, and their neglect or rejection immoral. It is customary, in most Western countries, to eat solid food with a knife and fork; but we do not call someone who fails to do this, preferring to use his fin-

gers, immoral—although we might well condemn him in some milder way. If on the other hand we moved among the Indian community of Singapore, we should find that it is customary among many educated Indians to eat their food with their fingers; but they would certainly not condemn a fellow-Indian as immoral for choosing to eat with a knife and fork. Again, we sometimes find ourselves condemning as immoral certain customs, either among our own community or (as is more frequently the case) among foreign communities, which are regarded as either perfectly moral or perhaps morally neutral by those who practise them. Finally, we often become seriously perplexed when, with the utmost tolerance and impartiality, we try to decide which of the customs of some "primitive" or non-literate people are to be

*From John Hartland-Swann, *An Analysis of Morals* (London: George Allen & Unwin, Ltd., 1960). Reprinted by permission of the publisher.

classed as forming part of their moral code and which are to fall into some other classification. . . .

It would be foolish to try to equate the customary with the moral. A simple piece of logical technique will serve to reinforce this point. It always makes sense to utter queries or comments like the following: "I know it's the custom here, but is it moral?" or "I gather that headhunting is an ingrained custom with this tribe, but don't you think it's a thoroughly beastly and immoral custom?" or "I wonder if fornication is really immoral?—it's customary in some communities and condemned in others." In short, despite the etymological origin of "moral," it clearly does not mean, today at least, the same as "customary" or "consonant with custom." What then is the significance of the apparent detachment of the "moral" from the "customary"?

Let us notice for a start that it is not so detached as we might at first think; simply because those actions or kinds of behaviour which are commonly regarded as moral, in any particular community, are not the unusual or the abnormal—on the contrary, they are the customary actions or kinds of behaviour, or, more precisely, those which have *become* customary. It is the general custom, in most communities, to tell the truth and refrain from lying, to keep and not break promises, to show kindness and not cruelty to other human beings, to protect the weak and aged, to show respect to parents and so on.

It is also, however, the custom in every community to do a lot of things—to eat food in certain ways, wear certain kinds of clothes, play certain kinds of games—none of which would be regarded as specifically moral by any member of the community concerned. What then is it that differentiates a moral from a morally neutral custom? To answer this will be to solve our problem. But the answer is a little complicated and has become overlaid with sophistication by some moral philosophers. . . .

In primitive societies certain customs, and certain patterns of behaviour, came to be regarded as *more important* than others—more important because they directly affected the lives and happiness of all members of the tribe, or because they indirectly affected the tribe's security, food supply, and general amenities. The observance of these customs, or the maintenance of these behaviour patterns, was therefore hedged about with taboos; and sanctions were imposed, of greater or lesser severity, for the neglect or violation of these taboos. . . .

In cases where the infringed customs are considered very important, then the sanctions take the form of actual physical punishment—a fine, imprisonment, or even the death penalty. Such infringements are covered by what we call the legal code of the community concerned. In other cases, where the custom infringed, though important, is considered less socially significant, the sanctions consist of overt blame or silent disapproval—which blame or disapproval is usually present, possibly in a more stringent form, in the case of infringements of customs whose violation brings the offender within the scope of legal sanctions. In yet other cases, where the customs violated are deemed to have far less, if any, social significance, disapproval will be of a far milder nature. It is these three types of cases which crystallize out into legal offences, moral misdemeanours, and lapses of etiquette. The trouble is, however, that what may be legally penalized in one community may only be morally condemned in another, and just mildly censured in yet another—according to the time and the place and the nature of the community or civilization concerned. . . .

Morality then—despite the sophistications often favoured by moral philosophers and which we shall discuss in a moment—is, I suggest, the term or concept which refers to the keeping or violating of customs considered socially important—important in the mutual relations between man and man and between a man and his community. We tend to lose sight of this simply because moral rules (positive and negative prescriptions) appear to have an independent existence and special authority which exempt us from enquiring into their *raison d'être;* but we can easily remind ourselves of the origin of moral rules by referring their content to our current social values. It is true that in any given community, ancient or modern, it is not always easy to determine how much of its morality is freely accepted and how much imposed by some powerful body of elders or by social tradition. But this does not affect the status of the moral. The moral will turn out to be what is regarded, freely or by conditioning, as the socially important as regards conduct and dispositions. If I see a small child drowning in a canal, and I have a new suit on and am due to meet a friend in a few minutes, then, while it is important for me to preserve my suit and keep my appointment, it is much more important for me, if I have a moral sense, to rescue the child and save its life; for I recognize that this is a moral duty, i.e., that it is *socially* important. . . .

We see at once how it *comes about* that one type of conduct is called moral by one community, since its performance is regarded as socially important and its neglect or violation socially disastrous; and how it is that the same type of conduct is not called either moral or immoral by another community, since neither its performance nor its neglect is regarded as socially important. Thus we see why a practice such as incest was not deemed immoral by the ancient Egyptians; for, wisely or unwisely, they did not regard its avoidance as important from a social point of view. Again, we can now see—although there is a lot more to be said about this later—how the specifically "immoral" can shade off into the "naughty" or the "unsportsmanlike," according to the degree of social importance attached to the type of conduct in question by the particular individual concerned. . . .

We can now see what it is that differentiates the moral from the non-moral whether problems or issues, judgments, or principles, or ends are at stake. And we can test our theory without much difficulty.

Suppose someone regards truth-telling and promise-keeping as moral issues; and suppose he asks himself why he and the community at large regard truth-telling and promise-keeping as moral issues, and choosing a motor car and playing cricket as non-moral issues. Provided he does not make an appeal to a religious authority of some sort, what answer can he give himself, if he thinks it out, other than to admit that truth-telling and promise-keeping derive their moral status from their preponderant social importance? Notice carefully that the question "Is truth-telling a moral issue?" is quite different from the question "Why should I tell the truth?" The answer to the second question depends on whether or not I have subscribed to the general moral prescription "One ought always (or generally) to tell the truth"—and if I have subscribed to that principle, then I am *logically* bound to tell the truth unless the situation is such as to enable me to invoke another general principle which I deem to absolve me from truth-telling in this particular case. Nevertheless, when a person subscribes to such principles as "The truth ought generally to be told," or "Promises made ought generally to be kept," he is in effect subscribing to such principles just because—even if he has forgotten this or never even knew about it—such principles have acquired or been endowed with a special authority on account of their being about issues of great social importance.

At the same time—as earlier arguments have been designed to show—there is nothing which is "intrinsically" or "unconditionally" or "absolutely" moral—or immoral; what is moral, or immoral, depends on the degree of social importance attached to its performance, or avoidance, by some particular community at some particular time and in some particular place. Or, where there is a divergence between individual and community moral appraisals, what is moral or immoral depends, so far as the individual is concerned, on what *he* regards as socially important and thus considers ought to be regarded as socially important by the community, or perhaps by humanity as a whole. That there is a large measure of agreement concerning what is to be regarded as socially important (to do or not to do) in the sphere of human conduct is something which is obvious. It is also something for which we may be thankful; for the general stability of social life depends on a widespread agreement—which is never, however, a universal agreement—that certain principles are to be called moral or immoral principles, and certain types of behaviour moral or immoral behaviour. But this same thesis explains—and it would be totally inadequate if it failed to do this—how it comes about that both communities and individuals differ, not only about what is morally justifiable or nonjustifiable, but about what is to be regarded as a moral issue at all. . . .

There are many more theories which have been propounded regarding the properties a rule or judgment *must* have in order to rank as moral; but all such theories are doing is to *stipulate* that this or that property must be present and to hope that we will agree with the stipulation. My own view must also be classed as a theory, but a theory of a very different kind. For it is a theory about what has in fact *caused* various communities to label certain rules moral and others non-moral, or, more broadly, it is a theory devised to account for the notion of morality which all or most of us have.

No doubt Hartland-Swann has given us a useful insight by showing that morality is closely related to socially important customs; yet, it is worth considering whether he overlooks the possibility that morality can be distinguished from both law (legal codes) and etiquette by features *other than* their relative social importance. In addressing this issue, we should be careful to avoid the conclusion that its resolution provides definitive reasons for completely rejecting Hartland-Swann's account. His account may need only minor correction and augmentation.

In the first place, it deserves notice that morality demands a whole way of life governed by certain acceptable principles and motives. Such broad and demanding requirements are not involved in law or etiquette. This seems to give morality greater importance than law or etiquette in one's personal life—even if not greater *social* importance. Further, because laws are often grounded in certain moral convictions that lead legislators to enact them, they may formalize or codify what is morally *already* of the greatest social importance. Laws against theft, murder, and discrimination are based upon moral beliefs about stealing, killing, and treating others as equals; and before they attained any legal status, these beliefs were of the highest social importance. Hartland-Swann would have us believe that moral rules occupy a secondary status of relative importance in comparison with legal rules (what he calls "the legal code of the community"). His comparison between legal offenses and "moral misdemeanours" is not implausible, but if some legal rules are structured on the basis of moral beliefs, then it is doubtful that legal codes can be said to be *more* socially important than moral codes. For example, let us suppose that no set of rules is more important to a society than its political constitution (and its subsequent development of constitutional law). But if the constitution itself is based on, and justified in terms of, moral standards, as constitutions commonly have been, how can it be argued that morality occupies a position of lesser social importance than law? We overturn, rewrite, or amend laws and constitutions when we see their moral deficiency or incompleteness; and we often refer to such laws, before their reformulation, as "unjust" and "morally impoverished." At most, then, it has been shown by Hartland-Swann that *some* moral offenses are less socially important than *some* violations of law.

Because many moral convictions seem to rank at least as high in the order of social importance as laws, it is difficult to accept Hartland-Swann's analysis without some modification of his claim that three levels of socially important customs "crystallize out into legal offenses, moral misdemeanours, and lapses of etiquette." However, on a more generous interpretation, it could be held that Hartland-Swann is concerned principally to distinguish morality from matters of etiquette and prudence and is not much interested in the distinctions between morality and law. Whatever the resolution of this interpretative question, we have not as yet found a need to reject his more general thesis that morality is to be understood in terms of socially important customs, beliefs, and rules. Let us now see whether this more general thesis also needs modification.

Defining Marks of the Moral

In some literature on the nature of morality, the social-institution analysis is augmented (or even abandoned) through an analysis of one or more of four criteria of moral judgments, principles, and ideals. These criteria will here be referred to as "marks of the moral," for each criterion has been presented as a factor which is centrally characteristic of moral beliefs. We shall see that the four marks of the moral, like the social-institution analysis, leave us with unresolved questions about the nature of morality, and therefore are not entirely satisfactory as an analysis of the concept. We can, however, learn much about what morality is and what it is not by critically examining these marks.

1. One of these criteria takes up where the "importance" part of Hartland-Swann's social-importance thesis left off. According to this first criterion, a judgment, principle, or ideal is moral only if a person (or alternatively a society) accepts it as *supremely authoritative or overriding* as a guide to action. To put it another way, this criterion says that morality must have priority over everything else in our lives. The secondary status ascribed to morality by Hartland-Swann will not do, according to the proponents of this criterion. For example, it can plausibly be maintained that principles which require avoidance of the harms that occurred in Zimbardo's experiment and that led to its premature termination are matters of such overriding importance that when they conflict with other objectives—such as the goals of Zimbardo's research—the authority of the principles prevails. For such reasons, Alan Gewirth—one representative of this approach—says that morality "purports to set, for everyone's conduct, requirements that take precedence over all other modes of guiding action, including even the self-interest of the persons to whom it is addressed."*

Morality has often been presented as Gewirth here depicts it, and there can be little doubt that it plays a central and important role in our lives. Nonetheless, it is doubtful that this first proposed mark or criterion is a necessary condition of morality. For one thing, it asserts that a principle or ideal is moral only if a person (or a society) is committed to its pursuit as overriding. Yet, as the discussion of Hartland-Swann's essay indicates, legal and other kinds of considerations can outweigh moral considerations when they are somehow in conflict. Moral considerations will often override other considerations, but not always. It is not evident that a moral principle must always override nonmoral principles even if society advances the principle as having the highest social importance. Most of us do not act as if we believed that moral demands ought always to take precedence over other demands; and social morality itself often seems to leave it an open question whether moral considerations override every other form of duty or demand. To hold that supremacy or "overridingness" is a necessary condition of morality is to prejudge the weight or priority that people must give moral principles when they are required to choose between them and other considerations—political, legal, religious, and prudential considerations, for example. As we shall see in Chapter 9 in some detail, moral considerations cannot be shown to outweigh or override all competing considerations merely *because* they are moral. This first criterion, then, is suggestive but hardly decisive.

2. According to a second criterion, moral statements are distinguished from others by their *prescriptive form;* that is, they are action-guiding imperatives that do not *describe* states of affairs in the way that "A basement at Stanford University housed Zimbardo's experiment" is descriptive. By this criterion, the injunction, "You ought not to continue the experiments," like all moral utterances, guides behavior by prescribing a particular restraint or course of action. Those who support this criterion (such as R. M. Hare, whose work is studied in Chapter 10) do not claim that morality *alone* is composed of prescriptive statements. Obviously, statements of law and etiquette, for example, can be prescriptive. The claim is merely that prescriptivity is a necessary condition of a moral judgment, principle, or ideal, and this is certainly an attractive proposal.

There are, however, problems with this second mark or criterion as well. Judgments such as "Zimbardo harmed his subjects" can constitute moral accusations, yet they are not obviously prescriptive, since their point is to blame or censure. Similarly, "Zimbardo's intentions were good" and "The character of a hero is praiseworthy" are evaluative statements, yet they do not issue clear imperatives to follow a course of action. Even such straightforward moral statements as "He is a morally virtuous man" or "His father failed in his moral upbringing" cannot easily be analyzed as prescriptive, for they do not clearly prescribe any actions. The supporter of the prescriptive thesis

---

*Alan Gewirth, *Reason and Morality* (Chicago: University of Chicago Press, 1978), p. 1.

will respond that these utterances are implicitly or subtly prescriptive, and can be restated in a more definitively prescriptive form. This claim is doubtful, however, for one may have to change the meaning of such utterances in order to *make* them prescriptive; and many doubts therefore linger in contemporary philosophy about this second criterion of morality. (We shall thoroughly explore this problem in Chapter 10.) On the other hand, most of the moral judgments, principles, and ideals that will be encountered in this text *do* prescribe, usually by specifying a duty. Therefore, this second criterion provides a useful insight into much moral discourse.

3. A third and widely accepted criterion for moral judgments, principles, and ideals is *universalizability*. According to this criterion, moral considerations should apply in a similar way to all people situated in relevantly similar circumstances. As Gewirth put it, morality sets rules "for everyone's conduct." We shall see in Chapter 3 that Immanuel Kant also maintains that moral principles impose unconditional, categorical demands on all alike, without regard to differences in persons.

It is quite plausible to hold that this third criterion is a necessary condition of morality, and many philosophers have accepted it. Nonetheless, its plausibility will depend on how tightly or loosely it is formulated. In some weak formulations, the criterion seems uncontroversially to capture a necessary condition of morality. For example, consistency requires that whenever we judge an act under a certain description to be right (or wrong), we are logically committed to judging *all relevantly similar* acts under the same description right (or wrong), whether or not we are interested in specifically moral rightness or wrongness. If a person holds that one act (such as Zimbardo's experiment) is right and another act (such as an identically designed experiment) wrong, but cannot point to any relevant differences between them, the judgment seems both arbitrary and without rational foundation.

It is less certain, however, that the criterion of universalizability is a necessary condition of morality if formulated differently. If we understand the criterion to hold that *all* moral principles apply universally to everyone alike and never apply solely to restricted groups or to individuals, then we have raised a hornets' nest of issues that must be put off until we come to the subjects of relativism and disagreement in Chapter 2. Suffice it to note here that many regard the criterion of universalizability as outlandishly provincial *under this second formulation*. Alasdair MacIntyre has argued, for example, that we are tempted to believe that moral judgments are universalizable in this sense only because we forget that moral judgments are tailored to particular cultures and systems of thought beyond which they are often not intended to apply. (MacIntyre's defense of this thesis appears in Chapter 2 of this text.) Some would also argue that many moral positions involve a significant measure of personal choice which even the individual making the choice would not wish to generalize for others. For example, Zimbardo himself indicates that he would not wish to generalize his conclusions about terminating his research for *all* social psychologists at all times. If another psychologist had continued the research, Zimbardo apparently would not have considered that decision immoral. As a second example, "I ought to terminate life-support systems for a seriously ill member of the family because she requests it of me" is not easily generalizable (on the second interpretation) for others or even for oneself in the case of other family members. Nonetheless, this third criterion, as it was formulated earlier, does provide one helpful way of understanding moral beliefs—a criterion that constitutes a necessary condition of moral judgments.

4. Finally, some philosophers have proposed a fourth mark or criterion of morality, one focused on moral content rather than on such formal considerations as those we have thus far encountered. These philosophers argue that it is necessary for a moral action-guide to have some direct reference to *human flourishing,* to consider the *welfare of others,* or at the very least to be concerned with *harm and benefit to other persons.* This condition excludes judgments, principles, or ideals pertaining exclusively to personal benefit, and it thus accords with common usage of the term "morality." The anthropologist Colin Turnbull argues, for example, that the African mountain people he studied, known as the Ik, have *no morality* even though they have social rules. He makes this claim on the basis of findings which showed that their lives are entirely oriented toward self-interest. Setting aside the matter of self-interested judgments, however, we can say that most moral principles and virtues do involve, at least obliquely, some reference to human welfare. We saw, for example, that virtually all the principles cited in the Zimbardo case centered on the welfare of his subjects. Moreover, many recognizable virtues, such as honesty, courage, temperance, justice, compassion, obedience, and reliability, clearly have something to do with the welfare of others. It seems attractive, then, to hold that anyone who makes a moral judgment must have the welfare of others in mind.

Yet, the reference to human welfare involved in moral rules or judgments is often so oblique or noncommittal that we may wonder about the exact requirements and implications of this proposed criterion. As it has generally been formulated, the criterion refers to the welfare or benefit of only *some* persons, not to *everyone's* welfare or even to the welfare of the majority. Codes of etiquette and systems of law, as we have seen, satisfy the criterion when formulated in this way. Furthermore, the criterion is compatible with many views that are blatantly immoral—various forms of discrimination giving preferential treatment to dominant and prejudiced groups being but one of many possible examples. Thus, in order to accept this fourth criterion, we must possess a well-developed conception of *how* morality makes reference to human welfare. Fortunately, we will have ample opportunity to pursue this goal, since much of this text deals with precisely that issue.*

*Many formulations of this fourth criterion also run the danger of asserting the correctness of substantive moral positions based on purely conceptual or definitional considerations about the concept of morality—although, as William Frankena has argued, this controversy again depends on how one formulates the fourth condition. The philosophical problem is whether the *concept* of morality can be analyzed without at the same time committing one to a moral position incompatible with certain other moral views that are excluded as moral by the analysis. Some have argued that any substantive restriction on what counts as a moral rule or reason in effect asserts a moral position rather than merely presenting an analysis of the concept of morality. W. K. Frankena, "What Is Morality?" in his *Thinking about Morality* (Ann Arbor: University of Michigan Press, 1980), pp. 1–40; "The Concept of Morality," *Journal of Philosophy,* **63** (1966), section 2, reprinted, together with his related article "On Defining Moral Judgments, Principles, and Codes," in Kenneth E. Goodpaster, ed., *Perspectives on Morality: Essays of William K. Frankena* (Notre Dame, Ind.: University of Notre Dame Press, 1976).

The Pluralist Solution

It remains controversial in contemporary philosophy whether these four marks of the moral, or some combination of them, can be sharpened enough to constitute jointly sufficient conditions distinguishing the moral from the nonmoral. We have seen thus far that no one of the marks clearly holds (depending on its formulation) for *all* moral judgments, principles, and ideals; and thus none is clearly a *necessary* condition of morality. This does not show definitively that all four together do not constitute a *sufficient* criterion of morality. Many have been skeptical, however, that they constitute jointly sufficient conditions or even that this is the best way to treat the four marks of the moral.

One alternative—which will here be referred to as a "pluralistic answer" to the question "What is morality?"—is that the term cannot be given any single exhaustive definition or analysis in terms of marks of the moral, because there are too many senses of "moral" and too many marks or criteria that we use to classify judgments or actions as moral. At least one philosopher (Alasdair MacIntyre) has argued that we no longer have a unified concept of morality, because it has been fragmented by different traditions. Another philosopher (C. H. Whiteley) has argued that there are so many different senses that no useful purpose can be served by attempting to unravel them. A more plausible view, however, is that there is no single *set* of marks that must always be present for a judgment, principle, or ideal to be moral, but there are nonetheless several marks that are frequently present and that are relevant to the classification of a judgment as moral. According to this approach, an intricate pattern of combinations of properties is sufficient for saying that we have a "concept" of morality. Any judgment, principle, or ideal that has *some* of these properties can be moral, though the absence of a property relevant to morality counts against a judgment's being moral. The following diagram illustrates this proposal:

MORALITY

M_1	M_2	M_3	M_4	M_5
ABCD	ABCE	ABDE	ACDE	BCDE

A = is accorded great social importance
B = harmonizes pro and con interests to reduce conflict in society
C = is derived from religious doctrines that guide conduct
D = is universalizable and prescriptive in form
E = is supremely authoritative and overrides nonmoral rules and principles

This diagram represents the view that morality is not one thing but many things in combination (M_1 through M_5), for no particular *set* of characteristics such as *A–E* and no *single* criterion such as *A*, *B*, *C*, *D*, or *E* is necessary for proper use of the term "moral"; and an unlimited variety of resembling combinations is sufficient. Because only *some* of these characteristics must be present, there can be different senses of morality, such as those found in theological ethics and professional ethics and the "personal morality" involved in sexual morals (as contrasted with the "social morality" of whole societies). What makes Zimbardo's case a moral matter, then, may be very different from what makes the Watergate scandal or polygamy a moral matter, and yet they may all involve genuinely moral problems.

Thus, the controversy discussed in this section on the concept of morality in the end apparently turns on whether an adequate treatment can be given of some combination of criteria, such as the four marks of the moral analyzed previously, perhaps in conjunction with a criterion of social importance. If a treatment cannot be given that shows some set of criteria both necessary and sufficient for morality—and most philosophers seem satisfied that it has not yet been given—then the pluralists' alternative must surely be judged an attractive one. On the other hand, we should not conclude this section without appreciating the attractiveness and significance of the four marks of the moral and of what has been learned by examining them. It is highly likely that if all four of these marks are present in any judgment, principle, or ideal, then we have a *moral* judgment, principle, or ideal. Thus, if some judgment has overriding social importance, prescribes a course of action, is universalizable, and pertains to the general welfare of a social group, we can be reasonably assured that the judgment is a moral one—or at least this is a plausible hypothesis to be held in mind as we encounter the many theories of ethics found in the subsequent chapters of this text.

THE CONCEPT OF A MORAL POSITION

This text contains a number of selections by philosophers who take a *moral position* on issues. While we now have some understanding of the nature of morality, virtually nothing has been said thus far about the distinction between taking a moral position and taking some other kind of position on, for example, a prominent social controversy. In this section, exclusive attention is given to the concept of a moral position. Examination of this concept will also provide us with a more adequate understanding of the concept of morality, for the two notions are clearly interconnected.

We all have some familiarity with puzzles about the nature of a moral position. People often act as if they had the weight of morality behind their pronouncements when others are suspicious that the "moral position" has anything to do with morality. For example, in the summer of 1980, a United States senator accused France of immorally providing nuclear capabilities to certain Arab countries in the middle east in return for rights to oil. The senator clearly held a position on an issue, but was it a moral one, or was it entirely rooted in some political, personal, or even prejudiced conception of foreign policy? Again, Zimbardo accused his critics of reacting emotionally to his research and thereby of confusing their *personal* views with a sober, properly distanced *moral* position. Can such a distinction be sustained, and if so, how? These questions lead us to reflect more generally on how a moral position is properly contrasted with merely prejudiced, personal, or political positions, as well as with positions rooted in emotion or rationalization.

To illustrate this problem further, consider an issue that will occupy us at length in Chapter 8: we will there encounter the view that laws should be passed to protect a society's most cherished and deeply embedded "moral" beliefs, especially its restrictions on sexual conduct. According to one prominent argument, advanced most notably by the English jurist Patrick Devlin, society has the right to enforce "public morality" because society cannot exist, or at least cannot remain secure, unless it preserves a basic community of "moral ideas" which determine how citizens must control their lives. Devlin maintains that society is justified, as a matter of principle, in legislating against private immoral conduct if that conduct is likely to be injurious to society by endangering any part of the moral order necessary for the preservation of that society. Adultery, for example, may legally be prohibited because it would undermine the institution of marriage, which Devlin takes to be indispensable for the stability of society. He also contends that homosexuality and prostitution undermine the moral fabric of society. Each can quite properly be legally restricted, then, using society's "moral position" as a basis.*

Some philosophers have objected that Devlin has a mistaken conception of both a social morality and a moral position in general. In the following essay, Ronald Dworkin, a prominent contemporary critic of Devlin, attempts to explain what a moral position is and how Devlin is confused in thinking that social morality constitutes such a moral position.

*See Patrick Devlin, *The Enforcement of Morals* (Oxford, England: Oxford University Press, 1965), especially chap. 1.

RONALD DWORKIN

The Concept of a Moral Position†

We might start with the fact that terms like "moral position" and "moral conviction" function in our conventional morality as terms of justification and criticism, as well as of description. It is true that we sometimes speak of a group's "morals," or "morality," or "moral beliefs," or "moral positions" or "moral convictions," in what might be called an anthropological sense, meaning to refer to whatever attitudes the group displays about the propriety of human conduct, qualities, or goals. We say, in this sense, that the morality of Nazi Germany was based on prejudice, or was irrational. But we also use some of these terms, particularly "moral position" and "moral conviction," in a discriminatory sense, to contrast the positions they describe with prejudices, rationalizations, matters of personal aversion or taste, arbitrary stands, and the like. One use— perhaps the most characteristic use—of this discriminatory sense is to offer a limited but important sort of justification for an act, when the moral issues surrounding that act are unclear or in dispute.

Suppose I tell you that I propose to vote

†From Ronald Dworkin, "Lord Devlin and the Enforcement of Morals," *Yale Law Journal,* **75** (1966), 994–999; republished as "Liberty and Morality," chap. 10 of *Taking Rights Seriously* (Cambridge, Mass.: Harvard University Press, 1978).

against a man running for a public office of trust because I know him to be a homosexual and because I believe that homosexuality is profoundly immoral. If you disagree that homosexuality is immoral, you may accuse me of being about to cast my vote unfairly, acting on prejudice or out of a personal repugnance which is irrelevant to the moral issue. I might then try to convert you to my position on homosexuality, but if I fail in this I shall still want to convince you of what you and I will both take to be a separate point—that my vote was based upon *a* moral position, in the discriminatory sense, even though one which differs from yours. I shall want to persuade you of this, because if I do I am entitled to expect that you will alter your opinion of me and of what I am about to do. Your judgment of my character will be different—you might still think me eccentric (or puritanical or unsophisticated) but these are types of character and not faults of character. Your judgment of my act will also be different, in this respect. You will admit that so long as I hold my moral position, I have a moral right to vote against the homosexual, because I have a right (indeed a duty) to vote my own convictions. You would not admit such a right (or duty) if you were still persuaded that I was acting out of a prejudice or a personal taste.

I am entitled to expect that your opinion will change in these ways, because these distinctions are a part of the conventional morality you and I share, and which forms the background for our discussion. They enforce the difference between positions we must respect, although we think them wrong, and positions we need not respect because they offend some ground rule of moral reasoning. A great deal of debate about moral issues (in real life, although not in philosophy texts) consists of arguments that some position falls on one or the other side of this crucial line.

It is this feature of conventional morality that animates Lord Devlin's argument that society has the right to follow its own lights. We must therefore examine that discriminatory concept of a moral position more closely, and we can do so by pursuing our imaginary conversation. What must I do to convince you that my position is a moral position?

(*a*) I must produce some reasons for it. This is not to say that I have to articulate a moral principle I am following or a general moral theory to which I subscribe. Very few people can do either, and the ability to hold a moral position is not limited to those who can. My reason need not be a principle or theory at all. It must only point out some aspect or feature of homosexuality which moves me to regard it as immoral: the fact that the Bible forbids it, for example, or that one who practices homosexuality becomes unfit for marriage and parenthood. Of course, any such reason would presuppose my acceptance of some general principle or theory, but I need not be able to state what it is, or realize that I am relying upon it.

Not every reason I might give will do, however. Some will be excluded by general criteria stipulating sorts of reasons which do not count. We might take note of four of the most important such criteria:

(*i*) If I tell you that homosexuals are morally inferior because they do not have heterosexual desires, and so are not "real men," you would reject that reason as showing one type of prejudice. Prejudices, in general, are postures of judgment that take into account considerations our conventions exclude. In a structured context, like a trial or a contest, the ground rules exclude all but certain considerations, and a prejudice is a basis of judgment which violates these rules. Our conventions stipulate some ground rules of moral judgment which obtain even apart from such special contexts, the most important of which is that a man must not be held morally inferior on the basis of some physical, racial or other characteristic he cannot help having. Thus a man whose moral judgments about Jews, or Negroes, or Southerners, or women, or effeminate men are based on his belief that any member of these classes automatically deserves less respect, without regard to anything he himself has done, is said to be prejudiced against that group.

(*ii*) If I base my view about homosexuals on a personal emotional reaction ("they make me sick"), you would reject that reason as well. We distinguish moral positions from emotional reactions, not because moral positions are supposed to be unemotional or dispassionate—quite the reverse is true—but because the moral position is supposed to justify the emotional reaction, and not vice versa. If a man is unable to produce such reasons, we do not deny the fact of his emotional involvement, which may have important social or political consequences, but we do not take this involvement as demonstrating his moral conviction. Indeed, it is just this sort of position—a severe emotional reaction to a practice or a situation for which one cannot account—that we tend to describe, in lay terms, as a phobia or an obsession.

(*iii*) If I base my position on a proposition of fact ("homosexual acts are physically debilitating") which is not only false, but is so implausible that it challenges the minimal standards of evidence and argument I generally accept and impose upon others, then you would regard my belief, even though sincere, as a form of rationalization, and disqualify my reason on that ground. (Rationalization is a complex concept, and also includes, as we shall see, the production of reasons which suggest general theories I do not accept.)

(*iv*) If I can argue for my own position only by citing the beliefs of others ("everyone knows homosexuality is a sin"), you will conclude that I am parroting and not relying on a moral conviction of my own. With the possible (though complex)

exception of a deity, there is no moral authority to which I can appeal and so automatically make my position a moral one. I must have my own reasons, though of course I may have been taught these reasons by others.

No doubt many readers will disagree with these thumbnail sketches of prejudice, mere emotional reaction, rationalization and parroting. Some may have their own theories of what these are. I want to emphasize now only that these are distinct concepts, whatever the details of the differences might be, and that they have a role in deciding whether to treat another's position as a moral conviction. They are not merely epithets to be pasted on positions we strongly dislike.

(*b*) Suppose I do produce a reason which is not disqualified on one of these (or on similar) grounds. That reason will presuppose some general moral principle or theory, even though I may not be able to state that principle or theory, and do not have it in mind when I speak. If I offer, as my reason, the fact that the Bible forbids homosexual acts, or that homosexual acts make it less likely that the actor will marry and raise children, I suggest that I accept the theory my reason presupposes, and you will not be satisfied that my position is a moral one if you believe that I do not. . . .

(*c*) But do I really have to have a reason to make my position a matter of moral conviction? Most men think that acts which cause unnecessary suffering, or break a serious promise with no excuse, are immoral, and yet they could give no reason for these beliefs. They feel that no reason is necessary, because they take it as axiomatic or self-evident that these are immoral acts. It seems contrary to common sense to deny that a position held in this way can be a moral position.

Yet there is an important difference between believing that one's position is self-evident and just not having a reason for one's position. The former presupposes a positive belief that no further reason is necessary, that the immorality of the act in question does not depend upon its social effects, or its effects on the character of the actor, or its proscription by a deity, or anything else, but follows from the nature of the act itself. The claim that a particular position is axiomatic, in other words, does supply a reason of a special sort, namely that the act is immoral in and of itself, and this special reason, like the others we considered, may be inconsistent with more general theories I hold.

The moral arguments we make presuppose not only moral principles, but also more abstract positions about moral reasoning. In particular, they presuppose positions about what kinds of acts can be immoral in and of themselves. When I criticize your moral opinions, or attempt to justify my own disregard of traditional moral rules I think are silly, I will likely proceed by denying that the act in question has any of the several features that can make an act immoral—that it involves no breach of an undertaking or duty, for example, harms no one including the actor, is not proscribed by any organized religion, and is not illegal. I proceed in this way because I assume that the ultimate grounds of immorality are limited to some such small set of very general standards. I may assert this assumption directly or it may emerge from the pattern of my argument. In either event, I will enforce it by calling positions which can claim no support from any of these ultimate standards *arbitrary,* as I should certainly do if you

said that photography was immoral, for instance, or swimming. Even if I cannot articulate this underlying assumption, I shall still apply it, and since the ultimate criteria I recognize are among the most abstract of my moral standards, they will not vary much from those my neighbors recognize and apply. Although many who despise homosexuals are unable to say why, few would claim affirmatively that one needs no reason, for this would make their position, on their own standards, an arbitrary one.

(*d*) This anatomy of our argument could be continued, but it is already long enough to justify some conclusions. If the issue between us is whether my views on homosexuality amount to a moral position, and hence whether I am entitled to vote against a homosexual on that ground, I cannot settle the issue simply by reporting my feelings. You will want to consider the reasons I can produce to support my belief, and whether my other views and behavior are consistent with the theories these reasons presuppose. You will have, of course, to apply your own understanding, which may differ in detail from mine, of what a prejudice or a rationalization is, for example, and of when one view is inconsistent with another. You and I may end in disagreement over whether my position is a moral one, partly because of such differences in understanding, and partly because one is less likely to recognize these illegitimate grounds in himself than in others.

Dworkin's essay offers many useful insights into the nature of a moral position, and we could easily apply his analysis to a moral controversy such as that between Zimbardo and his critics. In this case, we would probably decide that both parties are defending moral positions in Dworkin's sense. Nonetheless, there is reason to doubt that Dworkin's analysis is entirely adequate. In the earlier discussion of the fourth mark of the moral—consideration for human flourishing or social welfare—it was noted that a criterion requiring merely (oblique) reference to human welfare or to harm and benefit is compatible with views having nothing to do with morality. Similarly, in the case of Dworkin's theory, reasons for a belief can be defended thoughtfully, sincerely, and dispassionately, yet have little or nothing to do with morality. Such reasons may even be supported by what Dworkin refers to as "general" (normative) theories, yet the theories too may have little or nothing to do with morality. Dworkin could, of course, stipulate that these general theories must be *moral* ones, but then he risks begging the question of what a moral position is. How could we specify, *on Dworkin's grounds alone,* that a general theory is "arbitrary"? Are we forced to say that *any* theories which satisfy his criteria are thereby a sufficient basis on which to defend one's "moral positions"?

Perhaps what Dworkin means to say—and probably what he should say— is that only a certain restricted range of general ethical theories counts as providing "very general standards" and "ultimate grounds" for our more particular moral judgments. He does, of course, admit that moral reasons "presuppose positions" about immoral acts and indeed "presuppose some general moral principle or theory," but what seems additionally required is an analysis of an acceptable moral *theory*—an analysis that presumably would parallel Dworkin's analysis of what counts as an acceptable moral *position.* Even though Dworkin's argument is not expressed in quite these terms, this added requirement would seem a valuable addition to his other requirements. Chapters 3 through 5 in this book explore various dimensions of this problem.

THE OBJECT OF MORALITY

A question we shall explore in Chapter 9 is, "What is the object, point, or goal of morality?" This is an inquiry into the purpose of moral reasoning and the aim of having an institution of morality. Just as we can understand medical institutions in terms of their goal of improving health and combating disease, the function of businesses as producing a profit, and the function of social research as developing knowledge about social life, so we can attempt to understand the moral life in terms of its purpose. We can try to appreciate, for example, why moral judgments are made in the Zimbardo case by seeing why we make moral judgments at all. The assumption here, of course, is that there is some specifiable objective or purpose of morality. While this assumption may be mistaken, it is no more implausible than the assumption that the objectives of medicine, social research, and business can be made explicit.

Many philosophers have specified what they take the object of morality to be, though their discussions have generally been lamentably brief. For example, both John Stuart Mill and Aristotle, whose work we shall examine in Chapters 3 and 5, suggest that the object of morality is the creation and maintenance of conditions which allow the pursuit of a well-structured and happy life. By contrast, Immanuel Kant, whose philosophy is examined in Chapter 4, seems to hold that the purpose of morality should be to create in individuals what he calls a "good will," which in his view is the "supreme good" and the condition of every other moral good.

These theories, however, do not conform as closely as we might wish with the aforementioned idea that morality is an institution of fundamental social importance. G. J. Warnock has presented a thesis more consonant with this approach. He holds that morality functions to ameliorate or counteract the tendency for things to "go badly" in human relationships. Conditions naturally and inevitably deteriorate in human affairs, in his estimation, as a result of our limited resources, limited sympathy, and limited information. For example, we have institutions that house prisoners because they are the kind of persons who do not have enough of what they want in life, somehow fail in their responsibilities to others, and in general make things "go badly." Things go even worse, in many cases, when prisoners are placed in institutions where guards have "limited sympathy" for them. It is, of course, this particular situation of spiraling degeneration in human relations that Zimbardo studied. However, one need not go to the extreme of prison life to observe deteriorating human relationships. Child abuse, broken contracts, contested divorces, and dissolving partnerships are everyday examples. In the following selection, Warnock argues that the object of morality is to contribute to the betterment of this predicament by countering the limited sympathies that persons have for others and that can lead to unfortunate and even tragic situations.

G. J. WARNOCK

The Object of Morality*

It seems to me that to understand some species of evaluation (as contrasted perhaps with mastering it as a mere drill) is essentially a matter of grasping what its object is, what it is done *for;* and indeed if—*only* if—one understands this, can one be in any position to assess the appropriateness, or even relevance, of the standards and criteria employed.

Consider, for instance, the "grading" of candidates in a school-leaving examination. Clearly, in considering how this is or should be done, it is essential to be clear as to what it is being done for. Is it the object, for instance, to determine and indi-

*From G. J. Warnock, *The Object of Morality* (London: Methuen & Co., 1971), pp. 15–18, 21–23, 26.

cate how well candidates are judged to *have* done certain work at school? Or is it, differently, to indicate how well they are judged *likely* to do certain things in [the] future, for instance in employment or at universities? Conceivably one might hold that these come to the same, on the ground that what a candidate has done is the only sound, or only assessable, indicator of what he may be expected to do; but if that is not so, clearly the two objects would make appropriate and relevant the employment of different criteria. Then again, it might be the object, or part of the object, to reward or reprove, encourage or stimulate, the examinees themselves; and this too would make "grading" a different sort of exercise.

Now it is not impossible to raise the

question: what is *moral* evaluation for? What is its point? Why do we distinguish between, say, actions as morally right or wrong, between people or qualities of character as good or bad? Why do we teach children to do this, by precept or example? Why do we think it worth doing? What are we trying to achieve, or bring about, by doing it? Well, it is by and large—with qualifications already noted—evaluation *of* the actions of rational beings. It does not seem plausible that in doing this we are simply, so to speak, disinterestedly awarding marks, for no particular reason or purpose, to ourselves or others. There is, it seems obvious here, some general practical end in view; and if so, it may seem manifest that the general object must be to bring it about, in some way or other, that rational beings act, in some respects or other, *better* than they would otherwise be liable to do. Put more pompously, the general object of moral evaluation must be to contribute in some respects, by way of the actions of rational beings, to the amelioration of the human predicament—that is, of the conditions in which *these* rational beings, humans, actually find themselves. Accordingly, I take it to be necessary to understanding in this case to consider, first, what it is in the human predicament that calls for amelioration, and second, what might reasonably be suggested (to put it guardedly) as the specific contribution of "morality" to such amelioration. How are things liable to go wrong? And how exactly—or, perhaps, plausibly—can morality be understood as a contribution to their going better? . . .

It seems reasonable, and in the present context is highly relevant, to say, without necessarily going quite so far as Hobbes did,[1] that the human predicament is inherently such that things are liable to go

badly. This seems to be inherently so, but not completely hopelessly so; that is, there are circumstances, not in the least likely to change significantly or to be changed by our own efforts, which cannot but tend to make things go badly, but also something at least can be done, many different things in fact, to make them go at least somewhat better than they would do, if no such things were done at all. . . .

Now some human needs, wants, and interests are, special and exceptional circumstances apart, just naturally satisfied by the human environment and situation, and others frustrated. For instance, there is naturally available in the atmosphere of the planet, without any intervention of ours, enough air for everybody to breathe (not always clean air, but that is another matter); and there are doubtless some things that people want to do, or perhaps would like to do, or wish that they could do, which are simply physically impossible—either completely so, for everybody, or impossible in certain conditions, or for certain people. But, uncontroversially, over an enormous range of needs, wants, and interests, these are neither just naturally satisfied, nor naturally, ineluctably frustrated. In an enormous range of cases, something both needs to be done, and also at least in principle could be done. And of course this is where practical problems arise. . . .

What we need now to bring in might be called limited rationality, and limited sympathies. In the first place it may be said—certainly with extreme vagueness, but still with pretty evident truth—that human beings in general are not just naturally disposed always to do what it would be best that they should do, even if they see, or are perfectly in a position to see, what that is. Even if they are not positively neurotic or otherwise maladjusted, people are naturally somewhat prone to be moved by short-run rather than long-run considera-

[1] *Leviathan,* I, c. 13. [This work is examined in detail in Chap. 8 of this text.]

tions, and often by the pursuit of more blatant, intense, and obtrusive satisfactions rather than of those cooler ones that on balance would really be better. . . .

Next, limited sympathies. This may even be too mild a term for some of the things that I have in mind. One may say for a start, mildly, that most human beings have some natural tendency to be more concerned about the satisfaction of their own wants, etc., than those of others. A man who does not like being hungry, and who is naturally inclined to take such steps as he can to satisfy his hunger, may very well care less, even not at all, about the hunger of others, and may not care at all whether anything is done to satisfy them. Even if he does care to some extent about others, it is quite likely to be only about *some* others—family, friends, class, tribe, country, or "race." There is also, besides complete or comparative indifference, such a thing as active malevolence, perhaps even purely disinterested malevolence; a man will sometimes be not only unconcerned about, but actively malevolent towards, others whom he may see as somehow in competition with himself, and sometimes perhaps even towards some whose frustrations or sufferings are not even supposed to be for the advancement of any interest of his own. There are two obvious ways in which, consequentially, things in the human predicament are liable to go badly. For people are not simply confronted, whether as individuals or groups, with the problems of getting along satisfactorily in material conditions that may, in varying degrees, be ungenial or hostile. They are also highly vulnerable to other people; and they often need the help of other people. But, given "limited sympathies," it cannot be assumed that needed help will naturally be forthcoming; and it cannot even be assumed that active malevolence will *not* be forthcoming. And perhaps above all, there may be the

impossibility of trust. Whether, in pursuit of some end of my own, I need your help, or merely your non-interference, I may well be unable to trust you either to co-operate or to keep out of it, if I think that you are not only much less concerned about my ends and interests than your own, but possibly even actively hostile to my attainment of my ends. If so, then it may be impossible for either of us to do, either separately or together, things that would be advantageous to us both, and which perhaps we both clearly see would be advantageous to us both; and it may be necessary for us individually to do things, for instance in self-protection, the doing of which may be exceedingly laborious, wasteful, and disagreeable. It will be obvious that all this applies as fully to relations between groups as between individuals; and indeed that distrust and active hostility between groups has been, in the human predicament, as frequent and constant as between individuals, and vastly more damaging.

So far we have not, I think, said anything seriously disputable, or at all unfamiliar. It is obvious that human beings have, in general, an *interest* in the course of events in which they are involved: for, though they may indeed want some things which they would not be at all the better for having, they do have many entirely harmless and proper and reasonable wants; and they also have interests and actual needs, satisfaction of which may be absolutely necessary for their well-being. But the course of events is not at all likely, without their intervention, to go in a way at all satisfactory to them; and even with intervention, there is still so much that may go wrong. Resources are limited; knowledge, skills, information, and intelligence are limited; people are often not rational, either in the management of their own affairs or in the adjustment of their own affairs in relation to others. Then, finally, they are vulnerable to others, and dependent on others, and yet inevitably often in competition with others; and, human sympathies being limited, they may often neither get nor give help that is needed, may not manage to co-operate for common ends, and may be constantly liable to frustration or positive injury from directly hostile interference by other persons. Thus it comes about that— as Hobbes of course most memorably insisted—there is in what may be called the human predicament a certain "natural" tendency for things to go very badly; meaning thereby not, of course, in this connection, *morally* badly, but badly merely in the sense that, given the above-mentioned wholly indisputable facts about people and the circumstances in which they exist, there is the very evident possibility of very great difficulty in securing, for all or possibly even any of them, much that they want, much that it would be in their interest to have, even much that they need. And the facts that make this so are facts about the *human* predicament; there is probably no great interest in speculating about possible circumstances of other conceivable species of rational beings, but still it is worth bearing in mind that the facts we have so summarily surveyed are *contingent* facts. It is easy enough to see in general terms how very different the situation would be if the beings concerned were less vulnerable, less aggressive, less egotistical, less irrational, more intelligent, more self-sufficient, and more favoured by material circumstances. . . .

Now, the general suggestion that (guardedly) I wish to put up for consideration is this: that the "general object" of morality, appreciation of which may enable us to *understand* the basis of moral evaluation, is to contribute to betterment— or non-deterioration—of the human predicament, primarily and essentially by seeking to countervail "limited sympathies" and their potentially most damaging effects. It is the proper business of morality, and the general object of moral evaluation, not of course to add to our available resources, nor—directly anyway—to our knowledge of how to make advantageous use of them, nor—again, not directly—to make us more rational in the judicious pursuit of our interests and ends; its proper business is to expand our sympathies, or, better, to reduce the liability to damage inherent in their natural tendency to be narrowly restricted. We may note at once that, if this is, as I think, in a sense the most important of the built-in tendencies of things to go wrong, the present suggestion fits well with the common idea that there is something peculiarly *important* about morality.

If Warnock is correct in what he says about the general object of morality, as it is plausible to believe he is, then his analysis should help explain many pervasive features of the moral life. We are all aware that most persons are disposed to attend to the concerns of some favored persons to the exclusion of others, especially when personal ties are involved; we are similarly familiar with the human tendency not to intercede to prevent harm to other persons as the distance from those persons increases. That is, our natural sympathies for others expand and contract within bounds determined by our personal associations, and certainly one function of morality is to combat the deleterious consequences of these limitations on human sympathy. Moral judgments, we might say, function to condemn human plans and activities—such as lying, stealing, invading privacy, and depriving of freedom—that make things "go badly"; and, more generally, morality functions to limit selfish actions that cause harm to others. It is perhaps appropriate, then, to speak of moral judgments as fulfilling a preventive function, as condemning or demanding the avoidance of certain harm-producing human activities rather than as actually *contributing* to the betterment of the human predicament. But this suggestion may constitute only a small refinement of Warnock's thesis.

Warnock's account of the object of morality presupposes that *the* purpose of morality can be identified, and he will no doubt be accused by some of arbitrarily singling out one goal of the institution to the exclusion of its many other important purposes. Also, an objection could be raised that Warnock's discussion fails to account for the presence and significance of some moral standards besides those that condemn limited sympathies—such as the principles of justice discussed in Chapter 7 of this text and the principle of autonomy discussed in Chapter 4. At this point we are not ready to evaluate such objections, for the material in Chapters 3 through 5 provides critical background information necessary for such appraisals. We should take the time to observe now, however, that it is a matter of considerable importance for any ethical theory that *the* object of morality it presupposes or defends not be arbitrary or merely a matter of an author's personal preference. The hope in formulating the object of morality, after all, is to provide a perspective from which to justify a general ethical theory that properly applies to everyone alike.

APPROACHES TO THE STUDY OF MORALITY

The concept of morality, the idea of a moral position, and the object of morality have now been discussed. While this background is essential for later chapters of this text, the various ways in which morality and moral philosophy can formally be studied—including the approaches to the study of morality employed later—are also essential.

Four ways of either studying moral beliefs or moral philosophy have dominated the literature of ethics. Two of these approaches describe and analyze morality without taking moral positions. These approaches are therefore called "nonnormative." Two other approaches do involve taking moral positions, and are therefore called "normative." These four approaches, each of which will be characterized briefly in the remainder of this chapter, can be summarized in the following form:

Nonnormative approaches — Descriptive ethics
                        — Metaethics

Normative approaches — General normative ethics
                     — Applied ethics

It would be a mistake to regard these categories as expressing rigid and always clearly distinguishable differences of approach. They are often undertaken jointly by a single author in a single article, and, as will be seen in Chapter 10, important reservations have been expressed about some of these distinctions (especially the one between metaethics and normative ethics*). Nonetheless, when understood as broad polar contrasts exemplifying models of inquiry, these distinctions are important and serviceable.

Nonnormative Approaches

First among the two nonnormative fields of inquiry into morality is *descriptive ethics,* or the factual description and explanation of moral behavior and beliefs. Anthropologists, sociologists, and historians who study moral behavior employ this approach when they explore whether and in what ways moral attitudes, codes, and beliefs differ from person to person and from society to society. Novels about foreign lands in former times—such as James Clavell's popular book *Shōgun,* an account of medieval Japan—have often dwelled in great detail on the sexual practices, codes of honor, and rules governing permissible killing in a society. To a limited extent, Zimbardo too had descriptive objectives in mind, for he functioned as a social scientist studying the moral attitudes and behavior of his subjects. Descriptive ethics thus investigates a wide variety of moral beliefs and behavior, including methods of brutality, the treatment of the aged, kinship systems, morality in professional organizations, and abortion practices. Although philosophers do not generally range into descriptive ethics in their work, some have combined descriptive ethics with philosophical ethics by, e.g., analyzing the ethical practices of American Indian tribes. These philosophers, like many social scientists, have often raised interesting questions about the apparent relativity of moral judgments and rules. (These questions will be addressed in Chapter 2 of this text.)

Metaethics is the second nonnormative approach to morality. This approach involves (presumably nonevaluative) analysis of the meanings of central terms in ethics such as "right," "obligation," "good," "virtue," and "responsibility." The proper analysis of the term "morality" and the distinction between the moral and nonmoral, as explored earlier in this chapter, is a typical example of a metaethical problem. Attention will be paid to the meanings of such terms throughout this text. In addition to the analysis of central terms, the structure or logic of moral reasoning is examined in metaethics, including the nature of moral justifications and inferences. (These particular problems are explored in Chapters 9 and 10.)

Descriptive ethics and metaethics may of course not be the only forms of nonnormative inquiry. In recent years there has been considerable discussion of the biological bases of moral behavior and the ways in which humans do and do not differ from animals. This form of inquiry is quite different from the study of attitudes, codes, or beliefs. Nonetheless, descriptive ethics and metaethics have been more influential approaches, and they are the only nonnormative ones discussed in this book.

*A controversy exists as to whether a sharp distinction can be drawn between metaethics and normative ethics, largely because it is thought that metaethics incorporates normative views or at least presuppositions. See, for example, Philippa Foot, "Goodness and Choice," and J. R. Searle, "How to Derive 'Ought' from 'Is'," both in W. D. Hudson, ed., *The Is/Ought Question* (London: Macmillan & Co., 1969). See also Chap. 10 of the present text.

Normative Approaches

Let us now consider the third and fourth of the major approaches to the study of morality. *General normative ethics* is the philosophical attempt to formulate and defend basic moral principles and virtues governing the moral life. Ideally, any such ethical theory will provide reasons for adopting a system of moral principles or virtues and will defend claims about the range of their applicability. Before we turn to a detailed examination of these theories (in Chapters 3 through 5), it will be useful to consider broad introductory characterizations of the most prominent general normative theories.

Some philosophers have argued that there is one and only one fundamental principle determining right action. It is, roughly, the following: An action is morally right if, and only if, it produces at least as great a balance of value over disvalue as any available alternative action. This principle is known as the "principle of utility," and philosophers who subscribe to it are referred to as "utilitarians." Zimbardo at several points offers a utilitarian defense of his research by appealing to the favorable balance of goods over harms that resulted from it, though his is more an implicit than a direct appeal to utilitarianism. (A detailed analysis of utilitarianism is found in Chapter 3 of this text.) Nonutilitarians have argued that there are one or more fundamental principles of ethics which differ from the principle of utility. These are usually principles of strict duty, such as "Never treat another person merely as a means to your own goals." This principle means that it is immoral, for example, to deceive, coerce, or fail to consult with others merely in order to promote one's own goals. Philosophers who accept a nonutilitarian account of the principles of moral duty are referred to as "deontologists." (Deontological theories are examined in Chapter 4.)

Many regard utilitarian and deontological theories as the *only* competing options in contemporary normative ethical theory. This view has been so prevalent that deontological theories have sometimes been said to encompass all nonutilitarian theories. In recent years, however, some philosophers have come to appreciate the possibility that an ancient tradition dating from Greek philosophy presents an interesting contrast to utilitarian and deontological theories of ethics. This approach is variously called "virtue ethics" or the "ethics of character." Its adherents note that philosophy has long been concerned with the cultivation of character traits such as benevolence, honesty, compassion, faithfulness, and courage, and they argue that the specification of obligatory actions is less important than the cultivation of these character traits. (These theories will be studied in Chapter 5.)

The principles found in general normative ethics are also commonly applied to specific moral problems such as abortion, widespread hunger, and research involving human subjects. This use of ethical theory is referred to as "applied ethics." Philosophical treatments of medical ethics, engineering ethics, journalistic ethics, jurisprudence, and business ethics all involve such an application of general ethical principles to moral problems. Substantially the same general ethical principles apply to the problems across these professional fields and in areas beyond professional ethics as well. One might appeal to principles of justice, for example, in order to illuminate and resolve issues of taxation, delivery of health care, criminal punishment, and reverse discrimination. Similarly, principles of veracity (truthfulness) apply to debates about secrecy and deception in international politics, misleading advertisements in business ethics, balanced reporting in journalistic ethics, and the disclosure of the nature and extent of an illness to a patient in medical ethics. Moral problems about whether Zimbardo was truthful and whether he should have been truthful in obtaining the "consent" of his student subjects can be discussed by appeal to such principles. Presumably, greater clarity about the conditions in general under which truth must be told and when it may be withheld would enhance understanding of what is required in all these areas and would help us evaluate the moral dimensions of Zimbardo's study.

Applied moral philosophy has been frequently employed in recent years in contexts of public policy, where an interdisciplinary approach is required. Practitioners bring experience and technical information to the discussion, while moral philosophers bring familiarity with traditions of ethical reflection, insights into various distinctions and categories that can illuminate moral issues, and skill in probing presuppositions and the implications of positions. In the teaching of ethics in professional schools, moral problems have been examined through case studies, where the hope is to teach students how to identify the moral principles at issue in particular cases. The present text follows a similar procedure. Each chapter begins with a case that is relevant to the more abstract matters of theory discussed in the chapter, and the case is then invoked throughout the chapter to illustrate specific issues and principles. Zimbardo's case, we may note in passing, has been explored for some years by social scientists who teach courses on ethical issues involving research with human subjects.

THE REMAINDER OF THIS TEXT

Now that we have some idea of morality and its object, as well as some idea of how it can be studied, the remaining nine chapters can be outlined.

Chapter 2 completes the preliminary fundamental considerations begun in Chapter 1 by examining relativism, moral disagreements, moral pluralism, and egoism. It is useful to have studied these topics before considering the three classical theories of normative ethics: utilitarian theories, deontological theories, and virtue theories. Presentations of these theories in Chapters 3, 4, and 5 are woven together with a detailed analysis of the work of the three writers often regarded as the primary historical spokespersons for each of these approaches: the English philosopher John Stuart Mill, the German philosopher Immanuel Kant, and the ancient Greek philosopher Aristotle.

Chapters 6 through 8 then proceed to three topics that have been the focus of sustained inquiry in recent years: rights, justice, and liberty. These chapters are not developed in conjunction with a study of single historical figures of major influence; but some recent philosophical works of considerable impact, written by John Rawls, Robert Nozick, and Ronald Dworkin, are studied in detail, as are some of Mill's reflections on how the utilitarian theory applies to concerns of law and liberty. Finally, in Chapters 9 and 10, attention shifts from normative ethics toward predominantly metaethical considerations. Here the emphasis is on the justification of ultimate moral principles, theories of justification, the distinction between facts and values, and the justification of morality itself.

SUGGESTED SUPPLEMENTARY READINGS

Abelson, Raziel, and Kai Nielsen: "History of Ethics," in Paul Edwards, ed., *The Encyclopedia of Philosophy* (New York: Macmillan Company and Free Press, 1967), vol. 3, pp. 81–117.

Donagan, Alan: *The Theory of Morality* (Chicago: University of Chicago Press, 1977), chaps. 1–2.

Frankena, William K.: *Ethics,* 2d ed. (Englewood Cliffs, N.J.: Prentice-Hall, Inc., 1973).

———: *Thinking about Morality* (Ann Arbor: University of Michigan Press, 1980), chap. 1.

——— and John T. Granrose, eds.: *Introductory Readings in Ethics* (Englewood Cliffs, N.J.: Prentice-Hall, Inc., 1974), chap. 1.

———: *Perspectives on Morality: Essays of William K. Frankena,* ed. by Kenneth E. Goodpaster (Notre Dame, Ind.: University of Notre Dame Press, 1976), chaps. 10, 15.

Gert, Bernard: *The Moral Rules: A New Rational Foundation for Morality* (New York: Harper & Row, 1966), chap. 1.

Gewirth, Alan: *Reason and Morality* (Chicago: University of Chicago Press, 1978), chap. 1.

Hartland-Swann, John: *An Analysis of Morals* (London: George Allen & Unwin, 1960).

Ladd, John: *The Structure of a Moral Code* (Cambridge, Mass.: Harvard University Press, 1957).

MacIntyre, Alasdair: *A Short History of Ethics* (New York: Macmillan Company, 1966).

———: "How to Identify Ethical Principles," in National Commission for the Protection of Human Subjects of Biomedical and Behavioral Research, *The Belmont Report,* Appendix 1, selection 10, DHEW Publication (OS) 78-0013 (Washington, D.C.: Government Printing Office, 1978).

Mackie, John L.: *Ethics: Inventing Right and Wrong* (Harmondsworth, England: Penguin Books, Ltd., 1977).

Nielsen, Kai: "Problems of Ethics," in Paul Edwards, ed., *The Encyclopedia of Philosophy* (New York: Macmillan Company and Free Press, 1967), vol. 3, pp. 117–134.

Taylor, Paul W., ed.: *Problems of Moral Philosophy,* 3d ed. (Belmont, Calif.: Wadsworth Publishing Company, Inc., 1978), chap. 1.

Toulmin, Stephen: *An Examination of the Place of Reason in Ethics* (New York: Cambridge University Press, 1964).

Wallace, Gerald, and A. D. M. Walker, eds.: *The Definition of Morality* (London: Methuen & Co., Ltd., 1970).

Warnock, Geoffrey J.: *The Object of Morality* (London: Methuen & Co., Ltd., 1971).

CHAPTER TWO

Objectivity and Diversity in Morals

When the first European explorers sailed into the region of Hudson Bay in search of a "northwest passage" across the North American continent, they chanced upon some remarkable customs among certain tribal nations adjoining the bay. The members of the tribes there practiced a custom of killing their parents when they had become so old that they were incapable of supporting themselves by their labor. The specific custom was that elderly parents should be strangled by their children, who, it was believed, had an obligation to perform this ritual act. The explorers considered the manner of carrying out the duty as extraordinary as the practice itself: First, a grave for the old person was dug. The person would then descend into the grave, have a drink or two with his or her children, and perhaps smoke a pipe. When the old person signified a readiness to proceed, two of his or her offspring would put a thong around the neck of their parent and would pull violently from each side of the neck until the person was strangled. The children would then cover their parent in a way quite similar to the burial customs practiced in the lands of the explorers. Should a person have no children to perform this duty, it was the custom that he or she would request the services from friends. However, friends were not under the same obligation as children, and in some cases the request was flatly refused. Whatever the reason for this refusal, it seemed to count as something of a dishonor for the person making the request, as, in these tribes, dying for the sake of the group was a point of honor.

This example and many similar ones reported by the early explorers have been widely cited ever since.* This particular example even played a role in the history of

*This example is taken from Karl Duncker, "Ethical Relativity?" *Mind* **48** (1939), pp. 39–53. Duncker extracts it from Ellis's *Voyage for the Discovery of a North-West Passage*.

western philosophy; the eighteenth-century Scottish philosopher James Beattie employed it in arguing against certain doctrines that he despised in the writings of John Locke.

We are all so thoroughly familiar both with cultural differences, such as the one reported in this account of killing aged parents, and with disagreements with our friends over moral problems, such as abortion, that we may doubt the possibility of finding an objective position in morals. This doubt is fed by popular aphorisms that morality is more properly a matter of taste than reason, that one's beliefs are ultimately arbitrary, and that there is no neutral standpoint from which to view disagreements. Accordingly, we may be inclined to think that one's moral views are based simply on how one feels or on how a culture accommodates the desires of its people, not on some deeper set of objectively justifiable principles. On the other hand, and somewhat paradoxically, we tend to view morality as more than a matter of individual taste when we find ourselves feeling strongly about a particular moral position. Most of us have had the experience of being firmly convinced that another person or a certain nation is acting unjustly and ought to be punished, and we do not regard our convictions in these circumstances as mere matters of feeling or taste.

Tension between the belief that morality is purely subjective and the belief that it has an objective grounding is the source of several different issues we shall encounter in this chapter. These issues include problems of relativism, pluralism, disagreement, and egoism in morals. Each of these problems raises questions about whether an objective morality is possible and about whether reason has any substantial role to play in ethics.

RELATIVISM IN MORALS

One of the most common conceptions of morality is that all moral beliefs and principles are relative to individual cultures or individual persons. One person's or one culture's values, relativists maintain, do not or need not govern the conduct of others. The seventeenth-century explorers did not feel compelled, for example, to be governed by rules requiring the death of superannuated parents after visiting Hudson Bay, nor would any of us, reared in a different culture, feel constrained by such customs. Similar data have led to the conclusion that moral rightness and wrongness vary from place to place, without any absolute or universal moral standards that could apply to all persons at all times. It is frequently added that rightness is contingent on individual or cultural beliefs and that the concepts of rightness and wrongness are therefore meaningless apart from the specific contexts in which they arise.

Moral relativism is no newcomer to the scene of moral philosophy. Ancient thinkers were as perplexed by cultural and individual differences as moderns, as is evidenced by Plato's well-known battle with a relativism popular in his day. Nevertheless, it was easier in former times to ignore cultural differences than it is today, for there was once greater uniformity within cultures, as well as less commerce among them. The contrast between ancient Athens and modern Manhattan is evident; and any contemporary pluralistic culture is saturated with individuality of belief and life-style. Further, we are almost daily struck by differences between Anglo-American culture and, say, the customs prevalent in Iran, China, and India. The differences are sometimes so staggering that we can scarcely believe we live in the same world, or at least the same world of morals—as the Englishmen's reaction to practices in Hudson Bay indicates. At the same time, we wonder whether we are called upon by this diversity to tolerate racism, social caste systems, sexism, genocide, and a wide variety of inequalities of treatment that we deeply believe morally wrong but find sanctioned either in our own culture or in others.

Problems of apparent moral diversity offer a serious challenge to moral philosophy. If rightness and wrongness are completely determined or exhausted by particular contexts, a universal ethical system seems an unattainable ideal. Yet, as we saw in Chapter 1 and will study in detail in Chapters 3 through 5, one main goal of general normative ethics is to outline a system of moral norms applicable to everyone, independent of special contexts. Although it has at times been fashionable in the social sciences to view relativism as a correct and highly significant doctrine, moral philosophers have generally tended to discount this evaluation. They find relativistic views unconvincing, both because they seem irrelevant to the main task of moral philosophy and because the counterarguments appear to be at least as good as the arguments defending relativism. Furthermore, there are so many different notions subsumed under the rubric of relativism that the arguments often seem undirected and confused. In order to remain clear about the different types of relativism, we shall discuss its two main forms separately in the following pages.

Cultural Relativism

Anthropologists such as Ruth Benedict and M. K. Herskovits hold that patterns of culture can be understood only as unique wholes; moral beliefs and beliefs about normal behavior are thus closely connected in a culture to other cultural characteristics such as language and fundamental political institutions. From a wide variety of anthropological studies conducted in different cultures, these anthropologists infer that what is deemed worthy of moral approval or disapproval in one society varies, both in detail and as a whole pattern, from moral standards in other societies. They maintain that the anthropological evidence indicates at most that in all societies persons possess a moral conscience, a general sense of right and wrong; for, in every culture, some actions and intentions are approved as right or good, and others are disapproved as wrong or bad. On the other hand, the *particular* actions and motives that are praised and blamed vary greatly from culture to culture—the killing of aged parents being only one among thousands of examples.

This view is put forward on general theoretical grounds as the thesis that all moral standards are mere reflections of mores or folkways—i.e., behaviors customarily approved within a particular culture. From this perspective, a moral standard is simply a historical product sanctioned by custom. Psychological and historical versions of this thesis hold that the moral beliefs of individuals vary on the bases of historical, environmental, and familial differences. It is now a generally accepted psychological fact that moral beliefs, including our sense of conscience, are not innate and so must somehow be learned in a social context. Moreover, the evolution and transformation of these beliefs, over time, either in cultures or in individuals, can often be reconstructed by historians. The weight of anthropological, psychological, and historical evidence thus conspires to suggest that moral beliefs are relative to groups or individuals and that there are no universal norms, let alone universally *valid* ones. Indeed, argues Benedict, the term "morality" means "socially approved habits," and the expression "It is morally good" is synonymous with "It is habitual."*

Many philosophical arguments have been advanced against this form of relativism. Among the best known of these arguments is the contention that a universal *structure* of human nature, or at least a universal set of human needs, exists that leads to the adoption of similar or even identical principles in all cultures. This line of argument rests on empirical claims and raises a number of still unresolved questions, some of which are addressed in the following essay by Richard Brandt. His analysis links problems of cultural relativism with the problems of moral disagreement that will be discussed in the next section of this chapter. Brandt argues the interesting thesis that while relativism has little to commend it, ultimate disagreements in morals may be inevitable.

*Ruth Benedict, "Relativism and Patterns of Culture," in Richard B. Brandt, ed., *Value and Obligation* (New York: Harcourt, Brace, and World, 1961), p. 457.

RICHARD B. BRANDT

Relativism and Ultimate Disagreements about Ethical Principles†

Suppose that Eskimos, through their experience with the hardships of living, think of parricide as being normally the merciful cutting short of a miserable, worthless, painful old age. And suppose the Romans think of parricide as being normally the getting rid of a burden, or a getting one's hands on the parent's money—an ungraceful, selfishly motivated aggression against one whose care and sacrifices

†From Richard B. Brandt, *Ethical Theory* (Englewood Cliffs, N.J.: Prentice-Hall, Inc., 1959), pp. 100–103, 285–286, 287–288. Reprinted by permission of the author and the publisher, Prentice-Hall, Inc.

years ago have made the child's life a rich experience. The Eskimos are more-or-less unconsciously taking for granted that putting a parent to death is euthanasia under extreme circumstances; the Romans are more-or-less unconsciously taking for granted that putting a parent to death is murder for gain. In this case, although the Romans and the Eskimos may use the very same words to describe a certain sort of act—and then may express conflicting ethical appraisal of it—actually in some sense they have in mind quite different things. The Eskimos, perhaps, are accepting something of the kind *ABCD;* the Romans are condemning something of the kind *ABFG.* In this situation, we do not want to say there is necessarily any ultimate disagreement of principle between them.

When, then, do we want to say there is ultimate disagreement about ethical principles? . . .

It is not easy to answer the question whether there is ultimate disagreement on ethical principles between different groups. Most of the comparative material assembled, for instance by Westermarck, is of little value for this purpose, for in large part what it tells us is simply whether various peoples approve or condemn lying, suicide, industry, cleanliness, adultery, homosexuality, cannibalism, and so on. But this is not enough. We need, for our purpose, to know how various peoples *conceive* of these things. Do they eat human flesh because they like its taste, and do they kill slaves merely for the sake of a feast? Or do they eat flesh because they think this is necessary for tribal fertility, or because they think they will then participate in the manliness of the person eaten? Perhaps those who condemn cannibalism would not do so if they thought that eating the flesh of an enemy is necessary for the survival of the group. If we are to estimate whether there is ultimate disagreement of ethical principle, we must have information about this, about the beliefs, more or less conscious, of various peoples about what they do. However, the comparative surveys seldom give us this.

In view of the total evidence, then, is it more plausible to say that there is ultimate disagreement of ethical principle, or not? Or don't we really have good grounds for making a judgment on this crucial issue?

First of all, we must report that no anthropologists, as far as the writer knows, today deny that there is ultimate disagreement—although doubtless many of them have not posed the question in exactly the above form. (*Almost* no philosophers deny it either.) This seems a matter of importance, because, even if they have not explicitly argued the matter out, their intuitive impression based on long familiarity with some non-Western society should carry considerable weight. However, we must concede that no anthropologist has offered what we should regard as really an adequate account of a single case, clearly showing there is ultimate disagreement in ethical principle. Of course, we must remember that this lack of information is just as serious for any claim that there is worldwide *agreement* on some principle.

Nevertheless, the writer inclines to think there is ultimate ethical disagreement, and that it is well established. Maybe it is not very important, or very pervasive; but there is some. Let us look at the matter of causing suffering to animals. It is notorious that many peoples seem quite indifferent to the suffering of animals. We are informed that very often, in Latin America, a chicken is *plucked alive,* with the thought it will be more succulent on the table. The reader is invited to ask himself whether he would consider it justified to pluck a chicken alive, for this purpose. Or again, take the "game" played by Indians of the Southwest (but learned from the Spaniards, apparently), called the "chicken pull." In this "game," a chicken is buried in the sand, up to its neck. The contestants ride by on horseback, trying to grab the chicken by the neck and yank it from the sand. When someone succeeds in this, the idea is then for the other contestants to take away from him as much of the chicken as they can. The "winner" is the one who ends up with the most chicken. The reader is invited to ask himself whether he approves of this sport. The writer had the decided impression that the Hopi disapproval of causing pain to animals is much milder than he would suppose typical in suburban Philadelphia— certainly much milder than he would feel himself. For instance, children often catch birds and make "pets" of them. A string is tied to their legs, and they are then "played" with. The birds seldom survive this "play" for long: their legs are broken, their wings pulled off, and so on. One informant put it: "Sometimes they get tired and die. Nobody objects to this." Another informant said: "My boy sometimes brings in birds, but there is nothing to feed them, and they die."[1] Would the reader approve of this, or permit his children to do this sort of thing?

Of course, these people might believe that animals are unconscious automata, or that they are destined to be rewarded many times in the afterlife if they suffer martyrdom on this earth. Then we should feel that our ethical principles were, after all, in agreement with those of these individuals. But they believe no such thing. The writer took all means he could think of to discover some such belief in the Hopi subconscious, but he found none. So probably—we must admit the case is not definitively closed—there is at least one ultimate difference of ethical principle. How many more there are, or how important, we do not say at present.

Possibly we need not go as far afield as Latin America or the Hopi to establish the point. The reader *may* have argued some ethical point with a friend until he found that, as far as he could tell, there were just some matters of principle on which they disagreed, which themselves could not be debated on the basis of any further common ground. In this case, the conclusion is the same. Note, however, that we say only "may have argued." Some people say they cannot remember ever having had such an experience; and perhaps the reader has not. In this case, we do not need to go afield.

It is obvious that if there is *ultimate* disagreement of ethical opinion between two persons or groups, there is also disagreement in *basic* principles—if we mean by

[1] See the writer's *Hopi Ethics: A Theoretical Analysis* (Chicago: University of Chicago Press, 1954), pp. 213–215, 245–246, 373.

"basic ethical principle" . . . the principles we should have to take as a person's ethical premises, if we represented his ethical views as a deductive system. We have so defined "ultimate disagreement" that a difference in the ethical theorems of two persons or groups does not count as being "ultimate" if it can be explained as a consequence of identical ethical premises but different factual assumptions of the two parties. Since ultimate ethical disagreements, then, cannot be a consequence of the factual assumptions of the parties, it must be a consequence of their ethical premises. Hence, there is also disagreement in "basic" principles. Our conclusion from our total evidence, then, is that different persons or groups sometimes have, in fact, conflicting basic ethical principles. . . .

There are some more detailed questions, then, that we may well ask ourselves. For instance, we may ask: Is relativism true for *all* topics of moral assessment, for perhaps 50 percent, or perhaps for only 1 percent? Or again, is relativism true for all topics except perhaps for those about which we have no strong feelings anyway, or is it true also for some topics (for example, slavery) of strong concern to us? Or, and this is obviously the most important issue, on *exactly which topics* are conflicting ethical views supportable, and on which topics must we say that all valid views are in agreement? . . .

On this matter there has been a marked change of opinion among social scientists in the past twenty years. There was a time when anthropologists like Ruth Benedict proclaimed the equal validity of the most diverse modes of living and ideals for humanity. The megalomania of the Kwakiutl, the repressed sobriety of the Pueblo, and the paranoia of the Dobuan culture were different value systems; but it would be ethnocentric, she thought, to make judgments about the relative merits of the systems. Since that time, however, anthropologists have turned attention to the similarities between societies, and to the functioning of social systems, to the analysis of institutions in terms of their capacity to minister to essential human wants and the maintenance of the social group as a continuing entity. These new interests have led to the following results.

First, it has come to be agreed that certain features of a culture system are essential for the maintenance of life, and that a system of values that permits and sanctions these forms is inevitable in society.[2] For instance, every society must provide for mating and for the rearing of offspring. Again, it must provide for the education of the offspring in the performance of those tasks that are necessary for survival. Moreover, in a complex society there must be differentiation of jobs, assignment of individuals to these jobs and the means for training them for adequate performance, and provision of motivation to do the jobs. Sufficient security must be provided to prevent serious disruption of activities, for example, security against violent attack. And so on.

It must be no surprise, therefore, to find that certain institutional forms are present in all societies: such as the family with its responsibilities for training children and caring for the aged, division of labor between the *sexes* (and occupational differences in more complex societies), games or art or dance, and so on.[3]

Second, anthropologists have come to find much more common ground in the value systems of different groups than they formerly did. As Professor Kluckhohn recently put it:

> Every culture has a concept of murder, distinguishing this from execution, killing in war, and other ''justifiable homicides.'' The notions of incest and other regulations upon sexual behavior, of prohibitions upon untruth under defined circumstances, of restitution and reciprocity, of mutual obligations between parents and children—these and many other moral concepts are altogether universal.[4]

There are other universals we could mention: disapproval of rape, the ideal for marriage of a lifelong union between spouses, the demand for loyalty to one's own social group, recognition that the interests of the individual are in the end subordinate to those of the group. . . .

What is proved by these observations of anthropologists? First, that there is much agreement about values, especially important values, which provides some basis for the resolution of disputes, even if we set aside completely considerations of validity, and assume there is no such thing as a ''valid'' value. Second, some values, or some institutions with their supporting values, are so inevitable, given human nature and the human situation in society as they are, that we can hardly anticipate serious questioning of them by anybody—much less any conflicting ''qualified attitudes,'' that is, conflicting attitudes that are informed (and so on).

Thus, ethical relativism may be true, in the sense that there are *some* cases of conflicting ethical judgments that are equally valid; but it would be a mistake to take it as a truth with pervasive scope. Relativism as an emphasis is misleading, because it draws our attention away from

[2]See D. F. Aberle et al., "The Functional Prerequisites for a Society," *Ethics,* **49** (1949), 100–111.
[3]See G. P. Murdock, "The Common Denominator of Cultures," in R. Linton, ed., *The Science of Man in the World Crisis* (New York: Columbia University Press, 1945); and C. Kluckhohn, "Universal Categories of Culture," in A. L. Kroeber, ed., *Anthropology Today* (Chicago: University of Chicago Press, 1953).

[4]C. Kluckhohn, "Ethical Relativity: Sic et Non," *Journal of Philosophy,* **52** (1955), pp. 663–677.

the central identities, from widespread agreements on the items we care most about. Furthermore, the actual agreement on the central things suggests the possibility that, with better understanding of the facts, the scope of agreement would be much wider.

Brandt's article brings out the following important reason why many philosophers have not found cultural relativism to be persuasive: The fact that cultural or individual beliefs vary reveals nothing about whether people *ultimately* or *fundamentally* disagree about moral standards, as the example from the voyage to Hudson Bay can be exploited to illustrate. From an Anglo-American perspective, old people were killed at Hudson Bay, while they are treated quite differently in other cultures. Yet it does not follow from this divergence of belief and practice that the *ultimate* values in these different cultures are different. People in both cultures may adopt their different practices by appeal to a principle (of beneficence, say) that they share in common. That is, two cultures may agree about an ultimate principle of morality, yet disagree about the "ethics" of treating the aged and dying when called upon to *apply* the principle.

This possibility indicates that a *basic* conflict between cultural values can occur only if apparent cultural disagreements about proper principles or rules have occurred at a sufficiently fundamental level. Otherwise, the apparent disagreements can be understood in terms of, and perhaps be arbitrated by, appeal to higher rules. If a moral conflict were truly fundamental, then the conflict could not be removed even if there were perfect agreement about the facts of a case, about the concepts involved, and about background beliefs. In the Hudson Bay example, there would be a fundamental disagreement if persons from this and contrasted cultures agreed on all the facts surrounding old age, what happens in an afterlife, etc., and still disagreed over appropriate moral rules and judgments.

Anthropological or cultural relativists have never convincingly argued that conflicts are fundamental in this sense, and it would be a very difficult thesis to sustain. Indeed, much anthropological evidence suggests that there is no really basic or fundamental conflict between moral beliefs, because disagreements over critical *facts* or *concepts* are the underlying source of "moral" diversity. For example, in many cultures people believe that they are reborn in the condition in which they die. Persons who die in a senile and broken-hearted state will be reborn in the same state. To avoid this condition in the afterlife, people in these cultures execute their parents at what is considered an age immediately prior to senility. When the practices of the inhabitants of Hudson Bay are placed in this broader context of beliefs about death and reincarnation, they appear to be based on a principle of beneficent action that would uncontroversially be accepted in developed western cultures. What seemed to be a fundamental conflict turns out not to be fundamental, then, because both cultures appeal to a similar ultimate moral principle to justify their treatment of the aged.

Even if individuals in the same culture or persons from different cultures do not actually agree on the same ultimate norm or set of norms, it does not follow that there is no ultimate norm or set of norms in which everyone *ought* to believe. Consider an analogy to religious disagreement: From the fact that people have incompatible religious and atheistic beliefs, it does not follow that there is no single correct set of religious or atheistic propositions. Given anthropological data, one might be skeptical that there could be a compelling argument in favor of one system of either religion or morality. But nothing more than skepticism seems justified by the facts adduced by anthropology, and this judgment would hold even if *fundamental* conflicts of belief were discovered. Skepticism of course presents serious philosophical issues, but alone, it does not support relativism.

This philosophical point scarcely reaches beyond common sense. When we find two people arguing for or against some moral view—the morality of lying to children, killing animals, or practicing homosexuality, for example—we tend to think that at least one person is mistaken, or that some compromise may be reached, or we remain skeptical and uncertain. We are on the lookout for the one best argument to emerge, and we do not infer from the mere fact of a conflict between beliefs that there is no way to establish one view as correct, or at least as better than the other. The more absurd the position advanced by one party, the more convinced we become that the views embraced either are mistaken or require supplementation. We are seldom tempted, however, to conclude that there cannot be any correct moral theory that might resolve the dispute. Moreover, the existence of diverse and culturally bound customs is perfectly compatible with each of the nonrelativist ethical theories that will be presented later in this book—those of Kant, Mill, Aristotle, and others. The empirical findings of anthropology therefore seem to have nothing to say about the truth of an ethical theory, even if they do provide grounds for skeptical caution.

These considerations do not definitively refute all forms of relativism. They show only why philosophers have generally been disenchanted with *cultural* relativism. Let us now consider a second form of relativism.

Normative Relativism

Cultural relativists might reasonably be said to hold that "What is right at one place or time may be wrong at another." This statement is ambiguous, however, and can easily be interpreted as a second form of relativistic theory. Cultural relativists intend to report what is believed and how beliefs differ; their thesis is purely descriptive and in no sense normative. Some relativists, by contrast, interpret "What is right at one place or time may be wrong at another" to mean that it is *right* to act in a way in one context and *wrong* to act that way in another. What is right in Reno may be wrong in Salt Lake City; what *was* right at Hudson Bay three centuries ago may be wrong *now* at Hudson Bay, and may have been wrong *then* in London. This thesis is normative because it discloses standards of right and wrong behavior: Depending upon one's social attachments or personal beliefs, one *ought* to do what one's society determines to be right or what one personally believes. Thus there is a group or social form of normative relativism and an individual form of normative relativism.

This normative position has sometimes been crudely translated as "Anything is right or wrong whenever some individual or some group sincerely *thinks* it is right or wrong." Thus a national registry for the draft would be right for those who sincerely believe it is right and wrong for those who sincerely believe it is wrong. However, less crude formulations of the position can be given, and more or less plausible examples can be adduced. One can hold the slightly more developed view, for example, that in order to be right, something must be *conscientiously* and not merely customarily believed. Alternatively, it might be formulated as the view that whatever the belief, it is right if it is part of a well-formed traditional moral code of rules in a society. As an example of the first formulation, one may cite conscientious objection to war by individuals, and of the second, the obligation to obey constitutional law that is accepted in almost all cultures. Thus formulated, it seems quite plausible to say that a person ought to act on whatever he or she conscientiously believes; or, as a second case, that a person ought to obey a particular constitution because most people in that society believe it is morally right to do so. Both individual normative relativism and group normative relativism seem attractive in the light of such examples. What does not seem attractive is to mix the two forms of normative relativism, for individual beliefs too often conflict with group beliefs. In the very examples given, it is easy to imagine a conscientious objector strongly opposing a particular constitutional principle.

Support might be claimed for these relativist contentions in the widespread belief that it is inappropriate and ultimately indefensible to criticize one culture from within the limited blinders of another. Thus we must not criticize the inhabitants of Hudson Bay for their practices of mercy killing, and they must not criticize our prohibitions on active euthanasia. On the basis of such convictions, normative relativism has often been extended to include this thesis: Because moral norms are valid only when accepted by a group or an individual, it is morally illegitimate to apply any norm to another culture or individual. The idea is that the validity of norms is limited in scope and the norms themselves are binding only in a specific domain, much as principles of etiquette and custom are binding only in certain locations. Thus, no one may *legitimately* pass judgment on another's views, although we frequently regard our critical appraisals of others as valid.

Many counterexamples to normative relativism have been offered. It is pointed out, for example, that Jews in Germany were hardly obligated to follow the moral beliefs of the Nazi regime; and, because a dissident college student *believes* it is right to bomb a college dormitory in protest against a war, this belief does not prove that the act *is* right. It may, however, be possible to avoid such counterexamples by carefully refining and restricting the theory, and in any case, the more serious problems for normative relativism do not come directly from such counterexamples. The apparent inconsistency of this form of relativism with many cherished moral beliefs underlies such counterexamples and is the fundamental source of the major objections leveled against normative relativism. For example, almost all of us believe that better and worse moral beliefs can sometimes be identified, and that moral progress or moral retrogression sometimes occurs in cultures or individuals. Moreover, no theory of normative relativism is likely to convince us that we must tolerate *all* acts of others. At least some moral views seem relatively enlightened, no matter how great the variability of beliefs; and the idea that practices such as slavery cannot be evaluated across cultures by a common standard seems patently ridiculous to many persons. It is one thing to suggest that such practices might be *excused,* and quite another to suggest that they are *right*.

Perhaps the most serious philosophical objections to normative relativism turn on its claim to provide a *standard* for right belief. If a conscientious objector believed strongly, prior to World War II, that he or she must resist all wars, but after the beginning of World War II, changed this belief to cover only some wars, can one assume that one view was correct at one time and another correct at another time? If a person is forever changing beliefs, is it always morally right to act on each belief for the duration that it is held? Moreover, if we turn to the group form of normative relativism, what are we to think when a person belongs jointly to many groups or societies, each of whose moral standards conflicts with his or her beliefs? Suppose I am dying, and believe in assisted suicide, which is strictly prohibited in my society. What am I bound to do? If I am a Quaker of deep religious convictions that conflict with the generally accepted rules of war in my culture, wherein do my obligations lie? One of the problems involved in unraveling these puzzles is that the concept of a social group is itself difficult to interpret. Americans, for example, seem to differ in beliefs as often as they agree, and members of seemingly more homogeneous groups, such as Roman Catholics, often are in open conflict over matters of belief. Significant moral disagreement can emerge within all such groups, and it is sometimes unclear whether persons are or are not even members of a social group. All these matters need to be clarified before normative relativism can begin to appear a plausible and attractive ethical theory.

Finally, if we interpret normative relativism as *requiring* tolerance of other views, the whole theory is imperiled by inconsistency. The proposition that we ought to tolerate the views of others, or that it is right not to interfere with others, is precluded by the very strictures of the theory. Such a proposition bears all the marks of a *nonrelative* account of moral rightness, one based on, but not reducible to, the cross-cultural findings of anthropologists. If there can be relativity of belief in the case of every other ethical issue, then there certainly can be relativity over whether the practices of another society or person are to be tolerated. Alternatively, if the relativist holds that a principle of tolerance is demanded by "morality itself," then other fundamental normative propositions surely cannot be excluded from similar standing in the purportedly relativist theory. Indeed, we may suspect that something like a (universal) principle of respect for persons underlies and gives moral force to the normative relativists' appeal for tolerance and respect. But if this moral principle is recognized as valid, it can of course be employed as an instrument for criticizing such cultural practices as the denial of human rights to minorities and such beliefs as that of racial superiority. A moral commitment to tolerance of other practices and beliefs thus leads inexorably to the abandonment of normative relativism.

It may be possible to defend some form of relativism against these criticisms by various qualifications, but as yet, no compelling relativism of the forms studied here has emerged. Moreover, it would probably not repay the effort at this stage of our inquiry to concoct ingenious qualifications of relativist views. There will be many opportunities to compare relativism with nonrelative theories later in this book; and, as we shall presently see, concern about *relativism* probably mislocates the deepest moral problem. More bothersome are issues of moral pluralism and moral disagreement. As Brandt has indicated, problems of moral disagreement are different from (though closely related to) problems of relativism, even though they may be regarded as a natural outgrowth of the same anthropological data.

MORAL DISAGREEMENT AND MORAL PLURALISM

Two judges recently found themselves in an interesting disagreement when confronted with a murder trial popularly known as the Tarasoff case. A woman named Tarasoff had been killed by a man who had previously confided to a psychiatrist his intention to kill her as soon as she returned home from a summer in Brazil. Owing to obligations of confidentiality between patient and physician, a psychologist and a consulting psychiatrist did not report the threat to the woman or her family, though they did make one unsuccessful attempt to commit the man to a mental hospital. One judge held that the therapist could not escape liability, saying that, "When a therapist determines, or pursuant to the standards of his profession should determine, that his patient presents a serious danger of violence to another, he incurs an obligation to use reasonable care to protect the intended victim against such danger." Notification of police and direct warnings to the family were mentioned as possible instances of due care. The judge argued that although medical confidentiality must generally be observed by physicians, it was overridden in this particular case by a duty to the possible victim and to the "public interest in safety from violent assault." Despite the substantial importance of rules of professional ethics, the judge held that these rules cede priority to matters of greater importance, such as the protection of persons from violent assault. In the minority opinion, a second judge stated his firm disagreement. He argued that a patient's rights are violated when rules of confidentiality are not observed, that psychiatric treatment would be frustrated by nonobservance, that patients would subsequently lose confidence in psychiatrists and would fail to provide full disclosures, and that violent assaults would actually increase because mentally ill persons would be discouraged from seeking psychiatric aid.*

The Tarasoff case is an instance of a moral dilemma, for strong moral reasons support each of the quite opposite conclusions of the two judges. The most difficult and recalcitrant moral controversies are almost always similarly dilemmatic. This is a well-known feature of what Guido Calabresi has called "tragic choices." Everyone who has

---

*Tarasoff v. Regents of the University of California, California Supreme Court (17 California Reports, 3d Series, 425. Decided July 1, 1976).

been faced with a difficult decision, such as whether to have an abortion, to commit a member of one's family to a mental institution, to fire a failing but long-time employee, or to file for a divorce, knows through deep personal anguish what is meant by a personal dilemma and a tragic choice. Such dilemmas occur whenever good reasons for mutually exclusive alternatives can be cited; if any one set of reasons is acted upon, outcomes desirable in some respects but undesirable in others will result.

It is important to note that parties on both sides of dilemmatic controversies can *correctly* marshal moral principles in support of their substantially different conclusions. Consider, for example, the issue of whether prisoners should be involved as voluntary subjects of nontherapeutic drug research. Moral principles of autonomy, as we shall see in Chapter 4, dictate that prisoners should not be denied the opportunity to volunteer to participate. Yet moral principles requiring avoidance of the harm that might be caused by research or by exploitation of confined persons suggest the contrary conclusion that we should ban research in prisons, a prohibition most nations have now accepted. One moral resolution holds that prisoners should be free to volunteer under some prison conditions (e.g., where there are sanitary facilities, minimum security provisions, and consent referees) and be prohibited from volunteering under other prison conditions (e.g., where there exist powerful parole boards, unmonitored punitive possibilities, and undue influence through payments by drug companies). This ideal solution unfortunately leaves the actual dilemma largely unsettled. Current prison facilities exhibit an unstable mixture of these conditions, a mixture that is not likely to be changed merely to facilitate drug research.

Most moral dilemmas present a similar need to balance competing ideal claims in untidy circumstances. The reasons on each side of many moral problems are weighty, and none is obviously the right set of reasons. Indeed, there is a sense in which *all* the reasons ought to be acted on, for each, considered by itself, is a good reason. To summarize, situations involving moral dilemmas that lead to disagreements usually take one of two forms: (1) Some evidence indicates that an act is morally right, and some evidence indicates that the act is morally wrong, but the evidence on both sides is inconclusive. Abortion, for example, is sometimes said to be "a terrible dilemma" for women who see the evidence in this way. (2) It is clear to the agent that on moral grounds he or she both ought and ought not to perform an act. Some have viewed as dilemmatic in this second way debates about whether one ought to assist the suicide of a helpless, pain-ridden patient already near death. Perhaps a similar dilemma confronted persons in the Hudson Bay tribes who refused to strangle a friend despite the power of custom and the friend's overt request.

Dilemmas and disagreements such as the ones faced in the Tarasoff case and in the issue of prisoners' participation in research are familiar features of the moral life— at least as familiar as the legal controversies handled by courts. As we reflect on disagreements, we may increasingly come to stamp them as *irresolvable* moral dilemmas, much as we might find it impossible to arbitrate the differences between "mercy killing" at Hudson Bay and our own opposition to killing. Even if reason and rational deliberation play critical roles in moral arguments, when considered alone they seem insufficient to resolve disagreements over equally plausible solutions. Furthermore, different persons give different meanings to critical terms and principles invoked in these debates, and they attach different moral weights to the very same moral principles. Such disagreements are by no means confined to philosophy or to moral argument. The same sorts of problems appear in the natural and social sciences, for example, where controversies may be nourished and sustained for years, eventually terminating without real resolution of the disagreements. It is not at all implausible to maintain that the same degree of diversity and disagreement that infects morals also infects science, and that controversies are no more easily resolved in the one domain than in the other. Nonetheless, there is a peculiar intractability about some moral dilemmas and disagreements—one which suggests that a single ideal of moral objectivity may not be realizable.

One possible response to this problem is that we do not have, and are not likely ever to have, a single ethical theory or a single method for resolving disagreements. In any pluralistic culture, there may be many sources of moral value and consequently a pluralism of moral points of view on many issues: We will never agree about the morality of extramarital affairs, abortion, bluffing in business deals, providing national health insurance to all citizens, involuntarily committing the mentally disturbed, civil disobedience, etc. If this response is correct, it is obvious why there seem to be intractable moral controversies both within and outside professional philosophy.

The idea that there is an irreducible moral pluralism presently receives support from several moral philosophers, two of whom will now be encountered. The first argument, by Alasdair MacIntyre, reaches largely skeptical conclusions. MacIntyre believes that moral pluralism renders at least some moral disagreements systematically unresolvable, for the rival premises used by disputing parties simply cannot be made compatible, and there is no other rational way to assess the claims of one argument by comparison with those of another. This form of belief in ultimate disagreement could be used to support individual relativism, but MacIntyre does not argue in this direction. In the second article, Thomas Nagel develops a more optimistic position on moral pluralism, for he believes rational approaches can be taken to the resolution of controversial and even dilemmatic problems, despite what he sees as an ineliminable pluralism.

ALASDAIR MACINTYRE

Moral Disagreements*

I do not want to attend to the details of [moral] disagreements, so much as to the fact of disagreement. For I take it that the inability of professional moral philosophers to resolve disagreement about the concept of morality and the meaning of such words as ''moral'' and ''ethical'' through argument is related to the inability of ordinary moral agents to resolve their disagreements about which moral principles are the correct ones. Consider two important contemporary moral debates.

1. *A*: A just war is one in which the good to be achieved outweighs the evils involved in waging the war and in which a clear distinction can be made between combatants—whose lives are at stake—and innocent noncombatants. But in modern war, calculation of future escalation is never reliable and no practically applicable distinction between combatants and noncombatants can be made. Therefore no modern war can be a just war and we all *now* ought to be pacifists.

B: If you wish for peace, prepare for war. The only way to achieve peace is to deter potential aggressors. Therefore you must build up your armaments and make it clear that going to war on any scale is not ruled out by your policies. A necessary part of making this clear is being prepared both to fight limited wars and to go not only to, but beyond the nuclear brink on certain types of occasion. Otherwise you will not avoid war *and* you will lose.

C: Wars between the Great Powers are purely destructive and all of them ought to

be opposed by revolutionaries; but wars waged to liberate oppressed groups and peoples, especially in the Third World, are a necessary and therefore justified means for destroying exploitation and domination.

2. *A*: Everybody has certain rights over their own person, including their own body. It follows from the nature of these rights that at the stage when the embryo is essentially part of the mother's body, the mother has a right to make her own uncoerced decision on whether she will have an abortion or not. Therefore each pregnant woman ought to decide and ought to be allowed to decide for herself what she will do in the light of her own moral views.

B: I cannot, if I will to be alive, consistently will that my mother should have had an abortion when she was pregnant with me, except if it had been certain that the embryo was dead or gravely damaged. But if I cannot consistently will this in my own case, how can I consistently deny to others the right to life that I claim for myself? I would break the so-called Golden Rule unless I denied that a mother has in general a right on abortion. I am not of course thereby committed to the view that abortion ought to be legally prohibited.

C: Murder is wrong, prohibited by natural and divine law. Murder is the taking of innocent life. An embryo is an identifiable individual, differing from a new-born infant only in being at an earlier stage on the long road to adult capacities. If infanticide is murder, as it is, then abortion is murder. So abortion is not only morally wrong, but ought to be legally prohibited.

About these two arguments I want to make four major points. The first concerns

*From *The Belmont Report: Ethical Principles and Guidelines for the Protection of Human Subjects of Research,* Appendix I, DHEW Publication (OS) 78-0013 (Washington, D.C.: Government Printing Office, 1978).

the systematically unsettlable and interminable character of such arguments. Each of the protagonists reaches his conclusion by a valid form of inference from his premises. But there is no agreement as to which premises from which to start; and there exists in our culture no recognized procedure for weighing the merits of rival premises. Indeed it is difficult to see how there could be such a procedure since the rival premises are—to borrow a term from contemporary philosophy of science—incommensurable. That is to say, they employ and involve concepts of such radically different kinds that we have no way to weigh the claims of one alternative set of premises over against another. In the first debate an appeal to an Aristotelian concept of justice is matched against an appeal to a Machiavellian concept of interest and both are attacked from the standpoint of a Fichtean conception of liberation. We have no scales, no set of standards, by which to assess the weight to be given to justice thus conceived over against interest thus conceived or liberation thus conceived. Similarly, in the second debate an understanding of rights which owes something to Locke and something to Jefferson is counterposed to a universalizability argument whose debt is first to Kant and then to the gospels and both to an appeal to the moral law as conceived by Hooker, More, and Aquinas.

Secondly, in this unsettlable character, in this use of incommensurable premises, these debates are clearly typical of moral argument in our society. If the debates had been about euthanasia instead of abortion or social justice instead of war, the characteristics of the arguments would have been substantially the same. Perhaps not all moral disagreement in our society is of this kind, but much is and the more important the disagreement the more likely it is to have this character.

Thirdly—and this is the point of my excursion into the characteristics of moral disagreement—there are crucial links between this kind of disagreement among ordinary moral agents over which moral principles we are to adopt and the current disagreements between moral philosophers about how morality is to be defined. Indeed, one not uncommon type of argument used by contemporary moral philosophers has been of the form: if *X*'s account of morality is accepted, then such-and-such moral principles would be acceptable; but those moral principles are precisely unacceptable, and therefore *X*'s account of morality must be rejected. . . .

This conceptual connection between the content of moral principles and the definition of morality will perhaps be best elucidated by considering its historical explanation. When I characterized the rival moral premises of contemporary debates as Aristotelian, Machiavellian, Fichtean, and so on, I suggested something of the wide range of historical sources on which contemporary moral argument draws, but I did so by using the names of philosophers as a kind of allusive shorthand. Three points need to be made in a more extended way. The first is that the origins of contemporary moral debates are not to be found only or even mainly in the writings of philosophers, but in the forms of argument which informed whole cultures and which the writings of philosophers articulate for us in exceptionally clear and accessible ways: Aristotle is being treated here as a spokesman for at least a central strand in the culture of fourth-century Athens, Fichte as related in a similar way to [the] nineteenth century.

Secondly, the premises of contemporary moral debate have not merely been inherited; they have also been torn from the social and intellectual contexts in which they were originally at home, from which they derived such force and validity as they possess. What we have inherited are *only* fragments and one reason why we do not know how to weigh one set of premises against another is that we do not know what force or validity to grant to each of them in isolation.

Thirdly, as the conceptual connection between the content of morality and its definition would lead us to expect, this fragmented inheritance is embodied in our rival definitions of morality as well as in our rival sets of moral principles. . . .

Fourthly, . . . the peculiar function of evaluative expressions in our discourse is to refer us to impersonal standards of value, to give reasons whose force is independent of who utters them. The implication is that in this part of our discourse we ought to be able to arrive at rational agreements on central, if not always on peripheral, issues. Yet the state of moral argument in our culture shows this not to be so. We therefore seem to be in a dilemma: *either* we have to reject the presuppositions of the dominant culture of our own society *or* we have to reject the possibility of rationality in moral argument. But the roots of this dilemma are, so I have suggested, historical.

THOMAS NAGEL

The Fragmentation of Value*

The strongest cases of conflict are genuine dilemmas, where there is decisive support for two or more incompatible courses of action or inaction. In that case a decision will still be necessary, but it will seem necessarily arbitrary. When two choices are very evenly balanced, it does not matter which choices one makes, and arbitrariness is no problem. But when each seems right for reasons that appear decisive and sufficient, arbitrariness means the lack of reasons where reasons are needed, since either choice will mean acting against some reasons without being able to claim that they are *outweighed.*

There are five fundamental types of value that give rise to basic conflict. Conflicts can arise within as well as between them, but the latter are especially difficult. (I have not included self-interest in the group; it can conflict with any of the others.)

*From *Mortal Questions* (Cambridge, England: Cambridge University Press, 1979), pp. 128–137.

First, there are specific obligations to other people or institutions: obligations to patients, to one's family, to the hospital or university at which one works, to one's community or one's country. Such obligations have to be incurred, either by a deliberate undertaking or by some special relation to the person or institution in question. Their existence depends in either case on the subject's relation to others. . . .

The next category is that of constraints on action deriving from general rights that everyone has, either to do certain things or not to be treated in certain ways. . . .

The third category is that which is technically called utility. This is the consideration that takes into account the effects of what one does on everyone's welfare—whether or not the components of that welfare are connected to special obligations or general rights. . . .

The fourth category is that of perfectionist ends or values. By this I mean the intrinsic value of certain achievements or creations, apart from their value *to* individuals who experience or use them. Examples are provided by the intrinsic value of scientific discovery, of artistic creation, of space exploration, perhaps. . . .

The final category is that of commitment to one's own projects or undertakings, which is a value in addition to whatever reasons may have led to them in the first place. . . .

Obligations, rights, utility, perfectionist ends, and private commitments—these values enter into our decisions constantly, and conflicts among them, and within them, arise in medical research, in politics, in personal life, or wherever the grounds of action are not artificially restricted. What would it mean to give a system of priorities among them? A simpler moral conception might permit a solution in terms of a short list of clear prohibitions and injunctions, with the balance of decision left to personal preference or discretion, but that will not work with so mixed a collection. One might try to order them. For example: never infringe general rights, and undertake only those special obligations that cannot lead to the infringement of anyone's rights; maximize utility within the range of action left free by the constraints of rights and obligations; where utility would be equally served by various policies, determine the choice by reference to perfectionist ends; and finally, where this leaves anything unsettled, decide on grounds of personal commitment or even simple preference. Such a method of decision is absurd, not because of the particular order chosen but because of its absoluteness. The ordering I have given is not arbitrary, for it reflects a degree of relative stringency in these types of values. But it is absurd to hold that obligations can never outweigh rights, or that utility, however large, can never outweigh obligation.

However, if we take the idea of outweighing seriously, and try to think of an alternative to ordering as a method of rationalizing decision in conditions of conflict, the thing to look for seems to be a single scale on which all these apparently disparate considerations can be measured, added, and balanced. Utilitarianism is the best example of such a theory, and interesting attempts have been made to explain the apparent priority of rights and obligations over utility in utilitarian terms. The same might be tried for perfectionist goals and personal commitments. My reason for thinking that such explanations are unsuccessful, or at best partially successful, is not just that they imply specific moral conclusions that I find intuitively unacceptable (for it is always conceivable that a new refinement of the theory may iron out many of those wrinkles). Rather, my reason for doubt is theoretical: I do not believe that the source of value is unitary—displaying apparent multiplicity only in its application to the world. I believe that value has fundamentally different kinds of sources, and that they are reflected in the classification of values into types. Not all values represent the pursuit of some single good in a variety of settings. . . .

We appreciate the force of impersonal reasons when we detach from our personal situation and our special relations to others. Utilitarian considerations arise in this way when our detachment takes the form of adopting a general point of view that comprehends everyone's view of the world within it. Naturally the results will not always be clear. But such an outlook is obviously very different from that which appears in a person's concern for his special obligations to his family, friends, or colleagues. There he is thinking very much of his particular situation in the world. The two motives come from two different points of view, both important, but fundamentally irreducible to a common basis.

I have said nothing about the still more agent-centered motive of commitment to one's own projects, but since that involves one's own life and not necessarily any relations with others, the same points obviously apply. It is a source of reasons that cannot be assimilated either to utility, or perfectionism, or rights, or obligations (except that they might be described as obligations to oneself).

My general point is that the formal differences among types of reason reflect differences of a fundamental nature in their sources, and that this rules out a certain kind of solution to conflicts among these types. Human beings are subject to moral and other motivational claims of very different kinds. This is because they are complex creatures who can view the world from many perspectives—individual, relational, impersonal, ideal, etc.—and each perspective presents a different set of claims. Conflict can exist within one of these sets, and it may be hard to resolve. But when conflict occurs between them, the problem is still more difficult. Conflicts between personal and impersonal claims are ubiquitous. They cannot, in my view, be resolved by subsuming either of the points of view under the other, or both under a third. Nor can we simply abandon any of them. There is no reason why we should. The capacity to view the world simultaneously from the point of view of one's relations to others, from the point of view of one's life extended through time, from the point of view of everyone at once, and finally from the detached viewpoint often described as the view *sub specie aeternitatis* is one of the marks of humanity. This complex capacity is an obstacle to simplification.

Does this mean, then, that basic practical conflicts have no solution? The unavailability of a single, reductive method or a clear set of priorities for settling them does not remove the necessity for making decisions in such cases. When faced with conflicting and incommensurable claims we still have to do something—even if it is only to do nothing. And the fact that action must be unitary seems to imply that unless justification is also unitary, nothing can be either right or wrong and all decisions under conflict are arbitrary.

I believe this is wrong, but the alternative is hard to explain. Briefly, I contend that there can be good judgment without total justification, either explicit or implicit. The fact that one cannot say why a certain decision is the correct one, given a particular balance of conflicting reasons, does not mean that the claim to correctness is meaningless. Provided one has taken the process of practical justification as far as it will go in the course of arriving at the conflict, one may be able to proceed without further justification, but without irrationality either. What makes this possible is *judgment*—essentially the faculty Aristotle described as practical wisdom, which reveals itself over time in individual decisions rather than in the enunciation of general principles. It will not always yield a solution: there are true practical dilemmas that have no solution, and there are also conflicts so complex that judgment cannot operate confidently. But in many cases it can be relied on to take up the slack that remains beyond the limits of explicit rational argument.

This view has sometimes been regarded as defeatist and empty since it was expressed by Aristotle. In reply, let me say two things. First, the position does not imply that we should abandon the search for more and better reasons and more critical insight in the domain of practical decision. It is just that our capacity to resolve conflicts in particular cases may extend beyond our capacity to enunciate general principles that explain those resolutions. Perhaps we are working with general principles unconsciously, and can discover them by codifying our decisions and particular intuitions. But this is not necessary either for the operation or for the development of judgment. Second, the search for general principles in ethics, or other aspects of practical reasoning, is more likely to be successful if systematic theories restrict themselves to one aspect of the subject—one component of rational motivation—than if they try to be comprehensive.

To look for a single general theory of how to decide the right thing to do is like looking for a single theory of how to decide what to believe. Such progress as we have made in the systematic justification and criticism of beliefs has not come mostly from general principles of reasoning but from the understanding of particular areas, marked out by the different sciences, by history, by mathematics. These vary in exactness, and large areas of belief are left out of the scope of any theory. These must be governed by common sense and ordinary, prescientific reasoning. Such reasoning must also be used where the results of various more systematic methods bear on the matter at hand, but no one of them determines a conclusion. In civil engineering problems, for example, the solution depends both on physical factors capable of precise calculation and behavioral or psychological factors that are not. Obviously one should use exact principles and methods to deal with those aspects of a problem for which they are available, but sometimes there are other aspects as well, and one must resist the temptation either to ignore them or to treat them by exact methods to which they are not susceptible.

We are familiar with this fragmentation of understanding and method when it comes to belief, but we tend to resist it in the case of decision. Yet it is as irrational to despair of systematic ethics because one cannot find a completely general account of what should be done as it would be to give up scientific research

because there is no general method of arriving at true beliefs. I am not saying that ethics is a science, only that the relation between ethical theory and practical decisions is analogous to the relation between scientific theory and beliefs about particular things or events in the world.

In both areas, some problems are much purer than others, that is, their solutions are more completely determined by factors that admit of precise understanding. Sometimes the only significant factor in a practical decision is personal obligation, or general utility, and then one's reasoning can be confined to that (however precisely it may be understood). Sometimes a process of decision is artificially insulated against the influence of more than one type of factor. This is not always a good thing, but sometimes it is. The example I have in mind is the judicial process, which carefully excludes, or tries to exclude, considerations of utility and personal commitment, and limits itself to claims of right. Since the systematic recognition of such claims is very important (and also tends over the long run not to conflict unacceptably with other values), it is worth isolating these factors for special treatment. As a result, legal argument has been one of the areas of real progress in the understanding of a special aspect of practical reason. Systematic theory and the search for general principles and methods may succeed elsewhere if we accept a fragmentary approach. Utilitarian theory, for example, has a great deal to contribute if it is not required to account for everything. Utility is an extremely important factor in decisions, particularly in public policy, and philosophical work on its definition, the coordination problems arising in the design of institutions to promote utility, its connections with preference, with equality, and with efficiency, can have an impact on such decisions.

This and other areas can be the scene

of progress even if none of them aspires to the status of a general and complete theory of right and wrong. There will never be such a theory, in my view, since the role of judgment in resolving conflicts and applying disparate claims and considerations to real life is indispensable. Two dangers can be avoided if this idea of noncomprehensive systematization is kept in mind. One is the danger of romantic defeatism, which abandons rational theory because it inevitably leaves many problems unsolved. The other is the danger of exclusionary over-rationalization, which bars as irrelevant or empty all considerations that cannot be brought within the scope of a general system admitting explicitly defensible conclusions.

Nagel's conclusions about the fragmentation of value lead directly to moral pluralism. His argument and MacIntyre's argument together challenge the systems of general normative ethics that are introduced for discussion in Chapter 3, and the contentions of these two authors should be kept in mind when turning to those chapters. It is worth notice here, however, that even if MacIntyre comes close to defending a relativistic position, Nagel resists this alternative and concludes that a "romantic defeatism" that abandons "rational theory" is strictly to be avoided. Nagel obviously believes that reason has an essential role to play in moral thinking, that of critically reflecting on troublesome moral problems without attempting to unite them in a single moral theory. For him, fragmentation entails neither relativism, subjectivism, nor the ultimate disagreement that Brandt apparently accepts. On the other hand, if MacIntyre's challenge is taken up, and we ask how moral disagreement can be resolved—especially apparently deep ones such as those found by the Hudson Bay explorers—Nagel seems to leave us with only an undeveloped appeal to the importance of moral "judgment." Let us, then, address the question of whether reason and ethical theory can help to bring about a resolution of moral controversies.

THE RESOLUTION OF MORAL DISAGREEMENTS

Can we hope to resolve moral controversies in contexts of disagreements? And, if so, on what principles or procedures should we rely? Probably no single set of considerations will prove consistently reliable as a means of ending disagreement and controversy; and resolutions of cross-cultural conflicts such as those involved in the Hudson Bay case will always be especially elusive. Nonetheless, several methods for dealing constructively with moral disagreements have been employed in the past, and each deserves recognition as a method of easing and perhaps even settling controversies.

1. First, many moral disagreements can be at least partially resolved by obtaining critical factual information on which points of moral controversy turn. We have already seen how important such information can be in trying to ascertain whether cultural variations in belief are truly *fundamental*. Unfortunately, it has often been assumed that moral disputes are (by definition) produced solely by differences over

moral principles or their application, and not by a lack of scientific or factual information. This assumption is quite mistaken, for moral disputes—that is, disputes over what morally ought or ought not to be done—often have nonmoral elements as central ingredients. As we saw when considering cultural relativism, differences in factual belief over the nature of an afterlife or the harm that will be produced by some contemplated action may be at the heart of moral disagreements between cultures, though these are clearly not differences of moral principle.

Factual disagreements can also stall the resolution of moral disagreements that have nothing to do with cultural differences. For example, debates about capital punishment have foundered for decades on the factual issue of whether the threat of capital punishment functions effectively to deter potential criminals from committing certain especially hateful crimes. A great deal of factual evidence has been marshaled on both sides, as yet inconclusively. This key issue is again predominantly factual, not a dispute over a moral principle or its proper application (though this is not to say that *all* disputes about capital punishment are factual ones). In other cases, new information has made possible a move toward negotiation and even the resolution of controversies. New scientific information about the alleged dangers involved in certain kinds of scientific research, for example, have turned surging moral controversies over the public risks of science and the rights of scientific researchers in unanticipated directions. In one recent controversy (over so-called recombinant DNA research), it had been feared that the research might create an organism of pathogenic capability, against which known antibodies would be inefficacious and which might produce widespread contagion. Accusations of unjustifiable and immoral research filled the corridors of certain universities and even congressional hearing rooms. New scientific information to the effect that a bacterial strain used in the research was less dangerous than had been feared had a dramatic effect on the moral and political controversy about the justifiability of the risks to society presented by scientific research.

Controversies about saccharin, toxic substances in the workplace, nuclear plants, IQ research, fluoridation, and the swine-flu vaccine, among others, are similarly laced with issues over both values and facts. The arguments used by disagreeing parties may turn on some conception of liberty, and therefore may be primarily moral; but they may also rest on factual disagreements over, for example, the efficacy of a product or treatment. New information may have only a limited bearing on the resolution of some of these controversies, while in others it may have a direct and almost overpowering influence. The problem is that rarely, if ever, is sufficient information obtained to settle even these factual matters. This problem is identical to the one we encountered in noting that anthropological evidence is rarely complete enough to allow us to compare the factual and evaluative assumptions at work in such contexts as that of the beliefs and practices at Hudson Bay.

2. Second, controversies have been settled by reaching conceptual or definitional agreement over the language used by disputing parties. In some cases, stipulating a definition or clearly explaining what is meant by a term may prove sufficient, but in other cases, agreement will not be so easily reached. Controversies over the morality of euthanasia, for example, are often needlessly entangled because different senses of the term are employed. If one party equates euthanasia with mercy killing and another party equates it with voluntarily elected natural death, the "controversy" over the issue of the morality of euthanasia is lost in terminological problems. The Hudson Bay case presents similar problems, for it is doubtful that what we describe as "killing" would be the term chosen by the Hudson Bay tribes. It is unclear even what "killing" means in English, including the extent to which it carries moral censure. Thus, there may be no agreed-upon point of contention in some controversial cases, for the parties will be addressing entirely separate issues through their conceptual assumptions. Conceptual agreement provides no guarantee that a dispute will be settled, of course, but it may at least advance discussion of the issues.

3. Resolution of moral problems can also be facilitated if disputing parties can come to agreement on a common framework of moral principles. If this method required a complete shift from one moral point of view to another, starkly different one, resolution would rarely be achieved. Differences that divide persons at the level of their most cherished principles are deep divisions, and conversions are infrequent. MacIntyre, of course, concentrated on precisely this level of disagreement among philosophers, and he properly noted how naive it would be to suppose that moral theories can somehow be synthesized into one unified framework. On the other hand, various forms of discussion and negotiation can lead to the adoption of a new or changed moral framework that can serve as a common basis for discussion.

A recent United States national commission appointed to study ethical issues in research involving human subjects (of the sort we saw Zimbardo conducting in Chapter 1) began its deliberations by unanimously adopting a common framework of moral principles that provided the general background for deliberations about particular problems. Commissioners developed a framework of three moral principles: respect for persons, beneficence, and justice. These principles were analyzed in detail in the light of contemporary philosophical ethics and then applied to a wide range of moral problems that confronted the commission.* The transcripts of this body's deliberations provide ample evidence that the common framework of moral principles greatly facilitated discussion of the controversies the commissioners addressed and led to many agreements that might otherwise have been impossible.

4. Fourth, resolution of moral controversies can be aided by use of example and opposed counterexample. This form of debate is modeled after the legal reasoning that takes place in a court of law. Here precedent cases are detailed by a lawyer, and counterexamples are brought by a second lawyer against the claims of the first lawyer. Such use of example and counterexample serves as a format for weighing conflicting considerations and placing them in the proper perspective. This form of debate occurred, for example, when the aforementioned national commission came to consider the level of risk that can justifiably be permitted in scientific research involving children as subjects

---

*These principles and their analysis by the commission have been published as *The Belmont Report: Ethical Principles and Guidelines for the Protection of Human Subjects of Research*, DHEW Publication (OS)78-0012 (Washington, D.C.: Government Printing Office, 1978).

where no therapeutic benefit is offered to the child. On the basis of principles of acceptable risk used in their own previous deliberations, the commissioners were at first inclined to accept the view that only procedures involving very low or minimal risk could be justified in the case of children (where "minimal risk" refers analogically to the level of risk present in standard medical examinations of patients). However, examples from the history of medicine were cited that revealed how certain significant diagnostic, therapeutic, and preventive advances in medicine would have been unlikely, or at least retarded, if procedures that posed a higher level of risk had not been employed. Counterexamples of overzealous researchers who placed children at too much risk were then thrown up against these examples, and the debate continued for several months. Eventually, the majority of commissioners abandoned their original view that nontherapeutic research that presents more than minimal risk was unjustified; instead, they accepted the position that a higher level of risk can be justified by the benefits provided to other children (as when a number of terminally ill children become subjects in the hope that something will be learned about their disease that can be applied to other children). Once a consensus on this particular issue crystallized, resolution was quickly achieved on the entire moral controversy about the involvement of children as research subjects (although a small minority of commissioners never agreed).

5. Finally, one of the most important methods of philosophical inquiry in general is that of exposing the inadequacies and unexpected consequences of an argument. The nature of moral argument will be studied in Chapter 9, but we may observe here how this method of inquiry can be brought to bear on moral disagreements. If an argument is inconsistent, then pointing out the inconsistency to its advocates obviously can cause them to change their minds and shift the focus of discussion; but there are many more subtle ways of attacking an argument. For example, a number of writers have discussed the nature of "persons" when treating such issues as the problem of abortion and fetal rights; and some of these writers have not appreciated that their arguments about persons were so broad that they carried important implications for both infants and animals as well as for human fetuses. Their arguments provided them with previously unnoticed reasons for denying to infants rights that adults have, or for granting (or denying) to fetuses the same rights that infants have, or—in some cases—for granting (or denying) to animals the same rights that infants have. It may, of course, be correct to hold that infants have fewer rights than adults, or that fetuses and animals should be granted the same rights as infants. The present point is only that if a moral argument leads to conclusions which its proponent is not prepared to defend and did not previously anticipate, then part of the argument will have to be changed. Presumably, the distance between those who disagree will be reduced by this process. This form of argument is often supplemented by one or more of the four previously cited ways of reducing moral disagreement. Much of the work published in philosophical journals takes precisely this form of attacking arguments, citing counterexamples, and proposing alternative frameworks of principles.

Some moral disagreements may not be resolvable by any of the five means discussed here—as MacIntyre strongly hints in his essay. This conclusion may apply to the legal and moral problems of fetal status that plague the debate over abortion, and it may well apply to the beliefs about euthanasia and killing mentioned earlier. Some problems of theological ethics, particularly problems about premises resting on religious faith, may similarly be unresolvable. No contention has been made in this section that moral disagreements regarding either ethical theory or specific moral problems can always be resolved, or even that every rational person must accept the same method for approaching such problems. There is always a possibility of ultimate disagreement at the levels of both theory and practice. However, *if* something is to be done about these problems of justification in contexts of controversy, a resolution is most likely to be attained by using the methods outlined in this section. These strategies will often be invoked in later chapters of this book.

EGOISM

We have seen that relativism, pluralism, and disagreement challenge beliefs about the objectivity of morals. The problem of egoism similarly challenges claims of objectivity. Rather than place an emphasis on diversity, however, egoism features self-promotion. It raises critical questions about the relative merits that claims to self-interest do and ought to have in our lives.

The problem of egoism has familiar origins. We have all been confronted with occasions on which a choice must be made between spending money on ourselves or on some worthy charitable enterprise. For example, when one elects to purchase new clothes for oneself rather than contribute to a university scholarship fund for poor students, self-interest has been given priority over the interests of those students. Egoism generalizes beyond such familiar occasions of choices to all human choices. The egoist contends that all choices do involve or should involve self-promotion as their sole objective. Thus, a person's only goal and perhaps only moral duty is self-promotion; one owes no sacrifices and no obligations to others. The following list, which derives from C. D. Broad, illustrates the motives that egoists have in mind when they speak of desires for self-promotion:

Desire for self-preservation
Desire for one's own happiness
Desire to be a self of a certain kind
Desire for self-respect
Desire to get and keep property
Desire for self-assertion
Desire for affection*

*C. D. Broad, "Egoism as a Theory of Human Motives," in his *Ethics and the History of Philosophy* (London: Routledge & Kegan Paul, Ltd., 1952), pp. 218–231. Broad also notes that there are certain more special relationships which prompt egoistic desires. He refers to these as egoistic motive-stimulants. They include the relation of ownership, the relation of blood-kinship, love and friendship, and membership in institutions.

Egoism has had considerable currency among academic psychologists and political theorists, and many people both believe in egoism and behave as egoists. Yet, this theory has never fared well among moral philosophers, who have variously judged it to be unprovable, false, inconsistent, or utterly irrelevant to morality. We shall later consider objections to egoism, but let us first look at the nature of the theory, its two types, and the arguments advanced in its defense.

Two Types of Egoism   *descriptive*

Everyone has heard the advice that one should always try to maximize one's own personal good in any given circumstance. This counsel is generally put in somewhat looser terms by saying, "You're a sucker if you don't always look out for yourself first and others second." Such a proposal is clearly unacceptable in light of common moral requirements. Morality requires that we return a lost puppy to its owner even if we become quite enamoured of it, and that we correct bank statements containing errors in our favor. Yet, why should we look our for the interests of others on such occasions? This question has troubled many reflective persons, some of whom have concluded that acting against one's own interest is actually contrary to *reason.* These thinkers have seen conventional morality as tinged with irrational sentiment and indefensible constraints on the individual. They are supporters of *ethical egoism,* which may be roughly defined as the theory that the only valid moral standard is the obligation to promote one's own well-being above everyone else's.

This theory must be distinguished from a second type of egoism, which is a *psychological* rather than an *ethical* theory. The second is an account of what is contrary to human nature (in contrast to what is contrary to human reason), and hence is called "psychological egoism." This second theory concerns human motivation and offers an *explanation* of human conduct (as contrasted with a *justification* of human conduct). It says that people always do what pleases them or what is in their own interest. Sometimes it is even put in the stronger form that we not only *do* always maximize our own good but that we psychologically *cannot* act voluntarily against what we believe to be in our own best interest. For example, it could be maintained that the people of Hudson Bay who requested their own execution could not have acted otherwise, given their beliefs about how much they might suffer in the future and how they would fare in an afterlife. Regardless of whether the theory is formulated as "We *do* act egoistically" or as "We *must* act this way," some typical popular ways of expressing this viewpoint are these: "People are at heart selfish, even if they appear to be unselfish"; "people always look out for Number One first"; "in the long run, everybody always does what he or she wants to do or whatever is least painful"; and "no matter what a person says, everybody always acts for the sake of personal satisfaction."

Psychological egoism presents a serious challenge to moral philosophy, for, if correct, there could be no purely altruistic or moral motivation (as we commonly use the term "morality"). Normative ethics presupposes that one *ought* to behave in accordance with certain moral principles, whether or not such behavior promotes one's own interest. If people are so constituted that they always act in their own interest, then it would be absurd ever to ask them to act contrary to this self-interest. Moreover, if persons are so constituted that they can act only to promote their own interests, it is pointless and redundant to recommend what ethical egoism recommends; that is, it is pointless to tell them they should do so-and-so when they cannot avoid doing it anyway. Let us look in detail, then, at psychological egoism before turning to ethical egoism.

Psychological Egoism

Those who tend toward acceptance of psychological egoism do so because they are convinced by their observation of themselves and others that people are thoroughly self-centered. Conversely, those who reject the theory are likely to do so because they see such obvious examples of altruistic behavior in the lives of saints, heroes, and public servants, and because contemporary psychology offers many compelling studies of sacrificial behavior. Even if it is conceded that people are basically selfish, it seems undeniable that there are at least *some* outstanding examples of preeminently unselfish actions. Those who take this view often cite practices of euthanasia and suicide among the aged, as at Hudson Bay, as paradigmatically unselfish. They consider these acts sacrificial, performed for the sake of the younger and more productive members of society who otherwise would be short of food and housing.

The defender of psychological egoism, of course, is not impressed by the exemplary lives of saints and heroes or by social practices of sacrifice. The psychological egoist does not contend that people always behave in an *outwardly* selfish manner. No matter how self-sacrificing a person's behavior may be at times, these egoists maintain, the desire behind the action is always selfish; one is ultimately out for oneself—whether in the long or the short run. In their view, an egoistic action is perfectly compatible with behavior that we standardly refer to as altruistic. The clever person who is self-interested can appear to be the most unselfish person that we have ever known, for whether any person is really acting egoistically depends on the motivation behind the appearance of the behavior. Any apparently altruistic person may simply believe that an unselfish appearance best promotes his or her own long-range interests. The fact that some "sacrifices" (pseudo-sacrifices) may be necessary in the short run thus fails to count against egoism.

A politician, for example, may actively promote the appearance of unselfishness and may indeed work tirelessly for his or her constituents. But if the politician does so solely in order to be reelected—presumably the best way to promote his or her own objectives—then the person would have adopted an egoistic policy. There is no doubt that any clever egoist would act in this way, for an unselfish demeanor is almost universally praised and a selfish one, likewise almost universally, is condemned. The psychological egoist tries to show that all persons who spend a great deal of effort to help others, to promote the general welfare, or even to risk their lives for the welfare of others are really acting to promote themselves.

Perhaps the best way to investigate the claims made by this theory is to reflect on two relevant examples, one apparently in support of psychological egoism, the other in apparent conflict. The first example we shall consider is quite fictional, but it has long inspired philosophers who have been attracted to psychological egoism. It has its philosophical origins in a famous passage of Plato's *Republic* (Book 2). Plato there puts in the mouth of a figure named Glaucon a story about a young man who is able to get rid of all the normal conventions and cultural constraints that operate in society, and so is left to his basic human instincts. The story is the following: Gyges the shepherd was tending his flock when suddenly an earthquake split the ground before him into a deep chasm. After the earthquake passed, Gyges was astonished by the sight and entered the chasm, where he found a tomb in the form of a hollow brazen horse. Inside the tomb was a body naked save for a gold ring on one finger. Gyges took the ring, and later, while attending a meeting of the shepherds, innocently turned the top part of the ring to the inside of his hand. At once he became invisible, and his companions commented that he must have slipped out of the room. He found he could appear and disappear at will by manipulating the ring. After his discovery, this previously innocent and honest shepherd contrived to become a courier who took messages from small villages to the court of the king. Once inside the court, he seduced the queen, and with her help murdered the king and seized the throne.

Now, says Glaucon, suppose that there were two such rings and that one was given to the most just of all persons. How would that person behave? No one, suggests Glaucon, would have such iron strength of mind as to stand fast in doing right or to keep his or her hands off another's property—when the person could do anything and have anything he or she wanted with an utter maximum of ease. Such a person would have the powers of a god and would behave no better than the most unjust person. The conclusion Glaucon draws is that we do what is morally right only under social compulsion. For our purposes, the point is that all persons perform morally obligatory actions only because they are culturally conditioned to do so or because they seek personal gain by their performance. And this, of course, is just one way of stating psychological egoism.

The second example is not hypothetical. It is an actual, and in some ways a routine, story reported in the *Washington Post:*

Doorman Bequeaths $100,000

When you make $60 a week and you spend 42 years opening Mayflower Hotel doors for those much richer, you learn—by osmosis and advice—how to make a little money become a lot of money.

Until his death three weeks ago, William H. (Mike) Mann applied his lessons. When his will was submitted for probate there this week, it was Washington-area children and invalids who reaped the benefits.

Mann's will leaves $100,000 in stocks and savings to 10 area charities, in equal parts. The money has been building and multiplying—and has never been touched—since Mann joined the Mayflower as a busboy at the hotel's opening in 1925. He was doorman at the time of his death. . . .

Concentrating on blue-chip stocks and occasionally on the surefire dividends of savings accounts, Mann always handled his transactions himself. . . .

As a bachelor living in an $85-a-month apartment near the Mayflower, Mann had few expenses. "He never looked like he had a dollar or a friend," [Milton] Kronheim recalled. . . .

[The benefactors] are Children's Hospital, the Hebrew Home for the Aged, the Little Sisters of the Poor, St. Ann's Infant Asylum, the Men of St. John's, the Jewish Social Service Agency, the Ner Israel Rabbinical College in Baltimore, the Florence Crittenden Home, the Linwood Children's Center in Ellicott City, and the Columbia Lighthouse for the Blind.*

The egoist will delight, of course, in Glaucon's story, and then attempt to explain away Mike Mann's alleged altruism. The egoist will argue that even if Mann deceived himself into thinking that he was acting from a sense of charity or duty, he was really acting for a reward, for he knew his will would be publicly acclaimed and stories recounting it would appear in newspapers. He would receive fame and glamour as a memorial, and for him this was psychologically satisfying, a goal worthy of pursuit for that reason. He did not act for the sake of charities—rather, for the sake of people's remembrance of him and the pleasure their expected acclaim would bring him. The cynical egoist might even hypothesize that Mann acted as he did for the sake of rewards in heaven or for his own sense of pride and avoidance of shame, for his income did not approximate that of most people around him. But most plausibly of all, it will be argued, Mike Mann's greatest satisfactions were found in small daily kindnesses to others, such as opening doors for famous people, who responded with like kindnesses. Not all persons are out to derive maximal satisfaction from money and fame, Mike Mann being but one example, but they seek to derive satisfaction from doing something they believe in. Everyone always acts for his or her own greatest personal satisfaction, which is sometimes found, not in power, riches, and fame, but rather in doing such things for other people as making them happy. The underlying principle is to see that we do whatever we do not primarily for the sake of the action performed, but rather for the sake of the satisfaction derived or some ultimate state of personal happiness—at least so the psychological egoist argues.

Those who deny psychological egoism will argue that Mike Mann (let us assume for the moment that they knew him and have evidence) was always a retiring individual who shied away from public recognition in every way possible—and that, moreover, he did not believe either in the existence of God or in the possibility of an afterlife. Mike Mann and many like him, they will insist, stand as a definitive refutation of the conclusions drawn in Glaucon's hypothetical story. Moreover, they will note, to support altruism is not to insist that we are always altruistic. As David Hume maintained in arguing for the compatibility of self-love and altruism, the altruist insists only that "It is suffi-

---

The Washington Post (Nov. 11, 1970), p. A28. Reprinted with permission of *The Washington Post.*

cient for our present purposes, if it be allowed . . . that there is some benevolence, however small, infused into our bosom; . . . some particle of the dove kneaded into our frame, along with the elements of the wolf and the serpent."*

Nonegoists will also argue that there is an important confusion, and perhaps more than one confusion, involved in egoist arguments. To say a person *derives satisfaction* from doing something is markedly different from saying that something is done *for the sake of the satisfaction;* and, as they see it, Mike Mann did not act for the sake of the satisfaction. These critics of egoism will also insist that the egoistic argument confuses *self-motivation* with *selfish motivation.* In one respect, it is perfectly correct to say that every voluntary act is self-motivated and stands to be self-gratifying; the act, after all, involves doing something in order to achieve one's own goals, to satisfy one's desires, and to fulfill one's interests. Those who requested to be killed at Hudson Bay had certain desires and some definite goals in mind, and they may have been gratified by their children's or friends' responses. However, it does not follow from either self-motivation or the satisfaction of desire that an act is selfishly motivated or performed for the sake of satisfaction; that is, it is not inevitable that such acts disregard the interests of others for reasons of self-promotion.

Altruistic interests are correctly describable, then, as involving personal interests that are not selfish interests. While desire for personal gain is often the motivating factor in human actions, there are all sorts of desires, many of them directed toward the interests of others. For example, if I see a blind man being cheated by a clerk at a railroad station, I may be motivated by a desire to see justice done or at least to see the facts set straight—just as in studying philosophy I am motivated by the desire to know something about ethical values. But the fact that I am motivated by these desires does not prove that I am motivated by the satisfaction that follows the success of the venture. As Bishop Butler pointed out, the satisfaction of any desire is one's own satisfaction, whether the desire be for self-gratification, the welfare of a child, revenge, pity, or malice. But it is true neither that all impulses have for their objects "states of the self" nor that the object of any of such desires is the general happiness of the self who experiences them. For example, sympathy and malice are not directed at producing one's own happiness, though both certainly come from oneself and both may produce happiness for the self. But, in producing happiness or misery for another, there is no guarantee of pleasure, and there may even be—and be known to be—a loss of self-gratification.

If the arguments thus far are correct, psychological egoism is not a tenable doctrine. However, it is not easy to produce a definitive refutation of psychological egoism, owing to many unresolved questions about human motivation. As we have seen, every time a case of benevolent behavior is presented, the egoist responds by arguing that the person really acted for egoistic reasons and then suggests the presence of some egoistic motives. In Mike Mann's case, we saw how the egoist theory alleges that he saved and gave away all his money in order to be well regarded by others. When the nonegoist

*David Hume, *An Enquiry Concerning the Principles of Morals,* ed. L. A. Selby-Bigge, rev. by P. H. Nidditch (Oxford, England: Clarendon Press, 1975), par. 220.

provided evidence that Mann could not have cared less for matters of reputation, the egoist argued that he did it for rewards in heaven. When it was shown that he did not believe in God or immortality, the egoist said that he did it to remove the anxieties of a guilt complex. If a psychiatrist then argues against this thesis, the egoist may retrench and say, "Look, he passed up an opportunity to enjoy almost everything this world has to offer. Doesn't this prove that he must have done it for some kind of personal gain or perhaps for avoidance of some kind of displeasure? Surely there must be some unconscious desires or wishes that are operative."

Here the unargued and unarguable character of the egoist's strategy clearly comes into focus. No longer with any evidence and in the teeth of counterevidence, the egoist asserts an a priori thesis about an empirical question. The egoist is driven to cite unconscious motives because no plausible conscious motive remains. It may of course be true that all human behavior is unconsciously motivated, and that we have yet to discover its deepest causes. The point nonetheless remains that egoism has no proof of this thesis and defends it only in order to salvage what started out as an empirical account of human motivation. The salvaging operation winds up with an ad hoc, a priori, and quite unempirical defense.

always come up w/ a reason

Ethical Egoism

Many problems about psychological egoism stem from its status as a theory of motivation that lacks crucial supporting evidence. This problem does not attend ethical egoism, however, for it is a normative ethical theory independent of any particular psychological assumptions. Earlier, ethical egoism was loosely characterized as the theory that persons ought to desire their own well-being and only their own well-being as an end in itself. Let us now formulate this theory more tightly and consider arguments in its defense.

Because self-promotion is the sole valid standard of behavior recognized in ethical egoism, an ethical egoist would in any given circumstance assess the available options, calculating what he or she would favor and disfavor, and then perform whatever action promised to be maximally self-promoting. However, egoistic calculation of this sort is actually compatible with several different formulations of the basic egoistic position, and the formulation one accepts makes a major difference. One form of egoism is individualistic: "I ought to promote myself above others at all times." This assertion is more akin to a personal creed than to an ethical theory, for it is not held to apply beyond oneself. (In Chapter 9, we will consider whether one should adopt this personal creed.) It would be a self-defeating theory if one were to advocate it publicly, for to instruct others in its wisdom could lead them to accept it for themselves, and this acceptance would in turn undermine the promotion of one's own interests above theirs.

A second form of egoism is not so individualistic, yet it has many of the same problems: "Everyone ought to promote my interests above the interests of all others." This view too seems implausible as a moral theory, for others would never act voluntarily and exclusively to promote a specific individual's interests, whether the position was publicly advocated or not. The most plausible form of ethical egoism, then, is a third version: "Everyone ought to promote himself or herself above all others at all times." Hereafter, this universal form of egoism will be the only one under discussion. (*Note:* The egoist might not have a moral view about what ought to be the case, claiming only that clever, rational persons would place their own well-being first. This formulation too would never be publicly advocated and of course carries no prescriptive force. Thus it also can be ignored for present purposes.)

It is difficult to know what would count as an argument for ethical egoism, plausible as it may sound and widely believed as it may be. One might of course argue that if everyone acted to promote his or her own interests, the result would be the maximal realization of the interests of humanity as a whole. Adam Smith advanced a form of this argument for economic behavior, as will be seen in Chapter 7, and it might be applied to all behavior—though probably at the price of losing plausibility. Another problem with citing the interests of humanity as a whole as one's primary reason for adopting universal egoism is that this formulation makes the theory a species of utilitarianism—the main topic of Chapter 3—and not a distinctive egoistic theory at all. We would be better advised, then, to search for a more distinctive foundation for the theory.

Perhaps the most plausible foundation for ethical egoism is found in the writings of Thomas Hobbes, a well-known seventeenth-century British philosopher. Hobbes's work is difficult to interpret, and on one interpretation he is not an egoist at all, for, in his theory, once one has consented to the rules of civilized society (which it is to one's own advantage to do), there will be times when one *ought* to act altruistically, as altruism has previously been described. However, without too liberally abandoning important qualifications in his texts, we can attribute a foundation for ethical egoism to Hobbes. (An extended interpretation of Hobbes that situates his views in the context of a broad moral and political theory will be found in Chapter 8.)

For Hobbes, good and evil are closely connected with pleasure and pain for the individual person. The word "good" is associated with whatever is the object of a person's appetite or desire, and evil is the object of aversion. "Good and evil," he says, "are names that satisfy our appetites." The good is what we promote for ourselves, the evil what we wish to avoid. Considered independently of the social constraints in civilized society, our personal appetites alone "measure" good and evil, right and wrong, justice and injustice. Hobbes's rule of egoism is, in his own words, "It is natural, and so reasonable, for each individual to aim solely at his own preservation or pleasure."*

Hobbes's argument might be recast in the following form: Any clever person will realize that he or she has no moral obligations to others besides those he or she voluntarily assumes. One should accept moral rules and assume specific obligations only when doing so promotes one's self-interest. One may take the offensive and bring some benefit or liberty to oneself, or one may adopt a more defensive strategy by avoiding the enmity and limited sympathies of others; but any intelligent person will see that it is

---

*See Hobbes's *Leviathan,* chaps. 14–15, and *The Elements of Law,* chap. 1.

personally advantageous to make all such decisions using egoistic standards. Even if one agrees to live under a set of laws of the state that are binding on everyone, any obligation should be assumed only as a part of this general offensive and defensive strategy. Moreover, one should obey rules and laws only in order to protect oneself and to bring about a situation of communal living that is personally advantageous. One should also back down on an "obligation" whenever it becomes clear that it is to one's long-range disadvantage to fulfill the obligation. Thus, when confronted by a social revolution, the questionable trustworthiness of a colleague, or an incompetent administration at one's place of employment, one is under no obligation to obey the law, fulfill one's contracts, or tell the truth. These obligations exist only because one assumes them, and one ought to assume them only as long as doing so promotes one's interest.

What now can be said by way of criticism of this Hobbesian form of universal ethical egoism? One popular contention is that the theory gives incompatible directives in circumstances of moral conflict. If everyone acted egoistically, it seems reasonably certain that many circumstances of conflict would occur, just as many international conflicts now arise among nations primarily pursuing their own interests. According to universal egoism, both parties in a circumstance of conflict ought to pursue their own best interests exclusively, and it is morally permissible for both to do so. For example, suppose it is in the interest of an antiwar demonstrator to stop railroad shipments of dangerous chemicals used in the construction of bombs; yet, it is no less in the interest of the railroad to prevent the antiwar demonstrator from stopping the shipments. Egoism urges both parties to pursue their interests exclusively and holds both pursuits to be morally permissible.

The oddity of this situation can be brought out by imagining that the antiwar demonstrator is an egoist. In order to be a consistent egoist, the demonstrator must hold to a theory that the railroad ought to pursue its interest, which would involve thwarting his or her own antiwar objectives (for *all* ought to pursue their interests and thwart others if necessary). Yet, in thus striving for consistency, the egoist supports a theory that works against his or her own interest, and so seems to fall into inconsistency in the attempt. Another way of looking at this example is to see the egoist as having incompatible objectives. The egoist says that everyone ought to seek his or her own maximal satisfaction, yet this universalistic theory only implausibly would make it possible to maximize the egoist's satisfaction. (An *individual* egoism can escape this criticism, but at a price that has been previously noted.)

Perhaps the most plausible egoistic reply is that the objection springs from a misunderstanding of the rules and policies an ethical egoist would actually accept. If everyone were to act on more-or-less fixed rules such as those found in moral and legal systems, this arrangement would produce the most desirable state of affairs from an egoistic point of view. The reason is that such rules arbitrate conflicts and make social life more agreeable. These rules would include, for example, familiar moral and legal principles of justice that are intended to make everyone's situation more secure and stable. Only an unduly narrow conception of *genuine* self-interest, the egoist might argue, leads critics to think that the egoist would not willingly observe such rules of justice, for it is clearly in one's self-interest to do so. If society can be structured to resolve personal conflicts through courts and other peaceful means, the egoist will see it as in his or her interest to accept those binding social arrangements—just as the egoist will see it as prudent to treat other individuals well in his or her personal contacts with them. Notice that the egoist is saying not that his or her best interests are served by promoting the good of others—but rather, that one's personal interests are served by observing impartial rules irrespective of any favorable outcome whatever for others who live in society. The egoist, after all, does not care about the welfare of others except insofar as it affects her or his own welfare. (The egoist might extend this argument as follows: Egoism gives the best of all possible answers to the question, "Why be moral?" One ought to be moral because being moral is to one's long-range interest. Just as egoism supplies the final justification for doing anything, so it provides the final justification for adopting a moral way of life. This answer, however, leads straight to considerations that will be taken up in detail in Chapter 9.)

There has been much discussion of whether the egoist can escape from the clutches of arguments that attempt to locate some inconsistency or practical uselessness at the heart of the theory itself. However, these objections to egoism have never been thought the most decisive *moral* considerations. Many people have believed that egoism is an evil moral doctrine, if indeed it can be called a moral view at all. They have thought so because it advocates the overriding pursuit of selfish goals even when such pursuits would lead to the defrauding of others or to enormous suffering. For example, they have thought that egoism in principle supports extreme cruelties to animals whenever someone finds pleasure in inflicting pain on them. In principle, it advocates that a politician who can get away with stealing millions of dollars from taxpayers ought to do so, and that clever physicians should selectively lie to their patients and their families in order to save themselves minor embarrassments and additional efforts that would cost them time and money. Ethical egoism seems to advise us to ignore the welfare of others, not to pay legally uncollectable debts, to plagiarize where our theft cannot be detected, and to ignore commitments or avoid work through convenient excuses.*

Whether the sophisticated, long-run version of egoism previously discussed actually leads to the recommendation or support of such forms of immoral behavior is far from clear, and not a matter that can be pursued further at this point. However, it should be noted that in all the ethical theories opposed to egoism that we shall encounter in Chapters 3 through 5, these acts are treated as gross moral wrongs that egoism recommends to the prudent person. *Why* such acts are wrong will of course depend on the theoretical framework used to support the claim of their wrongness. In these chapters, the frameworks provided by three ethical theories of extraordinary historical and contemporary influence will be studied. Here, more than one philosopher will argue that any action required by a moral duty ought to be performed for reasons independent of

---

*See R. B. Brandt, *A Theory of the Good and the Right* (Oxford, England: Clarendon Press, 1979), p. 270, for a lengthy list of egoistic commitments and for an objection to egoism of the sort mentioned in this paragraph.

personal interest. Only after studying these three approaches can we determine whether this final objection to egoism is as compelling as some have claimed.

SUGGESTED SUPPLEMENTARY READINGS

Relativism

Benedict, Ruth: *Patterns of Culture* (New York: Pelican Books, 1946), especially chap. 7.
Brandt, Richard B.: *Ethical Theory* (Englewood Cliffs, N.J.: Prentice-Hall, Inc., 1959), especially chap. 11, "Ethical Relativism."
———: "Ethical Relativism," in Paul Edwards, ed., *The Encyclopedia of Philosophy,* (New York: Macmillan Company and Free Press, 1967), vol. 3, pp. 75–78.
Hartland-Swann, John: *An Analysis of Morals* (London: George Allen & Unwin, 1960).
Ladd, John, ed.: *Ethical Relativism* (Belmont, Calif.: Wadsworth Publishing Company, Inc., 1973).
Phillips, D. Z., and H. O. Mounce: *Moral Practices* (New York: Schocken Books, Inc., 1970), chap. 7.
Redfield, Robert: *The Primitive World* (Ithaca, N.Y.: Cornell University Press, 1953), especially chap. 6, "The Transformation of Ethical Judgment."
Taylor, Paul W.: "Four Types of Ethical Relativism," *Philosophical Review,* **62** (1954): 500–516.
Wellman, Carl: "The Ethical Implications of Cultural Relativity," *Journal of Philosophy,* **60** (1963): 169–184.
Westermarck, Edward: *Ethical Relativity* (Paterson, N.J.: Littlefield, Adams, & Co., 1960).

Disagreement and Pluralism

Beauchamp, Tom L.: "Ethical Theory and the Problem of Closure," in Arthur Caplan, H. T. Engelhardt, Jr., and Daniel Callahan, eds., *The Closure of Scientific Disputes* (New York: Plenum Press, 1982).
Glover, Jonathan: *Causing Death and Saving Lives* (New York: Penguin Books, Inc., 1977), chap. 2.
Griffiths, A. Phillips: "Ultimate Moral Principles: Their Justification," in Paul Edwards, ed., *The Encyclopedia of Philosophy* (New York: Macmillan Company and Free Press, 1967), vol. 8, pp. 177–182.
Harrison, Jonathan: "Ethical Objectivism," in Paul Edwards, ed., *The Encyclopedia of Philosophy* (New York: Macmillan Company and Free Press, 1967), vol. 3, pp. 71–75.

MacIntyre, Alasdair: "How to Identify Ethical Principles," in *The Belmont Report*, Appendix I (Washington, D.C.: Government Printing Office, DHEW Publication (OS)78-0013, 1978).

Nagel, Thomas: "The Fragmentation of Value," in *Mortal Questions* (Cambridge, England: Cambridge University Press, 1979).

Phillips, D. Z., and H. O. Mounce: *Moral Practices* (New York: Schocken Books, Inc., 1970), chap. 9, "Moral Disagreement."

Rachels, James: "Can Ethics Provide Answers?" *Hastings Center Report,* **10** (June 1980): 32–40.

Rescher, Nicholas: "Philosophical Disagreement," *Review of Metaphysics,* **32** (1978): 217–251.

Stevenson, Charles L.: *Facts and Values* (New Haven, Conn.: Yale University Press, 1963), chap. 1.

Egoism

Baier, Kurt: *The Moral Point of View* (Ithaca, N.Y.: Cornell University Press, 1958), chap. 8.

Baumer, W. H.: "Indefensible Impersonal Egoism," *Philosophical Studies,* **18** (1967): 72–75.

Baumrin, Bernard H., ed.: *Hobbes' Leviathan: Interpretation and Criticism* (Belmont, Calif.: Wadsworth Publishing Company, Inc., 1969).

Branden, Nathaniel: "Rational Egoism," *The Personalist,* **51** (1970): 196–211, 305–313.

Brandt, Richard B.: *Ethical Theory* (Englewood Cliffs, N.J.: Prentice-Hall, Inc., 1959), chap. 14.

Brunton, J. A.: "Egoism and Morality," *Philosophical Quarterly,* **6** (1956): 289–303.

Butler, Joseph: *Fifteen Sermons Preached at the Rolls Chapel,* in D. D. Raphael, ed., *British Moralists, 1650–1800,* vol. I (Oxford, England: Clarendon Press, 1969), pp. 323–377.

Campbell, Richmond, "A Short Refutation of Ethical Egoism," *Canadian Journal of Philosophy,* **2** (1972): 249–254.

Gauthier, David P., ed.: *Morality and Rational Self-Interest* (Englewood Cliffs, N.J.: Prentice-Hall, Inc., 1970).

Hospers, John: "Baier and Medlin on Ethical Egoism," *Philosophical Studies,* **12** (1961): 10–16.

Kalin, Jesse: "On Ethical Egoism," *American Philosophical Quarterly, Monograph Series No. 1: Studies in Moral Philosophy* (1968), pp. 26–41.

MacIntyre, Alasdair: "Egoism and Altruism," in Paul Edwards, ed., *The Encyclopedia of Philosophy* (New York: Macmillan Company and Free Press, 1967), vol. 2, pp. 462–466.

Medlin, Brian: "Ultimate Principles and Ethical Egoism," *Australasian Journal of Philosophy,* **35** (1957): 111–118.

Milo, Ronald D., ed.: *Egoism and Altruism* (Belmont, Calif.: Wadsworth Publishing Company, Inc., 1973).

Nagel, Thomas: *The Possibility of Altruism* (Oxford, England: Clarendon Press, 1970).

Nielsen, Kai: "Egoism in Ethics," *Philosophy and Phenomenological Research,* **19** (1959).

Nozick, Robert: "On the Randian Argument," *The Personalist,* **52** (1971): 282–304.

Olson, Robert G.: *The Morality of Self-Interest* (New York: Harcourt Brace Jovanovich, Inc., 1965).

Peters, Richard S.: *The Concept of Motivation* (London: Routledge & Kegan Paul, 1958).

Rachels, James: "Two Arguments Against Ethical Egoism," *Philosophia,* **4** (1974): 297–314.

Rand, Ayn: "The Objectivist Ethics," *The Virtue of Selfishness* (New York: Signet Books, New American Library, Inc., 1964), 13–35.

Slote, Michael: "An Empirical Basis for Psychological Egoism," *The Journal of Philosophy,* **61** (1964): 530–537.

PART TWO

Classical
Ethical Theories

CHAPTER THREE

Mill and
Utilitarian Theories

In the mid-1970s two professors at Harvard, Milton Weinstein and William B. Stason, became interested in facts and policies pertaining to high blood pressure in American society.* Few people in the United States know about, or pay much attention to, the fact that they themselves may have high blood pressure. The Harvard researchers noted that 17 percent of the adult American population, or 24 million persons, have problems with high blood pressure, that even minimally adequate treatment for these persons would cost over $5 billion annually (if all were treated), that close to 50 percent of the affected population are not even aware of the fact that they have problems, and that only about one-sixth of that group are receiving proper medical treatment and control.

The investigators became concerned with determining the most cost-effective way to tackle the problem of controlling hypertension in the American population. Data from screening programs that identify people who do not know that they have high blood pressure revealed that it is not cost-efficient to try to inform persons of their problem unless they are already under a physician's care. In general, people who were informed of their condition through massive screening and education programs were not likely to report to a physician for treatment. Among those who did subsequently see a physician, adherence to the recommended therapy turned out to be extremely poor.

As they further developed their research, Weinstein and Stason discovered (somewhat surprisingly) that, rather than to launch a communitywide campaign, it is more cost-effective to treat three classes of persons in the attempt to reduce the general public health problem of high blood pressure: (1) younger men, (2) older women, and

*See *Hypertension* (Cambridge, Mass.: Harvard University Press, 1976); *New England Journal of Medicine,* **296** (1977): 716–21; *Hastings Center Report,* **7** (October 1977).

(3) those patients with very high blood pressure. When the researchers combined these findings with their previous findings that large-scale, public screening and informational programs are not medically effective (and not cost-effective), they were led to conclude: "A community with limited resources would probably do better to concentrate its efforts on improving adherence of known hypertensives, even at a sacrifice in terms of the numbers screened. This conclusion holds even if such proadherence interventions are rather expensive and only moderately effective, and even if screening is very inexpensive. . . . Finally, screening in the regular practices [of physicians] is more cost-effective than public screening."

These investigators were bothered by their own recommendation because it implicitly meant that, if acted on by public policy experts in the government, the poorest sector of the country, which is also in greatest need of medical attention, would not be provided with any benefits of high blood pressure education and management. Public screening would be sacrificed in order to do a larger good for the whole community, where only persons known to have high blood pressure who were already in contact with a physician about their problem would be recontacted and new educational attempts made. These investigators were concerned because there seemed to them to be a possible injustice in excluding the poor and minorities by a public health endeavor aimed expressly at the economically better-off sector of society. Yet their statistics were very compelling: No matter how carefully planned the efforts, nothing worked except programs directed at those already in touch with physicians. They also discovered that a certain amount of money devoted to the education of physicians was quite cost-effective. Moreover, they knew that it was most unlikely, and perhaps undeserved in light of other health needs, that there would be new allocations of public health money to control high blood pressure. Yet it would take massive new allocations even to begin to affect the poorer sections of society.

These investigators therefore recommended what they explicitly referred to as a "utilitarian" set of criteria for allocation. As we will see in this chapter, their study is extremely useful for illustrating the utilitarian approach to morals as well as for noting certain disagreements that have emerged among utilitarians. It must not be taken, however, as perfectly representative of all forms of utilitarian thinking, for reasons that will now be considered.

THE UTILITARIAN CONCEPTION OF MORALITY

A structured normative ethical theory, it may be recalled from Chapter 1, is a system of moral principles by which people determine what they ought and ought not to do and what kinds of persons they ought or ought not to be. As we reflect on the nature of morality, the question arises as to whether there is some one supreme principle of morality which specifies all our duties and from which all our moral standards can be derived. Many prominent writers in moral theory, especially utilitarian thinkers, have taken the view that there is one supreme principle.

Utilitarianism is the most influential of several ethical theories that measure the worth of actions by their ends and consequences. These theories are commonly said to be "teleological" (derived from the Greek term *telos,* meaning "end") or consequentialist. While there are many types of utilitarian theory, they hold in common that the rightness and wrongness of actions and practices are determined solely by the consequences produced for the general well-being of all parties affected by the actions or practices. What makes an action morally right or wrong is the total good or evil produced by the act, not the mere act in itself. This contention sets utilitarianism off from many other moral theories, which hold that the act itself has moral value apart from the good or evil produced.

To understand utilitarianism, consider a person trying to decide whether he or she should attempt to rescue occupants of a burning building or, instead, notify the fire department. The utilitarian would counsel that one ought to choose the action that would lead to the production of the best consequences for all affected. If notification of the fire department would provide the best outcome, then that goal should be pursued. To use the example that begins this chapter, if a particular health program usefully affects more persons than an alternative program would, there are moral grounds for choosing it (unless other moral reasons prevent that choice). Utilitarianism, in short, is rooted in two connected theses: (1) that an action or practice is right (when compared with any alternative action or practice) if it leads to the greatest possible balance of good consequences or to the least possible balance of bad consequences in the world as a whole; and (2) that the concepts of duty and right are subordinated to or determined by that which maximizes the good (i.e., that which promises the best outcome determines what it is right to do).

Utilitarian views have been embraced throughout the history of ethical theory, but the earliest significant utilitarian philosophical writings were those of David Hume (1711–1776), Jeremy Bentham (1748–1832), and John Stuart Mill (1806–1873). Bentham, who was trained in law, regarded utilitarianism as a practical system for legislators, and not merely an abstract moral theory. Just as Weinstein and Stason were interested in a moral view appropriate for public policy, he was interested in a moral view to undergird legal reforms. Bentham's utilitarian views developed from a general disenchantment with the British legal system. He argued that the purpose of law is to promote the welfare of citizens, not to enforce divine commands, impose severe punishments, or protect so-called natural rights. He thought that the British system for classifying crimes, for example, was deficient because it based its determination of the gravity of offenses on outdated, brutal, and costly views about punishment (as exposited, for example, by Blackstone). As an alternative, Bentham suggested that crimes be classified according to the level of seriousness of offense, and that the levels of seriousness should be determined by the unhappiness and misery a crime causes to its victims and to society. His revisions in the classification scheme were thus intended to bring about revisions in the severity of criminal punishments. Bentham's fundamental rule was that the punishment for a crime should only be stringent enough to cancel the advantage gained by committing the crime, and should not be any greater than needed to deter the offender and others. Moreover, Bentham believed that an act should be classified as criminal only if it causes harmful consequences to others. He thus opposed criminal sanctions against sexual "crimes" between consenting adults, because they produce no harmful consequences to the parties involved. This line of thinking is typical of classical utilitarian writers.

While Bentham was among the earliest and most influential utilitarians, the major exposition of utilitarianism is generally regarded as that of John Stuart Mill in his work *Utilitarianism*. Mill was a member of parliament, and therefore was as heavily influenced as Bentham by legislative models of reasoning. Mill, who was born in London in 1806, was a person of legendary achievements in his youth. He apparently started to learn Greek at the age of three, and by age twelve he was sufficiently acquainted with Greek and Latin literature, history, and mathematics to enter what he called "more advanced studies," including logic. In 1819, at the age of thirteen, he studied political economy. During this period he read Adam Smith and Ricardo. At fifteen years of age, he had studied Roman law and had given serious consideration to the philosophy of Bentham, as well as to the works of other philosophers.

Mill's *Utilitarianism* was not an early work. It was not published until 1863, when, at the age of fifty-seven, he had corrected what he considered the flaws in Bentham's philosophy. In this work he gives what might be called two foundations of util-itarianism: (1) a *normative* foundation in the principle of utility and (2) a *psychological* foundation in a theory of human nature. The principle of utility, or the "greatest happiness" principle, is declared to be the basic foundation of morals: "Actions are right in proportion as they tend to promote happiness, wrong as they tend to produce the reverse of happiness, i.e., pleasure or absence of pain." His theory holds, then, that pleasure and freedom from pain are the only things desirable as ends, and that all desirable things (which are numerous) are desirable either for the pleasure inherent in them, or as means to the promotion of pleasure and the prevention of pain. Mill's second foundation of utilitarianism derives from his belief that all persons have a basic desire for unity and harmony with their fellow human beings. Bentham had tried to justify the principle of utility by claiming that it is in our own self-interest to promote everyone's interest, but Mill never attempts such a justification. He appeals instead to the social feelings of human beings. Just as we feel horror at crimes, he says, so we have a basic moral sensitiveness to the needs of others. His idea seems to be that we have a natural but very limited sympathy toward our fellows. The purpose of morality is at once to promote our natural sympathies and to combat their limitations, and the principle of utility is conceived as the best means to these ends.

In the following excerpt, Mill explicates both utilitarianism and its connection with a theory of justice.

JOHN STUART MILL

Utilitarianism*

Chapter I

General Remarks

There are few circumstances among those which make up the present condition of human knowledge, more unlike what might have been expected, or more significant of the backward state in which speculation on the most important subject still lingers, than the little progress which has been made in the decision of the controversy respecting the criterion of right and wrong. . . .

On the present occasion, I shall, without further discussion of the other theories, attempt to contribute something towards the understanding and appreciation of the Utilitarian or Happiness theory, and towards such proof as it is susceptible of. It is evident that this cannot be proof in the ordinary and popular meaning of the term. Questions of ultimate ends are not amenable to direct proof. Whatever can be proved to be good, must be so by being shown to be a means to something admitted to be good without proof. The medical art is proved to be good, by its conducing to health; but how is it possible to prove that health is good? The art of music is good, for the reason, among others, that it produces pleasure; but what proof is it possible to give that pleasure is good? If, then, it is asserted that there is a comprehensive formula, including all things which are in themselves good, and that whatever else is good, is not so as an end, but as a mean, the formula may be accepted or rejected, but it is not a subject of what is commonly understood by proof. We are not, however, to infer that its acceptance or rejection must depend on blind impulse, or arbitrary choice. There is a larger meaning of the word proof, in which this question is as amenable to it as any other of the disputed questions of philosophy. The subject is within the cognizance of the rational faculty; and neither does that faculty deal with it solely in the way of intuition. Considerations may be presented capable of determining the intellect either to give or withhold its assent to the doctrine; and this is equivalent to proof. . . .

Chapter 2

What Utilitarianism Is

The creed which accepts as the foundation of morals, Utility, or the Greatest Happiness Principle, holds that actions are right in proportion as they tend to promote happiness, wrong as they tend to produce the reverse of happiness. By happiness is intended pleasure, and the absence of pain; by unhappiness, pain, and the privation of pleasure. To give a clear view of the moral standard set up by the theory, much more requires to be said; in particular, what things it includes in the ideas of pain and pleasure; and to what extent this is left an open question. But these supplementary explanations do not affect the theory

*From John Stuart Mill, *Utilitarianism* (1863), chaps. 1, 2, 5.

of life on which this theory of morality is grounded—namely, that pleasure, and freedom from pain, are the only things desirable as ends; and that all desirable things (which are as numerous in the utilitarian as in any other scheme) are desirable either for the pleasure inherent in themselves, or as means to the promotion of pleasure and the prevention of pain.

Now, such a theory of life excites in many minds, and among them in some of the most estimable in feeling and purpose, inveterate dislike. To suppose that life has (as they express it) no higher end than pleasure—no better and nobler object of desire and pursuit—they designate as utterly mean and grovelling; as a doctrine worthy only of swine, to whom the followers of Epicurus were, at a very early period, contemptuously likened; and modern holders of the doctrine are occasionally made the subject of equally polite comparisons by its German, French, and English assailants.

When thus attacked, the Epicureans have always answered, that it is not they, but their accusers, who represent human nature in a degrading light; since the accusation supposes human beings to be capable of no pleasures except those of which swine are capable. If this supposition were true, the charge could not be gainsaid, but would then be no longer an imputation; for if the sources of pleasure were precisely the same to human beings and to swine, the rule of life which is good enough for the one would be good enough for the other. The comparison of the Epicurean life to that of beasts is felt as degrading, precisely because a beast's pleasures do not satisfy a human being's conceptions of happiness. Human beings have faculties more elevated than the animal appetites, and when once made conscious of them, do not regard anything as happiness which does not include their gratification. I do

not, indeed, consider the Epicureans to have been by any means faultless in drawing out their scheme of consequences from the utilitarian principle. To do this in any sufficient manner, many Stoic, as well as Christian elements require to be included. But there is no known Epicurean theory of life which does not assign to the pleasures of the intellect, of the feelings and imagination, and of the moral sentiments, a much higher value as pleasures than to those of mere sensation. It must be admitted, however, that utilitarian writers in general have placed the superiority of mental over bodily pleasures chiefly in the greater permanency, safety, uncostliness, &c., of the former—that is, in their circumstantial advantages rather than in their intrinsic nature. And on all these points utilitarians have fully proved their case; but they might have taken the other, and, as it may be called, higher ground, with entire consistency. It is quite compatible with the principle of utility to recognise the fact that some *kinds* of pleasure are more desirable and more valuable than others. It would be absurd that while, in estimating all other things, quality is considered as well as quantity, the estimation of pleasures should be supposed to depend on quantity alone.

If I am asked what I mean by difference of quality in pleasures, or what makes one pleasure more valuable than another, merely as a pleasure, except its being greater in amount, there is but one possible answer. Of two pleasures, if there be one to which all or almost all who have experience of both give a decided preference, irrespective of any feeling of moral obligation to prefer it, that is the more desirable pleasure. If one of the two is, by those who are competently acquainted with both, placed so far above the other that they prefer it, even though knowing it to be attended with a greater amount of discontent, and would not resign it for any quantity of the other pleasure which their nature is capable of, we are justified in ascribing to the preferred enjoyment a superiority in quality, so far outweighing quantity as to render it, in comparison, of small account.

Now it is an unquestionable fact that those who are equally acquainted with, and equally capable of appreciating and enjoying, both, do give a most marked preference to the manner of existence which employs their higher faculties. Few human creatures would consent to be changed into any of the lower animals, for a promise of the fullest allowance of a beast's pleasures; no intelligent human being would consent to be a fool, no instructed person would be an ignoramus, no person of feeling and conscience would be selfish and base, even though they should be persuaded that the fool, the dunce, or the rascal is better satisfied with his lot than they are with theirs. . . . Whoever supposes that this preference takes place at a sacrifice of happiness— that the superior being, in anything like the equal circumstances, is not happier than the inferior—confounds the two very different ideas, of happiness, and content. It is indisputable that the being whose capacities of enjoyment are low, has the greatest chance of having them fully satisfied; and a highly-endowed being will always feel that any happiness which he can look for, as the world is constituted, is imperfect. But he can learn to bear its imperfections, if they are at all bearable; and they will not make him envy the being who is indeed unconscious of the imperfections, but only because he feels not at all the good which those imperfections qualify. It is better to be a human being dissatisfied than a pig satisfied; better to be Socrates dissatisfied than a fool satisfied. And if the fool, or the pig, is of a different opinion, it is because they only know their own side of the question. The other party to the comparison knows both sides. . . .

I must again repeat, what the assailants of utilitarianism seldom have the justice to acknowledge, that the happiness which forms the utilitarian standard of what is right in conduct, is not the agent's own happiness, but that of all concerned. As between his own happiness and that of others, utilitarianism requires him to be as strictly impartial as a disinterested and benevolent spectator. In the golden rule of Jesus of Nazareth, we read the complete spirit of the ethics of utility. To do as one would be done by, and to love one's neighbour as oneself, constitute the ideal perfection of utilitarian morality. As the means of making the nearest approach to this ideal, utility would enjoin, first, that laws and social arrangements should place the happiness, or (as speaking practically it may be called) the interest, of every individual, as nearly as possible in harmony with the interest of the whole; and secondly, that education and opinion, which have so vast a power over human character, should so use that power as to establish in the mind of every individual an indissoluble association between his own happiness and the good of the whole; especially between his own happiness and the practice of such modes of conduct, negative and positive, as regard for the universal happiness prescribes: so that not only he may be unable to conceive the possibility of happiness to himself, consistently with conduct opposed to the general good, but also that a direct impulse to promote the general good may be in every individual one of the habitual motives of action, and the sentiments connected therewith may fill a large and prominent place in every human being's sentient existence. . . .

Chapter 5

On the Connexion between Justice and Utility

In all ages of speculation, one of the strongest obstacles to the reception of the doctrine that Utility or Happiness is the criterion of right and wrong, has been drawn from the idea of Justice. . . .

Each person maintains that equality is the dictate of justice, except where he thinks that expediency requires inequality. The justice of giving equal protection to the rights of all, is maintained by those who support the most outrageous inequality in the rights themselves. Even in slave countries it is theoretically admitted that the rights of the slave, such as they are, ought to be as sacred as those of the master; and that a tribunal which fails to enforce them with equal strictness is wanting in justice; while, at the same time, institutions which leave to the slave scarcely any rights to enforce, are not deemed unjust, because they are not deemed inexpedient. Those who think that utility requires distinctions of rank, do not consider it unjust that riches and social privileges should be unequally dispensed; but those who think this inequality inexpedient, think it unjust also. Whoever thinks that government is necessary, sees no injustice in as much inequality as is constituted by giving to the magistrate powers not granted to other people. Even among those who hold levelling doctrines, there are as many questions of justice as there are differences of opinion about expediency. . . .

Justice implies something which it is not only right to do, and wrong not to do, but which some individual person can claim from us as his moral right. No one has a moral right to our generosity or beneficence, because we are not morally bound to practise those virtues toward any given individual. And it will be found with respect to this as with respect to every correct definition, that the instances which seem to conflict with it are those which most confirm it. For if a moralist attempts, as some have done, to make out that mankind generally, though not any given individual, have a right to all the good we can do them, he at once, by that thesis, includes generosity and beneficence within the category of justice. He is obliged to say, that our utmost exertions are *due* to our fellow creatures, thus assimilating them to a debt; or that nothing less can be a sufficient *return* for what society does for us, thus classing the case as one of gratitude; both of which are acknowledged cases of justice. Wherever there is a right, the case is one of justice, and not of the virtue of beneficence: and whoever does not place the distinction between justice and morality in general where we have now placed it, will be found to make no distinction between them at all, but to merge all morality in justice. . . .

It is no objection against this doctrine to say, that when we feel our sentiment of justice outraged, we are not thinking of society at large, or of any collective interest, but only of the individual case. It is common enough certainly, though the reverse of commendable, to feel resentment merely because we have suffered pain; but a person whose resentment is really a moral feeling, that is, who considers whether an act is blamable before he allows himself to resent it—such a person, though he may not say expressly to himself that he is standing up for the interest of society, certainly does feel that he is asserting a rule which is for the benefit of others as well as for his own. If he is not feeling this—if he is regarding the act solely as it affects him individually—he is not consciously just; he is not concerning himself about the justice of his actions. This is admitted even by anti-utilitarian moralists. . . .

When we call anything a person's right, we mean that he has a valid claim on society to protect him in the possession of it, either by the force of law, or by that of education and opinion. If he has what we consider a sufficient claim, on whatever account, to have something guaranteed to him by society, we say that he has a right to it. If we desire to prove that anything does not belong to him by right, we think this done as soon as it is admitted that society ought not to take measures for securing it to him, but should leave it to chance, or to his own exertions. . . .

To have a right, then, is, I conceive, to have something which society ought to defend me in the possession of. If the objector goes on to ask why it ought, I can give him no other reason than general utility. If that expression does not seem to convey a sufficient feeling of the strength of the obligation, nor to account for the peculiar energy of the feeling, it is because there goes to the composition of the sentiment, not a rational only but also an animal element, the thirst for retaliation; and this thirst derives its intensity, as well as its moral justification, from the extraordinarily important and impressive kind of utility which is concerned. The interest involved is that of security, to every one's feelings the most vital of all interests. Nearly all other earthly benefits are needed by one person, not needed by another; and many of them can, if necessary, be cheerfully foregone, or replaced by something else; but security no human being can possibly do without. . . .

The principle, therefore, of giving to each what they deserve, that is, good for good as well as evil for evil, is not only included within the idea of Justice as we have defined it, but is a proper object of

that intensity of sentiment, which places the Just, in human estimation, above the simply Expedient.

Most of the maxims of justice current in the world, and commonly appealed to in its transactions, are simply instrumental to carrying into effect the principles of justice which we have now spoken of. That a person is only responsible for what he has done voluntarily, or could voluntarily have avoided; that it is unjust to condemn any person unheard; that the punishment ought to be proportioned to the offence, and the like, are maxims intended to prevent the just principle of evil for evil from being perverted to the infliction of evil without justification. The greater part of these common maxims have come into use from the practice of courts of justice, which have been naturally led to a more complete recognition and elaboration than was likely to suggest itself to others, of the rules necessary to enable them to fulfill their double function, of inflicting punishment when due, and of awarding to each person his right.

That first of judicial virtues, impartiality, is an obligation of justice, partly for the reason last mentioned; as being a necessary condition of the fulfilment of the other obligations of justice. But this is not the only source of the exalted rank, among human obligations, of those maxims of equality and impartiality, which, both in popular estimation and in that of the most enlightened, are included among the precepts of justice. In one point of view, they may be considered as corollaries from the principles already laid down. If it is a duty to do to each according to his deserts, returning good for good as well as repressing evil by evil, it necessarily follows that we should treat all equally well (when no higher duty forbids) who have deserved equally well of us, and that society should treat all equally well who have deserved equally well of it, that is, who have deserved equally well absolutely. This is the highest abstract standard of social and distributive justice; towards which all institutions, and the efforts of all virtuous citizens, should be made in the utmost possible degree to converge. But this great moral duty rests upon a still deeper foundation, being a direct emanation from the first principle of morals, and not a mere logical corollary from secondary or derivative doctrines. It is involved in the very meaning of Utility, or the Greatest-Happiness Principle. That principle is a mere form of words without rational signification, unless one person's happiness, supposed equal in degree (with the proper allowance made for kind), is counted for exactly as much as another's. Those conditions being supplied, Bentham's dictum, "everybody to count for one, nobody for more than one," might be written under the principle of utility as an explanatory commentary. The equal claim of everybody to happiness in the estimation of the moralist and the legislator, involves an equal claim to all the means of happiness, except in so far as the inevitable conditions of human life, and the general interest, in which that of every individual is included, set limits to the maxim; and those limits ought to be strictly construed. As every other maxim of justice, so this, is by no means applied or held applicable universally; on the contrary, as I have already remarked, it bends to every person's ideas of social expediency. But in whatever case it is deemed applicable at all, it is held to be the dictate of justice. All persons are deemed to have a *right* to equality of treatment, except when some recognised social expediency requires the reverse. And hence all social inequalities which have ceased to be considered expedient, assume the character not of simple inexpediency, but of injustice.

THE CONCEPT OF UTILITY

Utilitarianism is commonly recognized as having a strong intuitive appeal. After all, what could be wrong with the view that agents should perform those actions that will produce more good for people than any other action? Important objections have been raised against utilitarianism, however, and as a result many arguments in its defense have been developed. Both sides of this dispute will be assessed here, but it is worth noting from the outset that utilitarianism is a live option in contemporary ethics, and not simply a relic of the past. Indeed, its initial starting point is so plausible and its value for purposes of social policy so obvious that many have preferred to embrace it and to meet those objections, rather than to accept some alternative theory. With this in mind, let us now examine some unresolved issues about utilitarianism, as well as some of the different approaches taken by utilitarians.

All utilitarians share the conviction that human actions are to be morally assessed in terms of their production of maximal value. "Good" and "evil" are thus conceived from the start in terms of value and disvalue. But how are we to determine what things are valuable and to be achieved in any given circumstance? What does the notion of "utility" involve? Major disputes have erupted among utilitarians on this point, although they agree that ultimately we ought to look to the production of things that are *intrinsically,* rather than *extrinsically,* valuable. This distinction deserves elaboration.

An intrinsic value is one that we wish to possess and enjoy for its own sake and not for something to which it leads. These values are good in themselves and not merely good as a means to something else. Wealth is an example of a good that is strictly valuable as a means to other things. The possession of wealth is valued not for the sake of having stacks of currency, but rather, because the money can be used to purchase important goods and services in life. Money, we say, is good only as a means to other things. But some things that money will buy—e.g., artfully prepared meals and the pleasure they give us—seem good in themselves. They are valuable for their own sake, quite apart from any other consequences produced. Utilitarians believe that what we really ought to seek and promote in life are certain experiences and conditions that are good in themselves without reference to their further consequences, and that all extrinsic goods or instrumentally valuable things are ultimately to be produced for the sake of obtaining these intrinsic goods.

Because intrinsic values such as the pleasure of eating delicious food have no moral significance, what is *morally* good must be distinguished from what is *intrinsically* good. Utilitarians hold that the moral worth of actions is to be determined by our efforts to maximize the production of such *nonmoral* intrinsic values as pleasure and health. Consider again the example of hypertension with which this chapter begins: The pursuit of health is not in itself a moral endeavor, and seeking a normal blood pressure is not a moral good in the way virtuous conduct is. However, when public health officials act to promote or improve the health of others through public policies, the moral worth of their actions is determined by their efforts at maximally promoting the health of others while minimizing risks. For Bentham and Mill, moral theory is grounded in a theory of the general goal of life, which they claim is the pursuit of pleasure and the avoidance of pain. The production of pleasure and pain assumes moral and not merely personal significance for them when the consequences of actions importantly affect pleasurable or painful states of existence for others. Moral rules and moral and legal institutions such as criminal punishment, as they see it, are grounded in such a general theory of the goals and values of life, and morally good actions are determined by reference to these final values. Utilitarians have not always agreed on these goals and values, but one main task for any utilitarian is to provide an acceptable theory that explains why things are intrinsically good and that includes lists and categories of such goods.

Within utilitarian theories of intrinsic value, a major distinction is drawn between *hedonistic* utilitarians and *pluralistic* utilitarians. Bentham and Mill are hedonistic utilitarians because they conceive utility entirely in terms of happiness or pleasure. In effect, they argue that the good is equivalent to happiness, which is equivalent to pleasure (though they do not argue that the word "good" means happiness or pleasure in ordinary language). All other things are valuable only as means to the production of pleasure or the avoidance of pain. Hedonistic utilitarianism, then, holds that acts or practices which maximize pleasure, when compared with any alternative act or practice, are right actions.

Bentham viewed utility as that aspect of any action or practice which tends to produce different pleasures in the form of benefit, advantage, good, the prevention of pain, etc. Some crucial passages from Bentham will explicate this general conception of hedonistic utilitarianism:

Nature has placed mankind under the governance of two sovereign masters, *pain* and *pleasure*. It is for them alone to point out what we ought to do, as well as to determine what we shall do. On the one hand the standard of right and wrong, on the other the chain of causes and effects, are fastened to their throne. They govern us in all we do, in all we say, in all we think. . . . The *principle of utility* recognises this subjection, and assumes it for the foundation of that system, the object of which is to rear the fabric of felicity by the hands of reason and of law. Systems which attempt to question it, deal in sounds instead of sense, in caprice instead of reason, in darkness instead of light. . . .

By utility is meant that property in any object, whereby it tends to produce benefit, advantage, pleasure, good, or happiness, (all this in the present case comes to the same thing) or (what comes again to the same thing) to prevent the happening of mischief, pain, evil, or unhappiness to the party whose interest is considered: if that party be the community in general, then the happiness of the community: if a particular individual, then the happiness of that individual. . . .

To take an exact account then of the general tendency of any act, by which the interests of a community are affected, proceed as follows. Begin with any one person of those whose interests seem most immediately to be affected by it. . . . Sum up all the values of all the *pleasures* on the one side, and those of all the pains on the other. The balance, if it be on the side of pleasure, will give the *good* tendency of the act upon the whole, with respect to the interest of that *individual* person; if on the side of pain, the *bad* tendency of it upon the whole.

Take an account of the *number* of persons whose interests appear to be concerned; and repeat the above process with respect to each. *Sum up* the numbers expressive of the degrees of *good* tendency, which the act has, with respect to each individual, in regard to whom the tendency of it is *good* upon the whole: do this again with respect to each individual, in regard to whom the tendency of it is *bad* upon the whole. Take the *balance;* which, if on the side of *pleasure,* will give the general *good tendency* of the act, with respect to the total number or community of individuals concerned; if on the side of pain, the general *evil tendency,* with respect to the same community.*

The principle of utility for philosophers such as Bentham and Mill thus demands courses of action that produce the maximum possible happiness in a broad sense of the term. Mill went to considerable lengths to clarify his use of the term "happiness." He

*From Jeremy Bentham, *An Introduction to the Principles of Morals and Legislation* (Oxford, England, 1789).

insisted that happiness does not refer merely to "pleasurable excitement," but rather, encompasses a realistic appraisal of the pleasurable moments afforded in life, whether they take the form of tranquillity or passion. Because he believed both that pleasure and the freedom from pain are the only things desirable as ends and that pleasures and pains could be measured and compared, Bentham was led to argue (as in the passage just quoted) that pleasure and pain can be measured by using a hedonic calculus. To determine the moral value of an action, one is exhorted to add up the total happiness to be produced, subtract the pains involved, and then determine the balance, which expresses the moral value of the act. Thus one is enjoined literally to *calculate* what ought morally to be done.

A frequent objection against utilitarianism is that such quantification either is impossible or would take too long to be practical for determining what we ought to do in daily life. Whatever the merits of this objection, which is taken up in the final section of this chapter, Mill and Bentham realize that it is unrealistic in our daily practical affairs to pause and rationally calculate in detail on every occasion where choices must be made. They do not expect us to make the kind of formal calculations involved in Weinstein and Stason's study of hypertension. Instead, they maintain that we must rely heavily on our common sense, our habits, and our past experience. For example, we know that driving recklessly at high speeds is risky and that utility is maximized by careful driving. Mill and Bentham were agreed that we can ask for only reasonable predictability and choice—not perfect predictability or computerlike calculations.

Mill and Bentham were also aware that many human actions do not appear to be performed merely for the sake of happiness. For example, highly motivated professional academicians can work to the point of exhaustion for the sake of knowledge they hope to gain, even though they might have chosen different and more pleasurable pursuits. Mill's explanation of this phenomenon is that such persons are initially motivated by happiness, much in the way some students are attracted to a university by the prospects a college education holds out for a more satisfying life. Along the way, either the pursuit of knowledge may itself become intrinsically productive of happiness or else such persons may never stop associating the money or prestige they hope to gain with an ultimate goal of pleasure (despite their not actually deriving much, if any, pleasure).

Pluralistic utilitarian philosophers, in contrast with hedonists, have not looked kindly on the pleasure-centered conception of intrinsic value supported by Mill and Bentham. They have argued that there is no single goal or state constituting *the* good and that many values besides happiness possess intrinsic worth—e.g., the values of friendship, knowledge, love, courage, health, beauty, and perhaps even certain moral qualities such as fairness. According to one defender of this view, G. E. Moore, even certain states of consciousness involving intellectual activity and esthetic appreciation possess intrinsic value apart from their pleasantness.

The idea that there are intrinsic values other than pleasure has received widespread acceptance among utilitarians. These pluralistic utilitarians argue that if pleasure or happiness were the sole good, then goods such as knowledge, love, and beauty would be good only because they produce pleasure or happiness. Yet, they believe these goods are good independent of any pleasure they may produce. Imagine a world in which there is sexual pleasure, say, and no other good. In this hypothetical world, such goods as knowledge and beauty are totally absent, yet sexual pleasure produces more *total* happiness than exists in a world in which these goods are abundantly present. If the world involving only sexual pleasure offers more total happiness than the other world, a pure, quantitative hedonist must say it is a better or more desirable world. To many, this assumption seems a serious flaw in hedonistic utilitarianism, for they do not regard a world of abundant pleasure as being as *valuable* as a world having other forms of intrinsic value. Those who subscribe to a pluralist approach prefer to interpret the principle of utility as demanding that the rightness or wrongness of an action is assessed in terms of the total range of intrinsic values ultimately produced by the action, and not in terms of happiness and pleasure alone. The greatest aggregate good, then, will be determined by considering multiple intrinsic goods.

Both the hedonistic and the pluralistic approaches have seemed to some recent philosophers relatively useless for purposes of objectively aggregating widely different interests in order to determine where maximal value, and therefore right action, lies. It is difficult and perhaps impossible to determine objectively what is intrinsically good on any given occasion, and this problem leads many utilitarians to interpret the good as that which is subjectively desired or wanted: the *satisfaction* of desires or wants is seen as the goal of our moral actions. This third approach is based on individual *preferences,* and utility is analyzed in terms of an individual's actual preferences, not as intrinsically valuable experiences or states of affairs. To maximize an individual's utility is to maximize what he or she has chosen or would choose from the available alternatives. To maximize the utility of all persons affected by an action or a policy is to maximize the utility of the aggregate group. This maximization, of course, is exactly what Weinstein and Stason attempted to achieve through their recommendation about hypertension, though here, as elsewhere in the formulation of policies, it is difficult to know what individuals actually prefer—e.g., whether they wish to be let alone or to be notified about their health problems. Nonetheless, those who adopt the preference model believe it is far easier to determine aggregate needs based on preferences than to calculate maximal value in terms of some ad hoc or dubious general conception of pleasurable or objectively good states of affairs. This approach, then, is indifferent to hedonistic and pluralistic views of intrinsic value. What is "intrinsically" valuable is what each individual prefers to obtain, and utility is translated into the satisfaction of those needs and desires that individuals themselves choose to satisfy.

This utilitarian approach to value based on preferences is seen by many as superior to its predecessors for two main reasons. First, recent disputes about hedonism and pluralism have proved very difficult to resolve, even after protracted discussion. One's choice of a range of these values in constructing a general theory of utility seems decisively affected by unique personal experiences—a problem avoidable by using the preference approach, because on that model there is no general theory of value or utility that ranges across individuals. Second, in order to make utilitarian calculations and interpersonal comparisons in any literal sense, it is necessary to measure values. For Bentham and Mill, for example, we must be able to measure happy and unhappy states and then compare one person's level of happiness with another's in order to decide which is quantitatively greatest. Bentham devised his hedonic calculus for precisely this purpose. Later in this chapter, we will encounter a criticism of utilitarianism to the effect that we cannot objectively measure and compare the different intrinsic values of different individuals. Whatever the merits of this criticism of hedonistic and pluralistic utilitarianism, it does make sense to measure *preferences* more or less objectively by devising a utility scale that measures relative strengths of individual and group preferences. This procedure or roughly its equivalent is used whenever municipalities vote on increased spending proposals and whenever polls are taken to ascertain which candidate among a range of alternative choices for public office is preferred.

The preference-utility approach nonetheless is not trouble-free as a general theory of morals. A problem arises when individuals have morally unacceptable preferences (according to, say, standard norms of morality). For example, a person's strong sexual preference may be to rape young children, but such a preference is morally intolerable. We discount this preference because it may culminate in immoral acts. Utilitarianism based purely on subjective preferences is satisfactory, then, only if a range of *acceptable* values can be formulated. This latter task has proved difficult in theory, and it may even be inconsistent with a pure preference approach to attempt to limit or discount actual preferences. Nonetheless, some plausible replies to this objection are open to utilitarians. First, since most people are not perverse and do have morally acceptable (even if odd) values, utilitarians believe they are justified in proceeding under the assumption that the preference approach is not fatally marred by a speculative problem. As Mill noted, any moral theory whatever may lead to unsatisfactory outcomes if one assumes universal idiocy. Second, utilitarians can argue that acceptable values are restricted to the objects of a *rational* desire, i.e., objects which any individual might rationally desire. Privacy, for example, is rationally desirable, but chopping off one's neighbor's head in private is not (unless very peculiar circumstances prevail). Third, because perverse desires undercut the objectives of utilitarianism by creating conditions productive of unhappiness, the desires could never even be permitted to count. As Mill argued in the earlier selection from his *Utilitarianism,* the cultivation of certain kinds of desires is built into his formulation of the "ideal" of utilitarianism. Still, even if most persons are not perverse and the ideals of utilitarianism are well entrenched in society, some rational agents may have preferences that are immoral or unjust (by common standards); and the utilitarian may therefore stand in need of a supplementary criterion of value in addition to mere preference.

In summary, utilitarians seriously disagree about the nature of good and evil. They thus differ about the nature of utility, human welfare, and human detriment, as well as about how good and bad consequences are to be determined. Despite these problems, *if* utilitarianism could be fully worked out along the lines of any one consistent theory of utility, it would provide a definite and attractive procedure for making ethical choices. We would be able to determine the morally best actions among the various options open to us. We could do so by asking how much value and how much disvalue— as gauged by the preferences or values of those affected by our actions—would result in the lives of all affected, including ourselves. Knowingly to perform any action other than the one which could be expected to produce the most good would be more or less objectively condemnable.

ACT UTILITARIANISM

We have seen that utilitarians disagree about what counts as a good consequence. Let us now pursue this disagreement in a slightly different context.

A significant controversy has arisen over whether the principle of utility is to be applied to particular *acts* in particular circumstances or to *rules* of conduct which determine whether acts are right or wrong. For the *rule* utilitarian, actions are justified by appeal to rules such as "Don't deprive persons of freedom of opportunity." These rules, in turn, are justified by appeal to the principle of utility. An *act* utilitarian justifies actions simply by direct appeal to the principle of utility. To illustrate their differences, contrast legal reasoning with the reasoning of public officials charged with responsibility for decisions affecting citizens. Courts deliberate by reference to established laws and procedures (formal rules), and in an analogous way the rule utilitarian contends that morality is constituted by a set of rules. An act utilitarian, however, takes the view that the model of a public official is more appropriate for moral theory than the model of the courtroom. Public officials make particular decisions in particular cases, often by directly applying the principle of utility. Thus, for example, the decision whether or not to build a new dam should be made not by reference to systems of rules pertaining to when and under what conditions dams should be built, but rather, by reaching a decision in a particular case about the public interest in light of the desires of environmentalists, tourists, recreation enthusiasts, business interests, state officials, residents in the area, and other affected persons. Rule utilitarians, however, argue that it must first be decided which moral principles should be used to decide whether to build a dam. They hold that these principles form the necessary background for the moral life, just as laws form the background for courts when they arbitrate disputes about whether to go ahead with a projected dam.

The eighteenth-century Scottish philosopher David Hume perceptively noticed at least three differences between act and rule utilitarians, though he did not employ this terminology. First, he noticed that we are at times *motivated* to observe a moral rule because of that rule's position in a system of social rules. If there were no general scheme of rules of justice, for example, we might not be motivated to perform such morally praiseworthy actions as hiring new employees without respect to race, sex, or religion. Second, he noticed the distinction between the true claim that moral rules, such as that of truth-telling, generally have social utility and the false claim that every act of truth-telling has social utility. Moral rules condemn lying, according to this view, but occasionally lying to children or friends, for example, can have overriding utility. Third, he noticed that rules justified by their general utilitarian consequences may in particular circumstances require actions that do not maximize utility in those circumstances. Fulfilling a contract to spray a farmer's tract of land with a pesticide, for example, falls under a rule that one should keep one's promises and so one's contract. This is a commendable social rule justified by utility. Nonetheless, fulfilling one's obligations under this rule could endanger the public interest on some occasions. Hume expresses some of his thoughts about rules and the public interest as follows.

DAVID HUME

overall, society benefits even though individuals suffer

Utility and Justice*

A single act of justice is frequently contrary to *public interest;* and were it to stand alone, without being follow'd by other acts, may, in itself, be very prejudicial to society. When a man of merit, of a beneficent disposition, restores a great fortune to a miser, or a seditious bigot, he has acted justly and laudably, but the public is a real sufferer. Nor is every single act of justice, consider'd apart, more conducive to private interest, than to public; and 'tis easily conceiv'd how a man may impoverish himself by a signal instance of integrity, and have reason to wish, that with regard to that single act, the laws of justice were for a moment suspended in the universe. But however single acts of justice may be contrary, either to public or private interest, 'tis certain, that the whole plan or scheme is highly conducive, or indeed absolutely requisite, both to the support of society, and the well-being of every individual. 'Tis impossible to separate the good from the ill. Property must be stable, and must be fix'd by general rules. Tho' in one instance the public be a sufferer, this momentary ill is amply compensated by the steady prosecution of the rule, and by the peace and order, which it establishes in society. And even every individual person must find himself a gainer, on ballancing the account; since, without justice, society must immediately dissolve, and every one must fall into that savage and solitary condition, which is infinitely worse than the worst situation that can possibly be suppos'd in society. When therefore men have had experience enough to observe, that whatever may be the consequence of any single act of justice, perform'd by a single person, yet the whole system of actions, concurr'd in by the whole society, is infinitely advantageous to the whole, and to every part; it is not long before justice and property take place. Every member of society is sensible of this interest: Every one expresses this sense to his fellows, along with the resolution he has taken of squaring his actions by it, on condition that others will do the same. No more is requisite to induce any one of them to perform an act of justice, who has the first opportunity. This becomes an example to others. And thus justice establishes itself by a kind of convention or agreement; that is, by a sense of interest, suppos'd to be common to all, and where every single act is perform'd in expectation that others are to perform the like.

*From David Hume, *A Treatise of Human Nature*, L. A. Selby-Bigge, ed., rev. by P. H. Nidditch (Oxford, England: Clarendon Press, 1978), pp. 497ff.

Let us now explore this elementary formulation of the differences between act and rule utilitarians by a closer look at each of the two schools of thought.

Act utilitarianism is often characterized as a "direct" or "extreme" theory, because the act utilitarian asks only, "What good and evil consequences will result directly from this action in this circumstance?"—not, "What good and evil consequences will result generally from this *sort* of action?" An action is morally right if, and only if, it produces at least as great a balance of value over disvalue as any other action open to the person; or, in short, the right act is that which has the greatest utility *in the circumstances*. This posture seems natural for utilitarians, because utilitarianism aims at maximizing value, and the most direct way of achieving this goal would seem to be that of maximizing value on every single occasion.

This position does not demand, however, that every single time we act, we must determine what should be done without any reference to general guidelines. We clearly learn from past experience, and the act utilitarian does permit summary rules of thumb. The act utilitarian regards rules such as "You ought to tell the truth" as useful but not as unmodifiable prescriptions. However, the *main* question is always, "What should I do now?"—not, "What has proved generally valuable in the past"—for the simple reason that act utilitarians think observances of a general rule (of truth-telling in this case) would not on many important occasions be for the general good. An investigative reporter seeking facts for a newspaper, for example, might have to lie and break laws pertaining to privacy and confidentiality; yet the act utilitarian might find these acts justifiable in contexts where critical information could not otherwise be obtained. Since human situations are infinitely variable, rules of thumb that hold for previous cases may not serve well in a new circumstance. An act utilitarian thus would not hesitate to break such rules if a violation would undoubtedly lead to the greatest good for the greatest number in a particular case.

Consider the following case, which recently occurred in the state of Kansas: An old woman lay ill and dying. Her suffering was now too much for either her or her faithful husband of fifty-four years to stand, so she requested that he kill her. Stricken with grief and unable to bring himself to perform the act, the husband hired another man to kill her, and the agreement was consummated. An act utilitarian might reason that in this case, hiring another to kill the woman was justified even though in general such a practice would not be condoned. After all, only the woman and her husband were directly affected, and relief of her pain was the main issue. It would be unfortunate, the act utilitarian might reason, if the "rules" against killing failed to allow for selective killings of this sort, for it is extremely difficult to generalize from case to case. In a criminal trial, however, a jury convicted the husband of murder and sentenced him to twenty-five years in prison. An act utilitarian might maintain that such a legalistic application of rules of criminal justice inevitably leads to injustices and that rule utilitarianism cannot escape this consequence of a rule-based position.

As this example indicates, act utilitarians regard rule utilitarians as unfaithful to the fundamental demand of the principle of utility. As Hume points out, there are many cases in which abiding by a generally beneficial rule will not prove most beneficial to the persons involved in the circumstances. Why, then, ought the rule to be obeyed? After all, in the circumstance obedience does not maximize value. The contemporary act utilitarian J. J. C. Smart has argued that the rule utilitarian has no adequate reply to this criticism. The rule utilitarian fails to see, according to Smart, that there is another possibility between never obeying a rule and always obeying it—namely, that it should *sometimes* be obeyed.

J. J. C. SMART

An Outline of a System of Utilitarian Ethics*

We may choose to habituate ourselves to behave in accordance with certain rules, such as to keep promises, in the belief that behaving in accordance with these rules is generally optimific, and in the knowledge that we most often just do not have time to work out individual pros and cons. When we act in such an habitual fashion we do not of course deliberate or make a choice. The act-utilitarian will, however, regard these rules as mere rules of thumb, and will use them only as rough guides. Normally he will act in accordance with them when he has no time for considering probable consequences or when the advantages of such a consideration of consequences are likely to be outweighed by the disadvantage of the waste of time involved. He acts in accordance with rules, in short, when there is no time to think, and since he does not think, the actions which he does habitually are not the outcome of moral thinking. When he has to think what to do, then there is a question of deliberation or choice, and it is precisely for such

situations that the utilitarian criterion is intended.

It is, moreover, important to realize that there is no inconsistency whatever in an act-utilitarian's schooling himself to act, in normal circumstances, habitually and in accordance with stereotyped rules. He knows that a man about to save a drowning person has no time to consider various possibilities, such as that the drowning person is a dangerous criminal who will cause death and destruction, or that he is suffering from a painful and incapacitating disease from which death would be a merciful release, or that various timid people, watching from the bank, will suffer a heart attack if they see anyone else in the water. No, he knows that it is almost always right to save a drowning man, and in he goes. Again, he knows that we would go mad if we went in detail into the probable consequences of keeping or not keeping every trivial promise: we will do most good and reserve our mental energies for more important matters if we simply habituate ourselves to keep promises in all normal situations. Moreover, he may suspect that on some occasions personal bias may prevent him from reasoning in a correct utilitarian fashion. Suppose he is trying to decide between two jobs, one of which is more highly paid than the other, though he

*From J. J. C. Smart, "An Outline of a System of Utilitarian Ethics," in J. J. C. Smart and Bernard Williams, *Utilitarianism: For and Against* (Cambridge, England: Cambridge University Press, 1973). Reprinted with permission of Cambridge University Press.

has given an informal promise that he will take the lesser paid one. He may well deceive himself by underestimating the effects of breaking the promise (in causing loss of confidence) and by overestimating the good he can do in the highly paid job. He may well feel that if he trusts to the accepted rules he is more likely to act in the way that an unbiased act-utilitarian would recommend than he would be if he tried to evaluate the consequences of his possible actions himself. . . .

On these occasions when we do not act as a result of deliberation and choice, that is, when we act spontaneously, no method of decision, whether utilitarian or non-utilitarian, comes into the matter. What does arise for the utilitarian is the question of whether or not he should consciously encourage in himself the tendency to certain types of spontaneous feeling. There are in fact very good utilitarian reasons why we should by all means cultivate in ourselves the tendency to certain types of warm and spontaneous feeling.

Though even the act-utilitarian may on occasion act habitually and in accordance with particular rules, his criterion is, as we have said, *applied* in cases in which he does not act habitually but in which he deliberates and chooses what to do. Now the right action for an agent in given circumstances is, we have said, that action which produces better results than any alternative action. If two or more actions produce equally good results, and if these results are better than the results of any other action open to the agent, then there is no such thing as *the* right action: there are two or more actions which are *a* right action. However, this is a very exceptional state of affairs, which may well never in fact occur, and so usually I will speak loosely of the action which is *the* right one. . . .

It is true that the general concept of action is wider than that of deliberate choice. Many actions are performed habitually and without deliberation. But the actions for whose rightness we as agents want a criterion are, in the nature of the case, those done thinkingly and deliberately. An action is at any rate that sort of human performance which it is appropriate to praise, blame, punish or reward, and since it is often appropriate to praise, blame, punish, or reward habitual performances, the concept of action cannot be identified with that of the outcome of deliberation and choice. With habitual actions the only question that arises for an agent is that of whether or not he should strengthen the habit or break himself of it.

Smart's defense of act utilitarianism probably rests in the end on a more general belief that we will be better off in the moral life if we practice selective obedience to rules, because such behavior will not erode either moral rules, our general respect for morality, or our habituated tendencies to the common good.

Act utilitarianism of the sort defended by Smart has been subjected to sharp criticism in recent moral philosophy by rule utilitarians and other opponents. One major theoretical reason for its rejection is the claim that utilitarianism sometimes sanctions injustice and violations of rights. The argument here is not that act utilitarianism always sanctions unjust actions, but only that under certain imaginable conditions immoral acts seem "morally demanded" if utility considerations alone prevail. Bearing in mind that

ex. against
act utilitarian

act utilitarians take all the consequences of individual actions into account, consider the following classic counterexample that has been offered against act utilitarianism: A small town is highly disorganized and in economic distress. Unemployment is high and leadership is chaotic. The citizenry is depressed and unhappy. All the major social problems could be resolved by enslaving a small portion of this citizenry. The general level of happiness in the society would be increased by having a slave system, and even the slaves would be no worse off in material terms than they were previously. Yet, it is blatantly immoral to enslave a few in the service of the majority. The majority, we believe, has no right to treat the minority in this way. Direct use of the principle of utility strikes many as blatantly immoral if permitted by a moral theory to be put to such purposes.

Another standard form of counterexample to act utilitarianism is captured in the following imagined sequence of events: Suppose that you have made a promise to a close and faithful friend, a person whom you admire and respect, and from whom you have received many favors. Now suppose, however, that the utilitarian consequences of not fulfilling the promise are equal to the utilitarian consequences of keeping the promise. For example, your friend asks you to deliver money to an uncle who has helped him in the past. But you know that this uncle is very rich and will eventually squander the money. There is apparently no act-utilitarian reason requiring that you keep your promise, but in fact there does seem to be a good (nonutilitarian and rule-utilitarian) reason for keeping the promise—namely, that you promised.

The point of these counterexamples is to show that act utilitarianism is inconsistent with what might be called the "common moral consciousness." The fact that many have thought these criticisms sufficient to refute act utilitarians is of course no proof that the counterexamples are telling. The act utilitarian would reply that although promises ordinarily should be kept and rights carefully guarded in order to maintain a climate of trust and security, such considerations fail to apply in certain cases, because more good would be produced in extreme circumstances by breaking promises and setting rights aside. The act utilitarian willingly admits that such views may be inconsistent with ordinary moral convictions in some cases, but will add that we need to revise our ordinary convictions, not repudiate act utilitarianism. The act utilitarian also points out that *all* the consequences of slave-owning societies and broken promises would have to be taken into account when considering what should be done in single cases. Thus the act utilitarian finds these counterexamples exotic and unconvincing, for again they postulate speculative and highly implausible conditions.

Weinstein and Stason's study of hypertension, described at the beginning of this chapter, provides a useful example of this act-utilitarian reply. Ordinarily one would strongly resist (for moral reasons) excluding the poor and minority groups from receiving public health benefits. Indeed, it seems immoral not to include them. Yet, the recommendations proffered by Weinstein and Stason give us pause to reconsider our "ordinary moral convictions" precisely because we have been given solid utilitarian reasons for doing so.

LIKE THE ACADEMY

RULE UTILITARIANISM

The counterexamples and objections considered in the preceding section are directed exclusively at act utilitarianism. They do not work as well for refuting the rule utilitarian, who maintains that rules themselves have a central position in morality and cannot be compromised by the demands of a particular situation. Such a compromise would threaten the integrity and existence of moral rules, each of which was originally adopted because its general observance would maximize social utility better than would any alternative rule (or no rule). One popular way of expressing this view construes the principle of utility (somewhat negatively) as requiring that we generally not produce or otherwise promote undesirable consequences. According to this view, an action is morally wrong if the consequences of performing it are generally undesirable. It is morally wrong to cheat on examinations, income tax returns, and specifications for building houses, for example, because the consequences of permitting or neglecting such actions would be disastrous. Moral rules, then, are the formulations of our findings, based on experience, as to what is generally desirable and undesirable. Rules are justified when they are the rules that would maximize utility if there were general acceptance of and conformity to them. The conformity of an act to a socially valuable rule makes the action right—whereas, for the act utilitarian, the beneficial consequences of the act alone make it right or wrong.

The rule utilitarian believes this position is capable of escaping the counterexamples and objections to act utilitarianism encountered previously, because rules are not subject to the peculiar demands of individual circumstances. Rules are firm and protective of all classes of individuals—as human rights are rigidly protective of all individuals independent of social circumstances. If the basic moral rules composing morality as we know it are sanctioned by utility, then it is hard to see how we can be led by these rules to immoral actions in particular circumstances. This approach has seemed preferable to many because it at least attempts to answer the aforementioned criticisms of act utilitarianism.

Some rule utilitarians propose that we consider the utility of *whole codes* or *systems of rules* rather than independent rules, when considering which rules have the greatest social utility. Among the defenders of different versions of this position are Hume and the contemporary American philosopher R. B. Brandt. They believe the rightness or wrongness of individual acts is determined exclusively by reference to moral rules that have a place in a code or system of rules. The system is assessed as a whole in terms of its overall utilitarian consequences. This idea roughly parallels the notion that a political constitution is to be judged by all the articles and amendments it contains as a whole, for the strength of the constitution would not be proven by considering each article or amendment in isolation from the others.

This moral-code approach obviously bears a strong resemblance to simple rule utilitarianism, but it allegedly has its own unique advantages. We are more likely to act to maximize utility throughout a society by the public advocacy of a whole system of rules, rather than by merely testing and attempting to gain adherence to single rules, each considered in isolation from the consequences of other rules in the system. Most of us are motivated to the acceptance of a whole way of life that is moral, and we generally think of morality as a system of integrated principles and rules. This is a basic assumption of the following difficult but important essay by Brandt.

RICHARD B. BRANDT

Some Merits of One Form of Rule-Utilitarianism*

For convenience I shall refer to [my] theory as the "ideal moral code" theory. The essence of it is as follows: Let us first say that a moral code is "ideal" if its currency in a particular society would produce at least as much good per person (the total divided by the number of persons) as the currency of any other moral code. (Two different codes might meet this condition, but, in order to avoid complicated formulations, the following discussion will ignore this possibility.) Given this stipulation for the meaning of "ideal," the Ideal Moral Code theory consists in the assertion of the following thesis: *An act is right if and only if it would not be prohibited by the moral code ideal for the society; and an agent is morally blameworthy (praiseworthy) for an act if, and to the degree that, the moral code ideal in that society would condemn (praise) him for it.* . . .

For a moral code to have currency in a society, two things must be true. First, a high proportion of the adults in the society must subscribe to the moral principles, or have the moral opinions, constitutive of the code. Exactly how high the proportion

should be, we can hardly decide on the basis of the ordinary meaning of "the moral code"; but probably it would not be wrong to require at least 90 percent agreement. . . . Second, we want to say that certain principles *A*, *B*, etc., belong to the moral code of a society only if they are recognized as such. That is, it must be that a large proportion of the adults of the society would respond correctly if asked, with respect to *A* and *B*, whether most members of the society subscribed to them. . . .

We must now give more attention to the conception of an ideal moral code, and how it may be decided when a given moral code will produce as much good per person as any other. We may, however, reasonably bypass the familiar problems of judgments of comparative utilities, especially when different persons are involved, since these problems are faced by all moral theories that have any plausibility. We shall simply assume that rough judgments of this sort are made and can be justified.

(*a*) We should first notice that, as "currency" has been explained above, a moral code could not be current in a society if it were too complex to be learned or applied. We may therefore confine our consideration to codes simple enough to be absorbed by human beings, roughly in the way in which people learn actual moral codes. . . .

*From Richard B. Brandt, "Some Merits of One Form of Rule-Utilitarianism," a paper presented at a conference on moral philosophy, the University of Colorado, October 1965, revised and published in *University of Colorado Studies*, 1967, pp. 39–65. Reprinted by permission of the author and the University of Colorado Press.

(*b*) In deciding how much good the currency of a specific moral system would do, we consider the institutional setting as it is, as part of the situation. We are asking which moral code would produce the most good in the long run in this setting. One good to be reckoned, of course, might be that the currency of a given moral code would tend to change the institutional system.

(*c*) In deciding which moral code will produce the most per person good, we must take into account the probability that certain types of situation will arise in the society. For instance, we must take for granted that people will make promises and subsequently want to break them, that people will sometimes assault other persons in order to achieve their own ends, that people will be in distress and need the assistance of others, and so on. . . .

(*d*) It would be a great oversimplification if, in assessing the comparative utility of various codes, we confined ourselves merely to counting the benefits of people doing (refraining from doing) certain things, as a result of subscribing to a certain code. To consider only this would be as absurd as estimating the utility of some feature of a legal system by attending only to the utility of people behaving in the way the law aims to make them behave—and overlooking the fact that the law only reduces and does not eliminate misbehavior, as well as the disutility of punishment to the convicted, and the cost of the administration of criminal law. In the case of morals, we must weigh the benefit of the improvement in behavior as a result of the restriction built into conscience, against the cost of the restriction—the burden of guilt feelings, the effects of the training process, etc. . . .

It has been thought that the implications of rule-utilitarianisms for two types of situation are especially significant: (*a*) for situations in which persons are generally violating the recognized moral code, or some feature of it: and (*b*) for situations in which, because the moral code is generally respected, maximum utility would be produced by violation of the code by the agent. An example of the former situation (sometimes called a "state of nature" situation) would be widespread perjury in making out income tax declarations. An example of the latter situation would be widespread conformity to the rule forbidding walking on the grass in a park.

What are the implications of the suggested form of rule-utilitarianism for these types of situation? Will it prescribe conduct which is not utility maximizing in these situations? If it does, it will clearly have implications discrepant with those of act-utilitarianism—but perhaps unpalatable to some people.

It is easy to see how to go about determining what is right or wrong in such situations, on the above described form of rule-utilitarianism—it is a question of what an "ideal" moral code would prescribe. But it is by no means easy to see where a reasonable person would come out, after going through such an investigation. . . .

Far from "collapsing" into act-utilitarianism, the Ideal Moral Code theory appears to avoid the serious objections which have been leveled at direct [act] utilitarianism. One objection to the latter view is that it implies that various immoral actions (murdering one's elderly father, breaking solemn promises) are right or even obligatory if only they can be kept secret. The Ideal Moral Code theory has no such implication. For it obviously would not maximize utility to have a moral code which condoned secret murders or breaches of promise. W. D. Ross criticized act-utilitarianism on the ground that it ignored the personal relations important in ordinary morality, and he listed a half-dozen types of moral rule which he thought captured the main themes of thoughtful morality: obligations of fidelity, obligations of gratitude, obligations to make restitution for injuries, obligations to help other persons, to avoid injuring them, to improve one's self, and to bring about a just distribution of good things in life. An ideal moral code, however, would presumably contain substantially such rules in any society, doubtless not precisely as Ross stated them. So the rule-utilitarian need not fail to recognize the personal character of morality. . . .

The Ideal Moral Code theory has the advantage of implying that the moral rules recognized in a given society are not necessarily morally binding. They are binding only in so far as they maximize welfare, as contrasted with other possible moral rules. Thus if, in a given society, it is thought wrong to work on the Sabbath, to perform socially desirable abortions, or to commit suicide, it does not follow, on the Ideal Moral Code theory, that these things are necessarily wrong. The question is whether a code containing such prohibitions would maximize welfare. Similarly, according to this theory, a person may act wrongly in doing certain things which are condoned by his society. . . .

Let us examine the implications of the Ideal Moral Code theory by considering a typical example. Among the Hopi Indians, a child is not expected to care for his father (he is always in a different clan), whereas he is expected to care for his mother, maternal aunt, and maternal uncle, and so on up the female line (all in the same clan). It would be agreed by observers that this system does not work very well. The trouble with it is that the lines of institutional obligation and the lines of natural affection do not coincide, and, as a result, an elderly male is apt not to be cared for by anyone.

Can we show that an "ideal moral code" would call on a young person to take care of his maternal uncle, in a system of this sort? (It might also imply he should try to change the system, but that is another point.) One important feature of the situation of the young man considering whether he should care for his maternal uncle is that, the situation including the expectations of others being what it is, if he does nothing to relieve the distress of his maternal uncle, it is probable that it will not be relieved. His situation is very like that of the sole observer of an automobile accident; he is a mere innocent bystander, but the fact is that if he does nothing, the injured persons will die. So the question for us is whether an ideal moral code will contain a rule that, if someone is in a position where he can relieve serious distress, and where it is known that in all probability it will not be relieved if he does not do so, he should relieve the distress. The answer seems to be that it will contain such a rule: we might call it an "obligation of humanity." But there is a second, and more important point. Failure of the young person to provide for his maternal uncle would be a case of unfairness or free riding. For the family system operates like a system of insurance; it provides one with various sorts of privileges or protections, in return for which one is expected to make certain payments, or accept the risk of making certain payments. Our young man has already benefited by the system, and stands to benefit further; he has received care and education as a child, and later on his own problems of illness and old age will be provided for. On the other hand, the old man, who has (we assume) paid such premiums as the system calls on him to pay in life, is now properly expecting, in accordance with the system, certain services from a particular person whom the system designates as the one to take care of him. Will the ideal moral code require such a person to pay the premium in such a system? I suggest that it will, and we can call the rule in question an "obligation of fairness." So, we may infer that our young man will have a moral obligation to care for his maternal uncle, on grounds both of humanity and fairness.

Despite Brandt's attempt to put distance between rule and act forms of utilitarianism, one important and unresolved question remains: Can rule-utilitarian theories escape the very criticisms they advance against act utilitarianism? Moral rules themselves often come into conflict in the moral life; on some occasions, for example, one must steal in order to preserve a life, or lie in order to preserve a secret one vowed to keep, or break a rule of confidentiality in order to protect a person endangered by its maintenance. In all such cases, it must be decided which moral rule has priority over the moral rule with which it conflicts—e.g., whether the rule requiring that we not break confidences is to be given priority over the rule that we protect innocent persons endangered by others. Must there be rules, then, that determine the relevance of other moral rules, or must rule utilitarians admit that some moral decisions do not turn on rules?

If the moral life were so ordered that we always knew which rules should receive priority, there would be no serious problem for moral theory. Yet, such a ranking of rules seems clearly impossible, and in a pluralistic society there are many rules that some persons accept and others reject. But, even if everyone agreed on the same rules and on their interpretation, in one situation it might be better to break a confidence in order to protect someone, while in another circumstance it might be better to keep the information confidential. Mill briefly considered this problem of decision in the midst of conflict and argued, as one might expect, that the principle of utility should itself decide in any given circumstance which rule is to take priority over another rule. However, if this solution is accepted by *rule* utilitarians, then their theory seems to rely directly on the principle of utility to decide *in particular situations* which action is preferable to which alternative action in the absence of a governing rule. This problem has led some to say that whenever rule utilitarianism is applied to concrete problems and dilemmas in the moral life, it cannot be distinguished from act utilitarianism. If this assertion is correct, then all the same criticisms and counterexamples that rule utilitarians bring against act utilitarians may fit rule utilitarianism itself.

The rule utilitarian, however, need not capitulate to this reduction of a rule theory to an act theory. The rule utilitarian can reply that a sense of relative weight and importance should be built into the rules themselves, at least insofar as is possible. The weight and importance attached to a rule are based on the relative social utility produced by having the rule—a judgment that of course must be made in advance of particular circumstances. For example, the rule utilitarian would argue that rules which prohibit punishment of the innocent are of such vital social significance (i.e., have such paramount social utility) that they can never be overridden by appeal to rules protecting the public against criminal activities, even if grave problems of public safety are at stake.

This rule-utilitarian strategy of relative (a priori) weighting should be adequate to handle some problems of conflict, but even the rule utilitarian will acknowledge that weights cannot be so definitely formulated and built into principles that irresolvable conflicts among rules will never arise. What the rule utilitarian will *not* acknowledge is that this problem is unique to his or her position. Every moral theory, after all, has certain practical limitations in cases of such a conflict. This is a problem with the moral life itself, the rule utilitarian will argue, and so is not unique to a rule theory. Indeed, an act utilitarian seems faced with the same problem, for circumstances will arise where the principle of utility directs us to two equally attractive alternatives, only one of which can be pursued. The principle of utility itself obviously cannot resolve this problem of conflict, a problem that will occur whenever two possible actions produce equally utilitarian results but only one may be performed. In such cases, J. J. C. Smart argues, the act utilitarian will say, "There is no such thing as *the* right action: there are two or more actions which are *a* right action." Notice, however, that this same strategy is open to the rule utilitarian: In cases of an irresolvable conflict of equally weighted rules, there is no such thing as *the* right action; there are two or more right actions.

CRITICISMS AND DEFENSES OF UTILITARIANISM

We have seen that utilitarians, especially act utilitarians, have been criticized for allowing the interests of a majority to override the rights or legitimate interests of a minority. In conclusion, let us investigate three criticisms of utilitarianism advanced by contemporary philosophers, together with replies that utilitarians might offer.

The Problem of Quantifying Goodness ✓

One major criticism of utilitarians centers on their apparent commitment to the quan- *good* tification and comparison of goodness. Both hedonistic and pluralistic utilitarians have, *pt* at times, strongly suggested that goods can be measured, and yet neither type of utili- *against* tarianism has been very successful in defending this view. Utilitarians have also dis- *utilitar.* agreed among themselves about whether values can be measured and about the role of qualitative judgments about higher or more important goods. Mill argues that on Bentham's account of utility, it would be better to be a satisfied pig than a dissatisfied Socrates, thus raising problems about how to weigh qualitative considerations. Human experience, he contends, clearly reveals a belief that some pleasures are qualitatively better than others—e.g., that Socratic pleasures of the mind are qualitatively better than purely bodily pleasures. Mill thus had to grapple with an additional problem of assessing or measuring goodness qualitatively, since it is not at all obvious how "qualitative betterness" can be measured.

PROBLEM   A related problem is the difficulty of comparing goods. Because utility is to be maximized, one who makes a utilitarian choice must be in a position to compare the different possible utilities of an action. But can individual pleasures or units of happiness be quantified and compared so as to determine whether one is better than another? How does one compare the value of a good college education with the value of regular medical checkups—or even public health education with publicly funded clinics for checkups? In the hypertension study, how would one determine the public interest by quantifying and comparing the goods of affected parties? It is difficult for individuals to rank their own preferences, and still more difficult, if not impossible, to compare one person's preferences with those of other persons. Yet, at least a rough comparison is required if one is to *maximize* the utility of everyone affected by one's actions.

ANSWER   ——The utilitarian reply to these criticisms about quantification and comparison is as follows: Every day we make crude, rough-and-ready comparisons of values, including pleasures and pains. For example, we decide to go to the theater rather than a baseball game, because we think it will be more pleasurable or satisfy more members of a group than the game. At work, we devise systems of office management so that friction is minimized. More funds are allocated for cancer research than for the treatment of hypertension, etc. It is easy to overestimate the demands of utilitarianism, as well as the precision with which it may be employed. Making accurate measurements of the preferences of others can seldom be done because of our limited knowledge and scarce time, and often in everyday affairs we must act on severely limited knowledge regarding the consequences of our actions. Yet, the utilitarian does not condemn any sincere attempt to maximize value merely because the consequences turn out to be less than maximal. The important thing, morally speaking, is that one conscientiously attempts to determine the most favorable action, and then with equal seriousness attempts to perform that action. When judging the moral worth of an agent's performance of an action, motives as well as the consequences actually produced are obviously of moral significance. These motives must of course be aimed at maximizing valuable consequences, but the intention can deserve praise quite apart from what is produced in attempting to carry out the intent.

Moreover, it is often easier to achieve agreement in groups about how to *balance* different value interests than it is to reach agreements *in principle* on matters of moral rightness and wrongness. If so, utilitarianism is in no worse a position than any other moral theory. The fact that it is easier to reach agreement on an action does not make the action right, of course, but it may show that we have less difficulty in making these determinations than critics of utilitarianism acknowledge in attacking the notion of quantification.

The Problem of Unjust Distributions   ✓

Utilitarianism has also been challenged on grounds that it can lead to injustice, especially to unjust social distributions. We have already encountered one form of this criticism when we discussed two counterexamples against act utilitarianism: the slave *examples*

society and punishment of the innocent. Many philosophers believe this general line of argument can, with but slight reformulation, be extended as an objection against all forms of utilitarianism.

Consider again the example of the slave society. If a slave society in fact produced the greatest happiness for the greatest number, it would seem that even a rule utilitarian would have to say that the *practice* of slavery in that society is morally obligatory. Using examples paralleling this model, a number of moral philosophers have argued that it is not merely the production of some total amount of intrinsic value that counts in the moral life, but also how this amount is *distributed*. If everyone's utility were to be better in a slave-owning world than in a non-slave-owning world, it nonetheless seems plausible that the slave-free world is morally preferable. Such possibilities encourage the criticism that the principle of utility is not broad enough to capture our sense of distributive justice. If this criticism is sustainable, the principle of utility would have to be supplemented by certain principles of justice in order to have any hope of becoming an acceptable moral theory.

This argument has often been generalized further as follows: The action that produces the greatest balance of value for the greatest number of people affected may also bring about unjustified harm or disvalue to a minority. The action might involve breaking a promise, violating rights, or violating any moral rule whatever. Mill himself strongly resists this conclusion in his writings on social philosophy, suggesting that the power of government must be severely limited so that it cannot oppress a minority in the community. But his critics have often wondered how utilitarianism supports such protections of the individual. To the extent an ethical theory requires that the rights of individuals be surrendered in the interests of the majority, it seems deficient; and if even a fair opportunity is denied, as Weinstein and Stason's recommendation on hypertension seems to some to suggest, the theory supporting such a recommendation is clearly unfair.

Moreover, many political philosophers and legal theorists have argued that documents such as the Bill of Rights in the Constitution of the United States contain a set of rules based on nonutilitarian principles, for such rights rigidly protect citizens from invasions in the name of the public good. While utilitarians argue in response that the Bill of Rights can itself be justified on utilitarian grounds, the opponents of utilitarianism think that if the Bill of Rights did not lead to the greatest good for the greatest number, utilitarians would inevitably have to replace it with some document that did. In the following selection, Henry Sidgwick supports such a criticism by arguing that the principle of utility must be supplemented by a principle of justice.

[handwritten annotation: argues that utility must be supplemented w/ justice]

HENRY SIDGWICK

Justice and Utilitarianism*

It is evident that there may be many different ways of distributing the same quantum of happiness among the same number of persons; in order, therefore, that the Utilitarian criterion of right conduct may be as complete as possible, we ought to know which of these ways is to be preferred. . . . In all such cases, therefore, it becomes practically important to ask whether any mode of distributing a given quantum of happiness is better than any other. Now the Utilitarian formula seems to supply no answer to this question; at least we have to supplement the principle of seeking the greatest happiness on the whole by some principle of Just or Right distribution of this happiness. The principle which most Utilitarians have either tacitly or expressly adopted is that of pure equality—as given in Bentham's formula, "everybody to count for one, and nobody for more than

*From Henry Sidgwick, *The Methods of Ethics,* 7th ed. (London: Macmillan & Co., Ltd., 1962). The first edition was published in 1874.

one." And this principle seems the only one which does not need a special justification; for as we saw, it must be reasonable to treat any one man in the same way as any other, if there be no reason apparent for treating him differently. . . .

In short the self-evident principle strictly stated must take some such negative form as this; "it cannot be right for *A* to treat *B* in a manner in which it would be wrong for *B* to treat *A*, merely on the ground that they are two different individuals, and without there being any difference between the natures or circumstances of the two which can be stated as a reasonable ground for difference of treatment." Such a principle manifestly does not give complete guidance—indeed its effect, strictly speaking, is merely to throw a definite *onus probandi* on the man who applies to another a treatment of which he would complain if applied to himself: but Common Sense has amply recognised the practical importance of the maxim: and its truth, so far as it goes, appears to me self-evident.

Consider now a somewhat less speculative example than the well-worn slave-society example. Utilitarian reasoning is closely connected to that form of reasoning commonly known as cost-benefit analysis, which is widely used in contemporary business and government. According to cost-benefit models, an evaluation of all the benefits and costs of a potential program or action must be made in order to determine which among alternative programs or actions is to be recommended. The costs and benefits can include both economic and noneconomic factors. Opponents of utilitarianism and cost-benefit analysis argue as follows: At least some cost-benefit analyses will reveal that a particular government program or a new technology will prove highly beneficial as compared to its costs, and yet provision of this benefit might function prejudicially in a free market economy by denying basic medical or welfare services to the most disadvantaged members of society. Perhaps the disadvantaged ought to be subsidized as a matter of justice, either in terms of health services or financial awards—no matter what cost-benefit analyses reveal. Planning efforts employing cost-benefit analysis are morally mistaken, say these critics, because they fail to account for our sense of distributive justice; and Weinstein and Stason's study of hypertension is a perfect example.

The utilitarian reply to these objections begins by agreeing that it would not always be permissible to follow the dictates of *single, short-range* calculations of costs and benefits. For example, suppose that crop dusting were done with a new and technologically marvelous pesticide that significantly increased the profits of an agribusiness over the profits that would be realized by use of a less toxic and less effective pesticide. But suppose the far more profitable pesticide kills, on the average, 2 of every 295 farm workers exposed to the spraying for more than a year. A rule utilitarian would agree that it would be immoral to use the pesticide, even if statistical calculations indicate a highly favorable overall cost-benefit equation. The argument would be similar for Weinstein and Stason's recommendation about hypertension, which is squarely based on cost-benefit considerations: If deserving individuals would be harmed or unjustifiably neglected by government health programs, the programs must be modified. The rule utilitarian bases this reply on a framework of moral rules that follows from the quite general program of moral philosophy that defines rule-utilitarian thinking. For the rule utilitarian, Weinstein and Stason's study of cost-efficiency constitutes only *one* factor in a series of factors that must be considered in determining what public health officials ought to do. Findings about how to maximize health (per public dollar invested) for individuals must be considered *along with* moral rules governing just distribution and fair opportunity.*

This utilitarian reply rests on two strategies of argument. First, utilitarians insist that all the entailed costs and benefits must be considered. In the hypertension example, these costs would include protests from advocates of the poor and minorities, impairment to social ideals, further alienation of the poor from the government and public officials, etc. Second, rule-utilitarian analyses emphatically do not suggest that single cost-benefit determinations ought to be accepted. Such utilitarians propose that general rules of justice ought to constrain particular actions or uses of cost-benefit analysis in all cases. These rules themselves are derived from appeals to utility, and can be used to constrain overzealous employment of cost-benefit analysis such as might occur in a simple, direct application of the hypertension data.

The Problem of Requiring Supererogatory Acts ✓

Alan Donagan has offered an objection to all forms of utilitarianism by appealing to the distinction between (1) *morally obligatory actions* (those required by a moral duty)

---

*The point here is that there is an upper limit of risk of harm that can be permitted on any adequate rule-utilitarian theory by the utilization of immediate cost-benefit calculations, and we cannot pass beyond this limit without abusing basic rules of justice, themselves determined by larger considerations of social utility.

and (2) *supererogatory actions* (those over and above the call of moral duty and done from one's own personal ideals).* His strategy is that of imagining situations where it is our conventional moral conviction that an action would be supererogatory (beyond the demands of moral obligation) rather than obligatory, and yet, where utilitarians are committed by their theory to regard the action as a duty. They are so committed, Donagan says, because "there would be more good and less evil in society as a whole if the rule were adopted" or the action required. For example, Donagan imagines a society in which there would be utilitarian rules dictating occasions on which "one man should die for the people." Donagan would presumably regard rules requiring suicide for the elderly and the disabled who are no longer of use to society as one extreme illustration of such a supererogatory act. A less extreme example would be a requirement that large amounts of personal income be given to charity whenever utilitarian goals would be served. Donagan argues that such cases present the most difficult considerations that must be faced by *all* utilitarians, because none can rule out the ever-present possibility that what is now considered supererogatory will, through a changing social situation, become obligatory by utilitarian standards. As Donagan puts it, utilitarians cannot account for the everyday *distinction* between morally obligatory acts and supererogatory acts, because their theory tends to obliterate the distinction. If this criticism is sound, it shows that utilitarian arguments are too broad and demanding: they dictate such acts as altruistic suicide, which are at most optional matters of personal choice.

A rule utilitarian must of course allow for the possibility that any type of action whatever might become a matter of obligation, because the acceptance or rejection of a rule in utilitarianism depends upon existing social conditions. To this extent, Donagan is clearly correct. Nonetheless, under almost all social conditions, utility would not be served by having rules such as the one requiring suicide, even though one might in extreme cases be obliged to perform what would ordinarily be considered a supererogatory act. If this is correct, then utilitarianism will not deviate from conventional views about what is and what is not obligatory. Consider the following example of extreme "social" conditions: At the Treblinka concentration camp, some of those incarcerated were ordered to exterminate their fellow prisoners by opening the gas valves. Many committed suicide rather than carry out the order. Their reasons for suicide were that they had an obligation not to kill innocent persons and that suicide at their own hands was the only acceptable alternative, or at least was a less cruel fate than death at the hands of the Nazis. One might say that they felt obligated to commit suicide in order to preserve their own moral integrity. However, the reason for the obligation to suicide (let us suppose that suicide is here the only morally satisfactory alternative) in this case is the requirement *to protect* (themselves and others) *from harm,* not some rule that specifically requires suicide. Even in this extreme case, a rule utilitarian would

TRICKY.
READ CAREFULLY

*Alan Donagan, "Is There a Credible Form of Utilitarianism?" in Michael D. Bayles, ed., *Contemporary Utilitarianism* (Garden City, N.Y.: Doubleday & Co., 1968).

not propose a rule requiring suicide. The rule utilitarian holds that virtually all circumstances of obligation in bizarre cases can be handled in this way.

Normal or nonextreme social conditions are even easier to handle. The rule utilitarian holds that there is a point of diminishing returns in any moral code concerning how many rules can be or ought to be publicly promulgated. There ought not to be so many rules that people cannot acquaint themselves with all of them, or rules that apply only infrequently, or rules that are so heavily qualified with exceptions that their interpretation is difficult. Since moral rules restrict human freedom, the social value derived from the having of a rule must be greater than the value of the freedom that would be gained by not having the rule. Moreover, it is doubtful that any rule directly requiring what we generally take to be supererogatory actions could achieve any positive end that the basic and stable rules of morality could not. The kinds of examples envisaged by Donagan—such as "one man should die for the people"—would lead to considerable disutility because of the confusion, insecurity, and distrust they would introduce into society.

On the other hand, any rule utilitarian must leave open the question of whether, under some social conditions, a rule requiring such extraordinary acts as suicide might validly be made current. A rule utilitarian must, for example, applaud the Hudson Bay tribes' rule that required suicide by the elderly. Survival at a decent level of human existence depended upon the institutionalization of the rule in their moral code, and it was fairly applied. One can also imagine dire social circumstances that might involve any of us and thus similarly demand such a rule. For example, suppose that a large plane has been forced down in a remote, snowy region where it is invisible from the air. Outsiders do not know that the plane has crashed, so that rescue efforts are precluded. (Hume himself considers similar cases of shipwreck.) Imagine a moral code being devised in such a minisociety, where it is freely decided by all that in order for some to attempt escape after the spring thaw, cannibalism is necessary, that those who would die and be devoured would be chosen by a random method, that one so selected must commit suicide (so that none could later be prosecuted), and that normal rules against murder would prevail. Rule utilitarians would hold that under these and other unaccustomed circumstances, a rule requiring suicide should control everyone's conduct and ought to be given a prominent place in the moral code of that minisociety. Under these exotic circumstances, not committing suicide would encourage and perhaps even produce a general breakdown in the orderly system such that none could live—clearly the greatest disutility. Any utilitarian who took this line presumably would not be subject to Donagan's censure, for what in accustomed, conventional cases is either supererogatory or excusably wrong (because beyond a normal obligation) is here obligatory, even if desperate. The rule utilitarian thus argues that unpalatable rules are not dictated except in unpalatable circumstances beyond the normal bounds of morality, and thus that Donagan's objection fails to dent the most plausible version of the utilitarian philosophy.

CONCLUSION

Chapter 3 has shown that utilitarianism offers the broad outlines of a theory of moral justification and reform. The particulars must, of course, be sketched in by further utilitarian arguments as applied to particular cases. In conclusion, however, we should step back from this process and reflect on the utilitarian's approach to the moral life. Utilitarians invite us to consider the whole point or function of morality as a social institution, where the term "morality" is understood to include all our common rules of justice and the moral life. The point of the institution of morality, they insist, is to promote human welfare by minimizing harms and maximizing benefits: There would be no point at all in having moral codes and understandings unless they served this purpose. They see rules, or at least the principle of utility, as the means to the protection of individual rights and to the maintenance of broad social goals. How else, the utilitarian asks, could one in the end justify the requirements of the moral point of view if not by appeal to the goal of promoting human welfare or preventing evil?

Moreover, utilitarians often argue, any alternative ethic based on an inflexible conception of moral duty unchangeable by changing social circumstances is implausible. This contention brings to the surface one of the main areas of conflict between utilitarian and deontological theories, and we shall now pass on to the challenges that the deontological theories offer to utilitarian thinking.

SUGGESTED SUPPLEMENTARY READINGS

History

MacIntyre, Alasdair C.: *A Short History of Ethics* (New York: Macmillan Company, 1966), chaps. 12, 17.

Plamenatz, John: *The English Utilitarians* (Oxford, England: Humanities Press, 1949).

Stephen, Leslie: *The English Utilitarians,* 3 vols. (London: Kelley Press, 1900).

Classic Works

Bentham, Jeremy: W. Harrison, ed., *Introduction to the Principles of Morals and Legislation* (1789), with *A Fragment on Government* (Oxford, England: Hafner Press, 1948).

Hume, David: L. A. Selby-Bigge, ed., *Enquiries Concerning Human Understanding and Concerning the Principles of Morals,* rev. by P. H. Nidditch (Oxford, England: Clarendon Press, 1975), *Second Enquiry.*

Mill, John Stuart: *On Liberty* (London: J. W. Parker, 1859).

————: *Utilitarianism* (London: Longmans, Green, and Co., 1863). (There are many subsequent editions of these two works of Mill.)

Moore, George E.: *Principia Ethica* (Cambridge, England: Cambridge University Press, 1903).

————: *Ethics* (New York: Oxford University Press, 1965), especially chaps. 1, 2, 5.

Sidgwick, Henry: *The Methods of Ethics,* 7th ed. (London: Macmillan & Co., Ltd., 1890, 1963), especially I.9, II.1, III.11–13, IV.1–5.

Commentaries on Mill

Dryer, Douglas P.: "Mill's Utilitarianism," in John M. Robson, ed., *Collected Works of John Stuart Mill,* vol. 10, *Essays on Ethics, Religion and Society* (Toronto: University of Toronto Press, 1969).

Gorovitz, Samuel, ed.: *Mill: Utilitarianism, with Critical Essays* (New York: Bobbs-Merrill Company, Inc., 1971).

Martin, Rex: "A Defense of Mill's Qualitative Hedonism," *Philosophy,* **47** (1972): 140–151.

Raphael, D. Daiches: "Fallacies in and about Mill's Utilitarianism," *Philosophy,* **30** (1955): 344–357.

Smith, James M., and Ernest Sosa, eds.: *Mill's Utilitarianism: Text and Criticism* (Belmont, Calif.: Wadsworth Publishing Company, Inc., 1969).

West, Henry R.: "Reconstructing Mill's Proof of the Principle of Utility," *Mind,* **81** (1972): 256–257.

Contemporary Utilitarianism

Ayer, A. J.: "The Principle of Utility," in *Philosophical Essays* (London: Macmillan and Co., Ltd., 1954).

Bayles, Michael D., ed.: *Contemporary Utilitarianism* (Garden City, N.Y.: Doubleday & Co., Inc., 1968).

Blanshard, Brand: *Reason and Goodness* (London: George Allen & Unwin, Ltd., 1961).

Brandt, Richard B.: "In Search of a Credible Form of Rule-Utilitarianism," in H. N. Castañeda and George Nakhnikian, eds., *Morality and the Language of Conduct* (Detroit: Wayne State University Press, 1953).

————: *A Theory of the Good and the Right* (Oxford, England: Clarendon Press, 1979).

Braybrooke, D.: "The Choice between Utilitarianisms," *American Philosophical Quarterly,* **4** (1967): 28–38.

Cooper, Wesley E., Kai Nielsen, and Steven C. Patten, eds.: *New Essays on John Stuart Mill and Utilitarianism, Canadian Journal of Philosophy,* Suppl. vol. 5 (1979).

Diggs, B. J.: "Rules and Utilitarianism," *American Philosophical Quarterly,* **1** (January 1964): 32–44.

Duncan-Jones, A.: "Utilitarianism and Rules," *Philosophical Quarterly,* **5** (1957): 364–367.

Dworkin, Gerald: "Marx and Mill: A Dialogue," *Philosophy and Phenomenological Research,* **26** (1966): 403–414.

Feinberg, Joel: "The Forms and Limits of Utilitarianism," *Philosophical Review,* **76** (1967): 368–381.

Gibbard, A. F.: "Rule-Utilitarianism: Merely an Illusory Alternative?" *Australasian Journal of Philosophy,* **43** (1965): 211–220.

Gosling, J. C. B.: *Pleasure and Desire: The Case for Hedonism Reviewed* (Oxford, England: Clarendon Press, 1969).

Hare, Richard M.: *Freedom and Reason* (Oxford, England: Clarendon Press, 1963).

Hart, H. L. A.: "Bentham," in *Proceedings of the British Academy,* **48** (Oxford, England, 1962).

Hodgson, Dennis H.: *Consequences of Utilitarianism* (Oxford, England: Clarendon Press, 1967).

Lyons, David: *Forms and Limits of Utilitarianism* (Oxford, England: Clarendon Press, 1965).

———: "Utility and Rights," in Norman Bowie, ed., *Ethical Issues in Government* (Philadelphia: Temple University, 1981).

Margolis, Joseph: "Rule Utilitarianism," *Australasian Journal of Philosophy,* **43** (1965): 220–225.

McCloskey, H. J.: "An Examination of Restricted Utilitarianism," *Philosophical Review,* **66** (October 1957): 466–485.

Narveson, Jan: *Morality and Utility* (Baltimore: Johns Hopkins University Press, 1967).

Nowell-Smith, Patrick: "Utilitarianism and Treating Others as Ends," *Nous,* **1** (1967): 81–90.

Quinton, Anthony, ed.: *Utilitarian Ethics* (New York: St. Martin's Press, 1973).

Sartorius, Rolf E.: "Utilitarianism and Obligation," *Journal of Philosophy,* **66** (1969): 67–81.

———: *Individual Conduct and Social Norms: A Utilitarian Account of Social Union and the Rule of Law* (Encino, Calif.: Dickenson Publishing Company, Inc., 1975).

Schneewind, Jerome B.: *Sidgwick's Ethics and Victorian Moral Philosophy* (Oxford, England: Clarendon Press, 1977).

Sikora, Richard I.: "Utilitarianism: The Classical Principle and the Average Principle," *Canadian Journal of Philosophy,* **5** (1975): 409–419.

Smart, J. J. C.: "Extreme and Restricted Utilitarianism," *Philosophical Quarterly,* **6** (1956): 344–354.

——— and Bernard Williams: *Utilitarianism: For and Against* (Cambridge, England: Cambridge University Press, 1973).

CHAPTER FOUR

Kant and
Deontological Theories

a relevant principle of duty which determines what is right/wrong (U ⟹ consequences determine what is right/wrong).

As a simple example of some moral considerations that will be discussed in this chapter, let us look at a program of experimental research in social psychology conducted from 1960 to 1963 by Stanley Milgram at Yale University. The purpose of the experiment was to test ordinary citizens' obedience to authority. Subjects were solicited to participate in "a study of memory and learning" through an advertisement placed in a New Haven newspaper. Subjects of various occupations and levels of education between the ages of twenty and fifty were recruited. The announcement offered $4 (plus 50 cents carfare) for one hour of participation.

In the basic experimental design, two people were taken into the psychology laboratory to participate in what they were told was a "memory experiment." One person was a truly naive subject who had responded to the newspaper advertisement, while the other was really an accomplice in the experiment. The authority figure in the design of the research was a third person—the experimenter who greeted the subjects and instructed them about the study. The naive subject was designated as the "teacher" and the accomplice as the "learner." The experimenter explained that the study was concerned with the effects of punishment on the teaching and learning process.

The learning task conducted by the subject was a word-pair association. Punishment for a wrong answer came in the form of an electric shock from an apparently complicated machine. The learner receiving the shock was in an adjacent room, strapped into an "electric chair" apparatus. The teacher was placed before a shock generator ranging in voltage from 15 to 450 volts. The switches varied by increments of 15 volts and were labeled with verbal designators: "Slight Shock," "Moderate Shock," "Strong Shock," "Very Strong Shock," "Intense Shock," "Extreme Intensity

Shock," "Danger: Severe Shock," and finally *"XXX."* The subject (the "teacher") was given a sample shock of 45 volts prior to the experiment.

The study began after the experimenter gave full instructions to the teacher. Whenever the learner failed to designate the correct answer, the teacher was required by the authority (the experimenter) to administer a shock of increasing intensity for each incorrect answer. The learner, or accomplice, did not actually experience shocks, but the teacher did not know this, and fake verbal protests objecting to the electrical shocks were repeatedly heard from the learner. At the 75-volt shock, he grunted; at 120 volts, he shouted that the shocks were becoming painful; at 150 volts and thereafter, he demanded to be released, and at 270 volts, he let out an agonizing scream. As the voltage increased, his protests became more vehement and emotional. At 300 volts, he no longer provided answers to the memory test and fell into dead silence.

The so-called teacher reacted differently to the learner's responses. When the latter first protested, the teacher frequently asked the experimenter whether to go on. The experimenter adamantly insisted that the experiment must proceed despite the wishes of the learner. The experimenter stressed that the shocks were painful but not dangerous. The teacher was then torn between following the orders of the authority figure, the experimenter, and refusing to continue to inflict pain on the learner. As the voltage was increased, the conflict became more acute.

Milgram's findings in this study show that approximately 60 percent of his subjects were obedient to authority. They punished the victim until they reached the most potent shock lever, labeled *"XXX."* This finding is far from what was expected prior to the experiment. Four groups of people were asked to predict the outcome of the experiment: psychiatrists, graduate students and faculty in behavioral sciences, college sophomores, and middle-class lay adults. They forecast that virtually all subjects would refuse to obey the experimenter. Only a small percentage (approximately one-tenth of 1 percent) was expected to proceed to the highest voltage lever.

Once the teacher either reached the highest voltage lever *or* refused to proceed, the experimental session ended. After the experiment, an interview was held with all subjects at which they were "debriefed." Some subjects were asked to fill out questionnaires that allowed them to express their feelings about the "memory experiment"; but all were then told that the learner in fact had not received any shocks. A reconciliation with the unharmed victim followed. When the experimental series was complete, subjects received a report of the details of the experimental procedures and results. They also were asked to complete a follow-up questionnaire regarding their participation in the research.

Milgram's experiment was later replicated in Munich, Germany, where it was shown that 85 percent of the subjects were "obedient to authority," in contrast with the 60 percent level of obedience found in New Haven.

Milgram's research led to a protracted and bitter ethical controversy over his methodology. It was praised by many social scientists for the great contribution it made to social psychology, where it was thought to be research of the highest importance. But in other quarters, his research was condemned for its devastating psychological effects on some subjects and for the overt deception involved in his methods.*

THE DEONTOLOGICAL CONCEPTION OF MORALITY

As shown in Chapter 3, in modern ethical theory an important distinction is drawn between nonconsequentialist or deontological theories and consequentialist theories. Deontologists hold that an action is right when it conforms to a relevant principle of *duty.* (The Greek word *deon,* or "binding duty," is the source of the term "deontology." This term appears to have first been used with its current meaning in 1930 in C. D. Broad's *Five Types of Ethical Theory.*) One way to characterize deontological theories of ethics is to contrast them with consequentialist theories of ethics such as utilitarianism. While this method may reveal only what deontology is not, it provides a good way to begin this discussion of deontology. It also will allow us to draw direct comparisons between Mill's utilitarianism and Immanuel Kant's enormously influential deontological account of morals—around which this entire chapter is oriented. This procedure will show that Milgram's research is often defended on utilitarian grounds, while criticized on deontological grounds.

Utilitarianism conceives the moral life in terms of intrinsic value and means-to-ends reasoning. An act or a rule is right insofar as it produces or leads to the maximization of good consequences. This conception of the moral life, in terms of means to specifiable objectives, renders utilitarianism congenial to economics and public policy, for consequences and preferences can be studied by the empirical sciences. Deontologists, by contrast, argue that moral standards exist independently of utilitarian ends, that the moral life is wrongly conceived in terms of means and ends, and that congeniality to the empirical sciences is not a matter of major significance. An act or rule is right insofar as it satisfies the demands of some overriding (nonutilitarian) principle or principles of duty. For example, suppose someone defames the character of another and thereby damages that person's reputation and career. The action is that of defamation, and the damage is a consequence of that action. This consequence is clearly separable from a description of the action as one of defamation, for that type of action need not have any damaging consequences for another's character. A deontologist could offer the same appraisal of the deception involved in Milgram's experiment by distinguishing the act of lying to subjects from any harms to subjects that might have resulted from the act of lying.

*Sources used for this case study include: Robert A. Burt, "The Milgram Experiments: The Rule of Objectivity," *Taking Care of Strangers* (New York: Free Press, 1979); Stanley Milgram, *Obedience to Authority* (New York: Harper & Row Publishers, Inc., 1974); "The Perils of Obedience," *Harper's Magazine* (December 1973), pp. 62–77; and "Subject Reaction: The Neglected Factor in Ethics of Experimentation," *Hastings Center Report,* 7 (October 1977), pp. 19–23.

Deontologists urge us to consider that such actions are morally wrong not because of their consequences but, rather, because the action type—the class of which the actions are instances—involves a serious moral violation. A radical deontologist might go so far as to argue that consequences are irrelevant to moral evaluations: an act is right if, and only if, it conforms to the relevant moral duty, and it is wrong if, and only if, it violates the relevant moral duty. On this interpretation, the fact that a type of action generally brings about good consequences is insignificant. Many deontological theories are not so radical, however, holding only that some features of some actions other than their consequences determine their rightness or wrongness and that moral rightness is, at least in part, independent of some conception of goodness.

Several reasons have been offered in support of this deontological approach. Deontologists maintain that utilitarianism presupposes a greater capacity to predict and control future outcomes than human beings generally possess, and that the utilitarian goal of selecting efficient means to good ends distorts the moral life. Indeed, deontologists regard a consequentialist conception of morality in terms of means-to-ends reasoning as fundamentally mistaken. We can be very certain neither of our ultimate goals nor of the means that will get us there, they maintain. Rather, we often unpredictably encounter the claims, interests, and rights of others. It is in the context of such encounters that most moral decisions must be made. Deontologists thus typically believe that doing one's duty is a matter of satisfying the legitimate claims or needs of others as determined by applicable moral rules or claims. Promises must be kept and debts must be paid because such actions are one's duty—not because of the consequences of such actions.

This comparison between deontological and utilitarian theories can easily be applied to the debates over Milgram's research in social psychology. Those who defended his research appealed largely to utilitarian reasons: the research significantly advanced the field of social psychology and contributed important and unanticipated insights into obedience to authority. Furthermore, defenders suggested, the subjects were debriefed and often became intensely interested in the research; moreover, only minimal risk of serious or enduring harm seems to have been presented to the subjects. Critics of the research appealed largely to deontological considerations: They acknowledged the possible benefits and even the contribution to social psychology, yet they held that fundamental moral principles had been violated in conducting the research. These critics pointed both to the overt deception involved in explaining the experiment to subjects and to the way in which this treatment of them as a means to the researchers' ends failed to "respect the subjects as persons." They argued that even if the harm was "minor" on some scale of harms, this low level could not have been reasonably predicted in advance, and that many subjects experienced deep anguish and shame, even to the point of being horrified to discover the level of their own obedience to authority. It was further argued that experimental psychologists who create an environment in which "voluntary" subjects assist in the research have special and strong obligations to abstain both from deception and from disregard of their subjects' interests. These deontological considerations were thought by critics to overwhelm utilitarian reasons supporting the research, even if the direct benefits of the research did outweigh the costs to the subjects.

Our duties to others are thus recognized by deontologists to be manifold and diverse. While utilitarians hold that there is one peculiarly significant moral relationship between persons—the relationship of benefactor and beneficiary—deontologists consider other relations between people equally or more important. From these special relationships flow certain obligations and duties toward specific individuals that enrich the moral life. These include relationships between parent and child, promisor and promisee, lawyer and client, physician and patient, and employer and employee. Parents have obligations to their children that they do not have to other individuals; and children in turn incur special obligations to their parents. Thus, parents are held to have moral obligations to oversee and support the health and welfare of their children that they do not have in regard to other children in their neighborhood. This duty predominates even if the neighborhood would be better off in utilitarian terms if parents supported the health and welfare of all children equally.

In the view of deontologists, utilitarianism also gives little consideration to the past in moral judgments, because utilitarian reasoning applies mainly to the present and the future. Deontologists hold, however, that the performance of acts in the past creates obligations in the present. If I have promised or entered into a contract, then I am bound to the terms of the agreement, quite independently of the consequences of keeping or not keeping it. If I harm another, then I am bound to compensate that person whether the compensation serves utilitarian goals or not. These actions, according to deontologists, are right or wrong as such simply because of the personal relationships involved.

Deontologists are led by such reasoning to emphasize that the value of actions lies in motives rather than in consequences. (Utilitarians generally agree that motives are significant, but they insist that right motives are determined by the agent's intent to maximize good consequences.) To understand the role of motives for the deontologist, imagine three people who perform the same act: sending food supplies to a foreign nation faced with a critical food shortage and starvation. Suppose that one person performs the act in order to be elected to political office; the second believes that it will turn a profit for his or her business; and the third feels morally bound by a promise to give aid. Many would argue that the motive of the third person is praiseworthy, whereas the motives of the first two are not, even when the consequences flowing from the actions of the three agents are identical. It makes a significant difference, deontologists contend, whether one's motive is based on moral duty, on self-interest in the form of career advancement, or on the anticipated consequences for one's financial interests. Moral credit obviously derives from the motive of duty, but there may be no moral credit for actions based on the other two motives.

Deontologists also hold that at least some forms of utilitarianism lead to morally unacceptable conclusions. Suppose that two acts yield the same outcome in regard to their respective good and evil results. The scales are well balanced between them. But suppose that one act involves deception of the sort found in the Milgram experiment, while the other does not. An act utilitarian might say that the acts are equally right because the scale of consequences is perfectly balanced. Now suppose that the act involving deception is preferable on utilitarian grounds—as Milgram's defenders argued—because it offers a better cost-benefit outcome than the act not involving deception. According to act utilitarianism, the deceptive act is obligatory in such cases. The deontologist maintains that in such instances act utilitarianism can thus lead to morally unacceptable actions. Of course, a utilitarian may actually appeal to a great many other negative consequences of deception, and this simple example is intended only to exhibit the way a deontologist tends to conceive situations of the type found in Milgram's experiment. (It is worth notice at this point that many utilitarians would wholly reject the presentation of utilitarianism found thus far in this chapter. This presentation is meant to reflect how deontologists *conceive* utilitarians more than the way utilitarians themselves conceive their philosophy, which was the subject of Chapter 3.)

Deontologists thus believe an action is right when it conforms to a judgment or a rule of conduct which meets the requirements of some overriding nonutilitarian duty. However, what is the deontologist's conception of moral duty? Throughout the history of philosophy, deontologists have identified starkly different ultimate principles of duty as the final moral standard. It is therefore important to distinguish different types of deontological theory and to characterize the different grounds to which they have appealed.

Perhaps the best-known deontological account is the "divine command" theory. The will of God is the ultimate standard in this account, and an action or action type is right or wrong if, and only if, commanded or forbidden by God. Other deontologists hold that some actions or action types are right or wrong, good or evil in their very nature, not for any reason having to do with politics, religion, or social organization. As will be seen in Chapter 10, some of these deontologists claim that the moral value of actions can be known through reason, while others hold that their value can be known only through intuition (a form of self-evident apprehension). Finally, some deontologists appeal to a social contract reached under conditions of absolute fairness. The ultimate principle of duty is action in accordance with moral rules fairly derived from a situation of mutual agreement. The following selection from John Rawls's study *A Theory of Justice* is one influential social-contract approach to the deontological basis of morality that also helps to clarify the reasons why deontologists reject utilitarianism.

JOHN RAWLS

Justice, Utilitarianism, and Deontology*

My aim is to present a conception of justice which generalizes and carries to a higher level of abstraction the familiar theory of the social contract as found, say, in Locke, Rousseau, and Kant. In order to do this we are not to think of the original contract as one to enter a particular society or to set up a particular form of government. Rather, the guiding idea is that the principles of justice for the basic structure of society are the object of the original agreement. They are the principles that free and rational persons concerned to further their own interests would accept in an initial position of equality as defining the fundamental terms of their association. These principles are to regulate all further agreements; they specify the kinds of social cooperation that can be entered into and the forms of government that can be established. This way of regarding the principles of justice I shall call justice as fairness.

Thus we are to imagine that those who engage in social cooperation choose together, in one joint act, the principles which are to assign basic rights and duties and to determine the division of social benefits. Men are to decide in advance how they are to regulate their claims against one another and what is to be the foundation charter of their society. Just as each person must decide by rational reflection what constitutes his good, that is, the system of ends which it is rational for him to pursue, so a group of persons must decide

*From John Rawls, *A Theory of Justice* (Cambridge, Mass.: Harvard University Press, 1971), pp. 11–13, 30–31. Further passages from this work that serve as extensions of Rawls's views are found in Chapters 7 and 8 of this book.

once and for all what is to count among them as just and unjust. The choice which rational men would make in this hypothetical situation of equal liberty, assuming for the present that this choice problem has a solution, determines the principles of justice.

In justice as fairness the original position of equality corresponds to the state of nature in the traditional theory of the social contract. This original position is not, of course, thought of as an actual historical state of affairs, much less as a primitive condition of culture. It is understood as a purely hypothetical situation characterized so as to lead to a certain conception of justice. Among the essential features of this situation is that no one knows his place in society, his class position or social status, nor does any one know his fortune in the distribution of natural assets and abilities, his intelligence, strength, and the like. I shall even assume that the parties do not know their conceptions of the good or their special psychological propensities. The principles of justice are chosen behind a veil of ignorance. This ensures that no one is advantaged or disadvantaged in the choice of principles by the outcome of natural chance or the contingency of social circumstances. Since all are similarly situated and no one is able to design principles to favor his particular condition, the principles of justice are the result of a fair agreement or bargain. For given the circumstances of the original position, the symmetry of everyone's relations to each other, this initial situation is fair between individuals as moral persons, that is, as rational beings with their own ends and capable, I shall assume, of a sense of justice. The original position is, one might say, the appropriate initial status quo, and thus the fundamental agreements reached in it are fair. This explains the propriety of the name ''justice as fairness'': it conveys the idea that the principles of justice are agreed to in an initial situation that is fair. . . .

Our social situation is just if it is such that by this sequence of hypothetical agreements we would have contracted into the general system of rules which defines it. Moreover, assuming that the original position does determine a set of principles (that is, that a particular conception of justice would be chosen), it will then be true that whenever social institutions satisfy these principles those engaged in them can say to one another that they are cooperating on terms to which they would agree if they were free and equal persons whose relations with respect to one another were fair. They could all view their arrangements as meeting the stipulations which they would acknowledge in an initial situation that embodies widely accepted and reasonable constraints on the choice of principles. The general recognition of this fact would provide the basis for a public acceptance of the corresponding principles of justice. No society can, of course, be a scheme of cooperation which men enter voluntarily in a literal sense; each person finds himself placed at birth in some particular position in some particular society, and the nature of this position materially affects his life prospects. Yet a society satisfying the principles of justice as fairness comes as close as a society can to being a voluntary scheme, for it meets the principles which free and equal persons would assent to under circumstances that are fair. In this sense its members are autonomous and the obligations they recognize self-imposed. . . .

Utilitarianism is a teleological theory, whereas justice as fairness is not. By def-

inition, then, the latter is a deontological theory, one that either does not specify the good independently from the right, or does not interpret the right as maximizing the good. (It should be noted that deontological theories are defined as non-teleological ones, not as views that characterize the rightness of institutions and acts independently from their consequences. All ethical doctrines worth our attention take consequences into account in judging rightness. One which did not would simply be irrational, crazy.) Justice as fairness is a deontological theory in the second way. For if it is assumed that the persons in the original position would choose a principle of equal liberty and restrict economic and social inequalities to those in everyone's interests, there is no reason to think that just institutions will maximize the good. (Here I suppose with utilitarianism that the good is defined as the satisfaction of rational desire.) Of course, it is not impossible that the most good is produced but it would be a coincidence. The question of attaining the greatest net balance of satisfaction never arises in justice as fairness; this maximum principle is not used at all. . . .

The principles of right, and so of justice, put limits on which satisfactions have value; they impose restrictions on what are reasonable conceptions of one's good. In drawing up plans and in deciding on aspirations, men are to take these constraints into account. Hence, in justice as fairness, one does not take men's propensities and inclinations as given, whatever they are, and then seek the best way to fulfill them. Rather, their desires and aspirations are restricted from the outset by the principles of justice which specify the boundaries that men's systems of ends must respect. We can express this by saying that in justice as fairness the concept of right is prior to that of the good.

Rawls's social-contract theory represents only one type of deontological account. As with utilitarianism, the range of deontological positions is sufficiently broad to admit of sharp disagreements between particular philosophers, disagreements that frequently have nothing to do with their unified opposition to utilitarianism. Prominently situated among these disagreements is the controversy between act and rule deontologists, a topic to which we now turn.

ACT AND RULE DEONTOLOGY

Just as there are act and rule utilitarians, so there are act and rule deontologists. Act deontologists hold that the individual in any given situation must grasp immediately what ought to be done without relying on rules. Because they see each situation as potentially unique, and so not subsumable under general rules, they emphasize the particular and changing features of moral experience. An extreme view of this sort is that rules and general principles should play no role at all in moral judgments. Here it might be held that only individual intuition or conscience can discern what one ought to do. An act deontologist might argue, for example, that one's response to Milgram's experimentation is based on intuition about failures to respect others, and not on any abstractly formulated rules. Most act deontologists permit revisable rules of thumb reflective of past experience, but actions are not right or wrong *because* they conform to such rules. The British philosopher E. F. Carritt once defended such an act-deontological theory through appeal to the simple thesis that rules cannot be formulated in advance to apply to every circumstance. Rules are drawn from instances in which obligations are felt, he noted, but they may come in conflict. Carritt believed that it is senseless to have obligations to several rules, since only one can be fulfilled in any given situation in which rules are in conflict.*

Act-deontological theories have been criticized for several reasons. The most widespread doubt centers on whether morality can rest on a basis that is free of rules or at least free of general and permanent guidelines. Individual intuitions, conscience, faith, and the capacity to love have all been proposed as act-deontological standards, yet they seem inherently weak bases for normative ethics. How would one ever decide about the rightness or wrongness of Milgram's treatment of subjects, for example, if only faith or intuition were relied upon?† Furthermore, if one had no general guidelines in ethics, one could never offer moral reasons for preferring one act to another. This situation would leave us unable to resolve moral disputes, thereby promoting a general lack of respect for the capacity of moral thinking to resolve moral dilemmas. It has also

---

*See E. F. Carritt, *The Theory of Morals* (Oxford: Clarendon Press, 1928), pp. 69–71. Carritt later abandoned this theory and accepted a version of rule deontology, such as the one to be encountered later in this chapter in the theory of W. D. Ross.

†The possibility of using these bases is explored further in Chaps. 9 and 10.

been argued that to judge a particular act wrong implicitly involves an appeal to a general rule. If an act is indeed wrong, it seems to follow that all relevantly similar acts in relevantly similar cirumstances are wrong. For example, if it is wrong for a professor to lie to students about the grading standards used in a course, then it is always wrong to lie in relevantly similar circumstances. (But remember the problems encountered in Chapter 1 about universalizability.)

For rule deontologists, in contrast to act deontologists, types of acts are right or wrong because of their conformity or nonconformity to one or more principles or rules. Such guides are more significant than mere rules of thumb based on past experience, and they are valid independently of their general tendency to promote good consequences. Such a rule-deontological theory may envisage only one supreme principle (a *monistic* theory) or many (a *pluralistic* theory). Monistic deontological theories generally maintain that one fundamental principle provides the source from which all other moral rules and judgments can be derived. A simple theory of this sort is that all moral rules and duties ultimately derive from the golden rule that you should treat others as you would wish to be treated yourself. Pluralistic deontologists, in contrast, affirm two or more irreducible moral principles. For example, a deontologist who holds that duty is ultimately rooted in divine commands might well hold that we are obligated to observe the ten commandments, while arguing that there is no overarching principle of obligation from which these commandments can be derived.

Rule-deontological theories have generally enjoyed more support than act-deontological theories. Rule deontologists prefer their account of moral experience for several reasons. (These reasons are commonly shared in many cases by rule utilitarians.) First, rules facilitate decision making because we often have no opportunity or time to think through the steps from basic principles to conclusions. Second, act theories present serious problems for cooperation and trust. If social rules and expectations are forever changing in accordance with individual moral judgments, we cannot rely on others to act in accordance with our expectations. Lawyers, physicians, teachers, and friends would not be bound by any firm moral obligations, and a recognition of this fact would stand to diminish our trust that they will do the right thing. Third, act deontologists reduce all moral rules to mere rules of thumb approximating the (nonmoral) rule "Wash your hair once a day." Such rules obviously allow individual discretion. Rule deontologists find this view unsatisfactory as an account of moral rules, which they see as more binding than merely optional rules of thumb. Rules that prohibit murder, rape, torture, and cruelty, for example, cannot simply be set aside on any given occasion in the way "Wash your hair once a day" can be set aside. In the case of Milgram's research, it has been argued that codes of professional ethics should rule out, or at least set limits on, the use of human subjects that are not optional or open to individual discretion. (At the time of Milgram's experiment, however, there was no formal code for psychologists.)

The single most widely studied rule-deontological theory is the monistic theory developed by Immanuel Kant, an eighteenth-century German philosopher. By examining Kant's influential views in detail, we will come to understand both the nature and the limits of one important form of rule-deontological theory.

KANTIAN ETHICS

The goal for philosophical ethics, according to Kant, is to establish the ultimate basis for the validity of moral rules. He tries to show that the ultimate basis rests in pure reason, not in intuition, conscience, or the production of utility. Morality, as he sees it, provides a rational framework of principles and rules that constrains and guides everyone, quite apart from each individual's personal goals and interests: Moral rules apply universally to everyone, and rules qualify as universally acceptable only when no rational agent can reject them. The ultimate basis of morality, then, must be founded on principles of reason that all rational agents possess in common.

Kant's views are remote in the extreme from the utilitarian conviction that pleasure or some other intrinsic good is the object of morality. He believes that an action is right if, and only if, it conforms to a moral rule that a rational agent would necessarily follow if the agent were acting in accordance with reason. Kant thinks that we should put aside all considerations of utility and self-interest in our moral lives, because the moral worth of an agent's action depends exclusively on the moral acceptability of the principle out of which the person is acting—or, as Kant prefers to say, the principle that determines the agent's *will*. An action, therefore, has moral worth only when performed by an agent who possesses what Kant calls a "good will"; and a person has a good will only if moral duty based on a universally valid norm is the sole motive for the action.

Kant lays great emphasis on performing one's duty for the sake of duty and not for any other reason, and this emphasis is one indicator that he espouses a pure form of deontology. All persons, he insists, must act not only *in accordance with* duty but *for the sake of* duty. That is, the person's motive for acting must rest in a recognition that what he or she intends is demanded by a duty. It is not good enough, in Kant's view, that one discharge one's obligations by performing the morally correct action, for one could perform one's duty for self-interested reasons having nothing to do with morality. If one does what is morally right simply because one is scared, because one derives pleasure from doing that kind of act, because one is selfish, or because the action is in one's own interest, then there is nothing morally praiseworthy about the action. For example, suppose a teacher of philosophy despises his or her students because they invariably fail to write as well as Plato, but nonetheless treats them fairly and with all the respect required by morality *because* he or she fears the university will not otherwise grant tenure. Such a person acts rightly but deserves no moral credit, according to Kant.

When a person behaves according to binding moral rules valid for everyone, Kant considers that person to have an *autonomous* will. His concept of autonomy does not imply—as it does for some philosophers—personal liberty of action in accordance with a plan chosen only by oneself. Kant contrasts autonomy with what he calls "heteronomy"—the determination of the will by persons or conditions other than oneself. Autonomy of the will is present when one knowingly governs oneself in accordance with universally valid moral principles. Under heteronomy, Kant includes any source of determining influence or control over the will—internal or external—unless it is a determination of the will by moral principles.

This difference between governance of oneself by moral obligation and rule by coercive force is critical to Kant's moral theory. Coerced actions are obviously heteronomous; but Kant holds that actions done from desire, impulse, or personal inclination are also heteronomous actions. Thus, any person who acts heteronomously, rather than from moral principles, fails to act autonomously. Actions that are autonomous and morally right, by contrast, are based on moral principles that we accept (but could reject). This notion of self-determined actions based on valid moral principles accepted by the agent is central to Kant's moral philosophy.

It would, however, be easy to overstate his actual views. To say that an agent "accepts" a moral principle does not mean either that the principle is merely subjective or that each individual must create (author or originate) his or her own moral principles. As will be seen in the section on autonomy later in this chapter, such an extreme interpretation of Kant would require that we deny much that we know about the moral life. Kant seems merely to say that each individual must *will the acceptance* of the moral principles to be acted upon in the moral life. A person's autonomy consists in the ability to govern himself or herself through these moral principles. Moreover, Kant urges, moral relationships are contingent on mutual respect for autonomy by all the parties involved. As will be seen momentarily, he develops this notion into a fundamental moral demand that persons be treated as ends in themselves and never solely as means to the ends of others.

Kant often speaks in rather opaque language, at least by contemporary standards, and on most accounts there is also considerable profundity in his philosophy. The following selection exhibits both these facets.

IMMANUEL KANT

The Good Will and the Categorical Imperative*

Nothing in the world—indeed nothing even beyond the world—can possibly be conceived which could be called good without qualification except a *good will*. Intelligence, wit, judgment, and the other talents of the mind, however they may be named, or courage, resoluteness, and perseverance as qualities of temperament, are doubtless in many respects good and desirable. But they can become extremely bad and harmful if the will, which is to make use of these gifts of nature and which in its special constitution is called character, is not good. It is the same with the gifts of fortune. Power, riches, honor, even health, general well-being, and the contentment with one's condition which is called happiness, make for pride and even arrogance if there is not a good will to correct their influence on the mind and on its principles of action so as to make it universally comfortable to its end. . . .

Some qualities seem to be conducive to this good will and can facilitate its action, but, in spite of that, they have no intrinsic

*From Immanuel Kant, *Foundations of the Metaphysics of Morals,* Lewis White Beck, trans. (Indianapolis: Bobbs-Merrill Company, Inc., 1959), pp. 9–10, 16–19, 24–25, 28.

unconditional worth. They rather presuppose a good will, which limits the high esteem which one otherwise rightly has for them and prevents their being held to be absolutely good. Moderation in emotions and passions, self-control, and calm deliberation not only are good in many respects but even seem to constitute a part of the inner worth of the person. But however unconditionally they were esteemed by the ancients, they are far from being good without qualification. For without the principle of a good will they can become extremely bad, and the coolness of a villain makes him not only far more dangerous but also more directly abominable in our eyes than he would have seemed without it.

The good will is not good because of what it effects or accomplishes or because of its adequacy to achieve some proposed end; it is good only because of its willing, i.e., it is good of itself. And, regarded for itself, it is to be esteemed incomparably higher than anything which could be brought about by it in favor of any inclination or even of the sum total of all inclinations. Even if it should happen that, by a particularly unfortunate fate or by the niggardly provision of a stepmotherly nature, this will should be wholly lacking in power to accomplish its purpose, and if even the greatest effort should not avail it to achieve anything of its end, and if there remained only the good will (not as a mere wish but as the summoning of all the means in our power), it would sparkle like a jewel in its own right, as something that had its full worth in itself. Usefulness or fruitlessness can neither diminish nor augment this worth. . . .

An action performed from duty does not have its moral worth in the purpose which is to be achieved through it but in the maxim by which it is determined. Its moral value, therefore, does not depend on the realization of the object of the action but merely on the principle of volition by which the action is done, without any regard to the objects of the faculty of desire. . . . It is clear that the purposes we may have for our actions and their effects as ends and incentives of the will cannot give the actions any unconditional and moral worth. Wherein, then, can this worth lie, if it is not in the will in relation to its hoped-for effect? It can lie nowhere else than in the principle of the will, irrespective of the ends which can be realized by such action. . . .

Now, as an act from duty wholly excludes the influence of inclination and therewith every object of the will, nothing remains which can determine the will objectively except the law, and nothing subjectively except pure respect for this practical law. This subjective element is the maxim that I ought to follow such a law even if it thwarts all my inclinations.

Thus the moral worth of an action does not lie in the effect which is expected from it or in any principle of action which has to borrow its motive from this expected effect. For all these effects (agreeableness of my own condition, indeed even the promotion of the happiness of others) could be brought about through other causes and would not require the will of a rational being, while the highest and unconditional good can be found only in such a will. Therefore, the pre-eminent good can consist only in the conception of the law in itself (which can be present only in a rational being). . . .

But what kind of a law can that be, the conception of which must determine the will without reference to the expected result? Under this condition alone the will can be called absolutely good without qualification. Since I have robbed the will of all impulses which could come to it from obedience to any law, nothing remains to serve as a principle of the will except universal conformity of its action to law as such. That is, I should never act in such a way that I could not also will that my maxim should be a universal law. Mere conformity to law as such (without assuming any particular law applicable to certain actions) serves as the principle of the will, and it must serve as such a principle if duty is not to be a vain delusion and chimerical concept. The common reason of mankind in its practical judgments is in perfect agreement with this and has this principle constantly in view.

Let the question, for example, be: May I, when in distress, make a promise with the intention not to keep it? I easily distinguish the two meanings which the question can have, viz., whether it is prudent to make a false promise, or whether it conforms to my duty. Undoubtedly the former can often be the case, though I do see clearly that it is not sufficient merely to escape from the present difficulty by this expedient, but that I must consider whether inconveniences much greater than the present one may not later spring from this lie. Even with all my supposed cunning, the consequences cannot be so easily foreseen. Loss of credit might be far more disadvantageous than the misfortune I now seek to avoid, and it is hard to tell whether it might not be more prudent to act according to a universal maxim and to make it a habit not to promise anything without intending to fulfill it. But it is soon clear to me that such a maxim is based only on an apprehensive concern with consequences.

To be truthful from duty, however, is an entirely different thing from being truthful out of fear of disadvantageous consequences, for in the former case the concept of the action itself contains a law for me, while in the latter I must first look about to see what results for me may be connected with it. For to deviate from the principle of duty is certainly bad, but to be

unfaithful to my maxim of prudence can sometimes be very advantageous to me, though it is certainly safer to abide by it. The shortest but most infallible way to find the answer to the question as to whether a deceitful promise is consistent with duty is to ask myself: Would I be content that my maxim (of extricating myself from difficulty by a false promise) should hold as a universal law for myself as well as for others? And could I say to myself that everyone may make a false promise when he is in a difficulty from which he otherwise cannot escape? I immediately see that I could will the lie but not a universal law to lie. For with such a law there would be no promises at all, inasmuch as it would be futile to make a pretense of my intention in regard to future actions to those who would not believe this pretense or—if they overhastily did so—who would pay me back in my own coin. Thus my maxim would necessarily destroy itself as soon as it was made a universal law.

I do not, therefore, need any penetrating acuteness in order to discern what I have to do in order that my volition may be morally good. Inexperienced in the course of the world, incapable of being prepared for all its contingencies, I ask myself only: Can I will that my maxim become a universal law? If not, it must be rejected. . . .

Our concern is with actions of which perhaps the world has never had an example, with actions whose feasibility might be seriously doubted by those who base everything on experience, and yet with actions inexorably commanded by reason. For example, pure sincerity in friendship can be demanded of every man, and this demand is not in the least diminished if a sincere friend has never existed, because this duty, as duty in general, prior to all experience, lies in the idea of a reason which determines the will by a priori grounds.

It is clear that no experience can give occasion for inferring the possibility of such apodictic laws. . . .

Nor could one give poorer counsel to morality than to attempt to derive it from examples. For each example of morality which is exhibited to me must itself have been previously judged according to principles of morality to see whether it is worthy to serve as an original example, i.e., as a model. By no means could it authoritatively furnish the concept of morality. Even the Holy One of the Gospel must be compared with our ideal of moral perfection before He is recognized as such. . . .

From what has been said it is clear that all moral concepts have their seat and origin entirely a priori in reason. This is just as much the case in the most ordinary reason as in reason which is speculative to the highest degree. It is obvious that they cannot be abstracted from any empirical and hence merely contingent cognitions. In the purity of their origin lies their worthiness to serve us as supreme practical principles, and to the extent that something empirical is added to them just this much is subtracted from their genuine influence and from the unqualified worth of actions. Furthermore, it is evident that it is not only of the greatest necessity in a theoretical point of view when it is a question of speculation but also of the utmost practical importance to derive the concepts and laws of morals from pure reason and to present them pure and unmixed, and to determine the scope of this entire practical but pure rational knowledge (the entire faculty of pure practical reason) without making the principles depend upon the particular nature of human reason as speculative philosophy may permit and even sometimes find necessary. But since moral laws should hold for every rational being as such, the principles must be derived from the universal concept of a rational being generally.

The supreme principle or moral law, as emphasized by Kant, is the fundamental principle one recognizes (consciously or unconsciously) whenever one accepts an action or judgment as one's moral duty. It says: "I ought never to act except in such a way that I can also will that *my maxim should become a universal law*." This Kantian principle has often been compared favorably with the golden rule, but Kant himself calls it the "categorical imperative." Kant gives several examples of moral maxims made imperative by this fundamental principle: "Help others in distress," "Do not commit suicide," and "Work to develop your abilities." His example of deceitful promising in the above passage perhaps best illustrates his categorical imperative, and in reflecting on his analysis, one might consider whether he would categorically denounce the deception involved in Milgram's experimentation.

Kant's question in this passage is whether it is morally permissible to make a promise with every intention of breaking that promise. In order to answer this question, the categorical imperative demands that we ask further, "Can I will that making deceitful promises become a universal principle (or law) upon which everyone is permitted to act?" He answers no to the latter question. If the making of deceitful promises were to become a universally followed practice, then every promise would be conceived as possibly deceitful and might therefore be disregarded and received with hostility. In order for deceitful promise making to work at all, one would thus have to will simultaneously that deceitful promise making be a universal law (i.e., that everyone be permitted to promise deceitfully). But, according to Kant, a contradiction results from willing both promising and deceit as universal laws; and no rational being can will a contradiction, for it violates the nature of reason itself. The categorical imperative thus shows definitively that deceitful promise making is morally wrong. However, as nicely as this case works for deceit in the context of promising, it would not work nearly so well for deceit in the context of a social experiment such as Milgram's, where there is no direct parallel to a promise. Kant's philosophy seems to suffer from the fact that most immoral actions are not as easily pronounced "contradictory" as his own tidy examples are.

Kant's categorical imperative is *categorical* because it admits of no exceptions and is absolutely binding. It is *imperative* because it gives instruction about how one ought to act. Kant clarifies this basic moral law—the very condition of morality, in his view—by drawing an important distinction between a categorical imperative and a *hypothetical* imperative. A hypothetical imperative takes the form, "*If* I want to get to such and such an end, then I must do so and so." Such a prescription tells us what we must do provided that we already have certain desires or interests. An example would be, "If you want to get an 'A' on the next test in ethics, you must study Kant diligently." Such imperatives are obviously not commanded for their own sake; they are commanded only as *means* to an end which one has already willed or accepted. Hypothetical imperatives are not *moral* imperatives, which tell us what must be done quite irrespective of our desires: We must not commit suicide, for example, even if we wish to do so. Moreover, evil persons may employ hypothetical imperatives for their own ends, using such hypothetical imperatives as, "If I am to stay in power, I must kill anyone who wishes to take it away from me."

Categorical imperatives are held to be strikingly different. As Kant puts it, they are objectively necessary without reference to any purpose. That is, a categorical imperative tells one what must be done whether or not one wishes to perform the action. It prescribes which maxims are binding regardless of the circumstances. Kant expresses his views as follows:

> If the action is good only as a means to something else, the imperative is hypothetical; but if it is thought of as good in itself, and hence as necessary in a will which of itself conforms to reason as the principle of this will, the imperative is categorical. . . . The former present the practical necessity of a possible action as a means to achieving something else which one desires (or which one may possibly desire). The categorical imperative would be one which presented an action as of itself objectively necessary, without regard to any other end. . . .
>
> All sciences have some practical part which consists of problems of some end which is possible for us and of imperatives as to how it can be reached. These can therefore generally be called imperatives of skill. Whether the end is reasonable and good is not in question at all, for the question is only of what must be done in order to attain it. The precepts to be followed by a physician in order to cure his patient and by a poisoner in order to bring about certain death are

of equal value in so far as each does that which will perfectly accomplish his purpose. . . .

Skill in the choice of means to one's own highest welfare can be called prudence in the narrowest sense. Thus the imperative which refers to the choice of means to one's own happiness, i.e., the precept of prudence, is still only hypothetical; the action is not absolutely commanded but commanded only as a means to another end.*

Kant's fundamental moral principle presumably must be relied upon to derive all the rules of morality, for moral rules are binding if, and only if, they satisfy the conditions of the categorical imperative. However, his imperative is an unusual ultimate principle in that, by itself, it mentions nothing about the *content* of moral rules, and for this reason it is often said to be a purely formal principle. It does not, for instance, dictate a statement similar to "An action is right if and only if it produces the greatest good." The categorical imperative offers only the logical form that any rule must have in order to be an acceptable rule of morality. This idea of a logical form is somewhat obscure in Kant's philosophy, but on at least one interpretation, he has a worthy point— whatever its limits. One of the clearest cases of an immoral action occurs when a person attempts to make an exception for him- or herself, or when a group seeks a special exemption for itself. For example, a person may sell a car at a high price by lying about its actual condition, although that person would never accept such an act when buying a car whose owner was lying about it. For Kant, such "excepting" actions are necessarily immoral, irrespective of circumstances, for they cannot be made universal. Again one might profitably compare this claim with the demands of the golden rule.

It should be noted that Kant goes on to state his categorical imperative in a distinctly different formulation (which some philosophers take to be a wholly different principle). This later form is probably more widely quoted and endorsed in contemporary philosophy than the first form. Indeed, it has been repeatedly quoted by the critics of Milgram's research. Kant's later formulation stipulates: "One must act to treat every person as an end and never as a means only." This imperative insists that one must treat other persons as having their own autonomously established goals, and that one must never treat others purely as the means to one's self-determined goals. Milgram's critics of course argue that this is precisely what he did and what every experimenter who uses deception does with subjects.

It has been widely stated in contemporary textbooks that Kant is arguing categorically that we should never treat another as a means to our ends. This interpretation, however, seems to misrepresent his views. He argues only that we must not treat another *exclusively* as a means to our own ends. When secretaries are asked to type manuscripts, or human research subjects are asked to volunteer to test new drugs, for example, they are treated as a means to someone else's ends, but they are not used exclusively for others' purposes, because they do not become mere servants or objects. Kant does not prohibit this use of persons categorically and without qualification. His imperative

*Op. cit., pp. 30–33.

demands only that we treat such persons with all the respect and moral dignity to which every person is entitled at all times, including those times when they are used as means to the ends of others. To treat persons merely as means is to disregard their personhood by exploiting or otherwise using them without regard to their own thoughts, interests, and needs. We shall return to this topic in the section below on respect for persons and autonomy.

As appealing as his ethical theory may be, Kant has often been criticized on grounds that he leaves unresolved the question of how we are to determine our duty when two or more different rules demand duties that are in conflict. For example, if one rule demands truth-telling while another rule demands the protection of a person from serious harm, what is one to do when asked to disclose a piece of information that will bring the information seeker great harm—e.g., when the disclosure will cause a heart attack or the end of a treasured marriage? The categorical imperative appears to give no advice in this regard; it seems, in fact, to demand that both relevant duties be fulfilled.

Kant could possibly argue in such cases (though he does not) that it would be right to lie in order to prevent serious harm to persons. He might contend that one could will the maxim, "When lying is required in order to protect someone from serious harm, then lie," to be universally acted on in the limited situation specified. This argument would be all the more plausible if the maxim also required that the lying be fairly innocent and the prevention of harm desperately needed. Kant could go on to maintain that truth-telling is only hypothetically and not categorically imperative when it conflicts with an overriding categorical imperative such as protecting someone from serious harm. That is, lying would be conceived as a means to carrying out a firmly established categorical imperative. Kant, however, is reluctant to embrace this approach, and generally prefers the position that lies ought not to be spoken, come what may. But his argument is probably not adequate to support this conclusion, and the question of a conflict of duties has become a celebrated problem for his philosophy and for most rule deontologists (indeed for all rule theories, as we saw in Chapter 3).

It may be that no ethical theory can resolve this problem. But Kant's philosophy not only seems unable to help; it apparently *obliges* us to perform two or more actions when only one can be performed—an impossible demand. This issue will be treated in this chapter's concluding section on criticisms of deontology, where a possible way out for Kant will be proposed.

PRIMA FACIE DUTIES

W. D. Ross, a prominent twentieth-century British philosopher, has developed a *pluralistic* rule-deontological theory to assist in resolving this problem of a conflict of duties. Ross's views are based on an account of what he calls "prima facie duties." He argues that there are several different types of moral duties, and that they do not derive from either the principle of utility or Kant's categorical imperative. Thus, morality is composed of a number of basic principles. For example, our promises create duties of fidelity, wrongful actions create duties of reparation, and the generous gifts of our friends create duties of gratitude. Ross defends several additional duties as well, such as duties of self-improvement, nonmaleficence, beneficence, and justice. The principle of nonmaleficence, for example, enjoins us not to inflict harm directly on others—a principle frequently invoked in assessing Milgram's treatment of his subjects. Unlike Kant's system, Ross's list of duies is not based on any overarching principle, and he defends it simply as a reflection of our ordinary moral judgments.

According to Ross, we intuit our general duties; yet we do not intuit what is right in a particular situation, for here reason is required. He argues that we must find the "greatest duty" in any given circumstance by finding the "greatest balance" of right over wrong in that particular context. In the case of a conflict of duties, we must determine what action would actually bring about the greatest balance of right over wrong. In order to determine this balance, Ross introduces a most important distinction between *prima facie* duties and *actual* duties. He uses the phrase "prima facie duty" to indicate a duty that is always to be acted upon unless it conflicts on a particular occasion with an equal or stronger duty. A prima facie duty, we might say, is always right and binding, all other things being equal. "Prima facie duty" in this sense means "conditional on not being overridden or outweighed by competing moral demands." One's "actual duty" is determined by an examination of the respective weights of the competing prima facie duties. Prima facie duties are thus not absolute, since they can be overridden under some conditions; but at the same time, they have far greater moral significance than mere rules of thumb.

For example, Ross considers promise keeping a prima facie duty. Does this mean that one must always, under all circumstances, keep one's promise? No, for there certainly are situations in which breaking a promise is justified. Minor defaults on a promise are justified whenever disastrous harms would be inflicted on another if one were to keep the promise. To call promise breaking prima facie wrong means simply that insofar as an act involves promise breaking it is wrong, unless some more weighty moral consideration is overriding in the circumstances. Should the duty to keep promises come into conflict with the duty to protect innocent persons—as when one breaks a promise in order to protect someone from harm that would occur if the promise were kept—then the actual duty may be to protect innocent persons (thus overriding the prima facie duty of promise keeping).

As Ross admits, neither he nor any other deontologist has ever been able to present a system of moral rules free of conflicts and exceptions. This is no more of a problem for him than for anyone else, Ross claims, for the nature of the moral life simply makes an exception-free hierarchy of rules and principles impossible. He expresses his general views both on prima facie duties and on the correctness of a rule-deontological theory in the following passages.

W. D. ROSS

What Makes Right Acts Right?*

When a plain man fulfills a promise because he thinks he ought to do so, it seems clear that he does so with no thought of its total consequences, still less with any opinion that these are likely to be the best possible. He thinks, in fact, much more of the past than of the future. What makes him think it right to act in a certain way is the fact that he has promised to do so—that and, usually, nothing more. That his act will produce the best possible consequences is not his reason for calling it right. What lends colour to [utilitarianism] . . . is not the actions (which form probably a great majority of our actions) in which some such reflection as "I have promised" is the only reason we give ourselves for thinking a certain action right, but the exceptional cases in which the consequences of fulfilling a promise (for instance) would be so disastrous to others that we judge it right not to do so. It must of course be admitted that such cases exist. If I have promised to meet a friend at a particular time for some trivial purpose, I should certainly think myself justified in breaking my engagement if by doing so I could prevent a serious accident or bring relief to the victims of one. And the supporters of the view we are examining hold that my thinking so is due to my thinking that I shall bring more good into existence by the one action than by the other. A different account may, however, be given of the matter, an account which will, I believe, show itself to be the true one. It may be said that besides the duty of ful-

*From W. D. Ross, *The Right and the Good* (Oxford, England: Clarendon Press, 1930). Reprinted by permission of the Clarendon Press, Oxford.

filling promises I have and recognize a duty of relieving distress, and that when I think it right to do the latter at the cost of not doing the former, it is not because I think I shall produce more good thereby but because I think it the duty which is in the circumstances more of a duty. This account surely corresponds much more closely with what we really think in such a situation. If, so far as I can see, I could bring equal amounts of good into being by fulfilling my promise and by helping someone to whom I had made no promise, I should not hesitate to regard the former as my duty. Yet on the view that what is right is right because it is productive of the most good, I should not so regard it. . . .

I suggest "*prima facie* duty" or "conditional duty" as a brief way of referring to the characteristic (quite distinct from that of being a duty proper) which an act has, in virtue of being of a certain kind (e.g., the keeping of a promise), of being an act which would be a duty proper if it were not at the same time of another kind which is morally significant. Whether an act is a duty proper or actual duty depends on *all* the morally significant kinds it is an instance of. . . .

There is nothing arbitrary about these *prima facie* duties. Each rests on a definite circumstance which cannot seriously be held to be without moral significance. Of *prima facie* duties I suggest, without claiming completeness or finality for it, the following division.

(1) Some duties rest on previous acts of my own. These duties seem to include two kinds, (a) those resting on a promise or what may fairly be called an implicit promise, such as the implicit undertaking not to tell lies which seems to be implied

in the act of entering into conversation (at any rate by civilized men), or of writing books that purport to be history and not fiction. These may be called the duties of fidelity. (*b*) Those resting on a previous wrongful act. These may be called the duties of reparation. (2) Some rest on previous acts of other men, i.e., services done by them to me. These may be loosely described as the duties of gratitude. (3) Some rest on the fact or possibility of a distribution of pleasure or happiness (or of the means thereto) which is not in accordance with the merit of the persons concerned; in such cases there arises a duty to upset or prevent such a distribution. These are the duties of justice. (4) Some rest on the mere fact that there are other beings in the world whose condition we can make better in respect of virtue, or of intelligence, or of pleasure. These are the duties of beneficence. (5) Some rest on the fact that we can improve our own condition in respect of virtue or of intelligence. These are the duties of self-improvement. (6) I think that we should distinguish from (4) the duties that may be summed up under the title of "not injuring others." No doubt to injure others is incidentally to fail to do them good; but it seems to me clear that non-maleficence is apprehended as a duty distinct from that of beneficence, and as a duty of a more stringent character. It will be noticed that this alone among the types of duty has been stated in a negative way. An attempt might no doubt be made to state this duty, like the others, in a positive way. It might be said that it is really the duty to prevent ourselves from acting either from an inclination to harm others or from an inclination to seek our own pleasure, in doing which we should incidentally harm them. But on reflection it seems clear that the primary duty here is the duty not to harm others, this being a duty whether or not we have an inclination that, if followed, would lead

to our harming them; and that when we have such an inclination, the primary duty not to harm others gives rise to a consequential duty to resist the inclination. The recognition of this duty of non-maleficence is the first step on the way to the recognition of the duty of beneficence; and that accounts for the prominence of the commands "thou shalt not kill," "thou shalt not commit adultery," "thou shalt not steal," "thou shalt not bear false witness," in so early a code as the Decalogue. . . .

If the objection be made that this catalogue of the main types of duty is an unsystematic one resting on no logical principle, it may be replied, first, that it makes no claim to being ultimate. It is a *prima facie* classification of the duties which reflection on our moral convictions seems actually to reveal. And if these convictions are, as I would claim that they are, of the nature of knowledge, and if I have not misstated them, the list will be a list of authentic conditional duties, correct as far as it goes though not necessarily complete. The list of *goods* put forward by the rival theory is reached by exactly the same method—the only sound one in the circumstances—viz. that of direct reflection on what we really think. Loyalty to the facts is worth more than a symmetrical architectonic or a hastily reached simplicity. If further reflection discovers a perfect logical basis for this or for a better classification, so much the better.

It may, again, be objected that our theory that there are these various and often conflicting types of *prima facie* duty leaves us with no principle upon which to discern what is our actual duty in particular circumstances. But this objection is not one which the rival theory is in a position to bring forward. For when we have to choose between the production of two heterogeneous goods, say knowledge and pleasure, the "ideal utilitarian" theory can only fall back on an opinion, for which no logical basis can be offered, that one of the goods is the greater; and this is no better than a similar opinion that one of two duties is the more urgent. . . .

It is necessary to say something by way of clearing up the relation between *prima facie* duties and the actual or absolute duty to do one particular act in particular circumstances. If, as almost all moralists except Kant are agreed, and as most plain men think, it is sometimes right to tell a lie or to break a promise, it must be maintained that there is a difference between *prima facie* duty and actual or absolute duty. When we think ourselves justified in breaking, and indeed morally obliged to break, a promise in order to relieve some one's distress, we do not for a moment cease to recognize a *prima facie* duty to keep our promise, and this leads us to feel, not indeed shame or repentance, but certainly compunction, for behaving as we do; we recognize further, that it is our duty to make up somehow to the promisee for the breaking of the promise. We have to distinguish from the characteristic of being our duty that of tending to be our duty. Any act that we do contains various elements in virtue of which it falls under various categories. In virtue of being the breaking of a promise, for instance, it tends to be wrong; in virtue of being an instance of relieving distress it tends to be right. Tendency to be one's duty may be called a parti-resultant attribute, i.e., one which belongs to an act in virtue of some one component in its nature. *Being* one's duty is a toti-resultant attribute, one which belongs to an act in virtue of its whole nature and of nothing less than this. . . .

Our judgments about our actual duty in concrete situations have none of the certainty that attaches to our recognition of the general principles of duty. A statement is certain, i.e., is an expression of knowledge, only in one or other of two cases: when it is either self-evident, or a valid conclusion from self-evident premises. And our judgments about our particular duties have neither of these characters. . . .

The general principles of duty are obviously not self-evident from the beginning of our lives. How do they come to be so? The answer is, that they come to be self-evident to us just as mathematical axioms do. We find by experience that this couple of matches and that couple make four matches, that this couple of balls on a wire and that couple make four balls; and by reflection on these and similar discoveries we come to see that it is of the nature of two and two to make four. In a precisely similar way, we see the *prima facie* rightness of an act which would be the fulfillment of a particular promise, and of another which would be the fulfillment of another promise, and when we have reached sufficient maturity to think in general terms, we apprehend *prima facie* rightness to belong to the nature of any fulfillment of promise. What comes first in time is the apprehension of the self-evident *prima facie* rightness of an individual act of a particular type. From this we come by reflection to apprehend the self-evident general principle of *prima facie* duty. From this, too, perhaps along with the apprehension of the self-evident *prima facie* rightness of the same act in virtue of its having another characteristic as well, and perhaps in spite of the apprehension of its *prima facie* wrongness in virtue of its having some third characteristic, we come to believe something not self-evident at all, but an object of probable opinion, viz. that this particular act is (not *prima facie* but) actually right.

RESPECT FOR PERSONS AND RESPECT FOR AUTONOMY

In the earlier discussion of Kant's second formulation of the categorical imperative, we noted his injunction that persons must always treat one another as ends in themselves and never only as means. It was pointed out as well that Milgram's critics have complained that he violated this injunction in the way he treated his subjects, especially by not respecting their autonomy. Let us now look more closely at the notions underlying these claims—the notions of respect for persons and respect for autonomy.

Respect for Persons

Kant and many deontologists have maintained that only human beings intentionally perform actions that are motivated by moral rules. Animals—monkeys and cats, for example—do not act from moral reasons. They may perform quite ably in a laboratory experiment, and such performance might lead us to say that they act on reasons; but even so, their reasons would not be *moral* reasons. A rational will, in Kant's sense, is needed. Because humans act morally and have rational wills, they possess value independently of any special circumstances conferring value; and because all human beings and only human beings have such unconditional value, it is always inappropriate to treat them as if they had the merely conditional value possessed by animals and natural objects. One dimension of this view attained prominence in the writings of Charles Darwin, who observed that there are few distinguishing differences between humans and animals, the chief one being the human capacity to act morally. Human beings, as it is sometimes put, have an incalculable worth or moral dignity not possessed by other things or creatures, which are valuable only under certain conditions. Deontologists thus hold that a "species mistake" is made whenever human beings are treated as mere things or animals: persons are confused with things, and the species which has unconditional value and dignity is thereby confused with a species having only instrumental value.

An example of this deontological way of thinking is provided by the notion of a right to privacy—the "right to be let alone," as it is sometimes called. The deontologist holds that privacy is not merely one good appreciated by persons, a good to be balanced against other goods in the way suggested by utilitarianism (and, some would say, by the Supreme Court of the United States). The human right to privacy is beyond utilitarian measurement, for it is grounded in the basic moral tenet that each individual has an incalculable worth. Thus the interest that families and individuals have in respect for their privacy is a privileged value never to be weighed on the social scales of utilitarian evaluation. Deontologists claim that such rights ultimately derive from a principle of respect for persons.

This principle of respect for persons is frequently based on a deontological notion of moral agency. A moral agent, as Kant says, must not act merely *in accordance with* the demands of duty. The agent must act *for* moral reasons, or at least must have the capacity to act morally, and moral relationships between persons must always be characterized by a reciprocal respect for persons. (Immoral actors are "moral agents" in this sense if they have the capacity to know their duty, despite the fact that they act wrongly and reject their duty.) To respect persons is to see them as unconditionally worthy agents, and so to recognize that they should not be treated as mere conditionally valued things that serve our ends—a way some have complained that Milgram treated his subjects. To treat persons as mere means is to treat them in accordance with our own ends and thus as if they were not moral agents. To exhibit a lack of respect for persons, from this perspective, is either to reject a person's considered judgments or to deny the person the liberty to act on those judgments. Milgram's denial of information to his subjects, on the basis of which they might have decided not to participate in the research, is taken by some to involve just such disrespect (though, as others have pointed out, supplying the information would probably have invalidated the experiment).

This notion of respect for the human being demands that we allow persons the freedom to form their own judgments and perform whatever actions they choose (within other moral limits, of course). Such respect is demanded for no other reason than that those who possess moral dignity are rightfully the determiners of their own destinies. This consideration constitutes another point on which deontologists take exception to utilitarianism. They believe that utilitarianism fails to recognize our fundamental duty to respect other persons, for the doctrine conceives of individuals as having value because of the extrinsic worth they possess for others. Deontologists believe that this theory leads to the conclusion that, for example, company employees may be treated solely as means to achieve better productivity, parallel to the way machines and capital are means to the realization of the company's ends. (This is a dubious interpretation, however, since utilitarians treat each person as a source of the realization of intrinsic value and have rules requiring respect for the rights of others. This issue about the proper interpretation and defense of utilitarianism need not be pursued here, however.)

The idea of respecting persons has proved difficult to articulate clearly. However, a fine attempt that shows considerable sympathy for Kant's moral theories is made in the following selection by R. S. Downie and Elizabeth Telfer.

R. S. DOWNIE AND ELIZABETH TELFER

Respecting Persons*

It is now possible to make an attempt to explicate the concept of respect as it occurs in "respect for persons". . . . The expression "respect for persons" is used to indicate both an attitude which is commonly thought to be morally fundamental and a principle of action to be explained in terms of the attitude. . . . We shall be concerned here with analysing the nature of the attitude conveyed by the concept of respect. We can see what this attitude involves in the light of . . . the evaluative concept of a *person* (the concept which picks out those features of human nature which make it worthy of respect); this account [is best understood] in terms of rational will. In the exercise of rational will there are two main features, which we have called "self-determination" and "rule-following," and allowance must be made for the different nature of each in our shaping of the concept of respect. Let us first consider self-determination.

Kant provides an example in the *Groundwork* which hints at what is required as a morally fitting attitude towards self-determination. He takes the case of a man for whom things are going well but who sees others, whom he could help, struggling with hardships. Kant supposes that this man says to himself, "What does it matter to me? Let everyone be as happy as Heaven wills or as he can make himself; I won't deprive him of anything; I won't even envy him; only I have no wish to contribute anything to his well-being or to his support in distress." Now Kant holds that such an attitude is not the

worst possible, but he also holds that a will which decided to act in such a manner "would be in conflict with itself, since many a situation might arise in which the man needed love and sympathy from others, and in which . . . he would rob himself of all hope of the help he wants". . . .

Now if respecting persons as self-determining agents involves positive concern for them of this nature, it will involve what is best characterized by the concept of sympathy. . . .

It may be possible to go through the outward motions of actions which conform to duty without such sympathy, but the creative and imaginative exercise of the moral life is not possible without active sympathy. . . .

We might indeed wonder whether there is not a *conceptual* connexion between active and passive sympathy. For if passive sympathy involves sharing to some extent the feelings of others, must this not also mean sharing to some extent in the actions which are the expression of those feelings? If someone has a certain aim and we share with him his feelings about this aim, then, just as the existence of his own feelings implies the existence of a motivation to appropriate action, so we too will be motivated to take steps to fulfil the aim (to make his ends our own). In fact, the difficulty may be to prevent the identification of our feelings and his, and therefore of our policies, from becoming too complete; we may need to remind ourselves that the other man's aim is often not merely that he should in the end have something, but also that he should acquire it by his own efforts. The argument, then, is that active sympathy is necessarily connected with passive sympathy, and pas-

*From R. S. Downie and Elizabeth Telfer, *Respect for Persons* (New York: Schocken Books, Inc., 1970), pp. 23–29.

sive sympathy is a capacity which is the possession of all normal beings. It is therefore permissible to make active sympathy an ingredient in the attitude of respect, when that attitude is directed towards persons conceived as exercising self-determination in the pursuit of objects of inclination. . . .

If a man possesses the raw material of an attitude, in the form of some measure of the appropriate feelings, he can develop it by acting appropriately; and whereas the strength of an attitude may not always be under the direct control of a man's will, it is always possible for him to adopt the principle of action which will develop the germs of active sympathy which (we hold) everyone possesses, and thus strengthen his moral attitude.

It was argued that people are not only self-determining but also rule-following. This feature of persons also moulds the attitude of respect. . . .

Kant assumes that all men, insofar as they are rational, will legislate in the same way. Such a conception can be only an ideal, but the truth it exaggerates is that in dealing with others we ought to reveal in our attitudes a realization that the rules in terms of which they act may also be valid for us. Insofar as we are in moral disagreement with other persons our attitude towards them ought to display a realiza-tion that we could be mistaken, and that their rules could be the valid ones.

The same point can be made in terms of reasons. For, in seeing persons as essentially rule-following, we are conceiving of them as rational agents who are able to act or forbear because they can see good reasons for their actions. We ought therefore to consider how far their reasoning may apply to us.

Let us now try to tie together the various components in our attitude of respect. Insofar as persons are thought of as self-determining agents who pursue objects of interest to themselves, we respect them by showing active sympathy with them; in Kant's language, we make their ends our own. Insofar as persons are thought of as rule-following, we respect them by taking seriously the fact that the rules by which they guide their conduct constitute reasons which may apply both to them and to ourselves. In the attitude of respect we have, then, two necessary components: an attitude of active sympathy and a readiness at least to consider the applicability of other men's rules both to them and to ourselves. These two components are independently necessary and jointly sufficient to constitute the attitude of respect which it is fitting to direct at persons, conceived as rational wills.

Respect for Autonomy

The Kantian idea of respecting persons and the allied idea of self-determination, discussed by Downie and Telfer, have more than once in this chapter been linked to the principle of respect for autonomy, another important Kantian concept that deserves further attention, especially as it might be used to challenge the Kantian theory.

Many important writers in moral philosophy have held that respect for individual autonomy is a basic moral principle. Writers as diverse as Kant, Nietzsche, Sartre, and R. M. Hare—all encountered somewhere in this book—have urged this conclusion. Much of the literature in contemporary ethics is saturated with references to respect for autonomy, the right of self-determination, the right to choose, and the obligation to respect the decisions of others. Although we have seen that Kant does not conceive it in this way, the general idea of autonomy is often linked in this literature to several allied concepts, such as the freedom to choose whatever one wishes, choosing or creating one's own moral position, and accepting responsibility for one's moral views and actions.

Sometimes discussions of autonomy make the concept appear relativistic, or at least individualistic. For example, Sartre holds that "Man is nothing else but what he makes of himself," and goes on to speak of each person as having to "invent the law for himself."* While the word "autonomy" does literally mean "self-legislation," if every person invented his or her own moral law, some form of individual relativism or ultimate moral disagreement of the sort discussed in Chapter 2 would seem inevitable. We would then be quite discouraged about the possibilities for Kant's theory of universality in morals. Yet, as Henry Aiken notes, many traditional (non-Kantian) views of moral autonomy suggest that "Every moral principle must be regarded as nothing more than a first-personal precept."† Because of both the unclarity and the importance of the doctrine of moral autonomy, let us examine its connections with previous topics in this chapter and its importance for moral philosophy.

The most general formulation of autonomy is: A person is autonomous if, and only if, the person is self-governing. It is tempting to assimilate this notion of self-governance (and thereby autonomy) to that of the absence of constraint or freedom from constraint. Isaiah Berlin, however, has warned against this assimilation.‡ The question "*How* is the individual person governed?" Berlin suggests, is quite different from the question, "Is the person free from some governing body or force?" The autonomous person not only must be independent of external interference from some controlling factors (negative freedom), but must be in control in such a way as to govern his or her own person (positive freedom). This account is a thoroughly familiar one in the history of philosophy. Both Plato and Kant, for example, argue that human nature is divided into governing and nongoverning parts. Plato speaks of the ruling part and Kant of reason, where these aspects of the person are explicitly contrasted to purely appetitive factors or involuntary psychological causes of behavior. An autonomous being, under this conception, possesses internal governing capacities, beliefs, and values which can be identified as an integral part of the person and from which his or her actions spring.

Philosophers have characteristically associated this capacity for governance with human reason. Sometimes, as in Kant's account of heteronomy, it has been argued that reason is subject to the powerful influence of the passions or desires and must struggle to remain at the helm. For other moral philosophers, such as Hume and Mill, reason has been viewed more as the coordinator of already present desires and sympathies.

*Jean-Paul Sartre, "The Humanism of Existentialism," in *Essays in Existentialism* (Secaucus, N.J.: Citadel Press, 1965). A selection from this essay appears in Chap. 9.

†Henry Aiken, *Reason and Conduct* (New York: Alfred A. Knopf, Inc., 1962), p. 143.

‡In Isaiah Berlin, *Four Essays on Liberty* (London: Oxford University Press, 1969), p. 130.

Reason may thus guide us in assisting the infirm aged or in planning a marriage, but, according to this account, it is sympathy for the aged or love for another that leads reason into these ventures. Whichever view one takes of reason, there has been an almost uniform agreement in the history of philosophy that a person who lacks critical internal capacities for self-rule in some organized fashion—and not mere freedom from external constraint—lacks something integral to freedom and control. This form of control may reasonably be referred to as "autonomy." The important matter for our purposes is that the person be both *free of external control* and *in control of his or her own affairs*—positively free through internal governance and not merely negatively free. One is free and autonomous in this sense when one's ruling part is in control and is subject to no other governing conditions except those to whose control one has consented.

The autonomous person is thus capable of controlled deliberation and action and has at least some measure of independence, self-reliance, and ability to decide. A person of diminished autonomy, by contrast, is highly dependent on others, less than self-reliant, and, in at least some respect, incapable of choosing a plan on the basis of such deliberations. Institutionalized populations, such as prisoners and the mentally retarded, may have diminished autonomy in this sense, for psychological incapacitation may afflict the retarded and a restricted social environment may limit the autonomy of prisoners.

The idea that on at least some occasions human agents are autonomous is hardly troublesome or controversial. We noted earlier, however, that there are important issues about the extent to which the exercise of individual autonomy is compatible with moral objectivity or with the universality of moral principles. Many contend with Aiken that a principle of moral autonomy entails the reign of self-willed principles and choices in all important moral matters. In the following essay, Gerald Dworkin adresses this question of the connection between autonomy and moral objectivity. He argues that the apparent incompatibility between autonomy and objectivity is illusory, turning on a mistaken perception of the role of individuality and principled moral reflection. Dworkin's contentions should be considered both a criticism and an extension of Kantian ethics. Although he (elsewhere) finds Kant's views on autonomy obscure, Dworkin's own position is in a broad sense Kantian.

GERALD DWORKIN

Moral Autonomy*

I shall begin by distinguishing a number of ways of explicating the notion of moral autonomy. In the philosophical debate very different notions have been confused, and since they are involved in claims which range from the trivially true to the profoundly false, it is essential to distinguish them.

The most general formulation of moral autonomy is: A person is morally autonomous if and only if his moral principles are his own. The following are more specific characterizations of what it might mean for moral principles to be one's own.

1. A person is morally autonomous if and only if he is the author of his moral principles, their originator.

2. A person is morally autonomous if and only if he chooses his moral principles.

3. A person is morally autonomous if and only if the ultimate authority or source of his moral principles is his will.

4. A person is morally autonomous if and only if he decides which moral principles to accept as binding upon him.

5. A person is morally autonomous if and only if he bears the responsibility for the moral theory he accepts and the principles he applies.

6. A person is morally autonomous if and only if he refuses to accept others as moral authorities, i.e., he does not accept without independent consideration the

judgment of others as to what is morally correct. . . .

What could it mean to say that a person's moral principles are his own? We have already identified them as "his" when we referred to them as "a person's moral principles." But how do we make that identification? . . .

How could a person's moral principles not be his own? Not by being at the same time someone else's. For the fact that we share a common set of principles no more shows them not to be my own, than our sharing a taste for chocolate shows that my taste is not my own. . . .

One suggestion is that we create or invent our moral principles. Sartre speaks of a young man deciding between joining the Free French or staying with his aged mother as being "obliged to invent the law for himself."[1] Kant says the will "must be considered as also making the law for itself."

If this is what moral autonomy demands, then it is impossible on both empirical and conceptual grounds. On empirical grounds this view denies our *history*. We are born in a given environment with a given set of biological endowments. We mature more slowly than other animals and are deeply influenced by parents, siblings, peers, culture, class, climate, schools, accident, genes, and the accumulated history of the species. It makes no more sense to suppose we invent the moral law for ourselves than to suppose that we invent the language we speak for ourselves. . . .

*From Gerald Dworkin, in H. Tristram Engelhardt, Jr., and Daniel Callahan, eds., *Morals, Science, and Sociality* (Hastings-on-Hudson, N.Y.: The Hastings Center, 1978), pp. 156–171.

[¹This example is from the selection by Sartre found in Chapter 9 of this text.]

Does this imply that moral reform is impossible? Not at all. It just implies that moral reform takes place against a background of accepted understandings about our moral relationships with one another. And *these* are not invented. Moral reforms (almost?) always take the form of attacking inconsistencies in the accepted moral framework, refusals to extend rights and privileges that are seen as legitimate already. Analogy and precedent—the weapons of the conservatives—are the engines of reform as well.

If I do not and cannot make the moral law for myself, at least, so it is claimed, I can always choose to accept or reject the existing moral framework. It is up to me to decide what is morally proper. This is the proper interpretation of Sartre's claim that his young man is "obliged to invent the law for himself." Nothing in the situation he faces shows him what to do. The competing claims are equally compelling. He must simply decide.

Choice and decision do enter here but it is crucial to see how late in the game they enter. For Sartre (and the young man) already know they are faced with competing claims, and that these claims are of comparable moral force. That a son has obligations to his aged mother; that a citizen has a duty to defend his country against evil men; that neither of these claims is obviously more important or weighty than the other—none of these are matters of choice or decision. Indeed, the idea that they are is incompatible with the quality of tragic choice or moral dilemma that the situation poses. For if one could just choose the moral quality of one's situation, then all the young man would have to do is choose to regard his mother's welfare as morally insignificant, or choose to regard the Nazi invasion as a good thing, or choose to regard one of these evils as much more serious than the other. . . .

Underlying the notions of autonomy considered so far are assumptions about objectivity, the role of conscientiousness, obligation, responsibility, and the way in which we come to see that certain moral claims are correct. I shall argue that with respect to all of these issues the doctrine of autonomy in any of the interpretations (1–4) is one-sided and misleading.

These doctrines of autonomy conflict with views we hold about objectivity in morals. We believe that the answering of moral questions is a rational process not just in the sense that there are better and worse ways of going about it, but that it matters what answer we find. It makes sense to speak of someone as being mistaken or misled in his moral views. The idea of objectivity is tied up with that which is independent of will or choice. That a certain inference is valid, that a certain event causes another, that a certain course of conduct is illegal, that Bach is superior to Bachrach, that Gandhi was a better person than Hitler, that the manufacturer who substituted an inert substance for the active ingredient in ipecac did an evil thing, are independent of my will or decision.

There is a paradox for notions of autonomy that rely on the agent's will or decision. Consider the statement that moral agents ought to be autonomous. Either that statement is an objectively true statement or it is not. If it is, then there is at least one moral assertion whose claim to validity does not rest on its being accepted by a moral agent. If it is not, then no criticism can be made of a moral agent who refuses to accept it. . . .

The claim that all obligations are self-imposed does not fit the moral facts. That I have obligations of gratitude to my aged parents, of aid to the stranger attacked by thieves, of obedience to the laws of a democratic and just state, of rectification to those treated unjustly by my ancestors or nation are matters that are independent of my voluntary commitments. . . .

Consider the following bad argument . . . by Hare.

It might be objected that moral questions are not peculiar in this respect—that we are free also to form our own opinions about such matters as whether the world is round. . . . but we are free to form our own moral opinions in a much stronger sense than this. For if we say that the world is flat, we can in principle be shown certain facts such that, once we have admitted them, we cannot go on saying that the world is flat without being guilty of self-contradiction or misuse of language . . . nothing of the sort can be done in morals.[2]

This is mistaken on both counts. There are no facts—which are not logically equivalent to the roundness of the earth—which preclude a person from insisting upon an alternative explanation of them. Upholders of ad hoc and silly hypotheses are guilty neither of contradiction nor misuse of language. But if one wants to say this kind of

[2]From R. M. Hare, *Freedom and Reason* (Oxford, England: Clarendon Press, 1963), p. 2. [See Chapter 10 of this text for an interpretation of Hare's philosophy.]

thing, then one can say it in moral matters. To admit that I ran over your child's dog deliberately, without excuse, because I dislike both the dog and your child, and to go on saying that what I did was right, is as plausibly being guilty of self-contradiction or misuse of language.

We have not yet discovered an argument for the view that autonomy understood as critical, self-conscious reflection on one's moral principles plays a more distinctive or greater role in moral reasoning than it does elsewhere in our theoretical or practical reasoning, e.g., in scientific theorizing. Still, this conception of autonomy as critical reflection avoids the difficulties of the earlier interpretations. It is consistent with objectivity, for critical reflection is aimed at what is correct. It need not reject the view that some of us may be better at moral reasoning than others. It is compatible with the recognition of a notion of (limited) authority, and can accept the relevance (if not the conclusiveness) of tradition in moral life. . . .

It is only through a more adequate understanding of notions such as tradition, authority, commitment, and loyalty, and of the forms of human community in which these have their roots, that we shall be able to develop a conception of autonomy free from paradox and worthy of admiration.

The Kantian notion of self-directed action based on rational and universal principles is obviously consistent with Dworkin's general insistence on the compatibility of autonomy and objectivity. A broader view than Kant's is that so long as fundamental rules of morality are not violated, we must respect autonomous agents by duly recognizing their considered value judgments and outlook, including their right to their own views and their right to take actions based on those beliefs, even if those actions involve considerable risk and even if others consider them to be foolish. We respect the rights of those who wish to drive race-cars, for example, even if we think the risks excessive and the whole enterprise of racing foolish. Thus, in evaluating the self-regarding actions of others, we are obligated to respect them as persons with the same right to their judgments as we possess to our own, and they in turn are obligated to treat us in the same way.

Controversial problems with such a noble-sounding principle, as with other moral principles, arise when we must determine the limits of its application and how to handle situations when it conflicts with other moral principles, such as utility and justice. Again, one upshot of accepting a principle of autonomy is a presumption in any given context in favor of individual liberty; the burden of proof would therefore be on anyone who wishes to limit liberty. This presumption has led to debate over what Joel Feinberg calls "liberty-limiting principles"—a central controversy running through Chapter 8 in this book.

Through various applications of autonomy and respect for persons, some contemporary philosophers have enhanced other dimensions of deontological theory. For example, as will be seen in Chapter 6, they have used the principle of respect for persons as a foundation for a theory of moral rights. Because autonomous persons have unconditional worth, it has been argued, social institutions should be structured to protect individual rights from subversion or compromise in the broader public interest. It is just such a "subversion" of the rights of individuals in the interests of a more adequately developed social psychology that has bothered many about Milgram's research, which they believe violates rights of self-determination. Considerable controversy prevails, however, as to whether a conception of moral rights must have deontological roots, for many believe that utilitarianism is equally capable of grounding a theory of individual rights. Deontologists have also argued that a deontological account of justice provides a more adequate understanding of morality than the principle of utility, as the article by Rawls suggested earlier in this chapter; but this claim too has been challenged by utilitarians. Broad theories of justice based on deontological considerations will be further considered in Chapter 7.

CRITICISMS AND DEFENSES OF DEONTOLOGY

It was noted earlier that deontologists (especially act deontologists) have been criticized for a frequent reliance on such modes of judgment as intuition and conscience. In conclusion, let us investigate two additional criticisms of deontological theories that have been expressed in contemporary philosophy, most frequently by utilitarians, together with responses that deontologists might offer to these criticisms.

The Problem of Covert Consequential Appeals

Deontological theories vary in the consideration they give to the consequences of actions. Kant, as we have seen, asserts that actions are determined to be right or wrong independently of particular consequences, whereas Ross admits that consequences are relevant to moral thinking, even though they are not the only consideration. An important utilitarian criticism of deontology is that deontologists covertly appeal to consequences in order to demonstrate the rightness of actions. John Stuart Mill, for example, argues that Kant's theory does not avoid appeal to the consequences of an action in determining whether it is right or wrong. On Mill's interpretation of Kant, the categorical imperative demands that an action be morally prohibited if "the *consequences* of [its] universal adoption would be such as no one would choose to incur." Kant fails "almost grotesquely," as Mill puts it, to show that any form of *contradiction* appears when we universalize *immoral* rules of conduct. Mill argues that Kant's theory relies on a covert appeal to the utilitarian principle that if the consequences of the universal performance of a certain type of action can be shown to be undesirable overall, then that sort of action is wrong.

One possible defense of Kant against such charges is the following: It is not entirely accurate to say that Kant urges us to disregard consequences, or even that he believes an action is morally right (or wrong) without regard to its consequences. Kant holds only that the features of an action making it right are not dependent upon any particular outcome; he never advises that we disregard consequences entirely. The consequences of an action often cannot be separated from the nature of the action itself, and so they too must be considered when an agent universalizes the action in order to determine whether it is permissible. Kant occasionally overstates his views by too strongly condemning consequential reasoning, but many of his writings indicate that he was more than willing to consider the consequences as an integral part of the universalization process. Kant does not say, then, that an action can be universalized without universalizing its consequences, and few Kant scholars think otherwise.

Moreover, since one can universalize actions in particular circumstances, Kant, by this procedure, may be able to avoid the problem of a conflict of duties discussed earlier in this chapter. No action need be considered narrowly in terms of any one description. For example, an action of keeping a promise need not be *merely* an action of keeping a promise. Theoretically, one can avoid conflicts of duty by further specifying what the action involves overall, only then universalizing a rule for similar persons in similar circumstances.

The Problem of Nonsystematization

A second but related criticism has often been brought by utilitarians against *pluralistic* deontological theories. (Some monistic deontological thinkers have proposed the same criticism of pluralists.) The contention is that pluralistic theories lack unity, coherence, and systematic organization. These critics suggest that, whereas the principle of utility tells us what makes right actions right on all occasions, thinkers such as Ross merely provide a disconnected list of diverse right-making considerations. If one takes the basic task of philosophical ethics to be that of providing ultimate reasons for our moral judgments, then pluralistic deontological theories (and purely formal monistic Kantian theories that offer a plurality of categorically imperative principles) fail. They tend to retreat into an intuitionist theory where we either intuit on singular occasions which duty is the stronger, or else we must remain uncertain what our actual duty is on such occasions. Intuitionism seems to remove from philosophical ethics the task of constructing rational principles in terms of which actual duty can be determined.

Utilitarians who propose this criticism naturally believe that a unified theory requiring the maximization of value is superior to any pluralist deontological account. They contend not only that Ross is unsystematic but that he provides no criterion for determining one's duty. This general criticism is developed in the following selection by the American utilitarian Brand Blanshard. He argues that alleged deontological duties are more adequately grounded on a general principle of promoting good and preventing undesirable consequences—"a single characteristic of right acts"—than on some nonsystematic, pluralistic deontological basis.

BRAND BLANSHARD

Deontology*

"The sense of obligation to do, or of the rightness of, an action of a particular kind," says Prichard, "is absolutely underivative or immediate"; "our sense of the rightness of an act is not a conclusion from our appreciation of the goodness either of it or of anything else."[1] Ross writes: "It seems, on reflection, self-evident that a promise, simply as such, is something that *prima facie* ought to be kept. . . ."[2] "If any one asks us," says Carritt, " 'Why ought I to do these acts you call my duty?,' the only answer is, 'Because they *are* your duty,' and if he does not see this we cannot make him, unless by informing him about matters of fact; if he sees they are duties, he can no more ask why he ought to do them than why he should believe what is true."[3]

Now we have granted that the duty of promise-keeping, for example, does not rest merely on consequences; it is better that promises should be kept, even if no later advantage accrues from it. And it may be thought that this is what the deontologists too are saying. That would be a mistake. What they are saying is that promise-keeping is our duty, though in fact there is no good in it at all. According to Ross, "If I contemplate one of the acts in question, an act, say, in which a promise is kept . . . and ask myself whether it is good, apart both from results and from motives, I can find no goodness in it. The fact is that when some one keeps a promise we can see no intrinsic worth in that. . . ." And again: "We can see *no* intrinsic goodness attaching to the life of a community merely because promises are kept in it."[4] It is our duty to keep promises, not because, even with other things equal, the life of a community is *better* for promises being kept in it, but because . . . the

*From Brand Blanshard, *Reason and Goodness* (London: George Allen & Unwin, Ltd., 1961), pp. 149–150, 153.
[1] *Moral Obligation*, pp. 7, 9.
[2] *The Right and the Good*, p. 40.
[3] *Theory of Morals*, p. 29.
[4] *Foundations of Ethics*, pp. 142–143.

sentence cannot be completed. It is our duty, but there is no reason why. Our obligation is read off directly, and with self-evident necessity, from a set of neutral facts. So also of such duties as repaying debts, and telling the truth. Indeed most of the *prima facie* duties recognized by the deontologists rest not on the goodness of any state of things, but on the neutral and factual character of the act itself. For this reason, the ancient search of the philosophers for some single characteristic of right acts which serves to make them right is set down as misguided. There is *no* one thing that makes right acts right. Sometimes they are right because they are the keeping of promises, sometimes because they are the paying of debts. But between the rightness of an act and its tendency to bring into being any kind or degree of good there is no general relation at all.

Here I must dissent. This conclusion does not seem credible. We are being told that it may be a self-evident duty to choose one rather than another state of affairs even though, in respect to goodness, there is nothing to choose between them. But more; we are being told that state of things *A* may be definitely and admittedly *worse* than *B*, and that it may still be our duty to bring *A* into being. With a choice before us of making the world worse or making it better, we may have a moral obligation to make it worse. This is very hard to accept. A strong case has been carried too far. When the deontologists said that duty is not based always on a goodness that follows the act in time, but sometimes on the character of the act itself, they carried us with them. They did so because it seemed clear that a state of things in which promises were kept, gratitude recognized, and truth told, was a better state of things than one in which these were not done. But when we are now told that such obligations have nothing to do

either with the intrinsic goodness of the acts, or [with] the state of things they institute, let alone the goodness of their consequences, we feel as if the mat on which we had been approaching this school had been pulled out from under our feet. The obligations that were presented to us as rational insights take on an air of caprice. . . .

A further point may be mentioned which has troubled many moralists about this form of intuitionism: the duties with which it presents us are "an unconnected heap." Philosophers and scientists alike have generally felt that they should use Occam's razor whenever they can; it is their business to reduce apparent disorder to law, and diversity of fact to unity of principle. Moral philosophy has proceeded on the assumption that, if we searched resolutely enough, we should discover behind the great variety of acts that we call right and obligatory some unifying principle that made them so. Ethics has consisted very largely of the search for that principle. To be sure, moralists have disagreed in disappointing fashion as to what the principle was; we have been variously advised to order our conduct so as to secure survival, wisdom, self-realization, power, pleasure, the beatific vision, and much else. But the difficulty and disagreement in answering the question have not destroyed the conviction that some principle is there to be found, even if only a very abstract one like the rule of producing the greatest good. Now the new intuitionism says that there is *no* such unifying principle. There is *no* common reason for calling actions right or obligatory. Sometimes they are right because they produce the greatest good; sometimes because, though they produce a smaller good, they have the character of promise-keeping; sometimes because they have the character of debt-paying; and so on. And the deontologists are surely right in saying that we cannot be sure that when we set out in search of unity we shall find it, or even that it is there to be found. The fact that a theory is simpler than another is no proof in itself that it is nearer the truth. The world has not been ordered for the ease of our understanding.

In Chapter 2, Thomas Nagel defended the view that what Blanshard calls an "unconnected heap" of duties must be accepted as an ineradicable feature of morality, and thus that there can be no unifying principle. Nagel's position could be taken as one form of reply to Blanshard. Ross himself was well aware of at least the later parts of this criticism, and he too acknowledged that his catalogue of duties is unsystematic and probably incomplete. His response follows the lines drawn in one of his general criticisms of Kant's appeal to a single categorical imperative. He found that critics such as Blanshard (and Kant in attempting to describe a single categorical imperative) were forcing an "architectonic" of "hastily reached simplicity" on ethics. His reply attempts to turn the tables on his critics. Whereas they maintain that his views lack systematic unity, he sees that disunity as an integral feature of the moral life. Untidiness and complexity may be unfortunate features of morality, but if they nonetheless are true characterizations, his theory of morality can hardly be faulted for taking account of them. Indeed, it is the obligation of a moral philosopher, from Ross's perspective, to point out a lack of systematic unity if it is inescapable.

Ross might additionally have argued (though he does not) that deontological theories are no worse off than utilitarian theories in this regard. Rule utilitarians have an extremely general principle of duty based on certain views about goodness, from which a number of competing rules of duty are derived. These rules are not given systematic unity in utilitarian theories (beyond their derivation from the principle of utility itself). Ross could point out that the general demand to act on the most stringent prima facie duty is a rule that provides all the cohesion and unity that can be expected. Ross might conclude that this principle overrides all other principles on every occasion, and that this measure of systematic unity is all that one needs or can hope to find. (Not all deontologists have tried to escape this criticism in Ross's way. Rawls, for example, would argue that the criticism does not apply to his theory at all.)

CONCLUSION

Deontological theories bring together a wide variety of moral considerations. There is much that is attractive in these theories, and many of our most important moral beliefs may rest on the foundations they describe, even if no deontological theory has yet been shown to be free of error. For all its opacity, Kant's emphasis on treating persons as ends and on the moral responsibility of each person is a matter of fundamental importance. Few would deny that we must never make ourselves unique exceptions to the demands of moral rules or that it is immoral to treat another as only a means (though it is questionable whether doing so is *always* immoral). Ross's account of prima facie duty has also made an important contribution to ethical theory. Furthermore, it is widely believed that the considerations making actions right cannot be determined purely by appeal to a theory of intrinsic goodness, as utilitarians have maintained, and that utilitarianism cannot adequately account for the duties essential to any acceptable moral theory. For all these reasons, many contemporary philosophers believe that some form of deontology is more promising than utilitarianism.

On the other hand, many philosophers are also impressed with the nonsystematic, seemingly ad hoc character of deontological theories, and they have chosen to defend either utilitarianism or some other alternative approach to normative ethics. In Chapter 5, we shall encounter one such alternative approach that offers a quite different point of departure.

SUGGESTED SUPPLEMENTARY READINGS

Kant's Works

Kant, Immanuel: *Critique of Practical Reason,* Lewis White Beck, trans. (Indianapolis: Bobbs-Merrill Company, Inc., 1956).
———: *Foundations of the Metaphysics of Morals,* Lewis White Beck, trans. (Indianapolis: Bobbs-Merrill Company, Inc., 1959).
———: *Lectures on Ethics,* Louis Infield, trans. (New York: Harper Torchbooks, 1963).
———: *The Metaphysical Principles of Virtue,* James Ellington, trans. (Indianapolis: Bobbs-Merrill Company, Inc., 1964).
———: *The Metaphysical Elements of Justice,* John Ladd, trans. (Indianapolis: Bobbs-Merrill Company, Inc., 1965).

Commentaries on Kantian Ethics

Acton, Harry B.: *Kant's Moral Philosophy* (London: Macmillan & Co., Ltd., 1970).
Aune, Bruce: *Kant's Theory of Morals* (Princeton, N.J.: Princeton University Press, 1979).
Beck, Lewis White: *A Commentary on Kant's Critique of Practical Reason* (Chicago: University of Chicago Press, 1960).
Broad, Charlie D.: *Five Types of Ethical Theory* (London: Routledge & Kegan Paul, 1930), chap. 5.
Duncan, A. R. C.: *Practical Reason and Morality* (Edinburgh: Thomas Nelson & Sons, Ltd., 1957).
Harrison, Jonathan: "Kant's Examples of the First Formulation of the Categorical Imperative," *Philosophical Quarterly,* **7** (1957): 50–62.

Hutchings, Patrick A.: *Kant on Absolute Value* (Detroit: Wayne State University Press, 1972).

MacIntyre, Alasdair: *A Short History of Ethics* (New York: Macmillan Company, 1966), chap. 14.

Nell, Onora: *Acting on Principle, An Essay on Kantian Ethics* (New York: Columbia University Press, 1975).

Paton, Herbert J.: *The Categorical Imperative* (Chicago: University of Chicago Press, 1948).

Ross, William D.: *Kant's Ethical Theory* (Oxford, England: Clarendon Press, 1954).

Wolff, Robert P., ed.: *Kant: A Collection of Critical Essays* (Garden City, N.Y.: Anchor Books, 1967), part 2.

————: *The Autonomy of Reason: A Commentary on Kant's "Groundwork of the Metaphysics of Morals"* (New York: Harper & Row, Publishers, Inc., 1973).

Wood, Allen W.: *Kant's Moral Religion* (Ithaca, N.Y.: Cornell University Press, 1970).

Contemporary Deontological Writings

Baier, Kurt: *The Moral Point of View: A Rational Basis of Ethics* (Ithaca, N.Y.: Cornell University Press, 1958).

Ewing, Alfred C.: "Ethics and Belief in God," *The Hibbert Journal,* **39** (1941): 375–388.

Foot, Philippa: "Morality as a System of Hypothetical Imperatives," *Philosophical Review,* **81** (1972): 305–316.

Gert, Bernard: *The Moral Rules: A New Rational Foundation for Morality* (New York: Harper & Row, Publishers, Inc., 1970).

Grice, Geoffrey Russell: *The Grounds of Moral Judgement* (Cambridge, England: Cambridge University Press, 1967).

MacIntyre, Alasdair: "What Morality Is Not," *Philosophy,* **32** (1957): 325–335.

Olafson, Frederick A.: *Principles and Persons: An Ethical Interpretation of Existentialism* (Baltimore: Johns Hopkins Press, 1967).

Rawls, John: *A Theory of Justice* (Cambridge, Mass.: Harvard University Press, 1971).

Ross, William D.: *The Right and the Good* (Oxford, England: Clarendon Press, 1930).

————: *Foundations of Ethics* (Oxford, England: Clarendon Press, 1939).

Singer, Marcus George: *Generalization in Ethics: An Essay in the Logic of Ethics, with the Rudiments of a System of Moral Philosophy* (New York: Atheneum Press, 1971).

Warnock, Geoffrey J.: *The Object of Morality* (London: Methuen & Co., Ltd., 1971).

Autonomy and Respect for Persons

Beauchamp, Tom L., and James F. Childress: "The Principle of Autonomy," in *Principles of Biomedical Ethics* (New York: Oxford University Press, 1979), Chap. 3.

Darwall, Stephen: "Two Kinds of Respect," *Ethics,* **88** (1977): 36–49.

Downie, Robert S., and Elizabeth Telfer: *Respect for Persons* (London: George Allen & Unwin, Ltd., 1969).

Dworkin, Gerald: "Moral Autonomy," in H. T. Engelhardt, Jr., and Daniel Callahan, eds., *Morals, Science, and Sociality* (Hastings-on-Hudson, N.Y.: The Hastings Center, 1978).

Haezrahi, Pepita: "The Concept of Man as End-in-Himself," in Robert P. Wolff, ed., *Kant: A Collection of Critical Essays* (Garden City, N.Y.: Anchor Books, 1967).

Johnson, Oliver: "Heteronomy and Autonomy: Rawls and Kant," *Midwest Studies in Philosphy,* **2** (1977): 277–279.

CHAPTER FIVE

Aristotle and Virtue Theories

The case with which this chapter begins, unlike cases in other chapters, covers the entire life of a single individual, Jane Addams. This remarkable person was born in Cedarville, Illinois, in 1860. She lost her mother when she was only three years old, and by her own account her father was the "supreme affection" of her youth and easily the dominant influence on her life. He was a diligent, successful, and generous man—a mill owner, banker, and member of the state senate. While professing to be a Quaker, he had a considerable disdain for what he called "theological doctrine." He preferred, instead, to rely exclusively on "integrity, self-respect, and conscience." He was widely known in the state as a "virtuous man"—a person of "kindly spirit" and a "pillar of tolerance." He imparted his moral beliefs to his daughter, insisting on "mental integrity above everything else" and on "honesty whatever happens."

Jane Addams's stepmother held out somewhat different goals for her, hoping—in accordance with the family's prominent social position—that she would cultivate the traditional refinements and social graces of womanhood; but Jane Addams's social conscience was forever resisting this course. She worried that in "being educated," she had "lost that simple and almost automatic response" of sympathy in "the mere presence of suffering or of helplessness." In her postcollege years, her stepmother moved to Baltimore and introduced her to "the Johns Hopkins University society," complete with its wealthy traditionalism, its lavish home furnishings, and its dresses from Paris. Jane Addams, however, found the people she met in Baltimore wasteful and misdirected, and her exposure to them was on the whole a disillusioning experience. She came to feel "maladjusted," "nervous," and "useless." In 1887, when she had been out of college for several years and had done nothing she considered of importance, she went to Europe. On this trip she made an irrevocable decision that, despite her upbringing and the ambitions others held out for her, she could never lead a life of ease. She decided that she was "absolutely at sea so far as any moral purpose was concerned," and her trips to London in particular made her aware of "hideous human need."

In the midst of her crisis of conscience, she sat one day as a tourist in a German cathedral whose stained-glass windows, as she recalled, pictured "Greek philosophers as well as Hebrew Prophets, and . . . saints." One window, showing Luther affixing his decrees, particularly affected her. "The saints," she decided, "embodied fine action"; and that evening she formulated an idea that had been germinating for some time: the idea of a settlement house to serve immigrants and the poor. When she returned to the United States, she bought an old mansion on the West Side of Chicago. Owned by an affluent real estate dealer named Hull, the mansion, which had once been a grand and solitary estate, was now an isolated spot of affluence in a slum-ridden section of the city. It was there that, in 1889, Jane Addams established what was to become the world-famous Hull House, and in the process fixed the course of her life over the next forty years.

During these forty years she developed her settlement on Chicago's West Side into a great institution of social work—though she always considered it primarily a social experiment. In the initial year alone, over 50,000 needy persons visited Hull House for some form of attention, and in the second year the number exceeded 100,000. Her institution took care of hundreds of people every day. Its stated purposes were to provide a center for social and cultural life and to improve living conditions in the industrial districts of Chicago. Classes were taught from kindergarten to adult education, cooperative boarding houses were established, and an attempt was made to find employment for persons out of work. Though cautioned by police about the dangers of the neighborhood, Jane Addams went everywhere by herself, even at 3 o'clock in the morning. Her neighbors were at first suspicious of her efforts, but—as one of them later recalled—she won them over by her "uniform kindness and courtesy." As her operation expanded, she undertook formal lectures to the rich and to the middle class about "how the other half lives." She had debated William Jennings Bryan in her college days and was known for her quiet oratory. She desired above all to cultivate in the people she addressed, especially the women, what she regarded as a natural sympathy and tendency toward virtue. She also found time to lecture about, and campaign widely for, the abolition of child labor, improved factory laws, court reform, and women's suffrage.

Eventually, Jane Addams and Hull House each acquired a national reputation. She became politically active, seconding the nomination of Theodore Roosevelt for President, actively involving herself in a major Pullman strike, and continually promoting peace movements. She opposed the United States entry into World War I, and her stand on the issue tested some of her most important friendships, straining even her close association with the philosopher John Dewey.

Not everyone was convinced of her entire dedication to social ideals and to the poor, however. In the summer of 1896, she met the Russian writer Leo Tolstoy, who had renounced a life of wealth in favor of a peasant existence. The sleeves of Jane Addams's dress, said Tolstoy critically, had enough material in them to make a frock for a young girl. He also accused her of being an absentee landlord, for she had kept her family's property in order to support her work. She consequently resolved to move among working people even more than she had in the past; but, after reflecting on the encounter with Tolstoy, she determined that he was "more logical than life warrants."

Jane Addams wrote many books, several of her early writings being scholarly works. She was known among both academics and her peers as a first-rate theoretician, especially on matters pertaining to the fledgling fields of sociology and social work. One of her books, *Democracy and Social Ethics*, influenced American pragmatists as much as they had influenced her. By 1931, when she received the Nobel Peace Prize, she was both nationally and internationally famous. Characteristically, she refused to embrace the comfortable and well-to-do part of American society that only then welcomed her. Though always a gentle person, in 1932, at more than seventy years of age, she gave a strident address, entitled "Our National Self-Righteousness," at Swarthmore College. She denounced in particular what she saw as a deep mood of "impatience with differing opinions." These criticisms seemed only to enhance her image in certain academic and political circles. Bryn Mawr College awarded her its highest prize, and her close friend John Dewey traveled to the ceremony to see her receive it. In March 1934, the University of California celebrated its fiftieth anniversary by conferring honorary degrees on three persons: Herbert Hoover, Jane Addams, and a former Hull House resident named Frances Perkins, who had "risen" to become Secretary of Labor. Hoover and Perkins refused to be photographed together, but both were delighted to be photographed with Jane Addams.

Jane Addams has often been described as a saint; and in an article in the journal *Daedalus* (1964), she was praised as one of America's few true heroines. William James once wrote to her in admiration, "I do not know why you should always be right, but you always are. You inhabit reality." In 1935, at age seventy-five, she received the American Education Award for teaching "by precept and example." In that same year, she died of cancer. In England, John Burns eulogized her as a saint of the modern era, and in the United States, Walter Lippmann said that under her direction, Hull House has been a "cathedral of compassion." A Greek newspaper in Chicago asserted simply, "We of foreign birth have lost our best friend and the only one who understood us."*

THE CONCEPT OF AN ETHICS OF VIRTUE

In Chapters 3 and 4, principle-based or duty-based theories of right and wrong actions were examined. These theories discuss moral goods and evils by focusing on actions or principles that are good and evil. They do not emphasize the agents or actors who per-

*Sources for this case include Henry Steele Commager, Foreword to Jane Addams's *Twenty Years at Hull House* (New York: New American Library of World Literature, 1961), pp. vii–xvi; Jill Conway, *"Jane Addams: An American Heroine," Daedalus*, **93** (Spring 1964): 761–780; Christopher Lasch, ed., *The Social Thought of Jane Addams* (Indianapolis: Bobbs-Merrill Company, Inc., 1965), Introduction and Chronology, pp. xiii–xxxi; James Weber Linn, *Jane Addams* (New York: Greenwood Press, 1968).

form actions, have motives, and follow principles. Yet, we commonly make judgments about good and evil persons, their traits of character, and their willingness to perform actions. Jane Addams has certainly been studied as much for her saintly character as for her actions, and we make comparable judgments about the virtues and vices of persons we encounter by saying that they are saintly or heroic, hateful or lovable, noble or ignoble, etc. We thus judge the moral worth of persons as agents, and not merely their fulfillment of duty or their production of good consequences. Does the fact that we make such judgments indicate that we need a theory of virtue and character that adds content to, or even supplants, the theories we have previously encountered?

"Virtue ethics," as it will be called here, presents a challenge to deontological and utilitarian theories because the latter two approaches presumably offer accounts of what we ought to do, not of the kind of persons we ought to be. For all their differences, utilitarians and deontologists conceive moral philosophy and the demands of morality similarly: Ethics provides general guides to action in the form of principles and rules. Yet correct choices made from a proper sense of duty do not necessarily signify that a person is virtuous, for dutiful people sometimes despise and only grudgingly fulfill their moral obligations. It is this problem that invites closer attention to virtue and character.

In the classical Greek tradition represented by Plato and Aristotle, the virtue approach is dominant: they see the cultivation of virtuous traits of character as among the primary functions of morality. Their aim as writers in philosophy is not unlike the aim of Jane Addams's speeches—they appeal to whatever we possess in the way of a tendency to virtuous conduct. This approach has much to commend it, for two types of judgment are pervasively made in morality: (1) duty-centered judgments which assert that an *action* is right, wrong, obligatory, etc., and (2) character-centered judgments which assert that a *person* or *character* is good or bad, virtuous or vicious, praiseworthy or blameworthy, admirable or reprehensible. Whereas the first type of judgment is given primacy in utilitarian and deontological writings, the second is primary in virtue ethics.

It would of course be a mistake to suppose that we have not already encountered the second type of judgment in Chapters 3 and 4. Kant, after all, emphasizes the motives of the person of good will in his theory; and Mill was well aware of the distinction between these two types of judgment. Mill notes explicity that "utilitarian moralists have gone beyond almost all others in affirming that the motive has nothing to do with the *morality* of the action, though much with the *worth of the agent*."* He therefore argues that morally right actions are independent of, and to be distinguished from, morally right motives. His point is that we need know nothing about the quality of motives or character in order to know whether *actions* are right or wrong. In this contention Mill may be correct, but the exponent of virtue ethics will not be impressed. It is obvious that Mill's judgment is confined to actions, and in the case of both Jane Addams and her father, for example, we are at least as much interested in the moral quality of the person as in the moral quality of the action. While Mill goes on to maintain that "the object of virtue" is "the multiplication of happiness" and that a morality of actions is *primary*, he does not provide reasons sufficient to show that a morality based on virtues

*John Stuart Mill, *Utilitarianism* (1863), chap. 2, par. 19. (Italics added.)

compose
w/ mill?

and the evaluation of character is any less primary than a morality based on principles and the evaluation of actions. Moreover, since character is made manifest in action, there may not be as much as might at first be supposed to distinguish action-based theories from virtue-based theories. Mill's contention, then, seems less applicable to virtue theories than it is to deontological theories that make motives more significant to morality than actions.

An ethics of virtue obviously turns on an assessment of selected traits of character. These traits involve a tendency to perform certain actions on appropriate occasions—as Jane Addams's compassion, conscientiousness, and faithfulness attest. Such traits establish a person's moral character—much as certain traits of actors and actresses mark them as having a distinct character on stage (i.e., a distinct quality in acting). On some occasions, their performance on the stage will be better than on others, but this fluctuation will not change their "virtues" as performers and will not alter the traits that mark their performances. Most of us have a moral character that similarly varies over time in its strength and predictability, but even when variation results (e.g., from occasional moral weakness), we tend to retain our view of a person's typical moral behavior. A person may also, of course, be of virtuous character in some respects (e.g., possessing conscientiousness and trustworthiness), while suffering from deficiencies in other respects (e.g., lacking in patience and tolerance).

The word "virtue," thus far used rather freely, deserves a tighter definition. A "virtue" should not be confused with a principle or statement of what ought to be done, for it is a beneficial disposition, habit, or trait which a person possesses or aspires to possess. A moral virtue could, of course, be a habit or disposition to do what is morally *required,* but this characterization misleadingly associates moral virtue with duty. Accordingly, it is better to say that a moral virtue is a fixed disposition, habit, or trait to do what is morally commendable.* Any adequate general conception of virtue will also reflect the fact that there are virtues other than moral virtues. Those familiar with the "Christian virtues" know that faith, hope, and love are recognized as central virtues—so-called cardinal virtues; although primary virtues in a religious tradition need not be moral virtues. There also have been considerable differences even among philosophers over *which* virtues are central to the moral life—the Greek view being rather different from certain modern theories.

A general conception of virtue ethics that augments our discussion thus far, and which introduces the ancient Greek philosophers' approach to ethics, is found in the following essay by Bernard Mayo. He characterizes all traditional ethics that emphasize principles of duty as one-sided and concentrates on how an ethics of virtue adds an important perspective.

*Aristotle required that virtue involve deliberate purpose to pursue virtuous ends, a claim that is certainly subject to doubt (*Nichomachean Ethics*, Bk. 2, chap. 6). Thomas Aquinas additionally held that virtues can produce only good actions and cannot be put to bad use *(Summa Theologica,* 1a2ae question 56, article 5). This claim, too, is subject to doubt, as will be seen later.

? principles vs characteristics

BERNARD MAYO → good

Ethics and the Moral Life*

Attention to the novelists can be a welcome correction to a tendency of philosophical ethics of the last generation or two to lose contact with the ordinary life of man which is just what the novelists, in their own way, are concerned with. Of course there are writers who can be called in to illustrate problems about Duty (Graham Greene is a good example). But there are more who perhaps never mention the words duty, obligation or principle. Yet they are all concerned—Jane Austen, for instance, entirely and absolutely—with the moral qualities or defects of their heroes and heroines and other characters. This points to a radical one-sidedness in the philosophers' account of morality in terms of principles: it takes little or no account of qualities, of what people *are*. It is just here that the old-fashioned word Virtue used to have a place; and it is just here that the work of Plato and Aristotle can be instructive. Justice, for Plato, though it is closely connected with acting according to law, does not *mean* acting according to law: it is a quality of character, and a just action is one such as a just man would do. Telling the truth, for Aristotle, is not, as it was for Kant, fulfilling an obligation; again it is a quality of character, or, rather, a whole range of qualities of character, some of which may actually be defects, such as tactlessness, boastfulness, and so on—a point which can be brought out, in terms of principles, only with the greatest complexity and artificiality, but quite simply and naturally in terms of character.

*From Bernard Mayo, *Ethics and the Moral Life* (London: Macmillan & Co. Ltd., 1958; New York: St. Martin's Press, 1958). Reprinted by permission of the author, Macmillan, London and Basingstoke, and St. Martin's Press.

If we wish to enquire about Aristotle's moral views, it is no use looking for a set of principles. Of course we can find *some* principles to which he must have subscribed—for instance, that one ought not to commit adultery. But what we find much more prominently is a set of character-traits, a list of certain types of persons—the courageous man, the niggardly man, the boaster, the lavish spender, and so on. The basic moral question, for Aristotle, is not, What shall I do? But, What shall I be?

These contrasts between doing and being, negative and positive, and modern as against Greek morality were noted by John Stuart Mill; I quote from the *Essay on Liberty*:

> Christian morality (so-called) has all the characters of a reaction; it is, in great part, a protest against Paganism. Its ideal is negative rather than positive; passive rather than active; Innocence rather than Nobleness; Abstinence from Evil, rather than energetic Pursuit of the Good; in its precepts (as has been well said) "Thou shalt not" predominates unduly over "Thou shalt." . . . Whatever exists of magnanimity, highmindedness, personal dignity, even the sense of honour, is derived from the purely human, not the religious part of our education, and never could have grown out of a standard of ethics in which the only worth, professedly recognised, is that of obedience.

Of course, there are connections between being and doing. It is obvious that a man cannot just *be*; he can only be what he is by doing what he does; his moral qualities are ascribed to him because of his actions, which are said to manifest those qualities. But the point is that an ethics of Being must include this obvious fact, that Being involves Doing; whereas an ethics of Doing, such as I have been examining, may easily overlook it. As I have suggested, a morality of principles is concerned only with what people do or fail to do, since that is what rules are for. And as far as this sort of ethics goes, people might well have no moral qualities at all except the possession of principles and the will (and capacity) to act accordingly.

Principles and Ideals

When we speak of a moral quality such as courage, and say that a certain action was courageous, we are not merely saying something about the action. We are referring, not so much to what is done, as to the kind of person by whom we take it to have been done. We connect, by means of imputed motives and intentions, with the character of the agent as courageous. This explains, incidentally, why both Kantians and Utilitarians encounter, in their different ways, such difficulties in dealing with motives, which their principles, on the face of it, have no room for. A Utilitarian, for example, can only praise a courageous action in some such way as this: the action is of a sort such as a person of courage is likely to perform, and courage is a quality of character the cultivation of which is likely to increase rather than diminish the sum total of human happiness. But Aristotelians have no need of such circumlocution. For them a courageous action just is one which proceeds from and manifests a certain type of character, and is praised because such a character-trait is good, or better than others, or is a virtue. An evaluative criterion is sufficient: there is no need to look for an imperative criterion as well, or rather instead, according to which it is not the character which is good, but the cultivation of the character which is right. . . .

No doubt the fundamental moral question is just "What ought I to do?" And according to the philosophy of moral principles, the answer (which must be an imperative, "Do this") must be derived from a conjunction of premisses consisting (in the simplest case) firstly of a rule, or universal imperative, enjoining (or forbidding) all actions of a certain type in situations of a certain type, and, secondly, a statement to the effect that this is a situation of that type, falling under that rule. In practice the emphasis may be on supplying only one of these premisses, the other being assumed or taken for granted: one may answer the question "What ought I to do?" either by quoting a rule which I am to adopt, or by showing that my case is legislated for by a rule which I do adopt. . . . If I am in doubt whether to tell the truth about his condition to a dying man, my doubt may be resolved by showing that the case comes under a rule about the avoidance of unnecessary suffering, which I am assumed to accept. But if the case is without precedent in my moral career, my problem may be soluble only by adopting a new principle about what I am to do now and in the future about cases of this kind.

This second possibility offers a connection with moral ideals. Suppose my perplexity is not merely an unprecedented situation which I could cope with by adopting a new rule. Suppose the new rule is thoroughly inconsistent with my existing moral code. This may happen, for instance, if the moral code is one to which I only pay lip-service; if . . . its authority is not yet internalised, or if it has ceased to be so; it is ready for rejection, but its final rejection awaits a moral crisis such as we are assuming to occur. What I now need is not a rule for deciding how to act in this situation and others of its kind. I need a whole set of rules, a complete morality, new principles to live by.

Now according to the philosphy of moral character, there is another way of answering the fundamental question "What ought I to do?" Instead of quoting a rule, we quote a quality of character, a virtue: we say "Be brave," or "Be patient," or "Be lenient." We may even say "Be a man": if I am in doubt, say, whether to take a risk, and someone says "Be a man," meaning a morally sound man, in this case a man of sufficient courage. (Compare the very different ideal invoked in "Be a gentleman." I shall not discuss whether this is a *moral* ideal.) Here, too, we have the extreme cases, where a man's moral perplexity extends not merely to a particular situation but to his whole way of living. And now the question "What ought I to do?" turns into the question "What ought I to be?"—as, indeed, it was treated in the first place. ("Be brave.") It is answered, not by quoting a rule or a set of rules, but by describing a quality of character or a type of person. And here the ethics of character gains a practical simplicity which offsets the greater logical simplicity of the ethics of principles. We do not have to give a list of characteristics or virtues, as we might list a set of principles. We can give a unity to our answer.

Of course we can in theory give a unity to our principles: this is implied by speaking of a *set* of principles. But if such a set is to be a system and not a mere aggregate, the unity we are looking for is a logical one, namely the possibility that some principles are deducible from others, and ultimately from one. But the attempt to construct a deductive moral system is notoriously difficult, and in any case ill-founded. Why should we expect that all rules of conduct should be ultimately reducible to a few?

Saints and Heroes

But when we are asked "What shall I be?" we can readily give a unity to our answer, though not a logical unity. It is the unity of character. A person's character is not merely a list of dispositions; it has the organic unity of something that is more than the sum of its parts. And we can say, in answer to our morally perplexed questioner, not only "Be this" and "Be that," but also "Be like So-and-So"—where So-and-So is either an ideal type of character, or else an actual person taken as representative of the ideal, an exemplar. Examples of the first are Plato's 'just man' in the Republic; Aristotle's man of practical wisdom, in the Nichomachean Ethics; Augustine's citizen of the City of God; the good Communist; the American way of life (which is a collective expression for a type of character). Examples of the second kind, the exemplar, are Socrates, Christ, Buddha, St. Francis, the heroes of epic writers and of novelists. Indeed the idea of the Hero, as well as the idea of the Saint, are very much the expression of this attitude to morality. Heroes and saints are not merely people who did things. They are people whom we are expected, and expect ourselves, to imitate. And imitating them means not merely doing what they did; it means being like them. Their status is not in the least like that of legislators whose laws we admire; for the character of a legislator is irrelevant to our judgment about his legislation. The heroes and saints did not merely give us principles to live by (though some of them did that as well): they gave us examples to follow.

Kant, as we should expect, emphatically rejects this attitude as "fatal to morality"

(*Groundwork*, page 76). According to him, examples serve only to render *visible* an instance of the moral principle, and thereby to demonstrate its practical feasibility. But every exemplar, such as Christ himself, must be judged by the independent criterion of the moral law, before we are entitled to recognize him as worthy of imitation. I am not suggesting that the subordination of exemplars to principles is incorrect, but that it is one-sided and fails to do justice to a large area of moral experience.

Imitation can be more or less successful. And this suggests another defect of the ethics of principles. It has no room for ideals, except the ideal of a perfect set of principles (which, as a matter of fact, is intelligible only in terms of an ideal character or way of life), and the ideal of perfect conscientiousness (which is itself a character-trait). This results, of course, from the "black-or-white" nature of moral verdicts based on rules. There are no degrees of rule-keeping and rule-breaking. But there certainly are degrees by which we approach or recede from the attainment of a certain quality or virtue; if there were not, the word "ideal" would have no meaning. Heroes and saints are not people whom we try to be *just* like, since we know that is impossible. It is precisely because it is impossible for ordinary human beings to achieve the same qualities as the saints, and in the same degree, that we do set them apart from the rest of humanity. It is enough if we try to be a little like them.

Mayo's exposition of an ethics of virtue raises many important questions about the topics to be addressed in the remaining sections of this chapter: Aristotelian ethics, the exact nature of the relationship between an ethics of virtue and an ethics of duty, and the role of moral ideals in a moral theory—especially the ideals of saints and heroes. Each of these topics will be explored in turn, beginning with Aristotle because his work is still widely accepted as the most influential exposition of virtue ethics. (While Plato is better known than Aristotle for his treatment of certain virtues, Aristotle wrote more systematically and extensively on the general topic of virtue, and hence attention in this chapter is confined largely to his account.)

ARISTOTELIAN ETHICS

As with Mill and Kant in Chapters 3 and 4, we must begin with the philosophical foundations of Aristotle's ethics. In a famous passage, Aristotle says that ethics is a "branch of politics." This has a strange and misleading sound to modern ears and requires explication. First, the word *politikos* in Greek does not correspond well to our word "political." *Politikos* encompasses what is now meant by the political and the social jointly. Second, Aristotle holds that both politics and ethics are concerned to study the nature and promotion of human well-being, and that these topics can be studied only within the context of society. This orientation led W. D. Ross to quip, appropriately, that Aristotle's ethics are social and his politics ethical.* Whereas Mill and Kant often emphasize human individuality and autonomy, Aristotle sees individuals as essentially members of a social unit. He believes that moral actions can be promoted only by the support of a social group and that laws and the threat of punishment are required to foster morality and to elevate ideals of virtuous conduct. Moreover, Aristotle's approach to the general study of well-being and its promotion resembles that of a teacher and political leader. Ethics is the study of the conditions necessary for human well-being, and politics deals with how to order persons in a community so as to achieve well-being. Politics thus studies, for example, the constitution of the state and its fundamental institutions.

It might be said, then, that the task of one who administers the state or some part of it is to design and administer the institutions that make living well possible; the moral philosopher's task is the related one of determining how to live well and how to transmit this knowledge. It seems likely, given this approach, that Aristotle would have approved Jane Addams's way of proceeding in the study of ethics, especially the way in which she applied what she learned from John Dewey and other pragmatists. Because ethics is an essential dimension of political leadership for Aristotle, it should be studied by those who arrange and lead communities. The purpose of a community of free individuals, as he sees it, is to live together as well as possible—a view which Jane Addams too came to accept through her work in ward politics in Chicago.

Thus far, Aristotle's ethics in some ways is reminiscent of Mill's, for it is dominantly a consequential (or teleological) ethics. Morality is essentially bound up with bringing about human good, and Aristotle even proceeds, as does Mill, to search for that which is intrinsically good. He reasons that all human objectives lead to further objectives until finally we reach some supreme objective or end, an ultimate good for the sake of which all other goods are pursued. The ultimate good he of course conceives as well-being *(eudaimonia)*—a notion reminiscent of Mill's "happiness," when understood in the general sense of human flourishing. Aristotle also employs the same means-to-ends thinking that characterizes Mill's ethics: He looks for proper ends and the best means to achieve those ends.

We must be careful, however, not to let these similarities obscure some major differences between Mill and Aristotle. The function of ethics and politics for Aristotle is not to make people happy in the subjective sense in which Mill uses that term; Aristotle rather abruptly dismisses the pursuit of pleasure as a life fit for cattle (though here we may be reminded of Mill's dismissal of Bentham's form of hedonism, which Mill similarly criticizes as fit for a satisfied pig). Aristotle also rejects any close association between well-being and virtue, for well-being is a particular state of the person and virtue is a general disposition. The function of ethics and politics in Aristotle's vision is to teach people how to live well and prosperously; happiness or pleasure in Mill's sense presumably comes as something of a by-product of virtuous, correct living.

*W. D. Ross, *Aristotle*, 5th ed. (New York: Barnes & Noble, Inc., 1964), p. 183.

A more extreme view of the differences between Aristotle's ethical theory and more modern, duty-based systems, such as those of Mill and Kant, is that two fundamentally different enterprises are involved. Some philosophers have held that the Greeks, because of their emphasis on rationality and well-being, were not even concerned with what we would now call a *"moral"* way of life. This view is expressed by William Frankena as follows:

> . . . I have not spoken of Plato and Aristotle as having moralities or conceptions of morality. . . . The Greeks were seeking the *rational* way to live, without making special mention of the *moral* way to live; their solutions do not center on our relations to other persons. However, the moderns conceive of a specifically *moral* way to live that is largely a matter of our relations to our fellow human beings. A prevailing egoism in Greek ethics runs counter to the altruism featured in modern ethics.*

Although this is not a widely shared thesis, it has been defended in a somewhat different and more radical form by Alasdair MacIntyre (in accordance with his argument as presented in Chapter 2 of this text). It is in some respects, however, a difficult interpretation to defend, as can be exhibited by a single quotation from Aristotle: "The virtuous man will act often in the interest of his friends and of his country, and, if need be, will even die for them. He will surrender money, honor, and all the goods for which the world contends, reserving only nobleness for himself, as he would rather . . . perform one noble and lofty action than many poor actions. This is true of one who lays down his life for another; he chooses great nobleness for his own."†

Excellence and Moral Virtue

Aristotle's ethical theory and his account of human good and well-being are developed from his more general views regarding the activities and objectives that are characteristic of human life. He believes the good of any creature is found in the unimpeded exercise of capacities, tendencies, and functions peculiar to the species of which the creature is a member. Living well or living poorly is determined for any individual by success in pursuing these characteristic activities. One understands what it means for a human individual to live well, then, by identifying the capacities, tendencies, and functions that are characteristic of the human species and by determining how to be successful in pursuing these activities. Aristotle appeals in particular to the function or activity associated with membership in a given class. For example, the activity or function of a sculptor is to make statues, and the activity or function of the heart is to pump

---

*William K. Frankena, *Thinking about Morality* (Ann Arbor: University of Michigan Press, 1980), p. 11.

†Aristotle, *Nichomachean Ethics*, Bk. 9, chap. 8, Welldon, trans. (1892).

blood throughout the biological system. To this observation about characteristic functions, Aristotle adds that the good of a thing—its excellence or virtue—consists in its doing its work well, i.e., in functioning successfully: a good heart is one that functions to pump blood well, and a good sculptor is one who makes sculptures well.

From this minimal, almost commonsensical framework, Aristotle constructs a theory of the moral life and the virtues that attend it. His word for "excellence" or "virtue" in Greek is *arete*, a word which encompasses much more than moral virtue alone. He discusses not only the moral virtues, but also the virtues of magnificence, dignity, cheerfulness, and the excellences involved in activities requiring special skills. The breadth of virtues subsumed by the term *arete* is well illustrated by the range of excellences that Jane Addams possessed. Her oratorical skills, her devotion, and—above all for Aristotle's definition—her intelligence and the way she applied it to practical affairs are all forms of excellence. Such human excellences or virtues are fixed dispositions developed through the careful nurturing of one's capacities for living the human life well. Since we are not born morally virtuous, we must be trained so that virtuous activity becomes habitual—just as we must be trained in other technical skills. Because everyone can be, and should strive to be, *morally* virtuous, Aristotle distinguishes moral virtues from virtues or excellences that occur for one particular type of function or work in which persons engage. For example, the excellences that make cobblers good cobblers depend upon the goals of the craft. Moral virtues, by contrast, are universally praiseworthy features of human character that have been fixed by habituation. They are desirable dispositions and traits of the moral life (in a very broad sense); and a person who exhibits them is said by Aristotle to be a person of moral skill.

Aristotle also reasons that there must be some proper function and state of well-being for all human beings *as human beings*—as distinct from human beings as carpenters, dog trainers, or cooks, or who engage in any other function having characteristic virtues. He equates this proper function with what he sees as the distinctive attribute of the human species: reasoning or intelligence. Humans share many capacities and tendencies with other species in nature—e.g., processes of nutrition and growth—and it is the exercise of rational capacities, in Aristotle's philosophy, that is alone distinctive. The specifically *human* part of human excellence consists in the proper exercise of this faculty. Aristotle thus defines human well-being as "an active life in accord with excellence, or if there are more forms of excellence than one, in accord with the best and completest of them" (i.e., reasoning or intelligence).* Jane Addams's social theory exhibits this highest excellence unique to human beings, while her action from compassion is an excellence of a different order. (One possible flaw in Aristotle's theory is his failure to analyze "reason" and that which is unique to the human species more carefully. Bearing in mind the consequent difficulties of interpreting Aristotle, it is interesting to consider Charles Darwin's apparently contrasting argument that many animals reason and have "rationality," but that exhibiting moral virtues is unique to humans.)

*As translated by A. E. Taylor, in his *Aristotle* (New York: Dover Publications, Inc., 1955), p. 91.

Although Aristotle links the performance of a unique human function with human well-being and holds that life controlled by reason is the highest form of well-being, he does not infer that *only* a life of reason can promote human well-being. Any correct performance of a proper function should result in human well-being, even if not a form of well-being distinctive to the human species. Indeed, Aristotle describes the good for human beings in terms of activities that accord with a variety of virtues or excellences present throughout a whole life. He goes on to distinguish virtue of intellect from virtue of character, the latter constituting moral virtue. He also links goodness of character to the proper training and rational disciplining of feelings, impulses, and desires; thus such virtues as temperance, courage, and patience are to be developed through proper schooling. The ideal person would of course be one who exhibits all the virtues over a lifetime.

Practical Wisdom

A part of Aristotle's argument deserving special attention is his discussion of "practical wisdom," which he regards as intelligence engaged in directing human activities to the end of well-being. Although both are forms of intellectual excellence, Aristotle holds that excellence of pure thought is distinct from excellence of applied thought, as found in moral virtue. Since intellectual cleverness may lead to vicious actions, Aristotle declares, a person of practical wisdom knows which ends should be chosen and knows how to achieve them, at the same time keeping emotions within proper bounds and carefully selecting from among the range of possible actions that might be taken. Such a person of practical wisdom has the ability to see what should be done in particular circumstances. The required factor is the practical judgment that skilled and admired group leaders exhibit when they combine experience and good judgment. Such persons know, for example, both when to be courageous and how to use money for good causes, in each case without excess and without overreaction. Jane Addams is an example of such a person of good judgment, for she was at once courageous, efficient, prudent, innovative, and fiscally responsible.

The exercise of good judgment for Aristotle is not a skill that a rule utilitarian or rule deontologist would necessarily admire, for Aristotle does not conceive of moral reasoning as the skill of seeing how a particular case falls under a particular rule. Although Aristotle (like Nagel in Chapter 2) leaves his account of practical judgment largely undeveloped, we should note that if this account of judgment could be worked out as a practical decision theory, it would acquire a considerable advantage over rule-oriented theories. As repeatedly noted in previous chapters, the latter theories falter on the problem of how to handle a conflict of rules or obligations, leaving unclear what should be done and what counts as good judgment. It appears that the theory of practical judgment in Aristotle is specifically designed for those occasions where general guides to action either conflict or else do not provide sufficient guidance.

Aristotle does not, however, leave us completely uninstructed in the details of this practical moral judgment. In one of his most famous discussions of human excellence, he says that a training in virtuous conduct and good judgment involves learning to avoid two extremes: one is the vice of excess ("too much"), and the other is the vice of defect ("too little"). The virtuous person is one who aims at moderation between these extremes, and in Aristotle's conception, excess and defect are generally found in feeling and action. Just as we must learn that eating too much or too little food is bad for a person, so we must learn that courage, for example, is a mean between rashness and cowardice. We must learn not to fear so much as to be cowardly, and we must also learn not to be foolhardy or rash by neglecting to fear that which is dangerous. All virtues can be similarly analyzed, according to Aristotle. Every art and technique of skill likewise involve making judgments about the right amount, and such judgments too require learning about the mean between extremes. Finish carpentry, for example, involves the proper cutting of small pieces of wood and their proper positioning after they have been cut. Too short or too long a cut, and too much or too little of the wood displayed, are poor carpentry—and as with carpentry, so with other dimensions of life.

Aristotle does not claim, however, that the mean is the same for all persons and circumstances. It is, he says, "relative to ourselves" and "determined by reason, or as a right-minded person would determine it." In morality, the proper mean between extremes is best judged by persons of practical wisdom who have experience and great skill of judgment in facing situations that present new subtleties. They understand how to act with just the right intensity of feeling, in just the right way, at just the right time. These are virtuous persons in whom a right relation exists between reason, feeling, and desire. This is not an endorsement of relativism or subjective opinion, however, for Aristotle intends to offer an objective general standard of moral conduct: the right-minded or virtuous person serves as such a standard, much as the "reasonable person" serves as an objective standard for judges and juries. Undoubtedly, it was for roughly this reason that the American Education Award was given to Jane Addams for teaching "by precept and example." She was obviously a person of great experience and skill in precisely these Aristotelian senses, clearly exhibiting a proper relation between reason, feeling, and desire.

The following selection from Aristotle concentrates on the moral virtues and the mean between extremes. Despite its appearance here, in a context where it serves as an example of an ethics of virtue standing in contrast to an ethics of principle, it should be remembered that utilitarians and deontologists also support the cultivation of moral virtues, even though they differ over which virtues are most important. The virtue of benevolence, for example, will be of considerable importance to utilitarians, while the virtue of justice is likely to be of no less importance in many deontological accounts. Aristotle's theory of morality is sufficiently general that one may learn about the virtuous moral life regardless of one's preference for utilitarian, deontological, or virtue ethics.

One cautionary note deserves mention for those new to Aristotle's writings. The *Nichomachean Ethics* was not composed as a book, and Aristotle never published the work himself. It was originally little more than a set of outlines and lecture notes, and may have been compiled later from notes taken by students at his lectures. Aristotle's works lay decaying in a cellar owned by a private family for over a hundred years, and they were subsequently mistranscribed and issued in editions that contained many inaccuracies and gaps. Later scholarship has repaired most of these flaws, but the work unavoidably reads somewhat like well-prepared lecture notes and should be approached accordingly.

ARISTOTLE

Moral Virtue*

There are . . . two sorts of virtue: intellectual and moral. Intellectual virtue is mostly originated and promoted by teaching, which is why it needs experience and time. Moral virtue is produced by habit, which is why it is called "moral," a word only slightly different from our word for habit.

It is quite plain that none of the moral virtues is produced in us by nature, since none of the things with natural properties can be trained to acquire a different property. For example, the stone, which has a natural downward motion, cannot be trained to move upwards, not even if one "trains" it by countless upward throws. Similarly, fire cannot be trained to move downwards. In general, none of the things with a given natural property can be trained to acquire another.

The virtues, then, are neither innate nor contrary to nature. They come to be because we are fitted by nature to receive them; but we perfect them by training or habit. . . .

For example, people become builders by actually building, and the same applies to lyre players. In the same way, we become just by doing just acts; and similarly with "temperate" and "brave."

*From Aristotle, *Nichomachean Ethics*, Bk. 2, chaps. 1, 2, 4, 6, 7, 9, A. E. Wardman, trans., in Renford Bambrough, ed., *The Philosophy of Aristotle* (New York: Mentor Books, 1963).

There is further evidence in contemporary institutions: legislators make citizens good by training them. Indeed, all legislators aim at that, and those who do it incorrectly miss their objective. That is the point of difference between the institutions of a good and of a bad community.

Further, the very things that make virtue can also unmake it. Compare the techniques, where both good and bad players alike are produced by actually practicing. The same is true of building and all the skills: good building will make good builders, and so with bad. If this were not the case, there would be no need for an instructor, for all men alike would be born good or bad at their craft. Now, the same applies to the virtues. By acting in affairs that involve a contract with others, some of us become just, some unjust. . . .

Let us consider this first: it is in the nature of things for the virtues to be destroyed by excess and deficiency, as we see in the case of health and strength— a good example, for we must use clear cases when discussing abstruse matters. Excessive or insufficient training destroys strength, just as too much or too little food and drink ruins health. The right amount, however, brings health and preserves it. So this applies to moderation, bravery, and the other virtues. The man who runs away from everything in fear, and faces up to nothing, becomes a coward; the man who is absolutely fearless, and will walk into anything, becomes rash. It is the same with the man who gets enjoyment from all pleasures, abstaining from none: he is immoderate; whereas he who avoids all pleasures, like a boor, is a man of no sensitivity. Moderation and bravery are destroyed by excess and deficiency, but are kept flourishing by the mean. . . .

But the products of the virtues—i.e., actions—are not just or moderate according to the nature of the actions, but according to the disposition of the doer. Firstly, he must know; secondly, he must act from choice, choosing what he does for its own sake; and thirdly, he must act from a firm and unshakable disposition.

These factors, apart from knowledge, are not included when we consider whether someone has the other arts. But knowing contributes little or no strength toward having the virtues, whereas the other factors make no little difference. On the contrary, they make all the difference, since justice and temperance come about through frequent just and temperate acts.

Acts are called just and temperate when they are such as the just or temperate man would perform. The temperate and just man is not he who does these acts, but he who does them in the way in which just and temperate men do them. People are right when they say that the just man is formed by doing just acts, the temperate man by doing temperate acts: without doing them, no one would even be likely to become good. . . .

In this same way, everyone who knows, in any field, avoids excess and deficiency; he looks for the mean and chooses the mean, not the mean according to the thing, but the mean relative to us. Every art does its job well in this way, by looking to the mean and leading its products toward it—which is why people say of things well done that you cannot add anything or take anything away, since "well done" is

ruined by excess and deficiency and achieved by the mean; and good craftsmen, as we were saying, work with their eye on the mean. To resume: if virtue, like nature, requires more accuracy and is better than any art, then it will aim at the mean. I speak here of moral virtue, since that is concerned with emotions and actions; and excess, deficiency, and the mean occur in these. In feeling fear, confidence, desire, anger, pity, and in general pleasure and pain, one can feel too much or too little; and both extremes are wrong. The mean and the good is feeling at the right time, about the right things, in relation to the right people, and for the right reason; and the mean and the good are the task of virtue. Similarly, in regard to actions, there are excess, deficiency, and the mean.

Virtue is concerned with emotions and actions, where excess is wrong, as is deficiency, but the mean is praised and is right. Both being praised and being right belong to virtue. So virtue is a kind of mean, since it does at least aim at the mean. . . .

Virtue, then, is a disposition involving choice. It consists in a mean, relative to us, defined by reason and as the reasonable man would define it. It is a mean between two vices—one of excess, the other of deficiency. Also, virtue discovers and chooses the mean, whereas the vices exceed or fall short of the essential, in the spheres of both emotions and acts.

Therefore, as regards its essence and the definition of what it really is, virtue is a mean; but seen from the viewpoint of the supreme good and the best, it is an extreme. Not every act or emotion admits of the mean. The very names of some things imply evil—for example, the emotions of spite, shamelessness, and envy and such actions as adultery, theft, and murder. All these and their like get their name because they are evil in themselves, and not through excess or deficiency in them. In their case (i.e., in doing them), you can never be right; you must always be wrong. In such matters there is no good or bad in the sense of committing adultery with the right woman, at the right time, and in the right way. Quite absolutely, doing any of these things is wrong. One might in the same way claim that there is a mean, excess, and deficiency with regard to being unjust or cowardly or profligate. If so, there would be a mean of excess and of deficiency, an excess of excess, and a deficiency of deficiency. Now, there is no excess or deficiency of temperance or courage, since the mean is in a sense an extreme: similarly, there is no mean of the above vices (nor any excess or deficiency). They are wrong, however performed. In general, there is no mean of an excess or a deficiency, nor is there an excess or a deficiency of a mean.

We must not only put this in general terms but also apply it to particular cases. In statements concerning acts, general statements cover more ground, but statements on a specified point are more accurate. Acts are concerned with particulars, after all; and theory should agree with particular facts. Let us, then, take these particular virtues from our table.

Now, courage is the mean in matters of fearing and feeling brave. The man who exceeds in fearlessness has no special name (there are many vices and virtues that have no names). He who exceeds in confidence is overconfident, whereas the man who exceeds in feeling fear and falls short in confidence is a coward.

Concerning pleasures and pains (not all are involved, and indeed pains are less so), the mean is temperance, and the excess profligacy. . . .

Indignation is the mean between envy and malice. These concern the pleasure and pain experienced over what happens to neighbors. The indignant man feels pain when people prosper without deserving to; the envious man, who exceeds the former, feels pain at all good fortune; whereas the malicious man, so far from feeling pain, actually feels pleasure. . . .

We have said enough about moral virtue being a mean, and in what way it is a mean—i.e., between two vices, one of excess and one of deficiency. It is what it is because it aims at the mean both in feelings and in actions.

This is why it is a hard job to be good. It is hard to get to the mean in each thing. It is the expert, not just anybody, who finds the center of the circle. In the same way, having a fit of temper is easy for anyone; so is giving money and spending it. But this is not so when it comes to questions of "for whom?" "how much?" "when?" "why?" and "how?" This is why goodness is rare, and is praiseworthy and fine.

The man aiming at the mean should first keep clear of that extreme that is more the opposite of the mean. As Calypso says: "Keep your ship outside the spray and the waves." One of the extremes has more wrong in it than the other. Since hitting the mean just right is hard, we must take the least of the evils by way of second-best. This will happen in the following way.

We should see what we ourselves are most prone to (each of us has different natural tendencies). Now, this will be clear from the pleasure and pain we get. We should then drag ourselves off in the opposite direction. By moving to a long way from going wrong, we shall come to the mean, which is what people do who are straightening warped timber.

Above all, we should keep a sharp eye on pleasure and what is pleasant. The point is that we are not impartial judges of it. We should feel about pleasure as the old men in Homer felt about Helen, and say what they said all the time. In this way, as we send pleasure away, we shall go less wrong. In so doing, to put it briefly, we shall best be able to attain the mean. But it is certainly hard, and above all in particulars. It is not easy to decide how and with whom and about what and for how long one should be angry. At times we praise those who fall short and call them good-tempered, at other times we call those who are harsh real men. However, a slight deviation from the good is not blamed, either in the direction of excess or of deficiency; yet, the larger deviation is blamed, since it gets noticed. It is not easy to determine about blame, i.e., to what point and how far it should be applied. Nor is it easy to determine anything else that has to do with the senses; and such things as these depend on particulars, which are decided by perception. However, it is clear that the mean is always praiseworthy, but at times we should lean toward the excess, at other times to the deficiency. In this way, we shall most readily attain the mean, i.e., the good.

THE CORRESPONDENCE
BETWEEN VIRTUES AND PRINCIPLES

As Mayo suggested in the selection quoted earlier and as the selection from Aristotle clearly evidences, Greek philosophers conceived ethics in terms of virtuous conduct, not in terms of rules or principles of duty. They therefore presented moral theory as a theory of virtue rather than as a theory of obligation. Some contemporary philosophers have bluntly defended the view that virtue ethics should be primary in ethical theory. They believe that all we need to direct us in what we should do are fundamental directives about the kinds of persons we should be. In their view, morality does not consist in obedience to Kant's categorical imperative; rather, it is the expression of a virtuous character internal to the person—a character needing no external rules specifying right conduct.

Many prominent writers in philosophy have rejected such claims, of course, and have defended systems composed entirely of principles of duty. Kant represents a polar extreme, since he writes as though dedication to duty is the sole factor in determining a person's moral character and worth. But even philosophers as fascinated by virtue ethics as William Frankena reject the idea that virtue ethics has an independent or primary status—in his case, because he thinks "traits without principles are blind" and because we could not know which traits to encourage unless we already subscribed to some principles.* Philosophers who support this point of view do not deny that a study of moral virtues is important; they simply do not regard virtue ethics as making a fundamental contribution to the task of normative ethical theory. It is now appropriate to ask whether one of these two approaches captures the basic features of moral experience better than the other.

*William K. Frankena, *Ethics*, 2d ed. (Englewood Cliffs, N.J.: Prentice-Hall, Inc., 1973), p. 65.

Can virtue ethics be defended as primary or basic to moral theory? There are respects in which this position is inviting. We judge the successes and failures of people, not the successes and failures solely of their actions. Persons of generous character and warm personality are hardly judged by the way they live up to the demands of rules. Moreover, their virtue is determined as much by their innermost attitudes and outlook as by their performances or their principles. A person extremely conscientious in attending to the needs and deserts of others lies close to our ideal of moral praiseworthiness, especially when the person sets aside his or her own desires in order to promote the welfare of others. Consider, for example, the virtue of charity. Whereas, in Kant's view, all moral worth derives from a good will attempting to meet the demands of duty, we generally have less admiration for the person who acts charitably from duty than for the person who does so spontaneously from well-formed virtues without the prod of duty.

The compassion so obviously guiding Jane Addams's life is no matter of duty; and most of our celebrated figures of compassion have been persons moved solely by the plight of others. St. Francis of Assisi (Giovanni Benardone), for example, was best known for a tenderness and compassion exhibited in spontaneous displays of affection for others—such as his embracing a leper or giving away his only blanket on a cold evening. St. Francis many times expressed reservations about both appeals to reason and appeals to duty, for he found them simply irrelevant. Being so moved from natural sympathy, rather than duty, is undeniably virtuous, yet is a reaction for which there is no place in Kant's philosophy. As Philippa Foot puts this point, "The man who acts charitably out of a sense of duty is not to be undervalued, but it is the other who most shows virtue and therefore to the other that most moral worth is attributed." In this regard, Foot sees Aristotle's moral theory as far more prescient and acceptable than a duty-based theory, and she considers it superior in particular to Kant's account of "moral worth."*

Writers such as Foot therefore seek to reverse Kant's thesis that moral goodness, moral virtue, and moral worth *depend upon* the execution of duty. A morally good person, they say, has a prior disposition to do what is right. Such a person naturally assists and promotes the welfare of others, manifests prudence in matters of choice, and does so apart from any thought that these actions are matters of duty. We can again expect that Jane Addams will serve as a model instance of these claims. Throughout her writings she indicates that her objective is to tap natural responses in herself and others. The model she establishes by acting virtuously, moreover, sets the proper tone of the moral life for others—not some disembodied sense of duty. "Virtue par excellence," says Foot, is found in one who is prompt and resourceful in doing good, where this may be accomplished as much by one's "innermost desires" as by a deliberate action. In total retreat from Kant, she adds that "pleasure in the good fortune of others is, one thinks, the sign of a generous spirit; and small reactions of pleasure and displeasure often the surest signs of a man's moral disposition."†

*Philippa Foot, *Virtues and Vices* (Oxford, England: Basil Blackwell, 1978), pp. 12–14.

†Ibid., p. 5, and "Morality as a System of Hypothetical Imperatives," in the same volume.

Another argument that speaks in favor of giving primacy—or at the very least an independent status—to virtue ethics is the following: Even though we evaluate persons through our knowledge of their actions, we do not evaluate their moral worth or goodness simply by adding up all their actions. Rather, we take account of their total set of virtues (i.e., traits of character). It will not matter that morally good persons act from time to time from blameworthy motives, or that evil persons act occasionally from good motives. None of us is unfailingly good, and even saints and heroes, such as Jane Addams, can and do act out of character. If a person of veracity inexcusably lies on a given occasion, we will not brand the person a liar in general, and we will note that the act was out of character. This response shows that one can do what is wrong without being bad—as we all know from saying, "I don't think he's really a bad guy; he just got carried away." Notice that there is no attempt in this judgment to *excuse* the lie. The intent is, rather, to place the lie in the larger context of the person's moral worth and character. Only when it is discovered that telling a lie is "in character" do we appropriately use the label "liar." An overall assessment of the *person* thus depends fundamentally on whether we are confident that any given *act* exhibits the person's *character*; and even when we are certain that a person has acted wrongly on several occasions, we may still desist from judging the person's moral character until we get to know him or her better.

Despite the attractiveness of the arguments considered thus far, they do not seem sufficient to show virtue ethics to be primary or more fundamental than an ethics based on principles of duty. As we have seen, many utilitarians and deontologists support the cultivation of moral virtue. A morality that emphasizes duty and action can be assisted by a morality of character that promotes dispositions to act in accordance with one's duty; and at the same time, a morality of virtue and character will promote dispositions to *act* in certain ways. Moreover, moral virtues seem to correspond to many principles of moral duty; if so, there will of course be the same correspondence between acts prohibited by moral principles and those condemned as moral vices. The two approaches to morality may even be perfectly complementary: for every principle of duty there is a corresponding trait of character or virtue, which is a disposition to act in a certain way; and for every virtue of character there is a corresponding principle of duty. This program of correspondence can be diagrammed as follows, by reference to a few selected principles and virtues:

The principle or duty of	[corresponds to]	The virtue of
Beneficence		Benevolence
Justice		Fairness
Fidelity		Faithfulness
Nondeception		Nondeceptiveness
Nonmaleficence		Nonmalevolence
Confidentiality		Confidentialness
Gratitude		Gratefulness

According to this diagram, if a particular ethical theory recognizes the principles of beneficence and justice, for example, the theory can also recognize the corresponding

virtues of benevolence and fairness. Any theory based on principles, such as rule utilitarianism or rule deonotology, will therefore be able to derive corresponding virtues. If
this approach envisioned a *complete*, as distinct from a *partial*, correspondence theory,
then any principle of duty whatever, and also any principle capturing a moral ideal,
would have a corresponding virtue. The apparent fact that there seem to be vastly more
virtues than moral principles (think of modesty, humility, purity, integrity, loyalty, sincerity, and commitment*) could be accounted for by appeal to moral rules that are
derived from more fundamental principles and the diversity of types of acts that fall
under each rule or principle. This large program for exhibiting the correspondence
between virtue ethics and ethics of duty is at once too complicated and too speculative
to pursue here, but the basic idea may be presented in tabular form as follows:

	Theories of duty	[correspond to]	Theories of virtue
Common moral standards	Fundamental principles ↓ Derivative rules		Fundamental virtues ↓ Derivative virtues
Exceptional moral standards	Supererogatory ideals ↓ Derivative ideals		Ideal virtues ↓ Derivative virtues

The idea that there is a one-to-one correspondence between certain moral virtues
and moral principles is developed in the following selection from G. J. Warnock. His
argument expands the conclusions reached in his article in Chapter 1 of this book. It is
to be noted that Warnock does not say that his account of the virtues is Aristotelian
(which in some ways it certainly is not), and that he does not claim primacy for either
a virtue-based or a principle-based theory. Nor does he say that the virtues he mentions
are all the virtues that could conceivably play a role in a moral theory. His attempt is
the modest one of justifying a set of *fundamental* moral virtues which correspond perfectly to *fundamental moral principles of duty.*

*David Hume in effect regards the virtues as indefinitely large: "we . . . may pronounce *any* quality
of the mind virtuous, which causes love or pride; and *any* one vicious, which causes hatred or
humility" [Italics added]. David Hume, *A Treatise of Human Nature*, Bk. 3, part 3, sec. 1.

G. J. WARNOCK

Moral Virtues*

There are certain very general facts about the human predicament, including certain very general facts about human beings, which seem to be reasonably regarded as setting up, in ways already briefly sketched,† an inherent liability for things to go rather badly; what then, let us ask, is required, if things are to go better—or rather if, as by and large is the case, they are not actually to go quite so badly as they seem inherently liable to do? And where, among such requirements, might morality be seen as fitting in? . . .

If any of those things towards the amelioration of the human predicament which can be done are to be done in fact, then not only must people sometimes be *made* to do things which they are not just naturally disposed to do anyway; they must also sometimes voluntarily, without coercion, act otherwise than people are just naturally disposed to do. It is necessary that people should acquire, and should seek to ensure that others acquire, what may be called *good dispositions*—that is, some readiness on occasion voluntarily to do desirable things which not all human beings are just naturally disposed to do anyway, and similarly not to do damaging things. . . .

It seems to me reasonable to insist that . . . a certain absolute priority must be seen as attaching to human dispositions. We have already found, in an earlier chapter, some reason for thinking that, of the limitations which constitute (in a sense) the human predicament, the most important are those that might be called most

*From G. J. Warnock, *The Object of Morality* (London: Methuen & Co., Ltd., 1971), chap. 6, pp. 71–72, 75–77, 79–86.

†See Chapter 1 of this text [Ed.].

"internal" to human beings—that is, limitations of rationality and sympathy. It may now seem to be the case that, essentially for just the same reasons, what is crucial for betterment is the promotion of "good dispositions." All the other things—acquiring, disseminating, preserving, and transmitting knowledge, setting up and maintaining organizations and institutions, devising and operating means of making people do things—all of these things are things that people do; so that everything in the end depends on their readiness to do them, and to do them at least some of the time without being compelled to do so. . . .

The paradigmatic *moral* virtues [are] those good dispositions whose tendency is directly to countervail the limitation of human sympathies, and whose exercise accordingly is essentially—though indeed not, by itself, necessarily effectively—good *for* persons other than the agent himself. Let us see what profit we can extract from this proposition. . . .

We need now to consider in a little more detail what those particular ills are—that is, in what ways, in consequence of the limitedness of human sympathies, people are typically *liable* to act so as to worsen, or not to act so as to ameliorate, the predicament.

The first step on this path, at any rate, seems an easy one to take. If I am exclusively, or even predominantly, concerned with the satisfaction of my own wants, interests, or needs, or of those of some limited group such as my family, or friends, or tribe, or country, or class, with whose interests and ends I am naturally disposed to sympathize, then I, other members of that group, or the group as a whole, may be naturally prone to act directly to the detriment of other persons, nonmembers of the group, or of other groups. I may be inclined, from competitiveness or mere indifference or even active malevolence, to do positive harm to others, whether in the form of actual injury to them, or of frustration and obstruction of the satisfaction of their wants, interests, and needs. There is here, that is to say, a liability to act simply *maleficently*—harmfully, damagingly—to others, quite directly, either out of sheer unconcern with the damage so inflicted, or even out of a positive taste for the infliction of damage on persons or groups outside the circle of one's sympathies. That being so, it can scarcely seem controversial to say that *one* of the "good dispositions" we are in search of will be the disposition to abstain from (deliberate, unjustified) maleficence. . . .

The next step seems also, in general terms, scarcely more problematic. If we need, and if humans in general do not just naturally, regularly, and reliably have, the disposition of nonmaleficence, just the same can plainly be said of the disposition towards positive beneficence. The limitedness of sympathies tends often to make it not just natural to interest oneself directly in another's good; there is need, then, for cultivation of the disposition to do so, which will very often take the particular form of readiness to give *help* to others in their activities. . . .

I believe that we should now add, as an independent requirement, the disposition not to *discriminate*, as surely most humans have some natural propensity to do, to the disadvantage of those outside the limited circle of one's natural concern. If, for instance, twenty people have a claim upon, or are substantially in need of, some service or benefit that I can provide, it seems not enough merely to say that I should not refuse it; it must be added that I should not help or benefit some of them *less* merely because, for instance, I may happen to like them less, or be less well-disposed towards them. The general name for this good disposition is, I take it, fairness. . . .

Then one more thing. If we consider the situation of a person, somewhat prone by nature to an exclusive concern with his own, or with some limited range of, interests and needs and wants, living among other persons more or less similarly constituted, we see that there is one device in particular, very often remarkably easy to employ, by which he may be naturally more or less inclined to, so to speak, carve out his egoistical way to his own, and if necessary at the expense of other, ends; and that is *deception*. . . . Though deception is . . . not necessarily directly damaging, it is easy to see how crucially important it is that the natural inclination to have recourse to it should be counteracted. It is, one might say, not the implanting of false beliefs that is damaging, but rather the generation of the suspicion that they may be being implanted. For this undermines trust; and, to the extent that trust is undermined, all co-operative undertakings, in which what one person can do or has reason to do is dependent on what others have done, are doing, or are going to do, must tend to break down. . . .

We suggest, then, that, in the general context of the human predicament, there are these four (at least) distinguishable damaging, or non-ameliorative, types of propensity which tend naturally to emanate directly from "limited sympathies"— those of maleficence, non-beneficence, unfairness, and deception. If now we apply the supposition that the "object" of morality is to make the predicament less grim than, in a quasi-Hobbesian state of nature, it seems inherently liable to be, and to do so specifically by seeking to countervail the deleterious liabilities inherent in "limited sympathies," we seem to be led to four (at least) general types of good disposition as those needed to countervail the above-mentioned four types of propensity; and these dispositions will be, somewhat crudely named, those of (1) non-maleficence, (2) fairness, (3) beneficence, and (4) non-deception. We venture the hypothesis that these (at least) are fundamental *moral virtues*.

But we can now manipulate this conclusion a little. If it were agreed that we have here, in these "good dispositions," four moral virtues, it could scarcely be contentious to derive from this the proposition that we have here, by the same token, four fundamental moral *standards*, or moral *principles*. To have and to display, say, the moral virtue of non-deception could be said to be to regulate one's conduct in conformity to a *principle* of non-deception, or to refer to that as to a *standard* in one's practical decisions. But such a principle would be a principle of judgment as well as of decision. That is, if I accept a principle

of non-deception, I may judge others to be morally condemnable in so far as ('without excuse) their acts constitute breaches of it, or morally praiseworthy in so far as they (laudably) comply with it in practice. And thus we can say what a "moral reason" is. Namely, it is a consideration, about some person, or some person's character, or some specimen of actual or possible conduct, which tends to establish in the subject concerned conformity or conflict with a moral principle. That your act would inflict wanton damage on some other person would be a "moral reason" for judging that—at least "from the moral point of view"—you ought not so to act, since it tends to establish that your act would be in conflict with the moral principle of non-maleficence, or, to put just the same point in a different way, would be inconsistent with exercise of the moral virtue of non-maleficence.

Warnock's argument tempts one to conclude that virtue ethics is simply the mirror image of the ethical theories based on principles that we have previously studied (as the above tables of corresponding principles and virtues also suggest). His approach to the virtues *through a prior study of the object of morality* makes such a correspondence theory especially attractive. If the objectives of both a virtue ethics and a morality of principles are identical, a correspondence between the good actions and the good intentions which also promote that end should not be surprising. In agreement with Warnock, John Stuart Mill clearly saw matters in this way. As noted earlier, he held that the "object of virtue" is the "multiplication of happiness." We need not conclude that virtues and principles are interchangeable, or that one can be reduced to the other, but only that they may serve the same function or objective in a moral theory or code.

If there is some form of correspondence between the two types of theory, one may be skeptical that virtue ethics can add anything to normative moral philosophy. On the basis of the argument thus far, however, such skepticism would be premature. It may be that there are many virtues with no corresponding principles of duty—virtues such as modesty, friendship, sobriety, promptness, and prudence; and it may also be that the "supererogatory ideals" listed in the preceding diagram are in fact nothing but ideal *virtues* that cannot be squeezed under the label "theories of duty." To recall a few other virtues that were noted in discussing Jane Addams, to what principles of duty do the virtues of compassion, courage, conscientiousness, devotion, and caring correspond? Are these virtues not features of the moral life beyond all demands of duty? What would we mean if we should say that they "correspond to" supererogatory ideals in a theory of duty? And is Jane Addams not a perfect example of someone who is morally virtuous in those respects, even though utilitarianism and deontology have no adequate way of expressing her virtuous character? These questions lead straight to the subject of moral ideals.

MORAL IDEALS

Two Moralities?

good

The idea of a correspondence between an ethics of virtue and an ethics of duty, explored in the preceding section, leaves undecided the question whether either approach is more fundamental than the other. One optimistic resolution of this apparent struggle for preeminence is that one need not choose between the two, because they can be seen as two aspects of one and the same morality. An ethics of duty, according to this happy resolution, can be applied in those dimensions of the moral life where one has moral obligations, and an ethics of virtue can be applied to important areas of the moral life that are nonetheless beyond the call of duty. Thus, supererogatory actions, such as those performed by saints and heroes (terms denoting men and women alike), can be praised and counted toward a person's moral worth through a virtue ethics and at the same time judged beyond duty by an ethics of principles.*

If this resolution can be effected, two kinds of moral goodness should be distinguished: one for persons who do what is required by duty, and one for persons who perform praiseworthy actions beyond duty. This distinction naturally leads to the view that there are two forms of morality: the common morality within the reach of everyone who strives for it, and an uncommon morality within the reach of only a person of extraordinary talents, dedication, and drive. (From this perspective, there also are common virtues and extraordinary virtues, as well as common rules and extraordinary rules.) The general term "morality" would then be used to embrace both "moralities," but only one kind of morality would involve moral duties. Jane Addams, we could say, has a second morality beyond that practiced by most of us, one based on a set of moral ideals to which the rest of us are not only not faithful, but also not bound.

Moral ideals that transcend duties should be especially welcome to virtue ethics, because they are directed at the kind of person it is commendable to *be*, but do not state

---

*This thesis, we should note, has been anticipated in several previous chapters. For example, in Chapter I (when universalizability was discussed), the observation was made that moral judgments such as "I ought to terminate life-support systems for a seriously ill member of the family" are difficult to generalize as *duties* for others, even though one might see them as required of oneself; and in the final part of Chapter 3, attention was paid to the thesis that utilitarians cannot distinguish supererogatory moral ideals from moral duties, even though we all commonly acknowledge the distinction.

specifically what that person ought to *do.* To hold a moral ideal is no doubt to aspire to certain *actions*, but one can pursue them apart from all belief in a morality of obligations. Jane Addams's ideals again satisfy this description, but to understand this point we need not reach beyond the way most of us were introduced to morality through the lives of great saints, religious and nonreligious. While saints accept requirements for themselves well beyond ordinary moral duty, we nonetheless consider their demands worthy models for our own actions. On the other hand, we are often disposed to think that the saints—Jane Addams included—have led lives or proposed a morality for themselves that we could not come very close to satisfying. It is here that we resort to a morality of duty to specify what is minimally required in contrast with what is maximally excellent.

In opposition to the idea that there are two moralities, the defender of an ethics of duty will argue, in the words of William Frankena, that "if one's ideal is truly a moral one, there will be nothing in it that is not covered by the principles of beneficence and justice conceived as principles of what we ought to do in the wider sense."* As this comment crisply distinguishes the opposing positions, let us examine Frankena's contention further.

Saints and Heroes

Much recent literature on moral ideals explores the exemplary character traits of saints and heroic men and women. It is here that virtuous supererogatory acts present the sharpest challenge to Frankena's proposal. Do principles that assert "what we *ought* to do in the wider sense" indicate that we are morally obligated to act in accordance with the ideals of saints and heroes? These superhuman, sometimes legendary figures perform what *they* accept as their "duty," but most people would not and could not perform their heroic or saintly acts. Saints persevere where most people yield to desire or personal interest, while heroes overcome fears to which almost all others succumb. Some heroes, including Socrates (in an act recounted in detail in Chapter 8) and Jane Addams, even exceed requirements they had formerly assumed for themselves. Saints and heroes thus resist forces which others are unable to resist, and this very *inability* is one reason why saintly and heroic actions are not classified as actions that ought to be done because required by a duty.†

Our evaluations of saints and heroes seem to support much in the program for moral philosophy accepted in virtue ethics. First of all, the lives of saints are plainly virtuous, and yet their actions almost always exceed moral duties considered standard

---

*William K. Frankena, *Ethics*, 2d ed. (Englewood Cliffs, N.J.: Prentice-Hall, Inc., 1973), p. 68. He expresses an apparently different view in *Thinking about Morality* (Ann Arbor: University of Michigan Press, 1980), pp. 58–59.

†For some features of this paragraph and the subsequent analysis, I am indebted to J. O. Urmson, "Saints and Heroes," in A. I. Melden, ed., *Essays in Moral Philosophy* (Seattle: University of Washington Press, 1958), pp. 198–216.

by others than themselves. Saintly and heroic actions are usually, but not always beyond duty, since we sometimes view persons as saints or heroes because they do their moral *duty* in circumstances where others likely would not. Now it is of course true that many heroes and saints think they "ought" to do what they do, or "ought" to be certain kinds of persons. These men and women notoriously insist that they *had* to do what they did or they could not have lived with themselves had they lived some other kind of life. Thus they do not consider their actions or characters to be morally optional.

However, this explanation only shows that not all *requirements* related to morality are universal *duties,* or *obligations.* This way of understanding "what we ought to do in the wider sense" seems preferable to Frankena's depiction, for it places the "ought" and "must" language of saints and heroes where it belongs: in the realm of self-assumed moral ideals *beyond* the "ought" and "must" language of a duty. No doubt Frankena means to say that extraordinary ideals of beneficence and justice are simply the ideals accepted by saints and heroes, but the problem with this thesis comes in connecting it with "what we ought to do," for how wide can the "sense" be in an ethics of duty? Sometimes, of course, a hero or saint acts in a superbeneficent way, but there may be reasonable doubt that all the virtues can be ascribed to especially high levels of action based on principles of duty; and it is especially doubtful that the two principles mentioned by Frankena, however broad, will prove sufficient.

If people fail to fulfill their duties, we can blame or castigate them for nonperformance, but we cannot blame the saint or hero who fails to live up to his or her ideals. At most, it would be disappointing that the person did not turn out as we or the person had hoped. But reproach based on some principle of *duty,* such as beneficence or justice, seems plainly inappropriate. Our praise for saints and heroes is thus perfectly consistent with the view that their actions are morally optional acts based on ideals that transcend duties (i.e., are supererogatory).

A second way in which the lives of saints and heroes are ideally suited for virtue ethics is found in our judgments of character and motive. A person who acts in a manner normally deserving the accolade "saintly" or "heroic," but who does so purely for self-advancement or public recognition, is not a saint—and may not be a hero, depending on the exact motive involved. This contrast between a saint and a hero is particularly obvious in the case of character assessments. A saint *must* have a certain kind of character, with character traits that must consistently dispose him or her to proper deeds over a period of time. A hero, by contrast, may become a hero instantly by a single act. Nonetheless, we would likely deny someone the honorific title "saint" or "hero" if the person either were of despicable moral character or had acted for morally blameworthy reasons.

Finally, despite the fact that we have wound up discussing moral ideals by reference to saintly and heroic actions, we know from earlier discussions in this text that many actions exceed duty without being either heroic or saintly. For example, a teacher may put in extra hours of work that exceed normal duties without being saintly or heroic. On many occasions, it is also not clear where to draw the line between the dutiful and the supererogatory, and thus we may be unclear about the kind of action that would have to be performed in order to exceed duty. What is the teacher's duty to his or her students and to the entire school? Is it to grade tests and papers thoroughly? To serve as a friend or counselor? To assist all majors in the department in getting into graduate school? If the duty is merely that of spending, say, forty hours a week in conscientious performance of tasks, then the teacher can go beyond that duty just by working forty-five hours. On the other hand, if the duty is merely to perform such tasks as challenging a student to perform at a higher level, then a teacher who displays such "nonrequired" virtues as patience, fortitude, and friendliness will exceed the demands of duty. On some understanding of the teacher's responsibilities, these duties and more are required, but that is hardly to the point. We are simply observing now that many actions that exceed duty are genuine instances of living up to moral ideals, but not ideals so high that we wish to place the honorific titles "heroic" and "saintly" on them.

At the same time, it would be a mistake to think that the only persons who serve as models of virtue for us are saints and heroes. One reason a person becomes a saint or hero is that he or she possesses many virtues, and thereby is greatly admired and comes to influence us deeply. Yet we can and often do learn about virtuous conduct from persons with a more limited repertoire of virtues. Jane Addams learned about the virtuous life from her father, and by her own account, his influence became the dominant influence in her life. While we often learn conscientiousness from our parents and diligence from our teachers, neither our parents nor our teachers need, on the whole, lead virtuous lives to achieve such influence. We learn about virtue and how to practice it where we find it, and for most of us most of the time, our instructors are neither saints nor heroes.

This discussion can be concluded in Aristotelian terms by saying that we learn practical wisdom from all sorts of practically wise persons who help us learn how to avoid excessive extremes. The idea that one learns virtue from exemplary individuals is an attractive thesis about how we do and how we should learn moral behavior. Of course, there are excesses in this paradigm of moral instruction as well; following a "model person" often retards critical reflection and independent exercise of judgment. On the other hand, it seems foolish to abandon the idea that some persons have moral expertise, maturity, and authority and that they can serve as valid ideals of the moral life. Jane Addams can again serve as an ideal example, and her leadership is of the type Aristotle specifically commends.

CRITICISMS AND DEFENSES OF VIRTUE ETHICS

We have witnessed from the first page of this chapter a struggle between virtue ethics and moral theories based on principles of duty. Virtue ethics has been challenged to prove its independence as a moral theory, or at the very least to show that it adds a dimension lacking in other theories. Other criticisms may be offered besides those we have thus far encountered. In conclusion, we shall investigate two sweeping and important criticisms of virtue theories, together with some of the responses that could be made by defenders of them.

The Problem of a Basis for Obligations and Rights

We naturally expect a theory of moral *obligations* to be part of any adequate moral theory. In a virtue ethics, we presumably *ought* to be virtuous, but does this use of "ought" entail an obligation? If not, how are we to establish what our moral *obligations* to others are? Are we to suppose that in an ethics of virtue there are no obligations, merely some nonobligatory "oughts" issuing from the virtues themselves? Or are there no demands at all, so that all moral standards are merely ideals? At the same time, there is no mention of moral *rights* in virtue ethics. If both rights and obligations are systematically excluded from a virtue theory, then that theory would certainly seem to reflect inadequately the moral point of view as we know it.

These issues suffer particular neglect in Aristotle's philosophy. In his ethics, the best and highest human life is declared to be the one that maximally invests in reason. In both his *Ethics* and his *Politics*, he often writes as if one really should pursue fine literature, music, and the arts; and above all, one should pursue theoretical reasoning for its own sake, particularly such studies as metaphysics and physics, which deal with fundamental questions about the nature of the universe. Is it not paradoxical for an ethics devoted to the moral virtues to promote these particular human capacities, since the whole point of the *Ethics* and the *Politics* is presumably to show how life should be organized in a civilized community so as to make us good and effective persons? Aristotle thus not only seems to leave questions of rights and obligations entirely aside, but seems additionally to treat them as if they were not even matters of importance by comparison with other goals in life. His list of the virtues and his account of morality in general have often been criticized because they seem more a "code of a gentleman in ancient Greece" than a comprehensive moral theory, and this eccentricity is perhaps the root of the problem in his apparent inability to express obligations and rights.

The defender of an ethics of principles of duty will argue that these criticisms reveal a fatal deficiency in virtue ethics. After all, the utilitarian and deontological systems studied in Chapters 3 and 4 do explicitly offer an account of character, moral worth, and virtuous conduct *in addition to* an account of obligations (and rights, as will be seen in Chapter 6). For example, the discussion of deontological theories (in Chapter 4) noted that for many deontologists, the moral value of actions is found in the motives or intentions of the actors, not merely in the outcome of the actions. Praise, blame, and other assessments of character are all understood in terms of whether a person intends to do what is demanded by a principle of duty. As David Hume noted, almost all systems of morals are agreed that "virtuous actions derive their merit only from virtuous motives" and that "the external performance has no merit."* If this interpretation of a morality of principles is correct, then it seems more comprehensive and complete than a virtue theory, and not deficient in its appreciation of any particular moral category such as the categories of obligations and rights.

The most straightforward way to defend a virtue ethics against this objection is simply to deny that virtue ethics needs to provide a theory of obligation and rights.

---

*David Hume, *A Treatise of Human Nature*, Bk. 3, part 2, sec. I.

From this perspective, it is fundamentally wrong to conceive the whole moral life in terms of categories of requirements and protections. We have *legal* obligations and rights that are statements of obligation, and it is perhaps an analogy to law that explains why Kant often chooses the term "law" rather than "principles" when discussing moral obligation. Laws compel, "bind our will," and leave us "without choices"; but, from the point of view of a virtue ethics, morality is starkly different, for morality turns on character and the free exercise of will.

The difference between law and morality, on this conception, is instanced in the difference between *laws* that regulate the conduct of professionals such as physicians, legislators, and business people, and the *codes of ethics* voluntarily adopted by groups of physicians, legislators, and businesspersons themselves. It should come as no surprise that the former are always assertions of what must be done, and of course have attached penalties if conduct strays from the dictated course. But codes of ethics (unless, of course, they specify formal procedures, requirements, and penalties) are commonly matters of what the virtuous person does, not of what such a person must do. Hence, the defender of virtue ethics may argue that it is the law, not morality, that properly provides an account of rights and that makes certain conduct obligatory; morality only delineates the morally just person and urges people to be virtuous.

A subtle and restrained form of this general defense of virtue ethics is found in the following selection from Joel Feinberg. He defends the view that there is much more to the moral life than an ethics of obligation and that what we *ought* to do often cannot be translated into a statement of our *obligations*.

JOEL FEINBERG

Obligation and Supererogation*

The fundamental error commited by [philosophers who emphasize obligations] is the uncritical acceptance of jural laws and institutional "house rules" as models for the understanding of all counsels of wisdom and all forms of human worth. Many institutions have rules which allow persons to accumulate extra points of credit by oversubscribing their assigned quotas of cash or work. Merely acknowledging the existence of saintly and heroic actions

which go beyond duty will not help if they are understood on the model of these institutional oversubscriptions. To so understand them is to commit the same sort of mistake as that committed by philosophers who take the prohibitory rules of jural law and other institutions as a model for understanding all so-called moral rules which contain the word "ought" and thus commit themselves to identifying all meritorious actions with the performance of "duties." . . .

First, consider how the word "ought" differs from the word "duty." Suppose a stranger approaches me on a street corner and politely asks me for a match. Ought I

*From Joel Feinberg, "Supererogation and Rules," *Ethics*, **71** (1961), as reprinted in Feinberg, *Doing and Deserving* (Princeton, N.J.: Princeton University Press, 1970), pp. 3–7, 16.

to give him one? I think most people would agree that I should, and that any reasonable man of good will would, offer the stranger a match. Perhaps a truly virtuous man would do more than that. He would be friendly, reply with a cheerful smile, and might even volunteer to light the stranger's cigarette.

Now suppose that Jones is on the street corner and another stranger politely requests a light from him. Jones is in a sour mood this morning, and even normally he does not enjoy encounters with strangers. He brusquely refuses to give the stranger a match. I think we can agree that Jones's behavior on the street corner does not constitute an ideal for human conduct under such circumstances; that it is not what a perfectly virtuous man would have done; that it was not what Jones ought to have done.

If we reproach Jones, however, for his uncivil treatment of the stranger, he may present us with a vigorous self-defense. "Perhaps I was not civil," he might admit, "but surely I was under no *obligation* to give a match to that man. Who is he to me? He had no *claim* on me; he has no authority to *command* any performance from me: I don't *owe* him anything. It may be nice to do favors for people; but a favor, by definition, is nothing that we are legally or morally *required* to do. I am an honorable man. In this instance I did not fail to honor a commitment; neither did I fail to discharge an obligation, moral or legal; nor did I break any rule, of man or God. You have, therefore, no right to reproach me."

Jones's defense makes me think no better of him. Still, from a certain legal-like point of view, it appears perfectly cogent. Everything Jones said in his own defense was true. The moral I draw from this tale is that there are some actions which it would be desirable for a person to do and which, indeed, he *ought* to do, even though they are actions he is under no *obligation* and

has no *duty* to do. It follows logically that to say that someone has a duty or an obligation to do X is not simply another way of saying that he ought to do X.

We speak of duties and obligations in three different connections. First, there are actions required by laws and by authoritative command. These can be called "duties of obedience." Second, there are the assigned tasks which "attach" to stations, offices, jobs, and roles, which for some reason seem better named by the word "duty" than by the word "obligation." Third, there are those actions to which we voluntarily commit ourselves by making promises, borrowing money, making appointments, and so on. When we commit ourselves, we put ourselves "under an obligation" ("duty" seems to fit less comfortably here) to some assignable person or persons to behave in the agreed-upon way; and we do this by utilizing certain social countrivances or techniques designed for just this purpose. When a person invokes these procedures, he creates his own "artificial chains," dons them, and hands the key to the other. This act "binds" or "ties" him to the agreed-upon behavior and gives the other the authority to require it of him. The other can, if he chooses, release him from his chains, or he can, in Mill's much quoted words, exact performance from him "as one exacts a debt."[1]

All duties and obligations, whether imposed by authoritative injunctions and prohibitions, acquired through accepting or inheriting an office, job, or role, or voluntarily incurred through promises and other contractual agreements, share the common character of being *required*; and this in turn, while it may involve more than coercion or pressure, rarely involves less. In the legal sense, to have a duty or an

---

[1] John Stuart Mill, *Utilitarianism* (Indianapolis: Bobbs-Merrill Company, 1948), p. 60.

obligation is to be subject to civil liability or criminal punishment for nonperformance. In general, the law requires citizens to discharge their legal duties *or else* face up to the unpleasant legal consequences. Similarly, it follows from the rules of non-jural institutions (house rules) that a member who does not pay his dues can be dropped; an employee who fails to perform the duties of his job is liable to be fired; a negligent bureaucrat is liable to demotion, a wayward student to flunking, a disobedient soldier to court-martial.

That liability for failure to perform is an esential part of what we mean by "duty," when we talk of the duties of stations and positions, is suggested by our willingness to substitute in many contexts the word "responsibility" for the word "duty". To be assigned a task or a job in some organization is to be made responsible (answerable, accountable) for its performance. Without this associated accountability, I submit, we should be unwilling to speak of "the job" as involving any *duties* at all. . . .

We have seen that the word "ought" can be used to prescribe or give advice in particular cases. Singular pieces of advice, such as "You ought to keep your promise in this case," are often generalized into such principles as "you ought to keep your promises (generally)," "You ought to be kind," and "You ought to do favors." There is no harm in calling statements of generalized advice "rules"; indeed, it is consonant with usage to do so. But it is important to notice that these rules do not enjoin, prohibit, or confer obligations and duties. They are rules in a quite different sense, better named "maxims" or "precepts" than "injunctions" or "commands." Perhaps "counsels of wisdom" or "rules of advice" would be the most appropriate designations, since these names suggest, quite correctly, that these are rules of thumb rather than "laws" on some jural or institutional model.

Counsels of wisdom guide the wise man's conduct and sometimes, also, that of the fool; for to have the right precepts without knowing how to apply them in puzzling circumstances or where they come into conflict is to be merely sententious, not wise. The better part of wisdom is a kind of knack or flair which cannot be bottled up in simple formulas. A man is on his own when he must decide whether to stick safely by his station or do the "meritorious, abnormally risky nonduty," or whether to honor his duty or an opposing commitment of a different order—whether to stay with Mother or join the Free French forces. There are, unfortunately, no strict superrules for applying counsels of wisdom in such situations and no simple commands to obey.

The Problem of Judging Right and Wrong Actions

We have noted that virtue ethics does not concentrate on the morality of actions any more than on obligations. But now we may ask, "How can a virtue theory determine the rightness or wrongness of actions?" Suppose that in performing an action, an actor exhibits one or more virtues. It clearly does not follow that the action is right, or even that the actor is acting virtuously. For example, a quite misguided action may exhibit the virtues of loyalty and devotion. Even if a person has a virtuous character, it is not inevitable that the person's actions will be right. For example, a virtuous person may not know what should be done, and so may err by failing to act at all. What basis is there in virtue ethics, we may ask, for analyzing the moral quality of an action except by judging the moral quality of the person? And yet, as Mill pointed out earlier in this chapter, this assessment alone seems clearly unsatisfactory.

Why are cheating, breaking a fair contract, and intentionally inflicting harm wrong? Is it because they are vices? Because they are deficient in virtue? Clearly, not every act that fails in light of virtue or vice is morally wrong. There are many occasions on which I do no wrong by, for example, my foolhardiness or my failure to be compassionate. In what, then, does moral wrongness consist, and how is it to be distinguished from rightness? Especially unsettling would be any claim that if persons display a virtuous character, then their acts are therefore morally acceptable, or at least not prohibited. As has been seen, it is all too easy to act out of character, and thereby to do a moral wrong. Even so noble a person as Jane Addams occasionally failed to fulfill a promise, but her nobility and integrity did not turn the wrong into a right. Moreover, it is not open to the defenders of virtue ethics to maintain that justice and injustice, for example, consist in what just and unjust persons do. We could not pick out their acts as just or unjust without some independent criterion of justice and injustice; but any such criterion seems likely to be either utilitarian or deontological.

How might the defender of virtue ethics respond to this second line of criticism? It may first of all be pointed out that neither Aristotle nor any other careful advocate of the position has divorced a virtue ethics from an account of the *object* or *purpose* of morality. In Aristotle's theory, a distinction is drawn between the means and the ends of morality. The end of morals and politics is to produce a situation of well-being *(eudaimonia)*; the promotion of virtuous conduct is the means to this end. The person of practical wisdom must know both what constitutes proper ends and how to achieve them. Because acts may be wrong even though they exhibit a virtue, the morally virtuous person is one who keeps in mind the true goals of morality, and critical judgments of the person's actions are possible by reference to the adequacy of these actions in pursuing the moral goals. In conjunction with what he calls the "Aristotelian principle," John Rawls has expressed this view in the following terms:

> The excellences are a condition of human flourishing; they are goods from everyone's point of view.
>   The virtues are [moral] excellences.... The lack of them will tend to undermine both our self-esteem and the esteem that our associates have for us.*

It is also extremely important in this context to distinguish between having a moral virtue and having a morally virtuous character. One can exhibit a single virtue,

*John Rawls, *A Theory of Justice* (Cambridge, Mass.: Harvard University Press, 1971), pp. 443, 445.

and indeed a single *moral* virtue, while performing unspeakably evil actions. History reveals thousands of misguided assistants whose loyalty to evil leaders was flawless. Thorough display of the virtue of loyalty does not, of course, make one a virtuous person, and one may even possess many moral virtues while at the same time being an evil person. In order to have a morally virtuous character, multiple moral virtues must be exhibited, and even then the virtues must not be overbalanced by an extensive number of moral vices. A person who is faithful, conscientious, truthful, and committed cannot have a morally virtuous character if at the same time he or she is slothful, uncharitable, immodest, and overbearing. Naturally, there are many, many people who possess some moral virtues, but do not possess a morally virtuous character.

CONCLUSION

Good.
Go
Over

In the three chapters constituting Part Two of this volume, three broad-ranging approaches to morality have been discussed: utilitarian theories, deontological theories, and virtue theories. It is not entirely clear that one must accept only one of these approaches while rejecting the others. It is possible to conceive each general theory as developed from a different conception of the moral life, a conception which only partially captures the diversity of that life. The discussion of Aristotle in this chapter, for example, noted how his theory emphasizes statesmanship and the education of citizens in the state. He conceives ethics in terms of the way to promote the best form of life that is possible in a community, and his ethics is patterned with this objective in mind. Kant, by contrast, sees morality as springing from reason and as issuing categorical demands to individuals. He often refers to his supreme principle as the "moral law," and thus he conceives ethics in terms of categorical demands of duty. Mill and Bentham, on the other hand, came to morality from concerns about social welfare and social reform. They see morality as providing a set of means (in the form of actions or rules) to the end of certain human goods that are intrinsically desirable. Accordingly, they conceive ethics in terms of an overarching framework of maximizing benefits and minimizing harms.

Each of these conceptions of the moral life arguably offers a worthy perspective from which to reflect on morality. There is no reason why we should not be able to extract much of value from each approach, while rejecting whatever is excessively emphasized by the limited conception of the moral life it offers. Even though moral philosophy may often seem a very different enterprise in the hands of Mill, Kant, and Aristotle—the one neglecting what the other takes to be of chief importance—we have noticed many common themes and even many shared conclusions among these writers. Whatever their differences of approach and content, there is reason to believe that each has treated some important problems well and has provided insights not found in the other writers.

SUGGESTED SUPPLEMENTARY READINGS

Aristotle's Works

Aristotle: *Eudemian Ethics*, in William D. Ross, ed., *The Works of Aristotle*, J. Solomon, trans. (Oxford, England: Clarendon Press, 1925).

———: *Magna Moralia*, in William D. Ross, ed., in *The Works of Aristotle,* St. George Stock, trans. (Oxford, England: Clarendon Press, 1925).

———: *Nichomachean Ethics*, in William D. Ross, ed. and trans., *The Works of Aristotle* (Oxford, England: Clarendon Press, 1925), especially Books I–V, X.

Commentaries on Aristotle

Ackrill, J. L.: *Aristotle's Ethics* (New York: Humanities Press, 1980).

Adkins, W. H.: *Merit and Responsibility in Greek Ethics* (Oxford, England: Clarendon Press, 1960).

Allan, D. J.: "Aristotle's Account of the Origin of Moral Principles," *Proceedings of the Eleventh International Congress of Philosophy*, **12** ( ): 120–127.

Aquinas, St. Thomas: *Commentary on Aristotle's Nichomachean Ethics*, C. I. Litzinger, trans., 2 vols. (Chicago: Henry Regnery Company, 1964).

Barnes, Jonathon, ed.: *Articles on Aristotle, Vol. 2: Ethics and Politics* (New York: St. Martin's Press, 1978).

Cooper, John M.: *Reason and the Human Good in Aristotle* (Cambridge, Mass.: Harvard University Press, 1975).

Fortenbaugh, W. W.: *Aristotle on Emotion* (New York: Barnes & Noble, Inc., 1975).

Hardie, W. F. R.: "The Final Good in Aristotle's Ethics," *Philosophy*, **40** (1965): 277–295.

———: *Aristotle's Ethical Theory* (Oxford, England: Clarendon Press, 1968).

———: "Aristotle on the Best Life for a Man," *Philosophy*, **54** (1979): 35–50.

Joachim, H. H.: *Aristotle: The Nicomachean Ethics* (Oxford, England: Clarendon Press, 1951).

Randall, John H.: *Aristotle* (New York: Columbia University Press, 1960), chap. 12.

Ross, William D: *Aristotle,* 5th ed. (London: Methuen & Co., Ltd., 1949; New York: Barnes and Noble, Inc., 1964), chap. 7.

Sullivan, Roger: "The Kantian Critique of Aristotle's Moral Philosophy," *Review of Metaphysics*, **28** (1974): 24–53.

Walsh, James J., and Henry L. Shapiro, eds.: *Aristotle's Ethics: Issues and Interpretations* (Belmont, Calif.: Wadsworth Publishing Company, Inc., 1967).

Williams, B. A. O.: "Aristotle on the Good," *Philosophical Quarterly*, **12** (1962): 289–296.

Virtue Ethics

Baier, Kurt: "Moral Value and Moral Worth," *The Monist*, **54** (1970): 18–30.

Becker, Lawrence C.: *On Justifying Moral Arguments* (New York: Humanities Press, 1973), chap. 19.

———: "The Neglect of Virtue," *Ethics*, **85** (1975): 110–122.

Brandt, Richard B.: "Blameworthiness and Obligation," in Abraham I. Melden, ed., *Essays in Moral Philosophy* (Seattle: University of Washington Press, 1958).

———: "Traits of Character: A Conceptual Analysis," *American Philosophical Quarterly*, **7** (1970): 23–37.

Foot, Philippa: *Virtues and Vices* (Oxford, England: Basil Blackwell, 1978), chap. 1.

Frankena, William K.: *Ethics*, 2d ed. (Englewood Cliffs, N.J.: Prentice-Hall, Inc., 1973), chap. 4.

———: "Prichard and the Ethics of Virtue," *The Monist*, **54** (1970): 1–17.

Geach, Peter: *The Virtues* (Cambridge, England: Cambridge University Press, 1977).

Horsburgh, H. J.: "Prudence," in *Proceedings of the Aristotelian Society*, Supp. Vol. **36** (1962): 65–76.

Hudson, W. D.: *Ethical Intuitionism* (New York: St. Martin's Press, 1967), chap. 8.

Hunt, Lester: "Generosity," *American Philosophical Quarterly*, **12** (1975): 235–244.

Mabbott, J. D.: "Prudence," in *Proceedings of the Aristotelian Society*, Supp. Vol. **36** (1962): 51–64.

MacIntyre, Alasdair: "How Virtues Become Vices: Values, Medicine, and Social Context," in H. T. Engelhardt, Jr., and S. F. Spicker, eds., *Evaluation and Explanation in the Biomedical Sciences* (Dordrecht, Holland: D. Reidel Publishing Company, 1975), pp. 97–111.

———: *After Virtue* (Notre Dame, Ind.: University of Notre Dame Press, 1981).

Mayo, Bernard: *Ethics and the Moral Life* (London: Macmillan & Co., Ltd., 1958).

Prichard, Harold A.: "Does Moral Philosophy Rest on a Mistake?" in *Moral Obligation* (Oxford, England: Clarendon Press, 1949).

Richards, Norvin: "Moral Symptoms," *Mind*, **89** (1980): 49–66.

von Wright, G. H.: *The Varieties of Goodness* (London: Humanities Press, 1963).

Wallace, James D.: "Excellences and Merit," *Philosophical Review*, **83** (1974): 182–199.

———: *Virtues and Vices* (Ithaca, N.Y.: Cornell University Press, 1978).

Warnock, G. J.: *The Object of Morality* (London: Methuen & Co., Ltd., 1971), chap. 6.

Saints, Heroes, and Moral Ideals

Feinberg, Joel: *Doing and Deserving* (Princeton, N.J.: Princeton University Press, 1970), especially chap. 1.

———, ed.: *Moral Concepts* (Oxford, England: Oxford University Press, 1969), Selections 5–7, 9, and 11.

PART THREE

Topics in Moral and Social Philosophy

CHAPTER SIX

Rights

In the late 1960s (1965–1968) a sensational case about both the invasion and the promotion of rights emerged. A sociologist, Laud Humphreys, came to believe that the public as well as legal authorities and police hold dangerous, stereotyped attitudes toward men who commit impersonal sexual acts in public restrooms. "Tearoom sex," as fellatio in public restrooms is called, is the source of most arrests for "homosexuality" in the United States. Humphreys, who sympathized with the alienation suffered by those men, decided that it was a matter of considerable social importance that they be more objectively understood. He therefore set out to study the motivation for such impersonal sexual gratification, as well as the social position of those involved. Humphreys tried to answer his questions through direct observation and follow-up interviews. He first stationed himself in the so-called tearooms and served as "watchqueen"—the individual who keeps watch and coughs when a police car or stranger approaches. In that role he observed hundreds of acts of fellatio. He gained the confidence of some of the men he observed, revealed his true intentions as a sociologist, and persuaded them to tell him about the rest of their lives and about their motives. He also secretly followed others, recording the license numbers of their cars. A year later, while carefully disguised, Humphreys appeared at their homes, claimed (falsely) to be a health service interviewer, and interviewed them about their personal affairs.

Humphreys's findings destroyed numerous stereotypes in the minds of many who read his work. Fifty-four percent of his subjects were married and living with their wives, and his findings indicate that they lived normal lives in typical communities. Thirty-eight percent turned out to be neither bisexual nor homosexual, but most had marriages marked by tension and by rare, or at least infrequent, sexual relations. (Only 14 percent of Humphreys's subjects corresponded to stereotypic views of homosexuality.) Perhaps because of their place in the community, then, the source of sex for his subjects had to be inexpensive and impersonal. Most were motivated by the desire for a form of orgasm less lonely than masturbation and less committal than a love relationship.

Only after the completion of his research did certain other members of Humphreys's sociology department learn that it had been undertaken. Matters became heated when some objected that Humphreys's research had unethically invaded his subjects' right of privacy and involved gross violations of the right not to be deceived. The president of Washington University, where Humphreys had taken his doctorate, was asked to rescind it. The turmoil over Humphreys's alleged violations of the right of his subjects resulted in a furious exchange, including a fist fight among faculty members, and the exodus of approximately half the department members to positions at other universities. There was considerable public controversy as well. Many complained that Humphreys's deception failed to respect the right to self-determination of his subjects, most of whom did not consent to be subjects. A journalist, Nicholas von Hoffman, sharply condemned Humphreys's work as a violation of the right to privacy, because it invaded "our most private and secret lives."

Neither Humphreys nor the group he had studied, however, saw any serious violation of rights, although it was admitted that a certain amount of deception was involved and that the private lives of the subjects had been the arena of social science research. He argued that the importance of his research easily outweighed any violation of rights that might have been involved. Two sociologists came to his defense by arguing that Humphreys had a right to pursue and to communicate knowledge through the research process. Humphreys's work has also been widely praised by groups supporting "gay rights," on grounds that this research helps set the record straight about the members of a group whose rights have too long been denied.

In 1970 Humphreys's pioneering work was awarded the prestigious C. Wright Mills Award for the Study of Social Problems.*

PHILOSOPHICAL PROBLEMS ABOUT RIGHTS

It is only recently that western society has emphasized the importance of human rights. Appeals to rights are now commonplace, as the controversy over Humphreys's research indicates, and when rights are violated, we often become appropriately indignant. Yet, until the seventeenth and eighteenth centuries, even problems of political ethics were rarely discussed in terms of rights, perhaps because duties to lord, king, state, church,

---

*Relevant sources include: L. Humphreys, *Tearoom Trade: Impersonal Sex in Public Places* (Chicago: Aldine Publishing Co., 1975); Nicholas von Hoffman, "The Sociological Snoopers," *The Washington Post,* B1, col. 1, and B9, col. 5 (Jan. 30, 1970) and I. L. Horowitz and Lee Rainwater, "Journalistic Moralizers," *Trans-Action,* 7 (1970), both reprinted in *Tearoom Trade,* op. cit.

and God had been the predominant focus of political and ethical theory. However, in the 1600s and early 1700s crucial new ideas were introduced, including the notion of universal "natural rights." Documents such as the American Bill of Rights (1776) and the French Declaration of the Rights of Man (1789) incorporated these natural rights, safeguarding them by law.

These rights consisted primarily of rights not to be interfered with, or liberty rights. Proclamations of such rights as those to life, liberty, property, safety, a speedy trial, and the pursuit of happiness subsequently formed the core of major political and legal documents. One such document, the Universal Declaration of Human Rights of the United Nations General Assembly, adopted in 1948, reflects an extension of these developments, for the aforementioned national political documents formed part of the intellectual basis of the declaration. The United Nations document contains an extensive list of rights, moving beyond rights merely to liberty to include rights to benefits and services—e.g., rights to housing, clothing, medical care, and food. These rights require that other individuals or the society provide whatever is necessary to fulfill them. However, as we shall see, these goals are often better labeled aspirations than rights.

The idea that certain moral rights exist prior to and independent of social conventions and laws has led philosophers to speculate about the nature and source of rights. They ask questions such as: Are there rights independent of laws and conventions, or are rights merely cultural fictions? If they exist, are they grounded purely in the obligations of others? Do moral rights exist prior to and independent of what governments recognize as rights? What are the limits on the scope of such rights? What does it mean to say that "X has a right to Y," and what criteria would have to be satisfied for such a proposition to be true?

Everyone would agree that legal rights exist, but the status of moral rights is more puzzling. Philosophers differ significantly in their accounts of the nature and grounding of such rights. Also, the language of moral rights is still greeted with considerable skepticism by some thinkers. This skepticism has emerged from theories of ethical relativism (treated in Chapter 2 of this book), from general doubts that human rights are "self-evident" and "inalienable," and from a widespread belief that rights can be reduced to obligations owed to individuals by others (as treated extensively in Chapters 3 through 5). Others find absurd the proliferation of and conflict among claims about rights in recent political debates. The five or six rights claimed by contending parties in the debate over Humphreys's research illustrate this problem, but some rights that have been proposed seem in even sharper conflict than those present in this case. For example, some parties have claimed that there is a right to have an abortion, and other parties have argued that there is a right to life that precludes a right to have an abortion. Language about rights has been extended to include controversial rights to privacy, rights to health care, the rights of children, the rights of animals, the rights of the elderly, and the rights of other special groups. In the Humphreys case, his defenders argued in favor of a right to pursue and communicate knowledge that was contested by his critics. Such controversy about doubtful rights has emerged in celebrated cases over "smokers' rights" and "the right to own a pet."

For all these reasons, there has been a persistent tendency to reject the notion that there are moral rights independent of legal or conventional rights. On the other hand, those who reject moral rights may want to have matters two ways. Virtually everyone reacts in vigorous opposition when the recognition of cherished legal rights is removed from legal documents, even if valid legal or political processes are employed in eliminating the rights. "Those rights are fundamental," it is often said; yet this complaint cannot mean "legally fundamental," since the rights are not legal rights once validly removed from the books. Such complaints, then, seem to presuppose independent, nonlegal rights. This unresolved issue of the standing of rights remains among the most significant controversies to be discussed in this chapter. ·

While most socially influential claims about rights have appeared in political documents, carefully drawn distinctions pertaining to the nature and types of moral rights have been developed only in ethical theory. In order to discover the appropriate moral basis for rights, it is essential that we first examine some of these distinctions.

Prima Facie and Absolute Rights

Prima facie *duties* were discussed in Chapter 4 on deontological theories. We noted that moral philosophers generally regard duties not as absolute but, rather, as strong moral demands that may be validly overridden by more stringent competing demands in circumstances of high stakes. Such competition presumably could come in the form of rights as well, and this possibility raises the issue of whether rights may be overridden by competing rights (or some other moral claims). It has often been assumed, owing perhaps to political statements about fundamental human rights, that rights are absolute. Yet there appear to be many counterexamples to the thesis that they are absolute: parents have rights to rear their children as they see fit *unless* they abuse them; corporations have a right to increase productivity *unless* they become monopolies, etc. Accordingly, we may ask whether rights of any type are absolute and incapable of being validly overridden.

Consider the right to life. Sometimes it is assumed that this right is absolute, irrespective of competing claims or social conditions. This thesis is doubtful, however, as evidenced by common moral judgments about capital punishment, international agreements about killing in war, and beliefs about the justifiability of killing in self-defense. Most writers in ethics agree that we have only a right not to have our lives taken *without sufficient justification.* While there is disagreement concerning the conditions that are sufficient for taking another's life, most agree that some conditions can be specified. The right to life, according to this view, is not absolute: the right can be legitimately exercised and can impose actual duties on others only when the right has an overriding status. Thus claims of rights seem to be prima facie or presumptively valid standing claims, but ones which may have to admit other claims as equally valid.

Two or more rights can come into significant conflict if they are equally valid. In this situation, only one right can be overriding unless some compromise is appropriate. For example, persons who are potentially dangerous to society by virtue of a mental condition may assert their right not to be institutionalized for treatment. They have committed no crime and so appear to have the same right to liberty possessed by all other citizens. At the same time, other citizens have a right to be protected against dangerous attacks. Whose rights are overriding? Most now agree that no particular right always has primacy when rights come into conflict, but sharp debate often occurs as to which right ought to take precedence in particular circumstances.

The controversy over Humphreys's research is a case in point. Everyone would agree that rights to privacy and self-determination are important, and many believe that researchers have a right to do research; but whether the rights of researchers to accumulate data can override their subjects' rights to autonomy and privacy when the knowledge to be gained is of great social significance is far less clear. Rights to such services as health care and shelter, the right to die, and the right to be saved from starvation similarly must compete with other rights in many situations, thus producing protracted controversy and a need to balance with great discretion the competing claims. Such conflicts also explain why one is not always justified in attempting to exercise one's rights. One is entitled to the exercise of rights only if one's claim is not outweighed by competing considerations.

Legal, Moral, and Conventional Rights

We are most familiar with legal rights and their enforcement by the state, but there are also several types of nonlegal rights. Let us now investigate the differences between the various forms of rights.

Whereas legal rights are supported by existing legal principles and rules, moral rights are supported by moral principles and rules. There are substantial differences between these two types of rights, for legal systems do not formally require reference to moral systems for their understanding, nor do moral systems formally require reference to legal systems. One may have a legal right to do something patently immoral, or have a moral right without any corresponding legal guarantee. Legal rights are derived from political constitutions, legislative enactments, case law, and the executive orders of the highest government official. Moral rights, by contrast, exist independently of, and form a basis for, criticizing or justifying legal rights. Finally, legal rights can be eliminated by lawful amendments to political constitutions (or by a coup d'état), but moral rights cannot be eroded or banished by political votes, powers, or amendments.

Other rights are neither moral nor legal. Official organizations and professional societies are two types of groups that offer declarations asserting rights for the special populations they represent. The rights of employees in this or that industry have been a persistent topic of discussion by representative agencies, for example. Similarly, social practices and arrangements that define roles and responsibilities often confer rights, as in the case of the lawyer-client relationship. Private clubs and fraternal organizations also have rules and principles that confer rights; and participation in rule-governed games, such as board games and organized sports, confer rights. These conventional rights contrast with moral rights in that they do not exist independently of the set of conventions or rules governing the enterprise. They differ from legal rights in that they are not recognized as rights within juridical law.

It is sometimes assumed that claims addressed to the state or to the public at large must have legal standing in order to be valid. While it is generally true that rights requiring enforcement by the state have a legal basis, there may be a moral dimension distinct from the legal dimension. This is particularly true of the rights of liberty or of noninterference. If one has a moral right to practice one's religion freely, for example, then (as with all rights of liberty) one has a valid claim addressable to the public not to be prevented from engaging in religious practices. At the same time, one may have a claim against the state to provide protection from interferences, and so a claim to the legal protection of one's rights. Whenever moral rights are protected by law, one has both a legal right and a moral right rooted in the same claim. Of course, not every moral or legal right *is* protected by the state. Legal rights can exist even when there is no mechanism for enforcement; and within both law and morality, rights can be conferred or recognized, yet not actively protected.

In sum, then, some rights are moral and not legal; some rights are legal and not moral; some rights are neither legal nor moral; and some rights are at once both legal and moral. If there exist moral rights held in common by everyone, it is morally imperative that these rights not be violated by the laws of a community. Any law that infringes a fundamental right would be at least prima facie unjust. Governments have not always taken this imperative seriously, of course, and this neglect has formed one major basis for recent outpourings of international complaints about various violations of human rights.

In the following article, Ronald Dworkin explores both the consequences that might occur if governments were to take rights seriously and the exact character of the claim that rights are prima facie. He argues that some rights are so basic that ordinary justifications for interference by the state—such as lessening inconvenience or promoting utility—are insufficient justifications for overriding such rights. The stakes must be far more significant to justify such an invasion, he argues, for basic rights outweigh our general justifications for interference.

RONALD DWORKIN

Taking Rights Seriously*

1. The Rights of Citizens

Some philosophers, of course, reject the idea that citizens have rights apart from what the law happens to give them. Bentham thought that the idea of moral rights was "nonsense on stilts." But that view has never been part of our orthodox political theory, and politicians of both parties appeal to the rights of the people to justify a great part of what they want to do. I shall not be concerned, in this essay, to defend the thesis that citizens have moral rights against their governments; I want instead to explore the implications of that thesis for those, including the present United States Government, who profess to accept it. . . .

2. Rights and the Right to Break the Law

There is a clear difference between saying that someone has a right to do something . . . and saying that it is the "right" thing for him to do, or that he does no "wrong" in doing it. Someone may have the right to do something that is the wrong thing for him to do, as might be the case with gambling. Conversely, something may be the right thing for him to do and yet he may have no right to do it, in the sense that it would not be wrong for someone to interfere with his trying. If our army captures an enemy soldier, we might say that the right thing for him to do is to try to escape, but it would not follow that it is wrong for us to try to stop him. . . .

These distinctions enable us to see an ambiguity in the orthodox question: Does a man ever have a right to break the law? Does that question mean to ask whether he ever has a right to break the law in the strong sense, so that the Government would do wrong to stop him, by arresting and prosecuting him? Or does it mean to ask whether he ever does the right thing to break the law, so that we should all respect him even though the Government should jail him?

If we take the orthodox position to be an answer to the first—and most important—question, then the paradoxes I described arise. But if we take it as an answer to the second, they do not. Conservatives and liberals do agree that sometimes a man does not do the wrong thing to break a law, when his conscience so requires. They disagree, when they do, over the different issue of what the State's response should be. Both parties do think that sometimes the State should prosecute. But this is not inconsistent with the proposition that the man prosecuted did the right thing in breaking the law. . . .

Constitutional rights that we call fundamental, like the right of free speech, are supposed to represent rights against the Government in the strong sense; that is the point of the boast that our legal system respects the fundamental rights of the citizen. If citizens have a moral right of free speech, then governments would do wrong to repeal the First Amendment that guarantees it, even if they were persuaded that the majority would be better off if speech were curtailed.

*From Ronald Dworkin, *Taking Rights Seriously* (Cambridge, Mass.: Harvard University Press, 1977), chap. 7.

I must not overstate the point. Someone who claims that citizens have a right against the Government need not go so far as to say that the State is *never* justified in overriding that right. He might say, for example, that although citizens have a right to free speech, the Government may override that right when necessary to protect the rights of others, or to prevent a catastrophe, or even to obtain a clear and major public benefit (though if he acknowledged this last as a possible justification he would be treating the right in question as not among the most important or fundamental). What he cannot do is to say that the Government is justified in overriding a right on the minimal grounds that would be sufficient if no such right existed. He cannot say that the Government is entitled to act on no more than a judgment that its act is likely to produce, overall, a benefit to the community. That admission would make his claim of a right pointless, and would show him to be using some sense of 'right' other than the strong sense necessary to give his claim the political importance it is normally taken to have. . . .

The prospect of utilitarian gains cannot justify preventing a man from doing what he has a right to do, and the supposed gains in respect for law are simply utilitarian gains. There would be no point in the boast that we respect individual rights unless that involved some sacrifice, and the sacrifice in question must be that we give up whatever marginal benefits our country would receive from overriding these rights when they prove inconvenient. So the general benefit cannot be a good ground for abridging rights, even when the benefit in question is a heightened respect for law. . . .

I said that a state may be justified in overriding or limiting rights on other grounds, and we must ask . . . whether any of these apply. The most important—and least well understood—of these other grounds invokes the notion of *competing rights* that would be jeopardized if the right in question were not limited. . . .

It is true that we speak of the "right" of society to do what it wants, but this cannot be a "competing right" of the sort that may justify the invasion of a right against the Government. The existence of rights against the Government would be jeopardized if the Government were able to defeat such a right by appealing to the right of a democratic majority to work its will. A right against the Government must be a right to do something even when the majority thinks it would be wrong to do it, and even when the majority would be worse off for having it done. If we now say that society has a right to do whatever is in the general benefit, or the right to preserve whatever sort of environment the majority wishes to live in, and we mean that these are the sort of rights that provide justification for overruling any rights against the Government that may conflict, then we have annihilated the latter rights.

In order to save them, we must recognize as competing rights only the rights of other members of the society as individuals. We must distinguish the "rights" of the majority as such, which cannot count as a justification for overruling individual rights, and the personal rights of members of a majority, which might well count. The test we must use is this. Someone has a competing right to protection, which must be weighed against an individual right to act, if that person would be entitled to demand that protection from his government on his own title, as an individual, without regard to whether a majority of his fellow citizens joined in the demand. . . .

A government, [one] may argue, may be justified in abridging the personal rights of its citizens in an emergency, or when a very great loss may be prevented, or perhaps, when some major benefit can clearly be secured. If the nation is at war, a policy of censorship may be justified even though it invades the right to say what one thinks on matters of political controversy. But the emergency must be genuine. There must be what Oliver Wendell Holmes described as a clear and present danger, and the danger must be one of magnitude. . . .

If we allow speculation to support the justification of emergency or decisive benefit, then, again, we have annihilated rights. We must, as Learned Hand said, discount the gravity of the evil threatened by the likelihood of reaching that evil. I know of no genuine evidence to the effect that tolerating some civil disobedience, out of respect for the moral position of its authors, will increase such disobedience, let alone crime in general. The case that it will must be based on vague assumptions about the contagion of ordinary crimes, assumptions that are themselves unproved, and that are in any event largely irrelevant. . . .

I must emphasize that all these propositions concern the strong sense of right, and they therefore leave open important questions about the right thing to do. If a man believes he has the right to break the law, he must then ask whether he does the right thing to exercise that right. He must remember that reasonable men can differ about whether he has a right against the Government, and therefore the right to break the law, that he thinks he has; and therefore that reasonable men can oppose him in good faith. He must take into account the various consequences his acts will have, whether they involve violence, and such other considerations as the context makes relevant; he must not go beyond the rights he can in good faith claim, to acts that violate the rights of others. . . .

3. Controversial Rights

If a man has a particular moral right against the Government, that right survives contrary legislation or adjudication. But this does not tell us what rights he has, and it is notorious that reasonable men disagree about that. . . .

The institution of rights against the Government is not a gift of God, or an ancient ritual, or a national sport. It is a complex and troublesome practice that makes the Government's job of securing the general benefit more difficult and more expensive, and it would be a frivolous and wrongful practice unless it served some point. Anyone who professes to take rights seriously, and who praises our Government for respecting them, must have some sense of what that point is. He must accept, at the minimum, one or both of two important ideas. The first is the vague but powerful idea of human dignity. This idea, associated with Kant, but defended by philosophers of different schools, supposes that there are ways of treating a man that are inconsistent with recognizing him as a full member of the human community, and holds that such treatment is profoundly unjust.

The second is the more familiar idea of political equality. This supposes that the weaker members of a political community are entitled to the same concern and respect of their government as the more powerful members have secured for themselves, so that if some men have freedom of decision whatever the effect on the general good, then all men must have the same freedom. I do not want to defend or elaborate these ideas here, but only to insist that anyone who claims that citizens have rights must accept ideas very close to these.

It makes sense to say that a man has a fundamental right against the Government, in the strong sense, like free speech, if that right is necessary to protect his dignity, or his standing as equally entitled to concern and respect, or some other personal value of like consequence. It does not make sense otherwise. . . .

4. Why Take Rights Seriously?

The bulk of the law—that part which defines and implements social, economic, and foreign policy—cannot be neutral. It must state, in its greatest part, the majority's view of the common good. The institution of rights is therefore crucial, because it represents the majority's promise to the minorities that their dignity and equality will be respected. When the divisions among the groups are most violent, then this gesture, if law is to work, must be most sincere.

The institution requires an act of faith on the part of the minorities, because the scope of their rights will be controversial whenever they are important, and because the officers of the majority will act on their own notions of what these rights really are. Of course these officials will disagree with many of the claims that a minority makes. That makes it all the more important that they take their decisions gravely. They must show that they understand what rights are, and they must not cheat on the full implications of the doctrine. The Government will not re-establish respect for law without giving the law some claim to respect. It cannot do that if it neglects the one feature that distinguishes law from ordered brutality. If the Government does not take rights seriously, then it does not take law seriously either.

Fundamental and Derivative Rights

It has been argued in the literature of ethics that some rights are derived from more general rights. For example, the general rights to privacy and to self-determination so prominently mentioned in the debate over Laud Humphreys's research have been paraded in both law and ethics as the basis for the right to die, the right to commit suicide, and the right to have an abortion. Similarly, some have argued that the right to food is derived from the more general right to be protected from starvation, which in turn is derivative from the right to life. Underlying such claims about "more general" rights is the conviction that there is a significant difference between a fundamental right and a derivative right.

There are at least two senses in which rights can be fundamental. First, they may be fundamental because other rights are derived from them, while they are not derived from any more basic rights. For example, it might be argued that the right to an adequate standard of living is fundamental because it is *not* derived from more general rights such as the right to life, while nonfundamental rights, such as that to have a nutritionally sound diet, are derived from this right to an adequate standard of living. Second, it might be argued that certain rights are fundamental because they are preconditions or necessary conditions of *all* other rights. Life, liberty, and equality (of treatment and opportunity) have some claim to status as fundamental in this sense; and the right to food may be as fundamental as rights to life and liberty. Samuel Gorovitz has argued that the right to food is fundamental in this second sense, because "no right has meaning or value once starvation strikes." Starvation is the "ultimate deprivation," he holds, because "without food life ends, and rights are of value only to the living."*

It could be plausibly argued that most rights ultimately derive from fundamental rights to life, liberty, and equality. For example, Gorovitz's cryptic saying, "without food life ends," is indicative that the right to life may be the basis of our concerns about the right to food. Whether there are fundamental rights at all and the ways to determine which rights are fundamental are matters currently under discussion. One popular but controversial view is that only natural or human rights are fundamental—a topic to which we shall return soon.

The Nature of Rights

Rights in moral philosophy and political theory have traditionally been understood not as mere ideals, but rather, as rationally demonstrable holdings to some good, service, or liberty. Rights are thus to be contrasted with holdings received through privileges, personal ideals, group ideals, and acts of charity. None of the latter holdings can rightfully be demanded as one's due, but the bearer of rights is in a position to make demands based on what is deserved or due. For example, rights to food stamps or to Medicare are, as rights, no different from rights to receive an insurance benefit when required premiums have been paid: anyone *eligible* under fixed rules and requirements of eligibility for a program may validly demand due services and goods provided by that program. Similarly, if students have a right to appeal a teacher's failing grade in a course, then they are authorized by established procedures to a review, and they are not dependent merely upon the good will and friendly cooperation of the teacher or others in the institutional setting.

The foundation of any right is located in a justifying reason that directly supports a claim. One has a right, for example, to a particular seat in a particular section of a stadium if one holds a legitimate ticket to that location. But only persons with a *valid* entitlement or claim have such a right. Two people may have long-standing family claims to a plot of ground, but if only one person has a valid deed, that person alone has a right to the property. The fact that one can argue convincingly that one ought to receive a good or service does not always establish a right; for even a strong supporting argument may not be sufficient. For example, even if good arguments favor publicly funded food programs or public housing during periods of famine or natural disaster, it does not follow that one has rights to food or housing merely because these arguments have merit.

*Samuel Gorovitz, "Bigotry, Loyalty, and Malnutrition," in Peter G. Brown and Henry Shue, eds., *Food Policy: The Responsibility of the United States in the Life and Death Choices* (New York: Free Press, 1977), pp. 131 ff.

Rights are sometimes analyzed in terms either of *powers* possessed by persons or of the *interests* of persons. These analyses have considerable appeal for analyzing some dimensions of rights. To have a right to information is to be empowered to receive the information. If there is no actual power behind a legitimate demand, however, it would seem that we have only hollow rhetoric about rights, and no real right at all. If, for example, there exist "gay rights," as mentioned in the dispute over Humphreys's research, then homosexuals surely must be authorized to take action against those who disregard those rights. Rights without powers thus seem suspect in certain ways. Nonetheless, an analysis of rights exclusively in terms of powers seems insufficient, for we can have rights in the complete absence of powers; innocent persons have a right not to be punished for crimes they did not commit, yet they may have no power to prevent the punishment. Rights, then, seem not to entail powers at all.

Analyses of rights in terms of interests meet a similar fate. Most rights protect fundamental interests, but rights do not always entail interests and interests do not always entail rights. A person guilty of a crime has an interest in being found not guilty, but no right to such a verdict; and many people have a right to apply for employment in positions less attractive than their present positions, yet have no interest in doing so. Hence, analyses of rights in terms of either interests or powers are clearly insufficient.

An important dispute has emerged in recent philosophy regarding whether rights should best be analyzed as *entitlements,* as *valid claims,* or as both. This dispute captures problems about the nature of rights more adequately than analyses in terms of powers and interests (though one should consider how great the gulf really is between an entitlement and a valid claim). H. J. McCloskey explains the idea of rights as entitlements as follows:

> . . . A right is an entitlement to do, to demand, to enjoy, to be, to have done for us. Rights may be rights to act, to exist, to enjoy, to demand. We speak of rights as being *possessed, exercised,* and *enjoyed.* In these respects there is an affinity between our talk about rights and our talk about capacities, powers, and the like, and a distinct contrast with talk about claims, for we *make* claims but do not possess, exercise, or enjoy them. . . .
>
> We speak of our rights as being *rights to*—as in the rights to life, liberty and happiness—not as *rights against,* as has so often mistakenly been claimed.*

McCloskey's entitlement analysis has been disputed by Joel Feinberg. In the following article, he maintains that the notion of a *valid claim* provides a better analysis of rights—though he does not argue that the language of entitlements is entirely inconsistent with his analysis.

*H. J. McCloskey, "Rights," *Philosophical Quarterly,* **15** (1965), p. 118.

JOEL FEINBERG

The Nature of Rights*

Many philosophical writers have simply identified rights with claims. The dictionaries tend to define "claims," in turn, as "assertions of right," a dizzying piece of circularity that led one philosopher to complain—"We go in search of rights and are directed to claims, and then back again to rights in bureaucratic futility."[1] What then is the relation between a claim and a right?

As we shall see, a right *is* a kind of claim, and a claim is "an assertion of right," so that a formal definition of either notion in terms of the other will not get us very far. Thus if a "formal definition" of the usual philosophical sort is what we are after, the game is over before it has begun, and we can say that the concept of a right is a "simple, undefinable, unanalysable primitive." Here as elsewhere in philosophy this will have the effect of making the commonplace seem unnecessarily mysterious. We would be better advised, I think, not to attempt a formal definition of either "right" or "claim," but rather to use the idea of a claim in informal elucidation of the idea of a right. This is made possible by the fact that *claiming* is an elaborate sort of rule-governed *activity.* . . .

Even if there are conceivable circumstances in which one would admit rights diffidently, there is no doubt that their characteristic use and that for which they are distinctively well suited, is to be claimed, demanded, affirmed, insisted upon. They

are especially sturdy objects to "stand upon," a most useful sort of moral furniture. Having rights, of course, makes claiming possible; but it is claiming that gives rights their special moral significance. This feature of rights is connected in a way with the customary rhetoric about what it is to be a human being. Having rights enables us to "stand up like men," to look others in the eye, and to feel in some fundamental way the equal of anyone. . . .

Nearly all writers maintain that there is some intimate connection between having a claim and having a right. Some identify right and claim without qualification; some define "right" as justified or justifiable claim, others as recognized claim, still others as valid claim. My own preference is for the latter definition. Some writers, however, reject the identification of rights with valid claims on the ground that all claims as such are valid, so that the expression "valid claim" is redundant. These writers, therefore, would identify rights with claims *simpliciter.* But this is a very simple confusion. All claims, to be sure, are *put forward* as justified whether they are justified in fact or not. A claim conceded even by its maker to have no validity is not a claim at all, but a mere demand. . . .

There is one final kind of attack on the generic identification of rights with claims, and it has been launched with great spirit in a recent article by H. J. McCloskey, who holds that rights are not essentially claims at all, but rather entitlements. The springboard of his argument is his insistence that rights in their essential character are always *rights to,* not *rights against.* . . .

The argument seems to be that since

*From Joel Feinberg, "The Nature and Value of Rights," *Journal of Value Inquiry,* **4** (1970), pp. 243–257.
[1]H. B. Acton, "Symposium on Rights," in *Proceedings of the Aristotelian Society,* Supp. Vol. **24** (1950), pp. 107–108.

rights are essentially rights *to,* whereas claims are essentially claims *against,* rights cannot be claims, though they can be grounds for claims. The argument is doubly defective, though. First of all, contrary to McCloskey, rights (at least legal claim-rights) *are* held *against* others. . . .

If a general rule gives me a right of non-interference in a certain respect against everybody, then there are literally hundreds of millions of people who have a duty toward me in that respect; and if the same general rule gives the same right to everyone else, then it imposes on me literally hundreds of millions of duties—or duties towards hundreds of millions of people. I see nothing paradoxical about this, however. The duties, after all, are negative; and I can discharge all of them at a stroke simply by minding my own business. And if all human beings make up one moral community and there are hundreds of millions of human beings, we should

expect there to be hundreds of millions of moral relations holding between them. . . .

All rights seem to merge *entitlements to* do, have, omit, or be something with *claims against* others to act or refrain from acting in certain ways. In some statements of rights the entitlement is perfectly determinate (e.g., *to* play tennis) and the claim vague (e.g., *against* "some vague group of potential or possible obstructors"); but in other cases the object of the claim is clear and determinate (e.g., *against* one's parents), and the entitlement general and indeterminate (e.g., to be given a proper upbringing). If we mean by "entitlement" that *to* which one has a right and by "claim" something directed at those *against* whom the right holds (as McCloskey apparently does), then we can say that all claim-rights necessarily involve both, though in individual cases the one element or the other may be in sharper focus.

Common to the theories expounded by McCloskey and Feinberg is the concept of rights as expressing morally valid demands on human conduct. Both see rights as basically like property which one holds and over which one has discretion. If a person possesses a right, others are validly constrained from interferences with the exercise of that right and from failures to provide that which the person is owed. If, for example, a person engaging in "tearoom sex" has a right to be let alone (the right to privacy) or a right to remain anonymous, then Humphreys is validly constrained from interferences in their lives (assuming that he has no right of equal significance, of course). Henceforth, the language of both "valid claims" and "entitlements" will be used in discussing rights, but both these notions can be understood in terms of discretionary holdings that express morally valid demands on the actions of others. We shall also adopt Feinberg's thesis that claiming (or having an entitlement) is a form of rule-governed activity, and that systems of rights exist through systems of rules. These may be legal rules, moral rules, institutional rules, rules of games, etc.; but all rights of the relevant sort exist or fail to exist because the relevant rules either allow or do not allow the appropriate claiming or conferral of entitlements. In the case of moral rules and moral rights, the rules are our recourse to distinguish between valid claims and asserted claims that turn out to be invalid, and so between claims that amount to rights and those that do not.

POSITIVE AND NEGATIVE RIGHTS

Rights are commonly divided into two types: negative and positive. This distinction is based on the difference between the right to be free to do or believe something (a "liberty right") and the right to receive a particular action, good, or service (a "benefit right") from others. A *negative* right is a right to be free to hold a belief, to pursue a course of action, or to enjoy a state of affairs without interference; a *positive* right is a right to obtain a good, opportunity, or service. The many rights brought to our attention by the case of Laud Humphreys's research are negative, for they are all liberty-based. Many claims to liberty rights, as controversial and contested as those involved in Humphreys's study, come to our attention almost daily. For example, in the summer of 1980 a discussion erupted in the United States about travel to Iran when former Attorney General Ramsey Clark flew to Tehran in violation of an Executive Order issued by President Jimmy Carter. Clark claimed that a "right to travel" is protected by the Fifth Amendment to the United States Constitution. President Carter claimed a "power" to "prohibit any transactions in foreign exchange."*

Negative rights have sometimes been explicated as involving only omissions or forbearance on the part of others, hence not requiring active intervention. Yet, many liberty rights normally classified as negative rights do at least suggest a need for active intervention. For example, to assert a right to health (not health *care*) is to claim more than mere freedom from interferences that might cause others to be unhealthy. It asserts that the state is obliged to enforce the rights of citizens by protecting them against dangerous chemicals, emissions, polluted waterways, the spread of diseases, etc. A claim that some rights are rights both to freedom *and* to protection is perhaps best understood, then, as a dual claim to a negative right to freedom and to a positive right to active protection by the state. In this way, such rights can be treated as complex, containing both negative rights and positive rights within their broad sweep.

The political documents mentioned earlier as landmarks in the history of rights have generally been construed as affirming negative rights, because these documents were intended to be primarily protective of liberty. Broad declarations of positive rights, by contrast, have emerged largely in the twentieth century. In the early 1900s, for example, attention was focused in Europe and the United States for the first time on national health insurance schemes that confer a right to health care. In particular, Britain's National Health Insurance Act, passed in 1911, was much discussed in these and subsequent years. European programs were at that time seriously studied for their innovative nature by the American government and even by the American Medical Association, which established its own Committee on Social Insurance in 1916.

Extensive contemporary concern about this and other positive rights to such goods as food, shelter, and employment can probably be traced most directly to the aforementioned 1948 Universal Declaration of Human Rights of the United Nations

---

*"Is There a Right to Travel?" *Newsweek* (June 23, 1980), p. 87.

General Assembly. This document specifically mentions, for example, a right to a standard of living adequate to provide for one's health and well-being. On the other hand, the United Nations document does not appear to declare *entitlements* or presently valid claims, and it introduces no mechanism to protect these rights. This omission has created confusion as to what broad statements of positive rights actually do claim for individuals. Its preamble gives the impression that this document is a blueprint for future actions and declarations of entitlements, rather than an assertion of rights that persons in their native countries actually possess. One reason the United Nations document is difficult to interpret lies in its origins in political rhetoric and compromise. It includes rights taken from classic western declarations of independence, as well as rights to various goods and services that were adapted from statements by socialist states regarding minimum standards of living. Nonetheless, this document is historically significant because of its influence, its oft-cited extensive list of goods and services, and its assertion of positive (cross-national) rights for individuals to goods such as food supplies from foreign nations of which the individual recipient is not a citizen.

The position that rights are guiding ideals, rather than existing entitlements, has been given explicit recognition in many documents subsequent to the United Nations declaration. It might even be argued that this use of the term "rights" is the prevailing *political* use. Thus, in the report of the Symposium on Population and Human Rights at the World Population Conference in Bucharest (1974), also sponsored by the United Nations, it was formally recorded by some participants that "the right to an adequate standard of living . . . would remain a *distant ideal* for many developing countries unless their economic growth was accelerated."* The word "right" is here most plausibly functioning to set forth a commendable or perhaps obligatory target, but not to point to a specific obligation on the part of the state to protect a right of its citizens.

The writings of many religious organizations interested in rights also fit this pattern, and statements of the United States Congress invite a similar interpretation. The 1976 "Right-to-Food Resolution" in the House of Representatives, for example, says that "every person in this country and throughout the world has the right to food—the right to a nutritionally adequate diet—and this right is henceforth to be recognized as a cornerstone of United States policy." There is, however, no indication that individuals *now* have valid claims to food; rather, it is said that United States policy should be directed towards "assisting . . . the world's poorest people."† Such statements invariably employ the language of "rights" as a basis for a resolution or a policy statement, without further analysis of what it means to be a right and without explicit assertion of entitlements.

---

*"Report of the Symposium on Population and Human Rights" of the World Population Conference, August 19–30, 1974 (New York: United Nations, 1974), pp. 16, 19. [Italics added.]

† *The Right-to-Food Resolution, Hearings before the Subcommittee on International Resources, Food, and Energy of the Committee on International Relations of the House of Representatives,* 94th Congress, 2d Sess., on H. Cong. Res. 393, June 22–29, 1976 (Washington: Government Printing Office, 1976), p. 2.

The distinction we are exploring between positive and negative rights has recently been employed in political contexts in order to develop a position on the *limits* of claims about rights. For example, it has been argued that:

> A "right" [in classical historical writings] defines a freedom of action. . . . The greatest perversion of the concept of rights occurred during the Presidency of Franklin Delano Roosevelt, when "right" was surreptitiously transferred from the freedom to pursue a value to the value itself: now all Americans had the right to a job, the right to a house, [etc.] . . . Modern politicians have [subsequently] reduced the [idea of rights] to utter absurdity.*

It clearly makes sense to relate a modern conception of positive rights to Roosevelt, whose administration linked traditional liberty rights that are negative to the idea of freedom from want, fear, etc. This idea of "freedom from" is easily translated into the doctrine that human rights cover whatever is necessary to a decent life. Yet, as the above quotation indicates, there are philosophical problems with such programs. The analysis of exclusively negative rights reflected in this quotation rests in part on a position defended by John Stuart Mill: The state may, and in some cases ought to, intervene to restrict the liberty of a person or group if, and only if, that person or group is producing harm to others. It follows that the state is permitted to, and in some cases ought to, limit the freedom of action only of those who cause harm to others. Insofar as society as a unit *ought* to limit the liberty of those who cause harm, those who deserve protection have a right to be protected. The scope of valid intervention by the state, however, does not *surpass* the interventions permitted by this principle. There is thus no obligation for the state to provide benefits in the form of goods and services: at most, there exists a right to be protected from risks or hazards that are the result of the individual or collective actions of others.

Whether this heavily restricted view of rights, or the more expansive view expressed by the United Nations, or some position in between is the most appropriate view remains a matter of current controversy. As we have seen, one's general theory of moral and social obligations is certain to play a critical role in determining the list of rights accepted as legitimate—a problem to be considered in the final section of this chapter.

THE CORRELATIVITY THESIS

Rights have held a prominent place in political documents because they are powerful assertions of legitimate claims on others. They also demand respect and status. When someone appeals to rights, a response is demanded and we must either accept the per-

*R. Sade, "Is Health Care a Right?" *Image,* **7** (1974).

son's claim as valid, discredit the claim by countervailing considerations, or acknowledge the right but show how it can be overridden by competing moral claims. We saw this form of dialectic at work in the case of Laud Humphreys's research, where disputing parties either made concerted attempts to deny the validity of the other party's claims or argued that rights such as those to privacy and self-determination override such rights as the freedom to pursue and communicate knowledge through research. Some distressed research subjects claimed that their rights had been seriously violated, while Humphreys's defenders argued that restrictions on the freedom to do research would violate the rights of investigators.

How precisely are we to understand the language of rights in such discourse, and in what respect is there a relationship between one person's rights and another's obligations? Let us begin by asking how we should analyze the meaning of the general expression "*X* has a right to do or have *Y*." A plausible beginning is to say that one's right entails that others have an obligation not to interfere or to provide something. Thus, if a state promises or otherwise incurs an obligation to provide such goods as food or therapeutic care to needy citizens, then citizens can claim an entitlement to food or therapy when they meet the relevant criteria of need. If Laud Humphreys's subjects have an applicable right to privacy, then investigators such as Humphreys have an obligation not to snoop. The right to die, the right to privacy, the right to a healthy environment, and all negative rights whatever may be treated in parallel fashion as entailing the obligation to abstain from interfering with another person's intended course in life.

If this general analysis is correct, there is little distinctive about rights as a moral category. The moral basis for their assertion rests in the obligations of others (though it is controversial whether rights are generated from obligations or obligations generated from rights). "*X* has a right to do or have *Y*" simply means that the moral system (or the legal system where appropriate) imposes an obligation on someone to act or to refrain from acting so that *X* is enabled to do or have *Y* (if *X* wishes *Y*). This analysis accords with the widely accepted idea that the language of rights is translatable into the language of obligations—that is, that rights and obligations are logically correlative: One person's right entails someone else's obligation to refrain from interfering or to provide some benefit, and all obligations similarly entail rights.* It is of course not always easy to track down the obligation entailed by an assertion of right or the right that corresponds to an obligation, and there may be more than one obligation corresponding to any given right. Corresponding obligations may even derive from several different sources or persons.

The correlativity thesis has been challenged on grounds that several classes of obligations do not entail rights, and that certain rights do not entail obligations. Rights accorded to heads of corporations to expand operations, for example, do not seem to

---

*A weaker version of the correlativity thesis holds that rights entail obligations, though not all obligations entail rights.

entail obligations on others, and one's duty to obey the law does not obviously entail a right for anyone. Also, duties of charity, duties to be kind to animals, duties of love, and duties of conscience do not seem to confer correlative rights. It is important to note that such duties function more as services one requires of oneself than as universal moral requirements. This observation indicates that the words "duty" and "obligation" have come to refer to *any required action,* whether the requirement derives from a right, a matter of conscience, a supererogatory ideal, or some other source.

This problem has been treated in moral philosophy by distinguishing two classes of duties: duties of perfect obligation and duties of imperfect obligation. As John Stuart Mill describes them, duties of imperfect obligation are those obligatory acts left to our choice, as in the case of charity. We are bound to be charitable, says Mill, but not toward any particular person or at any particular time; rather, the persons and times are left to our discretion. By contrast, duties of perfect obligation entail a correlative right that some other person or persons possess. Mill argues that duties of perfect obligation are duties of justice that entail rights, while duties of imperfect obligation are rooted in other, less demanding moral principles than justice (such as beneficence), on the basis of which no one can claim a corresponding right. If this view is acceptable, then only duties of perfect obligation are correlative to rights, and the main problem for a theory of rights is how to specify which moral demands are based on perfect obligations and which on imperfect obligations. This task has proved a most difficult one, for, in a surprisingly large number of cases, it cannot be determined whether an obligation is perfect or imperfect.

Following Mill's general line of thought, it is possible to distinguish two senses of the word "required": (1) required by a universal moral duty and (2) required by some stricture one imposes on oneself, such as a rule of conscience or a commitment to charity. Many points in recent debates about rights turn on whether sense 1 or sense 2 is under consideration as the basis of the obligation. This matter, as well as a number of important issues in the analysis of the correlativity thesis, is taken up in the following essay by Joel Feinberg.

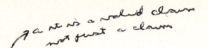

JOEL FEINBERG

The Correlativity of Rights and Duties*

[Let us] consider the so-called "doctrine of the logical correlativity of rights and duties." This is the doctrine that *(i)* all duties entail other people's rights and *(ii)* all rights entail other people's duties. Only the first part of the doctrine, the alleged entailment from duties to rights, need concern us here. Is this part of the doctrine correct? It should not be surprising that my answer is: "In a sense yes and in a sense no." Etymologically, the word "duty" is associated with actions that are *due* someone else, the payments of debts *to* creditors, the keeping of agreements with promises, the payment of club dues, or legal fees, or tariff levies to appropriate authorities or their representatives. In this original sense of "duty," all duties are correlated with the rights of those *to* whom the duty is owed. On the other hand, there seem to be numerous classes of duties, both of a legal and non-legal kind, that are *not* logically correlated with the rights of other persons. This seems to be a consequence of the fact that the word "duty" has come to be used for *any* action understood to be *required,* whether by the rights of others, or by law, or by higher authority, or by conscience, or whatever. When the notion of requirement is in clear focus it is likely to seem the only element in the idea of duty that is essential, and the other component notion—that a duty is something *due* someone else—drops off. Thus, in this widespread but derivative usage, "duty" tends to be used for any action we feel we *must* (for whatever reason) do. It

*From Joel Feinberg, "The Nature and Value of Rights," *Journal of Value Inquiry,* **4** (1970), pp. 243–257.

comes, in short, to be a term of moral modality merely; and it is no wonder that the first thesis of the logical correlativity doctrine often fails. . . .

A legal duty is not something we are implored or advised to do merely; it is something the law, or an authority under the law, *requires* us to do whether we want to or not, under pain of penalty. When traffic lights turn red, however, there is no determinate person who can plausibly be said to claim our stopping as his due, so that the motorist owes it to *him* to stop, in the way a debtor owes it to his creditor to pay. . . .

When we leave legal contexts to consider moral obligations and other extra-legal duties, a greater variety of duties-without-correlative-rights present themselves. Duties of charity, for example, require us to contribute to one or another of a large number of eligible recipients, no one of whom can claim our contribution from us as his due. Charitable contributions are more like gratuitous services, favors, and gifts than like repayments of debts or reparations; and yet we do have duties to be charitable. Many persons, moreover, in our actual world believe that they are required by their own consciences to do more than that "duty" that *can* be demanded of them by their prospective beneficiaries. I have quoted elsewhere the citation from H. B. Acton of a character in a Malraux novel who "gave all his supply of poison to his fellow prisoners to enable them by suicide to escape the burning alive which was to be their fate and his." This man, Acton adds, "probably did not think that [the others] had more of a right to the poison than he had, though he thought it his duty to give it to them." I am sure that there are many actual examples, less dramatically heroic than this fictitious one, of persons who believe, rightly or wrongly, that they *must* *do* something (hence the word "duty") for another person in excess of what that person can appropriately demand of him (hence the absence of "right").

Feinberg's arguments pertain exclusively to the problem of duties that seem to have no corresponding rights. It is at least as difficult to handle the problem of rights that seem to have no correlative duties. Positive rights to important goods and services provide the most obvious problem. Such goods as adequate housing, clothing, food, health care, education, and a clean environment populate the United Nations list of "human rights," yet does anyone have a corresponding duty? Rights as ideals, as discussed earlier, provide good examples of the use of the language of rights where there is no corresponding duty. Further, in a situation of scarce resources, where inadequate goods and services exist, it may be impossible to provide the goods and services. Some have suggested that although individuals in desperate need of food, housing, etc., have a valid claim, and so a right, the right often cannot be *exercised* simply because no one actually has a duty to provide the needed goods and services. On this analysis, if conditions of scarcity were to disappear, those with rights would become claimants because others would then have duties to supply them with the needed goods and services.

Some have thought, however, that this analysis fails. They have argued that in contexts where there are no duties, the term "rights" has no application because rights exist only if an obligation exists. Thus, the language of rights as ideals is regarded as misleading or mistaken, and in a famine, where food *cannot* be supplied, no one has a right to be supplied with food or even a right to be saved from starvation or a right to life. People may later come to have a right, but they have none where there is no possibility of fulfilling it. To accept this approach is to take the point of view that there are no rights without obligations.

Despite the problems that have been encountered with the correlativity thesis, many contemporary philosophers have defended it, usually with arguments paralleling Mill's. They have distinguished perfect from imperfect obligations and have argued that all perfect obligations entail rights, even if imperfect obligations do not. This approach has practical as well as theoretical significance. As we noted at the beginning of this section, a claim to a right obliges others either to accept the claim as valid or to discredit it by countervailing considerations. Whenever a person has a moral obligation to another, the person owed a performance is justified in demanding that the other fulfill the obligation, and a failure of performance may be justifiably criticized. Of course, when one person holds a certain right against another, the first is entitled but not required to press the claim against the second. The first can release the second, if he or she so wishes, for the claimant of a right is entitled to handle the claim as seems appropriate. In cases of *legal* rights, for example, one commonly has the option of suing for failure to discharge an obligation. Rights grounded in obligations thus play an enormously important role in our expectations and treatment of others, as well as in our demands for the protection of our rights.

NATURAL OR HUMAN RIGHTS

The expression "human rights" is a recent label for what has traditionally been referred to as "natural rights" or, in an older vernacular, the "rights of man." Such rights are often touted as inalienable and possessed equally by all persons, but there has been considerable confusion as to what such claims assert as well as to which rights qualify as "natural." The seventeenth-century philosopher John Locke maintained that the rights to life, liberty, and property are natural rights, while the United States Declaration of Independence holds that the rights to life, liberty, and the pursuit of happiness form the core of natural rights. The United Nations Declaration of Human Rights, as we have seen, interprets rights through a list of numerous basic needs required for a decent standard of living.

Human rights are supposedly those rights one possesses simply by being a person. This notion has been explained in different ways in different moral theories—perhaps the best known being the Kantian theory discussed in Chapter 4—but the question of how this idea is best explicated remains unresolved. One elementary point is that the concept of natural or human rights is rooted in a concept of natural or moral law that is to be sharply distinguished from constitutional law or other conventional social rules. Natural rights are thus said to be possessed by persons whether or not the rights are legally recognized in a society. Many rights prominently mentioned on lists of natural rights are, in fact, not universally recognized in law. These rights include protection against torture and assault, rights of due process, rights to free speech, and various rights to minimum subsistence conditions such as food, clothing, housing, medical care, and education.

Natural Rights Based on Natural Law

The doctrine of natural rights has a long history, the oldest tradition stretching back at least to ancient Greek and Stoic beliefs in natural law, an ideal or standard fixed by nature, binding on all persons, and taking precedence over the particular laws and standards created by human social conventions. In Greek philosophy, natural right or law was contrasted with conventional right or law. Philosophers such as Plato opposed any conventionalism that made human arrangements the measure and final source of authority in political and legal matters. Nature or the natural order was thought to contain normative standards, and Plato reasoned that it was quite possible for laws adopted by city-states to be unjust, or at least not perfectly just. If unjust laws prevail, as Plato apparently believed was the case in Athens, then the philosopher and lawmaker should seek a final normative standard of justice as found in nature.

This theory of natural law was refined and developed by philosophers during the Middle Ages. Thomas Aquinas identified natural laws with God-given rules that could be discovered by rational beings; he held that

> it is clear that the whole community of the universe is governed by divine reason. This rational guidance of created things on the part of God . . . we can call the Eternal Law. . . . But of all others, rational creatures are subject to the divine Providence in a special way . . . in that they control their own actions and the actions of others. . . . This participation in the Eternal Law by rational creatures is called the Natural Law.*

This theory of natural law allegedly provides divine standards against which the laws and policies of particular states are to be measured. These standards also constitute the foundation of rights and moral obligation.

Natural Rights Based on Human Nature

Aristotle, Aquinas, and other natural-law philosophers have also been responsible for a second tradition of natural rights, according to which human beings have a fixed nature or essence that is knowable by reason and that determines fundamental obligations and rights. This theory is based on a distinction between laws of nature and natural laws. Presumably, the former are descriptive statements derived from scientific knowledge of universal regularities in nature, while the latter are prescriptive statements derived from philosophical knowledge of the essential properties of human nature. In this theory, natural laws do not empirically describe behavior but, rather, limit or delineate the behavior which is morally appropriate for a human being. Activities proper to a human differ from what is to be expected from other creatures insofar as their "natures" differ; and their natures differ because they possess different essences with different potentialities. Natural laws stipulate which natural potentialities ought to be actualized, and these stipulations become moral action-guides. For example, suicide is said to be wrong because it violates a natural inclination to live, and from this perspective to commit suicide is to act against the laws of nature.

Many philosophers are skeptical of the validity of natural-rights theories as expressed in both traditions. Their criticisms have largely been epistemological. They have wondered how we can know the natural law so as to justify claims about rights and obligations. Unlike laws employed in scientific theories, these natural laws of "right reason" cannot be confirmed or falsified by any mode of factual reasoning. Nor do the rights often mentioned seem self-evident (not to mention the problem of the justification

*Thomas Aquinas, *Summa Theologica,* 1ae, 2ae, question 91, articles 1 and 2.

of claims to self-evidence). The idea behind natural-law theories is to provide an external and objective standard, yet the theory itself seems purely subjective to some critics. Questions have been raised as to whether there even is a fixed human nature. Some existentialists have argued that human beings have only a history, not a nature; and a number of prominent theories in psychology reach a similar conclusion. But, even if there is a fixed human nature, it would remain to be shown that one can draw *moral* conclusions from a theory of human *nature*. (This problem introduces the issue of the relationship between facts and values—a problem that will be encountered in Chapter 10.)

For these reasons among others, theories of natural rights have long perplexed philosophers. In the following treatment of the subject, Margarget Macdonald explains traditional reasons behind the acceptance of natural rights and her objections to them. She also proposes a way of interpreting the motives behind the arguments for natural rights that may make the theory more acceptable than many have found it in its classical forms.

MARGARET MACDONALD

Natural Rights*

The claim to "natural rights" has never been quite defeated. It tends in some form to be renewed in every crisis in human affairs, when the plain citizen tries to make, or expects his leaders to make, articulate his obscure, but firmly held, conviction that he is not a mere pawn in any political game, nor the property of any government or ruler, but the living and protesting individual for whose sake all political games are played and all governments instituted. . . .

Why should people have supposed, and, as I believe, continue to suppose, in obscure fashion, that they have "natural" rights, or rights as human beings, independently of the laws and governments of any

*From Margaret Macdonald, in *Proceedings of the Aristotelian Society*, **47** (1946–1947).

existing society? It is, surely, partly at least, because no existing social compulsion or relationship is self-justifying. Men may always ask why they should or should not endure it and expect a convincing answer. And, ultimately, it would seem, they may challenge the dictates of all existing governments and the pressures of every society if they find them equally oppressive, i.e., if they deny what the individual considers his fundamental "right." But since, *ex hypothesi*, this "right" is denied by every existing law and authority, it must be a right possessed independently of them and derived from another source. If, e.g., the laws of every existing society condemn a human being to be a slave, he, or another on his behalf, may yet hold that he has a "right" to be free. What sort of proposition is this and how is such a claim to be justified? . . .

Natural Law, Natural Laws, and Natural Rights

The answer lies in the peculiar status given to reason in the theory. Propositions about natural law and natural rights are not generalizations from experience nor deductions from observed facts subsequently confirmed by experience. Yet they are not totally disconnected from natural fact. For they are known as entailed by the intrinsic or essential nature of man. Thus they are known by reason. But they are entailed by the proposition that an essential property of men is that they have reason. The standard of natural law is set by reason and is known because men have reason. But that men have reason, i.e., are able to deduce the ideal from the actual, is a natural fact. And it is by having this specific, and natural, characteristic of being rational that men resemble each other and differ from the brutes. Reason is the great leveller or elevator. . . .

A person is accidentally a native of England, France, America; a Red Indian, negro or Jew. His social environment is determined by accident of birth. He may change his family by adoption and his citizenship by naturalization. And he is accidentally, or conventionally, a doctor, soldier, employer, etc. These conventionalities determine his civic and legal rights in a particular society. But he is not accidentally human. Humanity is his essence or nature. There is no essence of "being Greek" or "being English"; of "being a creditor" or "being an old age pensioner," all of which properties, however, might be the basis of civil rights. The nature of man determines his "natural" rights. And since, though not accidental, it also seemed to be a matter of fact that men exist and are rational, rights claimed on account of this fact seemed also to be natural and to follow from the essence of man, even though they might be denied. . . .

The Aristotelian dream of fixed natures pursuing common ends dies hard. It reappears in M. Maritain's account of the Rights of Man. . . .

> . . . there is a human nature and this human nature is the same in all men . . . and possessed of a nature, constituted in a given determinate fashion, man obviously possesses ends which correspond to his natural constitution and which are the same for all—as all pianos, for instance, whatever their particular type and in whatever spot they may be, have as their end the production of certain attuned sounds. If they do not produce these sounds, they must be attuned or discarded as worthless . . . since man has intelligence and can determine his ends, it is up to him to put himself in tune with the ends necessarily demanded by his nature.[1]

And men's rights depend upon this common nature and end by which they are subject to the natural or "unwritten" law. But this seems to me a complete mistake. Human beings are not like exactly similar bottles of whiskey each marked "for export only" or some device indicating a common destination or end. Men do not share a fixed nature, nor, therefore, are there any ends which they must necessarily pursue in fulfillment of such nature. There is no definition of "man." There is a more or less vague set of properties which characterize in varying degrees and proportions those creatures which are called "human." These determine for each individual human being what he *can* do but not what he *must* do. . . . Men are not created for a purpose as a piano is built to produce

[1]Jacques Maritain, *The Rights of Man and Natural Law*, p. 35.

certain sounds. Or if they are we have no idea of the purpose.

It is the emphasis on the individual sufferer from bad social conditions which constitutes the appeal of the social contract theory and the "natural" origin of human rights. But it does not follow that the theory is true as a statement of verifiable fact about the actual constitution of the world. The statements of the Law of Nature are not statements of the laws of nature, not even of the laws of "ideal" nature. For nature provides no standards or ideals. All that exists, exists at the same level, or is of the same logical type. There are not, by nature, prize roses, works of art, oppressed or unoppressed citizens. Standards are determined by human choice, not set by nature independently of men. . . .

One of the major criticisms of the doctrine of natural rights is that the list of natural rights varies with each exponent. For Hobbes, man's only natural right is self-preservation. More "liberal" theorists add to life and security: liberty, the pursuit of happiness and sometimes property. Modern socialists would probably include the right to "work or adequate maintenance." M. Maritain enumerates a list of nine natural rights which include besides the rights to life, liberty, and property of the older formulations, the right to pursue a religious vocation, the right to marry and raise a family, and, finally, the right of every human being to be treated as a person and not as a thing.[2] It is evident that these

"rights" are of very different types which would need to be distinguished in a complete discussion of the problem. My aim in this paper, however, is only to try to understand what can be meant by the assertion that there are some rights to which human beings are entitled independently of their varying social relationships. And it seems difficult to account for the wide variations in the lists of these "rights" if they have all been deduced from a fixed human nature or essence, subject to an absolutely uniform "natural law". . . .

The common thread among the variety of natural rights is their *political* character. Despite their rugged individualism, no exponent of the Rights of man desired to enjoy them, in solitude, on a desert island. They were among the articles of the original Social Contract; clauses in Constitutions, the inspiration of social and governmental reforms. But "Keep promises"; "Tell the truth"; "Be grateful" are not inscribed on banners carried by aggrieved demonstrators or circulated among the members of an oppressed party. Whether or not morality can exist without society, it is certain that politics cannot. Why then were "natural rights" conceived to exist independently of organized society and hence of political controversies? I suggest that they were so considered in order to emphasize their basic or fundamental character. For words like freedom, equality, security, represented for the defenders of natural rights what they considered to be the fundamental moral and social values which should be or should continue to be realized in any society fit for intelligent and responsible citizens.

[2]Loc. cit., p. 60.

THE GROUNDING OF RIGHTS IN MORAL THEORY

Our discussion of rights thus far suggests that they are grounded in obligations. If so, a theory of rights requires a theory of obligations for its justification. The issue of whether there are rights to food, shelter, privacy, property, or whatever would thus turn on whether there are certain moral obligations to provide these benefits or to ensure these liberties. The basis of the required obligations—if there are such obligations— could be justice, social utility, contractual agreement, or any of the ethical principles and theories studied in Chapters 3 through 5 of this book. While many different answers to this issue of the proper grounding of rights in moral theory have been offered, most answers have centered on the two principles previously mentioned while discussing perfect and imperfect obligations: The "principle of beneficence" and the "principle of justice." Let us look briefly at each.

Beneficence

The term "beneficence" has a broad usage in English, including among its meanings the doing of good, the active promotion of good, kindness, and charity. But in the present context, beneficence must be understood more restrictively as a directive to help others further their important and legitimate interests when we can do so with only minimal risk or inconvenience to ourselves. This duty includes providing benefits, preventing and removing harms, and balancing the benefits it is possible to produce against the possible harms that might result from their production. In the case of Humphreys's "tearoom" research, for example, this principle demands that the harms that might have been produced to his subjects by recording their license plates be balanced against the potential benefits that might result from the information he set out to acquire.

Firmly established in the history of ethics, in the practices of international relations, and in the formulation of public policy in most countries is the conviction that the failure to increase the good of others when one is knowingly in a position to do so is morally wrong. Preventive medicine and active public health interventions are illustrative of this conviction. Once methods of treating yellow fever and smallpox were discovered in early modern medicine, for example, it was universally agreed that governments ought to take positive steps to establish programs protective of public health. Many welfare programs presumably have a similar moral justification. The existence of both health and welfare programs is one reason why there is now so much discussion of the right to health care and various forms of welfare.

Still, there are problems with broad moral appeals to beneficence, some of which were implicitly encountered in discussing utilitarianism (in Chapter 3). Because beneficent behavior potentially demands extreme generosity in the moral life, some philosophers have argued that acting beneficently is commonly *virtuous,* but not a *duty;* or, as some prefer to say, beneficence asserts an imperfect, rather than a perfect, obligation. Those taking roughly this view treat many beneficent actions as approximating acts of charity, acts of conscience, and acts done from moral ideals (discussed in Chapter 5, on virtue ethics, and in Chapter 3, on utilitarianism and supererogatory moral ideals). They have therefore denied that *rights* can be based on beneficence. From this perspective, the positive benefiting of others by providing health and welfare services, for example, is based on personal ideals beyond the call of duty, and thus is supererogatory rather than obligatory. Following this argument, it was not morally obligatory to produce the valuable benefits deriving from Humphreys's research; the goal was quite optional, and thus we are not always morally required to benefit persons even if we are in a position to do so, and others have no rights to such beneficent actions. For example, we are not morally required to perform all possible acts of charity, even for people who are starving. In what respects and within what limits, then, is beneficence a duty (if it is)? And how does it apply to such problems as the distribution of food and allocation of health care?

Public support of medical, educational, and agricultural research and development has often been taken as indicative that some beneficent actions are demanded by social duties. This research is undertaken to benefit members of society in highly significant ways, including future generations; and the benefits produced are generally cited as the primary justification of all publicly funded research. Many similar examples of actions justified through the principle of beneficence could be cited. Still, it is one thing to maintain that actions or programs are morally *justified* and quite another to maintain that they are morally *required*. Even if Humphreys's research is justified, it is highly doubtful that it is required by the rules of morality. Thus, it remains to be demonstrated which, if any, beneficent actions are demanded by duties. This demonstration is of great importance because of the correlativity thesis. If rights can be derived only from duty-based premises, and beneficence is not a duty, no rights will flow from beneficence. Unfortunately, whether and how it can be shown that beneficence generates duties is a matter of ongoing controversy.

Justice

In light of the difficulties just discussed, some philosophers have sought to ground rights in a theory of distributive justice. Thinkers of this persuasion have held that principles of justice have a moral priority over other moral principles, as well as a priority over rights. For this reason, it has been common in recent moral theory to argue that controversial issues about the nature and types of rights can be grounded only within the broad framework of a theory of distributive justice, and that without such a theory to back up moral demands to rights, such assertions remain merely demands, not valid claims. Because Chapter 7 is devoted to the topic of justice, it would be redundant to treat all the issues about justice in detail in the present context. However, it may prove helpful at this point to see how certain issues of justice are related to discussions of rights.

The main idea behind the strategy of an appeal to distributive justice is to determine who deserves what, from which it presumably follows what persons have a right to. If distributive justice demands a reallocation of certain jobs to members of minority groups, for example, then some individuals in those groups can claim a right to the available positions. Just as rights are conceived as constraints on the way governments and individuals can act—as Dworkin argued in his essay—so the dictates of distributive justice can be seen as a constraint on government and a limitation on the actions of others.

The matters of central interest are whether positive rights to resources that the state or others would have to supply can be grounded in some account of distributive justice. Can the right to food, for example, be grounded in such an account, and does this "right" weaken for some persons when the use of resources to make it available would endanger, reduce, or extinguish the supply of goods and services to which other individuals can rightly make a claim (by virtue of some presumably equally justified allocational commitments)? It is hard enough to resolve such questions through moral theory when they are confined to the obligations of nation-states to their own citizens. It is still more difficult when questions of international justice come into play. Yet rights such as the right to food and others mentioned in the United Nations declaration must often be exercised at the international level, not just domestically within nation-states. Thus the moral justification of such rights seems in the end to require a theory of justice capable of transcending national concerns and boundaries.

There are, however, problems with this theory that parallel problems with the principle of beneficence. One might question whether principles of justice take priority over other moral principles, as this theory seems to assume; and whatever one's theory of distributive justice, there are many occasions on which abstract principles of justice will not in any decisive fashion determine appropriate allocations. Such occasions usually involve conflicting moral demands where no single moral principle is determinative. In such cases, a moral decision concerning the weight of competing moral claims is required, and this decision in turn establishes rights rather than being established by them. Moreover, many rights—especially negative rights—almost certainly cannot be justified by appeal to justice. The right to privacy and the right to self-determination mentioned in Humphreys's case, for example, seem at best only distantly related to justice. That a theory of justice can fully account for these decisions about rights is thus in doubt, a problem to which we shall return in Chapter 7.

CRITICISMS OF RIGHTS THEORIES

A number of criticisms of theories regarding rights have been encountered throughout this chapter. In conclusion, let us investigate two general and important criticisms, together with responses that exponents of these theories might wish to make.

Rights as Nonprimitive

One important criticism involves the correlativity thesis, the moral justification of rights, and the concept of fundamental rights. According to certain critics, rights themselves are not fundamental or primitive *in ethical theory* (even if some rights are fundamental relative to other rights). Rights are nonprimitive because their defense always requires some appeal to justifying reasons that are themselves rooted in a moral theory in which rights are not fundamental. Rights, on this account, tend to be recognized and asserted when we have achieved a sufficiently heightened sensitivity to the needs of individuals, but this moral sensitivity is rooted in more primitive and general views of moral duty. It is not that sensitivities are heightened because we notice that certain rights have been violated. To conceive of moral problems in terms of rights, then, is merely a way of placing claims within a moral framework; it is not to rely on a theory of rights to establish what is morally correct.

One form of this criticism is found in the following essay by Ruth Macklin.

RUTH MACKLIN

Moral Concerns and Appeals to Rights and Duties*

I should like to argue this: appeals to abstract notions of rights, in the absence of a moral theory in which appeals might be grounded, are bound to be arbitrary, *ad hoc*, or give rise to controversies that are impossible to settle, in principle. In addition, the attempt to *discover* the existence of human rights is an enterprise that is essentially misconceived. The existence and nature of human rights are matters for moral *decision*, not of empirical or *a priori* discovery. . . . In the absence of a broader moral theory—in particular, a theory of justice—a well-grounded account of human rights will not be forthcoming. It is, then, within the framework of an overall theory of justice that we might expect to resolve at least some of the debates and uncertainties about questions of rights. Without such a generally accepted theory, claims about the existence and nature of specific rights cannot be adequately grounded or justified; yet they may still serve as expressions of moral outrage or as

*From Ruth Macklin, "Moral Concerns and Appeals to Rights and Duties," *The Hastings Center Report* (October 1976): 31, 37–38.

demands for social and legislative reform. . . .

In an essay entitled "The Nature and Value of Rights," Feinberg alleges that a right is a kind of claim, and a claim is "an assertion of right"; he acknowledges the impossibility of giving what he calls a "formal definition" of the notion of a right. Feinberg asks us to accept the notion of a right as a "simple, undefinable, unanalysable primitive." It is best elucidated, he thinks, by viewing it in conjunction with the rule-governed activity of claiming. Feinberg offers not so much a theory for enabling us to know when rights properly can be said to exist, or how to resolve conflicts among them; but rather, as the title of his article reveals, he wants to explicate *the nature and value of rights*. . . .

But what Feinberg's account lacks—and what is sorely needed in applied moral contexts—is a normative ethical position stating criteria for the *validity* of claims, or a *justification* for the governing rules or moral principles that are used to validate claims. What reasons or grounds are *good* ones for engaging in the activity of making claims about rights? Feinberg does not give us an account of what these normative considerations should be like or where we may seek guidance. He has given an essentially pragmatic justification for viewing rights as valid claims of a certain sort. But in the absence of some further guidelines, we shall be unable to assess whether claims about the rights of the fetus or the rights of future generations or the rights of schoolchildren against drug researchers are *valid* claims or not.

I suspect that part of the problem with Feinberg's account stems from his starting point in taking the notion of a right as an "unanalysable primitive." As I indicated at the outset, I think the notion of a right is properly to be understood as a derivative moral concept. Following John Stuart Mill, I contend that the things we call rights are intimately bound up with the theory of justice we adopt. If systematic judgments about the existence of rights and objective resolutions of conflicts of rights can be made at all, it will only be possible when mediated by a well-worked-out theory of justice, such as that set out by the contemporary moral philosopher John Rawls in

his book, *A Theory of Justice*.[1] Indeed, I believe that treating the notion of rights as an "unanalysable primitive" is just what has led to the many and varied claims about rights that have been advanced in the past decade. If people disagree about the legitimacy of claims about rights, it is probably because they disagree about the basic precepts of social justice. And, it would seem, the reason such disagreements persist is that there *is* no generally accepted, fully worked-out theory of justice. . . .

If I am correct in viewing the concept of rights as a derivative notion—to be derived from some sound, well-articulated theory of justice—there will be as many disputes about rights as there are different conceptions of distributive and retributive justice. The different rights-claimers subscribe—implicitly or explicitly—to different conceptions or dictates of justice; hence, their views about the nature and existence of rights are bound to differ.

[1]John Rawls, *A Theory of Justice* (Cambridge, Mass.: Harvard University Press, 1971).

Equality and Fundamental Rights

A pervasive and important view about rights is the following thesis, which relates especially to the above account of "human rights": Some moral rights hold only in special, individual contexts. If I swear to you that I will tell the whole truth and nothing but the truth, for example, you acquire a right to be told the truth. Such special rights never have a claim to being fundamental or nonderivative, but there are fundamental rights held by all irrespective of merit and ability. We have these rights just because we are human. For example, our humanity confers rights to impartial treatment in matters of justice, freedom, equality of opportunity, and so on; and if our rights are violated, then our very humanity is violated. Anyone who challenges premises asserting an equality of rights begins with an extraordinarily strong presumption against his or her case that must be overcome by careful impartial reasoning; and any disagreements must be resolved not by weighing conflicting *interests,* but rather, by weighing conflicting *rights.*

This view is characteristic of exponents of natural rights, but it has been reflected in many different philosophical theories, including those of Kant and Aristotle.

Several types of challenge have emerged to this thesis. First, it has been asked why persons should be treated equally and granted equal rights when they demonstrate so many inequalities in ability, need, and merit. It will not do to say that all persons are equal in moral worth, for this reply only places the question one step further removed: What is it about persons that makes them equal in moral worth? What is it that all persons hold in common that renders them equal as claimants of rights? Many answers have been attempted to these questions. For example, it has been suggested that we are of equal moral worth because we are *rational* or because we are *capable of suffering pain.* Some philosophers have also attempted to provide Kantian reasons to explain our common human worth. They have argued that because we are rational creatures to be treated as ends and not means, as persons and not things, we are morally equal. Yet no theory along these lines has proved compelling, and such explanations have been criticized as again simply relocating the problem, for the way in which such a criterion establishes moral worth and equality must still be explained.

These questions of metaphysics and morals cannot be pursued further here, but suffice it to say that many believe the outlook is not bright that these notions can ground a theory of equal human worth and rights. This belief has led a number of writers to conclude, as Feinberg has put it, that "it may well be that universal 'respect' for human beings is, in a sense, 'groundless'—a kind of ultimate attitude not itself justifiable in more ultimate terms. . . . The 'respect' said by Kant and many others to be owed to every human being by his fellows . . . may well share this logical feature of ultimacy and 'groundlessness' with it."*

It is not easy to frame a response to this important problem. No prominent answers surpassing those found in the Kantian and Aristotelian theories previously studied have come forward, and this issue remains one of the more puzzling ones in contemporary moral philosophy. However, it is worth noting that a theory of rights can be defended even if this objection is entirely correct. Moral theories that do not appeal to natural laws, or to notions of personhood and respect, may nonetheless turn out to be sufficient to ground claims of rights if they are adequate as moral theories and if the correlativity thesis is correct. Thus, theories of rights may not be devastated by this criticism, as important as it is.

CONCLUSION

These two criticisms raise questions that lead naturally to a consideration of theories of justice—the subject of Chapter 7. While it is by no means obvious that a theory of justice can resolve the issues we have encountered about rights, many believe that justice is the deeper and more significant moral notion.

*Joel Feinberg, *Social Philosophy* (Englewood Cliffs, N. J.: Prentice-Hall, Inc., 1973), p. 93.

SUGGESTED SUPPLEMENTARY READINGS

Acton, H. B.: "Rights," in *Proceedings of the Aristotelian Society,* supp. vol. **24** (1950): 95–110.

Benn, Stanley I.: "Rights," in Paul Edwards, ed., *The Encyclopedia of Philosophy* (New York: Macmillan Company and Free Press, 1967), vol. 7, pp. 195–199.

———— and R. S. Peters, *Social Principles and the Democratic State* (London: George Allen & Unwin, 1959).

Brandt, Richard B.: *Ethical Theory* (Englewood Cliffs, N. J.: Prentice-Hall, Inc., 1957), chap. 17.

Braybrooke, David: *Three Tests for Democracy* (New York: Random House, 1968), part 1, "Personal Rights."

Brown, Stuart M., Jr.: "Inalienable Rights," *Philosophical Review,* **64** (1955): 192–211.

Cranston, Maurice: *What Are Human Rights?* (New York: Taplinger Publishing Co., Inc., 1973).

Dworkin, Ronald: *Taking Rights Seriously* (Cambridge, Mass.: Harvard University Press, 1977).

Feinberg, Joel: "Duties, Rights, and Claims," *American Philosophical Quarterly,* **3** (1966): 137–144.

————: *Social Philosophy* (Englewood Cliffs, N. J.: Prentice-Hall, Inc., 1973), chaps. 4–6.

————: "Rights," Warren T. Reich, ed., in *The Enclyclopedia of Bioethics* (New York: Free Press, 1978) vol. 4, pp. 1507–1511.

Flathman, Richard E.: *The Practice of Rights* (Cambridge, England: Cambridge University Press, 1977).

Frankena, William K.: "The Concept of Universal Human Rights," in *Science, Language and Human Rights* (Philadelphia: University of Pennsylvania Press, 1952), pp. 189–207.

————: "Natural and Inalienable Rights," *Philosophical Review,* **64** (1955): 212–232.

Golding, Martin P.: "The Concept of Rights: A Historical Sketch," in E. Bandman and B. Bandman, eds., *Bioethics and Human Rights* (Boston: Little Brown & Co., 1978), chap. 4.

Hart, H. L. A.: "Are There Any Natural Rights?" *Philosophical Review,* **64** (1955): 175–191.

————: "Between Utility and Rights," in Alan Ryan, ed., *The Idea of Freedom: Essays in Honour of Isaiah Berlin* (Oxford, England: Oxford University Press, 1979), pp. 77–98.

Hohfeld, Wesley Newcomb: *Fundamental Legal Conceptions* (New Haven, Conn.: Yale University Press, 1946).

Lyons, David: "Rights, Claimants, and Beneficiaries," *American Philosophical Quarterly,* **6** (1969): 173–185.

————: "The Correlativity of Rights and Duties," *Nous,* **4** (1970): 45–55.

————: *Rights* (Belmont, Calif.: Wadsworth Publishing Company, Inc., 1979).

McCloskey, H. J.: "Rights," *Philosophical Quarterly,* **15** (1965): 113–127.

Macdonald, Margaret: "Natural Rights," *Proceedings of the Aristotelian Society,* **47** (1946–1947): 225–250.

Mackie, John L.: "Can There Be a Right-Based Moral Theory?" *Midwest Studies in Philosophy,* **3** (1978).

Macklin, Ruth: "Moral Concerns and Appeals to Rights and Duties," *The Hastings Center Report,* **6** (1976): 31–38.

Marshall, G.: "Rights, Options, and Entitlements," in A. W. B. Simpson, ed., *Oxford Essays in Jurisprudence (2d Series)* (Oxford, England: Clarendon Press, 1973), pp. 228–241.

Melden, Abraham I.: *Human Rights* (Belmont Calif.: Wadsworth Publishing Company, Inc., 1970).

———: *Rights and Persons* (Berkeley, Calif.: University of California Press, 1977).

Murphy, Jeffrie G.: "Rights and Borderline Cases," *Arizona Law Review,* **19** (1977): 228–241.

Nelson, William N.: "Special Rights, General Rights, and Social Justice," *Philosophy & Public Affairs,* **3** (1974): 410–430.

Owens, Meirlys: "The Notion of Human Rights: A Reconsideration," *American Philosophical Quarterly,* **6** (1969): 240–246.

Raphael, D. D., ed.: *Political Theory and the Rights of Man* (Bloomington: Indiana University Press, 1967).

Singer, Marcus G.: "The Basis of Rights and Duties," *Philosophical Studies,* **23** (1972): 48–57.

Williams, Peter: "Rights and the Alleged Right of Innocents to Be Killed," *Ethics* **87** (1977): 383–394.

CHAPTER SEVEN

Justice

Antidiscrimination laws passed in the 1960s in the United States were addressed to many issues of social injustice. These laws subsequently had a dramatic effect on businesses throughout the United States. They required not only fair treatment of employees, but also documented proof of fair treatment. American Telephone and Telegraph Company (AT&T), the nation's largest private employer (providing jobs for more than one million people), was directly affected. In January of 1971, the Equal Employment Opportunity Commission (EEOC) brought charges of discrimination in hiring and promotion against AT&T. The EEOC filed a petition to block a rate increase of $385 million per year until the company ended its discriminatory practices. The petition alleged that job bias at AT&T kept rates from declining.

AT&T denied the charges, claiming that its record demonstrated equality of treatment for minorities and women. The company adduced statistics showing that (1) one-fourth of all employees hired from 1969 to 1971 were black, American Indian, oriental, or Hispanic; (2) while total employment since 1963 increased by 38 percent, the number of minority employees jumped by 265 percent; (3) 12.4 percent of the work force came from minority groups, a figure higher than the proportion of minorities in the United States population; (4) 55 percent of people on the payroll were women, and 33 percent of management positions were held by women. These statistics were marshaled to draw the conclusion that the company was in no respect guilty of the alleged injustices.

AT&T produced 100,000 pages of documents and statistics in support of these contentions, and the EEOC filed 30,000 pages of counterargument. The EEOC claimed that customers would pay lower phone rates if AT&T ended its discriminatory practices and that if AT&T had operated to minimize labor costs (i.e., if it had employed workers at the lowest possible wage regardless of sex), the company would have employed more women in all job categories, for a total reduction in rates of 2 to 4 percent.

While the EEOC pursued its charges, divisions arose between leaders of the Communication Workers of America and female members of that union. Many of these women union members remained on strike against the instructions of union officials because they were displeased with the settlement between union and management. While that settlement called for a 31 percent increase in wages and benefits over three years, it did not ensure *equal* pay for women.* A government study gave support to the women's charges of economic discrimination.†

AT&T eventually settled with EEOC out of court. The main provision was that AT&T would rectify past unjust treatment by paying lump sums of money, totaling $15 million, to 13,000 of its female and 2,000 of its male employees, and would grant $23 million in pay increases to 36,000 workers who had suffered injustice through job discrimination. Management agreed to alter the patterns of hiring and to upgrade female and minority employees. The stipulations of the settlement were met by the company before an established 1979 deadline. Virtually all parties were doubtful, however, that justice had actually been achieved through this settlement.‡

Moral controversies in contemporary society usually involve specific topical issues such as environmental responsibility, equal access to training programs, and famine relief. The AT&T case is illustrative of a number of such topical issues, but more general problems of justice are also clearly central to the case. Moral arguments about the case turn on the question of whether minorities and women were unjustly treated

---

*The female craft workers formerly earned 62 percent as much as the male craft workers, and the settlement proposed a reduction in that differential of only 3 percent. Women claimed that though 55 percent of the work force was female, the starting salaries for women were $30 per week less than for men in 96 percent of the cases.

†This study (by the Federal Commerce Commission) indicated that (1) women lost $950 million annually in wages because discriminatory practices kept them in low-paying jobs; (2) blacks lost $225 million in wages in the nation as a whole because AT&T did not hire them in numbers proportionate to their percentage in the population; (3) Spanish-surnamed Americans lost $137 million for the same reasons. The EEOC argued that AT&T systematically channeled women into operator jobs and men into management positions. It showed that 99 percent of all operators were female, while only 1 percent of craft workers were female.

‡Sources for this case include the following: "A.T.&T. Denies Job Discrimination Charges, Claims Firm Is Equal Employment Leader," *Wall Street Journal* (Dec. 14, 1970), p. 6; "A.T.&T. Makes Reparation," *The Economist*, **246** (Jan. 27, 1973), p. 42; Byron Calame, "Liberating Ma Bell: Female Telephone Workers Hit Labor Pact, Say Men Still Get the Best Jobs, More Pay," *Wall Street Journal* (July 26, 1971), p. 22; "FCC Orders Hearing on Charge that A.T.&T. Discriminates in Hiring," *Wall Street Journal* (Jan. 22, 1971), p. 10; "Federal Agency Says A.T.&T. Job Bias Keeps Rates From Declining," *Wall Street Journal* (Dec. 2, 1971), p. 21; Richard M. Hodgetts, "A.T.&T. versus the Equal Employment Opportunity Commission," in his *The Business Enterprise: Social Challenge, Social Response* (Philadelphia: W. B. Saunders Company, 1977), pp. 176–182.

in the distribution of positions and promotions. They also turn on the justice of salaries offered by the company. While no one would deny the wrongness of treating employees unjustly, there has been, and continues to be, strong disagreement about what, if anything, constitutes unjust treatment in this case. Such disagreement is not altogether surprising, for quite specific appeals to justice have proven sharply controversial. Common sense might lead us all to agree that it would be unjust to ask another person to accept an unfair share of the burdens society imposes, but common sense is insufficient to produce comparable agreement about the concept of an unfair share and its application to a wide variety of problems such as that presented in the AT&T case. Work on this problem may be begun indirectly by outlining how the terms "justice" and "distributive justice" are used in classical and contemporary moral philosophy. Some more substantive problems about the theory of social justice can then be explored.

THE NATURE AND TYPES OF JUSTICE

Justice is often explicated in terms of fairness, but perhaps the word most closely linked to the general meaning of "justice" is "desert." One has acted justly toward a person when one gives that person what is due or owed, and therefore what is deserved. If a position is available and an AT&T employee deserves to be promoted on the basis of past performance and ability, for example, justice has been done when that person is promoted. What persons deserve or can legitimately claim is based on certain morally relevant properties which they possess, such as being productive, having experience, or having been harmed by the acts of another. It is similarly wrong, as a matter of justice, to burden or to reward someone if the person does *not* possess the relevant property. For example, it is wrong or unjust of a university president to promote faculty members merely on the basis of personal friendship or religious affiliation rather than on public criteria of excellence in the profession (though this particular injustice seems to occur all too frequently).

The more restricted expression "distributive justice" refers to the proper distribution of social benefits and burdens. Paying taxes and being drafted into the armed services to fight a war are distributed burdens, while welfare checks, grants to do research, and a newly paved street for a neighborhood block are distributed benefits. Recent literature on distributive justice has tended to focus on considerations of fair *economic* distribution, especially unjust distributions in the form of inequalities of income between different classes of persons and unfair tax burdens on certain classes. But there are many problems of distributive justice besides strictly economic ones, including the issues raised in prominent contemporary debates over the busing of school children, reverse discrimination, distribution of health care, and international relations among advanced industrial and less developed countries.

Distributive Justice as Comparative

Issues of distributive justice often involve a comparison among many individuals in a society. Justice is said to be *comparative* when what one person deserves is determined by balancing the competing claims of other persons against his or her claims. Here the condition of others in society affects how much an individual is due. To take the example opening this chapter, the question whether a female employee of AT&T receives due compensation for her work probably must be decided by taking account of the compensation male employees at that institution and other employees at similar institutions receive for comparable work. Of course, comparisons to executive salaries may also be appropriate if one is searching for further injustices.

Not all problems of justice, however, involve a comparison among individuals. Issues of legal justice are essentially *noncomparative*. They concern the corrective actions or punishments due in return for various wrongs and crimes, as well as the legal procedures for fair trials and rights of appeal. In cases of legal justice, desert is judged by a standard which is quite independent of the claims of others (though comparative judgments may occasionally surface when, for example, the justice of a form of sentencing for a crime is in question). An innocent person does not deserve to be punished, and certain rules must be followed in hearing an appeal. The legal dictates of justice are never affected by the condition of other people in a society, such as other innocent people who may have been punished unjustly.

Distributive justice pertains to the distribution of benefits and burdens through society's major and pervasive institutions, including branches of government, laws of property ownership, lending institutions, and systems of allocating health-care benefits. Problems in legal justice are at once more technical and less controversial, and thus have naturally attracted less philosophical attention than issues of distributive justice, with its close ties to comparative claims in society at large. This chapter therefore deals predominantly with distributive justice.

Scarcity and Distributive Justice

Distributive justice applies only to the distribution of *scarce* benefits, where there is some competition for those benefits. If there were plenty of fresh water for industries to use in dumping their waste materials, with no subsequent problems of disease, patterns of restricted water use would not need to be established. It is only when we are worried that the supply of drinking water will be exhausted, that public health will be affected by the pollutants, or that certain forms of marine life will disappear, that limits are set on the amounts of permissible discharge. Similarly, the AT&T case would not have arisen if there had not been a scarcity of desirable jobs and monetary resources available for employees. There are, of course, various schemes which could be devised for distributing jobs, determining salaries, or setting limits on waste-water effluent; but this fact is secondary to our present discussion. We are merely observing that there are no problems of distributive justice, and there is no need for principles of distributive justice, until some measure of scarcity exists. Even when burdens rather than benefits are being allocated, there is competition for the least disadvantageous distribution.

David Hume pointed out that the concept of comparative justice was developed in order to handle problems of conflicting claims or interests.* Roughly speaking, his point is that rules of justice would have no point unless society were composed of persons with limited sympathy for others in the competition for scarce resources. The rules of justice serve to strike a balance between those conflicting interests and also between conflicting claims that repeatedly occur in society. Since law and morality are our explicit tools for balancing conflicting claims, there is a close link between the lawful society and the just society. Nonetheless, the law may be unjust—as we shall see in exploring issues such as civil disobedience in Chapter 8—and not all rules of justice are connected to the law or to legal enforcement. Accordingly, parties with conflicting claims often must justify their claims by appeal to basic moral rules. Consideration will now be given to such basic moral rules by exploring specific principles of justice.

PRINCIPLES OF JUSTICE

The Formal Principle of Justice

Justice has been analyzed in different ways in rival theories. But, common to all theories of justice is this minimal principle: Like cases should be treated alike—or, to use the language of equality, equals ought to be treated equally and unequals unequally. This elementary principle is referred to as the "principle of formal justice," or sometimes as the "principle of formal equality"—*formal* because it states no particular respects in which equals ought to be treated the same or unequals unequally. The principle merely asserts that whatever respects are under consideration, persons who are equal in those respects should be treated alike.

The formal principle of justice has traditionally been attributed to Aristotle, who treats the topic in Book V of the *Nichomachean Ethics*—perhaps the single most influential treatment of justice ever written. Aristotle there argues that justice can be equated with lawfulness in general, concluding that in this broad sense, justice is the whole of virtue and that the just person is simply the person who acts morally in dealing with others. But justice can also be seen as a part of virtue, according to Aristotle, and so as describing particular kinds of commendable moral behavior and proscribing particular vices. His examination of justice in this more restricted meaning reveals that it can assume three specific forms: justice in distribution, justice in correction or retribution, and justice in exchange. Aristotle maintains that in each of these forms, justice consists in an equality of proportion, and this basic equality is what has come to be

3 forms

*David Hume, *A Treatise of Human Nature*, L. A. Selby-Bigge, ed., 3d. ed., rev. by P. H. Nidditch (Oxford, England: Oxford University Press, 1978), pp. 490–500.

known as the "formal principle of justice." This influential starting point for all theories of justice is clearly expressed in the discussion of the distributive and corrective types of justice from the *Nichomachean Ethics*.

ARISTOTLE

Distributive and Corrective Justice*

... All men cling to justice of some kind, but their conceptions are imperfect and they do not express the whole idea. For example, justice is thought by them to be, and is, equality, not, however, for all, but only for equals. And inequality is thought to be, and is, justice; neither is this for all, but only for unequals. When the persons are omitted, then men judge erroneously. The reason is that they are passing judgment on themselves, and most people are bad judges in their own case. . . .

Now as an unjust man is unfair and an unjust thing unequal, it is clear that corresponding to the unequal there is a middle point or mean; namely, that which is equal; for any kind of action admitting of more or less also admits what is equal. . . . If the persons are not equal, they will not have equal shares; it is when equals possess or are assigned unequal shares, or persons who are not equal equal shares, that quarrels and complaints arise.

Moreover, the same point also clearly follows from the principle of assignment by merit. Everybody agrees that just distribution must be in accordance with merit of

*From Aristotle's *Politics,* Book III, chap. 9, Benjamin Jowett, trans., in *The Works of Aristotle,* vol. 2 (Chicago: Encyclopedia Britannica, Inc., 1952), p. 477; and *Aristotle's Ethics for English Readers,* chap. 5, rendered from the Greek of the *Nicomachean Ethics* by H. Rackham (1943). Reprinted by permission of Basil Blackwell, Publisher.

some sort, though everybody does not mean the same sort of merit. Democrats take merit to mean free status, adherents of oligarchy take it to mean wealth or noble birth, supporters of aristocracy excellence.

The just then is that which is proportionate and the unjust is that which runs counter to proportion; the man who acts unjustly has too much, and the man who is unjustly treated too little, of the good. In the case of evil, it is the other way about, as the lesser evil is accounted as good in comparison with the greater evil, because the lesser evil is more desirable than the greater, and what is desirable is a good, and what is more desirable a greater good. This then is one species of justice.

The species of justice that remains is the justice of redress, which operates in the case of voluntary and involuntary transactions. This form of justice has a different specific character from the preceding one. The justice that distributes common property always follows the kind of proportion mentioned above (because in the case of distribution from the common funds of a partnership it will follow the same ratio as that existing between the sums put into the business by the partners); and the unjust that is opposed to this form of the just is that which violates that proportion. But justice in transactions between individuals, although it is equality of a sort, and injustice inequality, does not go by the kind of proportion mentioned, but by arithmetical proportion.[1] It makes no difference[2] whether a good man has defrauded a bad one or a bad man a good one, nor whether a good man or a bad man has committed adultery; the law only looks at the nature of the injury, and treats the parties as equal if one has done and the other suffered a wrong or if one has inflicted and the other sustained damage. Consequently, in such cases the judge tries to equalize this injustice, which consists in inequality—for even in a case where one person has received and the other has inflicted a blow, or where one has killed and the other been killed, the suffering and the action have been distributed in unequal shares, while the judge's endeavor is to make them equal by means of the penalty he inflicts, taking something away from the gain of the assailant. The term "gain" is applied to such cases in a general sense, even though to some, for instance a person who has inflicted a wound, it is not specially appropriate, and the term "loss" is applied to the sufferer; at all events the terms "gain" and "loss" are employed when the amount of the suffering inflicted has been assessed. Consequently, while equal is intermediate between more and

less, gain and loss are at once both more and less in contrary ways—more of what is good and less of what is bad are gain, and more of what is bad and less of what is good are loss, intermediate between them being, as we said, the equal, which we pronounce to be just. Consequently the justice of redress will be what is intermediate between loss and gain. This is why when a dispute arises the parties have recourse to a judge; to go to a judge is to appeal to the just, inasmuch as a judge is virtually justice personified;[3] and they have recourse to a judge as intermediary—indeed, in some countries judges are called "mediators"—on the ground that if the litigants get the medium amount they will get what is just. Thus justice is a sort of medium, as the judge is a medium between the litigants. What he does is to restore equality; it is as if there were a line divided into two unequal parts, and he took away the amount by which the larger segment exceeded half the line and added it to the smaller segment. When the whole has been divided into two equal parts, people say that they "have got their own," having got an equal share. This is the arithmetical mean between the greater amount and the less.

Therefore the just is intermediate between gain and loss due to breach of contract; it consists in having an equal amount both before and after the transaction.

[1] I.e., two pairs of terms (e.g., 1, 3, 7, 9) the second of which exceeds the first by the same amount as the fourth exceeds the third. We do not call this "proportion," but if the third term also exceeds the second by the same amount (e.g., 1, 3, 5, 7), an "arithmetical progression."

[2] For corrective justice the merits of the parties are immaterial.

[3] Cf. our expressions "Mr. Justice So-and-So," "Justice of the Peace."

The formal principle of justice described by Aristotle would seem to be a rather minimal moral rule. It tells us that in retributive justice, punishment for crimes should be equal for different persons when their offenses are identical, and that when a distribution of burdens or goods is in question, people who are equal should receive equal shares. The formal principle of justice, however, does not tell us how to determine equality or proportion in these matters, and it therefore lacks substance as a specific guide to

[handwritten top margin: "? aristotles"]

conduct. In any group of persons, there will be many respects in which they are both similar and different, and thus Aristotle's account of equality must be qualified as "equality in relevant respects." Yet, clearly not *all* respects are relevant to justice—race and sex being widely discussed examples. In the AT&T case, for instance, the formal principle stipulates that the company ought to treat equally those among its employees who are equal; but it does not indicate whether differences in sex or race make employees unequal for purposes of distributing jobs and salaries. It is, of course, our modern conception that sex-based or race-based hiring is unjust, but nothing in Aristotle's bare principle commends this conclusion.

It is tempting to view the formal principle as entailing a general moral *presumption* in favor of *equal* treatment of individuals. In the words of Stanley I. Benn, "Impartiality implies a kind of equality—not that all cases should be treated alike but that the onus rests on whoever would treat them differently to distinguish them in relevant ways. . . . That is what is really meant by the right to equal consideration—to be treated alike unless relevant differences have been proved."* Yet some philosophers, such as Joel Feinberg, would argue that to see the formal principle as any sort of guide to conduct is to import an alien and invalid content into what is purely a formal principle. Feinberg believes that the formal principle gives no recommendation for action; on that principle alone, it cannot be presumed that all should be treated equally. In the following selection, he defends his view that a normative principle should not be presented in the guise of a purely formal principle.

*Stanley I. Benn, "Justice," in Paul Edwards, ed., *The Encyclopedia of Philosophy* (New York: Macmillan Company, 1967), vol. 3, p. 299.

[handwritten left: "Presume people to be equal, automatically to be fair to to treat people as equal, & if after they are unequal then treat them accordingly. you will be more fair if they are equal or unequal & treat them accordingly."]

[handwritten right: "acceptive not presumptive → if people are not equal than you should treat them as unequal. you have to make a decision early & determine"]

JOEL FEINBERG

The Presumption in Favor of Equal Treatment†

The principle that like cases should be treated alike is put too hastily by some equalitarian writers in the form of a "presumption for equality." It is commonly said, for example, that although it is absurd to think that justice requires us to treat all men exactly alike, it does require that we give them equal treatment until we have good reason not to do so, that "the burden of proof is on the person who wants to treat people differently from one another. . . . [1] But this presumptive principle is by no means identical in meaning or implications to the formal principle as we have formulated it. Our formal principle (which derives from Aristotle) would have us: (1) treat alike (equally) those who are the same (equal) in relevant respects, and (2) treat unalike (unequally) those

†From Joel Feinberg, *Social Philosophy* (Englewood Cliffs, N.J.: Prentice-Hall, Inc., 1973), pp. 100–102.

[1]Louis I. Katzner, "An Analysis of the Concept of Justice," (Ph.D. dissertation, University of Michigan, 1968), p. 37, paraphrasing S. Benn and R. S. Peters, *Social Principles and the Democratic State* (London: George Allen & Unwin, Ltd., 1959), p. 111.

who are unalike (unequal) in relevant respects, in direct proportion to the differences (inequalities) between them. The equalitarian presumptivist formulation completely ignores the second part of this principle in insisting that all and only departures from *equal* treatment need justification. Clearly, what needs justification according to the double formula above are: (1) departures from identical (equal) treatment when individuals seem to be the same (equal) in relevant respects, *and* (2) departures from different (unequal) treatment when individuals seem to be different (unequal) in relevant respects. Where the "burden of proof" actually lies in a given case, then, depends upon what is given (believed or known) about the relevant traits of the individuals involved, and also upon the particular context of justice and its governing norms and maxims. The presumption in favor of equal treatment holds when the individuals involved are believed, assumed, or expected to be equal in the relevant respects, whereas the presumption in favor of *unequal* treatment holds when the individuals involved are expected to be different in the relevant respects.

Consider some examples. If two pupils both violate the same rule but one is given a more severe penalty, we would *presume* (knowing no more facts) that a comparative injustice had been committed by the teacher. Unless some relevant difference between the two offenders or their offenses could be brought to light by the teacher, we would treat the presumption as decisive. On the other hand, consider the example cited by Louis Katzner to show that sometimes the "burden of proof" is on those who advocate equality of treatment. A testator whose sole survivor is his son leaves one half of his estate to that son and, "equally," one half to another person of the son's age. The two inheritors are different in a respect we normally take to be relevant in such contexts,

namely that one is a member of the testator's immediate family whereas the other is not. Because of this *given* relevant difference, the father has the burden of presenting a justification for *treating two people equally* that will override the presumption that they should be treated differently.

The equalitarian presumptivist principle, then, errs in overlooking cases in which our antecedent expectations about the existence of characteristics agreed to be relevant creates a presumption in favor of inequality. The disguised normative character of the principle ("disguised" when it is claimed to be the formal principle of comparative justice), and, more importantly, its ultimately arbitrary character, are shown by a consideration of how it would apply to cases where no expectation exists about the equal or unequal degree to which relevant characteristics are possessed by those subject to our treatment. The presumptive principle, in these cases, tells us to presume even in our ignorance that equal treatment is called for, that individuals about whom we know nothing should nevertheless be treated equally unless or until grounds for distinction between them can be found. In this instance, the presumptive principle clearly reveals itself as not "merely formal"; it purports to be a decisive guide to our conduct. Thus, a controversial (and indeed very doubtful!) normative principle is presented in the guise of a purely formal principle of reason supposedly definitive of the very nature of comparative justice. The moral of the story is this: Don't confuse an *exceptive principle* ("Treat all men alike *except* where there are relevant differences between them") with a *presumptive principle* ("Treat all men alike *until it can be shown* that there are relevant differences between them"). The exceptive principle is indeed formal, providing no guide to actions or grounds for presuming either equality or inequality in the case in which we are ignorant of the characteristics of the men to be treated. The presumptive principle has us presume equal treatment even in this case, and that would be to make a presumption every bit as arbitrary as the presumption in favor of *unequal* treatment in the absence of knowledge of the relevant similarities and differences of the persons involved.

Even for those who would dispute Feinberg's conclusion, the formal principle of justice is not a particularly informative guide to conduct, and it may be misleading by assimilating justice too closely to the more restricted notion of equality. Aristotle himself is not an egalitarian, as that term is conventionally used, for he does not demand equal treatment in all contexts; indeed, he often observes that justice must be governed by considerations of relative merit, and he admits wealth and noble birth, on some occasions, as causing relevant differences among persons. The formal principle, then, would, at most, specify a general presumption in favor of equal treatment, and it does not rule out all sorts of unequal treatments that are generally considered immoral. Many immoral "principles of distributive justice" could be applied quite equally to all— e.g., rules of taxation constructed to favor those who are already wealthy while penalizing the poor. This approach would lead to the unacceptable conclusion that some *just* acts or policies are *immoral*.

Theories of justice attempt to avoid such problems by systematically and precisely elaborating the notions of equality or proportion in distribution, specifying in detail what counts as a relevant respect in terms of which people are to be compared and what it means to give people their due. Philosophers achieve this specificity by developing *material* principles of justice, and it is to a consideration of such principles that we must now turn. *to each according to his needs, merit, its + contribution, + efforts.*

Material Principles of Justice *← why? answer*

As has been seen, the formal principle of justice is only a starting point for a theory of justice. That equals ought to be treated equally is not likely to stir disagreement. But who is equal and who unequal? Presumably, all citizens should have equal political rights, should possess equal access to public services, and should receive equal treatment under the law. But almost all of us would allow that distinctions based on such factors as experience, deprivation, merit, indebtedness, family membership, and social position sometimes justify differential treatment. If this belief is correct, how should the formal principle be supplemented?

The inadequacy of the formal principle as a sole principle of justice can be appreciated by imagining a system of distribution that takes no account of the respects in which people can differ. In a short story entitled "The Lottery in Babylon,"* Jorge Borges depicts a society in which all social benefits and burdens are distributed on the

*In Jorge Borges, *Labyrinths* (New York: New Directions Publishing Corporation, 1962), pp. 30–35.

basis of a lottery. Any person may, at the end of a lottery event, find himself or herself a slave, a factory owner, a priest, an executioner, a prisoner, etc. The lottery takes no account whatever of past achievement, training, or promise. It is a purely random selection system, without regard to contribution, need, or effort. In a sense, all the citizens of Borges's imaginary society are accorded equal treatment; everyone must participate in the lottery, with the result that each person has an equal chance to receive any particular outcome. Yet Feinberg's admonition seems appropriate here: The formal principle requires equal treatment for equals, but it is not to be presumed that all people are equal for purposes of distributing every social burden and benefit. Indeed, quite the contrary assumption may be in order. Different people possess different properties on the basis of which they deserve different social positions, and Borges's lottery system is unjust in its failure to recognize that salient moral point. We may strongly believe, for example, that certain employment practices at AT&T are unjust, but we do not attempt to rectify these injustices through a lottery for positions with the company. The latter action would seem only to compound the problem of injustice rather than to alleviate it.

Any plausible theory of justice, then, must specify relevant properties. And clearly, not just any proposed criteria are morally acceptable. If, at an AT&T facility, the fact that blacks do not live within five miles of the facility is judged a good reason for not hiring them, this fact introduces a *proposed* relevant difference for purposes of hiring. Yet, this difference is morally unacceptable. It allows a distribution of benefits based on the morally irrelevant property of living some distance away. Some of the most intractable questions about justice arise over how to specify the relevant respects in terms of which people are to be treated equally.

Principles that specify these relevant respects are said to be *material* principles of justice because they put material content into a theory of justice. Each material principle of justice identifies a relevant property on the basis of which burdens and benefits should be distributed. The following is a sample list of major candidates for the position of valid principles of distributive justice (though longer lists have been proposed): (1) to each person an equal share; (2) to each person according to individual need; (3) to each person according to that person's rights; (4) to each person according to individual effort; (5) to each person according to societal contribution; (6) to each person according to merit. There is no obvious barrier to acceptance of more than one of these principles, and some theories of justice accept all six as valid. Most societies use several in the belief that different rules are appropriate to different situations. In the United States, for example, unemployment and welfare payments are distributed according to need and individual rights (and to some extent on the basis of previous length of employment); jobs and promotions are in many sectors awarded on the basis of demonstrated achievement and merit; the higher incomes of wealthy professionals are allowed on the grounds of superior effort, merit, or social contributions; and, at least theoretically, the opportunity for elementary and secondary education is distributed equally to all citizens.

The diversity of these principles indicates that justice is an enormously broad normative concept; but might this diversity not also suggest that the concept is too

broad, possibly even incoherent? Consider the following example: A university professor
hires three male students to help move the furniture in her house to a new location,
promising each the standard hourly wage for professional movers in the city. One student turns out to be capable of lifting large items by himself, and is both more efficient
and more careful than either of the other students. The second, the professor learns
during conversation while driving the truck, is desperately in need of money owing to
a genuine and severe financial crisis that threatens the student's enrollment for the next
semester. The third student carelessly breaks two vases and scars a table, but otherwise
fulfills the conditions of the agreement, though in an undistinguished manner. The first
person deserves greater compensation on the basis of performance, the second needs a
larger share of the money to be divided among them though for no reason related to
performance, and the third deserves less on the basis of performance but deserves an
equal share on the basis of the agreement (if one overlooks the unnegotiated problem
of carelessly marred or broken items). The professor is therefore somewhat at a loss
about what reward to offer each student at the end of the day. Suppose she tries to call
on justice in general to tell her what ought to be done. It should be obvious by now that
invoking our most general notion of justice will prove quite worthless, for the professor
will have to accept one or more material principles of justice. She will perhaps wish for
a general account of justice that will order this fragmented array of considerations, but
if she is like most of us, no such account will be readily forthcoming. While we attach
some weight to each of the possible material principles, none clearly outweighs the
other.   4 TYPES

    Theories of distributive justice have been devised to handle not only such rela-
tively trivial situations as this example, but also to give general guidelines for the entire
scope of social justice. Such theories are commonly developed by systematically elaborating one or more of the material principles of distributive justice, perhaps in conjunction with other moral principles. *Egalitarian* theories emphasize equal access to primary
goods; *Marxist* theories emphasize need; *libertarian* theories emphasize rights to social
and economic liberty; and *utilitarian* theories emphasize a mixed use of such criteria so
that public and private utilities are maximized. The acceptability of any such theory of
justice is determined by the quality of its moral argument that some one or more
selected material principles ought to be given priority (or perhaps even exclusive attention) over the others. Consideration will now be given in turn to the libertarian theory,
some criticisms of that theory, and an egalitarian theory of justice. (The utilitarian
theory, in all essentials, is explained in Chapter 3.)

THE LIBERTARIAN THEORY OF JUSTICE

It has been noted earlier that most recent work on distributive justice has focused on
problems of distributing economic benefits and burdens. Libertarian theories are characterized by such a preoccupation with economic distribution. The libertarian concep-

tion of economic justice is often developed, as was suggested, by elaboration of a material principle that specifies rights to social and economic liberty to be the relevant respects in which people are to be compared for purposes of determining just distributions. What makes such theories *libertarian* is their advocacy of distinctive processes, procedures, or mechanisms for ensuring that rights are recognized in economic practice.

In the libertarian theory, those mechanisms are typically the rules and procedures governing economic acquisition and exchange in capitalist or free market systems. As Adam Smith classically described capitalist economic systems, people acting in an individually self-interested fashion exhibit behavior patterns that collectively further the interests of everyone in the larger society. Such a system presumes a model of economic behavior that attributes a substantial degree of economic freedom to individual agents. People are seen as freely entering and withdrawing from economic arrangements in accordance with a controlling perception of their own interest. A commitment to this model of individual freedom in economic activity accounts for the rubric of "libertarianism" that is applied to the theories presently under consideration. People choose to contribute in the ways they do to economic arrangements, and it is because contributions are freely chosen that they can be considered morally relevant bases on which to discriminate among individuals in distributing economic burdens and benefits. This feature lends support to Robert Nozick's characterization of the underlying material principle informing libertarian theories of justice: "From each as they choose, to each as they are chosen."

In seeing free choice as central to an account of justice in economic distribution, libertarian writers often commit themselves to a particular conception of economic production and value. That conception may be roughly described as individualist. Many libertarians maintain that people should receive economic benefits in proportion as they freely contribute to their production, and this variant of the theory assumes that it is possible to recognize meaningful distinctions between individual contributions to production. The industrious and imaginative business executive, for instance, would from this perspective be contributing far more to his or her company's success than the similarly exemplary assembly-line worker or secretary, and the executive therefore deserves—on grounds of justice—the proportionately greater share of the profits that he or she presumably receives.

The underlying assumption here probably corresponds fairly closely to important economic presuppositions in Anglo-American society, but many philosophers would nevertheless challenge it. They would maintain that, however great the differences between particular people's contributions initially appear to be, all individual contributions shrink to insignificance once the broader context of production is appreciated. On this account, economic value is generated through an essentially communal process which renders differences between individual contributions morally spurious. These critics might admit that it was once possible to identify more precisely the importance of an individual contribution to something of economic value when, for example, American frontier settlers turned virgin forests into productive farmland. But they would argue that this possibility has long since been eliminated by the complexity and interdependence of modern economic systems. Thus, the initiative and ideas of the business executive would be only one among a great many factors productive of a corporation's success, a factor itself reflecting a diversity of formative influences including family background, education, and interaction with professional colleagues. If this view of economic production and value were accepted, a material principle of contribution would result in broadly egalitarian or perhaps utilitarian distributions, since no single individual would be able to make a contribution to economic wealth distinguishable from the contributions of other members of the relevant social group.

Libertarian theorists explicitly reject the conclusion that egalitarian patterns of distribution represent a normative ideal. People may be equal in a host of morally significant respects (e.g., entitled to equal treatment under the law and equally valued as ends in themselves), but for the libertarian, it would be a basic violation of justice to regard people as a priori deserving of equal economic returns. This libertarian commitment to the importance of freely chosen differences between individuals accounts for the aforementioned libertarian conception of individual rights. As previously suggested, philosophers frequently supplement the material principles in a theory of justice by advocating other moral principles in conjunction with them. Notions of individual rights to life, liberty, property, etc., generally assume such a position in libertarian philosophies. In particular, people are seen as having a fundamental right to own and dispense with the products of their labor as they choose, and this right must be respected even if its unrestricted exercise leads to great inequalities of wealth within a single society.

Nozick's Theory

The role of individual rights in a libertarian theory of justice is emphasized by the contemporary philosopher Robert Nozick, whose *Anarchy, State, and Utopia* elaborates and defends many of the classic notions of the seventeenth-century philosopher John Locke. Nozick refers to the social philosophy presented in his book as an "entitlement theory" of justice. The appropriateness of that description is apparent from the provocative line with which he begins his work: "Individuals have rights, and there are things no person or group may do to them (without violating their rights)." Starting from that assumption, Nozick proceeds to develop a detailed defense of the minimal or "nightwatchman" state, a conception according to which government action is justified only when it *protects* the fundamental rights or entitlements of its citizens.

This theory of legitimate state power is meant as a challenge to many of the assumptions underlying political realities in contemporary industrial societies. It will therefore be helpful to keep those assumptions in mind while reading the following selection from Nozick's book. In both socialist and (impure) capitalist countries, a considerable degree of government activity beyond mere protection of individual rights is usually allowed on grounds of social justice. Governments take pronounced steps actively to *redistribute* the wealth that has been acquired by individuals exercising their economic rights in accordance with free market laws. Thus, the wealthy are taxed at a progressively higher rate than those who are less wealthy, with the proceeds underwriting state support of the indigent through welfare payments and unemployment compensation. The AT&T case too can be viewed from this libertarian perspective as illustrating a sphere of government intervention beyond the mere protection of individual rights. Here, the EEOC determined that a corporation was *not* free to employ whomever it wished, but that it had, instead, to take affirmative action in hiring people from historically disadvantaged populations. Again, the goal of interference by the state is the redistribution of the economic benefits that would accrue from the unchecked exercise of individual rights in the marketplace.* Nozick's libertarian theory of justice invites consideration of whether such common governmental activities are really what justice demands.

*It should be noted that Nozick's account of justice in rectification, in the following pages, could be construed to condone this instance of state interference. Given the extensive nature of the state action in question, however, this interpretation is not very plausible.

ROBERT NOZICK

The Entitlement Theory†

The term "distributive justice" is not a neutral one. Hearing the term "distribution," most people presume that some thing or mechanism uses some principle or criterion to give out a supply of things. Into this process of distributing shares some error may have crept. So it is an open question, at least, whether *re*distribution should take place; whether we should do again what has already been done once, though poorly. However, we are not in the position of children who have been given portions of pie by someone who now makes last minute adjustments to rectify careless cutting. There is no *central* distribution, no person or group entitled to control all the resources, jointly deciding how

†From Robert Nozick, *Anarchy, State, and Utopia* (New York: Basic Books, Inc., Publishers, 1974), pp. 149–154, 156–157, 159–163, 168, 174–175, 178–179, 182. Copyright 1974 by Basic Books, Inc., Publishers, New York. Reprinted by permission of Basic Books, Inc., and Basil Blackwell Publisher.

they are to be doled out. What each person gets, he gets from others who give to him in exchange for something, or as a gift. In a free society, diverse persons control different resources, and new holdings arise out of the voluntary exchanges and actions of persons. . . .

The subject of justice in holdings consists of three major topics. The first is the *original acquisition of holdings,* the appropriation of unheld things. This includes the issues of how unheld things may come to be held, the process, or processes, by which unheld things may come to be held, the things that may come to be held by these processes, the extent of what comes to be held by a particular process, and so on. We shall refer to the complicated truth about this topic, which we shall not formulate here, as the principle of justice in acquisition. The second topic concerns the *transfer of holdings* from one person to another. By what processes may a person transfer holdings to another? How may a person acquire a holding from another who holds it? Under this topic come general descriptions of voluntary exchange, and gift and (on the other hand) fraud, as well as reference to particular conventional details fixed upon in a given society. The complicated truth about this subject (with placeholders for conventional details) we shall call the principle of justice in transfer. (And we shall suppose it also includes principles governing how a person may divest himself of a holding, passing it into an unheld state.)

If the world were wholly just, the following inductive definition would exhaustively cover the subject of justice in holdings.

1. A person who acquires a holding in accordance with the principle of justice in acquisition is entitled to that holding.

2. A person who acquires a holding in accordance with the principle of justice in transfer, from someone else entitled to the holding, is entitled to the holding.

3. No one is entitled to a holding except by (repeated) applications of 1 and 2.

The complete principle of distributive justice would say simply that a distribution is just if everyone is entitled to the holdings they possess under the distribution. . . .

Not all actual situations are generated in accordance with the two principles of justice in holdings: the principle of justice in acquisition and the principle of justice in transfer. Some people steal from others, or defraud them, or enslave them, seizing their product and preventing them from living as they choose, or forcibly exclude others from competing in exchanges. None of these are permissible modes of transition from one situation to another. And some persons acquire holdings by means not sanctioned by the principle of justice in acquisition. The existence of past injustice (previous violations of the first two principles of justice in holdings) raises the third major topic under justice in holdings: the rectification of injustice in holdings. If past injustice has shaped present holdings in various ways, some identifiable and some not, what now, if anything, ought to be done to rectify these injustices? . . .

Historical Principles and End-Result Principles

The general outlines of the entitlement theory illuminate the nature and defects of other conceptions of distributive justice. The entitlement theory of justice in distribution is *historical;* whether a distribution is just depends upon how it came about. In contrast, *current time-slice principles* of justice hold that the justice of a distribution is determined by how things are distributed (who has what) as judged by some *structural* principle(s) of just distribution. A utilitarian who judges between any two distributions by seeing which has the greater sum of utility and, if the sums tie, applies some fixed equality criterion to choose the more equal distribution, would hold a current time-slice principle of jus-

tice. As would someone who had a fixed schedule of trade-offs between the sum of happiness and equality. According to a current time-slice principle, all that needs to be looked at, in judging the justice of a distribution, is who ends up with what; in comparing any two distributions one need look only at the matrix presenting the distributions. No further information need be fed into a principle of justice. It is a consequence of such principles of justice that any two structurally identical distributions are equally just. . . .

Most persons do not accept current time-slice principles as constituting the whole story about distributive shares. They think it relevant in assessing the justice of a situation to consider not only the distribution it embodies, but also how that distribution came about. If some persons are in prison for murder or war crimes, we do not say that to assess the justice of the distribution in the society we must look only at what this person has, and that person has, and that person has, . . . at the current time. We think it relevant to ask whether someone did something so that he *deserved* to be punished, deserved to have a lower share. . . .

Patterning

. . . Almost every suggested principle of distributive justice is patterned: to each according to his moral merit, or needs, or marginal product, or how hard he tries, or the weighted sum of the foregoing, and so on. The principle of entitlement we have sketched is *not* patterned. There is no one natural dimension or weighted sum or combination of a small number of natural dimensions that yields the distributions generated in accordance with the principle of entitlement. The set of holdings that results when some persons receive their marginal products, others win at gambling, others receive a share of their mate's income, others receive gifts from foundations, others receive interest on loans, others receive gifts from admirers, others receive returns on investment, others make for themselves much of what they have, others find things, and so on, will not be patterned. . . .

To think that the task of a theory of distributive justice is to fill in the blank in "to each according to his _____" is to be predisposed to search for a pattern; and the separate treatment of "from each according to his _____" treats production and distribution as two separate and independent issues. On an entitlement view these are *not* two separate questions. Whoever makes something, having bought or contracted for all other held resources used in the process (transferring some of his holdings for these cooperating factors), is entitled to it. . . .

So entrenched are maxims of the usual form that perhaps we should present the entitlement conception as a competitor. Ignoring acquisition and rectification, we might say:

> From each according to what he chooses to do, to each according to what he makes for himself (perhaps with the contracted aid of others) and what others choose to do for him and choose to give him of what they've been given previously (under this maxim) and haven't yet expended or transferred.

This, the discerning reader will have noticed, has its defects as a slogan. So as a summary and great simplification (and not as a maxim with any independent meaning) we have:

> *From each as they choose, to each as they are chosen.*

How Liberty Upsets Patterns

It is not clear how those holding alternative conceptions of distributive justice can reject the entitlement conception of justice in holdings. For suppose a distribution favored by one of these non-entitlement conceptions is realized. Let us suppose it is your favorite one and let us call this distribution D_1; perhaps everyone has an equal share, perhaps shares vary in accordance with some dimension you treasure.

Now suppose that Wilt Chamberlain is greatly in demand by basketball teams, being a great gate attraction. (Also suppose contracts run only for a year, with players being free agents.) He signs the following sort of contract with a team: In each home game, twenty-five cents from the price of each ticket of admission goes to him. (We ignore the question of whether he is "gouging" the owners, letting them look out for themselves.) The season starts, and people cheerfully attend his team's games; they buy their tickets, each time dropping a separate twenty-five cents of their admission price into a special box with Chamberlain's name on it. They are excited about seeing him play; it is worth the total admission price to them. Let us suppose that in one season one million persons attend his home games, and Wilt Chamberlain winds up with \$250,000, a much larger sum than the average income and larger even than anyone else has. Is he entitled to this income? Is this new distribution D_2, unjust? If so, why? There is *no* question about whether each of the people was entitled to the control over the resources they held in D_1; because that was the distribution (your favorite) that (for the purposes of argument) we assumed was acceptable. Each of these persons *chose* to give twenty-five cents of their money to Chamberlain. They could have spent it on going to the movies, or on candy bars, or on copies of *Dissent* magazine, or of *Monthly Review*. But they all, at least one million of them, converged on giving it to Wilt Chamberlain in exchange for watching him play basketball. If D_1 was a just distribution, and people voluntarily moved from it to D_2, transferring parts of their shares they were given under D_1 (what was it for if not to do something with?), isn't D_2 also just? If the people were entitled to dispose of the resources to which they were entitled (under D_1), didn't this include their being entitled to give it to, or exchange it with, Wilt Chamberlain? Can anyone else complain on grounds of justice? Each other person already has his legitimate share under D_1. Under D_1, there is nothing that anyone has that anyone else has a claim of justice against. After someone transfers something to Wilt Chamberlain, third parties *still* have their legitimate shares; *their* shares are not changed. By what process could such a transfer among two persons give a rise to a legitimate claim of distributive justice on a portion of what was transferred, by a third party who had no claim of justice on any holding of the others *before* the transfer? To cut off objections irrelevant here, we might imagine the exchanges occurring in a socialist society, after hours. After playing whatever basketball he does in his daily work, or doing whatever other daily work he does, Wilt Chamberlain decides to put in *overtime* to earn additional money. (First his work quota is set; he works time over that.) Or imagine it is a skilled juggler people like to see, who puts on shows after hours. . . .

The general point illustrated by the Wilt Chamberlain example is that no end-state principle or distributional patterned principle of justice can be continuously realized without continuous interference with people's lives. Any favored pattern would be transformed into one unfavored by the principle, by people choosing to act in various ways; for example, by people exchanging goods and services with other people, or giving things to other people, things the transferrers are entitled to under the favored distributional pattern. To maintain a pattern one must either continually interfere to stop people from transferring resources as they wish to, or continually (or periodically) interfere to take from some persons resources that others for some reason chose to transfer to them. . . .

Patterned principles of distributive justice necessitate *re*distributive activities. The likelihood is small that any actual freely-arrived-at set of holdings fits a given pattern; and the likelihood is nil that it will continue to fit the pattern as people exchange and give. From the point of view of an entitlement theory, redistribution is a serious matter indeed, involving, as it does, the violation of people's rights. (An exception is those takings that fall under the principle of the rectification of injustices.) . . .

Locke's Theory of Acquisition

Before we turn to consider other theories of justice in detail, we must introduce an additional bit of complexity into the structure of the entitlement theory. This is best approached by considering Locke's attempt to specify a principle of justice in acquisition. Locke views property rights in an unowned object as originating through someone's mixing his labor with it. This gives rise to many questions. What are the boundaries of what labor is mixed with? If a private astronaut clears a place on Mars, has he mixed his labor with (so that he comes to own) the whole planet, the whole uninhabited universe, or just a particular plot? Which plot does an act bring under ownership? . . .

Locke's proviso that there be "enough and as good left in common for others" is meant to ensure that the situation of others is not worsened. . . .

. . . I assume that any adequate theory of justice in acquisition will contain a proviso similar to [Locke's]. . . .

I believe that the free operation of a market system will not actually run afoul of the Lockean proviso. . . . If this is correct, the proviso will not . . . provide a significant opportunity for future state action.

CRITIQUES OF THE LIBERTARIAN THEORY

Types of Procedural Justice

Nozick's entitlement theory presents social justice in terms of fundamental rights and his three principles of acquisition, transfer, and rectification. On this libertarian account, it is a violation of justice to impose patterns of distribution which infringe individual economic rights. Indeed, though Nozick proposes a material principle of economic justice specifying free choice, his libertarian position is more accurately viewed as a rejection of *all* distributional patterns that might be imposed by material principles of justice. In his view, justice consists not in any particular distributional outcome, but in the unhindered operation of certain just procedures.

This feature of the theory suggests that the libertarian is committed to a form of *procedural* justice. That expression, however, has a variety of meanings, and these will have to be specified before the expression can be applied precisely. John Rawls, whose theory of justice will be discussed later (and whose work has already been encountered in earlier chapters), has identified three distinct forms of procedural justice.* The first is *perfect* procedural justice, a type easily illustrated by considering the rather trivial problem of how justly to divide a pizza. One possible solution to this problem would be to require that the person who cuts the pizza take the last piece. There would then be both an independent criterion or pattern of justice (i.e., each person should receive an equal share), and a procedure which guarantees that a just distribution is achieved. The person who cuts the pizza would be certain to receive the largest possible share only if he or she made every slice the same size. *Imperfect* procedural justice also has an independent criterion of just distribution, but it is not possible to design procedures that can guarantee outcomes in conformity with the criterion. An obvious example is the criminal trial. The independent criterion specifies that those who have committed crimes, and only those who have committed crimes, should be found guilty. The procedures of the criminal trial have been established as the most reliable means of achieving this outcome; yet however strictly those procedures are followed, just outcomes will not *always* result.

Pure procedural justice differs from both the perfect and imperfect forms in the absence of any criterion or pattern of justice independent of the demands of the procedure itself. With this type of justice, any outcome is just as long as it results from the consistent operation of the specified procedures. Gambling is an illustration of pure procedural justice; we consider the result of a lottery or a game of chance unjust only if the rules and procedures of those practices are violated (e.g., when a lottery is fixed or weighted rather than fully random). Thus, when a wealthy person wins big in Las Vegas, we do not say that it is unjust that he or she should win when so many poor people lost in the same game. We may think it unjust that the rich winner is not taxed more heavily, but this consideration of justice is quite separate.

Nozick's entitlement theory advocates procedural justice of this pure procedural type. There is no pattern of just distribution independent of the procedures of acquisition, transfer, and rectification, and justice is served whenever individual rights are respected in the protected operation of these procedures. This claim has been at the center of philosophical controversy over the extreme libertarian account; and many of the most influential theories of justice can be seen as reactions against a libertarian commitment to pure procedural justice. Philosophers who take this critical position often maintain that some independent substantive criterion or pattern is essential to an adequate account of justice, even if there are no procedures that always produce outcomes in conformity with the independent standard. Consideration will now be given briefly to some of these alternative theories of imperfect procedural justice.

Rights-Based Critiques of Libertarianism

Many objections to the libertarian theory take as their starting point assumptions which at least formally resemble the libertarian's own assumptions. It is possible, for instance,

*John Rawls, *A Theory of Justice* (Cambridge, Mass.: Harvard University Press, 1971), pp. 84–86.

to reach conclusions starkly different from Nozick's without abandoning his commitment to fundamental individual rights. For philosophers who adopt this approach, Nozick and other libertarians are correct to stress the importance of rights to a proper account of social justice. The mistake in the libertarian theory, claim these writers, is its ascription of overriding importance to a limited set of economic rights. The AT&T case, for example, involves economic rights beyond those Nozick envisages, for the right to a fair salary plays a major role in this case. Moreover, the rights of women and minorities to more positions bring in considerations of social equality and the right to equal treatment as well as economic rights. As seen in Chapter 6, the notion of a moral right has been given a remarkable variety of meanings. Some writers have considered the concept so vacuous as to have no significance independent of specific legal contexts, while others define the expression so broadly as to include claims to goods and states of life that are rarely possible to achieve.

Many philosophers would argue that a conception of fundamental individual rights more inclusive than Nozick's must be recognized in any adequate theory of justice. Even in strictly economic terms, these writers maintain, Nozick's conception of individual rights is excessively restricted. They would challenge the proponent of libertarianism to answer the following questions: Why should we assume that people's economic rights extend only to the acquisition and dispensation of private property according to the free market rules? Is it not equally plausible to posit more substantive moral rights in the economic sphere, say, to the material means necessary for a decent level of education, health, and welfare? Moreover, Nozick's ideal is most plausible for free transactions among informed and consenting parties. Often the world does not cooperate with this ideal. Contracts, voting privileges, ventures in the stock market, and even family relationships commonly involve manipulation and coercion that work systematically to disadvantage individuals. Does not such an individual have a right to be protected against coercion, fraud, and deception as well as the protections Nozick offers?

But if additional substantive rights are recognized, a far different picture of the requirements of justice comes into focus. The broader and more substantive conception of economic and noneconomic rights introduces a criterion of just distribution by which the outcomes of economic processes can be evaluated. The EEOC's conclusions critical of hiring and promotion at AT&T involve precisely such an evaluation of the justice of the company's policies and practices. Moreover, if people have a right to a minimal level of material means, their rights are violated whenever economic distributions leave some with less than that minimal level, and those distributions are themselves unjust. As seen in Chapter 6 on rights, declarations by the United Nations about human welfare seem to take this approach to justice and rights. A commitment to individual rights can thus result in a theory of justice that might require a far more activist role for government than Nozick's rights-based theory condones (at least, that is, to the extent that pure capitalist economic systems are considered unreliable mechanisms for distributing a decent minimum of material means). Progressive tax legislation to support some form of welfare would be but the most obvious policy implication of this alternative approach.

Marxist Critiques of Libertarianism

Many of the most prominent Marxist critiques of libertarian theories similarly challenge the adequacy of a pure procedural account of justice. Like objections based on rights, the Marxist critique is not formally incompatible with the libertarian account at the level of some general premises. Many Marxists would agree with Nozick that economic freedom of choice is a value deserving of respect and protection in an account of social justice. They would disagree, however, that the economic procedures Nozick and other libertarians advocate are capable of protecting that basic value. In particular, the Marxist critic finds libertarians naive in their assumption that anything like true freedom of choice in economic matters is compatible with systems of private property and capitalist exchange.

The Marxist attack on this critical libertarian assumption focuses on the relations between workers and the objects of their productive labor. As industrial society develops, industries adopt various forms of the division of labor. In consequence, men and women have little, if any, need for what they themselves produce. They work only for compensation. What they produce is simply a means to something else, and thus Marxists claim that workers are "alienated" from their product; one works only to acquire products produced by others, not for the sake of one's own product.

Under capitalist exchange, one's relations to other workers suffer as well, according to Marxists. Fellow workers and the fruits of their labor are regarded solely as a means for satisfying unfulfilled wants. We are interested neither in our fellow workers nor in their products as objects of value in themselves; our interest is purely instrumental. Moreover, our *only* interest in others occurs when they produce something we value; otherwise they are valueless to us. In this way, capitalist exchange based on private property restricts the most basic freedoms in the economic sphere; workers under capitalist systems are denied the freedom to attain a natural relation with the objects of their labor and with their fellow workers, and the range of their economic choices is therefore significantly restricted. The libertarian thus stands accused of ignoring a pernicious impoverishment of individual economic freedom intrinsic to capitalism.

Libertarians such as Nozick might respond by arguing that the justice of economic arrangements cannot be decided by assessing those arrangements at one particular moment. Rather, it is necessary to take multiple historical details into account, for those details alone enable us to determine whether existing inequalities are *deserved*. In the AT&T case, it would have to be determined whether individuals' rights had been violated, and no mere statistical correlations or base-salary figures will provide the needed facts. Thus, any diminution of economic choice entailed by contemporary capitalism—such as the choices left to executives at AT&T—would not be unjust if the present system arose by morally legitimate means. Here again, the Marxist would probably not deny the contention that historical details figure prominently in an adequate account of justice in economic distribution. Indeed, it is on precisely those grounds that Marxist (and many other) philosophers would mount a further challenge to the justice of existing economic arrangements. In what sense, they would ask, did former Vice-President Nelson Rockefeller, as the descendant of the wealthy capitalist John D. Rockefeller, deserve his privileged social status and accompanying enhancement of economic choice? And how do the indigent workers' children employed by the Rockefeller estate deserve their correspondingly disadvantaged position?

The Material Principle of Need

Such considerations lead Marxists and many non-Marxists as well to reject the pure procedural commitments of the libertarian theory of justice. In their place, these philosophers generally propose some form of material principle specifying need as the relevant respect in which people are to be compared for purposes of determining the justice of economic distributions. A similar material principle can also be seen as entailed by the aforementioned critiques of libertarianism that are based on rights. Of course, much will turn in both cases on how the notion of a need is delineated. Generally, to say that someone has a need for something is to say that the person will be harmed or detrimentally affected if that thing is not obtained. For purposes of justice, a material principle of need would be least controversial if it were restricted to *fundamental* needs. If malnutrition, serious bodily injury, and the withholding of critical information involve fundamental harms, then we have a fundamental need for nutrition, health-care facilities, and education. According to theories based on this material principle, justice would require that the satisfaction of fundamental human needs be a higher social priority than the protection of narrow Lockean economic freedoms or rights.

This construal of the material principle of need has provided a historically important alternative to the pure procedural theory of capitalist economic distribution. Yet there may be some room for reconciling theories that emphasize a supplementary principle of need with libertarian accounts of justice. The economies of many advanced industrial countries have the capacity to produce far more than is strictly necessary to meet their citizens' fundamental needs. (Questions of international justice will be set aside for the moment.) When they do so, a principle of need alone will be inadequate to govern the total distribution of economic goods produced. Some philosophers maintain that once everyone's fundamental needs have been satisfied, justice requires no particular pattern of distribution and will allow the operation of rule-governed procedures such as the free market mechanisms that libertarians support. Some current discussions of the right to health care and national health insurance are rooted in the idea of providing a decent minimum of health care in order to treat basic health needs—but no more than basic needs. In this way, a single theory of justice might require the maintenance of certain patterns in the distribution of basic goods (e.g., a minimum level of income, education, and health), while allowing the market to determine distributions of goods beyond those which satisfy fundamental needs. There is nothing necessarily inconsistent about this possibility; as noted earlier, most actual distributional schemes specify different material principles for different purposes. However, it is clearly a significant departure from Nozick's theory, and one he explicitly rejects. He thinks that his world of free transactions is a just world without any requirements of material equality or satisfaction of need.

The material principle of need thus suggests a way of supplementing, as well as fully replacing, the libertarian account of justice. As was noted, every capitalist economy in the modern world is supplemented in some degree by governmental activities designed to maintain patterns of distribution according to fundamental need. These activities are frequently explained in terms of the goal of social equality that Nozick rejects. In moral philosophy, too, many writers consider need-based theories of justice to be nothing more than plausible extensions of the more basic and important ideas in egalitarian theories of justice. Let us now turn directly to such egalitarian accounts.

THE EGALITARIAN THEORY OF JUSTICE

The idea of equality has an important place in most influential moral theories. Deontologists and utilitarians alike express a commitment to the equality of all persons, often for purposes of distributive justice. In the utilitarian view, different people are equal in the value accorded their wants, preferences, and happiness, while the Kantian considers all persons equally deserving of respect as ends in themselves. Also, as Ronald Dworkin suggested (in the first selection in Chapter 6), the notion that there are fundamental and inviolable moral rights is one way of giving expression to the idea of moral equality. In each of these theories, it is considered a requirement of morality that people be treated equally regardless of their individual differences. Nonetheless, as suggested earlier, a commitment to this basic equality is compatible with a belief that justice must be determined by attending to the relevant respects in which individual people differ. People may be considered fundamentally equal for some moral purposes (e.g., in their basic moral rights and obligations), yet startlingly diverse for the purpose of justly distributing certain social burdens and benefits.

It is precisely this contention, however, that the egalitarian theory most closely scrutinizes and to some extent rejects. In its radical form, egalitarianism is the thesis that individual differences are no more significant in an account of social justice than they are in the other domains of morality. Accordingly, distributions of burdens and benefits in a society are just to the extent that they are equal, and deviations from absolute equality in distribution can be determined to be unjust without consideration of the respects in which members of the society may differ. For example, the fact that roughly 20 percent of the wealth in the United States is owned by only 5 percent of the population, while the poorest 20 percent of the population controls only 5 percent of the wealth, would make American society unjust by this radical egalitarian standard, no matter how relatively deserving the people at both extremes might be (by a nonequalitarian standard of desert). For strict egalitarians, the possession of humanity is the sole respect in which people are to be compared in determining the justice of distributions.

Stated in so radical a form, egalitarianism seems highly implausible, for it leaves no room for the widespread conviction that some of the respects in which people differ entail differences in what they deserve. Most egalitarian accounts of justice, however, are heavily qualified and more carefully formulated than the extreme version just characterized. Thus, mere membership in the human species might not entitle people to absolutely equal shares of all social benefits, but it could recommend the equal distribution of those goods necessary to satisfy fundamental human needs.

Egalitarianism so construed is tied to some material principle of fundamental need. It points to a basic equality among individuals that takes priority over all differences in what people deserve by some other standard. On this view, it would be a misunderstanding of justice to think that any individual deserves anything less than the satisfaction of his or her fundamental needs, for desert cannot be judged until those needs have been met.

Some egalitarian accounts of justice move still further away from radical egalitarian commitments. Proponents of such accounts maintain that the equal possession of humanity does not legitimate even so minimal an equality of distribution as that involved in the satisfaction of everyone's fundamental needs. For these theorists, egalitarian considerations result in nothing more than a basic equality of *opportunity*. Justice would then require only that individuals each be given the opportunity to satisfy their fundamental needs and (more controversially) needs and desires that surpass the fundamental level. An egalitarianism of this sort is often invoked in support of contemporary affirmative action programs such as that illustrated by the AT&T case. Supporters of these programs maintain that true equality of economic opportunity can be achieved only if the government takes active, interventionist steps to promote the hiring of women and members of minority groups.

It is thus clear that egalitarian accounts provide an alternative to the libertarian endorsement of unhindered individual choice. One of the most powerful and influential egalitarian alternatives is that recently developed by John Rawls, whose theory of justice will be considered next.

Rawls's Theory

As seen in Chapter 4, Rawls's theory is a version of deontology. He presents his deontological theory as a direct challenge to utilitarianism, for he considers utilitarian accounts critically deficient in their treatment of social justice. It will be helpful to get a sense of his objections to utilitarianism (some of which were detailed in Chapter 4) before consideration is turned to his constructive proposals. His basic objection, shared with most similar critiques, is that the distributions produced by maximizing utility could entail violations of basic individual liberties and rights that ought to be guaranteed by social justice. In Rawls's own words, "Each person possesses an inviolability founded on justice that even the welfare of society as a whole cannot override."* Util-

*John Rawls, *A Theory of Justice* (Cambridge, Mass.: Harvard University Press, 1971), p. 3.

itarianism, being indifferent as to the *distribution* of satisfactions among individuals but not to the *total* satisfaction in society, would presumably permit the infringement of some peoples' rights and liberties if the infringement genuinely promised to produce a proportionately greater utility for others. For example, during a war or a circumstance of civil violence, it might be possible to justify restricting freedom of the press, confiscating weapons, searching private homes, denying the right to vote to certain groups, and even torturing prisoners, *if* there were sufficient utility for the great majority. This utilitarian approach to individual rights can lead, according to Rawls, to fundamental affronts to our conception of social justice. Utilitarianism thus becomes a kind of expediency incompatible with the central tenets of justice.

Of course, utilitarians have not been persuaded by such arguments; indeed, many have maintained that the principle of utility is alone sufficient to ground an adequate account of justice. These utilitarians argue that objections sketched by Rawls seem plausible only because they are abstracted from the actual conditions in which considerations of justice arise and because they appeal to excessively exaggerated examples. For these philosophers, a complete assessment of the social consequences in such cases reveals that the allegedly justified violations of common notions of justice do not genuinely satisfy the principle of utility. For example, though utilitarianism might seem to support slavery in certain contexts, enforced servitude would not appear justifiable once the destructive implications of such an act for important social and legal institutions are taken into account. Rule utilitarians, in particular, argue that adequate principles of justice are on the whole justifiable in view of their consequences, and that suspensions of those principles should not be permitted even if social utility seems to recommend them in special cases.

Rawls is as unmoved by these arguments as utilitarians are by pure egalitarian considerations. To him, it often seems enough that violations of justice could in principle be allowed on utilitarian grounds. The task, then, is to advocate an alternative ethical theory capable of grounding satisfactory principles of justice. As the first selection in Chapter 4 indicates, Rawls turns for this purpose to a hypothetical social contract procedure that is strongly indebted to what he calls the "Kantian conception of equality." According to this social contract account, valid principles of justice are those principles to which we would all agree if we could freely and impartially consider the social situation from a standpoint (the "original position") outside any actual society. Impartiality is guaranteed in this situation by a conceptual device Rawls calls the "veil of ignorance." This notion stipulates that in the original position, each person is (at least momentarily) ignorant of all his or her particular fortuitous characteristics. For example, the person's sex, race, IQ, family background, and special talents or handicaps are unrevealed in this hypothetical circumstance.

The veil of ignorance prevents people from promoting principles of justice that are biased toward their own combinations of fortuitous talents and characteristics— e.g., athletic, intellectual, or leadership skills. Rawls argues that under these conditions, people would unanimously agree on two fundamental principles of justice. The first requires that each person be permitted the maximum amount of equal basic liberty compatible with a similar liberty for others. The second stipulates that once this equal basic liberty is assured, inequalities in social primary goods (e.g., income, rights, and opportunities) are to be allowed only if they benefit everyone. Rawls considers social institutions to be just if they are in conformity with these two basic principles, as the following selection makes clear. (This selection, aimed exclusively at considerations of justice, reflects many of the ideas found in Rawls's selection in Chapter 4.)

JOHN RAWLS

An Egalitarian Theory of Justice*

The Role of Justice

Justice is the first virtue of social institutions, as truth is of systems of thought. A theory however elegant and economical must be rejected or revised if it is untrue; likewise laws and institutions no matter how efficient and well-arranged must be reformed or abolished if they are unjust. Each person possesses an inviolability founded on justice that even the welfare of society as a whole cannot override. For this reason justice denies that the loss of freedom for some is made right by a greater good shared by others. It does not allow that the sacrifices imposed on a few are outweighed by the larger sum of advantages enjoyed by many. Therefore in a just society the liberties of equal citizenship are taken as settled; the rights secured by justice are not subject to political bargaining or to the calculus of social interests. The only thing that permits us to acquiesce in an erroneous theory is the lack of a better one; analogously, an injustice is tolerable only when it is necessary to avoid an even greater injustice. Being first virtues of human activities, truth and justice are uncompromising.

*From John Rawls, *A Theory of Justice* (Cambridge, Mass.: Harvard University Press, 1971), pp. 3–4, 18–19, 60–62, 64–65, 100–104.

These propositions seem to express our intuitive conviction of the primacy of justice. No doubt they are expressed too strongly. In any event I wish to inquire whether these contentions or others similar to them are sound, and if so how they can be accounted for. To this end it is necessary to work out a theory of justice in the light of which these assertions can be interpreted and assessed. I shall begin by considering the role of the principles of justice. Let us assume, to fix ideas, that a society is a more or less self-sufficient association of persons who in their relations to one another recognize certain rules of conduct as binding and who for the most part act in accordance with them. Suppose further that these rules specify a system of cooperation designed to advance the good of those taking part in it. Then, although a society is a cooperative venture for mutual advantage, it is typically marked by a conflict as well as by an identity of interests. There is an identity of interests since social cooperation makes possible a better life for all than any would have if each were to live solely by his own efforts. There is a conflict of interests since persons are not indifferent as to how the greater benefits produced by their collaboration are distributed, for in order to pursue their ends they each prefer a larger to a lesser share. A set of principles is required for choosing among the various social arrangements which determine this division of advantages and for underwriting an agreement on the proper distributive shares. These principles are the principles of social justice: they provide a way of assigning rights and duties in the basic institutions of society and they define the appropriate distribution of the benefits and burdens of social cooperation. . . .

The Original Position and Justification

. . . The idea here is simply to make vivid to ourselves the restrictions that it seems reasonable to impose on arguments for principles of justice, and therefore on these principles themselves. Thus it seems reasonable and generally acceptable that no one should be advantaged or disadvantaged by natural fortune or social circumstances in the choice of principles. It also seems widely agreed that it should be impossible to tailor principles to the circumstances of one's own case. We should insure further that particular inclinations and aspirations, and persons' conceptions of their good, do not affect the principles adopted. The aim is to rule out those principles that it would be rational to propose for acceptance, however little the chance of success, only if one knew certain things that are irrelevant from the standpoint of justice. For example, if a man knew that he was wealthy, he might find it rational to advance the principle that various taxes for welfare measures be counted unjust; if he knew that he was poor, he would most likely propose the contrary principle. To represent the desired restrictions one imagines a situation in which everyone is deprived of this sort of information. One excludes the knowledge of those contingencies which sets men at odds and allows them to be guided by their prejudices. In this manner the veil of ignorance is arrived at in a natural way. . . .

Two Principles of Justice

I shall now state in a provisional form the two principles of justice that I believe would be chosen in the original position. . . .

The first statement of the two principles reads as follows.

First: each person is to have an equal right to the most extensive basic liberty compatible with a similar liberty for others.

Second: social and economic inequalities are to be arranged so that they are both (a) reasonably expected to be to everyone's advantage, and (b) attached to positions and offices open to all. . . .
[The Difference Principle]

By way of general comment, these principles primarily apply, as I have said, to the basic structure of society. They are to govern the assignment of rights and duties and to regulate the distribution of social and economic advantages. As their formulation suggests, these principles presuppose that the social structure can be divided into two more or less distinct parts, the first principle applying to the one, the second to the other. They distinguish between those aspects of the social system that define and secure the equal liberties of citizenship and those that specify and establish social and economic inequalities. The basic liberties of citizens are, roughly speaking, political liberty (the right to vote and to be eligible for public office) together with freedom of speech and assembly; liberty of conscience and freedom of thought; freedom of the person along with the right to hold (personal) property; and freedom from arbitrary arrest and seizure as defined by the concept of the rule of law. These liberties are all required to be equal by the first principle, since citizens of a just society are to have the same basic rights.

The second principle applies, in the first approximation, to the distribution of income and wealth and to the design of organizations that make use of differences in authority and responsibility, or chains of command. While the distribution of wealth and income need not be equal, it must be to everyone's advantage, and at the same time, positions of authority and offices of command must be accessible to all. One applies the second principle by holding positions open, and then, subject to this constraint, arranges social and economic inequalities so that everyone benefits.

These principles are to be arranged in a serial order with the first principle prior to the second. This ordering means that a departure from the institutions of equal liberty required by the first principle cannot be justified, or compensated for, by greater social and economic advantages. The distribution of wealth and income, and the hierarchies of authority, must be consistent with both the liberties of equal citizenship and equality of opportunity.

It is clear that these principles are rather specific in their content, and their acceptance rests on certain assumptions that I must eventually try to explain and justify. A theory of justice depends upon a theory of society in ways that will become evident as we proceed. For the present, it should be observed that the two principles (and this holds for all formulations) are a special case of a more general conception of justice that can be expressed as follows:

All social values—liberty and opportunity, income and wealth, and the bases of self-respect—are to be distributed equally unless an unequal distribution of any, or all, of these values is to everyone's advantage.

Injustice, then, is simply inequalities that are not to the benefit of all. Of course, this conception is extremely vague and requires interpretation.

As a first step, suppose that the basic structure of society distributes certain primary goods, that is, things that evey rational man is presumed to want. These goods normally have a use whatever a person's rational plan of life. For simplicity, assume that the chief primary goods at the disposition of society are rights and liberties, powers and opportunities, income and wealth. These are the social primary goods. Other primary goods such as health and vigor, intelligence and imagination, are natural goods; although their possession is influenced by the basic structure, they are not so directly under its control. Imagine, then, a hypothetical initial arrangement in which all the social primary goods are equally distributed: everyone has similar rights and duties, and income and wealth are evenly shared. This state of affairs provides a benchmark for judging improvements. If certain inequalities of wealth and organizational powers would make everyone better off than in this hypothetical starting situation, then they accord with the general conception.

Now it is possible, at least theoretically, that by giving up some of their fundamental liberties men are sufficiently compensated by the resulting social and economic gains. The general conception of justice imposes no restrictions on what sort of inequalities are permissible; it only requires that everyone's position be improved. . . .

Now the second principle insists that each person benefit from permissible inequalites in the basic structure. This means that it must be reasonable for each relevant representative man defined by this structure, when he views it as a going concern, to prefer his prospects with the inequality to his prospects without it. One is not allowed to justify differences in why not? Don't have a rt, torches

248   *Topics in Moral and Social Philosophy*

income or organizational powers on the ground that the disadvantages of those in one position are outweighed by the greater advantages of those in another. Much less can infringements of liberty be counterbalanced in this way. Applied to the basic structure, the principle of utility would have us maximize the sum of expectations of representative men (weighted by the number of persons they represent, on the classical view); and this would permit us to compensate for the losses of some by the gains of others. Instead, the two principles require that everyone benefit from economic and social inequalities. . . .

The Tendency to Equality

I wish to conclude this discussion of the two principles by explaining the sense in which they express an egalitarian conception of justice. Also I should like to forestall the objection to the principle of fair opportunity that it leads to a callous meritocratic society. In order to prepare the way for doing this, I note several aspects of the conception of justice that I have set out.

First we may observe that the difference principle gives some weight to the considerations singled out by the principle of redress. This is the principle that undeserved inequalities call for redress; and since inequalities of birth and natural endowment are undeserved, these inequalities are to be somehow compensated for. Thus the principle holds that in order to treat all persons equally, to provide geniune equality of opportunity, society must give more attention to those with fewer native assets and to those born into the less favorable social positions. The idea is to redress the bias of contingencies in the direction of equality. In pursuit of this principle greater resources might be spent on the education of the less rather than the more intelligent, at least over a certain time of life, say the earlier years of school.

Now the principle of redress has not to my knowledge been proposed as the sole criterion of justice, as the single aim of the social order. It is plausible as most such principles are only as a prima facie principle, one that is to be weighed in the balance with others. For example, we are to weigh it against the principle to improve the average standard of life, or to advance the common good. But whatever other principles we hold, the claims of redress are to be taken into account. It is thought to represent one of the elements in our conception of justice. Now the difference principle is not of course the principle of redress. It does not require society to try to even out handicaps as if all were expected to compete on a fair basis in the same race. But the difference principle would allocate resources in education, say, so as to improve the long-term expectation of the least favored. If this end is attained by giving more attention to the better endowed, it is permissible; otherwise not. And in making this decision, the value of education should not be assessed only in terms of economic efficiency and social welfare. Equally if not more important is the role of education in enabling a person to enjoy the culture of his society and to take part in its affairs, and in this way to provide for each individual a secure sense of his own worth.

Thus although the difference principle is not the same as that of redress, it does achieve some of the intent of the latter principle. It transforms the aims of the basic structure so that the total scheme of institutions no longer emphasizes social efficiency and technocratic values. . . .

The natural distribution is neither just nor unjust; nor is it unjust that men are born into society at some particular posi-

Diff. Principle?
Why not.?

tion. These are simply natural facts. What is just and unjust is the way that institutions deal with these facts. Aristocratic and caste societies are unjust because they make these contingencies the ascriptive basis for belonging to more or less enclosed and privileged social classes. The basic structure of these societies incorporates the arbitrariness found in nature. But there is no necessity for men to resign themselves to these contingencies. The social system is not an unchangeable order beyond human control but a pattern of human action. In justice as fairness men agree to share one another's fate. In designing institutions they undertake to avail themselves of the accidents of nature and social circumstance only when doing so is for the common benefit. The two principles are a fair way of meeting the arbitrariness of fortune; and while no doubt imperfect in other ways, the institutions which satisfy these principles are just. . . .

There is a natural inclination to object that those better situated deserve their greater advantages whether or not they are to the benefit of others. At this point it is necessary to be clear about the notion of desert. It is perfectly true that given a just system of cooperation as a scheme of public rules and the expectations set up by it, those who, with the prospect of improving their condition, have done what the system announces that it will reward are entitled to their advantages. In this sense the more fortunate have a claim to their better situation; their claims are legitimate expectations established by social institu-

tions, and the community is obligated to meet them. But this sense of desert presupposes the existence of the cooperative scheme; it is irrelevant to the question whether in the first place the scheme is to be designed in accordance with the difference principle or some other criterion.

Perhaps some will think that the person with greater natural endowments deserves those assets and the superior character that made their development possible. Because he is more worthy in this sense, he deserves the greater advantages that he could achieve with them. This view, however, is surely incorrect. It seems to be one of the fixed points of our considered judgments that no one deserves his place in the distribution of native endowments, any more than one deserves one's initial starting place in society. The assertion that a man deserves the superior character that enables him to make the effort to cultivate his abilities is equally problematic; for his character depends in large part upon fortunate family and social circumstances for which he can claim no credit. The notion of desert seems not to apply to these cases. Thus the more advantaged representative man cannot say that he deserves and therefore has a right to a scheme of cooperation in which he is permitted to acquire benefits in ways that do not contribute to the welfare of others. There is no basis for his making this claim. From the standpoint of common sense, then, the difference principle appears to be acceptable both to the more advantaged and to the less advantaged individual.

Rawls's theory is egalitarian in several ways. First, it makes equality a basic characteristic of the original position from which the social contract is forged. Equality is built into that hypothetical position in the form of a free and equal bargain among all parties, where there is equal ignorance of all individual characteristics and advantages that persons have or will have in their daily lives. Furthermore, people in such a position would choose to make the equal possession of a scheme of basic liberties the first commitment of their social institutions. Given the lexical ordering of the two principles, this commitment to equal liberty assumes a rigid priority in the Rawlsian account of justice. It can be said to express the inviolability of persons that utilitarian theories were criticized for ignoring. Finally, the second part of the second principle prescribes equality of opportunity as a subsidiary maxim of justice.

Because parties in the original position are said by Rawls to be free and *equal*, one might suppose that the overriding principle of distributive justice should be strictly equal distribution. No perfectly free and equal person, after all, would expect either more or less than an equal share of primary social goods. Rawls even notes that "the obvious starting point is to suppose that . . . social primary goods . . . should be equal: everyone should have an equal share."* Nevertheless, Rawls rejects radical egalitarianism, arguing that equal distribution cannot be justified as the sole primary principle. If there were inequalities rendering everyone better off by comparison to initial equality, these inequalities would be desirable—so long as they were consistent with equal liberty and fair opportunity. More particularly, if these inequalities work to enhance the position of the most disadvantaged persons as measured by a higher level of primary goods for them, then it would be self-defeating for the least advantaged or anyone else to seek to prohibit the inequalities. Rawls thus rejects radical egalitarianism in favor of his second principle of justice.

The first part of his second principle is called the "difference principle." This principle permits inequalities of distribution so long as they are consistent with equal liberty and fair opportunity. Rawls formulates this principle more precisely later in *A Theory of Justice* (and in several articles published subsequently), so that such inequalities would be justifiable only if they most enhance the position of the "*representative least advantaged*" person—that is, a hypothetical individual particularly unfortunate in the distribution of fortuitous characteristics or social advantages. Formulated in this way, the difference principle could allow, for instance, extraordinary economic rewards to entrepreneurs if the resulting economic stimulation were to produce improved job opportunities and working conditions for the least advantaged members of society. A strong egalitarian flavor is retained, however, in that such inequalities would be permissible only if it could be demonstrated that they worked to the greatest advantage of those who were worst off. Rawls even points out that the "first problem of justice" is to delineate principles of justice that can regulate inequalities and can be used to rearrange the long-lasting effects of social, natural, and historical contingencies. The difference principle rests on the view that because inequalities of birth, historical circumstance, and natural endowment are undeserved, society should correct them by improving the unequal situation of naturally disadvantaged members. "The idea," says Rawls, "is to redress the bias of contingencies in the direction of equality."†

*John Rawls, "A Kantian Conception of Equality," *Cambridge Review* (February 1975): 97.

†John Rawls, *A Theory of Justice* (Cambridge, Mass.: Harvard University Press, 1971), pp. 100 ff.

then we KNOW P2 is operant.
Justice is being served.

Critiques of Rawls's Theory

Rawls contends that people situated behind a veil of ignorance would adopt the difference principle as a way of protecting themselves against the unknown contingencies that could conceivably befall them. This contention has been among the most controversial in his theory. Some philosophers have argued that Rawls unjustifiably assumes that people would agree to the difference principle. That assumption implies a particular conception of the process of human deliberation in situations involving choice, and these critics maintain that Rawls's conception of the process of choice is inaccurate. Specifically, it is said to ignore the possibility that people would agree to a riskier system of basic rules which permitted more dramatic wins (as well as losses) in the distribution of social benefits. Other philosophers, including some utilitarians, suggest that the difference principle represents a departure from Rawls's commitment to the equal inviolability of all people. For it means in effect that the wants, preferences, and happiness of the most advantaged individuals do not count for as much as the wants, preferences, and happiness of those who are less advantaged.

A second line of criticism springs from Nozick's libertarianism, perhaps the single most visible alternative account of justice in contemporary philosophy. His theory, of course, guarantees equal liberties but without any attempt to compensate for advantages resulting from natural and social contingencies. He argues, specifically against Rawls, that a theory of justice should be structured to protect individual rights against state interference and should not promote patterning arrangements that in effect *redistribute* economic benefits and burdens. In *Anarchy, State, and Utopia,* Nozick argues against Rawls's views as follows:

> If things fell from heaven like manna, and no one had any special entitlement to any portion of it, and no manna would fall unless all agreed to a particular distribution, and somehow the quantity varied depending on the distribution, then it is plausible to claim that persons placed so that they couldn't make threats, or hold out for specially large shares, would agree to the difference principle of distribution. But is *this* the appropriate model for thinking about how the things people produce are to be distributed?*

Rawls no doubt would reply that Nozick fails to consider how the justice of acquisitions, holdings, transfers, and rectification is to be monitored by social institutions, thus ignoring problems of regulation and basic institutional structures in society. On the other hand, Nozick is accusing Rawls of neglecting the underlying reason for someone's having an entitlement to something in the first place, including the very significant reason that the person *produced* it. Rawls stands accused of incorrectly thinking of social goods as given, like manna, independently of a background history of individual effort.

*Robert Nozick, *Anarchy, State, and Utopia* (New York: Basic Books, Inc., Publishers, 1974), p. 198.

FAIR OPPORTUNITY

The difference principle expresses Rawls's conviction that the justice of social institutions is to be gauged by their tendency to counteract the inequalities caused purely by luck of birth (family and class origins), natural endowment, and historical circumstances (accidents at some point or over the course of a lifetime). This approach conforms with many common beliefs about justice, for it would generally be regarded as unjust if social burdens and benefits were distributed on the basis of such fortuitous characteristics. But why are fortuitous characteristics not considered appropriate as material principles of distributive justice? The most plausible reason is that to use principles based on fortuitous circumstances would be to treat "people differently in ways that profoundly affect their lives *because of differences for which they have no responsibility.*"* This reason for excluding various possible distributive arrangements, including Nozick's, has powerful implications. It implies that individual differences can fairly be made relevant differences for purposes of distribution only if those persons can be held responsible for the differences.

The "fair-opportunity principle," as it may be called, says that no person should be granted social benefits through (let us call them "advantageous") properties for which he or she is not responsible; and it says that no person should be denied social benefits on the basis of (let us call them "disadvantageous") properties for which he or she is not responsible. Such advantaging or disadvantaging properties are never grounds for morally acceptable discrimination between persons, because they are not the sorts of properties that one has a fair chance to acquire or overcome. While in many societies religion and social status are not acquired and can be overcome, race, sex, and IQ—those natural properties that plague justice more than any others—are not easily alterable and are the kinds of properties we must consider in addressing issues of fair opportunity.

Consider how the fair-opportunity principle could be applied to problems of very slow learners in the public schools. If IQ is something for which a child is not responsible, and if no person should be denied social benefits on the basis of this property, then it would be unjust not to distribute to these slow learners the benefits conferred upon all who share in the system of benefits. Any reflection at this point will be aided by considering the connected and more familiar example of the distribution of resources through which one may receive a basic education. This benefit is conferred on all citizens equally, and a person would be thought deprived or harmed if denied the benefit. Imagine a community in which an efficient school system provides a uniform opportunity for a quality education to all students with basic skills, regardless of sex, race, or religion. Suppose, too, that such a system does not offer any extra facilities to students with reading difficulties or mental handicaps, and therefore does not offer them an equal

---

*William K. Frankena, "Some Beliefs about Justice," in K. E. Goodpaster, ed., *Perspectives on Morality: Essays of William K. Frankena* (Notre Dame, Ind.: University of Notre Dame Press, 1976), p. 98. [Italics added.]

educational opportunity in *one* sense of "equal." Such students require special training in order to overcome their problems and to receive what for them is a minimally adequate education. If they were responsible for their slowness, we might say that they deserve no special training and simply must expend greater effort. But when we discover that they are not responsible, owing to IQ deficiencies or handicaps produced through injury, we often say that they deserve special consideration; hence, different levels of education are introduced for different kinds of students, regardless of the differential in cost (within reasonable financial limits).

At stake is not an *equal* distribution of economic resources to each individual. We do not say that slow learners with special reading problems or mental handicaps should be offered an equal amount of money or training or resources as other pupils on the ground that they are not responsible for their condition. Rather, we say they should receive a quality education, even if it costs more, because the principle of fair opportunity morally *requires* it. Any alternative distribution would lead to an undue burden for this group of persons. The burden would be undue because placed in violation of justice—or at least so it is claimed by those who support a principle of fair opportunity.

It should be observed that if one accepts this view of distributive justice, it can easily lead to a revised perspective on social policies of distribution. For the sake of moral consistency, it must be said that *whenever* people are not responsible for having certain disadvantageous properties, they should not be denied critical benefits simply because they possess those properties. But now suppose that almost all our chief abilities and disabilities are a function of what Rawls refers to as the "natural lottery." That is, suppose that almost all our talents and deficiencies are a causal function of heredity and environment and that we consequently are not responsible for them. Suppose, for example, that even one's ability to work long hours, one's competitive drive, and one's sense of dedication are environmentally produced. Advantageous properties, from this perspective, are not deserved any more than disadvantageous, handicapping properties. It follows that both advantageous and disadvantageous properties are irrelevant for purposes of distributive justice. If this theory of the causal origins of advantageous and disadvantageous properties were accepted along with the justification based on fair opportunity previously outlined, one would be led to views about distributive justice radically different from the ones we now generally acknowledge.

It is uncertain what the full implications of this approach would be, though roughly these assumptions and conclusions seem present in Rawls's work. He argues, for example, as follows (obviously against views such as Nozick's):

> [The liberal interpretation of] Free Market arrangements must be set within a framework of political and legal institutions which regulates the overall trends of economic events and preserves the social conditions necessary for fair equality of opportunity. . . .
>
> While the liberal conception seems clearly preferable to the system of natural liberty, intuitively it still appears defective. For one thing, . . . it still permits the distribution of wealth and income to be determined by the natural

distribution of abilities and talents. Within the limits allowed by the background arrangements, distributive shares are decided by the outcome of the natural lottery; and this outcome is arbitrary from a moral perspective. There is no more reason to permit the distribution of income and wealth to be settled by the distribution of natural assets than by historical and social fortune. Furthermore, the principle of fair opportunity can be only imperfectly carried out, at least as long as the institution of the family exists. The extent to which natural capacities develop and reach fruition is affected by all kinds of social conditions and class attitudes. Even the willingness to make an effort, to try, and so to be deserving in the ordinary sense is itself dependent upon happy family and social circumstances.*

Social rewards and punishments would clearly be conceived in a revisionary manner if Rawls's approach were generalized to many social contexts. Rather than allow radical inequalities based on effort, contribution, and merit, one would see justice as done when radical inequalities are diminished (so long as disadvantaged persons were advantaged by such a system of conferring benefits). On the other hand, as Bernard Williams has correctly pointed out,† this ideal procedure of reducing inequalities will have to stop somewhere, especially if it is assumed that everything about a person is environmentally controlled. The radical egalitarian ideal of complete equality is untenable. It thus remains uncertain what the broader implications of Rawls's approach would be. This problem also provides a reason why some have argued—Nozick, for example—that the principle of fair opportunity is not a valid principle at all.

CONCLUSION

Both Rawls and Nozick, as well as their utilitarian opponents, capture many of our intuitive convictions about justice. Rawls's difference principle, for example, describes a fairly common belief about the role of fortuitous human characteristics (i.e., those determined by natural or historical contingency). But Nozick's theory also makes a strong appeal in the domains of taxation and property ownership, while utilitarianism is widely used in the development of public policy. Here the discussion of moral pluralism in Chapter 2 may be recalled, for some have argued that there are several equally valid, or at least equally viable, theories of justice. Before this conclusion is accepted, however, attention should be addressed to some issues about liberty that have major implications for theories of justice.

*John Rawls, *A Theory of Justice* (Cambridge, Mass.: Harvard University Press, 1971), pp. 73 ff.

† Bernard Williams, "The Idea of Equality," reprinted in H. Bedau, *Justice and Equality* (Englewood Cliffs, N.J.: Prentice-Hall, Inc., 1971), p. 135.

SUGGESTED SUPPLEMENTARY READINGS

Concepts and Principles of Justice

Benn, Stanley I.: "Justice," in Paul Edwards, ed., *The Encyclopedia of Philosophy* (New York: Macmillan Company and Free Press, 1967), vol. 4, pp. 298–302.

Bowie, Norman E.: *Towards a New Theory of Distributive Justice* (Amherst: University of Massachusetts Press, 1971).

Feinberg, Joel: "Justice and Personal Desert," in Carl J. Friedrich and John W. Chapman, eds., *Nomos 6: Justice* (New York: Atherton Press, 1963), pp. 68–97.

———: *Social Philosophy* (Englewood Cliffs, N.J.: Prentice-Hall, Inc., 1973), chap. 7.

———: "Noncomparative Justice," *Philosophical Review* (1974): 297–338.

Frankena, W. K.: "Some Beliefs about Justice," in K. E. Goodpaster, ed., *Perspectives on Morality: Essays of William K. Frankena* (Notre Dame, Ind.: University of Notre Dame Press, 1976), pp. 93–106.

Lucas, J. R.: "Justice," *Philosophy,* **47** (1972): 229–248.

Perelman, Charles: *The Idea of Justice and the Problem of Argument,* John Petrie, trans. (New York: Humanities Press, 1963).

———: *Justice* (New York: Random House, 1967).

Plato: *The Republic,* Francis Cornford, trans. (New York: Oxford University Press, 1945).

Rescher, Nicholas: *Distributive Justice* (Indianapolis: Bobbs-Merrill Company, Inc., 1966).

Sterba, James: *The Demands of Justice* (Notre Dame, Ind.: University of Notre Dame Press, 1980).

———, ed., *Justice: Alternative Political Perspectives* (Belmont, Calif.: Wadsworth Publishing Company, Inc., 1980).

Libertarian Theories

Dworkin, Gerald, Gordon Bermant, and Peter G. Brown, eds.: *Markets and Morals* (Washington: Hemisphere Publishing Corp., John Wiley, 1977).

Friedman, Milton: *Capitalism and Freedom* (Chicago: University of Chicago Press, 1962).

Goldman, Alan H.: "The Entitlement Theory of Distributive Justice," *Journal of Philosophy,* **73** (1976): 823–835.

Hayek, Friedrich: *Individualism and Economic Order* (Chicago: University of Chicago Press, 1948).

Held, Virginia: "John Locke on Robert Nozick," *Social Research,* **43** (Spring 1976): 169–195.

Lyons, David: "Rights Against Humanity," *Philosophical Review,* **85** (1976): 208–215.

Mack, Eric: "Liberty and Justice," in John Arthur and William Shaw, eds., *Justice and Economic Distribution* (Englewood Cliffs, N.J.: Prentice-Hall, Inc., 1978), pp. 83–93.

Narveson, Jan: "Justice and the Business Society," in Tom L. Beauchamp and Norman Bowie, eds., *Ethical Theory and Business* (Englewood Cliffs, N.J.: Prentice-Hall, Inc., 1979).

Nozick, Robert: *Anarchy, State, and Utopia* (New York: Basic Books, Inc., Publishers, 1974).

Scanlon, Thomas M.: "Nozick on Rights, Liberty, and Property," *Philosophy and Public Affairs,* **6** (1976): 3–25.

Singer, Peter: "The Right to Be Rich or Poor," *New York Review of Books,* **6** (March 1976): 19–24.

Egalitarian Theories

Barry, Brian: *The Liberal Theory of Justice, a Critical Examination of the Principal Doctrines in a Theory of Justice by John Rawls* (Oxford, England: Clarendon Press, 1973).

———: "Rawls on Average and Total Utility: A Comment," *Philosophical Studies,* **31** (1977): 317–325.

Beauchamp, Tom L.: "Distributive Justice and the Difference Principle," in H. Gene Blocker and Elizabeth Smith, eds., *John Rawls' Theory of Social Justice: An Introduction* (Athens: Ohio University Press, 1980).

Bedau, Hugo, A., ed.: *Justice and Equality* (Englewood Cliffs, N.J.: Prentice-Hall, Inc., 1971).

Berlin, Isaiah: "Equality," in *Proceedings of the Aristotelian Society,* **56** (1955–1956): 301–326.

Blackstone, William T., ed.: *The Concept of Equality* (Minneapolis: Burgess Publishing Company, 1969).

Blocker, H. Gene, and Elizabeth Smith, eds.: *John Rawls' Theory of Social Justice: An Introduction* (Athens: Ohio University Press, 1980).

Daniels, Norman, ed.: *Reading Rawls: Critical Studies of a Theory of Justice* (New York: Basic Books, Inc., Publishers, 1975).

Gauthier, David: "Justice and Natural Endowment: Toward a Critique of Rawls' Ideological Framework," *Social Theory and Practice,* **3** (1974): 3–26.

MacIntyre, Alasdair: "Justice: A New Theory and Some Old Questions," *Boston University Law Review,* **52** (1972): 330–334.

McCloskey, Herbert J.: "Egalitarianism, Equality and Justice," *Australasian Journal of Philosophy,* **44** (1966): 50–69.

Nagel, Thomas: "Equality," in *Mortal Questions* (Cambridge, England: Cambridge University Press, 1979).

Raphael, David Daiches: "Equality and Equity," *Philosophy,* **21** (1946): 118–132.

Rawls, John: "Reply to Alexander and Musgrave," *Quarterly Journal of Economics,* **88** (1974): 633–655.

———: "Fairness to Goodness," *Philosophical Review,* **84** (1975): 536–554.

———: "Kantian Constructivism In Moral Theory: The Dewey Lectures 1980," *Journal of Philosophy,* **77** (1980): 515–572.

Richards, David: *A Theory of Reasons for Action* (Oxford, England: Clarendon Press, 1971).

Vlastos, Gregory: "Justice and Equality," in Richard B. Brandt, ed., *Social Justice* (Englewood Cliffs, N.J.: Prentice-Hall, Inc., 1962).

Williams, Bernard: "The Idea of Equality," in Peter Laslett and W. G. Runciman, eds., *Philosophy, Politics and Society,* 2d Series (New York: Barnes and Noble, 1962).

Socialist and Marxist Theories

Engels, Friedrich: "Socialism: Utopian and Scientific," reprinted in Arthur Mendel, ed., *Essential Works of Marxism* (New York: Bantam Books, Inc., 1961), pp. 45–82.

Gallie, W. B.: "Liberal Morality and Socialist Morality," in Peter Laslett, ed., *Philosophy, Politics, and Society* (Oxford, England: Blackwell Press, 1956), pp. 116–133.

Harrington, Michael: *Socialism* (New York: Bantam Books, Inc., 1973).

———: *The Twilight of Capitalism* (New York: Simon & Schuster, Inc., 1977).

Heilbroner, Robert: *Between Capitalism and Socialism* (New York: Random House, Inc., 1970).

Macpherson, C. B.: *The Life and Times of Liberal Democrats* (New York: Oxford University Press, 1977).

Marx, Karl: *Economic and Philosophical Manuscripts,* in T. B. Bottomore, ed., *Karl Marx: Early Writings* (London: C. A. Watts & Co., Ltd., 1963).

Miller, Richard: "Rawls and Marxism," *Philosophy and Public Affairs,* **3** (1974): 167–191.

Miller, David: *Social Justice* (Oxford, England: Clarendon Press, 1976).

Sweezy, Paul: *Modern Capitalism and Other Essays* (New York: Monthly Review Press, 1972).

Tucker, Robert C.: *The Marxian Revolutionary Idea* (New York: W. W. Norton & Company, Inc., 1969).

Utilitarian Theories

Becker, Edward F.: "Justice, Utility, and Interpersonal Comparison," *Theory and Decision,* **6** (1975): 471–484.

Braybrooke, David: "Utilitarianism with a Difference: Rawls' Position in Ethics," *Canadian Journal of Philosophy,* **3** (1973): 303–331.

Brock, Dan W.: "Contractualism, Utilitarianism, and Social Inequalities," *Social Theory and Practice,* **1** (1971): 33–44.

———: "Recent Work in Utilitarianism," *American Philosophical Quarterly,* **10** (1973): 241–276.

Frankel, Charles: Justice, Utilitarianism, and Rights," *Social Theory and Practice,* **3** (1974): 27–46.

Lyons, David: "Rawls versus Utilitarianism," *Journal of Philosophy,* **69** (1972): 535–545.

Mill, John Stuart: in A. D. Lindsay, ed., *Utilitarianism; On Liberty; Representative Government* (London: E. P. Dutton & Co., 1976).

Miller, Richard: "Rawls, Risk, and Utilitarianism," *Philosophical Studies,* **28** (1975): 55–61.

Ogden, C. K.: *Jeremy Bentham: The Theory of Legislation* (London: Routledge & Kegan Paul, 1931), Introduction.

Sartorius, Rolf: *Individual Conduct and Social Norms* (Encino, Calif: Dickenson Publishing Co., 1975), chap. 7.

Sidgwick, Henry: *The Methods of Ethics* (New York: Dover Publications, Inc., 1966).

Taylor, Paul W.: "Justice and Utility," *Canadian Journal of Philosophy,* **1** (1972): 327–350.

Some Applications

Arthur, John, and William H. Shaw: *Justice and Economic Distribution* (Englewood Cliffs, N.J.: Prentice-Hall, Inc., 1978).

Blackstone, William T.: "Reverse Discrimination and Compensatory Justice," *Social Theory and Practice,* **3** (1975).

English, Jane: "Justice between Generations," *Philosophical Studies,* **31** (1977): 91–104.

Gross, Hyman: *A Theory of Criminal Justice* (New York: Oxford University Press, 1979).

Held, Virginia: *Property, Profits, and Economic Justice* (Belmont, Calif.: Wadsworth Publishing Company, Inc., 1980).

Jagger, Alison: "On Sexual Equality," *Ethics,* **84** (1974): 275–291.

Nagel, Thomas: "Equal Treatment and Compensatory Discrimination," *Philosophy and Public Affairs,* **2** (1973): 348–363.

Olafson, Frederick A., ed.: *Justice and Social Policy* (Englewood Cliffs, N.J.: Prentice-Hall, Inc., 1961).

Phelps, Edmund S., ed.: *Economic Justice* (Baltimore: Penquin Books, Inc., 1973).

Singer, Peter: *Animal Liberation* (New York: Avon Books, 1977).

CHAPTER EIGHT

Liberty and Law

Several problems that will be discussed in this chapter can be introduced through a widely known obscenity case that came before the Supreme Court of the United States in 1973—a case known as *Paris Adult Theatre I v. Slaton.* The Court had previously handled several cases involving the control of pornography. In the now famous *Fanny Hill* case, the Court ruled that three elements must "coalesce" for a work to be "obscene": (1) The dominant theme must appeal to a "prurient" (shameful, morbid) interest in sex, (2) it must be "patently offensive" by prevailing "community standards," and (3) it must have utterly no "redeeming social value." Few were satisfied with this opinion. Such criteria are obscure and difficult to apply, and the "community standards" criterion seems to invite large-scale repression of publications by police, judges, and prosecutors.

This problem of standards dates back further to the 1957 landmark case of *Roth v. United States,* which *Fanny Hill* presumably clarified. Prior to *Roth,* many had supposed that in order to justify suppression of pornography, a showing of a "clear and present danger" of substantial harm to individuals in society would have to be offered. The Supreme Court held, however, that the "clear and present danger" test was not required in obscenity cases. Its grounds were narrowly legal: historical study of the Constitution shows that the First Amendment had never been intended to protect obscene materials. Consequently, the Court held that a state legislature could validly prohibit obscene materials and actions without any showing of their substantial harm.

Throughout its history, the Court has resisted defining pornography, tending to prefer the view expressed by Justice Potter Stewart in his famous opinion on the film *The Lovers;* while he had no definition of "obscenity" to offer, he said, "I know it when I see it." In 1973, the Supreme Court had an opportunity to answer those critics who had accused it of past legal, moral, and definitional unclarity. In that year, the Court heard the *Paris Adult Theatre* case. In this case, the State of Georgia sought to stop the showing of two films—*It All Comes Out in the End* and *Magic Mirror*. The State of Georgia charged that the films were obscene under appropriate Georgia legal standards, lacking any serious literary, artistic, political, or scientific value. A final trial court held that the showing of the films could be prohibited only if there was evidence to prove that they were shown to minors or nonconsenting adults. The Georgia Supreme Court reversed the decision of the trial court, and the United States Supreme Court upheld the reversal. Chief Justice Burger argued that there are legitimate state interests in controlling consenting adults' access to obscene materials, and he sought to "define" the area of interest. These interests were said to include the maintenance of a decent level of the quality of life in society, the tone of commerce in great cities, and "possibly" the public safety itself. While Chief Justice Burger acknowledged that there are no conclusive scientific data showing a causal connection between obscene material and antisocial behavior, he considered reasonable the commonsense belief that such a connection exists.

In a minority opinion, Justice Brennan acknowledged that it is theoretically possible that there might be a class of material—obscene material—which is not protected by any constitutional guarantee of free speech. He contended, however, that it is impossible to define "obscenity" in any legally acceptable manner, and that consequently citizens could not be given fair warnings that they might be in violation of laws. Further, he held that state efforts to suppress obscene material inevitably lead to the erosion of protected speech, thereby violating the Constitution in both the First Amendment and the Fourteenth Amendment; and he noted that in the past the Court had agreed that there was no evidence of a causal connection between exposure to obscene materials and deviant behavior or violence. Brennan saw no principled way to forestall "state-ordered regimentation of our minds" in general and thought "costly institutional harms" would be created by any such suppression. He analyzed the interest of states in suppressing obscene material, only to conclude that they are insufficient to "justify the substantial damage to constitutional rights and to this nation's judicial machinery." Brennan's larger philosophical point seems to be that restrictions on what one reads or sees is a serious and far-reaching control that governments ought not to possess (save perhaps in extreme cases).

The majority and minority opinions in this case clearly indicate that the debate over control of pornography will continue and that future court tests are virtually certain.*

THE CONCEPTS OF LIBERTY AND LAW

In Chapters 6 and 7, the fundamental concepts of justice and rights were explored. Now a third fundamental concept—liberty—is taken up. Here a move must inescapably be made further into the realm of social and political philosophy than is made anywhere

---

*The primary source for this case is *Paris Adult Theatre I v. Slaton*, 413 U.S. 49, 93 S. Ct. 2628 (1973).

else in this book. The moral roots of the theories that will be encountered will nonetheless be everywhere apparent.

Major ethical and social problems concerning liberty emerge when law and liberty intersect, as they dramatically do in *Paris Adult Theatre*. By protecting rights or liberties for one group, the law may create obligations on, or restrict the liberty of, others. Even the most protective law, by its very function, is restrictive; it places a limit on what was formerly an open option. It is generally accepted that some liberties should be judiciously traded off for various forms of state protection; but in circumstances where no valid justification is forthcoming, the law can easily become an instrument of oppression. This tension is clearly present in the history of the Supreme Court's discussion of restrictions on pornography. On the other hand, the law can also be so lax as to permit foolish exercises of liberty. Even strong advocates of liberty may change their position when they see others using their freedom to engage in repulsive or degrading actions. Questions then arise about when limiting individual liberty is justified and about when persons are justified in disobeying unjust laws.

Despite the threat to liberty and order that some systems of law present, most people would agree that laws are needed to restrict some types of behavior. As the seventeenth-century British philosopher Thomas Hobbes pointed out, without laws that bind everyone in society, life would be nasty and short in the extreme. Most people, in fact, believe that the rule of law is a necessary condition for the very possibility of a stable society of free individuals. But why exactly should one obey the law, if one should, and under what conditions would one be justified not to obey the law? What types of activities and behavior should be legally restricted? In what instances does protection of individual rights require that the freedom of others be restricted?

Various liberty rights are often said to be fundamental, perhaps because liberty is so intimately related to the very nature and dignity of human beings. However, if a right to liberty entailed a right to absolute freedom, then no restrictions on liberty would ever be justified. There could be no control of pornography or anything else. Justice Burger notes the impracticality of this view in *Paris Adult Theatre* when he writes that "Totally unlimited play for free will is not allowed in ours or any other society." The term "liberty" is better understood, then, to refer to actions in which people *ought* to be free to engage. Murder and theft, for example, would be excluded from the list of acceptable liberties. While it will be difficult to determine a set of right and wrong exercises of liberty, some solid restrictions surely must be found.

THE THEORY OF LEGAL OBLIGATION

The classic example of Socrates's conviction on charges of atheism and of corrupting the youth of Athens will help us understand the notion of our obligation to obey the law. The aura of a witchhunt surrounded this historic trial, and Socrates was unjustly sentenced to death. While awaiting the end, Socrates was visited in prison by his friend Crito, who informed him that an escape could be arranged. Crito offered several reasons to justify the escape: Socrates was innocent; he could continue his valuable work in philosophy; his friends would otherwise appear disloyal for not arranging his escape; he would not have to abandon his sons. Socrates, however, regarded such reasons as emotionally inflated and insufficient to justify his escape. He countered with his own reasons for remaining: Because he had always taught respect for the law, it would be hypocritical for him to disobey it; and if he refused to obey a law he disliked, his disobedience would foster general disobedience. The law, he argued, could not survive such disregard; one's tacit agreement to abide by the law was binding, even if on occasion unscrupulous persons could turn the law against those who had agreed to obey it. Socrates thus contended that what is now called an "act of civil disobedience" constitutes an expression of ingratitude and a violation of justice.

On the other hand, Socrates also expressed a second, somewhat conflicting view about one's obligations to the state. He maintained at his trial that if the court found him guilty and prohibited him from philosophizing (which in his accusers' eyes meant corrupting youth), he would disobey the sentence. Apparently, Socrates thought that some legal decisions were simply too unjust to be supported. They would therefore have to be disobeyed, though openly and without attempting to escape punishment for the disobedience. In the end, he left his followers with a nagging ethical question: How does one determine when obedience to the state is required and when it is not?

Situations such as that faced by Socrates raise questions about the extent of our obligation to the law and about the conditions, if any, under which it would be right to disobey an ostensibly legitimate order by the authorities who govern one's country. For example, if one could not, as a matter of deep conscientious objection, condone the showing of the pornographic film *Magic Mirror* in one's community, yet the state supreme court permitted its showing, would one be justified in taking action to shut down the theater, or would this action violate the liberties of theater owner and customer alike? Virtually everyone concedes that there have been moments in history when, had one been a citizen of a particular nation, one would have been justified in ignoring certain dictates of authorities. The period of Nazi rule in Germany is but one frequently cited example. On the other hand, there clearly are conditions under which one would not be justified in ignoring morally sound orders of the state.

Philosophers are interested in establishing criteria for justified and unjustified obedience, as well as for justified and unjustified disobedience. Attention will be turned first to the issue of the justification of obedience, then to the issue of the justification of disobedience.

The Justification of Obedience to Law

Socrates propounds two basic arguments in support of an obligation to obey the laws of the state: (1) Disobedience fosters an intolerable spread of disobedience throughout the state, and (2) tacit consent to the law is binding, and one's violation of that agreement is a violation of justice. In addition to Socrates's arguments, perhaps the most influential statement of the justification for obeying the law is the aforementioned argument offered by Thomas Hobbes. He took the view that if we were to exist in a complete state of unregulated liberty, without a system of impartial laws binding on everyone, our lives would be extremely unpleasant. It is thus to our advantage to trade our natural state of liberty for the protections afforded by law, and Hobbes thought that people should give up certain aspects of their natural state of liberty and their right to govern themselves. This constraint entails giving up the liberty of autonomously deciding which laws are good and to be obeyed and which are not to be respected. (Hobbes's argument is not too distant from some rule-utilitarian views encountered in Chapter 3.)

He argues that the great advantages secured through organized society are possible only if that society is subject to the constraints of rules that enforce contracts, prevent harms that one person might cause to another, provide procedures for settling disagreements, and so on. Hobbes thus sees the constraining arm of the law as critical, for law is the mechanism allowing us to move from a state of war to one of peace, and it is the repository of the rules under which the judicial and enforcement divisions of government must function in determining matters of justice and rights.

In the following selection from his work, Hobbes develops these views in detail.

THOMAS HOBBES

Liberty and Legal Obligation*

In the nature of man, we find three principal causes of quarrel. First, competition; secondly, diffidence; thirdly, glory.

The first, maketh men invade for gain; the second, for safety; and the third, for reputation. The first use violence, to make themselves masters of other men's persons, wives, children, and cattle; the second to defend them; the third, for trifles, as a word, a smile, a different opinion, and any other sign of undervalue, either direct in their persons, or by reflection in their kindred, their friends, their nation, their profession, or their name.

Hereby it is manifest, that during the time men live without a common power to keep them all in awe, they are in that condition which is called war; and such a war, as is of every man, against every man. For WAR, consisteth not in battle only, or the

act of fighting; but in a tract of time, wherein the will to contend by battle is sufficiently known: and therefore the notion of *time,* is to be considered in the nature of war; as it is in the nature of weather. For as the nature of foul weather, lieth not in a shower or two of rain; but in an inclination thereto of many days together: so the nature of war, consisteth not in actual fighting; but in the known disposition thereto, during all the time there is no assurance to the contrary. . . .

The desires, and other passions of man, are in themselves no sin. No more are the actions, that proceed from those passions, till they know a law that forbids them: which till laws be made they cannot know: nor can any law be made, till they have agreed upon the person that shall make it. . . .

To this war of every man, against every man, this also is consequent; that nothing

*From Thomas Hobbes, *Leviathan* (1651).

can be unjust. The notions of right and wrong justice and injustice have there no place. Where there is no common power, there is no law: where no law, no injustice. Force, and fraud, are in war the two cardinal virtues. . . .

The right of nature, which writers commonly call *jus naturale,* is liberty each man hath, to use his own power, as he will himself, for the preservation of his own nature; that is to say, of his own life; and consequently, of doing any thing, which in his own judgment, and reason, he shall conceive to be the aptest means thereunto.

By *liberty,* is understood, according to the proper signification of the word, the absence of external impediments: which impediments, may oft take away part of a man's power to do what he would; but cannot hinder him from using the power left him, according as his judgment, and reason shall dictate to him. . . .

Right, consisteth in liberty to do, or to forbare; whereas *law,* determineth, and bindeth to one of them: so that law, and right, differ as much, as obligation, and liberty; which in one and the same matter are inconsistent. . . .

Every one is governed by his own reason; and there is nothing he can make use of, that may not be a help unto him, in preserving his life against his enemies; it followeth, that in such a condition, every man has a right to every thing; even to one another's body. And therefore, as long as this natural right of every man to every thing endureth, there can be no security to any man, how strong or wise soever he be, of living out the time, which nature ordinarily alloweth men to live, and consequently it is a precept, or general rule of reason, that *every man, ought to endeavour peace, as far as he has hope of obtaining it; and when he cannot obtain it, that he may seek, and use, all helps, and advantages of war.* The first branch of which rule, containeth the first, and fundamental

law of nature; which is, *to seek peace, and follow it.* The second, the sum of the right of nature; which is, *by all means we can, to defend ourselves.*

From this fundamental law of nature, by which men are commanded to endeavour peace, is derived this second law; *that a man be willing, when others are so too, as far-forth, as for peace, and defence of himself he shall think it necessary, to lay down this right to all things; and be contented with so much liberty against other men, as he would allow other men against himself.* For as long as every man holdeth this right, of doing any thing he liketh; so long are all men in the condition of war. But if other men will not lay down their right, as well as he; then there is no reason for any one, to divest himself of his: for that were to expose himself to prey, which no man is bound to, rather than to dispose himself to peace. . . .

Whensoever a man transferreth his right, or renounceth it; it is either in consideration of some right reciprocally transferred to himself; or for some other good he hopeth for thereby. For it is a voluntary act: and of the voluntary acts of every man the object is some *good to himself.* . . .

The motive, and end for which this renouncing, and transferring of right is introduced, is nothing else but the security of a man's person, in his life, and in the means of so preserving life, as not to be weary of it. . . .

The mutual transferring of right, is that which men call *contract.* . . .

The final cause, end, or design of men, who naturally love liberty, and dominion over others, in the introduction of that restraint upon themselves, in which we see them live in commonwealths, is the foresight of their own preservation, and of a more contented life thereby; that is to say, of getting themselves out from that miserable condition of war, which is necessarily consequent to the natural passions of men, when there is no visible power to keep them in awe, and tie them by fear of punishment to the performance of their covenants. . . .

The only way to erect such a common power, as may be able to defend them from the invasion of foreigners, and the injuries of one another, and thereby to secure them in such sort, as that by their own industry, and by the fruits of the earth, they may nourish themselves and live contentedly; is, to confer all their power and strength upon one man, or upon one assembly of men, that may reduce all their wills, by plurality of voices, unto one will. . . .

This done, the multitude so united in one person, is called a *commonwealth,* in Latin *civitas.*

Although most philosophers would agree with Hobbes that we do have a prima facie moral obligation to obey the law, they would deny that the law must be obeyed under all circumstances. Some philosophers have also maintained that there is no moral obligation to obey any law to which one has not voluntarily consented. These issues would take us too deeply into political philosophy, but it should be noted here that the justice of laws and the political context in which they are enforced must be considered in any attempt to determine whether (morally) they ought to be obeyed. For example, in the aftermath of *Paris Adult Theatre,* one outraged publisher created a special and quite explicit issue of his sex-oriented journal with the intent of violating the Supreme Court's majority findings. In certain kinds of emergencies, we may even *expect* individual nonconformity to law. For exampe, we accept someone's swimming in forbidden waters in order to save someone else from drowning. Moreover, in the face of political repression and totalitarianism, we openly admire those who disobey the law. During the Vietnamese war, draft evasion was openly admitted in some quarters of the United States, and more recently it has been suggested that young persons should openly violate laws requiring registration for the draft. This problem of how to balance obedience and dissent takes us directly to the related topic of the justification of disobedience to law.

The Justification of Legal Disobedience

Civil disobedience is generally regarded as a grave threat to the democratic state and liberties within it, because such actions *by definition* violate a law, often a law upheld by a nation's highest court. Acts of disobedience threaten the civil order so critical in Hobbes's conception of the state. It has sometimes been argued that acts of civil disobedience may be justified only if a "higher law" provides moral support for the actions of the civilly disobedient. In other words, one has the right to disobey a law only if, in one's informed judgment, the law is invalidated by a higher law of the state. This claim raises fundamental issues concerning the proper analysis of the very concept of civil disobedience. Consideration, then, will be given to this idea of civil disobedience before turning to questions of the justification of disobedience.

The word "civil" has several distinct meanings, but if a constitution or body of laws were actually to sanction "disobedient" actions, it is hard to see how the acts would be civilly disobedient. If a higher law justifies disobedience to a law which is inconsistent or in contradiction with the higher law, then it would seem that one is not, in fact, breaking the law when one honors the higher law and disobeys the lower law. One could argue that one is legally obligated to break the lower law and obey the higher law. In other words, this sort of "disobedience" is justified. Most writers on civil disobedience agree that, by definition, an act is civilly disobedient only if it breaks a law considered invalid on moral (not legal) grounds. Civil disobedience presupposes a conflict between a legal obligation and a moral obligation, a conflict in which the moral obligation is held to take precedence over the legal obligation.

Appeals to Conscience

The problem of a sound justification of disobedience can now be broached. This problem is often associated with that of "duty to one's conscience." As was seen in Chapter 2 when discussing moral disagreement, there are powerful moral reasons favoring preserving considerable latitude of autonomous choice to individuals in circumstances of open social disagreements. In a society where such disagreements are allowed, autonomous agents would understandably appeal to their own reasons as grounds for various forms of resistance to social pressures and arrangements. There is a distinguished literature on conscientious objection that helpfully points to the importance of preserving autonomous disagreement in such contexts; in light of this literature, appeals to conscience cannot be set aside as merely an unjustifiable form of relativism or subjectivism.

Nonetheless, philosophers have generally judged appeals to conscience alone as untrustworthy. Consciences vary radically from person to person and time to time, and are often altered by circumstance and training. For example, views about pornography and the freedom of the press are matters of hot debate and deeply held conviction, but these alone seem hardly to advance or resolve the issues. Consciences seem subject to impulse and whim, and are rather more acute when, for instance, a police officer is sighted than when there are no enforcers nearby. Recent psychological theories have also been used by some writers to undermine the claim that there is a rational and impartial basis to appeals to conscience. Moreover, many appeals to the rightness of an action on the ground that "my conscience was my guide" seem to external observers to be rationalizations for an immoral act. Political assassins and terrorists, for example, commonly appeal to conscience as a source of justification for their actions. The reliability of conscience seems, then, not to be self-validating, for an external source of justification is needed.

The Conflict between Legal and Moral Obligations

One facet of this problem has almost certainly proved to be the central issue in the history of attempts to justify disobedience: What is the relationship between moral and legal obligations when they are in conflict? The central issue in determining whether or not we are ever at liberty to choose not to obey a law because of moral objections is the problem of the relationship between moral and legal obligations. The problem is most acute when the laws have been upheld by a nation's highest courts. On the one hand, we think we have an obligation (a prima facie moral one) to obey legally valid laws and to support generally the rule of law. On the other hand, we think this obligation is not so strong that it outweighs all other (prima facie moral) obligations. In most controversial cases, it is exceedingly difficult to determine which moral obligation is overriding.

In the following essay, John Rawls struggles with these issues in an attempt to present conditions of justified civil disobedience. Rawls finds grounds for one's moral obligation both to obey and to disobey the law in his theory of justice (see Chapters 4 and 7). Here, Rawls stipulates the conditions that must be met if disobedient acts are to be considered morally justified.

JOHN RAWLS

The Justification of Civil Disobedience*

The problem of civil disobedience, as I shall interpret it, arises only within a more or less just democratic state for those citizens who recognize and accept the legitimacy of the constitution. The difficulty is one of a conflict of duties. At what point does the duty to comply with laws enacted by a legislative majority (or with executive acts supported by such a majority) cease to be binding in view of the right to defend one's liberties and the duty to oppose injustice? This question involves the nature and limits of majority rule. For this reason the problem of civil disobedience is a crucial test case for any theory of the moral basis of democracy. . . .

Before I take up these matters, a word of caution. We should not expect too much of a theory of civil disobedience, even one framed for special circumstances. Precise principles that straightway decide actual cases are clearly out of the question.

Instead, a useful theory defines a perspective within which the problem of civil disobedience can be approached; it identifies the relevant considerations and helps us to assign them their correct weights in the more important instances. If a theory about these matters appears to us, on reflection, to have cleared our vision and to have made our considered judgments more coherent, then it has been worthwhile. The theory has done what, for the present, one may reasonably expect it to do: namely, to narrow the disparity between the conscientious convictions of those who accept the basic principles of a democratic society.

I shall begin by defining civil disobedience as a public, nonviolent, conscientious yet political act contrary to law usually done with the aim of bringing about a change in the law or policies of the government.[1] By acting in this way one addresses the sense of justice of the majority of the

*From John Rawls, *A Theory of Justice* (Cambridge, Mass.: Harvard University Press, 1971), pp. 363–376. (Wording as changed in the 9th printing, 1978.)

[1] Here I follow H. A. Bedau's definition of civil disobedience. See his "On Civil Disobedience," *Journal of Philosophy*, **58** (1961): 653–661.

community and declares that in one's considered opinion the principles of social cooperation among free and equal men are not being respected. . . .

It should also be noted that civil disobedience is a political act not only in the sense that it is addressed to the majority that holds political power, but also because it is an act guided and justified by political principles, that is, by the principles of justice which regulate the constitution and social institutions generally. In justifying civil disobedience one does not appeal to principles of personal morality or to religious doctrines, though these may coincide with and support one's claims; and it goes without saying that civil disobedience cannot be grounded solely on group or self-interest. Instead one invokes the commonly shared conception of justice that underlies the political order. It is assumed that in a reasonably just democratic regime there is a public conception of justice by reference to which citizens regulate their political affairs and interpret the constitution. The persistent and deliberate violation of the basic principles of this conception over any extended period of time, especially the infringement of the fundamental equal liberties, invites either submission or resistance. By engaging in civil disobedience a minority forces the majority to consider whether it wishes to have its actions construed in this way, or whether, in view of the common sense of justice, it wishes to acknowledge the legitimate claims of the minority.

A further point is that civil disobedience is a public act. Not only is it addressed to public principles, it is done in public. It is engaged in openly with fair notice; it is not covert or secretive. One may compare it to public speech, and being a form of address, an expression of profound and conscientious political conviction, it takes place in the public forum. For this reason, among others, civil disobedience is nonviolent. It tries to avoid the use of violence, especially against persons, not from the abhorrence of the use of force in principle, but because it is a final expression of one's case. . . .

Civil disobedience, so understood, is clearly distinct from militant action and obstruction; it is far removed from organized forcible resistance. The militant, for example, is much more deeply opposed to the existing political system. He does not accept it as one which is nearly just or reasonably so; he believes either that it departs widely from its professed principles or that it pursues a mistaken conception of justice altogether. . . .

With these various distinctions in mind, I shall consider the circumstances under which civil disobedience is justified. For simplicity I shall limit the discussion to domestic institutions and so to injustices internal to a given society. . . .

The first point concerns the kinds of wrongs that are appropriate objects of civil disobedience. Now if one views such disobedience as a political act addressed to the sense of justice of the community, then it seems reasonable, other things equal, to limit it to instances of substantial and clear injustice, and preferably to those which obstruct the path to removing other injustices. For this reason there is a presumption in favor of restricting civil disobedience to serious infringements of the first principle of justice, the principle of equal liberty, and to blatant violations of the second part of the second principle, the principle of fair equality of opportunity. Of course, it is not always easy to tell whether these principles are satisfied. Still, if we think of them as guaranteeing the basic liberties, it is often clear that these freedoms are not being honored. After all, they impose certain strict requirements that must be visibly expressed in institutions. Thus when certain minorities are denied the right to vote or to hold office, or to own property and to move from place to place, or when certain religious groups are repressed and others denied various opportunities, these injustices may be obvious to all. . . .

A further condition for civil disobedience is the following. We may suppose that the normal appeals to the political majority have already been made in good faith and that they have failed. The legal means of redress have proved to no avail. Thus, for example, the existing political parties have shown themselves indifferent to the claims of the minority or have proved unwilling to accommodate them. Attempts to have the laws repealed have been ignored and legal protests and demonstrations have had no success. Since civil disobedience is a last resort, we should be sure that it is necessary. Note that it has not been said, however, that legal means have been exhausted. At any rate, further normal appeals can be repeated; free speech is always possible. But if past actions have shown the majority immovable or apathetic, further attempts may reasonably be thought fruitless, and a second condition for justified civil disobedience is met. . . .

The third and last condition I shall discuss can be rather complicated. It arises from the fact that while the two preceding conditions are often sufficient to justify civil disobedience, this is not always the case. In certain circumstances the natural duty of justice may require a certain restraint. We can see this as follows. If a certain minority is justified in engaging in civil disobedience, then any other minority in relevantly similar circumstances is likewise justified. Using the two previous conditions as the criteria of relevantly similar circumstances, we can say that, other things equal, two minorities are similarly justified in resorting to civil disobedience if they have suffered for the same length of time from the same degree of injustice and if their equally sincere and normal political appeals have likewise been to no avail. It is conceivable, however, even if it is

unlikely, that there should be many groups with an equally sound case (in the sense just defined) for being civilly disobedient; but that, if they were all to act in this way, serious disorder would follow which might well undermine the efficacy of the just constitution. I assume here that there is a limit on the extent to which civil disobedience can be engaged in without leading to a breakdown in the respect for law and the constitution, thereby setting in motion consequences unfortunate for all. . . .

Suppose that in the light of the three conditions, one has a right to appeal one's case by civil disobedience. The injustice one protests is a clear violation of the liberties of equal citizenship, or of equality of opportunity, this violation having been more or less deliberate over an extended period of time in the face of normal political opposition, and any complications raised by the question of fairness are met. These conditions are not exhaustive; some allowance still has to be made for the possibility of injury to third parties, to the innocent, so to speak. But I assume that they cover the main points. There is still, of course, the question whether it is wise or prudent to exercise this right. Having established the right, one is now free, as one is not before, to let these matters decide the issue. We may be acting within our rights but nevertheless unwisely if our conduct only serves to provoke the harsh retaliation of the majority. To be sure, in a state of near justice, vindictive repression of legitimate dissent is unlikely, but it is important that the action be properly designed to make an effective appeal to the wider community. Since civil disobedience is a mode of address taking place in the public forum, care must be taken to see that it is understood. Thus the exercise of the right to civil disobedience should, like any other right, be rationally framed to advance one's ends or the ends of those one wishes to assist.

THE VALID RESTRICTION OF INDIVIDUAL LIBERTIES

The questions encountered thus far turn on the justification of obedience and disobedience to law. They concern our *moral obligations to law.* Beyond these issues, there are significant questions now to be considered about the *moral justification of legal restrictions* on personal liberty. This topic takes us in a new direction, but one no less oriented to the subject of liberty and law.

Almost anyone would agree that laws prohibiting such immoral actions as murder and theft are justified, and that they are justified by appeal to some moral point of view. Because persons are significantly harmed by these acts, we have no hesitation in legally prohibiting them, even at the "expense" of a loss of liberty to murderers and thieves. Liberties that cause serious harm to others do not deserve protection. Yet, what sorts of liberties do deserve protection? In particular, what are we to say of laws that prohibit conduct involving consenting parties—such as the consenting adults who went to see *Magic Mirror* at the Paris Adult Theatre? The remainder of this chapter considers these questions.

Liberty-Limiting Principles

Although liberty is among our most cherished values, it conflicts with other values such as the health and welfare of others. Because of this conflict, philosophers have been interested in establishing the proper limits of liberty for individuals, groups, and institutions. Thus, questions have arisen about the justifiability of limits placed on public nudity, the use of certain textbooks in public schools, the dissemination of pornography, high-risk behaviors, etc.

Various "moral" principles have been advanced in order to justify the limitation of individual human liberties. The following four "liberty-limiting principles" have frequently been defended in public debates and have played a significant role in recent philosophical controversies:

1. *The harm principle*—A person's liberty is justifiably restricted to prevent *harm to others* caused by that person.
2. *The principle of paternalism*—A person's liberty is justifiably restricted to prevent *harm to self* caused by that person.
3. *The principle of legal moralism*—A person's liberty is justifiably restricted to prevent that person's *immoral behavior.*
4. *The offense principle*—A person's liberty is justifiably restricted to prevent *offense to others* caused by that person.

The offense principle most directly relates to the *Paris Adult Theatre* case, but close examination of that case shows all four of these principles at work in the reasoning of Supreme Court justices. Indeed, the harm principle is repeatedly invoked in discussing "clear and present dangers" involved in pornography and "costly institutional harms" involved in controlling it. Each of these four principles represents a balancing of liberty with other values. Naturally, different people differently assess the weight of certain values in this balancing process. But the harm principle is almost universally accepted as a valid liberty-limiting principle—despite certain unclarities that surround the notion of a harm. There remains, however, much debate concerning whether any of the other three principles is a valid (morally justified) liberty-limiting one.

Each of these three supplementary principles proclaims that there is a valid limit on individual liberties, and therefore a valid limit on one's *right* to do something. The paternalistic principle limits one's right seriously to endanger oneself; the offense principle is commonly invoked to limit the right to disseminate certain forms of printed material; and legal moralism has been used to limit one's right to be sexually different. The immediate problem is whether such restrictions of liberty—even if highly qualified—may ever *validly* be invoked—and, if so, how the principles that stand behind these judgments are to be formulated. In order to answer such questions, a balance obviously must be reached between the firm belief that one ought to be free to do whatever one pleases (commensurate with a similar freedom for others) and an equally firm belief that there are limits to the scope of all freedoms when other parties are negatively affected by their exercise.

The Harm Principle

The scope of the four liberty-limiting principles has been often debated. But John Stuart Mill's monograph *On Liberty* (1859) continues to occupy the most prominent position in these discussions. In this work, Mill inquired after the nature and limits of justifiable social control over the individual. The following selection presents a summary and outline of his central theses regarding the harm principle, which he sees as the sole valid principle for placing restrictions on individual liberty.

so just don't hurt others, you can hurt yourself though

JOHN STUART MILL

On Liberty*

There is, in fact, no recognised principle by which the propriety or impropriety of government interference is customarily tested. People decide according to their personal preferences. Some, whenever they see any good to be done, or evil to be remedied, would willingly instigate the government to undertake the business;

*From John Stuart Mill, *On Liberty* (1859).

while others prefer to bear almost any amount of social evil, rather than add one to the departments of human interests amenable to governmental control. And men range themselves on one or the other side in any particular case, according to this general direction of their sentiments; or according to the degree of interest which they feel in the particular thing which it is proposed that the government should do, or according to the belief they entertain that the government would, or would not, do it in the manner they prefer; but very rarely on account of any opinion to which they consistently adhere, as to what things are fit to be done by a government. And it seems to me that in consequence of this absence of rule or principle, one side is at present as often wrong as the other; the interference of government is, with about equal frequency improperly invoked and improperly condemned.

The object of this Essay is to assert one very simple principle, as entitled to govern absolutely the dealings of society with the individual in the way of compulsion and control, whether the means used be physical force in the form of legal penalties, or the moral coercion of public opinion. That principle is, that the sole end for which mankind are warranted, individually or collectively, in interfering with the liberty of action of any of their number, is self-protection. That the only purpose for which power can be rightfully exercised over any member of a civilized community, against his will, is to prevent harm to others. His own good, either physical or moral, is not a sufficient warrant. He cannot rightfully be compelled to do or forbear because it will be better for him to do so, because it will make him happier, because, in the opinions of others, to do so would be wise, or even right. These are good reasons for remonstrating with him, or reasoning with him, or persuading him, or entreating him, but not for compelling him, or visiting him with any evil in case he do otherwise. To justify that, the conduct from which it is desired to deter him, must be calculated to produce evil to some one else. The only part of the conduct of any one, for which he is amenable to society, is that which concerns others. In the part which merely concerns himself, his independence is, of right, absolute. Over himself, over his own body and mind, the individual is sovereign.

It is, perhaps, hardly necessary to say that this doctrine is meant to apply only to human beings in the maturity of their faculties. We are not speaking of children, or of young persons below the age which the law may fix as that of manhood or womenhood. Those who are still in a state to require being taken care of by others, must be protected against their own actions as well as against external injury. . . .

This, then, is the appropriate region of human liberty. It comprises, first, the inward domain of consciousness; demanding liberty of conscience, in the most comprehensive sense; liberty of thought and feeling; absolute freedom of opinion and sentiment on all subjects, practical or speculative, scientific, moral, or theological. The liberty of expressing and publishing opinions may be seen to fall under a different principle, since it belongs to that part of the conduct of an individual which concerns other people; but, being almost of as much importance as the liberty of thought itself, and resting in great part on the same reasons, is practically inseparable from it. Secondly, the principle requires liberty of tastes and pursuits; of framing the plan of our life to suit our own character; of doing as we like, subject to such consequences as may follow: without impediment from our fellow-creatures, so long as what we do does not harm them, even though they should think our conduct foolish, perverse, or wrong. Thirdly, from this liberty of each individual, follows the liberty, within the same limits, of combination among individuals; freedom to unite, for any purpose not involving harm to others: the persons combining being supposed to be of full age, and not forced or deceived.

No society in which these liberties are not, on the whole, respected, is free, whatever may be its form of government; and none is completely free in which they do not exist absolute and unqualified. The only freedom which deserves the name, is that of pursuing our own good in our own way, so long as we do not attempt to deprive others of theirs, or impede their efforts to obtain it. Each is the proper guardian of his own health, whether bodily, or mental and spiritual. Mankind are greater gainers by suffering each other to live as seems good to themselves, than by compelling each to live as seems good to the rest. . . .

Again, there are many acts which, being directly injurious only to the agents themselves, ought not to be legally interdicted, but which, if done publicly, are a violation of good manners, and coming thus within the category of offences against others, may rightfully be prohibited. Of this kind are offences against decency; on which it is unnecessary to dwell, the rather as they are only connected indirectly with our subject, the objection to publicity being equally strong in the case of many actions not in themselves condemnable, nor supposed to be so. . . .

If all mankind minus one, were of one opinion, and only one person were of the contrary opinion, mankind would be no more justified in silencing that one person, than he, if he had the power, would be justified in silencing mankind. Were an opinion a personal possession of no value except to the owner; if to be obstructed in the enjoyment of it were simply a private injury, it would make some difference whether the injury was inflicted only on a few persons or on many. But the peculiar evil of silencing the expression of an opinion is, that it is robbing the human race; posterity as well as the existing generation; those who dissent from the opinion, still more than those who hold it. If the opinion is right, they are deprived of the opportunity of exchanging error for truth: if wrong, they lose, what is almost as great a benefit, the clearer perception and livelier impression of truth, produced by its collision with error. . . .

The strongest of all the arguments against the interference of the public with purely personal conduct, is that when it does interfere, the odds are that it interferes wrongly, and in the wrong place. On questions of social morality, of duty to others, the opinion of the public, that is, of an overruling majority, though often wrong, is likely to be still oftener right; because on such questions they are only required to judge of their own interests; of the manner in which some mode of conduct, if allowed to be practised, would affect themselves. But the opinion of a similar majority, imposed as a law on the minority, on questions of self-regarding conduct, is quite as likely to be wrong as right; for in these cases public opinion means, at the best, some people's opinion of what is good or bad for other people; while very often it does not even mean that; the public, with the most perfect indifference, passing over the pleasure or convenience of those whose conduct they censure, and considering only their own preference.

Mill thus writes in support of a general ethical principle limiting the social control of individual liberty—regardless of whether the controls are legal, religious, economic, or of some other order. Mill further defends his views with the utilitarian arguments that were discussed in Chapter 3. In particular, he argues that his general principle of social control, however dangerous to prevailing social beliefs, would produce the best possible conditions for social progress and for the development of individual talents. The notion of harm is never carefully analyzed in his essay, but presumably he allows more than mere physical and psychological pain and damages to count as harmful and does not count mere inconvenience as harmful. Often, harm seems to mean "serious injury to another's interests," for he speaks of certain important "interests" that should be protected by specific legal rights.*

Mill's position explicitly declares all allegedly valid liberty-limiting principles except the harm principle to be invalid (morally unjustified). His direct prohibition of legal moralism as well as the paternalistic and offense principles will be studied later in this chapter.

Mill's Critics

Some have attacked Mill's theory as useless on grounds that his principles are so broad as to support virtually any criminal legislation. These critics argue that Mill is too vague in drawing the line between harm and nonharm and between proper and improper government intervention, with the result that individuals and governments are free to draw that line wherever they wish. Presumably, these critics would criticize even the analysis of harm in terms of injury to interests. If Mill's notion of harm is construed narrowly (e.g., as bodily harm), it is argued, then even the most serious nonbodily invasions of a person's freedom would not be restricted. But if Mill's notion of harm is construed broadly, then virtually no freedom would be permitted and government regulation would extend to every phase of our lives. This criticism, if correct, is seriously damaging, because, if Mill provides no acceptable general principle or principles of liberty, he fails in his main goal of formulating an adequate statement of individual rights and social control.

Mill has also been attacked for failing to see that his arguments could justify the very paternalistic interventions that he opposes. In the following selection, Martin Golding argues that Mill does not, and probably cannot, adequately distinguish between "self-regarding" and "other-regarding" actions. This is a version of the familiar argument against Mill that "No man is an island." Golding, like others, also believes that Mill's arguments suffer from lack of clarity concerning the nature of such terms as "harm" and "damage."

*Taking the object of harm to be an "interest" has been a popular approach in recent times, especially in legal writings. The law deals with the broad notion of interests and protecting interests under many categories of finer description, such as property interests, privacy interests, and interests in reputation. Damage to interests can come through assault, battery, libel, defamation of character, negligence, theft, etc. Categories of harm broader than the merely legal would include certain kinds of insults, racial discrimination, and degradation. Under this broad analysis, Mill's harm principle asserts that a person's liberty is justifiably restricted only when the restriction is necessary to prevent or control injury to the significant interests of others.

MARTIN GOLDING

J. S. Mill on the Limits of Coercion*

Mill's intention is to supply a single principle, and a very simple one at that, which enables us to isolate those spheres of conduct that legitimately are beyond the reach of the law and the "coercion" of public opinion. Does it do this? There are a number of issues here: Are there any kinds of actions of the sort envisioned by Mill—namely, actions that do not harm others? Is his principle all we need, or does it require supplementation of some kind? Is the principle really "simple"?

We might begin by noticing that the last statement quoted does not seem to follow from the previous ones. It is not true, even on Mill's own terms, that an individual is, without qualification, sovereign over his own body. Shall a pregnant woman be permitted to take thalidomide? Shall a person be permitted to conduct bizarre genetic experiments upon himself? Such acts clearly may be matters that concern or harm others. Consider, also, a less exotic example. Most of the states, perhaps all, require a motorcyclist to wear a helmet. Arguing in a Millian fashion that the government lacks constitutional power to compel this, the Attorney General of New Mexico asserted that "it cannot be questioned that requiring a motorcylce rider to wear a helmet will render him less likely to be injured. However, if a motorcycle rider chooses to pursue his personal happiness by riding without a helmet it cannot be said that his choice will injure his fellow man." The latter statement, I think, is rather debatable. If the motorcyclist is injured, will not someone—a private party or the

state—have to bear the burden of caring for the addlepated rider? In our welfare state anyone who engages in a high-risk activity is likely to become a public charge if injured, and there is therefore a social interest in reducing the risk. In such cases there is no reason to confine the state's interference merely to conduct that is, as Mill says, "calculated to produce evil in someone else." Now, Mill might well concede that these cases do come under the purview of the state. But my general point is that considerations similar to the ones just mentioned can be brought against many of the cases which Mill and his spiritual descendents hold to be excluded from compulsion by his principle.

The difficulty with the assertion that an individual is sovereign over his mind and body is a special case of a more general difficulty. We simply cannot isolate, once and for all, spheres of conduct which inherently are not harmful to others or of no concern to others. (The terms "harmful to others" and "concerns others," while not literal equivalents, are used interchangeably by Mill.) This is to state in other words the notorious problem of distinguishing "self-regarding" from "other-regarding" actions, as Mill calls them. The issue is not merely whether there ever is conduct that is purely self-regarding (i.e., self-affecting), and thus beyond the reach of the law or "moral coercion." It may even be granted that instances of such conduct do occur. The question is, rather, whether the *kind* of conduct that is at issue is such that it is always self-regarding. For the legislator, at least, must work by and large in terms of rules.

Mill is aware of this difficulty, and I think ends up by abandoning his simple princi-

*From Martin Golding, *Philosophy of Law* (Englewood Cliffs, N.J.: Prentice-Hall, Inc., 1975), pp. 56–59, 62.

ple. Thus, in the fourth chapter of his essay, Mill allows that many persons will not admit the distinction on which the principle rests, and he agrees "that the mischief which a person does to himself may seriously affect, both through their sympathies and their interests, those nearly connected with him and, in a minor degree, society at large."[1] Nevertheless, Mill insists that such injury would be merely contingent, the *inconvenience* of which society must bear for the sake of the greater good of human freedom, unless the individual violates a "specific duty to the public" or a "distinct and assignable obligation to any other person or persons."[2] With this insistence, however, Mill has cut the ground from under his principle.

First, it does no good to say that such conduct is taken out of the "self-regarding" class in case of these violations, unless we have already determined what the duties and obligations are. But this is precisely what Mill's principle, with its distinction between self-regarding and other-regarding conduct, is supposed to help us determine. Second, in his reference to "inconvenience," Mill is in effect saying that what is required is a *weighing* of the inconveniences against the good of human freedom. Mill is convinced, of course, that the latter will always outweigh the former. But is this necessarily so? Consider the case of unsightly advertising billboards placed on private property adjoining a public highway. Suppose, now, that the legislature is deciding whether to prohibit entirely or to restrict the size of such billboards. There is no question yet of a duty to the public. Nor is there injury to "assignable" individuals, whatever that may mean. Is it clear, though, that the "inconvenience" is one that society can afford to

[1]Mill, *On Liberty*, p. 118.
[2]Ibid., pp. 119, 120.

bear for the sake of the greater good of human freedom? Not so long ago, in the state of California particularly, there were large billboards proclaiming "Impeach Earl Warren" (the then Chief Justice of the U.S. Supreme Court). Suppose these billboards had contained a well-known four-letter Anglo-Saxon word in place of "Impeach." Would this have been an "inconvenience" that the public could have afforded to bear for the greater good of human freedom?

In implicitly acknowledging that there must be a weighing of the public's inconvenience against the good of human freedom, Mill really abandons his "simple principle." But even more crucial, however, is the question of what, after all, is meant by such terms as "inconvenience," "concern," "harm," "definite damage," etc. Without a specification of these meanings no weighing can take place. Behind the use of these terms is a series of moral and social assumptions that need to be made explicit. . . .

[Moreover], I think it clear that the mere fact that an act is done in private is *not* sufficient to take it out of the realm of public concern. . . . Sex urges are natural and powerful, and the suppression of them causes pain or great discomfort. This may be true, yet no society has existed without some regulation of sex. The question is where to draw the line, and this is a very difficult matter. Perhaps the public only feels a small degree of distress in the case of in-private homosexuality, but intense distress in the case of in-private desecration of a human corpse, for example. . . . Ideals of proper conduct and living are not to be thrust completely aside. Certain sexual practices and "hard-core" pornography are humanly degrading, for they treat persons as things. There is, however, a very long step from morally condemning a practice to saying that it should be legally prohibited.

Golding's concluding comment leads us directly to the subject of the legal enforcement of moral beliefs.

LEGAL MORALISM

Everyone opposes the enforcement by an external authority of a moral view alien to his or her own. Hence, one may be skeptical that the legal enforcement of controversial moral positions can be justified. On the other hand, the justification of many commendable laws in our society is based on moral beliefs, and this uncontested fact indicates that our laws are already infused with moral content. It is clear, for example, that the Supreme Court's various decisions concerning pornography rest on moral appraisals about "fair warnings," the nature of "obscene conduct," matters of "redeeming social value," etc. The harm principle itself is a moral principle, one which provides the primary justification for a large number of laws; and certainly immoral conduct is not a matter that we usually consider beyond the bounds of law, as the public's usual reaction to the indiscretions of politicians evidences. Perhaps, then, moral views are legitimately enforceable when they are of overwhelming importance to moral stability in society.

The popular language of "moral offenses" and "offenses against morality and human decency" encourages the view that some actions should be subject to legal sanctions even if these actions do not harm the individuals involved. In supporting this conviction, the principle of legal moralism clearly moves beyond the harm principle. This principle raises questions regarding the *kinds* and *degree* of moral content, if any, that may properly underlie such laws. The issue is, What acts of deviant moral conduct can justifiably be outlawed in a pluralistic society? This issue has proved most troublesome when certain private sexual acts or depictions involving only consenting adults are widely regarded as perverse. Reservations of this order are clearly at work in the *Paris Adult Theatre* case, but the following are all categories that have been candidates for restrictive legislation:

Homosexual relations
Prostitution
Private use of pornographic films
Gambling
Private use of drugs having no socially harmful consequences
Voluntary euthanasia
Rational suicide

Morally Offensive Behavior without Victims

In considering these problems it is useful once again to distinguish between (1) morally offensive behavior in which there is no victim because no person is likely to be harmed and all involved voluntarily consent, and (2) morally offensive behavior in which there is a victim. Criminal sanctions against prostitution, homosexuality, gambling, the use of marijuana, and sexual stimulation in "massage parlors" are now familiar examples of laws designed to prohibit morally offensive behavior that may not directly harm those involved. By contast, rape—whether heterosexual or homosexual—is a crime that always has a victim, and as such, falls under the harm principle. The ethical issue is whether morally offensive behavior without victims should be considered crime at all. Perhaps legal restrictions on homosexuality and gambling, for example, constitute unwarranted restrictions of liberty. It may be that even if certain sexual acts are perverse, society should nonetheless allow individuals the personal freedom to engage in such conduct when only consenting adults are involved.

It is not because persons are harmed physically or psychologically that morally offensive behavior without victims is usually made illegal, but rather, because such behavior is thought to be inherently degrading, evil, or perverse. It has of course been argued that the sexual development of young children is harmed by some of these practices, but this argument is based on the harm principle, not legal moralism. For this reason, states that legislate against such acts seem to be straightforwardly involved in the enforcement of morals—that is, in maintaining a community's "moral" standards. Most people agree that such restriction of individual freedom should be limited to those situations involving extremely serious matters, if it is to be allowed at all; but the situation that is to count as a matter of such magnitude is seldom made clear, and consequently the issue of legal enforcement of morality can be applied to a wide range of sensitive issues.

Since the publication of Mill's *On Liberty,* there have been many sympathetic attempts to oppose the imposition of moral views or to eliminate existing restrictive legislation. The so-called Wolfenden Committee Report, issued in England in the 1950s, has now emerged as a landmark document in its own right. The committee itself was established in 1954 as a response to complaints that aspects of English law dealing with homosexuality and prostitution were ineffective and unjust. The committee recommended that English criminal law be amended so that homosexuality not be a crime for consenting adults, and that there be no change in existing laws permitting prostitution. These recommendations often stood noticeably in the shadow of Mill's proposals. The committee argued, for example, that firm distinctions should be drawn between crime and sin, and between public decency and private morality. Its members maintained that while the law must govern matters of public decency, private morality is not a matter to be legislated: "The function of the criminal law is to preserve public order and decency, to protect the citizen from what is offensive or injurious, and to provide sufficient safeguards against exploitation and corruption of others." They further maintained that the law should not function "to intervene in the private lives of citizens, or to seek to enforce any pattern of behavior" unless matters of public decency or harm are involved.

The clear message of the committee was that unless it could be shown that public indecency or personal exploitation are involved, the law should not prohibit activities such as homosexuality and prostitution. The committee's position is more ambiguous, however, when applied to a case such as *Paris Adult Theatre,* which requires reference to some criterion of "decency" of the sort the Supreme Court has struggled to supply. However, in contrast to the position of the Supreme Court, a general position warmly embraced by the Wolfenden Committee is that the state does not and should not have the right to restrict any private actions affecting only consenting adults. The state should not have this right, the committee argues, because of the supreme importance both social ethics and the law place on "individual freedom of choice and action in matters of private morality. . .which is, in brief and crude terms, not the law's business."

Arguments in Support of Legal Moralism

Mill and the Wolfenden Committee have by no means stood unchallenged. Two main arguments have been lodged against their views and in support of legal moralism. The first is an argument from democratic rule: There is no tradition in western democracies, ethical or legal, which stipulates that morality cannot be legislated. If some practice is regarded as outrageously immoral by the vast majority of citizens in a community, their reaction is in itself sufficient to justify the claim that the behavior should be illegal. Both democratic rule and the institution of morality must be protected at all costs, according to this argument, even at the expense of a risk to individual liberties. Community sentiment makes the law in democracies, and laws set forth the prevailing standards of justice. Any majority-sanctioned law is valid and appropriate, then, unless it is unconstitutional. Justice Burger considered this argument in *Paris Adult Theatre,* arguing that states have a right to maintain a "decent society" (though he does not invoke a majority standard). For all these reasons, the supporters of legal moralism conclude that a society is partially constituted by a set of moral ideas, and that if some practice is widely detested, society cannot be denied the right to restrict it.

A second argument for legal moralism is based on the social necessity and importance of morality. In the nineteenth century, it was argued against Mill that one of the law's primary functions is to promote virtue while discouraging vice—notions that cannot be reduced to mere benefit and harm. More recently, it has been argued that the legal enforcement of morals is justified whenever threats to moral rules challenge the social order. Just as law and order through government are necessary for a stable society, according to this view, so moral conformity is essential to a society's continuity. Individual liberties thus deserve protection only when they do not erode standards essential to the promotion of virtue and moral conformity in society. Precisely this line of argument was used (in June 1980) by the United States Navy in bringing formal discharge proceedings against sixteen suspected lesbians. Navy policy, stated in formal rules, stipulates that homosexuals "impair combat readiness, efficiency, security, and morals."

All supporters of this second argument agree that we ought to be cautious in declaring a practice intolerably immoral. But the point remains, they insist, that society has the *right* to pass criminal laws legislating morality in extenuating circumstances. The contention, in brief, is that the law may be used to preserve morality just as it is used to safeguard *anything* essential to its existence.

Arguments Opposed to Legal Moralism

The central objection to this defense of legal moralism is that it is intolerant and repressive of individual rights, thus failing to respect privacy and the differing views inevitably present in a pluralistic society. Justice Brennan, for example, repeatedly returns to considerations of protecting "privacy," "constitutional rights," "protected speech," and freedom of "private thoughts" in his minority opinion in *Paris Adult Theatre*. Although there are several forms of this argument against legal moralism, the consensus view is that any attempt to make immoral conduct illegal (criminal), when the conduct is not harmful to others, is unacceptable because it directly violates principles of individual liberty. If one is to be justifiably punished under law, it must be because one's action harms someone else, not because a particular moral practice is involved. That a moral practice is involved should be irrelevant as far as the law is concerned. According to this argument, the law should never be based on views that a certain moral perspective is intolerable, but rather, should be based on the view that harmful treatment is always intolerable. Though he never phrases his point in quite this way, Mill seems generally to suppport this line of thought.

H. L. A. Hart has been perhaps the leading critic of legal moralism, as well as a selective defender of both Mill and the Wolfenden Report. In the following selection, he argues—against the position of Patrick Devlin sketched in Chapter 1—that proof of moral wrongness is not sufficient justification for legislation against acts such as homosexuality, for laws create undue frustration and misery of a special degree for those legislated against. Hart sees legal moralism as a disguised conservative defense of the conventional moral order, one that attempts to sweep all legal restrictions against allegedly immoral practices (e.g., bigamy, killings, and dishonesty) under the same rug. This view purports that there is no morally relevant difference between them, and treats "morality" as if there were a single, indivisible whole without separate justifications for its separate principles. In this selection, Hart introduces an extremely important distinction between *positive* morality (that set of moral principles actually accepted in a culture) and *critical* morality (those principles of morality used to criticize both social institutions and rules of positive morality). He argues that the supporters of legal moralism seriously confuse the two by thinking that mere positive morality is sufficient justification for *legal* enforcement without consideration of critical morality.

H. L. A. HART

Law, Liberty, and Morality*

I do not propose to defend all that Mill said; for I myself think there may be grounds justifying the legal coercion of the individual other than the prevention of harm to others. But on the narrower issue relevant to the enforcement of morality Mill seems to me to be right. It is of course possible simply to assert that the legal enforcement by society of its accepted morality needs no argument to justify it, because it is a morality which is enforced. But Mill's critics have not fallen back upon this brute assertion. They have in fact advanced many different arguments to justify the enforcement of morality, but these all, as I shall attempt to show, rest on unwarranted assumptions as to matters of fact, or on certain evaluations whose plausibility, due in large measure to ambiguity or vagueness or inaccuracy of statement, dwindles (even if it does not altogether vanish) when exposed to critical scrutiny. . . .

It is plain that the question is one *about* morality, but it is important to observe that it is also itself a question *of* morality. It is the question whether the enforcement of morality is morally justified; so morality enters into the question in two ways. The importance of this feature of the question is that it would plainly be no sufficient answer to show that in fact in some society—our own or others—it was widely regarded as morally quite right and proper to enforce, by legal punishment, compliance with the accepted morality. No one who seriously debates this question would regard Mill as refuted by the simple dem-

onstration that there are some societies in which the generally shared morality endorses its own enforcement by law, and does so even in those cases where the immorality was thought harmless to others. The existence of societies which condemn association between white and coloured persons as immoral and punish it by law still leaves our question to be argued. It is true that Mill's critics have often made much of the fact that English law does in several instances, apparently with the support of popular morality, punish immorality as such, especially in sexual matters; but they have usually admitted that this is where the argument begins, not where it ends. I shall indeed later claim that the play made by some legal writers with what they treat as examples of the legal enforcement of morality "as such" is sometimes confused. But they do not, at any rate, put forward their case as simply proved by pointing to these social facts. Instead they attempt to base their own conclusion that it is morally justifiable to use the criminal law in this way on principles which they believe to be universally applicable, and which they think are either quite obviously rational or will be seen to be so after discussion.

Thus Lord Devlin bases his affirmative answer to the question on the quite general principle that it is permissible for any society to take the steps needed to preserve its own existence as an organized society,[1] and he thinks that immorality—even private sexual immorality—may, like treason, be something which jeopardizes a society's existence. Of course many of us may doubt this general principle, and

*From H. L. A. Hart, *Law, Liberty, and Morality* (Stanford, Calif.: Stanford University Press, 1963), pp. 5–6, 17–24.

[1] *The Enforcement of Morals*, pp. 13–14.

not merely the suggested analogy with treason. We might wish to argue that whether or not a society is justified in taking steps to preserve itself must depend both on what sort of society it is and what the steps to be taken are. If a society were mainly devoted to the cruel persecution of a racial or religious minority, or if the steps to be taken included hideous tortures, it is arguable that what Lord Devlin terms the "disintegration"[2] of such a society would be morally better than its continued existence, and steps ought not to be taken to preserve it. Nonetheless Lord Devlin's principle that a society may take the steps required to preserve its organized existence is not itself tendered as an item of English popular morality, deriving its cogency from its status as part of our institutions. He puts it forward as a principle, rationally acceptable, to be used in the evaluation or criticism of social institutions generally. And it is surely clear that anyone who holds the question whether a society has the "right" to enforce morality, or whether it is morally permissible for any society to enforce its morality by law, to be discussable at all, must be prepared to deploy some such general principles of critical morality. In asking the question, we are assuming the legitimacy of a standpoint which permits criticism of the institutions of any society, in the light of general principles and knowledge of the facts.

To make this point clear, I would revive the terminology much favoured by the Utilitarians of the last century, which distinguished "positive morality," the morality actually accepted and shared by a given social group, from the general moral principles used in the criticism of actual social institutions including positive morality. We may call such general principles "critical morality" and say that our question is one

[2]Ibid., pp. 14–15.

of critical morality about the legal enforcement of positive morality.

A second feature of our question worth attention is simply that it is a question of *justification*. In asking it we are committed at least to the general critical principle that the use of legal coercion by any society calls for justification as something *prima facie* objectionable to be tolerated only for the sake of some countervailing good. . . .

The unimpeded exercise by individuals of free choice may be held a value in itself with which it is *prima facie* wrong to interfere; or it may be thought valuable because it enables individuals to experiment—even with living—and to discover things valuable both to themselves and to others. But interference with individual liberty may be thought an evil requiring justification for simpler, utilitarian reasons; for it is itself the infliction of a special form of suffering—often very acute—on those whose desires are frustrated by the fear of punishment. This is of particular importance in the case of laws enforcing a sexual morality. They may create misery of a quite special degree. For both the difficulties involved in the repression of sexual impulses and the consequences of repression are quite different from those involved in the abstention from "ordinary" crime. Unlike sexual impulses, the impulse to steal or to wound or even kill is not, except in a minority of mentally abnormal cases, a recurrent and insistent part of daily life. Resistance to the temptation to commit these crimes is not often, as the suppression of sexual impulses generally is, something which affects the development or balance of the individual's emotional life, happiness, and personality.

Thirdly, the distinction already made, between positive morality and principles of critical morality, may serve to dissipate a certain misunderstanding of the question and to clarify its central point. It is sometimes said that the question is not whether it is morally justifiable to enforce morality as such, but only *which* morality may be enforced. Is it only a utilitarian morality condemning activities which are harmful to others? Or is it a morality which also condemns certain activities whether they are harmful or not? This way of regarding the question misrepresents the character of, at any rate, modern controversy. A utilitarian who insists that the law should only punish activities which are harmful adopts this as a critical principle, and, in so doing, he is quite unconcerned with the question whether a utilitarian morality is or is not already accepted as the positive morality of the society to which he applies his critical principles. If it is so accepted, that is not, in his view, the reason why it should be enforced. It is true that if he is successful in preaching his message to a given society, members of it will then be compelled to behave as utilitarians in certain ways, but these facts do not mean that the vital difference between him and his opponent is only as to the content of the morality to be enforced. For as may be seen from the main criticisms of Mill, the Utili-

tarian's opponent, who insists that it is morally permissible to enforce morality as such, believes that the mere fact that certain rules or standards of behaviour enjoy the status of a society's positive morality is the reason—or at least part of the reason—which justifies their enforcement by law. No doubt in older controversies the opposed positions were different: the question may have been whether the state could punish only activities causing secular harm or also acts of disobedience to what were believed to be divine commands or prescriptions of Natural Law. But what is crucial to the dispute in its modern form is the significance to be attached to the historical fact that certain conduct, no matter what, is prohibited by a positive morality. The utilitarian denies that this has any significance sufficient to justify its enforcement; his opponent asserts that it has. These are divergent critical principles which do not differ merely over the content of the morality to be enforced, but over a more fundamental and, surely, more interesting issue.

It must not be thought that Hart and Mill are attacking views that are now outmoded in liberal societies. It is arguably the case that in both English common law and American constitutional law, prohibitions based on legal moralism are permitted and in some cases even prevalent.

THE OFFENSE PRINCIPLE

It is not uncommon to encounter a newscast of the following description every year or so: "Publisher *X* was jailed last evening for the publication and distribution of pornographic materials. The decision to jail Mr. *X* followed an extensive police investigation into his traffic in pornography and other obscene materials." Such newscasts may be followed by either a favorable or an unfavorable editorial delivered by the local news station. Favorable reactions argue that the inherent offensiveness of the smut distributed by Mr. *X* shows that he deserves everything he got. Unfavorable reactions argue that Mr. *X*'s material may indeed be among the filthiest ever published but that its low quality is irrelevant: the relevant matter is that one ought to be free to publish whatever one wishes without restriction so long as it does not harm other persons. Here there is a straightforward moral problem: Is inherent *offensiveness* a ground for restricting liberty when there is no direct harm to individual persons?

This notion of offense should not be reduced to the notion of harm at work in the harm principle or to any idea of moral harm that might be operative in legal moralism (though the connections admittedly are at times quite close). Many of the morally offensive actions of concern to legal moralism are carried on in private between consenting adults, as was repeatedly seen in the discussion of the *Paris Adult Theatre* case. Offensive displays and the dissemination of offensive materials, by contrast with private showings in homes or theaters, are public and may be neither consented to nor avoidable. Justice Burger does argue that theaters are places of "public accommodation," but this characterization is not sufficient to make commerce that takes place in them public in the relevant sense. Publicly available books, pamphlets, and advertised appeals *are* public in the relevant sense, however.

When pornographic plays, novels, photographs, etc., are condemned, what is the meaning of the assertion that they are so "obscene" or "offensive" that they ought (on moral grounds) to be controlled? The word "obscenity" refers to something foul and disgusting, particularly when contrasted to chastity and modesty. The term has come to have definite associations with nudity, sexual display, and excretion. To say that instances of such matters are "offensive" is to say that they are obnoxious, revolting, and insulting. Both law and ethical theory use the terms similarly, but with an ethical import attached: To say that something is "obscene" is to say that *because of its offensiveness, it does not deserve to be protected from legal interference*. This judgment of course leaves open questions about precisely which criteria shall be used to define "offensiveness." The usual strategy is to appeal to community standards or sentiment, rather than to some more objective standard. However, these standards must be publicly testable and socially well entrenched in order to qualify as stipulating what is "offensive" for the purpose of law and ethics. This requirement is invoked to avoid the accusation that a judgment of offensiveness is purely "subjective," rather than being "objective" by reference to social beliefs.

The problem of obscene and offensive literature and displays has troubled many public bodies over the years, as was seen in the thinking of the Supreme Court. Another instructive instance arose in 1967 when the Congress of the United States, citing traffic in obscene and pornographic materials as "a matter of national concern," created the National Commission on Obscenity and Pornography. This commission, whose members were appointed by the President in 1968, was charged with thoroughly studying the issue of obscenity and pornography. Its eventual report might well have been written by Mill, and it contrasts sharply with the judicial findings of the Supreme Court. It recommended that all legal restrictions on the public sale, exhibition, and distribution of sexual materials to *consenting adults* be repealed, but that nonconsenting adults be protected from sexually explicit materials encountered through public displays and unsolicited mailings. The commission based its final recommendations more on factual findings than ethical arguments: There was no evidence to connect exposure to explicit sexual materials with antisocial behavior. It is worthy of notice that both the factual and the ethical theses of the commission are in agreement with Mill's claims.

The report of the Commission on Obscenity and Pornography was not well received in many quarters. Only twelve of the commission's eighteen members supported its striking final recommendations. Some members filed a minority report that challenged the factual findings, as well as the recommendations. President Richard Nixon, angered by the report, subsequently ignored it. Members of Congress and their constituents were less than enthusiastic, and consequently the commission's recommendations were never implemented. Still, this report and many similar documents, such as the Supreme Court's decision in *Paris Adult Theatre*, challenge us to consider seriously the conditions, if any, that would justify a government's limiting the access of informed and consenting adults to pornographic and other obscene materials.

The Arguments against Censorship

The case against censorship, as might be expected, is based on Mill's view that only harm to others provides proper grounds for the limitation of liberty. The argument usually employed, as in the case of the Commission on Obscenity and Pornography, is a consequentialist one based on the insufficiency of relevant evidence: there is no factual evidence to indicate that unrestricted dissemination of pornography and controversial displays will bring about a substantial social evil. For this reason it is regarded as unjustified to restrict access to printed materials of any sort, and even to curtail public displays that are offensive by prevailing standards. Because of lack of available evidence, Justice Brennan resorts to this argument several times in his dissenting opinion in *Paris Adult Theatre*, where he notes the Court's traditional view that there is "little empirical basis for" the claim that "exposure to obscene materials may lead to deviant sexual behavior or crimes of sexual violence." This form of reasoning is often expanded as follows: The government should never intrude in the private affairs of its citizens, both because every person possesses a right to privacy and because such interference is likely to produce more harm than it prevents. Furthermore, to enforce prevailing opinions about offensiveness would be to allow what Mill calls the "tyranny of the majority." Because there is no evidence that the access of consenting adults to offensive materials presents a "clear and present danger," censorship and similar restrictions are unwarranted. (The key words here are "access of consenting adults." Public displays and access by minors are not included in this limited case against censorship. Mill, too, explicitly exempts children.)

A quite striking argument in behalf of pornographic materials takes the optimistic view that they are positively beneficial to those exposed to them and to society as a whole. It is claimed, for example, that exposure to pornography sometimes promotes normal rather than deviant sexual development, that sexual relationships can be enhanced by it, and that for some people it provides a socially harmless release from sexual tension. Supporters of this point of view, therefore, favor easy access to pornography. Their arguments, if correct, provide maximally strong reasons in favor of free access, for they claim *benefits* for allegedly offensive materials, as well as *harms* from the loss of the liberty to acquire them.

The Arguments for Censorship

Only rarely is a case for censorship based purely on the principle of offense. Usually the appeal is to a mixture of the principles already discussed in previous sections of this chapter. Hence, several appeals must be considered in discussing limitations on pornography and other obscene materials or actions.

The harm principle is the moral basis for the common claim that exposure to pornography is a direct cause of such crimes as rape. Proponents of this position often cite studies or examples of persons exposed to pornographic material who subsequently commit a sex-related crime. Chief Justice Burger cites one report portending to show that "there is at least an arguable correlation between obscene material and crimes." The acknowledged problem with such examples is that they fail to establish that the crime, which *follows* exposure to pornography, is a direct *causal result* of the exposure itself. Sociological data indicating a causal relation are scarce. The Commission on Obscenity and Pornography claimed that, on the basis of the available data, there is virtually no evidence to support such causal claims. (The study cited by Chief Justice Burger is the only one found by the commission.) Of course, *if* a causal connection between the use of pornography and antisocial behavior could be demonstrated, the argument would have a solid basis in the *harm* principle; but then there would be no need for a supplementary offense principle. The principle of paternalism is also sometimes invoked on grounds that those exposed to pornography will harm themselves by such exposure—for example, exposure that reinforces their emotional problems or that renders them incapable of love and other distinctively human relationships—though it is again difficult to obtain sociological data to support such claims of harm.

According to some writers—e.g., Irving Kristol and Chief Justice Burger in his opinion—the rights of the community ought to occupy a prominent place in these discussions. Kristol believes that there is presently too much freedom to disseminate pornography and that it does have serious harmful social effects on children and on community standards. He further contends that pornography divides human responses from sexual responses, and thus affects basic sexual relationships between individuals by depriving those affected of "their specifically human dimension." In the end, he believes that "[w]hat is at stake [in the pornography discussion] is civilization and humanity, nothing less."* Chief Justice Burger offers a milder form of this same argument in *Paris Adult Theatre*.

*Irving Kristol, "Pornography, Obscenity, and the Case for Censorship," in *The Public Interest* (1972), as reprinted in Harry K. Girvetz, ed., *Contemporary Moral Issues*, 3d ed. (Belmont, Calif.: Wadsworth Publishing Company, Inc., 1974), pp. 150–160.

It is difficult to balance questions of liberty against problems of "mere" offense, but in the following selection, Joel Feinberg attempts to convince us that we ought to do so.

JOEL FEINBERG

"Harmless Immoralities" and Offensive Nuisances*

The American Civil Liberties Union, adopting an approach characteristic of both the friends and the foes of censorship in an earlier period, insists that the offensiveness of obscenity is much too trivial a ground to warrant prior restraint or censorship.[1] The A.C.L.U. argument for this position treats literature, drama, and painting as forms of expression subject to the same rules as expressions of opinion. The power to censor and punish, it maintains, involves risks of great magnitude that socially valuable material will be repressed along with the "filth"; and the overall effect of suppression, it insists, can only be to discourage nonconformist and eccentric expression generally. In order to override these serious risks, the A.C.L.U. concludes, there must be in a given case an even more clear and present danger that the obscene material, if not squelched, will cause even greater harm; and evidence of this countervailing kind is never forthcoming (especially when "mere offense" is not counted as a kind of harm).

The A.C.L.U. stand on obscenity seems clearly to be the position dictated by the [harm principle and its] corollary, the clear and present danger test. Is there any reason at this point to introduce the offense principle into the discussion? Unhappily, we may be forced to do just that if we are to do justice to all of our particular intuitions in the most harmonious way. Consider an example suggested by Louis B. Schwartz. By the provisions of the new Model Penal Code, he writes, "a rich homosexual may not use a billboard on Times Square to promulgate to the general populace the techniques and pleasures of sodomy."[2] If the notion of "harm" is restricted to its narrow sense that is contrasted with "offense," it will be hard to reconstruct a rationale for this prohibition that is based on a harm principle. It is unlikely that there would be evidence that a lurid and obscene public poster in Times Square would create a clear and present danger of injury to those unfortunate persons who fail to avert their eyes in time as

*From Joel Feinberg, "'Harmless Immoralities' and Offensive Nuisances," in *Issues in Law and Morality* (Cleveland: Case Western Reserve University Press, 1973), pp. 99–104, 133–34.

[1]"Obscenity and Censorship" (New York: American Civil Liberties Union, March 1963). The approach that was characteristic of the late fifties and early sixties was to assimilate the obscenity question to developed free speech doctrine requiring a showing of a "clear and present danger" of substantive harm to justify government suppression. Obscene materials pertaining to sex (but not excretion!) were taken to be dangerous, if at all, because they are *alluring* and thus capable of tempting persons into antisocial (harmful) conduct. As Herbert Packer points out (*Limits of Criminal Sanctions*, p. 319), the clear and present danger test is virtually certain to be passed by even the most offensive materials.

[2]Schwartz, "Morals Offenses," p. 681.

they come blinking out of the subway stations. And yet it will be surpassingly difficult even for the most dedicated liberal to advocate freedom of expression in a case of this kind. Hence, if we are to justify coercion in this case, we will likely be driven, however reluctantly, to the offense principle.

There is good reason to be "reluctant" to embrace the offense principle until driven to it by an example of the above kind. People take offense—perfectly genuine offense—at many socially useful or harmless activities, from commercial advertisements to inane chatter. Moreover, as we have seen, irrational prejudices of a very widespread kind can lead people to be disgusted, shocked, even morally repelled by perfectly innocent activities, and we should be loath to permit their groundless repugnance to override the innocence. The offense principle, therefore, must be formulated in a very precise way so as not to open the door to wholesale and intuitively unwarranted repression.

It is instructive to note that a strictly drawn offense principle would not only justify prohibition of public conduct and publicly pictured conduct that is in its inherent character repellent (e.g., buggery, bestiality, sexual sado-masochism), but also conduct and pictured conduct that is inoffensive in itself but offensive only when it occurs in inappropriate circumstances. I have in mind so-called indecencies such as public nudity. . . .

If we are to accept the offense principle as a supplement to the harm principle, we must accept two mediating norms of interpretation which stand to it in a way similar to that in which the clear and present danger test stands to the harm principle. The first is the *standard of universality* which has already been touched upon. The interracial couple strolling hand in hand down the streets of Jackson, Mississippi, with-

out question cause shock and mortification, even shame and disgust, to the overwhelming majority of white pedestrians who happen to observe them; but we surely don't want our offense principle applied to justify preventive coercion on that ground. To avoid that consequence let us stipulate that in order for "offense" (repugnance, embarrassment, shame, etc.) to be sufficient to warrant coercion, it should be the reaction that could reasonably be expected from almost any person chosen at random, taking the nation as a whole, and not because the individual selected belongs to some faction, clique, or party.

That qualification should be more than sufficient to protect the interracial couple, but, alas, it may yield undesirable consequences in another class of cases. I have in mind abusive, mocking, insulting behavior or speech attacking specific subgroups of the population—especially ethnic, racial, or religious groups. Public cross-burnings, displays of swastikas, "jokes" that ridicule Americans of Polish descent told on public media, public displays of banners with large and abusive caricatures of the Pope[3] are extremely offensive to the groups so insulted, and no doubt also offensive to large numbers of sympathetic outsiders. But still, there will be many millions of people who will not respond emotionally at all, and many millions more who may secretly approve. Thus, our amended offense principle will not justify the criminal proscription of such speech or conduct. I am inclined, therefore, simply to patch up that principle in an *ad hoc* fashion once more. For that special class of offensive behavior that consists in the flaunting of abusive, mocking, insulting

[3]For a penetrating discussion of an actual case of this description, see Zechariah Chafee, *Free Speech in the United States* (Cambridge, Mass.: Harvard University Press, 1964), p. 161.

behavior of a sort bound to upset, alarm, anger, or irritate those it insults, I would allow the offense principle to apply, even though the behavior would *not* offend the entire population. Those who are taunted by such conduct will understandably suffer intense and complicated emotions. They might be frightened or wounded; and their blood might boil in wrath. Yet the law cannot permit them to accept the challenge and vent their anger in retaliatory aggression. But again, having to cope with one's rage is as burdensome a bore as having to suffer shame, or disgust, or noisome stenches, and the law might well undertake to protect those who are vulnerable, even if they are—indeed, precisely because they are—a minority.

The second mediating principle for the application of the offense principle is the standard of reasonable avoidability. No one has a right to protection from the state against offensive experiences if he can easily and effectively avoid those experiences with no unreasonable effort or inconvenience. If a nude person enters a public bus and takes a seat near the front, there may be no effective way whatever for the other patrons to avoid intensely shameful embarrassment (or other insupportable feelings) short of leaving the bus themselves, which would be an unreasonable inconvenience. Similarly, obscene remarks over a loudspeaker, homosexual billboards in Times Square, pornographic handbills thrust into the hands of passing pedestrians all fail to be reasonably avoidable.

On the other hand, the offense principle, properly qualified, can give no warrant to the suppression of *books* on the grounds of obscenity. When printed words hide decorously behind covers of books sitting passively on the shelves of a bookstore, their offensiveness is easily avoided. The contrary view is no doubt encouraged by the common comparison of obscenity with

"smut," "filth," or "dirt." This in turn suggests an analogy to nuisance law, which governs cases where certain activities create loud noises or terrible odors offensive to neighbors, and "the courts must weigh the gravity of the nuisance [substitute "offense"] to the neighbors against the social utility [substitute "redeeming social value"] of the defendant's conduct."[4] There is, however, one vitiating disanalogy in this comparison. In the case of "dirty books," the offense is easily avoidable. There is nothing like the evil smell of rancid garbage oozing right out through the covers of a book whether one looks at it or not. When an "obscene" book sits on a shelf, who is there to be offended? Those who want to read it for the sake of erotic stimulation presumably will not be offended (else they wouldn't read it), and those who choose not to read it will have no experience of it to be offended by. . . .

I should like to take this opportunity to try one final example and to rest my case on it. It is an example that illustrates not just one but virtually all the categories of offensiveness mentioned in my article; and if the reader fails to concede that it provides a legitimate occasion for legal interference with a citizen's conduct on grounds other than harmfulness, then I must abandon my effort to convince him at all, at least by the use of examples. Consider then the man who walks down the main street of a town at mid-day. In the middle of a block in the central part of town, he stops, opens his briefcase, and pulls out a portable folding camp-toilet. In the prescribed manner, he attaches a plastic bag to its under side, sets it on the sidewalk, and proceeds to defecate in it, to the utter amazement and disgust of the passers-by. While he is thus relieving himself,

[4]William L. Prosser, *Handbook of the Law of Torts* (St. Paul, Minn.: West Publishing Company, 1955).

he unfolds a large banner which reads "This is what I think of the Ruritanians" (substitute "niggers," "Kikes," "Spics," "Dagos," "Polacks," or "Hunkies"). Another placard placed prominently next to him invites ladies to join him in some of the more bizarre sexual-excretory perversions mentioned in Krafft-Ebbing and includes a large-scale graphic painting of the conduct he solicits. For those who avert their eyes too quickly, he plays an obscene phonograph record on a small portable machine, and accompanies its raunchier parts with grotesquely lewd bodily motions. He concludes his public performance by tasting some of his own excrement, and after savoring it slowly and thoroughly in the manner of a true epicure, he consumes it. He then dresses, ties the plastic bag containing the rest of the excrement, places it carefully in his briefcase, and continues on his way.

Now I would not have the man in the example executed, or severely punished. I'm not sure I would want him punished at all, unless he defied authoritative orders to "move along" or to cease and desist in the future. But I would surely want the coercive arm of the state to protect passers-by (by the most economical and humane means) from being unwilling audiences for such performances. I assume in the example (I hope with some plausibility) that the offensive conduct causes no harm or injury either of a public or a private kind. After all, if the numerous tons of dog dung dropped every day on the streets of New York are no health hazard, then surely the fastidious use of a sanitary plastic bag cannot be seriously unhygienic.

Feinberg's views have much to be said for them, as do the somewhat contrasting conclusions of the Commission on Obscenity and Pornography. In particular, his standard of reasonable avoidability proposes a minimum requirement that we demand of offensive displays or actions. But how precisely is the boundary to be drawn between the avoidable and the unavoidable? What are the precise *conditions* (if any) under which restrictions of liberty are justified on grounds of offensiveness? Perhaps only general guidelines and not precise conditions governing such matters are possible in philosophy, as Rawls suggests in his essay earlier in this chapter. Be that as it may, philosophers have probably not struggled with this issue as much as they should have.

PATERNALISM

The word "paternalism" is broadly used to refer to the treatment of individuals as a parent treats his or her children. But in ethical theory, the word has the more narrow meaning of treatment that restricts the liberty of individuals, without their consent, where the justification for such action is either the prevention of some harm they might do to themselves or the production of some benefit for them which they might not otherwise secure. The principle of paternalism then claims that limiting a person's liberty is justified if, through his or her own actions, that person would seriously harm himself or herself or would fail to secure an important benefit.

Many actions, policies, and laws are commonly justified by appeal to the principle of paternalism. Two cases in American law governing the use of motorcycle helmets clearly illustrate the dilemma presented by paternalistic justifications. In one case, *American Motorcycle Association v. Davids*, Judge Miller cites Mill favorably and relies extensively on his views about liberty. Miller argues that requiring motorcyclists and their passengers to wear crash helmets for paternalistic reasons is an instance of reasoning that "could lead to unlimited [state] paternalism." He acknowledges that highway safety is a relevant reason for legal restrictions in cases where *other* persons are involved, but not where the cyclist alone is at risk. He also quotes Justice Brandeis on "the right to be let alone" to the effect that we ought to be especially careful to protect human liberty when government becomes overprotective through its beneficence. Much like the Wolfenden Report, Miller's legal opinion reads almost as if it were an immediate application of Mill's moral and social philosophy.

By contrast, in *State v. Eitel*, Judge Mann argues that "we ought to admit frankly that the purpose of the helmet [requirement] is to preserve the life and health of the cyclist"—not some other public purpose having to do with health or highway safety. He thus sees the issue as a case of justifiable paternalism. He finds at least some paternalistic laws to be acceptable, and points out that suicide, for example, has been "a common-law crime for centuries." Judge Mann even appeals for support to Mill, quoting him to the effect that "no person is an entirely isolated being," and therefore that one cannot perform actions free of responsibilities to other persons. These two opinions, and many others as well, tend to show that the issue of paternalism is as unsettled in contemporary American constitutional law as in philosophy.

The Nature and Types of Paternalism

Some disagreement persists in philosophy concerning the meaning of "paternalism." If use is made of a definition as loose as H. L. A. Hart's—"the protection of people against themselves"—misunderstandings can readily follow. Legislation intended to help citizens protect themselves from inadvertent acts, such as mutilating their hands in garbage disposals, would on this definition seem paternalistic. A more acceptable definition is the following: Paternalism is the limitation of a person's liberty of action or liberty of information justified by reasons referring exclusively to the welfare, needs, or values of the person whose liberty is limited.

Joel Feinberg has distinguished two types of paternalism, both of which fit the general definition. His distinction is between strong and weak forms of paternalism, where the *weak* form is explained as the form in which

> [one] has the right to prevent self-regarding conduct only when it is substantially nonvoluntary or when temporary intervention is necessary to establish whether it is voluntary or not.*

*Joel Feinberg, "Legal Paternalism," *Canadian Journal of Philosophy*, **1** (1971): 113.

The *strong* form holds that it is proper to protect or benefit a person by liberty-limiting measures even when his or her contrary choices are informed and voluntary.

A substantial problem is generated by this distinction. Virtually everyone acknowledges that some forms of weak paternalism are justified (e.g., preventing a person under the influence of LSD from self-inflicted death). If, then, *some* forms of paternalism are justified, the problem of paternalism for ethical theory is that of deciding under what conditions the principle of paternalism may be used and under what conditions it may not be used. The difficulty is that weak paternalism may not be paternalism in any interesting sense because it may not be a liberty-limiting principle which is *independent* of the harm principle. For this reason, some writers have restricted the meaning of the word "paternalism" to strong paternalism.

The Justification of Paternalism

Any careful exponent of a principle of paternalism will specify precisely which goods, needs, and interests deserve paternalistic protection, and the conditions under which intervention is warranted. In most recent formulations, it has been argued that the state (for example) is justified in interfering with a person's liberty if it thereby protects the person against such of his or her own actions that are extremely and unreasonably risky (waterfall-rafting and hang gliding, e.g.), or are potentially dangerous and irreversible in effect (as some drugs and some surgery are). Even supporters of paternalism widely accept the fact that a heavy burden of justification is needed to limit free actions by competent persons, especially since there is never direct subject consent (even if there might be proxy consent or direct consent by agreement to be placed under a paternalistic power). According to this position, paternalism is justified only when the evils prevented from occurring to the person are greater than the evils (if any) caused by interference with that person's liberty and when always treating persons in this way is universally justified under relevantly similar circumstances. This line of thought even emerged occasionally in the *Paris Adult Theatre* case, where it was argued that voluntary exposure to pornographic materials would lead to the development or reinforcement of emotional and sexual problems or would otherwise impair one's capacity for decent love relationships.

Gerald Dworkin defends one form of paternalism in the following selection. He regards paternalism as a form of "social insurance policy" that fully rational persons would take out in order to protect themselves. Such persons would be protecting themselves against actions which they might unguardedly take but which are potentially dangerous or irreversible—often when the persons do not sufficiently understand or appreciate the dangers involved.

GERALD DWORKIN

Paternalism*

I suggest that since we are all aware of our irrational propensities, deficiencies in cognitive and emotional capacities and avoidable and unavoidable ignorance it is rational and prudent for us to in effect take out "social insurance policies." We may argue for and against proposed paternalistic measures in terms of what fully rational individuals would accept as forms of protection. Now, clearly since the initial agreement is not about specific measures we are dealing with a more-or-less blank check and therefore there have to be carefully defined limits. What I am looking for are certain kinds of conditions which make it plausible to suppose that rational men could reach agreement to limit their liberty even when other men's interests are not affected.

Of course as in any kind of agreement schema there are great difficulties in deciding what rational individuals would or would not accept. Particularly in sensitive areas of personal liberty, there is always a danger of the dispute over agreement and rationality being a disguised version of evaluative and normative disagreement.

Let me suggest types of situations in which it seems plausible to suppose that fully rational individuals would agree to having paternalistic restrictions imposed upon them. It is reasonable to suppose that there are "goods" such as health which any person would want to have in order to pursue his own good—no matter how that good is conceived. This is an argument that is used in connection with compulsory education for children but it seems to me that it can be extended to

other goods which have this character. Then one could agree that the attainment of such goods should be promoted even when not recognized to be such, at the moment, by the individuals concerned.

An immediate difficulty that arises stems from the fact that men are always faced with competing goods and that there may be reasons why even a value such as health—or indeed life—may be overridden by competing values. Thus the problem with the Christian Scientist and blood transfusions. It may be more important for him to reject "impure substances" than to go on living. The difficult problem that must be faced is whether one can give sense to the notion of a person irrationally attaching weights to competing values.

Consider a person who knows the statistical data on the probability of being injured when not wearing seat belts in an automobile and knows the types and gravity of the various injuries. He also insists that the inconvenience attached to fastening the belt every time he gets in and out of the car outweighs for him the possible risks to himself. I am inclined in this case to think that such a weighing is irrational. Given his life-plans which we are assuming are those of the average person, his interests and commitments already undertaken, I think it is safe to predict that we can find inconsistencies in his calculations at some point. I am assuming that this is not a man who for some conscious or unconscious reasons is trying to injure himself nor is he a man who just likes to "live dangerously." I am assuming that he is like us in all the relevant respects but just puts an enormously high negative value on inconvenience—one which does not seem comprehensible or reasonable. . . .

*From Gerald Dworkin, "Paternalism," *Monist*, **56** (1): 78–84, with permission of the author and publisher.

Some of the decisions we make are of such a character that they produce changes which are in one or another way irreversible. Situations are created in which it is difficult or impossible to return to anything like the initial stage at which the decision was made. In particular some of these changes will make it impossible to continue to make reasoned choices in the future. I am thinking specifically of decisions which involve taking drugs that are physically or psychologically addictive and those which are destructive of one's mental and physical capacities.

I suggest we think of the imposition of paternalistic interferences in situations of this kind as being a kind of insurance policy which we take out against making decisions which are far-reaching, potentially dangerous and irreversible. Each of these factors is important. Clearly there are many decisions we make that are relatively irreversible. In deciding to learn to play chess I could predict in view of my general interest in games that some portion of my free time was going to be preempted and that it would not be easy to give up the game once I acquired a certain competence. But my whole life-style was not going to be jeopardized in an extreme manner. Further it might be argued that even with addictive drugs such as heroin one's normal life plans would not be seriously interfered with if an inexpensive and adequate supply were readily available. So this type of argument might have a much narrower scope than appears to be the case at first.

A second class of cases concerns decisions which are made under extreme psychological and sociological pressures. I am not thinking here of the making of the decision as being something one is pressured into—e.g., a good reason for making duelling illegal is that unless this is done many people might have to manifest their courage and integrity in ways in which they would rather not do so—but rather of decisions such as that to commit suicide which are usually made at a point where the individual is not thinking clearly and calmly about the nature of his decision. . . .

Using my argument schema the question is whether rational individuals would consent to such limitations. I see no reason for them to consent to an absolute prohibition but I do think it is reasonable for them to agree to some kind of enforced waiting period. . . .

A third class of decisions—these classes are not supposed to be disjoint—involves dangers which are either not sufficiently understood or appreciated correctly by the persons involved. Let me illustrate, using the example of cigarette smoking, a number of possible cases.

1. A man may not know the facts—e.g., smoking between one and two packs a day shortens life expectancy 6.2 years, the costs and pain of the illness caused by smoking, etc.

2. A man may know the facts, wish to stop smoking, but not have the requisite will-power.

3. A man may know the facts but not have them play the correct role in his calculation because, say, he discounts the danger psychologically because it is remote in time and/or inflates the attractiveness of other consequences of his decision which he regards as beneficial.

In case 1 what is called for is education, the posting of warnings, etc. In case 2 there is no theoretical problem. We are not imposing a good on someone who rejects it. We are simply using coercion to enable people to carry out their own goals. (Note: There obviously is a difficulty in that only a subclass of the individuals affected wish to be prevented from doing what they are doing.) In case 3 there is a sense in which we are imposing a good on someone since given his current appraisal of the facts he doesn't wish to be restricted. But in another sense we are not imposing a good since what is being claimed—and what must be shown or at least argued for—is that an accurate accounting on his part would lead him to reject his current course of action. Now we all know that such cases exist, that we are prone to disregard dangers that are only possibilities, that immediate pleasures are often magnified and distorted.

If, in addition, the dangers are severe and far-reaching, we could agree to allowing the state a certain degree of power to intervene in such situations. The difficulty is in specifying in advance, even vaguely, the class of cases in which intervention will be legitimate.

A related difficulty is that of drawing a line so that it is not the case that all ultra-hazardous activities are ruled out, e.g., mountain-climbing, bull-fighting, sports-car racing, etc. There are some risks—even very great ones—which a person is entitled to take with his life.

A good deal depends on the nature of the deprivation—e.g., does it prevent the person from engaging in the activity completely or merely limit his participation—and how important to the nature of the activity is the absence of restriction when this is weighed against the role that the activity plays in the life of the person? In the case of automobile seat belts, for example, the restriction is trivial in nature, interferes not at all with the use or enjoyment of the activity, and does, I am assuming, considerably reduce a high risk of serious injury. Whereas, for example, making mountain-climbing illegal prevents completely a person engaging in an activity which may play an important role in his life and his conception of the person he is.

In general, the easiest cases to handle are those which can be argued about in terms which Mill thought to be so important—a concern not just for the happiness or welfare, in some broad sense, of the individual, but rather, a concern for the autonomy and freedom of the person. I suggest that we would be most likely to consent to paternalism in those instances in which it preserves and enhances for the individual his ability to rationally consider and carry out his own decisions.

I have suggested in this essay a number of types of situations in which it seems plausible that rational men would agree to granting the legislative powers of a society the right to impose restrictions on what Mill calls "self-regarding" conduct. However, rational men knowing something about the resources of ignorance, ill-will, and stupidity available to the law-makers of a society—a good case in point is the history of drug legislation in the United States—will be concerned to limit such intervention to a minimum. I suggest in closing two principles designed to achieve this end.

In all cases of paternalistic legislation there must be a heavy and clear burden of proof placed on the authorities to demonstrate the exact nature of the harmful effects (or beneficial consequences) to be avoided (or achieved) and the probability of their occurrence. The burden of proof here is twofold—what lawyers distinguish as the burden of going forward and the burden of persuasion. That the authorities have the burden of going forward means that it is up to them to raise the question and bring forward evidence of the evils to be avoided. Unlike the case of new drugs where the manufacturer must produce some evidence that the drug has been tested and found not harmful, no citizen has to show with respect to self-regarding conduct that it is not harmful or promotes his best interests. In addition the nature and cogency of the evidence for the harmfulness of the course of action must be set at a high level. To paraphrase a formulation of the burden of proof for criminal proceedings—better ten men ruin themselves than one man be unjustly deprived of liberty.

Finally I suggest a principle of the least restrictive alternative. If there is an alternative way of accomplishing the desired end without restricting liberty then although it may involve great expense, inconvenience, etc. the society must adopt it.

Antipaternalistic Individualism

Many people believe that paternalism is never justified, whatever the conditions. It is now widely believed that Mill's argument to this conclusion fails in one or more crucial ways, but there have been repeated attempts to employ his strategy of permitting only the harm principle as the basis for justified limitations of liberty. Thus, many would maintain that the harm principle, when properly formulated, is all that is necessary in order to ensure adequate protection by the state against harms that might befall individuals, for this principle covers the full range of physical, psychological, and legal injuries and harms deserving protection.

A fairly common theme found among those who argue for this position is the following: We may (assuming objectivity and knowledge on our part) justifiably protect a person from harm that might result directly from partially nonvoluntary acts—e.g., those due to drunkenness or retardation. To the extent one protects a person from causes beyond his or her knowledge and control, to that extent (subject perhaps to further specific qualifications) one justifiably intervenes. If a person genuinely has "cloudy judgment" or is deceived by ignorance, his or her choices are not entirely voluntary. And if the person can be injured *because* of these conditions, we may justifiably restrain his or her action. Some would even say that intervention to restrict liberty is morally required in such a case, since disregard of the condition could imperil a person's future. But this justification for intervention is not paternalistic; the person who is informed of the dangers of this action and provided with a context in which voluntary choice is meaningfully possible cannot justifiably be further restrained. When persons become informed and capable of acting voluntarily, our obligations to them are altered, and coercion is no longer justified.

Mill believed that a person ignorant of a potential danger could justifiably be restrained, so long as the coercion was temporary and only for the purpose of rendering the person informed, at which point he or she would be free to choose whatever course seemed most satisfying. Such intervention limits liberty and is justified by antipaternalists on what might appear to be paternalistic grounds. Yet Mill regarded this intervention as no "real infringement" of liberty:

If either a public officer or anyone else saw a person attempting to cross a bridge which had been ascertained to be unsafe, and there were no time to warn him of his danger, they might seize him and turn him back, without any real infringement of his liberty; for liberty consists in doing what one desires, and he does not desire to fall into the river.*

According to this account, it is not a question of protecting men and women *against themselves* or of interfering with their *liberty of action*. The man in Mill's example is not acting at all in regard to the danger of the bridge. He needs protection from something which is precisely not himself, not his intended action, not in any remote sense of his own making. Mill goes on to say that once the person has been fully informed and understands the dangers of the bridge, then he should be free to traverse it, and it is thus that Mill's views on *temporary* interventions are sheltered from the incubus of paternalism.

Those who defend Mill's general libertarian point of view usually argue that the principle of paternalism ought not to be recognized as a valid principle for restricting liberty, because it allows (in principle) too much interference. The serious adverse consequences of giving such power to the state have led many to reject Dworkin's view that the fully rational person would accept paternalism. In the end, this disagreement between paternalists and antipaternalists seems to turn on whether acceptance of the principle of paternalism as valid would create a situation where, as Dworkin puts it, the "ignorance, ill-will and stupidity" of those in power might be used to override legitimate, though risky, exercises of freedom. Dworkin believes the risk of such unwarranted interference is worth taking in order to gain a kind of personal and social insurance policy, and the followers of Mill maintain both that the stakes are too high to justify the risk and that the harm principle alone will suffice.

CONCLUSION

In this chapter, the discussion has moved from moral problems of justifying legal obedience to paternalistic restrictions on individual freedoms. The sometimes narrowly legal character of these discussions may have led some readers to the conclusion that whatever ought to be legally permissible is morally permissible, a clearly questionable assumption. There are many immoral acts, such as breaking promises and violating another's trust, that we would not wish to see legally proscribed. As Aristotle, Kant, and Mill all recognized, legal coercion should not be allowed to reach into every dimension of the moral life.

Of all the topics in this book, the issues about liberty and law discussed here are probably most visible in our daily lives. Part Three now concludes, and a rather abrupt transition will be made from these matters of almost daily concern to philosophical

*John Stuart Mill, *On Liberty* (Indianapolis: Liberal Arts Press, Inc., 1956), p. 117.

issues of justification that underlie these problems. Many philosophers believe these problems of justification to be at once the most important and the most difficult problems in all ethical theory. Though more removed from our daily lives, they are the very heartland of moral philosophy in the twentieth century.

SUGGESTED SUPPLEMENTARY READINGS

Obligation to Law

Baier, Kurt: "The Justification of Governmental Authority," *Journal of Philosophy*, **69** (1972): 700–716.

Benditt, Theodore M.: *Law as Rule and Principle: Problems of Legal Philosphy* (Stanford, Calif.: Stanford University Press, 1978).

Bayles, Michael D.: *Principles of Legislation: The Uses of Political Authority* (Detroit: Wayne State University Press, 1978).

Bedau, Hugo A., ed.: *Civil Disobedience: Theory and Practice* (New York: Pegasus Books, 1969).

Flathman, Richard E.: *Political Obligation* (New York: Atheneum Publishers, 1972).

"Legal Obligation and Civil Disobedience," *Monist*, **54** (1970): 469–624.

Murphy, Jeffrie G., ed.: *Civil Disobedience and Violence* (Belmont, Calif.: Wadsworth Publishing Company, Inc., 1971).

Pennock, J. Roland, and John W. Chapman, eds.: *Political and Legal Obligation: Nomos* 12 (New York: Lieber-Atherton Press, 1970).

Singer, Peter: *Democracy and Disobedience* (Oxford, England: Clarendon Press, 1973).

Smith, M. B. E.: "Is There a Prima Facie Obligation to Obey the Law?" *Yale Law Journal*, **82** (1973): 950–976.

Walzer, Michael: *Obligations: Essays on Disobedience, War & Citizenship* (Cambridge, Mass.: Harvard University Press, 1970).

Wolff, Robert Paul: *In Defense of Anarchism* (New York: Harper Torchbooks, 1970).

Mill and Liberty-Limiting Principles

Bayles, Michael D.: "Legislating Morality," *Wayne Law Review*, **22** (1976): 759–780.

Berlin, Isaiah: *Four Essays on Liberty* (New York: Oxford University Press, 1969).

Golding, Martin P.: *Philosophy of Law* (Englewood Cliffs, N.J.: Prentice-Hall, Inc., 1975).

Hart, Herbert L. A.: *Law, Liberty, and Morality* (Stanford, Calif.: Stanford University Press, 1963).

McCloskey, H. J.: "Mill's Liberalism," *Philosophical Quarterly*, **13** (1963): 143–154.

Radcliff, Peter, ed.: *Limits of Liberty: Studies of Mill's* On Liberty (Belmont, Calif.: Wadsworth Publishing Company, Inc., 1966).

Rees, J. C.: *Mill and His Early Critics* (Leicester, England: University College, 1956).

Paternalism

Bayles, Michael D.: "Criminal Paternalism," in J. Roland Pennock and John W. Chapman, eds., *The Limits of Law: Nomos, 15* (New York: Lieber-Atherton Press, 1974): 174–188.

Dworkin, Gerald: "Paternalism," *Monist,* **56** (1972): 64–84.

Beauchamp, Tom L.: "Paternalism and Bio-Behavioral Control," *Monist*, **60** (1977): 62–80.

———: "Paternalism," in Warren T. Reich, ed., *Encyclopedia of Bioethics* (New York: Free Press, 1978), vol. 3, pp. 1194–1200.

Buchanan, Allen: "Medical Paternalism," *Philosophy and Public Affairs*, **7** (1978): 370–390.

Feinberg, Joel: "Legal Paternalism," *Canadian Journal of Philosophy*, **1** (1971): 105–124.

———: *Social Philosophy* (Englewood Cliffs, N.J.: Prentice-Hall, Inc., 1973), chaps. 2, 3.

Gert, Bernard, and Charles M. Culver: "Paternalistic Behavior," *Philosophy and Public Affairs,* **6** (1976): 45–57.

———: "The Justification of Paternalism," in W. Robison and M. Pritchard, eds., *Medical Responsibility* (Clifton, N.J.: Humana Press, 1979).

Murphy, Jeffrie G.: "Incompetence and Paternalism," *Archives for Philosophy of Law and Social Philosophy*, **40** (1974): 465–486.

Wikler, Daniel: "Paternalism and the Mildly Retarded," *Philosophy and Public Affairs*, **8** (1979): 377–392.

Moral Enforcement

Devlin, Patrick: "Law, Democracy, and Morality," *University of Pennsylvania Law Review*, **110** (1962): 635–649.

———: *The Enforcement of Morals* (Oxford, England: Oxford University Press, 1970).

Dworkin, Ronald: "Lord Devlin and the Enforcement of Morals," *Yale Law Journal*, **75** (1966): 986–1005.

Feinberg, Joel: *Rights, Justice, and the Bounds of Liberty* (Princeton, N. J.: Princeton University Press, 1980).

Hart, H. L. A.: *The Morality of the Criminal Law* (Jerusalem: Magner Press, 1964), Lecture 2.

Hughes, Graham: "Morals and the Criminal Law," *Yale Law Journal*, **71** (1962): 662–683.

Jenkins, Iredell: *Social Order and the Limits of Law* (Princeton, N. J.: Princeton University Press, 1980), chap. 19.

Wasserstrom, Richard, ed.: *Morality and the Law* (Belmont, Calif.: Wadsworth Publishing Company, Inc., 1970).

Wollheim, Richard: "Crime, Sin and Mr. Justice Devlin," *Encounter*, **13**: 5 (1959): 34–40.

Offensiveness

Bayles, Michael: "Comments on Feinberg: Offensive Conduct and the Law," in Norman S. Care and Thomas K. Trelogan, eds., *Issues in Law and Morality* (Cleveland: Press of Case Western Reserve University, 1973).

Berger, Fred R., ed.: *Freedom of Expression* (Belmont, Calif.: Wadsworth Publishing Company, Inc., 1980).

Feinberg, Joel: "'Harmless Immoralities' and Offensive Nuisances," in Norman S. Care and T. K. Trelogan, eds., *Issues in Law and Morality* (Cleveland: Press of Case Western Reserve University, 1973).

Leiser, Burton M.: *Liberty, Justice and Morals* (New York: Macmillan Company, 1973), chap. 6.

Morrow, Frank A.: "Speech, Expression, and the Constitution," *Ethics*, **85** (1975): 235–242.

The Report of the Commission on Obscenity and Pornography (Washington: Government Printing Office, 1970).

Scanlon, Thomas: "A Theory of Freedom of Expression," *Philosophy and Public Affairs*, **1** (1972): 204–226.

Simons, G. L.: *Pornography Without Prejudice* (London: Abelard-Schuman, Ltd., 1972).

PART FOUR

Moral Justification

CHAPTER NINE

The Justification
of Moral Beliefs

In a hospital in suburban New Jersey, thirteen patients died mysteriously during 1965 and 1966. Ten years later, a reporter for the *New York Times*, Myron A. Farber, revealed that mostly empty vials of a powerful muscle relaxant, curare, were found in the locker of a physician, whom Farber referred to as "Dr. *X*." Farber's investigation led authorities to reopen the case, and eventually they charged Dr. Mario F. Jascolevich (Dr. *X*) with administering lethal doses of curare to five patients, whose exhumed bodies were found to contain traces of the drug. The lawyer for the defense requested that the judge order Farber to turn over his files and notes, in order to ensure that Dr. Jascolevich receive a fair trial. Farber refused on grounds that his confidential sources would be compromised. To turn the material over to a judge, he argued, would be an offense against freedom of the press, which he considered legally guaranteed by the First Amendment and also defensible on moral grounds. The defense countered that not to turn over the files would deny a citizen the right to a fair trial, which it believed was both guaranteed by the Sixth Amendment and demanded by moral requirements of justice.

Judge W. J. Arnold ordered Farber's notes to be submitted for the judge's private inspection in order to determine whether they would be material and necessary. When Farber refused to deliver his files, he was cited for contempt of court. He was fined $2,000 and told he would be jailed until he agreed to release the material. The *New York Times* was fined $100,000 and $5,000 per day until the notes were turned over. The *Times* wholly supported Farber, paying for both the fines and a legal counsel. Newspapers across the country rallied in support of what they saw as an imperiled fundamental freedom. They appealed to First Amendment rights and cited the dangers to both press and society if reporters were forced to reveal sources.

After a 1972 court ruling which held that reporters who witness crimes must testify, many states, including New Jersey, passed "shield laws," which protect or shield journalists from having to give information in legal proceedings. Many judges, including Judge Arnold, interpret these laws as incomplete shields and order reporters to divulge information in the interests of the rights of the accused to a fair trial—rights the judge takes to be overriding in such cases.

Farber argued that he did not witness the crime and did not have any direct evidence that would establish guilt or innocence. "Placing my notes in the judge's hands would have the effect of turning me into an investigative arm of the law," he said. "At issue here is not Dr. X's right to fair trial, for he has access to the same people I interviewed. The issue is the right of the public to be informed through its press." The judge held that while the First Amendment offers some protection to the press, this protection is not absolute and can be superseded by overriding concerns, such as the right of a defendant in a criminal case to a fair trial.

Two weeks after his jailing, Farber's lawyers sought a writ of habeas corpus to have him released. Federal Judge F. Lacey accused Farber of having mixed motives for withholding evidence and of conflict of interest. Farber was then writing a book about the Jascolevich case, and therefore, Judge Lacey reasoned, had a personal financial stake in seeing Dr. X convicted. The judge said, "How can Farber justify revealing information to a publisher for profit but not to a court when a man's life is at stake? This is a sorry spectacle of a reporter who pretended to stand on his reporter's privilege when in fact he was standing on an altar of greed." Farber's lawyers claimed that the authors of books are also protected by the First Amendment: "No one argued for Woodward and Bernstein to reveal the identity of Deep Throat."

In November 1978, the jury acquitted Dr. Jascolevich of all charges. Farber was then released from jail, and the contempt penalties were suspended. The *New York Times* appealed to the United States Supreme Court in order to delineate clearly the commitments of the First and Sixth Amendments. The Supreme Court refused to review the case, leaving these legal issues of the clash between rights to a fair trial and rights of the press unresolved. The moral issues are scarcely more settled.*

Farber's case will be examined in this chapter by treating several interesting issues about justification that it raises. Although the first eight chapters of this book have been concerned with the justification of moral beliefs, they have also been concerned largely with general *normative* ethics. Parts of Chapters 1 and 2 constitute exceptions to this generalization, for there arguments in *metaethics* were introduced. Metaethics, as noted in Chapter 1, is commonly contrasted with normative ethics, on grounds that metaethics does not propound moral theses about what is right and wrong,

---

*Sources for this case include Ronald Dworkin, "The Rights of Myron Farber," *New York Review of Books* (October 26, 1978), pp. 34–36; Virginia Held, "An Exchange," ibid., p. 39; "A Jury Sets Dr. X Free," *Time*, **112**:48 (Nov. 6, 1978); "Farber Finis," *Time*, **112**:68 (Dec. 11, 1978); "Mixed Motives: Times Man Under Fire," *Time*, **112**:47 (Aug. 28, 1978); "Piercing a Newsman's Shield," *Time*, **112**:74 (Aug. 7, 1978); "First Amendment on Trial," *Newsweek*, **92**:87 (Aug., 7, 1978); and Thomas Griffith, "When the Law and the Press Collide," *Time*, **112**:60 (Sept. 11, 1978).

virtuous and vicious, or good and bad. Many philosophers are now skeptical that any sharp distinction can be drawn between metaethics and normative ethics, largely because metaethical discussions of moral justification so often wind up as accounts of *how to justify* moral claims. This problem will be repeatedly encountered in this chapter and in Chapter 10, and the Farber case will be used to illustrate features of both metaethics and normative ethics (to the extent they differ).

However one sees the differences between metaethics and normative ethics, some questions that have been thoroughly explored by those who hold the ideal of dispassionate metaethical reflection are of the utmost significance for moral philosophy. The three most general and important of these questions are the following:

1. Can answers about what is morally good and right be justified?
2. Can the claim that one ought to be moral be justified?
3. What are facts and values, and what role do they play in moral justification?

Questions 1 and 2 are addressed in this chapter; Chapter 10 focuses on question 3 as a way of attending to question 1.

As with the problem of relativism discussed in Chapter 2, these three questions recur again and again even in popular discussions of morality—especially when the skeptical question "Why should I be moral?" surfaces. Such questions of justification are at once matters of immediate practical significance and closely related to the most theoretical dimensions of philosophy. A good case can be made that philosophy in general is primarily concerned with the *justification* of a point of view—whether the justification is metaphysical, epistemological, ethical, or drawn from some other field of philosophy. Similarly, a good case can be made that the above three questions are the main ones to emerge from metaethical reflection, which has kept issues of meaning and justification at the forefront of moral philosophy. Thus far in this book, the metaethics encountered consists largely in discussions of the *meanings* of critical ethical terms. While this pursuit will again be followed in Chapter 10, the nature of justification itself and of the justification of ultimate moral principles is the main topic in this chapter.

MORAL ARGUMENTS AND MORAL JUSTIFICATION

Moral judgments are justified by giving reasons for them, as the Farber case that begins this chapter illustrates. From time to time, journalists such as Farber become embroiled with courts that subpoena files and other data used to write a story about a crime. These reporters routinely refuse to submit to the subpoena and wind up in jail, as Farber did. Commonly, they argue that they did nothing *morally* wrong even if there was a technical legal violation. When we hear this contention, we expect some further story about *why* the reporter's action was not morally wrong. A reporter, we think, is called upon to give justifying reasons. Suppose the reporter argues that freedom of the press is essential to any free society and must never be curbed because of the adverse consequences for freedom in general that would follow from such limitations. Suppose the reporter then points to a broad range of historical facts to support this contention—e.g., how many times and under what conditions freedom of the press has been curbed in the past and what extensive social consequences followed. The reporter will no doubt also note how *adverse* these consequences were for society. The reporter seems clearly to be offering both facts and values in this justification. Moral values about freedom of the press are joined with certain facts of history about what happens when the press is not left alone.

If the reporter's moral argument is not immediately convincing, the reasons offered may be considered in order to determine whether they should be accepted or rejected. The reasons that appear in the reporter's justification will then reappear in the deliberation about whether the press should be as free as the reporter suggests, though of course a few personal reasons may be added. In general, we *deliberate* about situations where alternatives are open to our choice; and we attempt to *justify* acts that have been performed or that we think ought to be performed. Moral *reasoning* occurs whenever a person either deliberates about or attempts to justify or condemn an action or judgment on moral grounds. An attempt at moral justification is successful if reasons are supplied that show a judgment morally right or at least defensible by appeal to reasons; to show that a judgment is unjustified, by contrast, one must provide reasons to show the judgment morally wrong or unsatisfactory.*

The Structure of Moral Arguments

Every belief we own is subject to rational challenge and therefore to justification by appeal to reasons. Not all reasons that are offered in support of a belief are good reasons, of course, and thus an alleged "reason" may provide no support at all for an intended conclusion. Logic is that branch of philosophy concerned in general with the relationship between reasons that can or cannot be given and the conclusions drawn from them; or, more precisely, logic is concerned with the relationship between premises and conclusions drawn from the premises, especially with how conclusions are *correctly* derived. Logic thus explains why arguments succeed and fail. But what is an argument—in particular, a moral argument— and what role do arguments play in justifications?

An argument is a group of statements standing in relation to one another; one statement in the group, the conclusion, is claimed either to be the consequence of or to be justified by the others, called variously "evidence," "reasons," "grounds," and

---

*This account of moral reasoning and justification does not insist that when deliberating or attempting to justify a position, one must have a full set of moral premises that are all well defended by overriding moral reasons. That ideal is rarely, if ever, satisfied. The point of the discussion thus far has been merely to explicate the nature of moral reasoning and justification—not to provide adequate moral standards for them or even to suggest that in the end there are adequate standards.

"premises." Thus, every argument consists of two parts: (1) one or more statements called the "premises" or "evidence," and (2) the conclusion, which supposedly follows from the premises and is supported by the evidence. An argument in this sense is different from a proof. The term "proof" refers to a *sound* argument, that is, one which *establishes* the truth of its conclusion. There are good and bad arguments, and one may argue adeptly for some conclusion and still not produce a sound argument or prove anything.*

In a newspaper interview several years ago, the millionaire oilman H. L. Hunt was asked to justify his statement that "I would starve if I earned less than a million dollars a week." Here is what he offered as his "reason" for the statement: "Our family spends 13 times that sum—$13 million—in keeping our food, oil, ranching, real estate, and other activities as going concerns." While some people may think Mr. Hunt has given a good reason for his conclusion about his potential for starvation, others will find it totally unconvincing and will try to show that, given the same premises (plus a few that may reasonably be added), conclusions utterly at odds with Mr. Hunt's can be drawn. While we distinguish arguments from claims for which no evidence is given, the distinction is not drawn in order to condemn the latter. In the case of some statements, we are willing to accept them as they stand, and thus the question of evidence does not arise. If, however, the statement is not one we are ready to accept, then problems of evidence and argument are inescapable. When relevant evidence has been supplied, the unsupported assertion is transformed into a supported conclusion, and an argument is available for scrutiny.

In general, every argument, no matter how complex, can be put into the following form:

X is correct; therefore, Y is correct.

Or:

Because X is correct, Y is correct.

Unfortunately, arguments are rarely presented as pictured in this simplified form. More often, we find them submerged in complex and intricate patterns of discourse—disguised by rhetoric, irrelevancies, redundancies, and subtle connections with other arguments (including what will be referred to in Chapter 10 as "noncognitive meanings"). A premise may be compounded with an exhortation, or a description, or an aside having no bearing on the point at issue. Then, too, people rarely argue so neatly that their premises are arranged in a logical order, all leading with obvious rigor to some clear

---

*In general, logic is not concerned with the soundness of arguments, because (with one exception) logic alone cannot determine whether the premises of an argument are true or false, and in order to know whether an argument is sound or not, one must be able to determine whether its premises are true. While this is not the business of *logic* (except in cases where the premises are logically true or logically false), it is the business of *ethics*, as will be seen throughout this chapter.

conclusion. Sometimes the conclusion is the first statement uttered; sometimes the conclusion is so obvious in the context that it is not even uttered at all. The same is true of premises; they may be left at the level of suggestion or only elliptically expressed. Such complexities obviously heighten the difficulty of finding an argument. Nonetheless, we can usually discover arguments if we search hard enough, especially if we are willing to shape and restructure their premises.

Levels of Justification in Moral Argument

When we engage in moral reasoning and argument, different levels of generality are involved. A moral *judgment*, for example, expresses a decision, verdict, or conclusion about a particular action or character trait. Moral *rules* are general guides indicating that actions of a certain kind ought (or ought not) to be done. Moral *principles*, by contrast, are both more general and more fundamental than such rules, and serve (at least in some systems of ethics) as the justifying reasons for accepting rules. A simple example of a moral rule is, "It is wrong to deceive your employees," while the principle of respect for persons (as discussed in Chapter 4), for example, may be the basis of several moral rules stipulating that deception in various circumstances is wrong. Finally, *ethical theories* (such as those discussed in Chapters 3 through 5) are bodies of both principles and rules, more or less systematically related.

The idea that there are different levels of generality involved in moral discourse can also be developed as an account of levels of justification. Judgments about what ought to be done can be viewed as justified (i.e., good independent reasons for the judgments are given) by rules, which in turn are justified (i.e., good independent reasons are given) by principles, which in turn are justified (i.e., good independent reasons are given) by ethical theories. This account may be diagrammed as follows (where "↑" describes a direction of *justification*, indicating that the particular or less general moral assertion is justified by appeal to the more general):

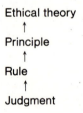

Some justifications advanced in the Farber case conform to this diagram. Farber judged that he ought not to submit to the court's demand for his records. He refused to submit to the court order on grounds of his right to protect the freedom of the press and society's correlative obligation to permit a free press. For convenience, this may be called the *rule* that "The press ought to be free to protect confidential information"—one among many rules of confidentiality. Farber justified this rule on grounds of a "right of the public to be informed"—a right that can be maintained only by a corps of journalists who must protect their sources. This is a more general principle about the gathering of information and the protection of its source. This principle, unlike the more specific rule, also applies to nonjournalistic contexts—e.g., to so-called freedom of information acts, which permit citizens to obtain confidential information about themselves that has been collected by government agencies. Both freedom of the press and the public's right to be informed were in turn given a consequentialist justification by Farber.

The direction of Farber's justification can be diagrammed as follows:

Consequential theory (perhaps utilitarianism)
↑
Principle of a right of the public to information
↑
Rule of the confidentiality of a reporter's information
↑
Judgment that Farber's confidential information should remain unreleased

That is, Farber's particular judgment is justified in terms of a rule, which is in turn justified in terms of a more general principle, which is in turn justified in terms of a consequentialist ethical theory.*

INTERNAL AND EXTERNAL JUSTIFICATIONS

The preceding conclusions might be summarized by saying that justification of a belief occurs in ethics (or anywhere else, for that matter) only if there is a successful appeal to a standard that is independent of the belief; the standard is necessary in order to validate the correctness of that which is *claimed* to be correct. Such a necessary condition of justification may not be sufficient, however; and it must now be asked how, if at all, one could justify *ultimate* or *final* moral claims.

---

*Sometimes the theory of levels of justification is expressed not merely in terms of the *justification* of the particular through appeal to the more general, but rather, in terms of the bolder thesis that there is an actual *deduction* of the particular moral judgment from general moral rules and principles. This notion is difficult to support as a theory about justification and argument. At least two critical reasons against it deserve mention. First, the most general action-guides in ethics are so general that it is implausible to maintain that much can be squeezed from them alone (or even from the entire set of moral action-guides constituting an ethical theory). Second, as seen elsewhere in this text, moral conclusions often cannot be reached without an understanding of relevant empirical facts. Indeed, in a consequentialist moral theory, such as utilitarianism, the principle of utility could almost never be applied accurately without considerable information about a situation.

This problem has been a major preoccupation of philosophers—not surprisingly—since the justification of ultimate knowledge claims is so central to philosophy generally. As every introductory student knows, philosophers ask whether our beliefs about the external world, the existence of minds and matter, causal powers, and our own abilities to choose freely can be justified. Philosophers even ask for a justification of the ultimate principles of logic—those normative principles determining the correctness of our reasoned inferences. Such fundamental beliefs and principles can be challenged, but ultimate principles in ethics seem more immediate to practical life and therefore in greater need of justification. One may skeptically doubt principles of logic or the existence of human selves, while at the same time recognizing both that it is almost impossible to act on such beliefs and that virtually no one actually will embrace such skeptical views in daily affairs. With ethics it is clearly otherwise. Since Chapter 2, this book has shown that moral disagreements of the most profound sort can be matters of immediate practical concern; and it can easily be doubted whether we know or can justify *anything* as objectively correct about morals. The problems of disagreement we have encountered indicate that beneath moral disputes there may be no common basis for an appeal to principle, and thus that moral disagreement may be unavoidable (as both Brandt and MacIntyre suggested in Chapter 2). This possibility naturally induces reflection on whether ultimate moral principles can be rationally justified.

The first thing to note in this connection is that *ultimate* moral principles cannot be justified by appeal to some rule or principle internal to morality itself. That procedure begs the question of ultimate justification, because it "justifies" morality in terms of morality; that is, it does not invoke a standard independent of the system of moral beliefs. Suppose we were to ask for a justification of the whole network of moral beliefs that Farber relies on to make his case, as the direction of his justification was previously diagrammed. Farber presumes principles of the right to gather information and protect sources, and these principles in turn rest on a consequentialist moral theory. If one challenges Farber's entire presentation by asking why he believes his principles justifiable, it would be insufficient merely to invoke rights to gather information and point to the consequences of restricting the press in a free society. This would patently beg the question. In order to meet the challenge, he must give a genuinely external justification by appeal to an independent standard, not an internal one that relies upon the very standards called into question.

The distinction between internal justification and external justification should be made more specific. Internal justifications occur within an established institution or system of thought. Thus there are principles and forms of justification appropriate to the fields of law, theology, history, science, etc., that are accepted by persons who work in those fields. They resolve problems of internal justification by reference to rules or standards of reasoning and argument that are accepted as governing their field. That is, the rational justification of a judgment or a rule can be accomplished by appeal to standards of reasoning considered applicable within an institution or field. To use another appeal to levels of generality in moral discourse, the idea of internal justification in the case of morality can be diagrammed as follows (where "↑" again indicates a relation of justification):

Ultimate principle(s) or theory governing the institution or system of thought
↑
Principle(s) internal to the institution or system of thought
↑
Rule(s) internal to the institution or system of thought
↑
Judgment (needing justification)

All internal problems of justification of particular moral judgments and principles thus assume the legitimacy of "higher" standards, which are the necessary conditions of their correctness. The higher standards have still higher necessary conditions of their correctness in the form of more fundamental principles. Obviously, this process of justification cannot go on forever, for at some point the highest or most fundamental level must be reached—the level of ultimate moral principles required for the correctness of all other principles.

External justification, by contrast to internal justification, attempts to address the problem of justifying principles at an ultimate level. It offers a way of showing the rational justifiability of an entire institution of beliefs and reasoning—i.e., an entire set of internal principles. To challenge an entire approach or institution is tantamount to challenging the rational defensibility of the most basic standards of the theory or institution. Thus, a challenge to scientific reasoning, theological reasoning, or legal reasoning that calls into question the complete structure of justifying principles in one of these disciplines can be answered only by showing that the ultimate principles defining the field can themselves be rationally justified. For moral philosophy, the challenge presented is that of providing an external justification of the basic standards at the roots of the moral way of life—the "institution of morality," as some have called it. Alternatively, we might be interested in the justification of the ultimate principles in a particular moral theory—such as Aristotle's, Kant's, or Mill's. In either case, we are requesting a justification at the upper level of principles in the institution or theory, and no appeal whatever to an internal principle will suffice.

These problems of justification, and the questions which often lead to them, have been thoughtfully captured in the following dramatic dialogue written by Herbert Feigl. In this dialogue, one participant holds that basic moral attitudes are the result of social conditioning in a culture. The other participant argues for the rational defensibility of moral standards and takes roughly the approach to the structure of justification found in the previous diagrams of levels.

HERBERT FEIGL

A Dialogue on Validation and Vindication*[1]

A.: Under what conditions can war be morally justified?

B.: Under no conditions. I am a convinced pacifist and conscientious objector. There is no greater evil than war and deliberate killing.

A.: Would you rather be killed or enslaved than do any killing? Are there no circumstances, such as a need for self-defense, that would justify killing?

B.: There are none.

A.: If you were saying that wanton killing and cruelty are to be condemned, I should heartily agree with you. But there are occasions in which killing is the only choice: a necessary evil, surely, but justifiable because it may be the lesser evil in the given circumstances.

The point of view of the radical pacifist is unreasonable. More lives might ultimately be saved, and greater happiness for a larger number of people might result if the innocent victims of aggression were to wage a victorious war upon the aggressor. This is essentially the same reasoning that I would apply to the situation in which, for example, a robber threatened my own life or that of a friend.

B.: I admit that all these are very unfortunate situations. My sincerest efforts would be devoted to prevent their very occurrence (by whatever suitable means: education, reform, arbitration, compromise, reconciliation, etc.). But once such a situation arises I still believe that one should not kill.

A.: How do you justify this position?

B.: How does one justify *any* moral judgment? Obviously by deriving it from the basic moral laws. Respect for the life, the rights, the happiness of others is surely such a basic norm, is it not?

A.: I shall be curious to find out how such basic moral laws are proved or established. But before we enter into this deep question, tell me how you defend such a rigid adherence to non-violence, even if you yourself may easily become the victim of aggression or war.

B.: I shall not invoke religious principles here. Perhaps I can convince you if I make you aware of the consequences of the pacifist attitude. Once practiced by many it would tend to spread by way of emulation and thus sooner or later eradicate the evil of killing altogether.

A.: This is an optimistic assertion concerning the probability of certain consequences. In any case it is a question of fact which is not easily decided. However, your disagreement with me seems to go beyond whatever we may think about the facts, namely the conditions and consequences of attitudes. True enough, in your last remark you have tried to establish a common basis of evaluation. You appealed to a humanitarian principle which I do share with you. Still, I think that to kill is morally better than to be enslaved. Since you disagree with me on this, it is

*From Herbert Feigl, in Wilfred Sellars and John Hospers, eds., *Readings in Ethical Theory*. Copyright, 1952, Appleton-Century-Crofts, Inc. Reprinted by permission of Prentice-Hall, Inc., Englewood Cliffs, N.J.

[1]This essay is a revision of an earlier (hitherto unpublished and altogether different) version of my essay "De Principiis Non Disputandum . . .?" included in *Philosophical Analysis*, edited by Max Black, Cornell University Press, Ithaca, N.Y., 1950.

obvious that we diverge in *some* of our basic norms. This divergence in attitude can apparently not be removed by considerations of fact.

B.: Are ethical principles then a matter of personal whim and caprice?

A.: I did not mean to imply this at all. As our own cases show, we tend to have very strong and serious convictions in these matters. Far from being chosen arbitrarily, our moral attitudes are a result of the culture and the subculture in which our personalities are formed.

B.: We are not necessarily conforming to the prevailing patterns. I for one, am certainly not. I arrived at my views by independent and serious reflection.

A.: I don't wish to dispute it. And yet your attitudes are a causal consequence of many factors: heredity, environment (physical, and especially social; the influence of parents, friends, teachers, attractive and abhorrent examples, crucial experiences, etc.) and, yes, your (more or less) intelligent reflection upon the facts as they impress *you-as-you-are.*

B.: If you are right, there are limits beyond which rational (i.e. logical and/or factual) argument cannot be extended. Intelligent reflection concerning means and ends, conditions and consequences operates within the frame of basic evaluations. Beyond those limits there could be only conversion by persuasion (rhetoric, propaganda, suggestion, promises, threats, re-education, psycho-therapy, etc.). There are also techniques of settlement of disagreements by way of compromise, segregation (separation, divorce) or higher synthesis. By "higher synthesis" I mean, for example, the abandonment or severe restriction of the sovereignty of individual nations and a transfer of all sentiments of loyalty to a world government. Only if none of these techniques succeeds, then indeed coercion by violence,

alas, seems inevitable.—(Universal pacifism is the only solution! But that's not my point at the moment.)

A.: You have expressed my point of view very well. But you are obviously unwilling to agree to it.

B.: Indeed not. Everything in me cries out for a belief in objectively and universally valid standards of moral evaluation.

A.: You will not get very far if you assume some theological or metaphysical absolutes. Any reference to the revealed commands of a divine authority is futile. For you would have to tell how you can know those imperatives as divine, and even if you were to know them as such you would have to state a reason as to why anybody should obey them. The same criticisms apply to any alleged metaphysical insight into what man ought to be. And if you dismiss theological and metaphysical foundations for morality you will find it difficult to argue for standards that are independent of human needs and interests.

B.: It's precisely human needs and interests that provide a solid foundation for moral standards. In all cultures that we call "civilized" there are essentially the same ideals of cooperation (as opposed to conflict), of helpfulness (as opposed to harmfulness), of love (as opposed to hatred), of justice (as opposed to inequity), and of perfection and growth (as opposed to stagnation and decay). Cultural relativity and the variability of human nature have been exaggerated. There is a significant core of essential features shared by all human beings. Human nature as it is constituted biologically and psychologically, and as it finds its existence in a context of interdependence with other human beings, could scarcely fail to develop just those ideals of morality. I admit that these ideals are only rarely fulfilled or even approximated in actual conduct. But they are *the* standards of ethical evaluation. It is with reference to this frame that we make our judgments of "good" and "bad," "right" and "wrong."

A.: Much as I share your ideals, I can't refrain from calling your attention to the fact that there are notable exceptions that restrict severely not only the universality of certain types of conduct (this is what you admitted), but also the universality of the very standards or ideals of morality. To many an ancient or oriental culture the idea of perfection or progress remained completely strange. The prevailing ideologies of capitalism and nationalism basically extol the ideals of competition over those of cooperation. Only superficially and often hypocritically do they pay lip service to humanitarian or Christian ideals. And the very principle of justice (in the sense of equal rights for all) has been flouted not only by tyrants, aristocrats and fascists but also by such eminent philosophers as Plato and Nietzsche. Our own divergence on the issue of radical pacifism is equally a case in point. There are countless further, possibly secondary and yet radical divergencies as regards attitudes toward civil liberties, sex and marriage, birth control, euthanasia, the role of religion (church and state), animals (vegetarianism, vivisection), etc., etc.

B.: Disregarding the secondary divergencies, I must say that the deviations from the more fundamental and true moral ideals are simply perversions and corruptions. Whoever denies the principles of justice and neighborliness is immoral. Kant was essentially right and convincingly logical in defining moral conduct by his categorical imperative. Only a principle that is binding for all and excludes any sort of arbitrary privilege and partiality can justifiably be called ethical. The ideals that I enumerated are the very essence of what is meant by "morality." To be moral consists precisely in placing oneself in the service of interests and ideals that transcend purely selfish purposes.

A.: That is what *you* mean by "morality." (And, of course, it is in keeping with traditional morality.) But Nietzsche, for example, explicitly proposed a revolution in all traditional morality. Clearly, he considered his own value-system as the "true ethics." Are you not aware that you are begging the very question at issue? You speak of "true moral ideals"; you call certain views "immoral," "perverse," "corrupt"; you say that only certain types of principles can "justifiably be called ethical." You are using persuasive definitions[2] here. You call "moral" or "ethical" only such doctrines or principles as agree with your own convictions about what is *right*. . . . You cannot by some verbal magic establish justifications for ideals which obviously are neither logically nor empirically unique. These ideals compete with genuine alternatives.

B.: I can't believe this. The ideals that I have listed are the ones that will benefit humanity in the long run. Not just a particular group, but all of mankind.

Moreover these ideals are comprised by the essence of *rationality*. Man, the rational animal, is by his very nature not only characterized by his capacity for adequate deductive and inductive thinking, but also by his sense of justice and his abhorrence of violence as a method for the settlement of disputes.

A.: You are still begging the question. Those who do not accept the principle of equality are not interested in *all* of mankind. Furthermore, your time-honored conception of human nature is clearly not an account of actual fact, but of an ideal (by

---

[2]This useful phrase was coined by C. L. Stevenson in his book *Ethics and Language* (Yale University Press, 1944), p. 210.

no means universally shared) which you utilize for a persuasive definition of MAN. You won't convince any serious opponents by mere *definitions*. But you might try to entice, persuade, educate or reform them in other ways. You may also hope that the increasing interdependence of all of mankind on this planet will eventually generate a fundamental uniformity in the principles of moral evaluation.

B.: You underestimate the role of experience in the settlement of moral conflicts and disputes. Those who have had an opportunity to experience different ways of life soon learn to discriminate between the better and the worse. Experience in the context of needs and interests, of claims and counter-claims, of existing and emerging rights and obligations in the social milieu soon enough mould the moral conscience of man. We do not live in a vacuum. The constant encouragements and discouragements of our actions and their underlying attitudes form the very atmosphere of the life in the family, the workshop, the market place, the tribunal, etc. Add to that the basic sympathy human beings feel for each other and you will have to admit that there is a large mass of empirical factors that operate in the direction of a common standard of social morality.

A.: If I may use a parallel drawn from the field of aesthetics, there are a great many people who prefer pulp-magazine stories to "good" literature; or swing (jazz, jive or whatever is the fashion) to "great" music. Similarly, there are plenty of people who

have had an opportunity to experience both the ruthless and the kindly way of life and yet subscribe to the principles of the former. Kropotkin rightly, though somewhat sentimentally, pointed out that despite the cruel struggle for existence in the animal kingdom there is also a good deal of mutual help and self-sacrifice. If human sympathy were as fundamental as (he and) you claim it is, there could hardly be such views as those of Nietzsche, Hitler, and Mussolini on the "greatness" of war. Only by endorsing one norm against other possible alternatives can you avail yourself of the premises by which to validate the special moral precepts which are dear to your heart.

B.: You still have failed to give me a single good reason why I or you or anyone should adhere to even those moral principles which we happen to share. Your position is a skepticism that could easily lead to moral indifference and cynicism.

A.: And what sort of a reason do you expect me to give you? If I provided you with premises from which you could *deduce* our moral standards, you would ask me for a justification of those premises. And you surely don't want a reason in the sense of a motive. You are motivated already. You do not seriously entertain doubt as long as this motivation prevails. And nothing that I've said was intended to undermine it. The aim of my remarks was clarification; not education, fortification or edification. Too many philosphers have sold their birthright for a pot of message.

This dialogue forces a confrontation with skepticism about matters of ultimate justification. One implication is that if *nothing* is permitted to constitute a justification of ultimate principles, one will be led to the conclusion that ultimate principles are arbitrary and rationally indefensible. In cases of moral disagreement, then, the disagreement could be resolved only by nonrational techniques such as indoctrination and propaganda. Feigl and Wesley Salmon have elsewhere argued* that skeptical challenges of many sorts to the justification of ultimate principles fail to consider what they call "pragmatic justifications"—a form of ultimate justification that deserves consideration at this point.

Feigl and Salmon sharply distinguish *validation* from *vindication*. Validation is internal justification, whereas vindication is external justification. To validate is to appeal correctly to principles already accepted within an institution or system of thought. Validating principles serve as the framework of principles for internal justification, and thus they warrant individual inferences. However, Feigl and Salmon maintain, it is always appropriate to ask for an external justification of these internal validating principles. To ask for such an external justification is to ask for a vindication of the entire approach, i.e., for a justification for the entire set of internal principles. Validation is totally unsuited to problems of externally justifying an ultimate principle, as can easily be seen from our earlier discussion of levels of justification. Lower-level rules and principles are validated through correct appeal to higher-level principles; but when the issue of justification is that of an ultimate or highest-level principle, there is no further (validating) principle by appeal to which the ultimate principle itself may be justified. Thus, if there is to be any possibility of rationally justifying ultimate moral principles, recourse must be made to some form of justification beyond validation. For this reason, the higher-level or supplementary form of justification called "vindication" is introduced.

For Feigl, vindication is pragmatic: once an operative purpose or objective of an institution or system of thought has been identified, a set of standards is considered most suitable (and therefore is vindicated) if it can be shown to be *better* for reaching these objectives than any other set of standards. *Whatever* set of principles best achieves a stated goal is the one that should be adopted. Consider an example of vindication that, though it is trivial and utterly unrelated to morals, usefully illustrates the pragmatic character of this general form of justification. There has always been considerable disagreement about the best strategy for playing football—i.e., the "theory of football" that ought to be adopted by coaches. Many kinds of plays and simple rules are taught to players, and behind these rules are more complex principles and, indeed, strikingly different "theories" of the game. Within each system or theory of the game, its rules and judgments can easily be internally justified; and the rules and principles of an alternative system or theory are not likely to be found justified by such an internal appeal. If a justification of coach *X*'s (Vince Lombardi's, say) entire theory of the game is requested, then only an external justification would be adequate, for the request in effect says, "Why this theory of football rather than that one?" According to the pragmatic

*Herbert Feigl, "De Principiis Non Disputandum . . .?" in Max Black, ed., *Philosophical Analysis* (Ithaca, N.Y.: Cornell University Press, 1950), pp. 119–56; Wesley Salmon, *The Foundations of Scientific Inference* (Pittsburgh: University of Pittsburgh Press, 1966); "Should We Attempt to Justify Induction?" *Philosophical Studies* (1957), pp. 38–42; and "Symposium on Inductive Evidence," *American Philosophical Quarterly*, **2** (1965): 265 ff.

theory of justification (vindication), that set of principles or that theory is best which is most suitable for fulfilling the objectives of the game of football. Suppose a condition that is probably true: the simple objective of football games is winning. In that case, a theory is pragmatically justified when shown to be most effective in deploying (similarly talented) players in such ways that it enables a team to win more often than the same players would if following any other theory of the game.

The same line of argument may be used to justify externally a *moral* framework of rules or guides to action. The external justification of a moral theory finally rests on its suitability for fulfilling the objectives the institution of morality is intended to serve. If there is a set of standards best adapted for achieving this objective, then that set and no other is justified. The assumption here is, of course, that there is a single goal or purpose of moral reasoning, but, as we saw in Chapter 1, this is not an implausible assumption. As G. J. Warnock argued in that chapter—to take one theory of the objectives of morality with which we are already familiar—the fundamental objective of morality is to ameliorate or counteract the tendency for things to "go badly" in human affairs as a result of the limited resources, sympathy, information, and intellectual abilities of our fellow human beings. In this theory, the object of morality is to better the human predicament by countervailing those limited sympathies that lead to social conflicts.* If this view of the *goal* of morality is correct, then Feigl's pragmatic approach says that any system of moral guides is rationally justified if, and only if, it is the most suitable means for achieving the goal.

It is, however, not clear that Feigl's *pragmatic* scheme to handle the problem of external justification is entirely satisfactory. His account presupposes that one can identify both the meaning and the purpose of "morality," formidable tasks despite Warnock's useful proposals. If morality is actually a complex enterprise with many different goals, some framework of principles best suited to achieve some single goal (such as Warnock's) may be quite unsuited to achieving other goals of morality. Additionally, if there is no set of standards that clearly leads to (or that can reliably be predicted to lead to) the goals of morality, then it seems an arbitrary matter which set of standards among the alternatives one adopts. Note, too, that it is of the highest importance for this pragmatic theory that *the* goal or objective of morality not be an arbitrary matter of personal choice; for then any goal one chose would be permissible, and consequently any "moral theory" whatever could be justified merely by specifying the goal of morality so that the desired theory is the best means to that goal.

Another important objection is that pragmatic arguments beg one of the most substantial questions about justification in ethics, namely, the controversy examined in Chapters 3, 4, and 5 between consequentialist (utilitarian) and nonconsequentialist theories. Because pragmatic justifications assume that a theory of morality must be justified as the best *means* to a particular *end* (goal), this account of justification runs the risk of presupposing without argument the truth of a consequentialist theory. While

---

*G. J. Warnock, *The Object of Morality* (London: Methuen & Co., Ltd., 1971), especially pp. 26, 61, 85 ff, as found in Chap. 1 of this text.

some form of consequentialism may of course ultimately be the correct moral theory, no theory can be justified by presupposing its own correctness. Along the same lines, there is one further problem for pragmatic vindication theories: They are developed to stop the regress of justification, so that one can no longer ask the question, "But in terms of what is that principle or theory justified?" Yet one certainly can raise the question, "What justifies a pragmatic scheme of justification?"—and hence it may be doubted that the regress really has been stopped by this theory.

Whatever one's final views on the acceptability of pragmatic theories of justification, it has not been the purpose of this section to deal exclusively or even primarily with them. Rather, the point has been to show the difference between an internal and an external justification, so as to emphasize that it is always appropriate to ask for both an internal and an external justification of any moral belief, principle, code, or theory. In this regard, the distinction between validation and vindication has served us well; for it is precisely the distinction we need in order to address what some people have called the ultimate question about external moral justification: "Why be moral?"

THE JUSTIFICATION OF MORALITY ITSELF

The ultimate problem of moral justification is whether the moral way of life itself can rationally be justified: can one rationally justify the belief that one ought to be a person of good moral character or ought to live a moral way of life? Despite the "ought" in this statement, this question is not a *moral* one, for it does not ask what one ought *morally* to do. The question asks, rather, for a rational justification of our bothering with the moral life at all, especially since it may conflict with our own self-interest and with other important commitments. This question, then, is a request for an external justification of the moral way of life—as opposed, for example, to some egoistic approach to life or perhaps to some purely aesthetic, political, or religious approach.

In philosophical writings on this topic, the challenge is often put in the blunt form of "Why be moral?" This question will here be construed as a request for an answer that lies entirely outside all internal justifications; it is thus not to be confused with the provision of good *moral* reasons. Because internal justifications of moral claims by definition provide only good moral reasons, and because morality itself is challenged by requests for ultimate justification, the sole reasons that can qualify as acceptable are nonmoral reasons. In short, the question is, "Even if one can determine by reference to morality what one morally ought to do, why ought one to do what is morally required?"

It is sometimes said in response to such a request that it is senseless because it asks for a good reason for doing something when such a reason has already been provided. From this perspective, if a reason is indeed a good *moral* reason, then it is a good reason—period; and it makes no sense to ask questions when good answers are already known. To ask such senseless questions would be tantamount to asking what one ought to do when one already knows what one ought to do; it would be like asking Farber why he thought he ought to keep his files confidential when he already had every good reason that could be wanted for doing so. The philosopher P. H. Nowell-Smith defends this point of view thus:

> The question "Why should I do what I see to be [morally] right?" is not just an immoral question, but an absurd one. In ordinary life we should be puzzled by a man who said, "Yes, you have convinced me that it is the right thing to do; but ought I to do it?" We shouldn't know how to answer him, not because we could not think up any new arguments, but because, in conceding that it is the right thing to do, he has already conceded that he ought to do it. . . . He seems to think that there is an extra step to be taken.*

Critics of this line of argument insist that there is an extra step to be taken and that Nowell-Smith has confused internal and external justification. The question, after all, is not, "Why, from a moral (internal) point of view, should one be moral?" Rather, it is, "Why, from a nonmoral (external) point of view, should one be moral?" Though this may seem, as Nowell-Smith suggests, an odd question from the moral point of view, it is not a particularly odd question when we consider all the kinds of conflict that life presents between a moral way of life and other ways of life, or even between moral decisions and decisions made on nonmoral bases. All of us have often been tempted to cast aside moral reasons in favor of attractive nonmoral reasons. We occasionally encounter a combination of *moral* reasons, *religious* reasons, and *self-interested* reasons for or against performing action *X*. Some pacifists in World War II, for example, found themselves with strong religious reasons and reasons of self-interest against participation in the war effort, while seriously entertaining moral reasons in favor of participation. In Farber's case, he had legal reasons inclining him in one way and moral reasons inclining him in another. Had he been in a no-win situation (as some have asserted that he was), his self-interest might have best been served by simply quitting his position with the *Times* and turning over his files. Why should he, or anyone else, act on moral reasons in such circumstances rather than on legal reasons or on reasons of self-interest? Why, indeed, should we not act immorally? Is there no reason that could help us answer this question that is not itself a moral reason? (Psychological questions about why we *do* act morally in the face of such conflicts are of course not at issue here; our present questions are strictly philosophical requests for external justifying reasons.)

As now framed, "Why be moral?" is a nonmoral question about how to justify the claim that the moral approach or way of life has priority over conflicting approaches. It is thus a question not only about ultimate justification but also about the depth of our commitment to morality. This problem is not as unfamiliar as it may at first seem. As we grow up, we are taught that religion or morality or both should take precedence over every other demand in life, and most explicitly we are taught that

*P. H. Nowell-Smith, *Ethics* (Baltimore: Penguin Books, Inc., 1954), pp. 41 ff.

moral demands take precedence over self-interest. Many people attempt to structure every phase of their lives in conformity with this conception of life's proper priorities. A morally good character, for example, is given priority over everything else; or perhaps the (moral) duty to raise and take care of one's children is given precedence over a promising career. The question is how we can justify a whole way of life that places morality in such a commanding position of overriding importance.

The question "Why be moral?" admits of two different interpretations, and we should be clear about the possible meanings of the inquiry before proceeding further. The question might be construed as asking why we should, as a group of people or as a whole society, adopt a moral way of life. Why should society adopt action-guiding standards for its members which dictate that a moral way of life rightly overrides law, religion, and self-interest? Here the answer seems relatively clear when morality is in conflict with self-interest, for it is the answer effectively sketched by Thomas Hobbes (as discussed in Chapter 8 of this book). Hobbes, it will be recalled, argues that a moral way of life, buttressed by a political and legal framework, overcomes many disadvantages that would be present without such a system of rules; circumstances that allow us to pursue our objectives would not be possible apart from the civilized state of affairs that morality promotes. Hobbes's approach is not unlike the pragmatists' approach to justification that was earlier encountered, and together they offer a strong *external* justification of morality (since nothing moral per se is presupposed)—that is, of society's acceptance of a moral code of behavior for its members. (This justification works much better, of course, for morality in contrast with self-interest than for morality in contrast with law or religion. The demands of law and religion may function as well as morality to the *pragmatic* benefit of society, and even better in some societies.)

However, the question "Why be moral?" has never been taken as focusing centrally on why a *group* should give priority to morality; rather, it has been seen as a question about why an *individual* person should adopt and give supremacy to a moral way of life. One might attempt again to adopt the Hobbesian or pragmatist approach to this question by arguing that a moral way of life pragmatically overcomes many disadvantages that one would have to encounter if one did not live by moral standards. Society, after all, treats moral offenders much as it treats criminal offenders, and a moral way of life seems clearly preferable to a life of punishment, rejection, and isolation.

This time, however, Hobbes's answer seems less than compelling, for such a justification of morality in terms of self-interest is subject to the following damaging objection: While it is true that I would be advantaged by everyone else's acting morally and that I should attempt to escape the sanctions that would be imposed for my immoral acts, these considerations provide no compelling reason why I should act morally or be moral instead of merely pretending to act morally; nor do they explain why I should *always* act morally in cases of conflict with alternative standards, including self-interest. Indeed, if one could succeed in making one's own self-interest paramount while inducing others to make the demands of morality paramount in their lives, would this not seem the best possible world for oneself?

One precaution about the interpretation of this question must first be mentioned. The question is generally construed as asking whether it is to an individual's personal *advantage* to be moral; but on certain interpretations of the word "advantage," a satisfactory answer favoring morality cannot possibly be provided. What is permitted to count as being toward one's "advantage"? If the question is, "Should I act morally, *or* should I act to my personal advantage (self-interest) *in cases of conflict?*" the decks are unfairly stacked. *Only* an answer showing that it is in one's self-interest or advantage is permitted, and morality therefore cannot be victorious. That is, framing the issue in this way begs at least one important question about external justification, for it is assumed from the start that only an answer in favor of self-interest will be satisfactory.

Let us suppose, however, that the absurd question, "Is it to my self-interest (advantage) to act morally *instead* of self-interestedly?" is *not* the one before us. Instead, suppose we want to know whether, on grounds of self-interest, morality should be adopted. The following question clearly does make sense: "Can my acceptance of the demands of morality—including the sacrifices it sometimes demands—be (externally) justified in terms of the advantages my moral behavior will bring to me?" In the following probing essay, David Gauthier argues compellingly that this question probably cannot be answered affirmatively, and hence morality probably cannot be justified on grounds of self-interest.

DAVID P. GAUTHIER

Morality and Advantage*

Let us examine the following proposition, which will be referred to as "the thesis": *Morality is a system of principles such that it is advantageous for everyone if everyone accepts and acts on it, yet acting on the system of principles requires that some persons perform disadvantageous acts.*

What I wish to show is that this thesis *could be true,* that morality could possess those characteristics attributed to it by the thesis. I shall not try to show that the thesis is true. . . .

*From David P. Gauthier, "Morality and Advantage," *Philosophical Review,* **76** (1967): 460–475.

It will be useful to examine in some detail an example of a system which possesses those characteristics ascribed by the thesis to morality. This example, abstracted from the field of international relations, will enable us more clearly to distinguish, first, conduct based on immediate interest; second, conduct which is truly prudent; and third, conduct which promotes mutual advantage but is not prudent.

A and *B* are two nations with substantially opposed interests, who find themselves engaged in an arms race against each other. Both possess the latest in weaponry, so that each recognizes that the actual outbreak of full scale war between them would be mutually disastrous. This recognition leads *A* and *B* to agree that each would be better off if they were mutually disarming instead of mutually arming. For mutual disarmament would preserve the balance of power between them while reducing the risk of war.

Hence *A* and *B* enter into a disarmament pact. The pact is advantageous for both if both accept and act on it, although clearly it is not advantageous for either to act on it if the other does not.

Let *A* be considering whether or not to adhere to the pact in some particular situation, whether or not actually to perform some act of disarmament. *A* will quite likely consider the act to have disadvantageous consequences. *A* expects to benefit, not by its own acts of disarmament, but by *B*'s acts. Hence if *A* were to reason simply in terms of immediate interest, *A* might well decide to violate the pact.

But *A*'s decision need be neither prudent nor reasonable. For suppose first that *B* is able to determine whether or not *A* adheres to the pact. If *A* violates, then *B* will detect the violation and will then consider what to do in the light of *A*'s behavior. It is not to *B*'s advantage to disarm alone; *B* expects to gain, not by its own acts of disarmament, but by *A*'s acts. Hence *A*'s violation, if known to *B*, leads naturally to *B*'s counterviolation. If this continues, the effect of the pact is entirely undone, and *A* and *B* return to their mutually disadvantageous arms race. *A*, foreseeing this when considering whether or not to adhere to the pact in the given situation, must therefore conclude that the truly prudent course of action is to adhere.

Now suppose that *B* is unable to determine whether or not *A* adheres to the pact in the particular situation under consideration. If *A* judges adherence to be in itself disadvantageous, then it will decide, both on the basis of immediate interest and on the basis of prudence, to violate the pact.

Since *A*'s decision is unknown to *B*, it cannot affect whether or not *B* adheres to the pact, and so the advantage gained by *A*'s violation is not outweighed by any consequent loss.

Therefore if *A* and *B* are prudent they will adhere to their disarmament pact whenever violation would be detectable by the other, and violate the pact whenever violation would not be detectable by the other. In other words, they will adhere openly and violate secretly. The disarmament pact between *A* and *B* thus possesses two of the characteristics ascribed by the thesis to morality. First, accepting the pact and acting on it is more advantageous for each than making no pact at all. Second, in so far as the pact stipulates that each must disarm even when disarming is undetectable by the other, it requires each to perform disadvantageous acts—acts which run counter to considerations of prudence.

One further condition must be met if the disarmament pact is to possess those characteristics ascribed by the thesis to a system of morality. It must be the case that the requirement that each party perform disadvantageous acts be essential to the advantage conferred by the pact; or, to put the matter in the way in which we expressed it earlier, both *A* and *B* must do better to adhere to this pact than to a pact which is similar save that it requires no disadvantageous acts. In terms of the example, *A* and *B* must do better to adhere to the pact than to a pact which stipulates that each must disarm only when disarming is detectable by the other.

We may plausibly suppose this condition to be met. Although *A* will gain by secretly retaining arms itself, it will lose by *B*'s similar acts, and its losses may well outweigh its gains. *B* may equally lose more by *A*'s secret violations than it gains by its own. So, despite the fact that prudence requires each to violate secretly, each may well do better if both adhere secretly than if both violate secretly. Supposing this to be the case, the disarmament pact is formally analogous to a moral system, as characterized by the thesis. That is, acceptance of and adherence to the pact by A and B is more advantageous for each, either than making no pact at all or than acceptance of and adherence to a pact requiring only open disarmament, and the pact requires each to perform acts of secret disarmament which are disadvantageous. . . .

We may now return to the connection of morality with advantage. Morality, if it is a system of principles of the type characterized in the thesis, requires that some persons perform acts genuinely disadvantageous to themselves, as a means to greater mutual advantage. Our example shows sufficiently that such a system is possible, and indicates more precisely its character. In particular, by an argument strictly parallel to that which we have pursued, we may show that men who are merely prudent will not perform the required disadvantageous acts. But in so violating the principles of morality, they will disadvantage themselves. Each will lose more by the violations of others than he will gain by his own violations.

Now this conclusion would be unsurprising if it were only that no man can gain if he alone is moral rather than prudent. Obviously such a man loses, for he adheres to moral principles to his own disadvantage, while others violate them also to his disadvantage. The benefit of the moral system is not one which any individual can secure for himself, since each man gains from the sacrifices of others.

What is surprising in our conclusion is that no man can ever gain if he is moral. Not only does he not gain by being moral if others are prudent, but he also does not gain by being moral if others are moral. For although he now receives the advantage of others' adherence to moral principles, he reaps the disadvantage of his own adherence. As long as his own adherence to morality is independent of what others do (and this is required to distinguish morality from prudence), he must do better to be prudent.

If all men are moral, all will do better than if all are prudent. But any one man will always do better if he is prudent than if he is moral. There is no real paradox in supposing that morality is advantageous, even though it requires the performance of disadvantageous acts.

On the supposition that morality has the characteristics ascribed to it by the thesis, . . . is it possible to answer the question "Why should I be moral?"

I take it that this question, if asked seriously, demands a reason for being moral other than moral reasons themselves. It demands that moral reasons be shown to be reasons for acting by a noncircular argument. Those who would answer it, like Baier, endeavor to do so by the introduction of considerations of advantage.

Two such considerations have emerged from our discussion. The first is that if all are moral, all will do better than if all are prudent. This will serve to answer the question "Why should we be moral?" if this question is interpreted rather as "Why should we all be moral—rather than all being something else?" If we must all be the same, then each person has a reason—a prudential reason—to prefer that we all be moral.

But, so interpreted, "Why should we be moral?" is not a compendious way of asking, for each person, "Why should I be moral?" Of course, if everyone is to be whatever I am, then I should be moral. But a general answer to the question "Why should I be moral?" cannot presuppose this.

The second consideration is that any individual always does better to be prudent rather than moral, provided his choice does not determine other choices. But in so far as this answers the question "Why should I be moral?" it leads to the conclusion "I should not be moral." One feels that this is not the answer which is wanted.

We may put the matter otherwise. The individual who needs a reason for being moral which is not itself a moral reason cannot have it. There is nothing surprising about this; it would be much more surprising if such reasons could be found. For it is more than apparently paradoxical to suppose that considerations of advantage could ever of themselves justify accepting a real disadvantage. . . .

It is possible that there are systems of principles which, if adopted and adhered to, provide advantages which strictly prudent men, however rational, cannot attain. These advantages are a function of the sacrifices which the principles impose on their adherents.

Morality may be such a system. If it is, this would explain our expectation that we should all be worse off were we to substitute prudence for morality in our deliberations. But to characterize morality as a system of principles advantageous to all is not to answer the question "Why should I be moral?" nor is it to provide for those considerations of fairness which are equally essential to our moral understanding.

Gauthier's conclusions might be generalized beyond considerations of personal advantage. It is always possible that in some other sense of a "better life," some persons will have a better life if they do not live up to the demands of morality. This might be a "better life" from a religious or political standpoint. One would, of course, have to supply the crucial sense of a "better life" and argue for the point of view that it is better than morality. This problem will be again considered near the end of this chapter (in the selection by W. K. Frankena).

ULTIMATE JUSTIFICATION AND PERSONAL CHOICE

A point about moral justification made in earlier sections may now be brought to bear on the question, "Why ought I to be moral?" Justification, it was seen, requires giving reasons, and reasons can continually be challenged right up to the highest level of reasons. Even at the highest level, it is appropriate to ask for a justification, and thus the regress of justification seems unstoppable. The question, "Why should I be moral?" seems to challenge morality at the highest level by demanding an external justification. If so, we cannot advance further to some still higher level, and we therefore must *choose* to live either a moral way of life, a nonmoral way of life, or a partially moral way of life. This would be a choice for which no *further* (i.e., no higher-level) reasons can be given—in other words, a choice where no further justification is possible. This possibility merits exploration.

A long philosophical tradition holds that acceptance of morality and other forms of obedience to principle in life are not matters of reason or rational justification at all;

rather, they are matters of commitment and choice of the most abiding and significant sort. Many theologians have offered such an appraisal of religious faith, which they construe as a commitment to religious demands for which there are no justifications beyond a certain point. Perhaps morality is similar: Ultimate choices and commitments must be made by each individual, and the individual must thereafter accept responsibility for the choice and abandon the hope for some higher level of justification. Farber might ultimately be committed to freedom of the press and to any justification this belief requires, including a justification of the moral way of life that (let us suppose) he has chosen. Yet, can he show that his ultimate commitment to a moral way of life is more justified than, say, the ultimate commitments of someone who rejects morality? Must not both at some point choose and give up hope for a higher-level justification of the choice?

An extreme version of this thesis is found in the writings of Jean-Paul Sartre, who maintains not only the necessity of such choice about morality, but also that whatever we are and become is a matter of our own choosing and responsibility. We are free to choose or to reject morality, and "Why be moral?" is, in the end, a question each of us must answer in the knowledge that there is no hope of any external justifying reason. Although he is not directly discussing the question, "Why be moral?" Sartre develops this thesis about external justification in a most striking way in the following article on moral dilemmas and moral creativity.

JEAN-PAUL SARTRE

The Humanism of Existentialism*

[I begin with] the case of one of my students who came to see me under the following circumstances: his father was on bad terms with his mother, and, moreover, was inclined to be a collaborationist; his older brother had been killed in the German offensive of 1940, and the young man, with somewhat immature but generous feelings, wanted to avenge him. His mother lived alone with him, very much upset by the half-treason of her husband and the death of her older son; the boy was her only consolation.

*From Jean-Paul Sartre, *Essays in Existentialism* (Secaucus, N.J.: Citadel Press, 1965), pp. 42–45, 54–56.

The boy was faced with the choice of leaving for England and joining the Free French Forces—that is, leaving his mother behind—or remaining with his mother and helping her to carry on. He was fully aware that the woman lived only for him and that his going off—and perhaps his death—would plunge her into despair. He was also aware that every act that he did for his mother's sake was a sure thing, in the sense that it was helping her to carry on, whereas every effort he made toward going off and fighting was an uncertain move which might run aground and prove completely useless; for example, on his way to England he might, while passing through Spain, be detained indefinitely in a Spanish camp; he might reach England or Algiers and be stuck in an office at a desk job. As a result, he was faced with two very different kinds of action: one, concrete, immediate, but concerning only one individual; the other concerned an incomparably vaster group, a national collectivity, but for that very reason was dubious, and might be interrupted en route. And, at the same time, he was wavering between two kinds of ethics. On the one hand, an ethics of sympathy, of personal devotion; on the other, a broader ethics, but one whose efficacy was more dubious. He had to choose between the two.

Who could help him choose? Christian doctrine? No. Christian doctrine says, "Be charitable, love your neighbor, take the more rugged path, etc., etc." But which is the more rugged path? Whom should he love as a brother? The fighting man or his mother? Which does the greater good, the vague act of fighting in a group, or the concrete one of helping a particular human being to go on living? Who can decide *a priori?* Nobody. No book of ethics can tell him. The Kantian ethics says, "Never treat any person as a means, but as an end." Very well, if I stay with mother, I'll treat her as an end and not as a means; but by virtue of this very fact, I'm running the risk of treating the people around me who are fighting, as means; and, conversely, if I go to join those who are fighting, I'll be treating them as an end, and, by doing that, I run the risk of treating my mother as a means.

If values are vague, and if they are always too broad for the concrete and specific case that we are considering, the only thing left for us is to trust our instincts. That's what this young man tried to do; and when I saw him, he said, "In the end, feeling is what counts. I ought to choose whichever pushes me in one direction. If I feel that I love my mother enough to sac-

rifice everything else for her—my desire for vengeance, for action, for adventure—then I'll stay with her. If, on the contrary, I feel that my love for my mother isn't enough, I'll leave."

But how is the value of a feeling determined? What gives his feeling for his mother value? Precisely the fact that he remained with her. I may say that I like so-and-so well enough to sacrifice a certain amount of money for him, but I may say so only if I've done it. I may say "I love my mother well enough to remain with her" if I have remained with her. The only way to determine the value of this affection is, precisely, to perform an act which confirms and defines it. But, since I require this affection to justify my act, I find myself caught in a vicious circle.

On the other hand, Gide has well said that a mock feeling and a true feeling are almost indistinguishable; to decide that I love my mother and will remain with her, or to remain with her by putting on an act, amount somewhat to the same thing. In other words, the feeling is formed by the acts one performs; so I cannot refer to it in order to act upon it. Which means that I can neither seek within myself the true condition which will impel me to act, nor apply to a system of ethics for concepts which will permit me to act. You will say, "At least, he did go to a teacher for advice." But if you seek advice from a priest, for example, you have chosen this priest; you already knew, more or less, just about what advice he was going to give you. In other words, choosing your adviser is involving yourself. The proof of this is that if you are a Christian, you will say, "Consult a priest." But some priests are collaborating, some are just marking time, some are resisting. Which to choose? If the young man chooses a priest who is resisting or collaborating, he has already decided on the kind of advice he's going to get. Therefore, in coming to see me he knew the answer I was going to give him, and I had only one answer to give: "You're free, choose, that is, invent.". . .

We are told, "So you're able to do anything, no matter what!" This is expressed in various ways. First we are accused of anarchy; then they say, "You're unable to pass judgment on others, because there's no reason to prefer one configuration to another"; finally they tell us, "Everything is arbitrary in this choosing of yours. You take something from one pocket and pretend you're putting it into the other."

These three objections aren't very serious. Take the first objection. "You're able to do anything, no matter what" is not to the point. In one sense choice is possible, but what is not possible is not to choose. I can always choose, but I ought to know that if I do not choose, I am still choosing. Though this may seem purely formal, it is highly important for keeping fantasy and caprice within bounds. If it is true that in facing a situation, for example, one in which, as a person capable of having sexual relations, of having children, I am obliged to choose an attitude, and if I in any way assume responsibility for a choice which, in involving myself, also involves all mankind, this has nothing to do with caprice, even if no *a priori* value determines my choice.

If anybody thinks that he recognizes here Gide's theory of the arbitrary act, he fails to see the enormous difference between this doctrine and Gide's. Gide does not know what a situation is. He acts out of pure caprice. For us, on the contrary, man is in an organized situation in which he himself is involved. Through his choice, he involves all mankind, and he cannot avoid making a choice: either he will remain chaste, or he will marry without having children, or he will marry and have children; anyhow, whatever he may do, it is impossible for him not to take full responsibility for the way he handles this

problem. Doubtless, he chooses without referring to pre-established values, but it is unfair to accuse him of caprice. Instead, let us say that moral choice is to be compared to the making of a work of art. And before going any further, let it be said at once that we are not dealing here with an aesthetic ethics, because our opponents are so dishonest that they even accuse us of that. The example I've chosen is a comparison only.

Having said that, may I ask whether anyone has ever accused an artist who has painted a picture of not having drawn his inspiration from rules set up *a priori?* Has anyone ever asked, "What painting ought he to make?" It is clearly understood that there is no definite painting to be made, that the artist is engaged in the making of his painting, and that the painting to be made is precisely the painting he will have made. It is clearly understood that there are no *a priori* aesthetic values, but that there are values which appear subsequently in the coherence of the painting, in the correspondence between what the artist intended and the result. Nobody can tell what the painting of tomorrow will be like. Painting can be judged only after it has once been made. What connection does that have with ethics? We are in the same creative situation. We never say that a work of art is arbitrary. When we speak of a canvas of Picasso, we never say that it is arbitrary; we understand quite well that he was making himself what he is at the very time he was painting, that the ensemble of his work is embodied in his life.

The same holds on the ethical plane. What art and ethics have in common is that we have creation and invention in both cases. We cannot decide *a priori* what there is to be done. I think that I pointed that out quite sufficiently when I mentioned the case of the student who came to see me, and who might have applied to all the ethical systems, Kantian or otherwise, without getting any sort of guidance. He was obliged to devise his law himself. Never let it be said by us that this man—who, taking affection, individual action, and kind-heartedness toward a specific person as his ethical first principle, chooses to remain with his mother, or who, preferring to make a sacrifice, chooses to go to England—has made an arbitrary choice. Man makes himself. He isn't ready-made at the start. In choosing his ethics, he makes himself, and force of circumstances is such that he cannot abstain from choosing one. We define man only in relationship to involvement. It is therefore absurd to charge us with arbitrariness of choice.

As he notes, Sartre's approach to creation and invention in morality has often been accused of irrationality and arbitrariness. His morality is accused of being like a game of chance in which one blindly feels out the alternatives. In at least some respects, however, this analogy to a game of chance is inaccurate and unfair. First, a person can choose as best he or she is able in light of a wealth of information about what it would be like to live *different* ways of life that involve the acceptance of quite different principles. Such a person could then debate the options with others, and could choose in light of both the available information and the perspectives on that information provided by others. In one sense of the term "rational justification," this process surely qualifies, even if it is true that in the end one must choose and cannot evade the choice. Of course, one could always ask (as we have seen through our analysis of levels of moral justification), "Why should I adopt this method of choice?"—i.e., "Why should I engage in rational deliberation and justification at all?" But if this is the question to which this discussion has led, then a skeptical terminus, beyond which one cannot proceed, has been reached. A justification of rational deliberation itself is now being asked; and the only way to satisfy this demand is to engage in rational deliberation in order to muster an answer. Here a *commitment* of some sort is inescapable, and it must be a commitment to rational inquiry if the questions that have been posed are to be answered.

Let us return, then, to the question, "Why should I adopt this method of choice?" which need not be interpreted as a question about why an involvement in *rational* inquiry is necessary. An alternative construal of the question is the following: at first, a search was begun to find a nonmoral justification of morality, and now it looks as though there is no ultimate *reason* that can be given—only a *choice* that is up to each individual. Earlier in this chapter, however, it was seen that a pragmatic vindication of morality offers an attractive form of external justification based on an understanding of the object or purpose of moral reasoning. Yet, this proposal also seems to presuppose the correctness of a consequential approach to justification, and it is possible to ask, "What justifies a pragmatic scheme of justification?" With this question, another level seems to have been reached; beyond it, one cannot advance without *choosing* for or against the pragmatist approach to justification. This choice would not in itself be a moral one, but it is a choice for or against a form of justification to which the question, "Why be moral?" has led.

The analysis of justification in terms of levels thus indicates that the ultimate justification of any way of life—moral, religious, egoistic, or whatever—or any method of justification raises the problem that at some point a choice simply has to be made. For this reason, the choice of a moral way of life has seemed to some writers neither more rational nor ultimately more justifiable than the choice of an alternative way of life. Some of these writers have argued that the analogy to religious commitment that was considered earlier is perfectly appropriate: in the end, they claim, a religious way of life and a moral way of life both rest on faith. The contention that a *philosophical* defense of morality as a way of life rests in some important respect on faith is defended in the following article by William Frankena. He "postulates" that one would choose to be moral if one knew clearly what one wanted and what the facts of one's situation are. He admits that his own postulation rests on an "article of faith," though he also holds that "this faith is rational" because a process of rational justification can be given that stands behind the choice.

WILLIAM K. FRANKENA

Why Be Moral?*

[Suppose one] asks what is the rational thing to choose, all things considered: prudence, morality, and whatnot. Then one is asking what one *would* choose, as far as one can see, *if* one were completely clearheaded and fully knowledgeable about oneself and everything involved. What could be more rational than such a decision? If I am right, then something is rational for one to choose if one would choose it under those conditions. *Rational* thus means "would be chosen under such conditions." And then it is an open question, not only whether being moral is rational, but also whether being prudential or self-interested is. . . .

I [wish to dispute] the assumption that a course of action or a way of life, to be rational for me to adopt, must be such as

*From William K. Frankena, "Lecture Three: Why Be Moral?" *Thinking about Morality* (Ann Arbor: University of Michigan Press, 1980), pp. 85–94.

to give me the best or highest score in the long run, or for the time I can reasonably expect to have, in terms of something like pleasure, satisfaction, fulfillment, happiness, flourishing, or achievement of excellence—in short, that it is never rational to pursue a course that involves any sacrifice on one's part or results or may be expected to result in anything less than such a highest score for oneself. . . .

What worries me is the assumption that one can show being moral to be rational only if one can show that it gives one the best score for one's life, all things considered. It would, after all, be paradoxical if the only way to justify a nonegoistic enterprise like morality were by use of an egoistic argument. Besides, I do not believe that being moral will always give one the best score even if one considers the contribution that being moral makes to one's good or happiness, though I agree that this contribution is a great one. I believe, rather, that morality sometimes requires genuine sacrifice, and may even require self-sacrifice. . . .

If, in order for an individual to be rational, being moral must yield him or her the best score in some longrun way, then the rationality of genuine sacrifice, supreme or not supreme, cannot be proved, even if one has strong, deeply-rooted interests in one's fellows. For genuine sacrifice means taking a course of action that makes one's total score in life less than it would be otherwise. It can therefore be rational for a person only if it represents a course that person would choose "on the whole if all the consequences of all the different lines of conduct open to him were accurately foreseen and adequately realized in imagination at the present point of time," to borrow words Sidgwick used in defining the notion of "a man's future good on the whole."[1]

It may be thought that I am making a distinction without a difference. Not so. There is a difference between the life that gives one the best score and the life one would prefer given complete knowledge and a perfect realization of what is involved. One might, all things considered, prefer a life that does not yield one the best score, precisely on the ground that it has morality on its side. To give me my best score, a life must include my being around to collect the results, but a life involving self-sacrifice may not allow me to do this. Nevertheless, I might prefer it if I knew all about myself and the world. . . . We cannot know for certain that being moral is rational either for anyone or for everyone. We are, however, still ahead *if* we can say more in favor of believing *this* than we can in favor of believing that being moral is for the

good of everyone in the sense of always giving him or her the better score. I am convinced that we can. In the first place, we can, of course, say for it everything that can be said for the coincidence of being moral with self-interest, which is a great deal. Here I would stress both of the lines of argument mentioned earlier, i.e., the one that points out how much happiness there is in relating well to others, and the one that centers on the thought that virtue is its own reward. The good life for anyone consists primarily of enjoyments of various kinds and of the achievement of such excellence as one is capable of; the first argument emphasizes the former component, the second the latter. To make the second clearer, I may observe that being moral entails achieving a certain kind of excellence, namely excellence as judged from the moral point of view; that this is a kind of excellence which requires no special ability or gift, as artistic and athletic excellence do (even a person of ordinary talents can become a very good person); and that it is a peculiarly important sort of excellence just because it is excellence in one's relations to other persons and sentient beings as well as to oneself. The facts about mental illness show how significant for human life such relations and performing well in them are. . . .

I think one can also claim, judging by the case of Socrates and many others, that those who have been moral would choose to be so again if they could look back over their actions from the vantage point of perfect hindsight.

Finally, there is the matter of self-respect. Moral philosophers have been making much of its importance lately, but they were anticipated by Aldo Leopold who wrote, "Voluntary adherence to an ethical code elevates the self-respect of the sportsman, but . . . voluntary disregard of the code degenerates and depraves

[1]Henry Sidgwick, *Methods of Ethics,* 7th ed. (London: Macmillan & Co., Ltd., 1907), pp. 111–112.

him.''[2] His point is that self-respect pre-supposes that one sees oneself as moral. What is self-respect? I suggest that it is a conviction that one's character and life will be approved by any rational being who contemplates it from the moral point of view. One can claim that having this belief about oneself is a primary human good, as John Rawls does in his widely read and much discussed book, *A Theory of Justice,* but it is not just a good that is to be added in, along with other goods or evils, in determining one's score. Rather, I believe, it is a judgment about oneself that one cannot make if one sees oneself as always looking for the best score for oneself, as never willing to make a genuine sacrifice, however small. The importance of self-respect is not so much that it improves one's score as that it may lead one to prefer a life in which it is present to one from which it would be absent but which would yield a better score. Why can it do this? I believe it is because we are so constituted that we cannot clear-headedly respect ourselves unless we perceive ourselves as respecting others. At any rate, our need for self-respect and its dependence on our being moral are important evidence that we may prefer being moral to having the highest score. . . .

We can safely assert, although we cannot know, that at least some people are so

built that they would choose to be moral if they were clear-headed and logical and knew all about themselves and the alternative lives open to them. For them, being moral is rational, even if it involves sacrifice. This is an important result. We can then infer that for certain kinds of persons it is rational to be moral. But, of course, this leaves open the possibility that for others it is not. Are we left with the conclusion that whether one should be moral or not depends on what kind of a person one is, as some, including myself, have suggested? That is all we can be sure of, and it is important, because no one of us can know with certainty what kind of a person he or she is at any point in time (or only in a Day of Judgment, if there will be one, when it will be too late). However, in view of what has been said, it seems to me reasonable to *postulate* that everyone is so constituted by nature, antecedently to any conditioning he or she may receive, that he or she would choose to live a moral life if the stated conditions were fulfilled. This cannot be proved, and so must remain a postulate, but it also cannot be disproved, and one who would be moral must affirm it. Why then should one be moral? Why is it rational to be moral? Because one would choose to be moral if one clearly knew what one was about. This is an article of moral faith. Being moral is rational if this faith is rational, i.e., if one would espouse it if one knew what everything is about—a possibility that at least cannot be ruled out.

[2]Aldo Leopold, *A Sand County Almanac* (New York: Ballantine Books, Inc., 1970), p. 232.

At least two possible problems surround Frankena's approach, and both deserve momentary consideration. Frankena's several reasons for choosing a moral way of life seem dominantly to be moral ones. This feature of his argument risks begging the question by providing a moral, rather than a nonmoral, justification of morality. The second and more important issue, however, is whether these matters can be decided by *reason* or by appeals to *rationality* at all. Frankena's final appeal is clearly to rationality and not to faith: he holds that it is rational to be moral because the rational person would choose to be moral on the basis of comprehensive knowledge and deliberation. This claim about what a rational person would choose is reminiscent of John Rawls's strategy for justifying his principles of justice (as was seen in Chapter 7). Rawls has been broadly criticized for unjustifiably assuming that rational individuals (in what he calls the "original position") would agree to his second principle of justice. Rawls's critics insist that some rational individuals would agree to a riskier system of basic rules, a system permitting more dramatic wins as well as losses in the distribution of social benefits. Frankena seems open to the same criticism, for some rational individuals may not choose in favor of morality (even if they already have long lived a moral way of life), preferring, instead, the criterion of a "best score."

An alternative to Frankena's argument is that in the end one's choice for or against morality in light of comprehensive knowledge and deliberation is not justifiable by any appeal to reason or rationality. At the same time, it may be doubted that a bold appeal to "faith" is satisfactory either. As Sartre hints, our decisions may instead be based on whether we have a sufficiently strong *desire* to live the moral life—a stronger desire than we have to live some alternative form of life. A philosophical attempt at rational justification may provide all the data needed to generate a comprehensive view of the nature and consequences of living a moral way of life, and one's desire may be based on this comprehensive view. Yet, it is clearly possible that two rational individuals possessing an identical comprehensive view will choose opposite courses, depending upon how deeply they are attracted to the moral life and how much they therefore want to live it.

This suggestion cannot be pursued here, but it is worth noting that it is not remote from common sense. We all recognize that some persons, by disposition, are of better moral character and are more deeply committed to morality than others—just as some persons are deeply moved by the plight of others around the globe when others are not at all moved. The desire to see injustices rectified and human suffering reduced thus may be the deepest cause of our living moral lives (though such a psychological motivation of course constitutes no rational justification); and it may not be a rationally defensible desire at all. This conclusion, together with others reached earlier in this section about choice and commitment, provides a reason for questioning whether it is even possible to adduce ultimate rational grounds in favor of morality.

CONCLUSION

The account of levels of justification that are seemingly forever in need of an external justification, as discussed in this chapter, would be rejected by many philosophers. They would hold that such "justificationism" or "foundationalism" inevitably leads to the stultifying skeptical thesis that there can be no justification in ethics, for in the end one would still have to provide an external justification for one's method of justification and for all possible premises—an ideal that seems hopeless. As an alternative to "justificationism," some philosophers have suggested that human society is governed by a set of moral rules and principles that form the terms of cooperation in the society—the implicit and explicit terms under which individuals are obligated to cooperate with others. While new experience and changes in the organization of collective life lead to modifications in the terms of cooperation, one need not look for a "level" beyond the established general terms of cooperation when attempting to justify a moral judgment. Morality simply is not structured in a neatly layered system of principles and rules. Some have even argued that a distinction cannot be successfully drawn between internal and external justifications, because moral knowledge—like scientific and other forms of knowledge—is a unit that stands or falls as a whole and so cannot be justified in bits and pieces.

While this suggestion offers a simple and inviting way to escape some of the problems encountered in this chapter, it fails to provide any systematic method for justifying and criticizing moral beliefs. In effect, it cuts justification adrift at all levels. On the other hand, this objection has one point in its favor: Skepticism would be the inevitable and unfortunate outcome of a *too rigid* understanding of the theory of levels of justification. If the requirements of an "ultimate justification" compel us to go on forever searching for more general principles that justify our less general beliefs and principles, and if the requirements insist that without reaching an ultimate level there is no justification, then skepticism about the justifiability of moral beliefs is indeed inevitable. No matter what levels of justification we reach, we cannot in principle terminate the search, for the whole process of justification is triggered again at each level, thus leading to the conclusion that no position or principle is ultimately justifiable. One of the most valuable features of the pragmatic vindication approach discussed earlier in this chapter is that it provides one rational means to avoid this skeptical implication of a general theory of justification.

We may conclude that the arguments in this chapter need not lead inevitably to any form of a despairing skepticism. The only firm conclusion here is that one's commitment to a moral way of life may ultimately be a matter for autonomous choice and that reason, completely independent of desire and volition, may not be able to make that choice alone. While sufficient to constitute an article of skepticism in the minds of some, this conclusion does not entail that volition unaided by reason is equipped to or ought to make such a choice; nor does it entail the impossibility of providing a theory of moral justification that is capable of showing moral judgments to be based on knowledge. As will be seen in Chapter 10, other theories of justification lead constructively beyond any skeptical conclusions encountered in this chapter.

SUGGESTED SUPPLEMENTARY READINGS

Moral Justification

Aiken, Henry David: *Reason and Conduct: New Bearings in Moral Philosophy* (New York: Alfred A. Knopf, Inc., 1962), especially chaps. 3–5.

————: "Morality and Ideology," in Richard T. DeGeorge, ed., *Ethics and Society* (Garden City, N.Y.: Anchor Books, 1966), pp. 149–172.

Baier, Kurt: "Good Reasons," *Philosophical Studies,* **4** (1953): 1–15.

————: "Reasons for Doing Something," *Journal of Philosophy,* **61** (1964): 198–203.

Becker, Lawrence C.: *On Justifying Moral Judgments* (New York: Humanities Press, 1973).

Beehler, Rodger: *Moral Life* (Totowa, N.J.: Rowman and Littlefield, 1978).

Brennan, John M.: *The Open-Texture of Moral Concepts* (New York: Barnes & Noble, Inc., 1977).

Falk, W. D.: "Goading and Guiding," *Mind,* **62** (1953): 145–171.

Findlay, J. N.: "The Methodology of Normative Ethics," in *Language, Mind, and Value* (London: George Allen & Unwin, 1963), pp. 248–256.

Held, Virginia: "Justification: Legal and Political," *Ethics,* **86** (1975): 1–16.

Phillips, D. Z., and H. O. Mounce: *Moral Practices* (New York: Schocken Books, Inc., 1970).

Raz, Joseph: *Practical Reason and Norms* (London: Hutchinson Publishing Group, Inc., 1975).

Rawls, John: "Outline of a Decision Procedure for Ethics," *Philosophical Review,* **66** (1957): 177–197.

Wheatley, Jon: "Reasons for Acting," *Dialogue,* **7** (1969): 553–567.

Ultimate Justification: Why Be Moral?

Baier, Kurt: *The Moral Point of View: A Rational Basis of Ethics* (Ithaca, N.Y.: Cornell University Press, 1958), especially chaps. 8, 11, 12.

Gauthier, David P.: *Practical Reasoning: The Structure and Foundations of Prudential and Moral Arguments and Their Exemplification in Discourse* (Oxford, England: Clarendon Press, 1963), especially chaps. 6–8.

————, ed.: *Morality and Rational Self-Interest* (Englewood Cliffs, N.J.: Prentice-Hall, Inc., 1970).

Gert, Bernard: *The Moral Rules: A New Rational Foundation for Morality* (New York: Harper Torchbooks, 1973), especially chap. 10.

Nielsen, Kai: "Is 'Why Should I Be Moral?' an Absurdity?" *Australasian Journal of Philosophy,* **36** (1958): 25–32.

————: "Why Should I Be Moral?" *Methodos,* **15** (1963): 275–306.

Pahel, Kenneth, and Marvin Schiller, eds.: *Readings in Contemporary Ethical Theory* (Englewood Cliffs, N.J.: Prentice-Hall, Inc., 1970), sec. 4.

Phillips, D. Z.: "Does It Pay to Be Good?" in *Proceedings of the Aristotelian Society,* **65** (1964–1965): 45–60.

Prichard, H. A.: "Does Moral Philosophy Rest on a Mistake?" *Mind,* **21** (1912): 21–37.

Rawls, John: *A Theory of Justice* (Cambridge, Mass.: Harvard University Press, 1971), especially chap. 9.

Richards, David A.: *A Theory of Reasons for Action* (New York: Oxford University Press, 1971), especially chap. 14.

Scriven, Michael: *Primary Philosophy* (New York: McGraw-Hill Book Company, 1966), especially pp. 238–265.

Singer, Marcus G.: *Generalization in Ethics* (New York: Atheneum Publishers, 1971), chap. 10.

Taylor, Paul W.: *Normative Discourse* (Englewood Cliffs, N.J.: Prentice-Hall, Inc., 1961), especially pp. 142–150.

CHAPTER TEN

Facts and Values

In June of 1978, Robert McFall, thirty-nine years old and a Pittsburgh asbestos worker, entered Mercy Hospital with an uncontrollable nosebleed. Physicians diagnosed his condition as aplastic anemia, a rare and usually fatal disease in which the bone marrow fails to produce enough red and white blood cells and platelets. McFall's physician recommended a bone-marrow transplant on the ground that it would increase his patient's chance of surviving for one year from 25 percent to 40 to 60 percent. The search for a compatible transplant donor began with McFall's six brothers and sisters. After they were located in various parts of the country, none turned out to be compatible.

The search continued and McFall's first cousin, David Shimp, aged forty-three, agreed to undergo some preliminary tests. He was a perfect match for tissue compatibility; but then suddenly he refused to be tested for genetic compatibility. He had decided that he would not donate bone marrow to his cousin, even if he was a perfect match. Apparently, some family discussions and disagreements had influenced Shimp's decision. He told his cousin that his wife was angry because he had undergone the first tests without telling her. Shimp's mother also appeared to be bitter about a decades-old disagreement in the family, and she too asked him to stop the testing.

Friends and other of McFall's relatives believed that disagreements of the past should not affect the present, and they tried to persuade Shimp to change his mind. When McFall called his cousin and told him, "You're killing me," Shimp responded that his wife had to come first. Even Shimp's four children tried to persuade him that he would be responsible for his cousin's early death, and they volunteered to be tested themselves; but Shimp would not be moved.

McFall then filed suit to compel his cousin to undergo the bone-marrow transplant. McFall's attorney argued in court that the procedure is essentially harmless to the donor and that the marrow would be replenished, just as blood is replenished after donation. He also cited English common law, dating back to the thirteenth century, which upheld society's right to force an individual "to help secure the well-being of other members of society." Shimp's attorney argued that his client's right to refuse could not be invaded, and that "no one could be forced to submit to an operation." Shimp told reporters that he refused to be a donor because he was afraid of becoming paralyzed during the procedure and feared that his marrow might fail to regenerate.

Judge John Flaherty denied McFall's request to force Shimp to undergo the transplant. The judge based his decision on United States common law precedents, which do not recognize a legal duty to take action to save another person's life. "This would defeat the sanctity of the individual," he argued. "Our society is based on the right and sanctity of the individual. It would require forcible submission to the medical procedure. Forcible extraction of bodily tissues causes revulsion to the judicial mind. The rights of the individual must be upheld, even though it appears to be a harsh decision." The judge also declared irrelevant the argument by McFall's attorney that in English law, court-ordered transplants are permitted. Although he thus held that Shimp had no legal obligation to donate his marrow, Judge Flaherty nevertheless called Shimp's refusal "morally indefensible."

After the ruling, McFall told the press, "I feel sorry for my cousin because he and I are friends and he was under a lot of pressure." Shimp made no comment, but his mother said, "He's not a coward the way they are trying to make him out to be. When you get on the table there is no guaranteeing how much bone marrow they will take. It could be my son's death sentence. The doctors don't care about the donors; they care about patients."

On August 10, 1978, Robert McFall died of a cranial hemorrhage. His last request was that his family forgive his cousin, whose actions he found understandable even if not justifiable. A hospital spokesperson said that cranial hemorrhage is a common complication for people with aplastic anemia and that it might have occurred even with the bone-marrow transplant. The day after his cousin died, Shimp said, "I could throw up right now. I feel terrible about Robert dying, but he asked me for something I couldn't give. That's all I can say now. I feel sick."*

PROBLEMS OF MEANING AND JUSTIFICATION

In Chapters 2 and 9, it was briefly pointed out that both facts and values can properly be used to justify moral positions. In the case just recounted, an attempt is made to use *facts* about McFall's medical condition to justify moral *value* judgments about what

*Sources for this case include Barbara J. Culliton, "Court Upholds Refusal to Be Medical Good Samaritan," *Science,* **201** (Aug. 18, 1978): 596–597; "Bone Marrow Transplant Plea Rejected," *American Medical News,* **21**: 31 (Aug. 11, 1978): 13; "Anemia Victim Dies, Asks Forgiveness for Cousin," *International Herald Tribune* (Aug. 12–13, 1978); "Judge Upholds Transplant Denial," *The New York Times* (July 27, 1978), p. A10; Dennis A. Williams and Lawrence Walsh, "The Law: Bad Samaritan," *Newsweek,* **92**: 6 (Aug. 7, 1978): 35.

Shimp ought to do. This chapter will explore in detail the question, "What are facts and values, and what role do they properly play in moral justification?"

The contrast between facts and values raises the following four much discussed questions:

1. What is the *difference,* if any, between facts and values?
2. Can values be *derived* from facts, i.e., can a value judgment be derived from a factual judgment?
3. Do value statements assert either factual or nonfactual *knowledge?*
4. Are value judgments either *true* or *false?*

These questions are clearly interconnected, and they have equally clear connections to the discussions of rational justification in Chapter 9. At stake is the determination of whether value judgments (including moral judgments) can ultimately be proved, verified, or justified in terms of either facts or rational argument. We understand reasonably well, so some have argued, how conclusions in science are supported by factual evidence. But how does one objectively support conclusions in ethics? What constitutes evidence and what constitutes proof?

Issues about facts and values concern the question of what, if anything, can be known in such a way that a rational justification for the knowledge can be provided. One important issue is whether reason has any role at all to play in moral justifications: does ethics involve a rational appeal to facts and values, or is it merely the expression of emotion and personal attitudes? If emotions and attitudes are the source of our values, then it is doubtful that reason plays any significant role in moral inquiry and justification. A different view is that ethics is based on some uniquely ethical properties of actions, traits of character, or situations that are known by intuition. In this case too, many have wondered what the role of reason could be if it should turn out that moral rightness and wrongness, virtue and vice, appropriateness and inappropriateness are simply matters of intuition.

In the present chapter, these problems are examined by considering in turn five major schools of thought on problems of facts and values: naturalism, intuitionism, noncognitivism, prescriptivism, and descriptivism. Some of these approaches to facts and values explicitly offer answers to problems of *moral* judgments and justification. Other approaches, however, are less concerned with moral judgments per se than with the more general topic of values and value judgments (of which moral values and moral judgments are only one species). Much significant philosophical literature in this area has therefore not been focused exclusively on morality—perhaps understandably, since the topic of facts and values would naturally seem to encompass issues that arise in a broad range of contexts. In any case, the reader should be prepared to endure discussions of good strawberries, courageous behavior, positive attitudes, and value predicates along with discussions of morally good persons, moral courage, moral attitudes, and moral predicates.

NATURALISM

The first school of philosophy to be studied in this chapter is generally referred to as "naturalism." According to this theory, value judgments can be justified through a factual method (sometimes called the "rational method" by naturalists)—one that parallels methods of historical and scientific justification. Indeed, in philosophy the naturalist holds that values are a type of fact (a "natural thing"), and that value properties are natural properties. The naturalist thus believes that value statements are subject to confirmation or disconfirmation in the way all factual statements are; and in the naturalistic view, justification therefore does not differ from justification in history, science, or any domain where conclusions are defended by marshaling factual evidence. The naturalist holds that this process of justification is the only way to save moral judgments from arbitrariness and relativism.

The following is the line of argument taken by the naturalist in defense of this view: In value judgments, a value property is attributed to a subject. In "McFall was courageous," for example, the value of courage is attributed to McFall; that is, the value predicate "courageous" is applied to, or conjoined with, the subject "McFall." The naturalist holds that all value predicates, such as "courageous," can be defined in terms of, or translated into, factual predicates; moral language can thus be defined in terms of, or translated into, factual, nonvaluational words. For example, a naturalist might hold that "Shimp acted wrongly" can be translated as "Shimp acted against the ideals of behavior adopted by his family and culture"—a factual and, in principle, a confirmable statement. Different naturalistic theories provide different definitions or translations of value predicates, but they are united in believing that value words can, without loss, be understood in terms of factual predicates. They are also united in believing that value problems are factual problems whose solution depends on empirical evidence and research.

The simple idea behind naturalism is that if we can only understand what value words mean or refer to, we can determine how to go about justifying them. If the word "good," for example, means "that which is desired by the majority in a culture," we can show that something *is* good by showing that it is in fact desired in a culture. Thus, if someone asserts that "freedom of the press is good," the claim can be justified (in this view of the meaning of "good") by showing that a free press is desired by the majority in the culture in question. Or, to take a different example, if the word "right" means "is commanded in the ten commandments," then we can show that an action is right by showing that it *is* commanded in the ten commandments—something it is usually easy to verify or to disprove.

Naturalists do not necessarily hold that a natural property exists in nature or in the world apart from subjective human attitudes. There are many subjectivist (and even relativist) types of naturalism. Some naturalists have held that "right" can be defined in terms of the personal approvals of the individuals who utter statements about what is right; and, as suggested already, some naturalists have proposed that what is good or right is to be understood exclusively in terms of what is accepted in a society's code. Some naturalistic theories, however, are more objective. Bentham, for example, tends to understand "evil" as meaning "causing pain or displeasure," and some writers, influenced by Darwin, have suggested that "right" means "conforming to the course of human evolution." These subjectivist and objectivist views are alike naturalistic because of their proponents' common belief that the presence of value properties can be ascertained by empirical tests and hence that justifications in morals are factual in character. (Certain theories of natural rights that were studied in Chapter 6 hold that the expression "human rights" refers to standards of conduct existing in nature; in these theories, however, the "natural" standards are generally not considered empirically confirmable, because they are derived from a metaphysical theory.)

In all naturalistic theories, it becomes possible to derive an "ought" or value statement from an "is" or factual statement, for "ought" can be defined in terms of "is." Given a naturalistic definition, one can proceed logically from an "is" to an "ought"—or, more precisely, one can simply reduce an "ought" to an "is," thus formally eliminating the "ought" statement while retaining its meaning. For example, if "One ought to do X" means "One is required by the legal and moral code of one's society to do X," then "One ought to stop one's car at red lights" can be deduced from "One is required by the legal and moral code of one's society to stop one's car at red lights." One major issue about naturalism is whether values can be correctly defined in terms of facts, but it is indisputable that values can be logically derived from facts once a naturalistic definition has been given. This problem of "is" and "ought" will be again examined in the next section.

Among the philosophers studied earlier in this book, Aristotle and Bentham can plausibly (though not without controversy) be interpreted as naturalists. Aristotle seems to define the good as "that towards which we aim," and his view that "well-being is the highest good" seems to be reducible to, or translatable in terms of, certain facts about human nature. Bentham too tends to define the good in terms of happiness and evil in terms of unhappiness. However, it is harder to find unambiguous assertions of naturalism in these classical theories than in some more recent accounts.

One of the most plausible arguments in favor of naturalism is that developed by the twentieth-century American philosopher R. B. Perry. Although he is a subjective naturalist, his theory resembles Bentham's in many respects. He begins by noticing how value terms such as "good" and "bad" are closely connected with things, events, or states of mind that persons like and dislike, approve and disapprove, or love and hate. These are, of course, psychological states, and Perry's naturalism is thus rooted in psychological fact. His strategy is to define goodness in terms of persons' positive interests in things, and to define badness in terms of negative interests. He then defines *moral* goodness as "harmonious happiness"—a definition based on his broader conception of the nature and function of morality. The following selection is a representative statement of Perry's naturalism.

RALPH BARTON PERRY

The Definition of Value, Morality, and Moral Concepts*

The Definition of Value

Some philosophers, unfortunately, put the question concerning value in the form "What *is* meant by 'value'?" or "What *does* one mean by 'value'?" as though that meaning were already determined, and it was only necessary to call attention to it. Those who approach the matter in this way are accustomed to challenge a proposed definition of value by saying, "But this is not what is meant by 'value'" or "This is not what one means by 'value.'" The fact is, however, that there is no such established and universal meaning. Different people mean different things in different contexts. The problem is not to discover a present meaning—there are only too many meanings.

The problem is not solved, however, by simply enumerating these many meanings. This job is already done by the unabridged dictionaries which list, in fine print, all the varieties of meaning which appear in literature and ordinary speech. Theory of value is in search of a preferred meaning. The problem is to define, that is, *give* a meaning to the term, either by selecting from its existing meanings, or by creating a new meaning.

But one must not then leap to the conclusion that this giving of a meaning to the term "value" is an arbitrary matter, dictated by the caprice, or mere personal convenience, of the author. One can, it is

true, make the term mean "anything one likes," but this would not advance knowledge, or be of the slightest importance, or be capable either of proof or of disproof. The man who said "When I say 'value' I mean a purple cow" would not even be listened to, unless by a psychiatrist or a kindergarten teacher. There must, in other words, be a control or set of criteria, by which the definition is justified or rejected.

According to the definition of value here proposed, *a thing—any thing—has value, or is valuable . . . when it is the object of an interest—any interest.* Or, *whatever is object of interest is ipso facto valuable.* Thus the valuableness of peace is the characteristic conferred on peace by the interest which is taken in it, for what it is, or for any of its attributes, effects, or implications.

Value is thus defined in terms of interest, and its meaning thus depends on another definition, namely, a definition of interest. The following is here proposed: *interest is a train of events determined by expectation of its outcome.* Or, *a thing is an object of interest when its being expected induces actions looking to its realization or non-realization.* Thus peace is an object of interest when acts believed to be conducive to peace, or preventive of peace, are performed on that account, or when events are selected or rejected because peace is expected of them.

Both of these definitions require clarification and elaboration; but these summary statements will suffice for the present purpose of indicating the criterion by which the definitions are to be justified. . . .

*From Ralph Barton Perry, *Realms of Value: A Critique of Human Civilization* (Cambridge, Mass.: Harvard University Press, 1954), pp. 2–3, 90–91, 101, 104, 106, 109, 119, 134. Reprinted with permission of Harvard University Press.

The Meaning of Morality

Morality is man's endeavor to harmonize conflicting interests: to prevent conflict when it threatens, to remove conflict when it occurs, and to advance from the negative harmony of non-conflict to the positive harmony of cooperation. Morality is the solution of the problem created by conflict—conflict among the interests of the same or of different persons. The solution of the personal problem lies in the substitution for a condition of warring and mutually destructive impulses a condition in which each impulse, being assigned a limited place, may be innocent and contributory. For the weakness of inner discord it substitutes the strength of a unified life in which the several interests of an individual make common cause together. The same description applies to the morality of a social group, all along the line from the domestic family to the family of nations. . . .

The Interpretation of Moral Concepts

There are certain terms of discourse, such as "good," "right," "duty," "responsibility," and "virtue," which are commonly recognized as having to do with morality, and to which a theory of morals must assign definite meanings.

Two meanings have already been assigned to the term "good." In the most general sense, it means the character which anything derives from being the object of any positive interest: whatever is desired, liked, enjoyed, willed, or hoped for, is *thereby* good. In a special sense, "morally good" is the character imparted to objects by interests harmoniously organized. . . .

An object . . . is *morally good* in the special sense when the interest which makes it good satisfies the requirement of harmony, that is, innocence and cooperation. . . .

The "good life," morally speaking, may be described as a condition of *harmonious happiness*—a condition in which, through the increase and cooperation of its members, all interests tend to be positive. This description throws light on the meaning of the familiar but obscure idea of "happiness," and on the traditional claim of happiness to rank as the supreme moral end. . . .

According to the theory here proposed, "right" means conduciveness to moral good, and "wrong" means conduciveness to moral evil: the one to harmony, and the other to conflict. . . .

On the level of everyday discourse what ought to be done is what is called for by some end; it is the converse of the right. The moral ought is what is called for by the end of the moral good, that is, by harmonious happiness. . . .

The moral good has been defined as harmonious happiness, or as that organization of interests in which each enjoys the non-interference and support of the others, whether within the personal life or the life of society. This becomes the moral "first principle." It sets the standard by which objects are deemed morally good or bad, and is the premise from which right, duty, and virtue are to be derived. It provides the most general predicate of moral judgment and the basic concept of moral knowledge. . . .

The theory here proposed reaffirms the standard virtues of antiquity—courage, temperance, wisdom, and justice. The good of harmonious happiness requires, like any end, a brave will that is not dismayed by obstacles, and effort sustained without complaint through long stretches of time. It requires a moderation of appetites lest in their excessive indulgence they should rob one another. It requires enlightened mediating judgments, that is, a true representation of ends and an intelligent choice of means. It requires a distribution of goods to each interest in accordance with a judgment which represents all interest. Christianity did not reject these virtues, but added faith, hope, and love; and these, also, are endorsed by the present theory. . . .

Perry argues for a general theory of value (moral, aesthetic, political, religious, etc.) which would answer the question, "What is *value?*" He then specifies those features which differentiate moral values from other values. His theory is often called the "interest theory of value," because value is defined in terms of interest. Interest is in turn defined in terms of positive attitudes and negative attitudes. For Perry, "interest" is thus a class term designating such combinations of positive and negative attitudes as "liking-disliking," "desiring-avoiding," "approving-disapproving," and "loving-hating."

To explain further: I am interested in something, according to Perry, if I take either a positive attitude toward it ("I like nurses in my classes") or a negative attitude toward it ("I avoid old men with scraggly beards"). I am *not* interested in something if I am either indifferent to it ("I don't care who is crowned Miss America") or interested in a sense other than that of having a positive or negative attitude ("I am fascinated by Shimp's refusal to donate bone marrow to McFall, but I neither favor nor disfavor Shimp's actions"). If someone takes a positive attitude toward something, then it is good, and particular judgments growing out of such attitudes are positive value judgments; if someone takes a negative attitude toward something, then it is bad, and particular judgments growing out of such attitudes are negative value judgments. What distinguishes this interest theory of values from certain others is that it makes values both subjective and naturalistic. The value of objects depends strictly on the presence of someone's or some group's pro or con attitudes. Thus, something is good because one likes or approves of it; one does not like or approve of it because it is somehow good in itself.

Addressing the problem of how to define "morality," Perry argues that whenever there are conflicts between pro attitudes and con attitudes, morality provides a set of rules that attempts to bring such conflicts into harmony. (Think, for example, of "Honor your father and mother.") A moral interest, then, is one that satisfies the requirement of harmony when more than one person is affected by the interest. On this analysis, it is possible that Perry would regard Shimp's children as most clearly having a moral interest in the transplant case, for, more than anyone else, they attempted to harmonize conflicting pro and con attitudes held by members of the two families.

Perry is not merely arguing for a metaethical theory of the meaning of words and of how facts (such as interest) play a role in justifications. He uses his account of the meaning of moral language to propose a broad normative theory—one with close affinities to utilitarianism but also expressing conclusions about the nature and role of virtues. However, it is Perry's naturalistic metaethical theory that is of interest here, and his normative views will therefore be set aside in order to evaluate his naturalism critically.

Many objections have been offered against Perry's theory. With the exception of the "naturalistic fallacy," which will be examined momentarily, the two most prominent objections directed specifically against his views are the following: First, it is said that Perry's theory makes it possible for something to be both good and bad at the same time. If I take a positive interest in bone-marrow transplants and you take a negative interest, then bone-marrow transplants are good for me and bad for you. This outcome of his theory has led many to offer the following objection: " 'Good' and 'bad' are usually considered to be *contraries*. That is, something can be neither good nor bad, but nothing can be both good and bad."* The criticism seems to be that nothing can really be both good and bad at the same time, though Perry's theory permits this absurdity. It is unclear, however, that this criticism is telling. Perry is actually offering a *revisionary* account of value predicates through his subjectivism. Whatever has traditionally been meant by the words "good" and "bad," Perry would not regard such meanings as constraining a philosophical theory. On his subjectivist view, it makes perfectly good sense to say that the same thing can be both good and bad when two or more parties take an interest in it.

This response can be better understood if a second criticism is considered. It is that Perry uses the word "good" in an extraordinarily counterintuitive fashion, for anything whatever becomes good if someone takes a positive interest in it. Failure to help a needy cousin, hatred of an enemy, love of the "perverse," and cynicism about morals all become good if someone takes a positive attitude toward them. No doubt this is a highly undesirable outcome for a *normative* theory of morality, because anything whatever can be asserted to be good. Still, it is not clear that this objection decisively refutes Perry's *metaethical* theory. Perry himself anticipated such criticisms and admitted that his theory leads to surprising and paradoxical results. He conceded specifically that when any proposition is analyzed as relative to a person or persons, and their interests are specified, then *conflict* may result between two opposed views; but he did not think any logical mistake occurs. Thus, if Jones takes a positive attitude toward Nazi concentration camps, for example, then one is bound by Perry's analysis to say that they are good, though one will understand this judgment exclusively to mean good *relative to Jones's positive interest*. This may be a *morally* absurd conclusion, but it is not *logically* absurd, and it shows no metaethical defect in Perry's theory. Furthermore, his normative theory (about harmonizing interests) would reject such a moral conclusion.

Whatever one may think of these two criticisms of Perry, they are but minor complications when compared with what almost everyone considers the major stumbling block for naturalists. This criticism is known as the "naturalistic fallacy," and it is an argument so important that it deserves independent treatment.

*Fred Feldman, *Introductory Ethics* (Englewood Cliffs, N.J.: Prentice-Hall, Inc., 1978), p. 182.

THE NATURALISTIC FALLACY

The two most widely discussed criticisms of naturalism originated in the eighteenth-century work of David Hume and the early twentieth-century writings of G. E. Moore. What Hume actually intended to say remains a matter of scholarly disagreement, but he has been widely interpreted to hold that value statements cannot be derived from purely factual statements because at least one nonfactual value premise is logically required. Hume's embryonic contentions were developed with a novel twist at the beginning of the twentieth century by G. E. Moore, whose book *Principia Ethica* (1903) quickly became a classic in moral philosophy. Much of Moore's book, unlike Hume's work, was directed specifically against naturalism, and it was Moore who coined the now common expression "naturalistic fallacy." His open-question argument pertaining to this alleged fallacy encompasses some of the territory covered by Hume, but, for purposes of clarity, the discussions of the two philosophers will be kept separate (and will be historically reversed in order of appearance in this discussion).

The expression the "naturalistic fallacy" is generally used (and will be used here) to refer to both (1) Moore's open-question argument and (2) Hume's argument about facts and values. In a way, it is strange that Moore's critique of naturalism has thus been connected to Hume's discussion of the problem of facts and values and that both have been linked to the naturalistic fallacy, for no extended discussion of facts and values appears in the writings of either philosopher. Accordingly, while tribute is paid to their considerable historical influence, the problem must be reconstructed by reaching somewhat beyond what either has to say on the subject.

Moore's Open-Question Argument

It has been noted that, for Perry, the word "good" means, or can be defined in terms of, a natural property, namely, "being an object of desire" (or positive interest), while the word (morally) "right" means the empirical property of "being conducive to harmonious happiness." Perry's thesis about meaning and definition, then, is that value predicates can be defined in terms of natural properties. It is precisely this claim that Moore attacks with his open-question argument:

> Ethics aims at discovering what are those other properties belonging to all things which are good. But far too many philosophers have thought that when they named those other properties they were actually defining good; that these properties, in fact, were simply not "other," but absolutely and entirely the same with goodness. This view I propose to call the "naturalistic fallacy." . . .
>
> When they say "Pleasure is good," we cannot believe that they merely mean "Pleasure is pleasure" and nothing more than that. . . .
>
> No difficulty need be found in my saying that "pleasure is good" and yet not meaning that "pleasure" is the same thing as "good," that pleasure *means*

good, and that good *means* pleasure. . . . There is no meaning in saying that pleasure is good, unless good is something different from pleasure. . . .

Whoever will attentively consider with himself what is actually before his mind when he asks the question "Is pleasure (or whatever it may be) after all good?" can easily satisfy himself that he is not merely wondering whether pleasure is pleasant.*

What does Moore mean by this rather dark way of stating his point? First, he is attacking the naturalistic method of *defining* a value predicate such as "good." A definition, for Moore, is an analysis of that which a word stands for, and he has an almost chemical conception of "analysis": to analyze something is to break it down into its component parts. To analyze "goodness," if it were analyzable, would be to break it down into its component parts. To appreciate this point, it is useful to consider an example Moore gives of the difference between the words "good" and "horse." The term "horse," he says, can be understood through those component properties making up horses: legs, head, heart, liver, etc., all arranged in a definite order and proportion. That is, one can define the term "horse" by identifying and distinguishing the various components constituting that which the term designates. But "good" cannot be analyzed in this way, because it has no parts, and certainly no factual parts.

Moore's central contention in the preceding quotation is that the meaning of value predicates is not identical with that of factual predicates, for values cannot be broken down into factual units without losing their sense. Moore's complaint is this: Many writers in ethics, having claimed to discover the properties belonging to all things which are in fact good, believe that by naming these properties they have defined the word "good." This is precisely what Moore means by the "naturalistic fallacy." To illustrate his point, he provides another example, that of yellowness. Suppose a physicist declares that since the appearance of yellow is always accompanied by a certain vibration, the meaning of yellow is that vibration. This pronouncement, Moore declares, would be nonsense. When we assert that something is yellow, we do not mean anything about vibrations. The color word is the name of a property perceptible to the normal eye, not the name of something measured by physics. Moore argues that the word "good" is similar, for it is impossible to state what, besides being good, all good things are. Should it turn out that all good things are pleasant, even this correlation would not indicate that "good" *means* pleasant. To identify light waves with color or pleasantness with goodness is equally to commit a fallacy in his view, for it betrays a misunderstanding of the meaning of the terms.

Suppose, for example, that "good" and "right" are held to mean, or to be identical respectively to, "being an object of desire" and "being conducive to harmonious happiness." This is Perry's proposal. If these claims about identity and meaning were correct, then the value word could be substituted without alteration of meaning for the

*G. E. Moore, *Principia Ethica* (Cambridge, England: Cambridge University Press, 1903), pp. 10, 12, 13, 14, 16.

word or words that define it; but this substitution cannot be made, according to Moore, without committing a mistake. By substituting the defining words, one would alter the meaning of the sentence. It is here that Moore's well-known open-question test is applied. If "good" simply meant "desired," he holds, we could never raise the question, "Is it good?" about anything that is desired. This query would be like asking, "Is that which is desired desired?" (for, remember, we are supposing that "good" and "desired" have the same meaning). Moore's contention is that for anything whatever that is desired—or that has any value property discussed by naturalists—one can always ask meaningfully, "But is it good?" "But is it right?" etc. Thus we can always sensibly say, "This is desired, but is it good?" If this open question holds of all natural properties whatever, Moore argues, then naturalism must be false.

One way to understand Moore's open-question strategy is through the opposite notion of a closed question. Suppose that the word "wife" means "woman joined in marriage to a man," and someone says, "I know she is Don's wife, but is she married to him?" This is a nonsensical and closed question—closed because the meaning of the word "wife" is identical to the meaning of "woman joined in marriage to a man." If the question had been phrased in the following way, however, it would clearly have been an open question: "I know Don treats her like a wife, but is she married to him?" Thus, whenever we have a correct definition and a definitional question is raised, the question is closed, because the two terms linked by the definition have the same meaning. Without such a definitional linking, on the other hand, the question always remains open. In the case of "good," Moore argues, it is always an open question in just this sense of whether anything is good. Thus, "Is it good to be happy?" is a sensible open question no matter how strongly we believe that it is good to be happy.

One final example: Moore takes Mill to hold that "good" means "pleasant." If "good" meant "pleasant," then whenever we had a sentence which contained the word "good," we could substitute the word "pleasant" without any loss of meaning, because the two are identical in meaning. If I were to say, for example, "Exercise is good," I should be able to substitute "Exercise is pleasant" without any loss of meaning. But, according to Moore, we can always ask, "Even if exercise is pleasant, is it good?" If good just meant pleasant, there would be no open question at all. To ask if something pleasant is good would be tantamount to asking if something pleasant is pleasant. Moore does not take this argument to refute Mill's utilitarianism, but he does conclude that Mill's analysis of "good" is mistaken.

There are several possible responses to Moore's line of argument, some of which were anticipated in our discussion of Perry. First, Moore's claim that "good" in *ordinary* language cannot be equated with any naturalistic term (or terms) seems flawless. However, most naturalists have probably not thought otherwise. They have regarded the great body of ethical terms, such as "good," "right," and "duty," to be vague, ill-defined words in ordinary language and thus unsuited to rigorous ethical theory. They hold that words such as "good" and "right" therefore need a clarifying and even revisionary definition. Any substituted meaning will not be entirely the same as the original, and yet, closer examination will show the revisionary meaning to be adequate for purposes of ethical theory. Mill himself made such a suggestion, and Perry quite explicitly maintains that his purpose is to refine or sharpen value terms on the basis of a theoretical analysis of their meanings. Accordingly, Perry offers his definitions of value terms as revisions of the ordinary understandings of such terms. As was seen previously, Perry dismisses Moore's argument in these words:

> Theory of value is in search of a *preferred meaning*. The problem is to define, that is, *give a meaning* to the term, either by selecting from its existing meanings, or by *creating a new meaning*.*

One might say that Perry proposes to do with "good" precisely what Moore warns against (perhaps fallaciously) through his example of a physicist's changing the meaning of "yellow" by linking it to wave vibrations. Perry and any similarly revisionary naturalist thus can reply that Moore is entirely correct in everything that he says in the open-question argument (which applies to ordinary language), but is entirely wrong in his interpretation of naturalism (which rejects ordinary language for theoretical reasons). The naturalist never supposes that theoretical definitions of value predicates accurately capture ordinary meanings; but this discrepancy provides no reason for not adopting the proposed definitions. Perry would no doubt find Moore's example of "yellow" absurd, for physicists have ample justification for giving "yellow" a revised meaning in light of a compelling physical theory about vibrations. Thus the naturalists accuse Moore of begging the question by failing to appreciate that theoretical revision was their objective all along, not mere analysis of value language. Moore argues that it is *fallacious* to assimilate or reduce goodness to some other property, but perhaps the fairest procedure is to determine whether any given naturalist is correct in arguing that goodness *should* be reconceived by identifying it with some particular natural property. If so, the naturalist must first be allowed to speak his or her piece before the soundness of the claims advanced can be determined.

Hume's Argument about Facts and Values

Attention will now be turned to the relation of facts and values, and to Hume's argument in particular. From the discussion in Chapter 9, we know that both factual and evaluative reasons are commonly cited in defending moral views. An appeal to both is made, for example, in the judgment, "Refusing a bone-marrow transplant in order to please one's wife and mother is wrong because of the *fact* that it will kill another person." This "fact" clearly functions as a justifying reason. However, the moral contention that dynamiting laboratories is wrong does not (obviously, anyway) rest on fact alone. Underlying the contention is the claim that "acts which intentionally kill innocent people are wrong," and this is a value statement.

*Ralph Barton Perry, *Realms of Value* (Cambridge, Mass.: Harvard University Press, 1954), pp. 2 ff. [Italics added.]

Many kinds of facts and values are commonly appealed to in the context of a single argument or controversy. The facts in the Shimp case, for example, are historical ("Disagreements have always divided this family"), psychological ("Shimp just can't face his wife's rejection"), and medical ("Without a transplant McFall will die"). The values functioning as justifying reasons may be equally diverse and need not always be moral values, even though they may be closely connected to moral reasons. They can, for instance, be legal ("No one can be required in American law to submit to surgery") or religious ("God demands that one sacrifice for one's relatives and friends").

It initially seems only too obvious that there are stark differences between factual judgments and value judgments. If someone says, "Students in American universities generally turn away from religion during their college years," it is testable whether and to what extent this factual judgment is true or false. Both the methods and the facts that govern its truth or falsity are understood. If, however, someone adds that this state of affairs is "tragic" or "sinful" or "morally evil," a value judgment has been introduced, and it is far less clear what evidence could be adduced to show the truth or falsity of such a statement, if indeed it is true or false. It is also unclear that facts have any bearing on decisions of whether to accept such judgments. Yet, people constantly make strong assertions that they believe correct by using such value terms as "evil," "good," "right," "duty," and "virtue." How are we to interpret these so-called value predicates? And what are "facts" and "values"?

While this matter is controversial, a fact may be assumed to be an empirically confirmable or falsifiable statement about some aspect of the world. Such a statement either describes or asserts the existence of some event or object. Its objective is presumably to say what is true, and factual statements are thus either true or false. A value, by contrast, is taken to be an evaluative statement or judgment concerning what is, for example, good, right, or virtuous. (In many, but not all, cases, value judgments are concerned with what therefore ought to be the case.) It is unclear whether such judgments are true or false. "Robert McFall died in June of 1978" is a factual statement, while "Robert McFall died courageously" and "His cousin Shimp ought to have undergone further testing" are evaluative statements, though not necessarily moral evaluations. The last two statements appraise and assess events, while the first statement merely describes some aspect of the event and does not appraise or assess it.

While nothing is more common in the attempt to justify a moral position than appealing to such facts and values, there are problems about *justifying* moral views (or evaluative views) by appeal merely to facts. In a much debated passage in his philosophy, Hume raises this problem as follows.

DAVID HUME

"Is" and "Ought"*

Reason is the discovery of truth or falshood. Truth or falshood consists in an agreement or disagreement either to the *real* relations of ideas, or to *real* existence and matter of fact. Whatever, therefore, is not susceptible of this agreement or disagreement, is incapable of being true or false, and can never be an object of our reason. . . .

As reason can never immediately prevent or produce any action by contradicting or approving of it, it cannot be the source of the distinction betwixt moral good and evil, which are found to have that influence. Actions may be laudable or blameable; but they cannot be reasonable or unreasonable. . . . Moral distinctions, therefore, are not the offspring of reason. . . .

Nor does this reasoning only prove, that morality consists not in any relations, that are the objects of science; but if examin'd, will prove with equal certainty, that it consists not in any *matter of fact,* which can be discover'd by the understanding. This is the *second* part of our argument; and if it can be made evident, we may conclude, that morality is not an object of reason. But can there be any difficulty in proving, that vice and virtue are not matters of fact, whose existence we can infer by reason? Take any action allow'd to be vicious: Wil-

ful murder, for instance. Examine it in all lights, and see if you can find that matter of fact, or real existence, which you call *vice.* In which-ever way you take it, you find only certain passions, motives, volitions and thoughts. There is no other matter of fact in the case. . . .

I cannot forbear adding to these reasonings an observation, which may, perhaps, be found of some importance. In every system of morality, which I have hitherto met with, I have always remark'd, that the author proceeds for some time in the ordinary way of reasoning, and establishes the being of a God, or makes observations concerning human affairs; when of a sudden I am surpriz'd to find, that instead of the usual copulations of propositions, *is,* and *is not,* I meet with no proposition that is not connected with an *ought,* or an *ought not.* This change is imperceptible; but is, however, of the last consequence. For as this *ought,* or *ought not,* expresses some new relation or affirmation, 'tis necessary that it shou'd be observ'd and explain'd; and at the same time that a reason should be given, for what seems altogether inconceivable, how this new relation can be a deduction from others, which are entirely different from it. But as authors do not commonly use this precaution, I shall presume to recommend it to the readers; and am persuaded, that this small attention wou'd subvert all the vulgar systems of morality, and let us see, that the distinction of vice and virtue is not founded merely on the relations of objects, nor is perceiv'd by reason.

*From David Hume, *A Treatise of Human Nature,* L. A. Selby-Bigge, ed., 3d ed. rev. by P. H. Nidditch (Oxford, England: Oxford University Press, 1978), pp. 458, 468–470.

Hume is arguing (or at least may reasonably be interpreted as arguing) that anyone who tries to move in an ethical argument from purely factual premises—so-called "is" statements—to purely evaluative conclusions—so-called "ought" statements—owes us an explanation of how this move can be made. It has very often been asserted in philosophy that as a matter of logic, "ought" statements cannot be deduced from "is" statements. According to this common line of thought, when presenting a moral argument one must somehow include "ought" statements in one's premises independently of factual citations if one is to have any hope of having "oughts" in one's conclusion. For example, one can cite the facts about Shimp's psychological state (his fears and feelings of deference to his wife) and family history (of disagreements), but from those facts nothing ensues about what Shimp ought to do until further (value-based) premises are added—premises such as "Shimp ought to follow his wife's directives" or "Shimp shouldn't do anything for a family that already dislikes him."

One who holds with Hume that a gap separates facts from values asserts that (purely) factual statements do not *entail* moral statements. This gap between facts and values, the "is" and the "ought," may be called the "entailment gap," and it is generally agreed in contemporary philosophy that this gap prevails; that is, it is agreed that there is a logical gap between factual statements and evaluative statements, and thus that "ought" statements cannot be logically deduced from statements of fact. This point about logic, however, is not decisive as a point about justification, and it is not at all agreed that values cannot ultimately be justified in terms of purely factual premises, as we have seen in studying naturalism.

It follows from Moore's theory of definition and analysis of value terms that no list of facts or descriptions of what is the case could ever determine what ought to be the case or what is good. It is this contention that relates his open-question argument to Hume's argument about facts and values. Moore and his followers in effect maintain that it is fallacious to deduce value statements from factual statements, because value predicates are not identical in meaning with factual predicates. Therefore, no factual term entails a value term, and no factual judgment entails a value judgment (one way to characterize the entailment gap).

The following example of an argument illustrates the problem that concerns both Moore and Hume:

McFall cannot survive without Shimp's bone marrow.
Therefore, Shimp ought to donate his bone marrow.

Here, an "ought" statement is allegedly derived from an "is" statement, but it is unclear how the "derivation" is grounded. Shimp himself did not make this inference, and it hardly seems to follow as a matter of logic. Indeed, so far as logic is concerned, it is no worse to draw from this premise the conclusion "Shimp ought not to donate his bone marrow." The sheer fact that McFall cannot survive is not alone logically powerful enough to entail anything about what Shimp ought to do. A further value premise is needed to make the argument valid, as is illustrated by the following example:

McFall cannot survive without Shimp's bone marrow.

Everyone ought to help others survive through transplant donations involving minimal risk.

Therefore, Shimp ought to donate his bone marrow.

By adding a new value premise, it is possible to deduce a value conclusion; a value conclusion is thus derived from a factual premise together with a value premise. The new value premise bridges the (logical) gap between a factual premise and a value conclusion. But, prior to adding the value premise, it was possible to assert the first premise while denying the conclusion, and no use of logic alone could convince us otherwise.

If correct, this important argument seems to show that naturalism is mistaken, for the naturalist holds that value judgments are a species of factual judgments. But is the argument correct? It has been noted that it is compelling both as a logical thesis and as a claim about ordinary language (though "descriptivists" challenge the latter view, as will be seen below). Once again, however, it is possible to adopt Perry's strategy and to revise our value terms so as to turn them by definition into factual terms. If "right action," for example, were defined by a naturalist as "any action that helps others survive or promotes their welfare," then the argument about Shimp's obligations could be accepted on purely naturalistic grounds. Moreover, it would do no good in this case to object that the naturalist's definition is mistaken as a matter of ordinary language; it is a *naturalistic* definition, and thus the objection would simply beg the question. Accordingly, Perry's response to his critics, as discussed previously, also qualifies as one form of response to Hume and to Moore. As will now be seen, however, this response may not be entirely satisfactory.

INTUITIONISM

Those opposed to naturalism may collectively be referred to as "antinaturalists." Antinaturalists believe that evaluative statements are not factual statements, and that value predicates are not definable in naturalistic terms. One influential type of antinaturalism is "intuitionism," an alternative theory that will now be explored. (Intuitionism is sometimes referred to as "nonnaturalism." It is best to avoid this term, however, because of its subtle but false suggestion that nonnaturalism covers *all* theories that are not naturalistic.)

While intuitionists agree with naturalists that value predicates are attributed to subjects in moral judgments, they regard value properties as distinct in kind from factual properties. Thus, they believe that terms such as "good," "right," and "courage" do not refer to something that can be known through sense experience or through the empirical methods of the social sciences. One can check the hardness of setting concrete by pressing one's finger on its surface or test for lying through a lie-detector machine, but no such method is or could be available for value properties. To take a further example, if I say, "Pumpkin pie is orange," then I have cited a natural property of pumpkin pie. However, intuitionists argue, statements such as "Pumpkin pie is good" assert no parallel natural property. Things that are good have the *property* of goodness, but there is no way to test empirically for this property, and in this critical respect, goodness is unlike a natural property.

"What is the property of goodness?" ask intuitionists. Is it visible? Tangible? How shall we characterize it and analyze it? Intuitionists argue that any proposition of the form "*X* is good" refers to a unique property (namely, goodness), and when we speak of something as "good," we are ascribing this property to it. We cannot, however, define "good" through other terms in the dictionary; we can say only that "good" refers to goodness, which is an ultimate, unobservable, untestable, and unanalyzable property. In a noteworthy passage in recent philosophy rivaling his related views on the naturalistic fallacy, G. E. Moore expressed this view as follows:

> If I am asked "What is good?" my answer is that good is good, and that is the end of the matter. Or if I am asked "How is good to be defined?" my answer is that it cannot be defined, and that is all I have to say about it. . . .
>
> My point is that "good" is a simple notion, just as "yellow" is a simple notion; that, just as you cannot, by any manner of means, explain to any one who does not already know it, what yellow is, so you cannot explain what good is. . . . You can give a definition of a horse, because a horse has many different properties and qualities, all of which you can enumerate. But when you have enumerated them all, when you have reduced a horse to his simplest terms, then you can no longer define those terms. . . . But yellow and good, we say, are not complex: they are notions of that simple kind, out of which definitions are composed and with which the power of further defining ceases.*

Because goodness cannot be directly experienced in sensory terms, Moore labels it "nonnatural." His general view is that "good" names the simple property "goodness" which is shared by all things that are good. Since the property is simple (noncomplex), the word is indefinable (not analyzable into smaller units). Value judgments can be true or false on this intuitionistic theory, because subjects referred to as good, virtuous, etc., either do or do not have the value property attributed to them. Intuitionists, of course, disagree with the naturalist's contention that "ought" statements can be directly derived from "is" statements. Because value premises are themselves considered fundamental, there is no temptation to search for nonevaluative premises from which they can be derived.

One critical question about intuitionism is, "How can it be *known* that a particular value judgment is either *true or false?*" Since value judgments cannot be supported

*G. E. Moore, *Principia Ethica* (Cambridge, England: Cambridge University Press, 1903), pp. 6–8.

by factual evidence—the empirical method of discovering truth—what method could there be for testing the correctness of a value judgment? Intuitionists answer this challenge by arguing that basic value principles are known to be true or false by intuition or self-evidence. To use a favored mathematical analogy involving self-evidence and intuition: Just as we intuitively see that if a triangle is equilateral, then it is equiangular, so we see that if an act is the keeping of a promise, then it is right. The claim is that we directly apprehend the presence of a value property without the aid of any form of direct sensory experience or empirical testing. This view is familiar in the abstract to all people who know the United States Declaration of Independence, which asserts, "We hold these truths to be self-evident."

Perhaps the intuitionist theory of evidence and justification can best be explained by an analogy (and it is strictly an analogy) to religious theories of divine revelation. Considering that a fundamental religious proposition—a divine commandment, say— is known to be authoritative and ought therefore to be followed, religious leaders have for centuries maintained that such claims are revealed truths. Unlike knowledge acquired by tasting, touching, surveying opinions by telephone, performing an experiment, or looking at detecting instruments, knowledge of theological truths is thus said to be gained by a unique method of knowing (i.e., revelation). Analogously, intuitionists hold that directly apprehending the truth of moral principles is a method unto itself. The principle that "one ought not to harm an innocent person intentionally" provides an example. We do not feel, see, touch, taste, or otherwise empirically experience the quality of wrongness, according to the intuitionist; rather, we immediately grasp the truth of the statement and are directly aware of the wrongness of the acts it prohibits.

At times in the history of philosophy, this view has been the dominant one in ethical theory. Major philosophers have suggested that we possess a mental faculty of moral intuition, and that through this faculty we come to apprehend the moral truths that save our moral principles from being the products of mere guesswork or subjective feeling. In this tradition, many analogies have been made to mathematical thinking, where basic truths are said to be intuitively known with certainty and to be obvious to any person of requisite mathematical background and development. W. D. Ross, who was studied in Chapter 5, is a modern exponent of this traditional point of view (as is A. C. Ewing in the next selection). He holds that the basic principles of ethics are known only after a person has achieved an appropriate stage of moral development or maturity. Just as a scientist can "see" or "interpret" many things that baffle a nonscientist, so a person of moral experience can "see" the rightness, wrongness, or virtuousness of basic moral principles. (This is reminiscent of Aristotle's account of practical wisdom, but Aristotle can hardly be counted among the ethical intuitionists, as was earlier noted.)

Even where there may appear to be unresolvable moral disagreements, the problem, according to intuitionists, may simply be that disputants are at different stages of moral development. As in mathematics, self-evident propositions require reflection and insight. Even the greatest mathematicians had to be instructed in basic mathematics by others, and there is no reason, according to Ross, why we should trust less in reason and its inner capacities when it comes to morality than we trust a mathematical axiom. In both domains, he says, we accept propositions that cannot be proved and that need no proof.

The discussion of intuitionism thus far may now be summarized. The intuitionist supports the following theses:

1. Basic terms in moral and all evaluative statements refer to nonnatural properties (a thesis about the metaphysics of morals).
2. Moral principles are intuitively or self-evidently discovered to be true or false (a thesis about moral epistemology).
3. Nonnatural properties are objective, and evaluative statements are either true or false.
4. "Ought" statements cannot be derived from "is" statements.

Persons not attracted to intuitionism have always been greatly puzzled as to why anyone would believe it. It seems to be a theory on the basis of which anything at all can be justified, including highly prejudiced conclusions; and it seems so opposed to the forms of moral reasoning and justification that were discussed in Chapter 9 that many have regarded it as an abandonment of critical thinking about morality. Far from providing a basis on which moral beliefs could be known or ultimately justified, intuitionism has struck many as a way of treating mere opinion as if it were justified and true. While intuitionists have maintained that only *general* moral principles are known intuitively, there is plenty of leeway for this criticism even when confined to the level of general principles. Consider, for example, the claim (made by McFall's attorney) that one person may validly be compelled to undergo a transplant procedure in order to "help secure the well-being of other members of society." If this statement is held to be a moral principle justified on the basis of intuition, does it amount to anything more than mere opinionated rationalization? Is there not a need for further justification by appeal to nonintuitionistic principles?

Moreover, it has often been suggested that intuitionism is worthless for arbitrating differences in a context of moral disagreement—where justification is of course most needed. Here one person's intuition seems as good as the next person's. If Shimp's supporters in the transplant case argue that their intuitions inform them that there is no valid moral or judicial grounds requiring a person "to secure the well-being of others," how could it possibly be determined that one party is right and the other wrong? To those who accept this criticism, intuitionism provides no method of knowing moral truths or justifying a position, for intuition is virtually the antithesis of objective methods of justification. Thus, there is no remaining assistance in the attempt to arbitrate moral disagreements.

Despite these serious and important reservations, it is possible to explain the appeal of intuitionism to generations of philosophers. The best way to understand intuitionism is to view it as a general theoretical approach toward the resolution of timeless problems in moral philosophy. One obvious feature of moral discourse, noticed by naturalists and intuitionists alike, is that it appears to involve objectively true or false assertions. As noted in Chapter 2, merely believing that something is right or virtuous does not make it so, and there is a tendency to think that some judgments and actions can be shown to be immoral, misguided, and flatly mistaken. The intuitionist is keenly sensitive to these features of moral thought, and at the same time knows that mere subjective opinion about right and wrong justifies nothing at all. For example, one who believes Shimp cowardly or morally in the wrong does not believe Shimp's moral views are as justified as, say, the moral views of his children; and none of Shimp's avowed beliefs will alter this firm conviction. But, because the intuitionist regards the naturalist belief in natural moral properties as hopelessly indefensible and at the same time wants to preserve objectivity and justifiability, the idea of a nonnatural objective property known by intuition becomes powerfully attractive. As was seen earlier, naturalists allege that theirs is the *only* theory by which objectivity and nonarbitrary justification are preserved. This claim is clearly false, according to the intuitionist, for naturalism can be rejected while holding to the truth and justifiability of moral statements. The intuitionist appeal, then, is to something beyond what is subjectively believed, and thus to the objective nonnatural properties of things that make judgments true or false.

The viability of intuitionism as an ethical theory is of course crucially dependent on the ability of its proponents to defend it against its critics. In the following selection, a leading intuitionist presents such a defense.

A. C. EWING

The Role of Intuition*

Probably the principal reason which makes people inclined to deny the objectivity of ethics is the fact that in ethical argument we are very soon brought to a point where we have to fall back on intuition, so that disputants are placed in a situation where there are just two conflicting intuitions between which there seem to be no means of deciding. However, it is not only ethics but all reasoning which presupposes intuition. I cannot argue A, [therefore] B, [therefore] C without seeing that A entails B and B entails C, and this must either be seen immediately or require a fur-

*From A. C. Ewing, *The Definition of Good* (New York: Macmillan Company, 1947), chap. 1, pp. 25–27.

ther argument. If it is seen immediately, it is a case of intuition; if it has to be established by a further argument, this means that another term, D, must be interpolated between A and B such that A entails D and D entails B, and similarly with B and C, but then the same question arises about A entailing D, so that sooner or later we must come to something which we see intuitively to be true, as the process of interpolation cannot go on *ad infinitum*. We cannot therefore, whatever we do, get rid of intuition if we are to have any valid inference at all. It may, however, be said that in subjects other than ethics people at any rate agree in their intuitions. But outside mathematics or formal logic this is by no means universally true. There is frequent disagreement about matters of fact as to what has happened or will happen or concerning the causes of something, and when we have exhausted the arguments on a given point in these matters there still remains a difference between the ways in which these arguments are regarded by the disputants. In any science where you cannot prove your conclusions but only make them more or less probable there will be different estimates as to the balance of probability. . . . In ethics you have to balance different values against each other in order to decide what you ought to do, . . . and in order to do this you must rely at some point or other on an estimate of their strength which cannot itself be further justified by mediate reasoning. Yet, when everything has been said in the way of argument, people may not all agree. Some will attribute more weight to one consideration, others to another, as they do in ethical questions about what is the right action in a given case. Our decision as to which of two probable arguments is the stronger may be influenced by other arguments in turn; but in order to deal with the situation rationally we must also estimate the weight of these other arguments, so that in the last resort it is a matter of insight into their nature which cannot be settled by other arguments *ad infinitum.* . . .

It is the case here that . . . we are often confronted with a situation in which we either see or do not see, and cannot logically prove, that what we seem to see is true. Yet we cannot surely therefore conclude that the . . . propositions under discussion are really only propositions about the state of mind of the people who assert them, or that they are neither true nor false, or that we have no justification whatever for believing any of them!

We must therefore have intuition, and in a subject where infallibility is not attainable, intuitions will sometimes disagree. Some philosophers indeed prefer not to call them intuitions when they are wrong, but then the problem will be to distinguish real from ostensible intuitions, since people certainly sometimes think they see intuitively what is not true. . . .

The methods I have suggested will not always be successful, but then is there any sphere in which human efforts always do succeed? Even the methodology of physical science cannot lay down rules which will guarantee that any scientist can make discoveries or show him in detail in advance how to prove to others the truth of the discoveries when made. I am not claiming that it is possible in practice to remove all ethical differences, but how do we know that it could not be done if there were a will on each side to listen to what the other had to say and an intelligence to discern the best methods to adopt in order to facilitate a decision? A person cannot be brought into agreement even with the established truths of science if he will not listen to what the scientist says, and there is no reason to think even with ethical intuitions that there are not describable processes by which any cause of error can on principle be removed. I insert the words "on principle" simply because it will still often be the case that none of the disputants thinks of the right way of removing the error or that the person in error will not or cannot take it, as also occurs in disputes about questions of fact outside ethics.

Some skepticism about intuitionist reasoning was previously expressed, but other reservations about an intuitionism such as Ewing's now deserve consideration. First, to what is one committed in believing that there are simple, nonnatural properties? What evidence is there that moral discourse refers to such properties, let alone evidence that they exist? Intuitionists seem burdened with a peculiar and indefensible theory of language according to which moral judgments ascribe properties that are mysterious; and the faculty of intuition involved seems no less shrouded in mystery. The difficulty here is not merely the inability to find goodness through a sensory experience of it. Many properties and concepts cannot be confirmed empirically by sensory experience—e.g., mathematical and logical concepts. The difficulty is that there is no way to find simple value properties at all, much less to discover them objectively; and this problem makes it difficult to accept the claim that such properties exist. Moreover (as will be seen below), value language has numerous functions, not all of which *ascribe properties* to things. For example, moral discourse may function to guide action, to commend, and to express attitudes. An intuitionist could of course hold that moral discourse has all these functions and nonetheless refers to nonnatural properties; but this assertion seems an ad hoc and unconvincing response.

Second, questions may be raised about the intuitionist's claims to *know* something to be the case. To say that one knows something is not only to say that it is true and believed, but that one has a method or means for justifying one's claim. There are many such means that entitle one to make a knowledge claim. Presumably, the intuitionist's means of knowing something is intuition itself. Yet, unaided intuition seems a matter of mere belief that does not confer any additional entitlement. In other words, if one cannot show that an intuition is something distinct from a strongly held belief, then one does not seem entitled to the knowledge claim so critical to intuitionism. We also commonly retract our knowledge claims when new evidence indicates that a once-held belief is false. But what conceivably could show an intuition false except a counterintuition? This question leads back to the previously discussed problem of how intuitionism could hope to resolve competing moral intuitions.

NONCOGNITIVISM

Many philosophers have rejected both naturalism and intuitionism and have adopted, instead, a theory known as "noncognitivism" (or, in an older terminology, the "emotive theory"). Controversy between these three approaches often turns on an understanding of different functions served by the language of morals. Each theory might be said to develop a metaethical account of the meaning of *moral* language and to rely on an underlying *general* theory of the meaning of words. In particular, naturalists and intuitionists both believe that the language of morals reports something to be the case and has a function of referring to a property. While differing over *how* moral judgments are known to be true, they both believe that moral propositions *are* either true or false. These two theories are cognitivist theories, then, for they believe in moral knowledge and truth. Noncognitivism, by contrast, denies that moral language reports something to be the case, that moral assertions are either true or false, and that there is moral knowledge.

The noncognitivist sees a quite different function for moral (and all value) discourse. Sometimes value language can be used to express our feelings directly, as when we say, "Ah, how sweet it is!" after a victory, or "More, more!" after hearing a stirring violin performance. Sometimes, we use moral language for exhorting, pleading, or expressing our feelings; on other occasions, we are attempting to persuade others; and on still other occasions, we issue commands. In carrying out these objectives, say noncognitivists, we are not making true or false claims, not reporting or knowing something to be the case, and not referring to value properties. It is the element of not knowing that gives this approach the distinctive title "noncognitivism."

The following table summarizes the differences between cognitivists and noncognitivists:

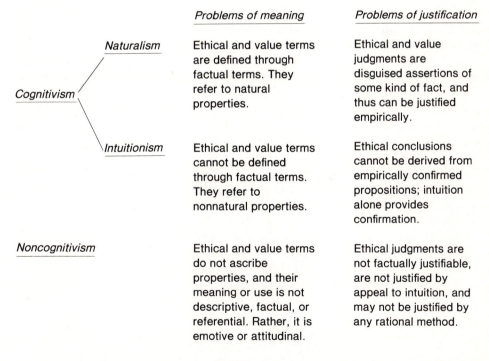

		Problems of meaning	*Problems of justification*
	Naturalism	Ethical and value terms are defined through factual terms. They refer to natural properties.	Ethical and value judgments are disguised assertions of some kind of fact, and thus can be justified empirically.
Cognitivism	*Intuitionism*	Ethical and value terms cannot be defined through factual terms. They refer to nonnatural properties.	Ethical conclusions cannot be derived from empirically confirmed propositions; intuition alone provides confirmation.
Noncognitivism		Ethical and value terms do not ascribe properties, and their meaning or use is not descriptive, factual, or referential. Rather, it is emotive or attitudinal.	Ethical judgments are not factually justifiable, are not justified by appeal to intuition, and may not be justified by any rational method.

Noncognitivism and the problems of facts and values exposed in this diagram have recently been major issues in both continental European and Anglo-American moral philosophy. The movement often called "existentialism," as represented by the selection from Sartre in Chapter 9, is united with the followers of Hume in holding that no property possessed by a state of affairs determines by itself the *value* of that state of affairs. "Noncognitivism," then, is a quite general label covering a wide variety of theories, some of which have little in common. They are all united, of course, by their acceptance of the view that ethical judgments are not fact-asserting and are noncognitive; but beyond this initial point of agreement, opinion diverges sharply over the role, if any, for reason and rational justification in moral argument. Thus, in order to discuss this diverse array of theories fairly, each form of noncognitivism must be treated separately.

The Emotive Theory

At once the starkest and most extreme of the noncognitivist views is *emotivism*—a theory that has an extraordinarily strong appeal to many nonphilosophers. This theory, once brought to notoriety by Alfred Ayer, holds that moral utterances are like ejaculations or displays of emotion. "Abortion, boo" and "Women's rights, yeah" function in this theory as models of moral disapproval and approval, and hence as models of moral wrongness (in the case of abortion) and moral rightness (in the case of women's rights). A sentence such as "Shimp's children did what they ought to have done" expresses feelings of approval or disapproval, but such judgments are neither true nor false. They also cannot rationally be defended, because they are merely expressions of emotional disapproval. The emotive theory is not always stated strictly in terms of emotion, for some emotivists believe that moral language expresses ambitions, will, commitments, or personal decisions. Nonetheless, the result is much the same: Moral utterances are neither objective nor cognitive, and there is no role for reason in moral expression and argument.

To say, however, that there is no role for *reason* is not to say that there is no role for *argument* in an emotive theory. On the contrary, emotivists such as Ayer recognize that we are forever trying to resolve disputes by persuading other persons to accept our point of view. In such contexts, say emotivists, we are operating on the assumption that the persons with whom we are disputing already share our more fundamental commitments. Hence we hope to point out certain facts, anecdotes, motives, or beliefs that we think the person may not know about or may have overlooked. In the attempt to persuade Shimp in the transplant case, for example, many appeals were made to McFall's serious medical condition and his remoteness from old family quarrels. The hope was that Shimp was a person who would respond to certain kinds of appeals because of his own commitments to morality and family. McFall's explanation that "he was killing me" seems calculated to persuade Shimp in this way. Since disputants in moral arguments are generally shaped by similar environments and often hold similar basic attitudes, these attempts at persuasion frequently meet with success—though, of course, McFall and his family were not successful. However, if we ever run into a fundamental moral disagreement—one in attitude, emotion, or commitment—then emotivists claim that facts cannot resolve the dispute, and we must abandon all attempts to convince an opponent by argument.

The Attitude Theory

A second and less extreme theory is also frequently designated an emotive theory, yet it is so different from Ayer's theory that it deserves separate treatment and a different label. It will here be referred to as the "attitude theory." This account was developed by C. L. Stevenson, who held that moral judgments express speakers' attitudes and are generally uttered with the intention of evoking similar attitudes in others. Stevenson adopts a pragmatic or psychological account of meaning that clearly distinguishes his theory from earlier emotive theories. His technique is to show a dual, interconnected use for value terms, and he refers to the two constituents of this usage as the *emotive meaning* and the *descriptive meaning* of value terms. The emotive meaning is the power or tendency a word has acquired, through historical association in emotional situations, to express emotional attitudes or to evoke effective responses. Examples are "death sentence," as used by Shimp's mother, and "socialized medicine," which in some hearers evokes powerful negative responses and in others powerful positive attitudes. The descriptive meaning is the tendency of a word to affect cognition (after a process of conditioning in the proper use of the word), i.e., the tendency to express a characterization of something. "Cousin" and "cranial hemorrhage" are nonvalue terms which illustrate this descriptive function, though they too can have an attached emotive meaning.

Stevenson argues that value terms need never be completely emotive in the way the terms "alas" and "hurrah" are. Consider, for example, the value predicate "good." He contends that sometimes "This is good" has the descriptive meaning of "This has qualities or relations *X, Y, Z.*" For example, a good college president may be one who (*X*) is an industrious executive, (*Y*) is honest and tactful with university personnel, and (*Z*) commands wide respect for his or her intellectual abilities. This usage might be thought to constitute a *purely* descriptive use of value predicates, but Stevenson rejects this possibility too. His claim is that the descriptive part of the pattern (i.e., the possession of properties *X, Y,* and *Z*) is *always* accompanied, either explicitly or implicitly, by a "laudatory emotive meaning which permits it to express the speaker's approval, and tends to evoke the approval of the hearer."*

Stevenson admits that his views about the meaning of value statements reduce the descriptive element to a minimum. But he also says that in some cases, such as the example of the college president, reference to attitudes of approval may be only "suggested" and not central to the value judgment. Stevenson seems to mean that descriptive meaning here overshadows, but does not entirely displace, emotive meaning. In general, he argues that there is a continuum in our usage of value terms, from pure emotive expressiveness to nearly pure descriptive reference. There is a linguistic requirement that we either impoverish or enrich the descriptive meaning in value judgments, he says, but it is an "elastic requirement of 'natural English usage,'" and the basic emphasis may broadly fluctuate between descriptive and emotive meanings even for the same value predicate. Nonetheless, Stevenson often writes as if descriptive meaning plays

---

*C. L. Stevenson, *Ethics and Language* (New Haven, Conn.: Yale University Press, 1944), pp. 9, 33, 207 ff.

only a subordinate role in value judgments. He stresses, instead, the role of attitude, emotive meaning, persuasive definition, and subtle influence. Notice, for example, where the prize ("major use") is awarded in the following statement:

> Doubtless there is always *some* element of description in ethical judgments, but this is by no means all. Their major use is not to indicate facts but to *create an influence*. Instead of merely describing people's interests, they *change* or *intensify* them. They *recommend* an interest in an object, rather than state that the interest already exists. ... *Reasons* which support your ethical judgment are simply a means of facilitating your influence.*

Stevenson draws an important distinction between disagreement in attitude and disagreement in belief. Disagreements in belief concern what is in fact the case, while disagreements in attitude turn on some evaluation of a state of affairs. In the transplant case, Stevenson would regard virtually all the disagreements as ones in attitude, not in belief. In ethics generally, disagreements occur when there are conflicting attitudes (which are of course neither true nor false), not when there are conflicting beliefs (which are either true or false); beliefs can modify attitudes only to the indeterminate extent that attitudes depend on beliefs. Consider attitudes toward marriage, for example. A person may hold strong attitudes of approval toward the whole institution, but upon experiencing a failed marriage and seeing how a relationship can easily go sour, the person may change his or her attitude. The new attitude depends on the new beliefs, but neither the new nor the old attitude is true or false. Stevenson develops this thought in the following classic expression of noncognitivism.

*C. L. Stevenson, "The Emotive Meaning of Ethical Terms," in *Facts and Values: Studies in Ethical Analysis* (New Haven, Conn.: Yale University Press, 1963), p. 16.

CHARLES L. STEVENSON

The Nature of Ethical Disagreement†

When people disagree about the value of something—one saying that it is good or right and another that it is bad or wrong—by what methods of argument or inquiry can their disagreement be resolved? Can

†From Charles L. Stevenson, "The Nature of Ethical Disagreement," *Sigma*, **8–9** (1948), as reprinted in *Facts and Values: Studies in Ethical Analysis* (New Haven, Conn.: Yale University Press, 1963), pp. 1–8.

it be resolved by the methods of science, or does it require methods of some other kind, or is it open to no rational solution at all?

The question must be clarified before it can be answered. And the word that is particularly in need of clarification, as we shall see, is the word "disagreement."

Let us begin by noting that "disagreement" has two broad senses: In the first sense it refers to what I shall call "disagreement in belief." This occurs when Mr. A believes *p*, when Mr. B believes *not-p*, or something incompatible with *p*, and when neither is content to let the belief of the other remain unchallenged. Thus doctors may disagree in belief about the causes of an illness; and friends may disagree in belief about the exact date on which they last met.

In the second sense the word refers to what I shall call "disagreement in attitude." This occurs when Mr. A has a favorable attitude to something, when Mr. B has an unfavorable or less favorable attitude to it, and when neither is content to let the other's attitude remain unchanged. The term "attitude" is here used in much the same sense that R. B. Perry uses "interest"; it designates any psychological disposition of being *for* or *against* something. Hence love and hate are relatively specific kinds of attitudes, as are approval and disapproval, and so on. . . .

Suppose that the representative of a union urges that the wage level in a given company ought to be higher—that it is only right that the workers receive more pay. The company representative urges in reply that the workers ought to receive no more than they get. Such an argument clearly represents a disagreement in attitude. The union is *for* higher wages; the company is *against* them, and neither is content to let the other's attitude remain unchanged. *In addition* to this disagreement in attitude, of course, the argument may represent no little disagreement in belief. Perhaps the parties disagree about how much the cost of living has risen and how much the workers are suffering under the present wage scale. Or perhaps they disagree about the company's earnings and the extent to which the company could raise wages and still operate at a profit. Like any typical ethical argument, then, this argument involves both disagreement in attitude and disagreement in belief.

It is easy to see, however, that the disagreement in attitude plays a unifying and predominating role in the argument. This is so in two ways:

In the first place, disagreement in attitude determines what beliefs are *relevant* to the argument. Suppose that the company affirms that the wage scale of fifty years ago was far lower than it is now. The union will immediately urge that this contention, even though true, is irrelevant. And it is irrelevant simply because information about the wage level of fifty years ago, maintained under totally different circumstances, is not likely to affect the present attitudes of either party. To be relevant, any belief that is introduced into the argument must be one that is likely to lead one side or the other to have a different attitude, and so reconcile disagreement in attitude. Attitudes are often functions of beliefs. We often change our attitudes to something when we change our beliefs about it; just as a child ceases to *want* to touch a live coal when he comes to *believe* that it will burn him. Thus in the present argument any beliefs that are at all likely to alter attitudes, such as those about the increasing cost of living or the financial state of the company, will be considered by both sides to be relevant to the argument. Agreement in belief on these matters may lead to agreement in attitude toward the wage scale. But beliefs that are likely to alter the attitudes of neither side will be declared irrelevant. They will have no bearing on the disagreement in attitude, with which both parties are primarily concerned.

In the second place, ethical argument usually terminates when disagreement in attitude terminates, even though a certain amount of disagreement in belief remains. Suppose, for instance, that the company and the union continue to disagree in belief about the increasing cost of living, but that the company, even so, ends by favoring the higher wage scale. The union will then be content to end the argument and will cease to press its point about living costs. It may bring up that point again, in some future argument of the same sort, or in urging the righteousness of its victory to the newspaper columnists; but for the moment the fact that the company has agreed in attitude is sufficient to terminate the argument. On the other hand: suppose that both parties agreed on all beliefs that were introduced into the argument, but even so continued to disagree in attitude. In that case neither party would feel that their dispute had been successfully terminated. They might look for other beliefs that could be introduced into the argument. They might use words to play on each other's emotions. They might agree (in attitude) to submit the case to arbitration, both feeling that a decision, even if strongly adverse to one party or the other, would be preferable to a continued impasse. Or, perhaps, they might abandon hope of settling their dispute by any peaceable means. . . .

Having discussed disagreement, we may turn to the broad question that was first mentioned, namely: By what methods of argument or inquiry may disagreement about matters of value be resolved?

It will be obvious that to whatever extent an argument involves disagreement in belief, it is open to the usual methods of the sciences. If these methods are the *only* rational methods for supporting beliefs—as I believe to be so, but cannot now take time to discuss—then scientific methods are the only rational methods for resolving the disagreement in *belief* that arguments about values may include.

But if science is granted an undisputed sway in reconciling beliefs, it does not thereby acquire, without qualification, an undisputed sway in reconciling attitudes. We have seen that arguments about values include disagreement in attitude, no

less than disagreement in belief, and that in certain ways the disagreement in attitude predominates. By what methods shall the latter sort of disagreement be resolved?

The methods of science are still available for that purpose, but only in an indirect way. Initially, these methods have only to do with establishing agreement in belief. If they serve further to establish agreement in attitude, that will be due simply to the psychological fact that altered beliefs may cause altered attitudes. Hence scientific methods are conclusive in ending arguments about values only to the extent that their success in obtaining agreement in belief will in turn lead to agreement in attitude.

In other words: the extent to which scientific methods can bring about agreement on values depends on the extent to which a commonly accepted body of scientific beliefs would cause us to have a commonly accepted set of attitudes.

How much is the development of science likely to achieve, then, with regard to values? To what extent *would* common beliefs lead to common attitudes? It is, perhaps, a pardonable enthusiasm to *hope* that science will do everything—to hope that in some rosy future, when all men know the consequences of their acts, they will all have common aspirations and live peaceably in complete moral accord. But if we speak not from our enthusiastic hopes but from our present knowledge, the answer must be far less exciting. We usually *do not know*, at the beginning of any argument about values, whether an agreement in belief, scientifically established, will lead to an agreement in attitude or not. It is logically possible, at least, that two men should continue to disagree in attitude even though they had all their beliefs in common, and even though neither had made any logical or inductive error, or omitted any relevant evidence. Differences in temperament, or in early training, or in social status, might make the men retain different attitudes even though both were possessed of the complete scientific truth. Whether this logical possibility is an empirical likelihood I shall not presume to say; but it is unquestionably a possibility that must not be left out of account.

To say that science can always settle arguments about value, we have seen, is to make this assumption: Agreement in attitude will always be consequent upon complete agreement in belief, and science can always bring about the latter. Taken as purely heuristic, this assumption has its usefulness. It leads people to discover the discrepancies in their beliefs and to prolong enlightening argument that *may* lead, as a matter of fact, from commonly accepted beliefs to commonly accepted attitudes. It leads people to reconcile their attitudes in a rational, permanent way, rather than by rhapsody or exhortation. But the assumption is *nothing more*, for present knowledge, than a heuristic maxim. It is wholly without any proper foundation of probability. I conclude, therefore, that scientific methods cannot be guaranteed the definite role in the so-called normative sciences that they may have in the natural sciences.

Despite his view that value judgments are neither true nor false, Stevenson obviously provides a role for reason or rational argument in ethics. Because attitudes depend to some extent on beliefs, the whole point of moral argument may be to change attitudes by citing beliefs that will have a psychological impact on attitudes. For example, if I disfavor restrictive legislation requiring all persons to wear seat belts in automobiles, I may be influenced heavily by the beliefs of others who cite new research indicating that thousands of lives and millions of dollars have been saved by such legislation. Moral "reasoning" occurs through the citation of such facts with the expressed intent of changing the attitudes (views) of others. Stevenson does not, however, regard moral arguments as *purely* factual, for the acceptance of new data itself depends on an attitude approving or favoring the use of the data in arguments. If one holds a negative attitude toward the research by means of which certain data are assembled, then one will not be impressed by the data and will never back down in an argument that employed the data findings. Of course, this characteristic is not unique to evaluative claims, because disagreements in belief too cannot be aided by new data unless an attitude prevails favoring use of such data.

Moral language thus has an appearance of objectivity and of factual justification, according to Stevenson, because facts may causally affect attitudes. Despite this appearance, reasons do not in the end justify moral statements or show them either true or false. Stevenson concludes that our *fundamental* moral judgments and principles rest on attitudes which may themselves lack the support of any factual beliefs—in which case there is no way that we can either be persuaded rationally to abandon them or provide an ultimate justification of them. However, one might argue that exactly the same problem infects disagreements in beliefs—a possibility Stevenson does not seriously entertain.

PRESCRIPTIVISM

In the last three or four decades, emotivism and the attitude theory, together with naturalism and intuitionism, have undergone sustained criticism and emendation in ethical theory. One view to emerge from these discussions, generally considered at least a first cousin to noncognitivism, is referred to as "prescriptivism." It too is associated largely with the name of a single philosopher, R. M. Hare. In developing his theory, Hare has modified his own views almost as much as he has criticized and modified the claims of his noncognitivist predecessors, and hence generalizations about his overall theory are dangerous. Nonetheless, a general description of his prescriptivism (one that relies at least as much on his early writings as on his later work*) will be attempted here.

Let us return momentarily to the naturalistic fallacy in order to appreciate the historical development of Hare's views. Many believe that one of Moore's great contributions was to show that value judgments are distinct from, and not reducible to, empirical judgments. Hare accepts this part of Moore's argument, but he resists Moore's assertion that value judgments report properties of things. This is precisely what Hare thinks they do not do. Accordingly, he sees Moore as having been led to the threshold of an adequate theory in morals, especially through his open-question argument against naturalism, but as having gone astray in then proposing intuitionism as a substitute.

Hare also follows Hume and other noncognitivists by distinguishing facts and values. Value judgments are seen as having a prescriptive or action-guiding function that is totally absent in purely factual judgments; and evaluative language in general is said to function to *commend* or *condemn* particular courses of action. The foundations of normative ethics as well as all value judgments are thus *prescriptive*. Factual discourse, by contrast, is not action-guiding, dealing, instead, with descriptions and causal explanations of human or natural phenomena. The statements in these two domains thus display an unbridgeable logical difference, according to prescriptivism.

To say that something is right or obligatory or good is, in the prescriptivist view, to attempt to guide choice and action by commending or condemning. Sometimes this objective is attempted in a subtle and almost caressing fashion; sometimes it is direct and blunt. But, in all cases, the language of values is prescriptive. Consider, for example, the recommendation of McFall's physician: "I recommend a bone-marrow transplant." The physician could have said, "You ought to have a bone-marrow transplant," without altering the content or objective of his message. This utterance is of course a nonmoral value judgment; but the language of values is everywhere the same for prescriptivism, whose program is to provide an account of value judgments in general. The moral judgments that "Shimp's mother was an evil influence" and that "No one ought to be forced to submit to an operation" conform to the same action-guiding and choice-instructing

*The explanation offered relies heavily on Hare's book *The Language of Morals* (Oxford, England: Oxford University Press, 1952) and assorted essays in response to critics of this work.

model. Such utterances commend or condemn certain actions and thereby guide us in deciding about our own rules, character traits, and behavior.

In Hare's view, moral language functions quite differently from language expressing an emotion or an attitude; a person who commends or condemns something uses specifiable *criteria* for value words, and thus can support value judgments by appeal to reasons. Several features of this prescriptivist doctrine merit consideration in more detail.

Meaning and Criteria

Hare focuses in particular on moral judgments that use the word "good." Above all other words, this one functions explicitly to commend, and so is especially important to the study of ethics and values. However, Hare points out, many other words in our language function similarly in certain contexts to commend or condemn. Consider the word "brilliant," for example, as used in the statement, "She is a brilliant student." To know whether a person is using this word to commend, one must examine the *context* of the statement to see if the word is actually serving this function.

Hare believes that the naturalists' great mistake lay in their supposition that a single set of characteristics attends every good thing, from which assumption they inferred that "good" means this set of characteristics. Hare challenges anyone to indicate what "good" means by pointing to a set of natural (or nonnatural) properties. Consider, for example, the statement, "That's a good strawberry." This assertion is not identical in meaning to "That's a strawberry, and it is sweet, juicy, firm, red, and large." These are factual properties which the strawberry possesses, and they often are the features leading us to say that a strawberry is good. Nonetheless, terms describing these factual properties do not mean what "good" means, and "good" cannot be reduced to a list of such properties. For one thing, says Hare, if a lengthy list were prepared of all the factual properties of strawberries—redness, sweetness, firmness, juiciness, etc.— then the strawberry would be described but not evaluated. Some term having commending power, such as "good," must be employed to serve the value function. If all value words are dropped, this commending power disappears with them.

Hare also argues that the general meaning of "good" is the same regardless of the context. Otherwise, we could not understand the commending force of the term in unfamiliar contexts. He therefore introduces an extremely important distinction between the *meaning* and the *criteria* of value terms. His suggestion is the following: The word "good" has a common meaning in all its uses, functioning as "the most general adjective of commendation." "Good" has this meaning in every context, regardless of the items involved in the evaluation. But, says Hare, while the meaning of "good" is always the same, the criteria of goodness shift from context to context and from type to type; the criteria for something's being a good cactus are different from the criteria of something's being a good sunset or a good surgical procedure. Learning the criteria of goodness applicable to a new class of items may always be a new lesson, but we are able to use "good" for entirely new classes of objects, and a different lesson in *meaning* is never involved once we understand the word's commending function. The *criteria* for the application of "good" of course do vary in relation to the class of objects being evaluated. Thus, the criteria of a good pencil are different from those of a good strawberry, but in both cases the meaning of "good" is that of commendation.

Hare qualifies this line of thought by arguing (in a way reminiscent of Stevenson) that words, such as "good," whose primary function is evaluative may in some limited contexts be used almost entirely as descriptive words. If I say, "This is a blue pencil," then I am stating a fact and using language descriptively. But when I say, "This is a good pencil," I may also be using the sentence primarily to describe, for I may be saying that the pencil has all the properties that pencils in working order have (it writes smoothly, has an eraser, the point does not break easily, etc.). This judgment proclaims that the criteria for good pencils are satisfied in this particular case, and thus the term "good" is not used *primarily* to commend.

Moral Justification

Hare's prescriptivism also offers an analysis of the justification of moral judgments that differs from that of his noncognitivist predecessors. It follows from the prescriptivist analysis of "good" that it is always appropriate to solicit a person's reasons for believing that something is good. Such a request asks explicitly for the item's good-making characteristics (and assumes implicitly that one has criteria for its goodness). Thus, "Why do you believe the judge's legal opinion was good?" may be answered by citing features of its structure, argument, and relation to past opinions. These features are good-making characteristics and are the reasons justifying one's belief. Such reasons will be confirmable by factual or conceptual investigation, because evaluated items either do or do not have such properties; but the choice of criteria will of course not be a factual matter. For example, "The judge in the case of the bone-marrow transplant gave a good legal argument" is a value judgment that can be justified by pointing to the features of legal justification that make arguments good under some assumed set of criteria—e.g., precedents in the law are followed, the judge does not let personal moral views interfere with the responsibilities of being a judge, the opinion is tightly formulated using strict definitions, etc. The initial *selection* of criteria of goodness—such as the assumed set of criteria in this case—depends on value judgment, but whether the properties satisfying the criteria are present in any given case is a matter not of values but of fact.

Any final or ultimate justification of value judgments or standards would of course involve *defending* one's criteria, not merely *appealing* to them—as was seen throughout Chapter 9 when discussing internal and external justifications. If, for example, one believes the characteristics of a good automobile are compactness, gas economy, maneuverability, standard transmission, a high rear bumper, and sleek lines, one's use of these criteria can be challenged. When the criteria are challenged and someone asks why one should not substitute such criteria as heavy weight, a stereo system, and a wide wheel base, one cannot go on pointing just to the compactness and gas economy in cars as an argument to meet the challenge. Rather, one must provide an argument for one's initial selection of criteria. This same problem attends the justification of ethical standards governing human conduct, which Hare refers to as "principles." Moral principles can be challenged, and it is always logically and morally appropriate to ask for a justification of even our ultimate standards of conduct (as was discussed in the concluding sections of Chapter 9).

How, then, does a prescriptivist suggest that we justify moral principles? This problem of justification can be phrased as "Why should one accept a principle as action-guiding?" In a well-known discussion of "decisions of principle," Hare considers how we learn about general action-guides. He points out that the "learning of principles" (Hare's expression) is not the learning of individual acts; in the case of principles, we learn to do acts of a certain kind in a certain kind of situation. For example, a teacher instructing someone to drive an automobile does not teach by saying, "Do this now." He or she teaches that whenever one reaches a particular level of speed or a particular kind of sign, a certain kind of act should be performed. Otherwise, a person would never learn to drive, for each individual act would have to be commanded on each separate occasion. However, says Hare, in most cases teaching cannot consist in merely getting a learner to perform faultlessly a fixed, habitual drill. In any but the most elementary kind of instruction, an opportunity must be provided for the learner to make decisions for himself or herself, and in so doing, to examine and sometimes to modify the principles being taught. Clever people can often find new and better ways of doing things; for this reason, we should think of principles as provisional. That is, one should be taught principles and how to use them, but with the tacit understanding that should one find better principles, one should be prepared to decide in favor of the new principles and to give up the old ones.

The factor of personal decision, Hare argues, is no less crucial to the *morally* good person than to the good driver. That is, one's moral principles are also provisional, and thus may require modification in unforeseen circumstances. Such decisions Hare refers to as "decisions of principle," because a principle is modified or a precedent set which is not adequately covered by an old principle or a set of principles. In ethics we are taught certain principles, but as we mature and encounter unanticipated circumstances, we begin to question our old principles and sometimes are forced to make decisions of principle. How, then, are we to justify the decisions we make in ethics? Ordinarily, says Hare, we justify our decisions by appeal to the probable effects of an action and to principles governing the action. But if we are asked for a full and complete justification (internal and external, as those terms are used in Chapter 9), we will deliberate about both effects and principles, as well as about the effects which invariably accompany the *use* of certain principles. Thus a complete justification of a decision would consist in a complete account of its effects, the principles employed, and the effects of always observing the principles. Such a justification seems to require a complete specification of some general way of life.

But suppose, further, that even after giving this complete specification, a person is still not satisfied and asks, "But why should I live like that?" This question is similar to "Why be moral?" as discussed in Chapter 9. Here, claims Hare, there is no further answer to give, because we have already said everything we can by way of justification. We can only ask the person to make up his or her own mind about which way one ought to live. In the end, everything pertaining to the choice of retaining one's old principles or finding new ones rests upon such a decision of principle. Hare thus defends the view that individuals must decide for themselves whether to accept a course of conduct such as the moral life; if one accepts it, one can justify decisions within the framework. If one rejects it, some alternative way of life must be found. These decisions, however, should not in any sense be conceived as arbitrary, in Hare's view, for they may be extremely well informed decisions, just as a good driver may be well informed when modifying a principle of how to drive an automobile.

In short, Hare suggests that our only recourse in the matter of ultimate justification is to consider whether a whole way of life is desirable. He apparently does not believe that once principles and ways of life have been critically examined and compared, any given way of life resting on careful decisions of principle can be shown better as a whole than another way of life based on decisions of principle, for we must decide to commit ourselves at some point to one or the other. Such commitments can nonetheless be justified through deliberation about the consequences of certain acts. Because of the emphasis on effects, Hare's arguments bear a close resemblance to utilitarian theories of justification, and in recent years he has explicitly embraced one form of utilitarianism. His line of thought on ultimate justification in ethics is expressed in the following celebrated passage from his book *The Language of Morals*. Certain similarities both to pragmatic justification and to Sartre's views on personal choice, as studied in Chapter 9, are also evident in this passage.

> A complete justification of a decision would consist of a complete account of its effects, together with a complete account of the principles which it observed, and the effects of observing those principles. . . . If pressed to justify a decision completely, we have to give a complete specification of the way of life of which it is a part. This complete specification it is impossible in practice to give; the nearest attempts are those given by the great religions. . . . If the inquirer still goes on asking "But why *should* I live like that?" then there is no further answer to give him, because we have already, *ex hypothesi*, said everything that could be included in this further answer. We can only ask him to make up his own mind which way he ought to live; for in the end everything rests upon such a decision of principle.*

Hare's prescriptivism has been broadly discussed for over three decades, and numerous arguments have emerged which challenge the view that the prescriptivist model can accommodate all forms of moral discourse. It has been maintained, for example, that we not only prescribe with ethical language but also advise, exhort,

---

*R. M. Hare, *The Language of Morals* (Oxford, England: Oxford University Press, 1952), p. 69.

implore, deplore, and confess. These sometimes tedious discussions are not unimportant, but they may be set aside while we consider the most sweeping, concentrated, and influential criticism of prescriptivism yet to emerge. This criticism derives from a group of philosophers who believe that moral language is no more prescriptive than descriptive.

DESCRIPTIVISM

"Descriptivism" boasts the ability to account more adequately than prescriptivism for the language of morals, the relation between facts and values, and certain features of moral choice. The writings of Philippa Foot have been especially prominent in the recent discussion of these questions, and the presentation here generally follows her treatment of them.*

Foot's case rests heavily on an analysis of the language and logic of morals. It would be impossible to appreciate the force of descriptivism without having some understanding of this orientation. Foot specifically attacks two major assumptions in Hare's thought: (1) that the descriptive or factual component of meaning and the prescriptive or value component of meaning are separable—as Hare suggests in distinguishing (prescriptive) meaning and (descriptive) criteria; and (2) that individuals may accept criteria for evaluating things which no one else accepts as criteria (and may do so without logical error). These two challenges to prescriptivism may be referred to as the "descriptivist thesis" and the "closed-criteria thesis."

The Descriptivist Thesis

Let us begin with assumption 1. Foot and others have wondered why, when we offer a value judgment such as "McFall is courageous," a prescription is involved (or entailed) just because it is a value judgment. Foot thinks it untrue that we necessarily commend persons in judging them courageous or that we must accept an imperative on the order of "let me be courageous" in doing so. Her view is that one can recognize the virtue of courage in another even though one is a complete and unreformable coward; and one can consistently commend others for being courageous without prescribing for oneself or for anyone else. For example, one can judge McFall courageous without prescribing anything for him, for Shimp, or for oneself.

Other examples of Foot's thesis include words which are generally used to *describe* objects but which, by their logic, also *require* one's taking negative attitudes

---

*Foot is ranked as a descriptivist because she seeks to undermine prescriptivism by attacking Hare's sharp distinction between facts and values. She wants to restore the naturalistic perspective of a close relation between facts and values, and she is therefore sometimes referred to as a neo-naturalist. One might loosely characterize the point of her arguments as a return to traditional beliefs that in ethics we describe what is the case.

whenever one uses them. The word "dangerous" is typical of the examples she has in mind. When we use the word "dangerous," we can supply factual evidence for an object's being dangerous—such as a threat offered to human life—but one kind of "evidence" required for the proper use of "dangerous" is that there be a threatening *evil*, as she puts it. "Danger" is thus not evaluatively neutral, for use of this concept entails an appeal to such value concepts as harm and evil. That is, "danger" and many concepts like it have so-called facts and values so intertwined that the concepts cannot be sorted into "factual" and "evaluative" components. The whole idea of two sorts of components is thus under attack in Foot's philosophy. Such examples indicate, according to descriptivists, that descriptions are often logically inseparable from modes of evaluation; descriptions cannot be provided without already having logically determined the appropriateness of attitudes that might be taken toward the objects or persons involved.

In light of earlier discussions in this chapter, however, it is worth noting that descriptivism is not merely one form of naturalism, for descriptivists do not say that values actually *are* facts. Values are not reduced to facts any more than facts are reduced to values. Rather, the claim is that conceptual considerations (a study of the nature of concepts) show values logically connected to facts so that it makes no clear sense to distinguish them into two different types with different "functions." The descriptivist is maintaining that action-guiding features and factual features of concepts are not distinguishable in such a way that they can be separated into factual and evaluative components. Some descriptivists even maintain the strong thesis that there is *no distinction* at all to be made between facts and values.

These descriptivist conclusions can be challenged from a prescriptivist's point of view on grounds that they presuppose culturally or linguistically determined views about morality. Such an objection would take the following form: The prescriptivist would not deny the descriptivist thesis if construed purely as an account (logical or conceptual) of the way moral concepts reflect moral beliefs. Indeed, the prescriptivist holds that we should expect the incorporation of values into the concepts and language of every culture. Terms such as "harmful," "dangerous," or "courageous," it can be argued, are not so much descriptive as they are complex repositories of positive and negative cultural attitudes toward certain types of events, objects, and persons. A particular chemical is "harmful" or "dangerous" to human health or to the environment only because of ways in which health and the environment are valued. Many concepts require such attitudes, but from this fact nothing follows to indicate that values *cannot* logically be distinguished from facts. It has been shown, as we all know, only that our concepts are complex structures, sometimes containing both descriptive and prescriptive components.

Consider as an example of this objection the statement, "Shimp's refusal of further testing killed McFall." Without a context to determine how the word is being used, it is not clear whether "killing" is a descriptive or an evaluative term (or some combination of the two). In some contexts, however, the term is unambiguously used with evaluative connotations, including prescriptive force. When McFall called his cousin Shimp and told him "You're killing me," he was using moral language in an attempt to guide action. Here the descriptive component of "killing" is "causing death" and the prescriptive component is a condemnation of the behavior. By contrast, the statement, "The loss of bone marrow is killing McFall," has no such action-guiding, prescriptive, or condemning force. Even though McFall's life is endangered, and the danger is suggested (but only suggested) by "The loss of bone marrow is killing McFall," this statement is evaluatively neutral and in no respect prescriptive. (Moreover, if death were considered by McFall a peaceful release from life and not an "evil," as Foot puts it, then even the suggestion of danger would disappear.) From the prescriptivist's point of view, such examples confirm that our evaluative usage of terms is context-bound (requiring a background of values making up a moral way of life) and that the evaluative use or meaning of words can be analyzed independently of their factual (or neutral) meaning.

The Closed-Criteria Thesis

Another critical question Foot directs at Hare is the following: "Is it open to us to *choose* what the criteria for determining moral goodness shall be?" Put another way: Are we free to choose what counts as evidence for moral goodness, or is what counts as evidence given and restricted by the institution of morality itself? This is a question about whether morality permits the latitude of autonomous choice that Hare seems to think it does. As Foot sees it, Hare's philosophy leads to the implausible position that anything at all can be counted as a "good reason" for a value judgment (moral or nonmoral) if only we choose to *make* it a good reason. Her interpretation and criticism are expressed in this example:

> [According to prescriptivism] one man may say that a thing is good because of some fact about it, and another may refuse to take that fact as any evidence at all, for nothing is laid down in the meaning of "good" which connects it with one piece of "evidence" rather than another. It follows that a moral eccentric could argue to moral conclusions from quite idiosyncratic premises; he could say, for instance, that a man was a good man because he clasped and unclasped his hands, and never turned NNE after turning SSW. He could also reject someone else's evaluation simply by denying that his evidence was evidence at all.*

If someone asks for moral reasons in the context of moral justification, Foot thinks Hare's view allows the citation of anything at all as a reason. She proposes to argue for the quite opposite view that "Criteria for the goodness of each and every kind of thing . . . are always determined, and not a matter for decision." In support of her contentions, she points out that we cannot in general choose criteria for the goodness of something; for example, we cannot choose criteria for a good knife, a good farmer, or

---

*From Philippa Foot, "Moral Beliefs," in *Proceedings of the Aristotelian Society*, **59** (1958–1959), pp. 83 ff.

a good reader. Latitude in the selection of criteria for good knives, she says, is not permitted by "the language of mankind." In these evaluations, and in moral evaluations as well, the point of the activity and the function of the objects involved impose a limit upon what the criteria of goodness can be. If someone does not adhere to these standards in commending relevant items, Foot believes, we cannot understand that person as speaking from a moral point of view. G. J. Warnock, who has openly associated himself with Foot's position on this point, argues for this thesis with more direct reference to morality:

> ... Not just anything can function as a criterion of *moral* evaluation. ... That there *are* such limits seems to me perfectly evident. ... The limits are set somewhere within the general area of concern with the welfare of human beings. ... The *relevance* of considerations as to the welfare of human beings *cannot*, in the context of moral debate, be denied. (Again, of course, we do not *choose* that this should be so; it *is* so, simply because of what "moral" means.)*

Again, responses to Foot are open to the prescriptivist: Perhaps the most effective response is that it is not a *logical* impossibility that some criteria can be replaced in "the language of mankind" by other criteria; the real problem is that certain criteria are implausible as moral or evaluative standards, given the evaluative and conceptual background assumed in the language or culture. The argument, thus far, follows from the prescriptivist response mentioned earlier. Hare himself has argued against Foot that our moral choices are (conceptually) restricted by what we select as contributing to our survival, growth, and procreation. We call things good because we take them to be relevant to ends satisfying what we conceive as "fundamental human needs." Hare insists, however, that nothing *must* be called a fundamental human need. From the fact that something is called (by some people in some contexts) a fundamental need, and therefore that other things can appropriately be called good which satisfy the need, it is not inevitable that any particular things *must* be called "needs" or that other things satisfying needs *must* be called "goods." Hare thinks his opponents confuse *truths about words* with *truths about things*. He develops this line of thought in the following discussion of Foot and descriptivism.

*G. J. Warnock, *Contemporary Moral Philosophy* (New York: St. Martin's Press, 1967), pp. 67 ff.

R. M. HARE

Descriptivism*

There are some things which, if wanted or thought good by somebody, seem to call for no explanation (for example, food, a certain degree of warmth, etc.). Other things, if wanted or thought good, require explanation. The explanation can perhaps be given: a man who wants a flat pebble may want it to play ducks and drakes with, and think it good for this purpose; but, as we progress to more and more bizarre examples, the explanation gets harder and harder to give. It therefore seems to be open to the descriptivist to take a very extraordinary imaginary example, and ask rhetorical questions about it, such as "Suppose that a man says that somebody is a good man because he clasps and unclasps his hands, and never turns NNE. after turning SSW.; could we understand him?" It is implied that an anti-descriptivist has to claim that he can understand such an absurd statement, and this is treated as a *reductio ad absurdum* of his position.

This type of argument rests on a confusion between, on the one hand, logical absurdity and its various weaker analogues, and, on the other, various sorts of contingent improbability. . . . It is contingently extremely unlikely, to say the least, that I should become able to lift a ton weight with my bare hands; but it is not logically impossible for this to happen, nor is it logically absurd, in any weaker way, to claim that it has happened. By this I mean that if a man claimed to be able to do this, there would be no ultimate obsta-

*From R. M. Hare, "Descriptivism," in *Proceedings of the British Academy*, **69** (1963), as reprinted in *Essays on the Moral Concepts* (Berkeley: University of California Press, 1972), pp. 70–72.

cle to our understanding him. Admittedly, we might well think at first that we had misunderstood him; it is so improbable that anybody should even think that it had happened, that, if a person claimed that it had happened, we should think at first that he could not be meaning the words in their literal senses. We might think that he meant, for instance, that the weight in question was counter-balanced, so that he could put his hands underneath it and lift, and make it go up. That is to say, when a man says something which is sufficiently improbable (as we think the universe to be constituted), we tend to assume that he cannot mean it literally, and that therefore we have to search for some non-literal meaning if we are going to understand him. But for all that, what he says has in its literal sense nothing *logically* wrong with it. It follows that no conclusions whatever are to be drawn concerning the meanings or uses of words from the oddity of such a remark; what is odd is not the use of words, but that anybody should think such a thing.

The case before us is much the same. If a man said that somebody was a good man because he clasped and unclasped his hands, we should, indeed, at first find ourselves wondering whether we had understood him. But the reason is that, although what has been said is perfectly *comprehensible* in its literal sense, it is very odd indeed for anybody to think it. We should therefore look around for non-literal senses or contrived explanations, and should be baffled if we failed to find any. Why would it be odd for anybody to think this? For a reason which can, indeed, be gathered from the writings of descriptivists, who have given a tolerably correct account of it, vitiated only by their assumption that it can teach us anything about the uses or meanings of words, and that therefore it can support, or discredit, logical theses. The reason is that very few of us, if any, have the necessary "pro-attitude" to people who clasp and unclasp their hands; and the reason for this is that the pro-attitudes which we have do not just occur at random, but have explanations, albeit not (as the descriptivists whom I am discussing seem to think) explanations which logic alone could provide. To think something good of its kind is, let us say, to have at least some disposition to choose it when, or if, choosing things of that kind, in actual or hypothetical circumstances. After what I have said earlier, you will not, I know, confuse this thesis with the thesis that for something to *be* good is for us to have a disposition to choose it. Now we do not have, most of us, any disposition to choose, or to choose to be, men who clasp and unclasp their hands. We do not, accordingly, think that men who do this are good.

The explanation of our not thinking this is that such choices would hardly contribute to our survival, growth, procreation, etc.; if there have been any races of men or animals who have made the clasping and unclasping of hands a prime object of their pro-attitudes, to the exclusion of other more survival-promoting activities, they have gone under in the struggle for existence. I am, I know, being rather crude; but in general, to cut the matter short, we have the pro-attitudes that we have, and therefore call the things good which we do call good, because of their relevance to certain ends which are sometimes called "fundamental human needs."

To call them this, however, is already to make a *logical* connexion between them and what it is good for a man to have. This, indeed, is why descriptivists have fallen into the trap of supposing that, because the word "good" is logically tied in certain contexts to the *word* "needs," it is therefore logically tied to certain concrete *things* which are generally thought to be needs.

CONCLUSION

This chapter has surveyed the most influential issues and writings yet to emerge from metaethics. As noted at the beginning of the chapter, these theories, more than any others encountered in this book, range beyond moral judgments into the broader domain of all kinds of value judgments. Contemporary literature in metaethics itself has led the discussion in this more general direction. This literature, somewhat surprisingly, has had a greater impact on philosophy in the twentieth century than the literature surveyed in any of the other chapters in this book except Chapters 3, 4, and 5 on classical ethical theories. The far-ranging influence of metaethics is a matter of regret in some quarters in philosophy, largely because the work in this area has often been so remote from the rest of ethical theory and from any direct applications to moral problems.

On the other hand, the effects of a body of literature on a field are sometimes as significant as the intrinsic quality of the literature itself. Metaethics arguably has introduced a commendable measure of clarity and rigor into moral philosophy, and its very generality has led to closer relations among ethics, epistemology, aesthetics, and the general theory of value. Metaethics is also in some respects the youngest and least

advanced of all the fields of ethical theory. It is hoped that in coming years this literature will develop so as to make a greater contribution both to the analysis of fundamental concepts in normative ethical theory and to the problems of moral justification
that were encountered in Chapter 9.

SUGGESTED SUPPLEMENTARY READINGS

The Issue of Facts and Values and General Background

Hancock, Roger N.: *Twentieth-Century Ethics* (New York: Columbia University Press,
1974).
Harrison, Jonathan: *Our Knowledge of Right and Wrong* (New York: Humanities
Press, 1971).
Hudson, W. D., ed.: *The Is/Ought Question: A Collection of Papers on the Central
Problem in Moral Philosophy* (New York: St. Martin's Press, 1970).
————: *Modern Moral Philosophy* (New York: Anchor Books, Doubleday and Co.,
Inc., 1970).
Monro, David H.: *Empiricism and Ethics* (Cambridge, England: Cambridge University
Press, 1967).
Warnock, Geoffrey J.: *Contemporary Moral Philosophy* (New York: St. Martin's
Press, 1967).

Naturalism

Lewis, Clarence Irving: *An Analysis of Knowledge and Valuation*, Book 3 (LaSalle, Ill.:
Open Court Publishing Co., 1946).
Perry, Ralph Barton: "Value as an Objective Predicate," *Journal of Philosophy*, **28**
(1931): 477–484.
————: *General Theory of Value: Its Meaning and Basic Principles Construed in Terms
of Interest* (Cambridge, Mass.: Harvard University Press, 1950).
Sesonske, Alexander: *Value and Obligation: The Foundations of an Empiricist Ethical
Theory* (New York: Oxford University Press, 1964).

The Naturalistic Fallacy

Foot, Philippa, ed.: *Theories of Ethics* (Oxford, England: Oxford University Press,
1967).
Frankena, William K.: "The Naturalistic Fallacy," *Mind*, **48** (1939): 464–477.
Nakhnikian, George: "On the Naturalistic Fallacy," in H. N. Castañeda and George
Nakhnikian, eds., *Morality and the Language of Conduct* (Detroit: Wayne State
University Press, 1963).

Prior, A. N.: "The Naturalistic Fallacy: The Logic of Its Refutation," in R. Ekman, ed., *Readings in the Problems of Ethics* (New York: Charles Scribner's Sons, 1968).

Searle, John R.: *Speech Acts: An Essay in the Philosophy of Language* (Cambridge, England: Cambridge University Press, 1970).

Intuitionism

Broad, C. D.: "Is 'Goodness' a Name of a Simple Non-Natural Quality?" in *Proceedings of the Aristotelian Society*, **34** (1933–1934): 249–268.

Ewing, Alfred C.: *The Definition of Good* (New York: Macmillan Company, 1947).

Hudson, W. D.: *Ethical Intuition* (New York: St. Martin's Press, 1967).

Moore, George Edward: *Principia Ethica* (Cambridge, England: Cambridge University Press, 1903).

————: "A Reply to My Critics: Ethics," in Paul Arthur Schilpp, ed., *The Philosophy of G. E. Moore* (Cambridge, England: Cambridge University Press, 1942).

Nowell-Smith, P. H.: *Ethics* (Baltimore: Penguin Books, Inc., 1954).

Ross, William David: *The Right and the Good* (Oxford, England: Oxford University Press, 1930).

————: *Foundations of Ethics* (Oxford, England: Clarendon Press, 1939).

Strawson, P. F.: "Ethical Intuitionism," *Philosophy*, **24** (1949): 23–33.

Noncognitivism

Ayer, Alfred J.: *Language, Truth and Logic*, 2d ed. (New York: Dover Publications, Inc., 1936), especially chap. 6.

Edwards, Paul: *The Logic of Moral Discourse* (Glencoe, Ill.: Free Press, 1955).

Stevenson, Charles L.: *Ethics and Language* (New Haven, Conn.: Yale University Press, 1944).

————: *Facts and Values: Studies in Ethical Analysis* (New Haven, Conn.: Yale University Press, 1963).

Urmson, J. O.: *The Emotive Theory of Ethics* (New York: Oxford University Press, 1969).

Prescriptivism

Hare, Richard M.: *The Language of Morals* (Oxford, England: Oxford University Press, 1952).

————: *Freedom and Reason* (Oxford, England: Oxford University Press, 1963).

Descriptivism

Anscombe, G. E. M.: "Modern Moral Philosophy," in J. J. Thomson and G. Dworkin, eds., *Ethics* (New York: Harper & Row, Publishers, Inc., 1968).

Beardsmore, R. W.: *Moral Reasoning* (New York: Schocken Books, Inc., 1969).

Foot, Philippa: "Moral Arguments," *Mind*, **67** (1958), as reprinted in *Virtues and Vices* (Oxford, England: Basil Blackwell, 1978).

——: "Goodness and Choice," in *Proceedings of the Aristotelian Society*, Suppl. Vol. 35 (1961), as reprinted in *Virtues and Vices* (Oxford, England: Basil Blackwell, 1978).

Phillips, D. Z., and H. O. Mounce: *Moral Practices* (New York: Schocken Books, Inc., 1969), especially chap. 5.

Warnock, Geoffrey J.: *The Object of Morality* (London: Methuen & Co., Ltd., 1971).

Index